HENRY V

by the same author

(Ed.) Society at War: The Experience of England and France during
the Hundred Years War
Lancastrian Normandy, 1415–1450: The History of a Medieval
Occupation
The Hundred Years War: England and France at War,
*c.*1300–*c.*1450
(Ed.) Power, Culture and Religion in France, *c.*1350–*c.*1550
(Ed. with C. A. J. Armstrong) English Suits before the Parlement of
Paris, 1420–1436

HENRY V

Christopher Allmand

Professor of History, University of Liverpool

METHUEN LONDON

First published in Great Britain in 1992
by Methuen London
an imprint of Reed Consumer Books Ltd
Michelin House, 81 Fulham Road, London sw3 6rb
and Auckland, Melbourne, Singapore and Toronto

A CIP catalogue record for this book
is available from the British Library

isbn 0 413 53280 1

Photoset in Great Britain by
Rowland Phototypesetting Ltd
Bury St Edmunds, Suffolk
Printed and bound by
Clays Ltd, St Ives plc

To
Bernadette,
Catherine,
Sarah,
Celia
and
Alison

CONTENTS

LIST OF ILLUSTRATIONS

MAPS

GENEALOGICAL TABLE

Acknowledgements and thanks for permission to reproduce the photographs are due to Aerofilms for plate 3; to All Souls College, Oxford, for plate 16; to the Bodleian Library, Oxford, for plate 24; to the British Library for plates 1, 5, 14, 15, 19, 20 and 21; to the Trustees of the British Museum for plate 13; to the Dean and Chapter of Canterbury Cathedral for plates 8 (photo by the British Tourist Authority) and 23; to Martin Collins for plate 22; to the Master and Fellows of Corpus Christi College, Cambridge, for plate 10; to Archives Générales, Dijon, Côte d'Or, for plate 7; to Lambeth Palace Library for plate 12; to C. S. Middleton for plate 26; to William Powell for plate 25; to the Public Record Office for plates 4, 11, 18 and 27; to the Royal Commission on the Historical Monuments of England for plate 2; to the Dean and Chapter of Westminster Abbey for plates 9, 29 and 30; to the Dean and Chapter of Winchester Cathedral for plate 6 (photo John Crook); and to the Warden and Scholars of Winchester College for plate 17 (photo John Crook).

The maps and genealogical table were redrawn from the author's roughs by Neil Hyslop.

ACKNOWLEDGEMENTS

This book could not have been written without the practical help accorded me by many persons and institutions. Professor Jack Scarisbrick, General Editor of the English Monarchs series, having invited me to write this study, the University of Liverpool gave me two terms' leave, and the Leverhulme Trust generous financial support, to begin work on it. As will become apparent below, I have made use of manuscript evidence found in French archives and libraries, in particular in Paris, Rouen, Caen, Dijon, Orléans and Amiens. In England, I consulted manuscripts at the Chancery Lane branch of the Public Record Office, where Margaret Condon gave me every assistance, and at the British Library. I was also able to make use of the records of the Duchy of Cornwall (thanks to the Secretary and Keeper of the Records and Dr Graham Haslam); the muniments of Westminster Abbey (by courtesy of the Dean and Chapter and the kind assistance of the Keeper, Dr Richard Mortimer); the archives of the Worshipful Company of Mercers of London (with the help of Miss Anne Sutton); and those of the College of Arms (made available to me by Mr R.C. Yorke). I was also made welcome at the Corporation of London Record Office; the Guildhall Library, London (where I saw records belonging to the Worshipful Company of Brewers and to the Master and Wardens of the Grocers' Company); the Lincolnshire Archives Office; the Hereford and Worcester Record Office; Canterbury Cathedral Archives; the Bodleian Library and All Souls College, Oxford; and the libraries of Corpus Christi College and Trinity College, Cambridge. My sincere thanks are due to all who gave me help on my visits.

Dr Carole Rawcliffe and Dr Linda Clark did all that they could to smooth my path through the work which I needed to do on the parliamentarians of the reign. I owe them, and the Trustees of the History of Parliament Trust, a considerable debt of gratitude. My friend Dr David Bowsher offered a diagnosis of the malady which carried off the subject of this book: I am grateful to him for his help in this matter. With the generosity happily so often found among scholars, Caroline Barron, Anne Curry, Ian Friel, Robert Massey, Nigel Saul and Jenny Stratford shared their knowledge of useful sources with me. Those whose theses I consulted and, in some cases, cited are listed at the end of the bibliography.

I began to write this book during two visits, sponsored by the P.H. Holt Trust of Ocean Transport and Trading Ltd, to the peaceful haven of St Deiniol's Library at Hawarden. Jeremy Catto, Christopher Crowder, Rhidian Griffiths, Gerald Harriss, Margaret Harvey, Neil Jamieson and Edward Powell read parts of the book and I have benefited considerably from their constructive comments. The preparation of the typescript was completed with exemplary speed, efficiency and cheerfulness by Mrs Pat Thompson, to whom I am deeply indebted. The friendship, interest and, particularly in the last phase of preparation, the encouragement not only of the General Editor but also of Maurice Keen and Elizabeth Danbury, who all read the entire text, were invaluable in getting the typescript to the publishers, for whom Ann Mansbridge, Ann Wilson and William Powell did a fine job in overseeing its transformation into more presentable form. I am happy to acknowledge that the production of this book has been, in more senses than one, an exercise of co-operation among friends.

LIST OF ABBREVIATIONS

Add. Ch.	Additional Charter
Add. Ms	Additional Manuscript
AHR	*American Historical Review*
AN	Archives Nationales
Annales ESC	*Annales: Economies, Sociétés, Civilisations*
Arch. comm.	Archives communales
Arch. dép.	Archives départementales
BBCS	*Bulletin of the Board of Celtic Studies*
BEC	*Bibliothèque de l'Ecole des Chartes*
BIHR	*Bulletin of the Institute of Historical Research*
BJRL	*Bulletin of the John Rylands Library*
BL	British Library
BN	Bibliothèque Nationale
CCR	*Calendar of Close Rolls*
CPR	*Calendar of Patent Rolls*
CS	Camden Society
C&YS	Canterbury and York Society
DCO	Duchy of Cornwall Office
DL	Duchy of Lancaster
DKR	*Reports of the Deputy Keeper of the Public Records*
EETS	Early English Text Society
EconHR	*Economic History Review*
EHR	*English Historical Review*

Foedera	T. Rymer, *Foedera* (The Hague edn, 1739–45)
LQR	*Law Quarterly Review*
PPC	*Proceedings and Ordinances of the Privy Council of England*
PRO	Public Record Office
RHistS	Royal Historical Society
RP	*Rotuli Parliamentorum*
RS	Rolls Series
SHF	Société de l'Histoire de France
SHN	Société de l'Histoire de Normandie
TRHistS	*Transactions of the Royal Historical Society*
VCH	*Victoria County History*
WAM	Westminster Abbey Muniments

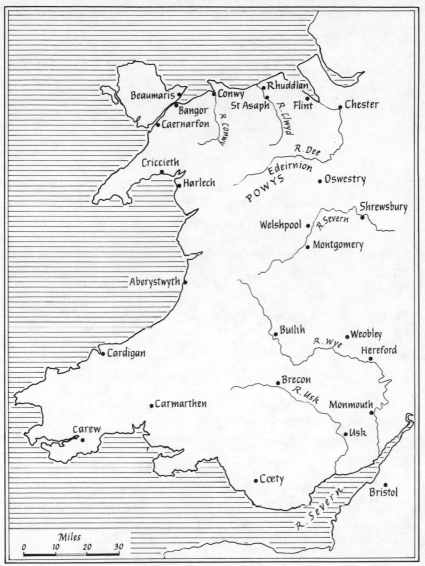

Wales and the Glyn Dŵr revolt.

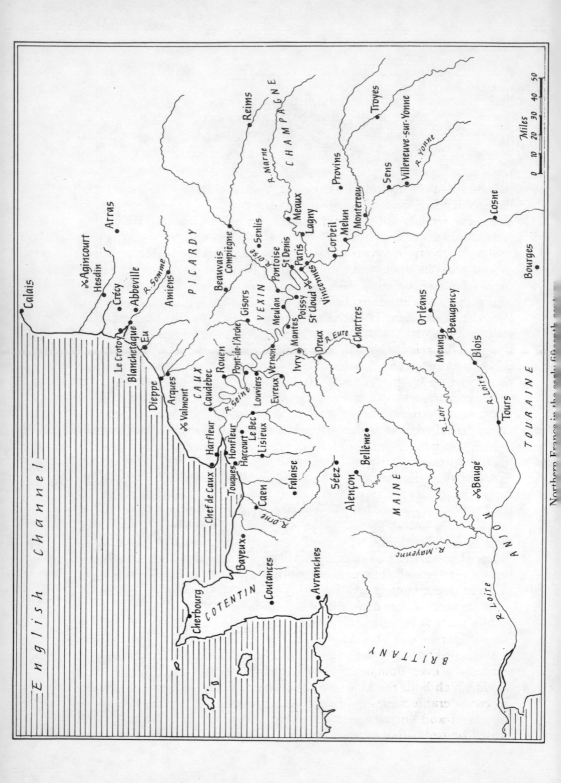

Northern France in the early fifteenth century

INTRODUCTION

The student of the man who ruled England as Henry V faces a number of problems. Ever since his own day, he has been seen as an outsize king, the recipient of praise and adulation, which makes it difficult to judge him objectively. Furthermore, he died relatively young, probably only thirty-five years old. Inevitably, the unanswerable questions about what he might have done had he lived longer are left lingering at the back of the mind. Reaction to him takes several forms. On the one hand, there is admiration for his military skills and achievements. On the other, there is criticism of what is regarded as his ambition, which, according to some, he pursued hypocritically in the name of justice; and reluctance, too, to admit outstanding ability, even greatness, because our age is disinclined to give its blessing to a reputation built largely on the exploits of war. Shakespeare was not alone in concentrating upon Henry's war against the French. Almost all who have written about him in more recent times have done the same. A story based on war is one based on action: it appeals. It is a story which can be told with confidence: the sources for it abound, mainly in the chronicles written at the time. The war was also the central issue of the reign, around which almost all other activity turned. It was a factor of vital significance to men of the early fifteenth century: Henry used it to help harness the country and, not least, the nobility behind him in an effort to bring unity to the kingdom. In addition, war provides a thread with which to follow Henry's career, that of a man who, having had early military experience in Wales, developed into a very remarkable, possibly an outstanding soldier. We can learn a great deal about Henry by seeing how he responded to the needs and demands of conflict.

Yet there is more to Henry than the soldier, however successful a war leader he may be thought to have been. His fulfilment of that role turned in large measure upon adequate supply, financial and material – even human. The raising of money depended on political skills which both the king and others who helped him rule possessed in considerable measure. Parliament, the great provider, had to be managed and encouraged to develop a sense of cohesion so that it might be persuaded to meet the king's requests for financial support

whenever he made them. But that was not all. The size of the military
effort which England undertook could only lead to success if it were
properly organized: it is arguable that Henry's administrative and
planning skills as a soldier were greater than the tactical ones which
he showed on the field. In all these aspects of kingship, Henry was
not afraid to delegate, while insisting on keeping overall control for
himself. He was lucky that he had capable men to assist him, men
upon whose abilities he drew and to whose loyalties he appealed to
assist him in the arduous tasks of ruling. Not the least of his skills
was that of forging a bond between those who were responsible for
the government of England during the nine and a half years of his
rule.

    More than half this book is concerned with emphasizing the signifi-
cance of Henry's contribution to, and achievement in government,
which was complementary to war. Generally speaking no great innovator, Henry showed that the system which he inherited was sound
if it were not abused. An important part of kingship was the attention
which the ruler paid to the details of making the system work. [1] Henry
appreciated detail: before Henry VII ever did so, he would check the
accounts of departments to see that the finances were in order. [2] He
wanted to be master of every aspect of government and rule, because
he was responsible for it all. That was part of his vision of the 'job'.
Henry had an exalted sense of his high responsibility to God for the
good of his people, a sense accentuated by his recognition, shared by
many, that his father had not fulfilled the hopes and promises of the
beginning of his reign. For the past forty years or so, England had
been ruled by an old king in his dotage (Edward III), a king with
unusually autocratic views and tendencies (Richard II) and, most
recently, by Henry V's own father (Henry IV), a man never strong
enough morally, politically or physically to give a firm lead to his
countrymen. In 1413 England lived in hope of better days, and the
main reason why Henry V came to be so well regarded was that he
revitalized his country and its people, partly through his personality,
partly through his very 'professional' approach to the tasks in hand.
The contemporary view of Henry recognized that he was, in every
sense of the word as it was then understood, a real king.

    His achievement depended on very much more than apparent suc-
cess in war, and the reader who wants to understand what the man

----

    [1] See the paper, perhaps a lucky survival from Henry's 'memo-pad', on which,
under the heading 'Memoires', he sets out administrative tasks to be done. Most of
the text is in French, and may have been dictated. At the end, in another ink and
hand (that of Henry himself?) are two points in English. (PRO, E 30/169; probably
autumn 1420.)
    [2] G.L. Harriss (ed.), *Henry V. The practice of kingship* (Oxford, 1985), p. 177.

did must be asked to accept that his death and burial are recorded even before the mid-point of this book has been reached. A crucial part of the study is contained in the pages which follow the description of those events. For this, I have relied a great deal upon the work, much of it recent, of other scholars, to whom I am much indebted, as the footnotes will indicate. The debate whether Henry was 'the greatest man that ever ruled England'[3] will continue, as will that concerning the wisdom of making war against France, the morality of killing prisoners at Agincourt, or the execution of the 'pre-mature reformers', the Lollards. This book is one in a series concerned with 'English monarchs'. The question to be asked, then, is what was Henry's status as a monarch? It is from this point that I have begun, and to this question that I have tried to give an answer.

[3] K.B. McFarlane, *Lancastrian Kings and Lollard Knights* (Oxford, 1972), p. 133.

PART I

A Royal Apprenticeship

Chapter 1

EARLY YEARS

The historian can be more confident about the place which witnessed the birth of the boy who would one day become Henry V than he can be about its date. He was born, as a financial document of Henry VI's reign informs us, in the chamber of the gatehouse tower of Monmouth castle,[1] then part of the lands of the duchy of Lancaster, to which the baby's father, also called Henry, was heir. As to the date, there is no absolute certainty about it, although either 9 August or 16 September always features. The year, however, remains unresolved: was it 1386 or 1387? Virtually every combination has had its supporter, influenced by one near contemporary or another. Modern authorities have clashed. Even the co-authors of the three-volume study of Henry as king, published between 1914 and 1929, differed in their views, while, hardly surprisingly, the modern quality press is divided on the issue.[2]

In choosing 1386, on the grounds that the baby's parents were in Monmouth in the summer of that year, we should recognize that the choice is based more on likelihood than absolute certainty, although the

[1] R. Somerville, *History of the Duchy of Lancaster, I, 1265–1603* (London, 1953), 176, n.1, citing PRO, DL 37/12, m.6d. In February 1445 the 'Yatehous' was said to be 'multum debilis et ruinosa'.

[2] The uncertainty about Henry's date of birth stems from the different ways of expressing it chosen by writers of the time. These are as follows: (a) a clear date, e.g. 16 September 1386 (John Rylands University of Manchester Library, French Ms 54). (b) Henry is said to have been in his twenty-sixth year (i.e. he was twenty-five years old) when he was crowned in April 1413 (*Titi Livii Foro-Juliensis Vita Henrici Quinti Regis Angliae*, ed. T. Hearne (Oxford, 1716), p. 5). (c) Henry's death on 31 August 1422 occurred in a particular year of his life (e.g. in the thirty-sixth year of his age (i.e. he was thirty-five years old), *First English Life of King Henry the Fifth*, ed. C.L. Kingsford (Oxford, 1911), p. 182). If he was born on 9 August, this gives the year as 1387, if on 16 September (the feast of St Edith, as some contemporaries pointed out), Henry must have been born in 1386. See C.L. Kingsford, 'The early biographies of Henry V', *EHR*, 25 (1910), 62. (d) Writing in 1896, J.H. Wylie chose August 1386 (*History of England under Henry the Fourth* (4 vols, London, 1884–98), iii, 323–4). W.T. Waugh, author with Wylie of *The reign of Henry the Fifth* (3 vols, Cambridge, 1914–29, iii, 427), claimed 16 September 1387 as 'correct'. *The Times* used to favour 16 September; the *Independent* recorded both the August and September dates (for 1387).

astrological evidence contained in a treatise on his birth written during Henry V's reign favours 16 September 1386, the time of birth being 11.22 a.m.[3] The doubt, irritating as it is, hides a significant point: Henry's birth was not recorded with greater formality because no one expected him to become king. Although a great-grandson of Edward III, others stood between him and the throne. His father was the son of John of Gaunt, duke of Lancaster, the third surviving son of Edward III who, when his long reign ended in June 1377, had been succeeded by his ten-year-old grandson, Richard, whose father, Edward, the Black Prince, was already dead. Richard was to marry young; his bride, Anne of Bohemia, was of the same age. When Henry of Monmouth was born there seemed to be little reason why Richard II, then some twenty years old, should not be succeeded by a son of his own.

Meanwhile, John of Gaunt remained the country's leading nobleman.[4] By the time that Richard II inherited the throne, Gaunt was the eldest of Edward III's sons still alive. Much the most effective of three brothers who survived almost to the end of the century (he was outlived only by Edmund, duke of York, who did not die until 1402), and some twenty-five years older than his nephew, Richard II, he was the senior figure on the political field in these years. A man who enjoyed a European reputation and had, for a while, borne a Spanish royal title, his power was based on the great wealth which came to him from the duchy of Lancaster, endowed with extensive lands in many parts, notably in the north, the midlands and Wales. In 1380, in lieu of 5000 marks (£3333 13s. 4d.) owed to him by Richard II for war services, Gaunt secured the right to arrange the marriage of Mary de Bohun, second daughter of Humphrey, earl of Hereford, Essex and Northampton, a rich co-heiress in her own right with important estates in the marches of Wales and a member of one of the oldest noble families in medieval England.[5] That year, or in the next, in spite of opposition from his brother Thomas, duke of Gloucester (who had taken her sister, Eleanor, as his wife), Gaunt married Mary to his son, Henry. Perhaps because of her extreme youth (she was probably only eleven or twelve at the time) their first child, a boy, died at birth in 1382. But a few years later their efforts to rear a family were successful. Between 1386(?) and 1394 six chil-

---

[3] See Oxford, Bodleian Library, Ashmole Ms 393, fos 109–11; Ms 192, pt iii, fos 26–36; and H. Carey, 'Astrology and divination in later medieval England' (Univ. of Oxford D.Phil. thesis, 1984), p. 19. Dr M.H. Keen kindly drew my attention to this recent work.

[4] '. . . le plus grant seigneur et plus haute persone del roialme apres mon seignur liege le roy' (cited by A. Goodman, 'John of Gaunt', *England in the Fourteenth Century*, ed. W.M. Ormrod (Woodbridge, 1986), p. 77, n.70).

[5] J.L. Kirby, *Henry IV of England* (London, 1970), pp. 17–18.

dren were born to Henry and Mary. First came four boys, Henry, [6] Thomas, John and Humphrey, all born by 1390, followed by Blanche in 1392 and Philippa in 1394. However, in giving birth to the last, Mary died, leaving six young children, the oldest probably no older than eight, and their father, himself only twenty-seven at the time.

What sort of a man was the father, known at this time as earl of Derby? Like his own father, John of Gaunt, he fulfilled the role expected of a great nobleman. Inevitably, as a first cousin of Richard II (who was almost exactly his contemporary in age) he played a part of significance in the turbulent politics of the reign. What emerges from the evidence is that Henry of Derby, in spite of opposing him in 1387–88, was loyal to his sovereign, and that this appears to have been appreciated by the king. His instinct for action was to be satisfied in the spring of 1390 when he took part in the well-publicized tournament at St Inglevert, not far from Calais, where he achieved a certain reputation and met other leaders of European chivalry. Soon afterwards, with his wife awaiting the birth of their fourth child, he set out on an expedition against the Lithuanians. In 1392 he repeated the experience, returning home only after he had travelled from northern Germany through what is now Austria to Venice (where he was received by the Doge), down the coast of Dalmatia to Corfu, then to Rhodes and, finally, to the Holy Land and Jerusalem. The return journey, completed about a year after he had left the shores of England, was made through Cyprus, northern Italy and France. [7] It was notable for the way in which the earl gave charity to those who needed it; notable, too, for the lavish expenditure which he allowed himself in the acquisition of silver and gold collars and other items of jewellery. Henry liked to be seen living in style, as befitting a man with a growing European reputation.

Meanwhile, what of his children? We know very little about their upbringing. Henry had a nurse, Joan Waryn, who was paid 40s. a year to look after him. He must have had respect and affection for her for, in June 1415, he made her a grant of £20 for life to be taken from the royal manor of Isleworth; the obligation was still being honoured as late as May 1431, when Joan must have been quite an old lady. [8] In the absence abroad of their father, and after the death of their mother, they were placed in the care of their maternal grand-

[6] He was said to have been named after the first duke of Lancaster ('Annales Ricardi secundi et Henrici quarti, Regum Angliae', J. de Trokelowe et H. de Blaneforde, *Chronica et Annales*, ed. H.T. Riley (RS, London, 1866), p. 287).

[7] Kirby, *Henry IV*, pp. 38–40.

[8] Wylie, *Henry the Fourth*, iv, 177; *CPR, 1413–1419*, p. 329; *CPR, 1422–1429*, pp. 200, 322. She was described as his 'nutrix' in PRO, E 403/698, m.4 (a reference which I owe to Dr Jenny Stratford).

mother, Joan, countess of Hereford, who lived at Bytham, in Lincolnshire. The young Henry may have spent part of his early years there,
perhaps in the care of a governess, Mary Hervy. [9] The brothers
probably also spent part of their time on some of their father's estates,
particularly at Tutbury, in Staffordshire, and at Kenilworth, in Warwickshire, for which Henry was later to show a particular liking.
They were also to be found at Leicester, one of the main centres of
Lancastrian authority, and the town in which their mother, Mary,
was buried. [10] It was while he was here, in the spring of 1395, that
the young Henry was taken ill and a physician, Thomas Pye, had to
be summoned from London. It is said that the boy was puny at birth,
and this lack of physical strength may have marked his early years.
If so, it certainly disappeared as he entered his teens.

The year 1395 was to witness the first attempt to arrange his marriage. His prospective bride was to be Marie, daughter of John IV,
duke of Brittany, and his duchess, Joan. The plan fell through, however, and the girl was married to the count of Perche. Yet the Breton
link was not lost. In 1403 Henry's own father was to marry the duchess
Joan, by then widowed. Thus the lady who might have become our
subject's mother-in-law became his stepmother instead.

His education in these years was probably that of the very highest
ranks of the aristocracy. Henry would have learned to ride and to
fight, to hunt and to use the falcon. [11] His father, we know, revelled
in the outdoor life and in physical activity. His sons, too, were all
to show both skill and courage when their moment came to prove
themselves in adult wars. But education went wider than that. Henry
learned grammar, as the purchase of seven Latin books in London in
1396 (when he was some ten years old) indicates. It seems that he
may also have learned to play the harp at this early stage, for both
his parents were lovers of music. [12] Later in life, even when engaged
in war, Henry was to value the services of musicians around him,
whether those in the chapel royal or those who played the harp or
organs which accompanied him on his French campaigns. [13] As earl

[9] PRO, DL 28/1/4–5; Wylie, *Henry the Fourth*, iii, 327; iv, 163, 171; N. Orme,
From Childhood to Chivalry. The Education of the English Kings and Aristocracy, 1066–1530
(London/New York, 1984), p. 13 and references therein.
    [10] Within a short time of becoming king, Henry V was to have an image of his
mother placed upon her tomb in the church in Leicester (*Issues of the Exchequer . . .
from King Henry III to King Henry VI inclusive*, ed. F. Devon (London, 1837), p. 321).
    [11] He was later to own books on hunting (ibid., p. 368, and ch. 19 below).
    [12] Orme, *Childhood to Chivalry*, pp. 183, 146, 166; McFarlane, *Lancastrian Kings*,
p. 115.
    [13] See, for example, PRO, E 403/644, m.2; C.L. Kingsford, *Henry V. The typical
medieval hero* (London/New York, 2nd edn, 1923), pp. 82–3; Devon, *Issues of the
Exchequer*, pp. 363, 367.

of Derby, Henry's father had given the poet Chaucer an annuity; later in life, Henry, too, would patronize writers, while his two youngest brothers, John and Humphrey, were to be in the forefront of royal patronage of the arts in the first half of the fifteenth century.

As Henry approached his eleventh birthday, the tempo and temperature of English political life rose rapidly. Richard II, who had already faced a major crisis of authority in 1387–88, but had since ruled in a more discreet manner, began once again to reassert himself. Those, like Derby, who had opposed him earlier, only to be pardoned, felt that they had cause to fear for their safety. Thomas of Gloucester, youngest uncle of the king and one of 'the undivided trinity' who had given Richard so much trouble a decade earlier, was arrested and sent to Calais, where he died in mysterious circumstances while in the custody of Thomas Mowbray, earl of Nottingham. Although Nottingham was to be created duke of Norfolk at the same time (September 1397) as Derby became duke of Hereford (three other dukes, a marquis and four earls were created simultaneously), he felt, as he told Hereford in casual conversation, that they were soon to be undone by the king, as he had in the past undone others. Whether this was treasonable talk or not, it was foolish to have spoken in this way. Hereford reported the matter to his father, Gaunt, who perhaps to avenge himself on Norfolk for the death of his brother, Gloucester, passed it on to the king, who, in his turn, commanded Hereford into his presence to repeat the entire conversation. As a result, Hereford was made to confront Norfolk before the king, who ordered an appearance in the court of chivalry, Norfolk in the meantime being kept in custody while Hereford was allowed his freedom on receipt of sureties. At the meeting of the court further accusations were made, and it was decided that the two should meet in the lists at Coventry to settle the matter.

The occasion – trial by battle – was intended to be more than that, a veritable spectacle attended by all the English nobility and by others from beyond the sea. However, the expected encounter never took place. Instead, Richard condemned the two men to banishment, Norfolk for life, Hereford for ten years, soon to be reduced to six. Preparations for departure were made and persons authorized to receive the revenues of Hereford's already large estates were appointed. On 13 October 1398 Hereford left London on his exile. Less than four months later, on 3 February 1399, his father, John of Gaunt, duke of Lancaster, died at Leicester. Hereford should have been heir not only to his Bohun revenues, but to those of the vast Lancastrian estate as well. However, his rights were now dramatically revoked by the king when the possessions of the duchy of Lancaster were, in effect,

declared forfeit to the crown.[14] Could the exiled duke allow this to
happen without response? What was he to do?

The challenge could not go unanswered. The problem was to know
what form the response should take. The matter, as contemporaries
saw it, was that action of this kind perpetrated by the king against
one of the most powerful figures in the land suggested that no man
was entirely safe in his inheritance. As such, Hereford's quarrel with
the king over the future of his estates became the quarrel of every
owner of land in the country. In these circumstances, how far did
loyalty to the king stretch? Could such action on his part be tolerated?
The implications of Richard's act against Hereford attacked the very
stability of political and social society in England.

There was a further, vital problem. In 1399 the king, who on the
death of his first wife, Anne, in 1394 had married Isabelle, a daughter
of the king of France, still had no heir. His designated successor,
Roger Mortimer, earl of March, whose claim was based on being
descended from Lionel, duke of Clarence, second son of Edward III
(John of Gaunt had been the third) but through the female line, had
been killed in July 1398, leaving a young son, Edmund, scarcely seven
years old. If anything were to happen to the king or if he acted in a
manner which the nobility, above all, regarded as unacceptable, what
would occur to the succession to the crown? It is clear that, to many,
both Hereford's problem and that of the uncertain succession might
be resolved by the duke taking the crown for himself.

The thought probably crossed the minds of many in the spring of
1399. It may even have occurred to Richard that he was in danger.
As it was, events turned out badly for him. A crisis in Ireland
demanded his personal attention. At the end of May Richard crossed
over the sea, taking with him not only a sizeable army but, among
others, Hereford's young son, nearly thirteen and the recipient of £500
per annum from Hereford's revenues. Henry had probably been living
at court since at least his father's departure into exile late in the
previous year. Was the king taking him as a hostage? Although
Richard treated the boy well, and indeed knighted him on this
occasion,[15] the idea that he was under royal control as some sort of
surety for his father's good behaviour cannot be discounted.

Richard's departure for Ireland was to cost him dear. Hereford,
seeking friends in France (he made one, in particular, in the person
of Louis, duke of Orléans), decided to use the opportunity presented
by the king's absence to return home to seek the return of the inheritance, both his and that of his wife, of which he had been deprived.

---

[14] *RP*, iii, 372, 419.
[15] BL, Harley Ms 1319, fos 4v–5 (including the illumination).

Early in July 1399, accompanied by only a small force of 300 or so men, he landed at Ravenspur, in the east riding of Yorkshire. As he advanced through the county, men, many from duchy of Lancaster estates, came to join him. It was later said that he had claimed to be seeking only his inheritance, and that he had undertaken to continue to recognize Richard as king and the young Edmund, earl of March, as his heir. Did Hereford see himself as simply using the support which was gathering about him as a means of regaining his own, and of obliging the king to be reconciled to him? Perhaps. But the numbers coming to him were beginning to change all that. It was becoming increasingly evident that Richard was an unpopular king, and that the movement which Hereford was leading, whatever had been its original intentions, was now taking on the proportions of a national uprising which, by the end of July, had won the approval of many of the king's erstwhile and most powerful supporters.

Meanwhile Richard, informed of events in England, dithered in Ireland. It was said later that when he heard of Hereford's invasion, he called the young Henry to him and told him that, regrettably, such action by his father might cost him his patrimony. Henry is said to have replied, in an adult way, that he was innocent of any conspiracy, a fact which Richard readily acknowledged. None the less he had Henry and the son of the duke of Gloucester, one of a number of young men of noble family whom he had taken to Ireland with him to hold against any future trouble, imprisoned in the castle of Trim, some thirty miles north-west of Dublin.[16] Then, sending part of his army back to north Wales, he delayed for a while before crossing over to land in south Wales towards the end of July. Here he found that many were deserting him. Yet, in spite of this, he marched north through Wales to Conwy where Hereford, then at Chester, made contact with him. None can tell what was in Hereford's, or indeed, in Richard's mind at this stage. Hereford invited the king to restore his inheritance to him and to come to a meeting of parliament. (It had been in the context of a parliament that Hereford had been exiled the previous year.) But hardly had Richard set out when he was ambushed by Henry Percy (until recently his supporter) and taken by him to meet Lancaster, as he now styled himself, at Flint castle. He was, in effect, his opponent's prisoner.

That opponent, however, still observed the formalities. Official letters were sent out in the king's name, although they were written 'by the advice' of Lancaster and his supporters. Parliament was summoned to meet at Westminster on 30 September and the last week of August was spent travelling from Chester to London, where Richard

[16] Trokelowe et Blaneforde, pp. 247-8.

was lodged in the Tower. At about this time the young Henry of Monmouth was brought over from Ireland where he had been left in the castle of Trim.[17] He was entering upon a decisive moment in his country's history. By the time the act was played out, at the end of September, his father would be king and he himself declared heir to the throne.

The final act was to take place within the space of a few days. On 29 September a special committee of churchmen, nobles and lawyers visited Richard in the Tower and asked him to abdicate, as they claimed he had previously promised to do. He asked to see Lancaster and archbishop Thomas Arundel, and in their presence he signed the instrument of abdication, saying that he would have wished Lancaster to be his successor, and giving him his signet as a symbol of his abdication and transfer of authority. So the official, pro-Lancastrian account was made to read. On the next day, when parliament met, the royal throne was vacant and covered by a large cloth of gold. How was Lancaster to justify his seizure of it? By hereditary right? His descent from Henry III was undoubted, but his own ancestor, Edmund of Lancaster, had been younger than Edward I whose claim to succeed his father had been undoubted. By conquest? This was a very dangerous approach, which might be used by others in the future to justify the use of force to depose Lancaster himself. By parliamentary title? Possibly, according to the practice and doctrine of the day. Yet, once more, difficulties might be foreseen. Besides, it could be asked, if the throne were vacant, or the legal king forcibly prevented from being present, could such an assembly be called a genuine 'parliament'? What legal powers did those assembled on this historic occasion actually possess? The right to depose? The right to elect or create?

None can have doubted that on this particular day Lancaster was the most powerful man in England. But did power confer right? That was the question which needed to be addressed. To satisfy the waverer and to guard himself against future claimants, Lancaster required some firm justification of the legality of what he was doing. This was difficult to achieve through direct appeal to any one of the methods referred to above. But he could at least refer to his descent from Henry III ('I that am disendit be right lyne of the Blode comyng fro the gude lorde Kyng Henry therde');[18] to his claim which came from God and which his friends had helped him to fulfil; and to the failure of good government for which Richard had been responsible and for which Lancaster was now taking on responsibility. Nor would he wish

[17] PRO, E 404/16/394.
[18] *RP*, iii, 423.

to deprive any man of what was his (the parallel between Richard II being deprived of his kingdom and Hereford losing the duchy of Lancaster was an amazingly and embarrassingly close one) except if he failed to achieve 'the gude purpose and the commune profyt of the Rewme'.[19] Richard had been made to abdicate his throne because he had not acted for the common good. It was a sentiment which would have appealed to the times. And, as archbishop Arundel said in his homily, England would now be ruled not by boys, but by men.

Richard might be said to have destroyed himself, politically at least. None the less there remained the uncomfortable fact that the new king's de facto possession of the throne was his only true claim to power. He might be the head of by far the richest family in England, happily endowed with four male heirs; he might also claim much sympathy and support as the result of Richard's illegal acts against the house of Lancaster. Yet his possession of the throne of England had stemmed from a decision to use force to secure it. Early on the young man whose right to use the title 'Prince of Wales' depended upon his acceptance, albeit tacit, of his father's act of usurpation had learned that a legal claim was always rendered stronger if military might was there to support it. As his father had done in England in 1399, so the future Henry V would do in France some twenty years later.

[19] Ibid., iii, 423.

Chapter 2

WALES

It was on the day of his father's coronation that Henry of Monmouth (or Henry de Lancaster, as he was referred to in a duchy document of 1397)[1] first stepped properly into the limelight of history. His father's new role was to bring about a radical change in the position of his children, in particular in that of his eldest son and heir. The boy had been brought back from Ireland, together with members of Richard II's chapel, by Henry Dryhurst, probably in September.[2] Now he was to take part in the ceremonies of his father's coronation. On the eve of that day the king, accompanied by his eldest son and many knights, rode through London to Westminster, where he spent the night at the abbey. The next day, 13 October 1399, had a double significance. It was the feast of St Edward the Confessor, founder of the abbey, whose shrine lay behind the high altar; it was also exactly a year to the day since the new king (or Hereford, as he had then been) had left London to go into exile, banished by the very man whom he had now deposed. As Adam of Usk was to recall, four swords were carried in procession: a sheathed one representing military power, borne by the earl of Northumberland; two covered ones representing twofold mercy, carried by the earls of Somerset and Warwick; and a fourth, unsheathed and without a point, representing the execution of justice, which was held by the king's eldest son.[3]

Two days later, on 15 October, in response to a petition laid before it, parliament agreed that Henry of Lancaster should be created Prince of Wales, Duke of Cornwall and Earl of Chester, dignities habitually conferred upon the king's eldest son. The Commons voted to accept the Prince (as he had come to be known and as we shall now call him) as his father's heir in the event of the king's death. Such decisions made it clear that the right of the house of Lancaster

---

[1] Cited by Goodman, 'John of Gaunt', p. 86, n.125.

[2] '. . . pour amesner notre trescher filz le Prince en Engleterre ovesque la chapelle de notre trescher seigneur et cousin le roy Richard que Dieux assoille' (PRO, E 404/16/394).

[3] *Chronicon Adae de Usk A.D. 1377–1421*, trans. E.M. Thompson (London, 1904), p. 187; J. Froissart, *Chroniques*, ed. K. de Lettenhove (25 vols, Brussels, 1870–77), xvi, 205; *Chronicles of London*, ed. C.L. Kingsford (Oxford, 1905), p. 49.

to the crown of England had been accepted by the Commons. Seated upon his throne in full parliament, the king placed a coronet ('un cercle') upon his son's head, put a gold ring upon his finger, gave him a golden rod, and kissed him. The duke of York then led the new Prince to the seat reserved for him by virtue of his principality.

On the following day the Prince gave his assent to the first political question formally put to him. With a large number of bishops, abbots, lords and others, he is recorded as having given his assent to the imprisonment, in secret, of the former king, Richard. On the same day, at the request of Thomas Arundel, archbishop of Canterbury, it was agreed that the Prince should be granted the title of duke of Aquitaine.[4] On 10 November the last act was played out when the king himself proposed that the title of duke of Lancaster, borne by his honourable ancestors, and with all its ancient privileges, should not be allowed to die, but should be conferred upon his eldest son, the Prince, to be borne by his heirs separately from the crown of England. With the king's agreement it was now accorded that the Prince should be known as 'Prince of Wales, duke of Aquitaine, Lancaster and Cornwall, earl of Chester, and heir apparent to the kingdom of England'.[5]

These were more than simply sources of honour granted to the king's eldest son. Great lords, in particular the heir to the throne, had to live in style, and the lordships given to them were intended to support the style which was a reflection of their position in society. Lordships required looking after, and this important task demanded the assistance of men experienced in government and administration, in particular when the lord was only in his teens.[6] Lands and titles were also a source of responsibility. If neither the duchy of Lancaster nor that of Cornwall was to be a source of political trouble to the Prince, his principality of Wales was certainly to be so, his earldom of Chester was not altogether peaceful, while the military position of Aquitaine was such that, in 1401, the possibility that the Prince might serve there was yet far from being ruled out.[7] The Prince was being asked to accept his share of the wider responsibility which his father had assumed with the crown.

[4] Trokelowe et Blaneforde, pp. 311–12; Thomas Walsingham, *Historia Anglicana, ii, 1381–1422*, ed. H.T. Riley (RS, London, 1864), p. 240. Walsingham added that the Prince was also recognized as heir to the throne. The last holder of the dukedom had been Edward, the Black Prince.

[5] *RP*, iii, 426–8. He was given only the liberties and franchises of Lancaster, not the duchy itself (Somerville, *Duchy of Lancaster*, i, 144, n.4).

[6] On 14 April 1401 'le conseil de nostre trescher filz le Prince' discussed military affairs in north Wales (PRO, E 404/16/452).

[7] M.G.A Vale, *English Gascony, 1399–1453* (London, 1970), p. 43.

It was not long before the ambiguous circumstances in which Henry had come to the throne manifested themselves all too brutally. Some undoubtedly felt that Richard II had been unjustly deposed, whilst others would try to regain for themselves rank and position lost through the former king's deposition. A group of noblemen, including the dukes of Exeter and Surrey, and the earls of Salisbury and Rutland, plotted to seize the king while he was at Windsor for the Epiphany celebrations of 1400. The plot was betrayed by Rutland, through his father, the duke of York, and by rapid action Henry IV was able to come to London, win its support and move against the rebels. The events constituted an inauspicious beginning to the reign, [8] and were to lead to an almost inevitable decision. The man in whose name the rebels had acted must be removed from the scene. Within a month or so Richard II was dead. His spirit, however, would not die so quickly, and would reappear several times to trouble the future.

Meanwhile, all was not at peace elsewhere in England. In Cheshire, a county whose loyalty to Richard II in his time of troubles had been well rewarded, supporters of the late king carried out attacks upon property and persons. On the Scottish border, too, trouble was brewing. The new king took his responsibilities towards Scotland with great seriousness, and doubtless wished to mark the start of his reign with a success against the old enemy. With this intention in mind, he organized a force which he led into southern Scotland in August 1400; but his call for the king, Robert III, and the Scottish nobility to give homage was not answered. Lacking adequate military and financial support, Henry could only withdraw across the border. The expedition into Scotland, in which the Prince and archers from Cheshire took part, was but the first organized during the reign against both Scotland and France. None was to be outstandingly successful. [9]

The main military effort of the reign was to be directed almost at once against rebellion in Wales. Such activity could not but affect the Prince closely and personally. On 19 September 1400, when the king was on his way south from Scotland, and had reached Northampton,

___

[8] In February 1400 the Prince was given several silver pieces confiscated from a rebel, Sir Thomas Shelley, who, along with others, was executed (*CPR, 1399–1401*, p. 198; *An English Chronicle of the Reigns of Richard II, Henry IV, Henry V, and Henry VI, written before the year 1471*, ed. J.S. Davies (Camden Soc., London, 1856), p. 22).

[9] A.L. Brown, 'The English Campaign in Scotland, 1400', *British Government and Administration. Studies presented to S.B. Chrimes*, ed. H. Hearder and H.R. Loyn (Cardiff, 1974), p. 46. On 1 July Henry Percy, Justiciar of Chester, wrote in the Prince's name to summon archers to resist the threatened invasion by the Scots. Men held in gaol could be released for this service (PRO, CHES 2/74, m.15d).

he heard of the rising which had begun three days earlier in north-east Wales. The reasons behind it may never be known with exactitude. It may have arisen out of a local rivalry and disagreement between Reginald, Lord Grey of Ruthin, and one of his neighbours, an important landowner, Owain Glyn Dŵr. But the fundamental causes of the rising went much deeper than that, as its ten-year duration clearly indicates.[10] National in character from its very origins, the revolt was a protest against English rule and against the lack of respect shown by the English to native Welsh leaders, as well as being an attempt to fill a 'vacuum of lordship and loyalty'[11] created, through the death of some leading marcher lords, in the preceding three years.

In the first, dramatic step towards filling that vacuum and restoring the honour of his country and countrymen, Glyn Dŵr, who was descended on both sides from distinguished princely stock, had himself proclaimed Prince of Wales on 16 September 1400, called his retainers, friends and relations together, and two days later set fire to the town of Ruthin, this act being followed by an attack on Denbigh and places in Flintshire. Moving quickly southwards, they then attacked Oswestry and Welshpool; on 24 September, however, they were met and defeated by a force raised by Hugh Burnell. Within a few days a number of captured rebels were executed. It looked as if the rebellion might already be over.

Whether, at this early stage, the troubles constituted much more than the overspill of a local quarrel, it is difficult to tell. At this point the rising may have reflected an element of sympathy for those in Cheshire (so close at hand) who had earlier expressed their protest against the new dynasty. That, indeed, may have been the reason why it was not long after the return of his father to London that the Prince travelled to Chester to make his first acquaintance with the place which, for a while, would be one of his main bases of operation. Just fourteen, he was at this time in the charge of the Northamptonshire knight, Hugh le Despenser, whom the king had appointed his governor. To help him rule his principality and county, the Prince also had a council, filled with royal nominees, while Henry Percy, the son of the earl of Northumberland, had been appointed Justiciar of Chester and north Wales on 29 October 1399, in effect becoming the chief executor of policy in that area.[12]

[10] Particularly useful are: R.R. Davies, *Conquest, Coexistence and Change. Wales, 1063–1415* (Oxford, 1987), ch. 17; 'Owain Glyn Dŵr and the Welsh Squirearchy', *Trans. Honourable Soc. of Cymmrodorion* (1968), 150–69; J.E. Lloyd, *Owen Glendower* (Oxford, 1931); E.F. Jacob, *The Fifteenth Century, 1399–1485* (Oxford, 1961), ch.2; D. Walker, *Medieval Wales* (Cambridge, 1990), ch.8.
[11] Davies, *Conquest, Coexistence and Change*, pp. 442–3.
[12] PRO, CHES 2/74, m.7.

Probably to counter the local influence of a number of people who
had been granted annuities by Richard II, and in response to a
Commons' petition that a greater proportion of Cheshire's revenue
should be made available to the Prince for the upkeep of his dignity
and estate, it was decided that those who had been released from their
debts by Richard should now be made to pay them, while annuities
granted merely under privy seal or by word of mouth, rather than by
official grant under the great seal, should be revoked.[13] Such a policy
was bound to create local hostility to the Prince. On the other hand,
it would enable the new dynasty, if it wished, to replace Ricardian
sympathizers by its own; and it certainly made good sense, in time of
uncertainty, to maximize the Prince's revenues from the area.

The king and the Prince would have to make the most of their
landed revenues; parliament had announced that it would not be
profligate with financial support. Whether it would stick to its point
would be tested if war were to occur, particularly in Wales, for which
parliament, at this moment, appeared to show scant sympathy. That
Glyn Dŵr's short-lived rising in September 1400 would probably not
be the last was apparent to those who attended parliament at Westminster in January 1401. Welsh scholars at Oxford, it was reported,
were leaving the university to return to their country, and labourers,
carrying arms, were doing the same. The Prince was asked to be
careful about any Welshman in his employment, and on 2 March
1401 he was one of those who voted that traitors should forfeit their
lands. Anti-Welsh sentiment was on the increase; parliament was at
the centre of it, urging that those who lived in the march should be
wary about the rustling of cattle by enemy sympathizers, and that
marcher lords should take steps against Welsh traitors, keeping all
castles in Wales well provisioned and at the ready.[14]

Vigilance was an ideal not always achieved. On Good Friday, 1
April 1401, as the garrison was at prayer, Conwy castle was captured
by a group of insurgents led by Gwilym and Rhys ap Tudur, who
had previously been excluded from a pardon. The English were the
undisputed April Fools of that year. The daring exploit was of some
military significance; furthermore, its psychological effect was considerable, for it served to rekindle the flame of revolt which appeared
to have been extinguished.[15] The spring and summer of 1401 witnessed increased military activity in Wales, first in the north and

[13] *RP*, iii, 441–2.
[14] See R.A. Griffiths, 'Some Partisans of Owain Glyn Dŵr at Oxford', *BBCS*, 10
(1962–64), 282–92; *RP*, iii, 457, 459, 474; PRO, CHES 2/74, m.14 (wheat from
Ireland).
[15] K. Williams-Jones, 'The Taking of Conwy Castle, 1401', *Trans. Caernarvonshire
Hist. Soc.* (1978), 7–43.

then, later, in the south. The Prince himself took part in the siege to recapture Conwy;[16] Percy was active in Merionethshire; while in late May or early June John Charlton, Lord Powys, nearly captured Glyn Dŵr, probably in central Wales. If he failed to take the arch-rebel himself, he had the satisfaction of seizing his armour and a cloth painted with maidens with red hands, as well as his assistant ('son henxman') whom, he reported to the Prince, he was sending to the king.[17]

The rebellion was spreading. In July the Prince may have returned to London, but by September he was back in Shrewsbury, not having won much support with which to resist the Welsh. With both Aberystwyth and Harlech threatened, and Glyn Dŵr now moving to the south, the king advanced into those parts,[18] while the Prince may have been among those who joined Sir Richard Aston at Harlech. By the end of the year, when the king wrote to the Prince, he had precious few successes to report, other than the capture and execution, in Hereford, of a number of rebels. More important to the Prince was the death, probably in October, of his governor, Despenser. To replace him the royal council considered four names, those of Thomas Percy, earl of Worcester, Sir Thomas Erpingham, Lord Lovell and Lord Say, all supporters of the house of Lancaster. In the end it was Worcester who was appointed.[19]

Later, on 31 March 1402, Worcester was also named king's lieutenant in south Wales (thereby making his relationship with the Prince more formal than real), while his nephew, Henry Percy, was named lieutenant in the north by the king and council.

In terms of the war against the rebels, English military effort appeared to be achieving precious little. In May 1402 Henry Percy sealed indentures with Sir John de Pullen and Sir William Stanley to serve him at sea for a fortnight. The contribution was small, yet the idea was sound, reflecting as it did an appreciation that the sea was a way of taking the rebels from the rear, as well as a means of supplying the coastal fortresses, such as Conwy, Beaumaris, Caernarfon, Harlech and Aberystwyth, should these come under attack by land. The Prince may not have been in the north-west of England in the first half of the year, the administration of his earldom being left in

---

[16] W.R.M. Griffiths, 'Prince Henry, Wales, and the Royal Exchequer', *BBCS*, 32 (1985), 202; *Chronicon Adae de Usk*, pp. 61, 226. On terms of surrender, see *PPC*, i, 145–6.

[17] '... un drape de teille, peinte des pucelles ov rouge mains, et son henxman' (*Anglo-Norman Letters and Petitions*, ed. M.D. Legge (Oxford, 1941), no.226).

[18] PRO, E 404/16/766; 17/314; *Anglo-Norman Letters*, no.227.

[19] *Anglo-Norman Letters*, no.215; *PPC*, i, 178; Trokelowe et Blaneforde, p. 361.

the hands of bishop Trevor and others.[20] In May he was probably in London to meet the ambassadors of Eric VII, king of Denmark, who had arrived to negotiate terms for a marriage between him and Henry IV's youngest child, his second daughter, Philippa, as well as the possibility of a match between the Prince and Eric's sister, Katharine. After long drawn-out negotiations, Philippa's marriage was arranged; the discussions involving the Prince were brought to an earlier, but negative, conclusion.

The Welsh war that summer was still conspicuous for its lack of success. Just as serious were the first signs of loss of confidence in the Percies, and of their growing disaffection. The Percies, it should be recalled, were the greatest family of the Scottish border region, an area where all was far from peaceful. In 1402 that border was the scene of much military activity in which Henry Percy was personally involved. His absence had the result of making the Prince a more important figure in the war against the Welsh. On 26 July, while he was at Lichfield, the king gave effective control of the march, from north to south, to the earls of Arundel and Stafford, of much of south Wales to Lord Grey of Codnor, and of the area around Welshpool, in Powys, to Edward, Lord Charlton.[21] However, a letter sent by the king to the Prince at about this time made it clear that Arundel and Stafford were to be subordinated to the Prince's command and overall view of the strategy required, and that the Prince and his council were to be responsible for formulating policy and taking the necessary decisions, the king merely asking to be informed from time to time what those decisions were.[22] At a time when the rebels were extending their area of activity to the very south of Wales, and little could be done against them, a change of approach to the rebellion was badly needed.

It was one thing to understand this. It was quite another to know what should be done and to put a new plan into effect. A start could be made over the critical matter of command. We have seen how, in the previous year, the Prince was beginning to take at least nominal charge of the Welsh operations; he now became the focus of authority for those who opposed the rebels. This was an important development which helped military efficiency by breaking down local barriers in an area of traditional loyalty to the local lord. In a real sense the English crown was playing the Welsh at their own game of filling the vacuum of loyalty which lay at the heart of the rebellion. The inden-

[20] J.E. Messham, 'The County of Flint and the Rebellion of Owen Glyndŵr in the Records of the Earldom of Chester', *Flintshire Hist. Soc. Publications*, 23 (1967–68), 4.
[21] *CPR, 1401–1405*, pp. 138–9.
[22] *Anglo-Norman Letters*, no.216.

ture system, which bound those in the Prince's service to him, gave expression to the fact that it was his cause which they were serving and his orders which they were accepting. Little by little the Prince was making a reality of the words addressed to him by his father in 1401 after the capture of Conwy castle by the Welsh, that responsibility for military success lay with him, as Prince of Wales.[23] Slowly, as he grew into his late teens, his practical ability to control the war from a position of overall command grew.[24] He would learn things which could be used against the French in later years.

The manner in which the command structure was being developed came to be seen on 1 April 1403, when a further important step was taken with the Prince's first appointment, for a period of a year, as royal lieutenant for the whole of Wales.[25] Significantly, this was followed three weeks later by his own appointment of John Trevor, bishop of St Asaph, chamberlain of Chester, and Sir William de Brereton as his lieutenants during his periods of absence, with instructions to resist and destroy the malice of the enemy.[26] The Prince was appointing lieutenants because, from now on, his chief base would no longer be Chester. As royal lieutenant in Wales, his military responsibilities would take him with growing frequency up and down the border, more often than not in a southerly direction, where the war against the Welsh was increasingly to be fought. For the moment, Chester appeared relatively safe (or so it was thought) and might be left in the hands of able and loyal lieutenants.

The move was also an attempt, at a time of growing financial stringency, to place greater responsibility for the payment of garrisons upon the Prince and his patrimony. As it was, a large proportion of his revenue was now being spent on the war.[27] Almost all that came from Chester was being turned to this purpose; the effect was to make it difficult for him to make ends meet, in particular as his revenue from the principality had dropped from about £5000 a year to almost nothing as a result of the effects of the rebellion, and he was having

[23] *Royal and Historical Letters during the Reign of Henry the Fourth*, ed. F.C. Hingeston (RS, London, 1860), i, 71–2.

[24] The point is emphasized by Davies, *Conquest, Coexistence and Change*, p. 455.

[25] PRO, E 404/18/300; Griffiths, 'Prince Henry and Wales', p. 54.

[26] PRO, CHES 2/76, m.4d.

[27] A.E. Curry, 'Cheshire and the Royal Demesne, 1399–1422', *Medieval Cheshire (Trans. Hist. Soc. Lancs & Cheshire*, 128, 1978), p. 122. On 6 November 1402 all men living in Chester holding land valued at £20 or merchants holding 100 marks (£66 13s. 4d.) of merchandise were to assume responsibility, under pain of fine of £50, for the defence of the city (PRO, CHES 2/76, m.13d.). The injunction was renewed for £20 landholders and merchants worth £40 in February 1404 (CHES 2/77, m.4d). In March 1406 archers and men-at-arms were to be raised in the county to serve against rebels (CHES 2/78, m.2.).

to rely heavily on his more buoyant revenues from the duchy of Cornwall, amounting to some £3700, to support his household.[28]

Where was the money going? The year 1403 saw not only a change of leadership, but a change of policy to go with it. The activities of the previous two years had made it clear that the manner of conducting the war through raids was inefficient and wasteful. Raids might do damage: the season's crops could be destroyed in late summer, forcing the rebels into trying to obtain provisions (and horses) for themselves from sympathizers living in Cheshire and elsewhere along the border.[29] Yet the rebels could always withdraw into the hills when the English were known to be advancing, and once they had gone, the land fell into rebel hands again until the next campaigning season, the English thereby losing the military initiative, administrative control and the ability to raise revenues. Clearly what was needed were permanent garrisons in as many places as possible, which would serve as bases from which attacks upon the rebels could be made, as well as providing forcible reminders of the presence of English lordship. The Prince was ordered to do this with 500 men-at-arms, including four barons and bannerets and twenty knights, along with 2500 archers 'bien montez'. Since his revenues had been destroyed by the war, he was to be paid £8108 2s. od. by the royal exchequer for the first quarter, 4000 marks (£2666 13s. 4d.) at once, £2738 4s. 8d. at Shrewsbury on 1 April, and the remainder (£2703 4s. od.) on the first day of the third month (1 June), once again at Shrewsbury.[30]

Garrisons, however, required permanent finance. The coastal castles of Conwy, Caernarfon, Criccieth and Harlech, for instance, had garrisons totalling 271 men (fifty-one of them being men-at-arms) and their annual cost was £2421 3s. 4d., while the revenue was only £1333 6s. 8d., leaving a deficit of £1087 16s. 8d. In addition, the chamberlain of Chester was responsible for the wages of the soldiers at Flint and Rhuddlan, which added a further £568 15s. 10d. to expenditure. In spite of such deficits, military activity in Wales could not be excluded altogether. Some raids there would have to be, such as that conducted by the Prince himself from Shrewsbury into Glyn Dŵr country in May 1403. These served to show that the English

[28] Griffiths, 'Prince Henry and Wales', p. 57.
[29] PRO, CHES 2/76, mm.8, 10; 2/77, m.4; 2/78, mm.1, 4d; *PPC*, ii, 70. This was a constant problem for the English authorities on the border with Wales.
[30] The Prince was held 'de faire une frontiere de fortz garnisons de gentz darmes et archers par entre Northgales et Southgales es lieux especifiez es dites endentures, et si bien pur estuffer les ditz garnisons come pur chivacher en dit pais de Gales sur la sauve garde dycel et iustification des rebelx que y purrient estre trovez . . .' (PRO, E 404/18/300).

were still active; they may even have deterred the Welsh from advancing into England itself, always a possibility, as had been shown by the royal licence granted to the inhabitants of Leominster in July 1402 to strengthen their defences with walls, pales and ditches against the rebels.[31] A flag-showing visit by the Prince to Harlech and Aberystwyth in May and June 1403 showed that trouble could occur almost anywhere at almost any time. It underlined, too, the importance of having access to these great castles by sea, since so much of Wales was a 'no-go' area as far as Englishmen were concerned. Yet all the time costs were mounting. In the quarter running from 17 April to 18 July 1403, the central exchequer contributed £5323 6s. 8d., and the Prince himself £1851 to the outgoings on war. During this period the king was bearing almost three-quarters of the expenses in Wales.

In the summer of 1403, however, events were to occur which made such matters pale into relative insignificance. Early in July news was brought to the king that Henry Percy and his uncle, the earl of Worcester, had raised the standard of revolt, claiming that Richard II was still alive. Their grievances against the king were numerous: not least among them was the manner in which their positions as office-holders of the crown in Wales had been diminished in the past year or so.[32] It is more than likely, indeed, that Percy was in contact with Glyn Dŵr, and it was to be recalled that two years earlier he had proposed to the king that he should try to come to terms with the Welsh leader. Now Percy and Worcester, who had gathered men from the north to support them, turned against the king. Hoping to capture the Prince in Shrewsbury, they came there quickly, but not quickly enough to beat the king in the race. Before they could be joined either by the Welsh or by supporters sent by Percy's father, the earl of Northumberland, the king forced them to battle.

On the rebel side were important contingents from Cheshire and Flintshire, where Percy influence had only recently been strong, many, no doubt, encouraged to fight in support of the erstwhile royal patron of Cheshire, Richard II, whose badge, the white hart, some wore.[33] On Saturday, 21 July, the two sides prepared for battle, although they continued to negotiate to the last.[34] The conflict itself probably began only in the late afternoon; the king's army enjoyed greater numbers, while that of the rebels was in the hands of men of greater military experience. At first the Percies appeared to have the advantage, many

[31] *CPR, 1401–1405*, p. 139.
[32] J.M.W. Bean, 'Henry IV and the Percies', *History*, 44 (1959), 212–27.
[33] *English Chronicle*, p. 28.
[34] E.J. Priestly, *The Battle of Shrewsbury, 1403* (Shrewsbury, 1979), provides a brief summary of the battle and events surrounding it.

in the royal army being killed by a large force of rebel archers. It may
have been at this time that the Prince suffered a nasty wound in
the face from an arrow; he refused, however, to leave the field.[35] A
counter-attack then took place, during which Henry Percy was killed.
His death marked the decisive moment in the battle. From the time
that the news got round, there was little doubt about the day's outcome. Many must have been killed as they tried to flee, for they were
later buried over a wide area of land. Others could not, or did not,
do so. Among them were many from Cheshire, some of them notable
members of that county's society.[36] The most famous prisoner, however, was Henry Percy's uncle, Thomas, earl of Worcester, who could
expect no mercy. Two days later, on the Monday, justice was done:
Worcester and some of his leading Cheshire supporters were publicly
executed in Shrewsbury. As a means of recompensing his son, the
king gave him all the silver vessels which had been forfeited by Worcester; in March 1404 the Prince paid £14 to a London goldsmith
'pour la faisure d'une coler de Sir Thomas de Percy' which he had
received from his father.[37] At a time when money for war was becoming increasingly scarce, such a gift might one day prove useful as a
guarantee for a loan.

The battle over, and the king now master of the situation,[38] the
Prince left the area, others assuming his responsibilities against the
Welsh.[39] It is likely that he was affected by the wound to his face,
and in the coming months he may have been in Worcestershire and
Gloucestershire, not directly involved in action against the Welsh, but
close enough if called upon in an emergency. In mid-September he
was at Kenilworth;[40] it may have been from here that he wrote to the
king asking that the men of Cheshire be formally pardoned the support which they had given the Percies, in return for a fine of 3000
marks (£2000) from the county, and from the city either a fine of £200
or the provision of ships to convey soldiers being sent to rescue the
castle of Beaumaris on Anglesey.[41] Although the fine was due to the

[35] Trokelowe et Blaneford, p. 368; Walsingham, ii, 258; *English Chronicle*, p. 29. See
R. Theodore Beck, *The Cutting Edge* (London, 1974), pp. 117–18, for the description
of an instrument devised by John Bradmore to remove an arrow head from the
Prince's cheek, a reference which I owe to Dr Carole Rawcliffe.

[36] Messham, 'County of Flint', 9 and n.2.

[37] PRO, E 404/18/598; E 101/405/1; *CPR, 1401–1405*, p. 249.

[38] On 25 July the king, then at Stratford, ordered the punishment of rebels in
Cheshire, Flintshire and Denbighshire (PRO, CHES 2/75, m.10d).

[39] On 16 September he appointed Sir John Stanley, his seneschal, to take charge
around Chester against the rebel Welsh (PRO, CHES 2/76, m.11).

[40] Ibid., m.11.

[41] PRO, CHES 2/77, m.3; W. Rees, *Calendar of Ancient Petitions relating to Wales*
(Cardiff, 1975), p. 380.

king, in the following August (1404) it was formally assigned to the Prince, together with the custody of Denbigh castle, previously granted to Henry Percy but forfeited after the battle of Shrewsbury. In the meanwhile, the Prince betook himself on pilgrimage to Canterbury and Walsingham.

Not all was yet well with the English war effort, and the years 1404 and 1405 were to be difficult ones. The king faced an acute financial crisis. Attempts to quell the Welsh rebellion had so far failed. No fully effective command structure had emerged. In the first of two parliaments held in 1404, attended by the Prince, the command against the Welsh was once again split, Thomas, earl of Arundel, being appointed to the north, Edward, duke of York, acting in the south, and the Prince being given general oversight of the war. At the end of June 1404, on the king's orders, he was in Worcester.[42] From July until late in the year he and his household (or at least part of it) were based on Hereford and Leominster, principally to keep the Welsh at bay and to guard the valley of the river Wye.[43] In November the Prince, with his brother, Thomas (both had received the commendation of parliament a month earlier), moved into south Wales and later assisted at the relief of Coety, in Glamorgan.[44]

This period may perhaps be said to mark the nadir of English fortunes in Wales. Glyn Dŵr had become strong in south Wales; while in the north bishop Trevor, chamberlain of Chester, had abandoned the English for the Welsh in the summer of 1404, his place going to Thomas Barneby.[45] We have seen how English military policy had appeared to alter during the years 1401–04. In part this reflected changing attitudes to the rebellion and, consequently, how it should be dealt with. At the beginning, in 1400 and 1401, it had seemed to be a local difficulty and, as such, the responsibility of the Prince of Wales. Writing to his son (probably in June 1401) the king had not been afraid to say as much: Conwy castle had been lost through the negligence of one of the Prince's officers, and it was the Prince's responsibility to retake it. None the less, the king did recognize the great expenses which the rebellion was causing his son, and he was willing to contribute half the costs which the recapture of Conwy would incur.[46]

The letter is important as signifying several aspects of the problem

---

[42] *PPC*, i, 229–32.
[43] The household account (PRO, E 101/405/17) refers to his 'petit hostiel'. The importance of guarding the valleys, including that of the Wye, is stressed in Griffiths, 'Prince Henry and Wales', p. 56.
[44] *RP*, iii, 547.
[45] Lloyd, *Owen Glendower*, p. 90; Messham, 'County of Flint', 18–19.
[46] *Royal and Historical Letters*, i, 71–2.

as they were seen by the early summer of 1401. The king was in
financial difficulties; parliament was unsympathetic to Wales; and
there were the competing military claims of Ireland and Scotland to
be considered. Yet the king was showing his appreciation that the
Welsh problem was growing in dimension and significance, and that,
since the principality's revenues would be the first to suffer from the
effects of rebellion, alternative means of financing the war would have
to be found. By 1402 money from the central exchequer was being
paid to the Prince for the payment of his soldiers on service in Wales.
In 1403 the appointment of the Prince as the king's lieutenant in
Wales, in addition to witnessing a growing sense of royal responsibility
for Welsh affairs, implied that the new lieutenant would draw wages
from royal resources; he also received the first quarter's wages for his
soldiers which had been promised him in his indentures. Yet, by the
summer of 1403, the moment which witnessed the revolt of the Percies,
money was becoming very short again, and it is likely that the Prince's
withdrawal from military activity that summer to some extent
reflected an inability on the part of the crown to pay him.[47]

In financial terms, the year 1404 was one of crisis. Revenue from
the principality was almost non-existent, scarcely sufficient to maintain the wages of the garrisons of some of the castles. Chester and
Flint brought in small sums, and the fine imposed upon the county
for its part in the Percy revolt would have helped; but most was spent
on the upkeep of the castles.[48] The Prince, active on the border and
the southern march, had to pay his soldiers from household funds,[49]
some of the revenue used for war coming from the estates of the duchy
of Cornwall (which were producing well in these years), some, too,
from a very heavy programme of loans incurred by the Prince at
this period.[50] Such moneys were administered by the Prince's own
household staff, some, in the form of a secret fund, by John Waterton,
while John Spenser, called 'controller of the household of the lord
Henry, Prince of Wales, assigned to pay wages of war', dealt with
this essential function through the Prince's chamber, a branch of his
household.[51] It is evident that, for the years 1403–05 at least, the war
which was a threat to the king of England's authority was largely
being paid for by moneys provided by his son. The point was made
in two letters sent by the Prince to the chancellor, Thomas Arundel,
asking him to use his influence and good offices to raise further finan-

[47] Griffiths, 'Prince Henry . . . and the Royal Exchequer', p. 208.
[48] *PPC*, i, 236.
[49] The garrison at Carmarthen was paid in kind (ibid., i, 234).
[50] Ibid., i, 237.
[51] See W.R.M. Griffiths, 'The Military Career and Affinity of Henry, Prince of
Wales, 1399–1413', (Univ. of Oxford M. Litt. thesis, 1980), pp. 119, 124–5.

cial support from the crown to support the soldiers whom he was
having to pay through his household. In the second, dated June 1404,
he emphasized that he was serving the king in Worcester and the
country around, although he had no formal indenture of service; this
was being done out of love for his father and his recognition that
the rebels must be kept out of the border counties, Herefordshire in
particular. Money had been raised by mortgaging a small silver vessel,
and by members of his council entering into bonds for their lord.[52]
This was not the way to finance a successful war.

The Prince probably spent the winter of 1404–05 in the southern
march, parliament, which had thanked him and his brother, Thomas,
for their effort, having also requested that the area and the border
counties be properly guarded.[53] We can probably date to 27 January
1405 a letter sent by the Prince to his father from Hereford in which
he reported that his spies and people of the march had informed him
that rebels were meeting at Builth in preparation for an attack on
Hereford. The dangers were only too apparent: most of the leading
members of his retinue were away in London and elsewhere at that
moment, so the county would be weak in defence if soldiers did not
come to resist and chastise the rebels.[54] Only very recently parliament
had emphasized the need to guard the Herefordshire and Shropshire
borders with special care, and the earl of Arundel and others had
been named to do this work.[55] Significant, too, was parliament's
authorization of the appointment of two treasurers for war, with the
implication that finances for the payment of forces might be forthcoming. The account roll of John Wynter, the Prince's receiver-
general, shows that between November 1404 and May 1405 he was
in receipt of £12,375, some of it for use in the south, some in the
north. 'There can be little doubt, therefore, that the appointment of
treasurers of war eased the financial situation by ensuring more regular supply.'[56]

Such a change of attitude and, above all, of practice, led almost
immediately to success. On 11 March the Prince wrote to the king
from Hereford to report the good news of a success won at Grosmont
against 8000 rebels, a victory achieved in large measure by members
of his household or others closely associated with him in the defence
of the march. Not surprisingly, the king ordered his council to inform
the city of London of the victory achieved, as the Prince had written

[52] *Anglo-Norman Letters*, nos 293, 296.
[53] *RP*, iii, 552.
[54] BL, Cotton Ms Vespasian F xiii, fo.41.
[55] *RP*, iii, 552.
[56] Griffiths, 'Prince Henry . . . and the Royal Exchequer', p. 211; B.P. Wolffe, *The Royal Demesne in English History* (London, 1971), p. 81.

to his father, not by numbers but by the hand of God. Then, early in May, Gruffydd, Glyn Dŵr's eldest son, was taken prisoner at Usk. Welsh morale, reported in February never to have been higher, must have suffered a severe dent.[57] In the north, however, matters were going less well for the English, and on 6 March the Prince was appointed lieutenant in that part at the head of 3000 men. Late in the following month he moved northwards, to take up his base once again in Chester.

Not all activity in 1405, however, was to be centred on Wales. The year was to bring further and wider developments to the story. For some time Glyn Dŵr had been in touch with the French court, in the hope of receiving help from that quarter, help which eventually came in the form of an expedition which landed in south Wales in early August. This was accompanied by a revolt in the north of England involving not only Percy, but also Richard Scrope, archbishop of York, and others. In June and July the Prince was in those parts, at Newcastle on 25 June and very likely at the siege of Berwick in the following month. Scrope was captured, tried for treason, and executed; Percy, however, escaped into Scotland. On the Welsh border a French force got almost as far as Worcester.[58] These had been months of crisis, but the king and his family survived.

The year of survival, wrote a Welsh annalist, was also the turning point.[59] In parliament the Prince was praised as a young man of 'bone coer et corage', obedient to his father's will, as good a prince as might be found anywhere, who should be thanked for his achievements against the Welsh rebels.[60] Just before Christmas, at the very end of this lengthy parliament, further steps were taken to ensure the smooth succession to the crown in the event of the king's death.[61] Nearly three years earlier, in February 1404, after the Percy conspiracy, Henry IV had been recognized as the legitimate king, and the Prince as his heir, and as recently as 7 June 1406 the entire matter had been debated and a declaration made.[62] Now the settlement of the crown was formally exemplified with a very long list of witnesses, the decision having been taken that the succession should be through the heirs general of each of the king's four sons in turn. This not only

[57] *PPC*, i, 247–50, translated in F.S. Flood, 'Prince Henry of Monmouth, his Letters and Despatches during the War in Wales, 1402–1405', *TRHistS*, new series, 4 (1889), 136–7; Lloyd, *Owen Glendower*, pp. 95–6.

[58] *Anglo-Norman Letters*, no.334.

[59] Lloyd, *Owen Glendower*, p. 152.

[60] *RP*, iii, 569, 573–4, 577. The royal council said that the Prince was now to make decisions how money allocated to Wales should be spent (*PPC*, i, 265–6).

[61] *RP*, iii, 580–3.

[62] Ibid., iii, 525, 574–6.

strengthened the dynasty by allowing daughters to succeed; it gave the king of France, with whom Henry IV was negotiating for a bride for the Prince, the assurance that any daughter born of the union would have precedence over the Prince's brothers and their sons.[63]

The year 1406 saw the Welsh revolt 'brought to a standstill'.[64] In April parliament thanked the Prince for his successes. He had been appointed his father's lieutenant in Wales for three months from 1 February, and on a number of occasions during the parliamentary sessions of that year the Speaker expressed gratitude for what he was doing in the war.[65] At the end of September 1406 terms were agreed whereby he was to continue as the king's lieutenant in Wales for a further three months with 500 men-at-arms and 1500 archers. He was to go in person against the rebels to cause them maximum hurt and, if God so willed, to conquer them. Other soldiers, 120 men-at-arms and 360 archers, were to be left in garrisons while their fellows were out on active service.[66] Whether the Prince served in person is not certain; he was present in parliament on 7 June and again in December when a petition against Lollards was presented.[67] At this time, too, he began to appear on his father's council.[68] Early in the new year of 1407 archbishop Thomas Arundel became chancellor of England for the fourth time. Among those who witnessed him take the oath of office was the Prince, now twenty years old and a military commander of growing experience.

By then, the war was certainly going in favour of the English. Not only had the Welsh revolt run out of steam, but financial reforms were also beginning to have an effect.[69] Even if there was not much money to spare, the sense of crisis hitherto found in the military organization was now being fast overcome. In May and December 1406 substantial cash payments had been made to the Prince as royal lieutenant, and the surviving evidence of payments from the exchequer for soldiers in Wales shows that these rose after 1405, almost twice as much (£47,808 1s. 1d.) being paid out in the years 1406 to 1413 as had been (£24,762 9s. 8 1/2d.) in the critical period 1401 to 1405.[70] This was done in spite of the fact that in November 1407 the

[63] Kirby, *Henry IV*, p. 205.
[64] Lloyd, *Owen Glendower*, p. 126.
[65] *RP*, iii, 569; *CPR, 1405–1408*, p. 140 (By king and council).
[66] PRO, E 404/21/310; *CPR, 1405–1408*, p. 215.
[67] *RP*, iii, 574, 583–4.
[68] J.L. Kirby, 'Councils and councillors of Henry IV, 1399–1413', *TRHistS*, fifth series, 14 (1964), 64. See also below, ch.3, n.1.
[69] *RP*, iii, 569, 580. For the restoration of authority and economic order in the earldom of Chester, see Messham, 'County of Flint', 24 seq.
[70] Calculated from Griffiths, 'Prince Henry . . . and the Royal Exchequer', pp. 214–15.

notion that the war should be the concern mainly of those who held lands in Wales or on the march had again been put forward by the Speaker, together with the plea that parliament should, in future, be discharged from the responsibility of providing money for the Welsh campaigns.[71]

However, it was not solely a question of the money supply. In the first months of 1407 the Prince appeared more than once in the royal council. On 12 May he indented to serve for six months in south Wales with 200 men-at-arms and 600 archers,[72] and by July he was before Aberystwyth, with some notable commanders, including the duke of York, the earl of Warwick, John Talbot, Lord Carew and Sir John Oldcastle in his company. On 28 June orders were issued for the conveying of cannon stones and gunpowder from the Tower of London, where they were stored, to Bristol, and then by sea into Wales, the exchequer assuming responsibility for the costs of transport.[73] However, the siege of Aberystwyth, for which they were destined, was to fail. There appear to have been divisions among the English as to the best course to follow (perhaps a sign that the Prince could not yet impose his command over others, older and more experienced than he?), so that the Prince later felt obliged to emphasize before parliament the role played there by the duke of York.[74] Nor was the artillery, brought up at the cost of so much effort, as effective as had been hoped; one cannon, the 'Messenger', exploded when it was fired.[75] Terms of surrender were reached on 12 September, according to which it was agreed that the castle would surrender if not relieved by Glyn Dŵr by 1 November.[76] That relief, in fact, did come, and the besieging force was not able to prevent the Welsh leader re-entering the castle. The English were forced to withdraw and the Prince, who was probably at Hereford by the beginning of October, went to attend parliament which met that month in Gloucester, there to be thanked for his efforts.[77]

In the first half of 1408 the Prince's household was based on a number of places, none of them far from the Welsh border.[78] We

---

[71] *RP*, iii, 610.
[72] PRO, E 404/22/503; WAM, no.12230. The indenture was sealed with the council's approval.
[73] PRO, E 404/22/551.
[74] *RP*, iii, 611–12.
[75] R.A. Griffith, *Boroughs of Medieval Wales* (Cardiff, 1978), p. 31.
[76] Lloyd, *Owen Glendower*, pp. 130–3; text in *Foedera*, IV, i, 120, and *St Albans Chronicle, 1406–20*, ed. V.H. Galbraith (Oxford, 1937), pp. 22–7.
[77] PRO, E 101/405/17; *RP*, iii, 611–12.
[78] The Prince appeared at Pershore, Kenilworth, Worcester, Bromyard and Hereford between Christmas 1407 and May 1408 (PRO, E 101/405/17).

cannot be certain that the Prince always remained with his household; it is likely, for instance, that he was in Yorkshire, on pilgrimage to Beverley and Bridlington, in May.[79] But the king and his council must have felt that victory was within their grasp. In October 1407, and again in February 1408, money, some of it originally earmarked for use in Aquitaine, was provided for the garrison at Strata Florida, some fifteen miles to the south-east of Aberystwyth, while on 8 March 1408 the Prince again agreed to serve in Wales for a period of six months beginning on 1 April, with 500 men-at-arms and 1500 archers.[80] The funds from which he and his men were to be paid were to come in large measure from clerical and lay taxation to be raised in April and May. Any surplus was to be used on artillery, cannon stones, saltpetre and gunpowder, and on making artillery usable. This time efforts against Aberystwyth were successful. The capture of Harlech, which followed, took considerably longer. Money owed to the Prince to pay his besieging force, which included 'canoners et autres artificers', was being paid in February 1409, when the siege was thought, by those in London, to be still in progress.[81]

With the loss of these two fortresses, Glyn Dŵr's cause was doomed. His wife, children and grandchildren fell into English hands and were taken to London, where some of them had died by the early months of the next reign. Glyn Dŵr himself escaped, leaving behind him little hope that his cause would progress any further. In 1410 (in all probability) he made a final attempt with an unsuccessful raid on the border of Shropshire.[82] In 1412, in one of the last references we have to him, Glyn Dŵr was holding prisoner Dafydd Gam of Brecon, whose release was eventually secured and who would one day achieve fame at Agincourt.[83] The revolt which had come in with a bang 'simply petered out',[84] although Glyn Dŵr became the subject of legends and prophecies. As late as mid-July 1415, when he was about to embark on his first expedition to France, Henry made one last attempt to come to terms with the old rebel: Sir Gilbert Talbot was empowered to offer him a pardon. Henry could do this from a position of strength, but his intentions came to nothing, for Glyn Dŵr could be neither

[79] St John of Bridlington was the Prince's special patron (*St Albans Chronicle*, p. 25). In his will Thomas, earl of Arundel (d.1415), recalled that he had been to Bridlington with the Prince before his accession and that he, Arundel, had undertaken either to visit the place or to pay 5 marks every year. (*The Register of Henry Chichele, Archbishop of Canterbury, 1414–1443*, ed. E.F. Jacob (C&YS, 4 vols, Oxford, 1938–47), ii, 74.)
[80] PRO, E 404/23/109–11, 235, 310.
[81] PRO, E 404/24/231, 275.
[82] Lloyd, *Owen Glendower*, pp. 141–2, 153–4.
[83] *CPR, 1408–1413*, p. 406; *St Albans Chronicle*, pp. 61, 67.
[84] Davies, *Conquest, Coexistence and Change*, p. 447.

found nor drawn. He had, in effect, disappeared; in all likelihood, he died shortly afterwards, perhaps in September of that year. His burial place remains, to this day, unknown.[85]

The outbreak of the Welsh revolt in 1400 had coincided almost exactly with the Prince's fourteenth birthday. It was to occupy him, to a greater or lesser degree, for almost a decade, and may thus be said to have been one of the formative influences upon his development as a young man, and upon the way in which he was to face up to and tackle problems in the future, when he would be king of England. In what ways was this so? As Prince, he was responsible for that part of Wales which formed his principality, and indeed for that which formed the march. His personal interest in the first (which included Flintshire, Anglesey, Caernarfonshire, Merioneth in north Wales, with Cardiganshire and Carmarthenshire in south Wales) is easily understood. As Prince of Wales (a title which went back to 1301) he held no sinecure and, as both his father and parliament were to remind him on more than one occasion, he had the responsibility to rule these counties, at least in time of peace, from the revenues of his principality. What Glyn Dŵr's revolt did was to deprive him of effective authority within those parts and of the means, in terms of both manpower and financial support, to re-establish himself as Prince and to reassert the authority of the English crown in areas which had supported the rebellion. For the Prince the significance of this war was that he was fighting to regain his patrimony, granted him in October 1399, from the control of 'rebels'.[86] The use of this word is not insignificant; it would be used freely only a few years later to describe those who opposed English rule in Normandy and in other parts of France. As Prince, and later as king, Henry spent much of his time in conflict with those who opposed him. Conflict was to be a determining factor in his career and in the formation of his character.

As earl of Chester Henry was also responsible for a county which had been much favoured by Richard II and which, as the troubles of 1400 and the Percy rising of 1403 showed, was still far from loyal to the house of Lancaster. However, with the defeat of the Percies in 1403, political life in the county became more settled. In the years to come the county was to play an important role in supplying money and men for war; money principally for the garrisons of north Wales, men both for garrison service and more active warfare against rebels

---

[85] *CPR, 1413–1416*, pp. 342, 404; *CPR, 1416–1422*, pp. 89, 335; J. Beverley Smith, 'The last Phase of the Glyndŵr Rebellion', *BBCS*, 22 (1968), 250–60; J.R.S. Phillips, 'When did Owain Glyndŵr die?', ibid., 24 (1970–72), 59–76.

[86] E.g., BL, Cotton Ms Vespasian F xiii, fo.41; PRO, E 404/16/766; 17/282; 18/300; *Anglo-Norman Letters*, nos 216, 227, 296.

all over Wales. Along with Lancashire and Derbyshire, Cheshire provided a large number of the soldiers who served in north Wales in these years, as well as in France in the years to come.

More immediately, the scene of the war moved to south Wales, thereby involving the Prince increasingly in the defence not only of his principality but in that of the march, too. In this large area of southern and eastern Wales, English influence was stronger. In the towns in particular, the burgesses played an important role (just as parliament had urged them to do) in the defence of the English cause and interest, especially in those places where loyalty was suspect. The need to help in that defence was now better understood by those English lords who held substantial lands in those parts of Wales. Since marcher revenues could be considerable, certain of them had a direct interest in safeguarding parts of their larger patrimonies threatened or, as was sometimes the case, controlled by the Welsh. In this they made common cause with the Prince. So it was that members of several great English families found themselves fighting on the march, and doing so not only for the king or the Prince, but for themselves, too. The frequent parliamentary appeals for direct military aid and action from those families were finally being answered.[87]

In addition we should recognize those closely associated with the Prince, some as annuitants, others as recipients of fees for offices performed within the household or administration, men who helped to create a coterie known personally to him within the force which he was leading, many of whom were present when the terms for the surrender of Aberystwyth were drawn up before the town on 12 September 1407.[88] The Welsh rebellion had an important effect in the manner in which it united men from different groups and different localities around the persons of the king and the Prince. John of Gaunt, it has been observed, had encouraged continuity of service by maintaining and strengthening family bonds among those who served him.[89] As king, Henry IV continued to employ men who had already served him as earl of Derby or duke of Hereford, some of whom belonged to families whose members had been in Gaunt's service. The young Prince followed this tradition. The list of those in his service in Wales in the second quarter of 1403 (which finished with the Percy rebellion) shows how the lands of which he was lord

[87] Ibid., iii, 501 (1402), 552 (1404).
[88] They included Richard Beauchamp, John Talbot, Thomas, Lord Carew, and Sir John Oldcastle (*St Albans Chronicle*, p. 23).
[89] A. Goodman, 'John of Gaunt: Paradigm of the late Fourteenth-Century Crisis', *TRHistS*, 5th series, 37 (1987), 136–8. The point is underlined by S. Walker, *The Lancastrian Affinity, 1361–1399* (Oxford, 1990)

provided him with a supply of men who were ready to join him in war. John Chetwynd received an annuity from Henry IV from the duchy of Lancaster and a fee from the Prince as duke of Cornwall; while John Waterton was both an annuitant and a feed man of the duchy of Cornwall.[90] John Stanley was a Cheshire knight loyal to the Prince, who was later to appoint him Lord of Man; while Sir Thomas Tunstall, Sir William Harrington and Hugh Standish were among those from the duchy of Lancaster who were with the Prince that summer.[91] As already noted, Shropshire and Herefordshire, counties which stood to suffer more than most from the threat of Welsh incursions, provided the Prince with a number of followers, notable among whom was Sir John Oldcastle,[92] who was an annuitant of the duchy of Lancaster in Henry IV's reign. A close study of those in the Prince's service would show that the war was the cause for the entry of many into that service, as well as the reason for them remaining in it. It tells us something about the Prince that from an early age he liked soldiers whose loyalty he was ready to reward.

What military lessons may the Prince have learned from these formative years as a young soldier and leader of men? We may think that he had come to appreciate the importance of the control of fortified towns and castles. The great Edwardian strongholds of Beaumaris, Conwy and Harlech were not merely prestigious symbols of authority, against whose loss the English should beware and whose capture a Welsh annalist could record with pride.[93] To both sides they were effective instruments of power, not least in the way in which, when linked to the use of ships, they enabled men, provisions and equipment to be brought, in the case of the English, from Bristol or Chester, or, on behalf of the Welsh, from other parts of Wales or, even, from France. The importance placed upon keeping these great castles in loyal hands shows how clearly Henry IV's advisers appreciated the practical value to the English cause of retaining control of them: the large ones were significant for the garrisons which they might contain; the smaller ones, situated mainly inland, could act as sally points from which rebel lands might be controlled or their forces obliged to come to action. In both cases it was essential to deny use of these castles to the enemy, to give him no vantage point, and to keep him, as far as possible, on the run. The failure, up to 1403, fully to appreciate that Wales could not be subdued from the English border was to be rectified by a conscious attempt to regain and main-

[90] PRO, DL 42/16; DCO, Rolls Series, 94/201.
[91] PRO, E 101/404/24, fos 4–11v.
[92] PRO, DL 42/16.
[93] Lloyd, *Owen Glendower*, p. 152.

tain control of strongholds in both the march and the principality. The Prince appears to have understood the significance of this major change of policy.

The need to uphold the English presence in the Welsh strongholds, once these had been taken, was to place emphasis upon the siege as an essential part of the war's strategy. What the English were aiming to achieve was not only military control but political dominance as well. This could never be done if, for example, the town and castle of Caernarfon, the administrative and judicial centre of the northern principality, were to be lost to the rebels. The uprising was given a boost in 1401 when the castle of Conwy was seized from English control under the very noses of its garrison. Likewise, however, once Aberystwyth and Harlech had capitulated to the English, the uprising was to come to a virtual end. Both in 1401 and in 1407/8 the Prince was to be involved in those actions which led to the recapture of Conwy and Aberystwyth by the English. From these he would have learned both the military and the political importance of being able to bring sieges to a successful conclusion.[94]

Siege warfare was associated with two further factors of relevance: the use of specialist weapons (with which, it may be noted, the Welsh were ill-provided)[95] and the vital necessity of keeping the besiegers supplied with food and other forms of provisioning and equipment which they required. The military accounts for the war show that the period of conflict witnessed a considerable increase in the use of cannon of different kinds and its accompanying requirements: cannon stones, saltpetre and gunpowder. The transport of these was difficult and dangerous, and this in turn was to lead to growing importance being attached to controlling the means of access for this cumbersome weaponry, much of which had begun its journey to destination from the Tower of London. The principal lesson to be learned was that the sea provided the easiest and safest method of access to the Edwardian castles; weapons might be taken by road from London to Bristol, but would then be put aboard ship to be conveyed to the appropriate places in Wales which, in 1407 and 1408, were Aberystwyth and Harlech. Likewise it would be wrong to ignore the significance of the rivers and their valleys (such as those of Wye and Usk) as means of access into Wales, but equally as roads along which rebels might travel to attack the border shires. In terms of their ability to help or hinder movement of soldiers inland, the control of castles on these rivers was also of great importance. The Prince would have learned that control of the means of access (and even withdrawal), whether by

[94] D. Seward, *Henry V as Warlord* (London, 1987), p. 25.
[95] Davies, *Conquest, Coexistence and Change*, pp. 454–5.

land or by sea, was a factor upon which victory in some considerable measure depended.

The war would have taught him yet another lesson. The main problem faced by the Prince in these years was that of securing regular amounts of money to pay his men's wages and other military expenses. He was to take practical steps to overcome these difficulties: the creation of his private treasure, kept by John Waterton, was one such. What it taught him was that a measure of planned finance was a necessary prerequisite of a successfully waged war and of effective government. The difficulties which confronted him as Prince, and to which solutions were found, were to have an influence upon his approach to government when he took over control of it later in his father's reign, and upon his way of organizing war against the French once he had become king. The Welsh experience had been a valuable one.[96]

[96] Griffiths, 'Prince Henry and Wales', pp. 57–60.

Chapter 3

THE PRINCE IN
GOVERNMENT, 1406–13

Wales was not to be the Prince's sole concern. By 1406, aged twenty and with considerable experience of war and decision-making already behind him, he was ready to take part in the more routine activities of government. The parliament of 1406, which, with two adjournments, lasted from March to December, found itself in dispute with the king over the twin matters of membership of his council (should the king be forced to reveal the names of those whom he consulted over questions of policy?) and the voting of subsidies to carry out government, not least the war against the Welsh. In May the names of seventeen councillors were made known. Later in the year, in November, a new council was nominated, this time sixteen in number. In the following month a third list was published. This one contained the names of twelve men who swore to observe thirty-one articles which set out what were, in effect, instructions for their conduct, attendance and responsibilities. The aim of these measures (a sign that parliament did not fully trust the king?) was the establishment of good governance, the king having to undertake (for that is what the oath taken by his councillors implied) to rule with the advice of a known group of men according to principles of responsible government set out by parliament. Having achieved this notable victory, parliament voted the subsidy which the king needed.

It was in December 1406, at the latest, that the Prince began his service as a regular member of his father's council.[1] The body which he was joining was a very different one from that which the king had consulted in previous years. Those who took the oath on 22 December constituted what was essentially an aristocratic council,[2] a number of knights appointed as recently as November being unceremoniously dropped, although not for the reason that they were out of favour.[3]

[1] A list of those present at the council held at Hereford on 4 September 1405 begins with the Prince's name (misplaced: now PRO, C 81/1542/41).
[2] P. McNiven, 'Political developments in the second half of the reign of Henry IV, 1405–13' (Univ. of Manchester Ph.D. thesis, 1977), p. 231.
[3] A.L. Brown, 'The Commons and the Council in the Reign of Henry IV', *EHR*, 79 (1964), 25.

Furthermore, it appears that the king's ability to seek advice from persons neither recognized nor, in the case of a number of them, paid as members of his council was curtailed by the disappearance of 'fringe' members from conciliar meetings.

What was happening, and what clearly pleased the Commons, was that those responsible for advising the king were, to a man, persons of substance and background, one of them being the heir to the throne. Two men were now to dominate the council. One was the Prince who, in 1407, was present at about two-thirds of its known meetings, and attended even more frequently in 1408 and 1409, his increasingly regular attendances reflecting the welcome fact that his presence in Wales was required less and less.[4] The other was Thomas Arundel, archbishop of Canterbury, who, having served Richard II three times as chancellor, accepted the seals of office on 30 January 1407 at a ceremony which the Prince himself attended. It has been traditional to see these men as rivals, but, at this stage at least, nothing was further from the truth. Until 1409, in all probability, the Prince was concerned with affairs in Wales; Arundel, whose presence in his see meant that he was never very far from London, saw to matters of 'bone et substanciall gouvernance'.

In the context of the reign of Henry IV this phrase constituted a request for responsible government, in which special attention should be paid to financial considerations. For a few years the problems of the government of England were to be dominated by a search for means of re-establishing the effective control of the crown over expenditure, which had to be organized and overseen in a manner which lived up to the call for responsible government. In this situation two not necessarily contradictory influences were at work. There was the natural anxiety of the Prince, starved of funds with which to wage the war against the Welsh, to ensure, now that he was a leading member of the king's council, that money in sufficient quantity to meet his military needs should be diverted in his direction, all the more so as the resistance of the rebels seemed on the point of being broken by 1407. On the other hand, the inclination of the council's most regular member, the chancellor, Arundel, may have been to exercise greater restraint over spending, for he would have recognized that the goodwill of parliament depended upon evident signs that money made available to the king should be spent with a sense of responsibility.

There was, furthermore, a limit to what could be spent. The parliament of 1406, having wrung concessions about membership of the

---

[4] T.E.F. Wright, 'Royal finance in the latter part of the reign of Henry IV of England, 1406–13' (Univ. of Oxford D.Phil. thesis, 1984), p. 113.

council from the king, voted only 'a modest supply' of a single tenth and fifteenth.[5] It is not unlikely, too, that the spirit of economy was intended to be enforced through the appointment of Sir John Tiptoft, the Speaker of the very same parliament and a member of the royal household since early in the reign, as treasurer of that household in December 1406. There was no question of the king being made to accept a man who was hostile to him: indeed the opposite was probably the case. But the household had been prominent in the minds of those who had criticized excessive and unnecessary royal expenditure in the past, and the appointment of the man who had spoken up for parliament in these – and other – matters suggested that days of relative austerity were not far away. It is evident that, under Arundel (in particular) and the Prince, much time was spent by members of the council in the regulation of financial affairs, and that the council imposed its will increasingly upon the exchequer, at the same time making inroads into the financial independence of the king and his household.[6] That the policy was making a favourable impression in parliament seems likely: the parliament which met at Gloucester in October 1407 made increased provision for government, in addition to taxes on skins, wool and wine which were allowed for the defence of the sea and trade.[7]

The fact that no parliament met until January 1410 (a period of just over two years) suggests that the council's careful control of the finances was working sufficiently well to make the summons of another parliament unnecessary. Certainly the long gap between parliaments was giving government by council a chance, a chance which was to be accentuated by the near-fatal illness of the king in the winter of 1408–09, when, seemingly on the point of death, he hurriedly made his will. It was evident that, in the circumstances, the council was bound to have to take on more and more of the decision-making and policy-fixing of everyday government. Circumstances, as much as anything else, pushed the Prince, now freed from his military commitments in Wales, to the fore, and gave him a valuable practical lesson, before his time, of the problems faced by those in authority.

Is it possible that the power which he thus came to wield gave the Prince a desire to exercise it yet further? By 1409 he was well into his twenties, and he had, at last, almost put down the rebellion in Wales. Whether, by this time, he was still getting on well with his main partner in government, the chancellor, Arundel, may be open to

---

[5] J.S. Roskell, *The Commons and their Speakers in English Parliaments, 1376–1523* (Manchester, 1965), pp. 147–8.

[6] Wright, 'Royal finance', p. 322.

[7] *RP*, iii, 612.

question. At first, after they had been given power early in 1407, the two had worked in tandem, each doing what he was best at. Yet from very early days there were signs that the Prince was bringing forward and encouraging members of his family: John Beaufort, earl of Somerset; Henry Beaufort, bishop of Lincoln from 1398 to 1404 and now bishop of Winchester, who had been chancellor from February 1403 to March 1405; and Thomas Beaufort, who was to be chancellor later in the reign. All three were the king's half-brothers, their mother being Katherine Swynford, John of Gaunt's third wife. In February 1407 their legitimation was confirmed by the king, but a clause excluding them from claiming the crown ('excepta dignitate regali') was added, as many believed, at the request of Arundel, who thus lost their friendship. Certainly Henry Beaufort attended the council fairly regularly between 1407 and 1409 (more often indeed than the Prince), and John Beaufort was not far behind.[8] Notable, too, as a sign of the rising influence of the Prince and his Beaufort supporters, was the election of Thomas Chaucer as Speaker of the last three Parliaments of the reign (1407, 1410, 1411). As a son of the poet he merited a certain claim to fame; but it is more important in this context to appreciate that, through his mother, Philippa Roet, sister to Katherine Swynford, he was a first cousin to the Beauforts and their natural political ally. The links of family were thus being built up in favour of the Prince.

   This was of great importance for him since certain differences may have made a good working relationship with archbishop Arundel difficult to achieve. There was, for instance, a generation gap between the two men. Arundel, more than thirty years older than the Prince, had already been Richard II's chancellor for almost a year before Mary Bohun had borne her first surviving son at Monmouth. Furthermore there may have been differences of emphasis over the financial policy to be pursued after 1407, although these were not significant. Yet we should not hasten to regard the king and the archbishop as natural allies against the Prince. Although three times chancellor under Richard II, Arundel had had to wait seven years before Henry IV had called him to assume that office again. This may have been because he had not always shown himself to be a strong supporter of the king. It is possible, too, that Henry may not have fully appreciated that the archbishop's restrictive financial practices were being pursued in the best interests of the crown. We cannot ignore the fact that, by the end of 1409, Arundel may not have been high in the royal favour.

   The changes in the council which occurred in the last days of 1409

---

[8] Kirby, 'Councils and councillors', 64.

and the early days of 1410 have never been satisfactorily explained. Yet we may be reasonably sure that they would not have happened without the acquiescence of the king, now back in at least reasonable health, but still lacking the energy to resist the taking over of power by his son. [9] The king may have been resentful of the restrictions thus placed upon him, while the Prince may have found his activities in Wales in 1409 curtailed by lack of money, thus making him, in this, his father's natural ally. May one conclude that the immediate cause of the 'crisis' was financial, perhaps a demand from the king, backed by the Prince, that more money be made available for government and war? On 21 December 1409 Arundel, having lost the confidence of his royal master, was relieved of his office. [10]

Personality and differences over policy lay behind the changes brought about at this time. These factors probably explain the delay of about five weeks or more before a new chancellor, approved by the king, could be named. The post went not to bishop Henry Beaufort, who had already held it between 1403 and 1405, but to his able younger brother, Thomas, who thus entered the council for the first time. The Prince, with his Beaufort allies (both of whom were to serve him faithfully when he became king), had secured the effective reins of power.

That power was to be exercised for a period of almost two years, during which time relations between the Prince and his father appear to have remained outwardly cordial. The immediate concern was a meeting of a new parliament, originally summoned to meet in Bristol only to have its venue changed to Westminster at the last moment. When it met, Thomas Beaufort had not yet been appointed chancellor, and the task of making the opening address, which would normally have fallen to him, had to be carried out by his brother, the bishop of Winchester. Taking as his theme the necessity to make England a land of justice, he stressed the need for the law to be obeyed by all, for the Church to be maintained in her liberties, and for the kingdom to live in harmony under the rule of a king who was loved and respected by his people. The major danger to the country's security was presented by the duke of Burgundy who, having control of the government of France, was threatening Calais, England's outpost over the Channel. What was required was financial aid, in return for which Beaufort promised good government. [11] On the following day, 28 January, the Commons elected Thomas Chaucer as their Speaker,

[9] P. McNiven, 'The problem of Henry IV's health, 1405–1413', *EHR*, 100 (1985), 763–4.
[10] Wright, 'Royal finance', pp. 196, 200.
[11] *RP*, iii, 622.

a choice which must have given satisfaction to the Prince and his friends.

The formal record of this parliament reveals something of what was in the minds of those present. Petitions refer to the need of achieving 'bone et substanciall gouvernance'.[12] In part, this referred to the desire that the borders with Scotland and Wales be properly guarded by those with local territorial responsibilities,[13] in part that riots and acts of violence within England be controlled. The need for proper defence of England's maritime interests was also emphasized. But it is clear, too, that the Commons were particularly concerned with financial matters, and for the king to live within his means. A demand was made that all with military responsibilities in Calais, Guyenne and Ireland should reside there and fulfil their obligations without further payment, thereby helping to cut down costs. Furthermore, lands which came into the king's hands should not be granted away, but their revenues more appropriately used to support the king's household, while sums voted for defence and war should be spent for that purpose, and that purpose alone.[14]

In almost every case the demands of the petition were met. This was not a sign of weakness. Rather, it was a recognition that what was now being sought, in the aftermath of the campaigns in Wales, was a greater degree of local responsibility for the defence of the marches, that those who had benefited from the royal bounty in the past owed something to the defence of the realm. The Prince could claim to have given his country value for money in terms of his personal commitment to the war in Wales; his brother, John, could say the same of his activity on the Scottish border.[15] The curious entry in the parliamentary record underlines the feeling that the king's second son, Thomas, was not really pulling his weight.[16] Such inactivity could bring only discredit upon the crown. The call was clearly one for all, in particular those holding office from the crown, to accept their responsibilities.

Behind the responses 'Le roy le voet' and 'Le roy soy voet adviser' lay, in all probability, the voice of the Prince and the council.[17] In the parliament of 1410, following the precedent of 1407, the king was

[12] Ibid., iii, 623, 624.
[13] See above, p. 35 (for Wales); RP, iii, 474, 624.
[14] RP, iii, 624–5.
[15] E.C. Williams, My Lord of Bedford, 1389–1435 (London, 1963), ch.3; S.B. Chrimes, 'Some letters of John of Lancaster as Warden of the East Marches towards Scotland, 1399–1412', Speculum, 14 (1939), 3–27.
[16] RP,iii, 625; PPC, i, 313–17.
[17] RP, iii, 632, 626.

asked to name those who formed this body. On 2 May he did so.[18] At the head of the list was the Prince, followed by three bishops: Henry Beaufort of Winchester (his uncle); Thomas Langley of Durham (both of whom had already acted as chancellor earlier in the reign, and doubtless enjoyed the personal confidence of the king); and Nicholas Bubwith of Bath and Wells, together with four nobles: Thomas, earl of Arundel (who had given the Prince much assistance in the war against the Welsh, and had sealed indentures of service for life with him in February 1408);[19] Ralph Neville, earl of Westmorland, brother-in-law to the Beauforts; Hugh, Lord Burnell (who had served in Wales and had been close to the centres of power as a councillor since 1405); and Henry, Lord Scrope, the treasurer. A week later it was announced that Langley and Westmorland, whose commitments took them to the north of England, were to be replaced by Henry Chichele, bishop of St David's, and Richard Beauchamp, earl of Warwick, both relative newcomers to this kind of work.[20] Such were the men who, under the leadership of the Prince, were nominated by the king to advise him and, in effect, to see to the everyday government of England, a task which they swore to accomplish but only on condition, as the Prince specifically set out, that money should be made available by parliament for the completion of this work.[21] If it were not, he said, they reserved the right to resign at the end of the current parliament.

What were the responsibilities of this newly formed body? The record describes them as the king's 'continual council',[22] appointed to carry out the decisions made in parliament, provided that the necessary financial backing was given them. They were to take an oath in parliament undertaking to give the king good and impartial advice, free of all favour, in the search for 'good and effective rule, along with the good of the king and the kingdom'.[23] Baldwin suggested that they took their oaths and received their commissions 'in a manner suggesting their responsibility to parliament'.[24] Was this an attempt to make the council, as a body, assume responsibilities which would only be broken if parliament failed to provide financial

[18] Ibid., iii, 632.
[19] PRO, CHES 2/79, m.3.
[20] *RP*, iii, 634.
[21] '. . . Le Prince . . . pria de leur avoir pur excusez en cas que ne pourroit estre trovez de quoi pur supporter les charges necessairs' (ibid., iii, 632).
[22] 'consail continuel' (ibid., iii, 632).
[23] 'bone & substanciall Gouvernance, & la Bien de Roy & de Roialme' (ibid., iii, 623).
[24] J.F. Baldwin, *The King's Council in England during the Middle Ages* (Oxford, 1913), p. 162.

support?' Or was it simply an attempt to get the lords to attend more regularly?[25] In all likelihood the oath was a more general one, given to the king, from which the Prince was exempted, 'because of the highness and excellence of his honourable person'.[26] None the less, the position of the Prince and the council remained ambiguous: to whom, in the final analysis, were they responsible? Two years later the king would give his answer to the question.

The new council of 1410–11 was entirely noble and clerical; the knights and courtiers had been carefully omitted. It was an experienced, active and united body of men (some having seen service in Wales) whom the Prince had around him, even more partisan towards him after bishop Henry Chichele and Richard, earl of Warwick, had been added to its number.[27] What was to be its policy? Reform, certainly. Yet, at the same time, as bishop Beaufort's opening speech in January made clear, rising expenses could scarcely be avoided when the country was threatened from outside. Parliament was expected to provide. On its part, the council was sympathetic to the desire for harmonious relations between king and people, and between the people themselves.

In all this, it was recognized that the tone of petitions submitted by the Commons was critical of the organization of the royal finances and, principally, of the king's household. Yet the subsidy voted on 8 May 1410, although seemingly adequate, was in fact less than so since the last of the three equal parts into which it was divided was not to be raised until the autumn of 1412, some two and a half years later. Such limitations, which would force the council to look very closely at all expenditure, were bound to lead to a drive not only for economies, but for efficiency as well.[28] Savings were one thing, and could be achieved (as they were) by imposing restrictions upon the payment of annuities by the crown in 1410 and 1411. Efficiency in matters of finance was another. One step towards its achievement was the establishment of priorities, and this involved the making of political decisions. The guarding of the sea (the subject of a Commons' petition in 1410) was at first placed low on the list;[29] some money was spent on Scotland and Ireland, and considerable sums on the army in Wales,[30] while French pressure upon Guyenne was to elicit a sizeable financial commitment for defence. The threat to Calais was that which

[25] Ibid., p. 101.
[26] '. . . a cause del hautesse & excellence de son honurable persone' (RP, iii, 632).
[27] Baldwin, King's Council, p. 162.
[28] Wright, 'Royal finance', p. 203 seq.
[29] See, however, PPC, i, 346–7; ii, 17.
[30] Griffiths, 'Prince Henry . . . and the Royal Exchequer', p. 215; PPC, i, 338–9; ii, 14, 38; PRO, E 404/25/381.

was taken most seriously of all, the appointment of the Prince as captain in March 1410 probably having much to do with that decision. Financial planning, with estimates looking further into the future, and the cutting of the costs of government (which were already falling), meant that government was being tailored to the availability of financial resources to support it.

Surviving records are instructive about conciliar activity at this time. Between January 1410 and December 1411 fourteen meetings are recorded, at all of which the Prince was present.[31] It is evident that financial matters were among the council's top priorities:[32] the payments of money for the keeping of the sea and the defence of Wales, the Scottish border and Guyenne; the answering of a petition from Thomas, duke of Clarence, for money due to him for Ireland and Guines; the guaranteeing of loans made by bishop Bubwith, the earl of Warwick, Lord Scrope and the Prince's grandmother, the countess of Hereford; while on 29 July 1410 decisions had to be taken on the value of the coinage.[33] It is clear that the king was not receiving in revenue as much as his council thought he needed. The difficulties faced by the council were symbolized by what may have been an ill-advised request that the crown should receive a clerical tenth and a fifteenth from the laity every year irrespective of whether parliament met or not.[34] Thomas Walsingham, the monk of St Albans who reported this, had little sympathy for the scheme. And when parliament made its financial grant to the king that year, it did so, he reported, rather grudgingly.

The re-establishment of the king's finances was the single most important problem which faced the Prince and his fellow councillors in 1410 and 1411. But in 1411 a second problem, already foreseen in bishop Beaufort's speech before parliament in the first days of 1410, was to assume growing significance: relations with the kingdom of France and, in particular, with the main factions struggling for supremacy within that country. Ever since the last years of the fourteenth century France, ruled by Charles VI, a king prone to periods of mental instability, had been the prey of factions which, by the early years of the new century, centred on the leaders of two of the greatest princely houses in the land, those of Burgundy and Orléans, the latter being linked by marriage to that of Armagnac, by whose name it was often known. In 1407 John, duke of Burgundy, had plotted the murder

---

[31] His appointment as royal lieutenant in Wales, on 19 June 1410, was largely formal (*CPR, 1408–1413*, p. 202). See also Kirby, 'Councils and councillors', 65.

[32] McNiven, 'Political developments', pp. 595–6.

[33] *PPC*, i, 346–7, 339–46, 347–9, 349–51.

[34] '. . . sine Parliamento tenendo' (Walsingham, ii, 283).

of Louis, duke of Orléans, in the streets of Paris, and the political rivalry between the two houses had been intensified by the personal hatred which the assassination had caused between John of Burgundy, Charles, the new duke of Orléans, and his three main allies, the dukes of Berry, Bourbon and Alençon. Murder, it must be recognized, had given Burgundy power: it was he who controlled Paris and the main policy-making organs of the French state. In 1411, however, the opposition to him began to assume considerable proportions, with military attacks upon his main sphere of influence, the area which lay to the north-east of Paris, stretching a 100 miles or more from the capital. To meet the threat, Burgundy sought the help of allies.

In July 1411 the first approach was made to the king by ducal envoys. According to one chronicler, when they asked the king for help against the duke of Orléans it was not accorded: only when they approached the Prince was it decided to give a favourable response, and to consider the possibility of an alliance with Burgundy.[35] In return, duke John offered the possibility of a marriage between his fifth daughter, Anne, and the Prince. In certain respects, such an alliance made sense. Burgundy was, if not the undisputed master of France, at least the most politically powerful of the royal princes; an alliance with the effective ruler of Flanders might help resolve the commercial disputes between Flemish interests and their English counterparts which had sometimes led to violent incidents and much mutual recrimination over the past years. Furthermore, as warden of the Cinque Ports and constable of Dover since 1409, and now as captain of Calais, the Prince may have preferred to have the duke of Burgundy as an ally rather than as an enemy, for his threat to the English enclave could be menacing and expensive to oppose.

But these were not the only factors to be considered in deciding where England's best interests lay. Both the king and the Prince were anxious to pursue the fulfilment by the French of the terms of the treaty of Brétigny of 1360 by which France had conceded Aquitaine in full sovereignty on condition that the king of England should abandon his claim to the crown of France. The emphasis on the narrower question of Aquitaine, rather than that of the English claim to the whole kingdom of France, was one shared by father and son not, as has sometimes been alleged, one which divided them.[36] With this aim in mind, negotiations were also held with Berry in 1411. Both sides expressed a desire for peace, which might last for a period of years.

---

[35] *Chronicle of London from 1089 to 1483*, ed. N.H. Nicolas and E. Tyrrell (London, 1827), p. 93; *The Brut*, ed. F.W.D. Brie (2 vols, EETS, London, 1906, 1908), ii, 371.
[36] The distinction made by Vale (*English Gascony*, p. 58) is, in my view, a little too sharp.

The French wished to include the allies of each side, a condition which the English could not accept, as this would mean an implicit recognition of Glyn Dŵr, seen by the English as a traitor.[37] Nor could the English agree that Normandy should be one of those parts of France to be included in a general truce, as this would leave them with no way of entering France.[38]

At the same time, negotiations were also being carried out with Burgundy by ambassadors friendly to the Prince, including Henry Chichele, bishop of St David's, the earl of Arundel, Hugh Mortimer, former comrade-in-arms in Wales, and John Catterick, a friend of the Prince. On 1 September they were instructed to discuss the possibilities of a marriage for the Prince and what lands and valuables the princess might bring with her. The English, however, had more than a marriage in mind. Would Burgundy give help against Orléans and Berry and, most significant question of all, would he give the king of England military assistance to recover lands wrongfully withheld in France?[39]

Such a question, asked on the instructions of the king and his council, is a clear indication of the fact that there was no real division of aim in English policy in relation to France. Both king and Prince were united in seeking the fulfilment of English rights in Aquitaine as set out in the treaty of 1360; it even looked as if the king himself might lead a military expedition into northern France, for which shipping was prepared.[40] In the end, probably because of illness, he did not do so. In its place, at the end of September a force of men, unauthorized by the king but led by Thomas, earl of Arundel, the Prince's close associate and member of the royal council, crossed over to France. In his company were a number who would later serve in Normandy.[41] These helped Burgundy to defend Paris, and on 9 November, at St Cloud, south-west of the capital, played a leading part in the defeat of the Armagnacs who were hoping to isolate and capture Paris. Some days later Arundel was feasted in the Louvre by the duke of Burgundy, and money was collected to pay for the service of those who had come to help him.[42]

In the meanwhile the French dukes, Orléans, Berry and Alençon

---

[37] Oxford, Bodleian Library, Ashmole Ms 789, fos 132v-33; Ms fr. b.3, fos 1–2. The English refused to include 'Yvain Glaindor ne les Galoys' because 'c'estoient leurs traitres ausquelx nul noble prince ne devroit bailler aide ne confort'.

[38] '. . . ilz n'auroient par ou entrer ou royaume de France' (Ms fr. b.3, fo.1).

[39] PPC, ii, 19–24; Le Cotton Manuscrit Galba BI, ed. E. Scott and L. Gilliodts-van Severen (Brussels, 1896), pp. 322–6.

[40] Wylie, Henry the Fourth, iv, 37–40.

[41] Ibid., p. 57 seq.

[42] Brut, ii, 371; English Chronicle, p. 36.

sought English help against their rival. The queen, Joan, whose father
was Burgundian in sympathies, asked Henry IV not to interfere in
the quarrel.[43] Although the king and the Prince shared the common
aims of securing England's historic interests in Aquitaine, they were
not at one as to the best way of achieving this. A French chronicle,
favourable towards Burgundy, reported that a letter from Charles VI,
then in Burgundian control, encouraged Henry not to give help to
Orléans who was, in effect, a traitor to his king. Instead, Henry was
urged, both by the French court and by his queen, to allow the Prince
to marry Burgundy's daughter.

At the moment at which English troops were winning success at
St Cloud, parliament was meeting at Westminster. It was an assembly
which was to witness a strange turn of events. On the third day
Thomas Chaucer, friend to both the Prince and the Beauforts, was
elected Speaker for the third consecutive time. In response to a request
for money, the wool subsidy was extended for a year, and a tax of
6s. 8d. on every £20 of income from lands and rents was voted: all
this, it was none the less made clear, was not to be a precedent for
the future.[44] Of that sum, three-quarters was to be expended on the
defence of Calais and the surrounding area, as well as on the defence
of the sea: in such decisions one may see the influence of the Prince
and his council at work. Yet their days at the centre of power were
numbered. On 30 November, as the rather bland account in the Rolls
of Parliament reveals, the Commons asked the king to thank the
Prince and his fellow councillors for their work and effort.[45] The
Commons felt that they had accomplished their task well, as they had
sworn they would. Kneeling before the king, the Prince, speaking on
behalf of the others, claimed that they had done their best to fulfil the
task given to them, for which the king thanked them. To this he added
that he recognized that if more money had been made available, as
the Prince had said, they could have done more for the good of the
kingdom and its defence. He finished by thanking them for the loyal
work which they had done as members of the council.

It seems that the king, as was his right, had relieved the whole
council of its duties. What had happened? That there were frictions
between some of the leading characters is clear; between which of
them is less clear. The Prince's relationship with his father, if not
warm, always appears to have been good. Yet the king, largely

[43] 'Le livre des trahisons de France envers la maison de Bourgogne', *Chroniques
relatives à l'histoire de la Belgique sous la domination des ducs de Bourgogne*, ed. K. de
Lettenhove (Brussels, 1873), p. 72 seq.
[44] *RP*, iii, 648–9; Roskell, *Speakers*, p. 153.
[45] *RP*, iii, 649.

because of the illness which dogged him and which had caused him to make his will in a moment of fright early in 1409, may have resented his son's energy and the apparent ease with which he had assumed leadership of the council at the beginning of 1410. At the time when Henry planned to lead the expedition into France in September 1411, and then failed to do so, he suffered the humiliation of a man whose ability to rule actively seemed to be diminishing and who had witnessed the initiative, in a matter which concerned relations with a foreign power, taken out of his hands. The fact that the Burgundian envoys who had come to England in September 1411 were authorized to negotiate with 'the king and the Prince' may have given Henry the impression that their master was no longer struck by the degree of authority which he appeared to exercise, authority which seemed to rest effectively in the hands of his son and heir.[46] His pride, naturally enough, would have been hurt. It was at this moment that bishop Beaufort may have suggested that he should abdicate in favour of his son; in 1426 the bishop had to maintain before parliament that he had always acted with complete loyalty towards his half-brother, the king: 'I was [a] trewe man to Kyng Henry fourth'.[47] Differences of how best to pursue English interests in France (not the interests themselves) may have helped to widen the gap which appears to have been growing between the king, on the one hand, and the Prince and the council who formed policy, on the other. Nor is it impossible that Thomas, the Prince's brother, may have felt aggrieved by the treatment accorded him by the council. As royal lieutenant in Ireland, Thomas had hardly been outstandingly successful: one reason for this was his irregular residence in Ireland itself (and likewise in Guines, where he was captain), something which had been tactfully commented on in the parliament of 1410.[48]

Behind the changes, certainly behind the summoning of parliament, lay the lack of a successful financial policy. The parliament of 1410 had not been generous in its grant: by the autumn of 1411, when the next assembly met, the second of three instalments voted in 1410 was just due. It seems likely that the need for more money lay behind the decision to call another parliament a whole year before the final instalment of the subsidy voted by its predecessor had come due.[49] As the king implied in thanking the Prince's council for its services, more might have been achieved if greater sums of money had been

[46] *English Chronicle*, p. 37.
[47] *RP*, iv, 298.
[48] Ibid., iii, 625.
[49] In the parliament of January 1410 the Prince had threatened to resign if money for government were not provided (ibid., iii, 632. See above, n.21).

made available.[50] If the council had, in a sense, been a failure, responsibility for that failure was being laid at parliament's door.

At the root of the explanation of the events of November-December
1411, however, must lie the king's fear that his position was being
threatened, and that the Prince, if not directly responsible for this,
was not protecting his father with sufficient vigour. Signs of royal
unease, possibly of disapproval, were to be found in the speech made
by the chancellor, Thomas Beaufort, at the beginning of the session.
Calling for 'bon Governance' of the kingdom, Beaufort maintained
that this depended on loyal and unprejudiced counsel being given, as
well as honour and respect for the king himself.[51] Two days later,
replying to a request made by the Speaker, Thomas Chaucer, that he
might express his mind as his predecessors had been allowed to do,
the king said that he might do so, but that he would tolerate no
'novellerie' in this assembly, nor would he allow the liberties and
franchises which belonged to him as king, and which had previously
belonged to his predecessors, to be diminished.[52]

Such a reaction reflected what was undoubtedly a period of tension
in the relationship between king and Prince. With the departure of
Arundel's force to help the duke of Burgundy in September 1411, the
whole matter of who was really in charge of national affairs had come
to a head. What was the status of the Prince and the Council?[53] The
Prince, after all, held no real or recognized office. Could he act much
as he wanted, even if the king were opposed to his policies? Was he
thought to be acting in this way? Did 'abdication' mean the formal
surrender of the throne, or simply allowing others to assume the
realities of power without such a transfer? Any thought of the first
was dangerous. Richard II was said to have abdicated his regal
power; Henry IV, of all people, could not allow himself to be forced
into doing the same. Even an informal act of commission allowing the
Prince to rule on the king's behalf would do neither monarchy nor
dynasty any good. Henry appears to have been determined not to
allow things to happen this way. The critical moment had probably
already passed by the time parliament met in November 1411, when
he could assert publicly that he would tolerate no 'novellerie'. The

[50] 'Et dist outre, q'il savoit bien que s'ils eussent eue plus de quoy q'ils n'avoient
. . . ils vorroient avoir fait leur devoir pur avoir fait plus de bien que ne feust fait . . .'
(ibid., iii, 649).

[51] Ibid., iii, 647.

[52] '. . . il ne vorroit aucunement avoir nulle manere de Novellerie en cest Parlement'
(ibid., iii, 648); P. McNiven, 'Prince Henry and the English political crisis of 1412',
History, 65 (1980), 2.

[53] McNiven, 'Political developments', p. 674 seq.

Prince had gone too far, and he paid the political price. His father was still king.

For the remaining fifteen months of the reign the Prince and most of his former associates were excluded from the exercise of power. But we should not see the change in the administration, now a kind of second XI, as a clean sweep of those who had worked with the Prince. While archbishop Arundel was restored to the position of chancellor and leading councillor, Thomas Langley and Nicholas Bubwith, who had worked with the Prince in the intervening period, were retained as paid councillors. Moreover, the records present evidence that at least some of those who lost their positions were granted 'douceurs' by a probably not altogether ungrateful king.[54] The fact remains, however, that such payments could not hide the strains and stresses which existed in the relationships between Henry IV and his two eldest sons. The king undoubtedly felt vulnerable. In the circumstances, his natural ally was his second son, Thomas, who had also suffered at the hands of the Prince and members of his council, in particular bishop Beaufort, when they had been in control of affairs. In June 1410, when Thomas had requested the payment of sums owed to him as royal lieutenant in Ireland, he had been told that he would be paid only on condition that he went to Ireland and did his duty there.[55] At about the same time, his marriage to Margaret, widow of John Beaufort and sister-in-law to the bishop, encountered the latter's opposition and refusal, as an executor of his brother's will, to satisfy certain financial demands made of him, a stand in which he appears to have had the backing of the Prince. Personal animosities thus played their part, and probably continued to do so after the Prince and bishop Beaufort had left the council late in 1411.

The differences between the Prince, on the one hand, and his father and brother on the other were to develop in the course of the spring and summer of 1412. The matter at issue was how England should react to political events in France partly brought about by the victory of the Burgundians at St Cloud in November 1411, and to requests from the leaders of the defeated party for help against Burgundy. Early in 1412 negotiations with them were already under way, and on 18 May terms agreed at Bourges received final approval in London. These have usually been regarded as a deliberate decision by the king, approved, probably, by his son Thomas and archbishop Arundel, to pursue an approach to France contrary to that which had led to

[54] Not only the Prince but also Scrope, Arundel and Warwick received such financial rewards (PRO, E 404/27/168–9, 214, 268).

[55] *PPC*, i, 319–20, 339–41.

participation in the victory at St Cloud only a few months earlier.[56] The fact was that Henry, having dismissed his son for pursuing his own policy which involved an understanding with Burgundy, could not go down the same path and demonstrate his independence at one and the same time.[57] Moreover, the Armagnacs were offering him terms which he could scarcely turn down: help in the furtherance of all his quarrels in France, including that of his claim to Aquitaine; promise of the cession to him of twenty specified towns and castles; an undertaking to hold certain lands as fiefs of the English crown; and the giving of homage by Berry for the county of Poitou. In return for these concessions, Henry was not to make any alliance with Burgundy, and was to send 4000 men, whose wages would be paid by his allies, to assist in Burgundy's defeat. Such terms could not be refused, even if it meant abandoning the alliance which the Prince had struck up with Burgundy and which had led to the expedition being sent to France the previous autumn, an expedition which had won both success and reputation for English arms.

The king was laying himself open to criticism at home; Sigismund, King of the Romans, would not be alone in thinking that it was wrong to deal almost simultaneously with both parties in a civil war. Henry was also banking on achieving some kind of military success in France before the rival French parties should patch up their differences. He would have to do this without the support of the Prince who, granted his well-known support for the Burgundians, and the negotiations at that very moment in progress regarding a possible marriage between himself and Anne, daughter of the duke of Burgundy, would not take the part of Burgundy's enemies.[58] That the Prince had much the same diplomatic aim as his father is strongly hinted at by part of the contents of a letter, sealed by him in London on 30 May, in which he informed the duke of Burgundy that he was particularly concerned with the possibility of regaining the duchy of Aquitaine, together with his hereditary lands and rights there. What this suggests is that the difference between the Prince and the king was not so much one of

[56] Arundel's approval is strongly suggested by the order issued to the clergy of the Canterbury province to exhort the faithful to pray for the success of the expedition aimed at recovering the duchy of Aquitaine, which belonged to the king by hereditary right – a very traditional approach to the 'French problem' (Vale, *English Gascony*, p. 58; Jacob, *Fifteenth Century*, p. 113). The policy was condemned by Sigismund, emperor-elect, as irresponsible (R. Vaughan, *John the Fearless. The Growth of Burgundian Power* (London, 1966), p. 94).
[57] McNiven, 'Political developments', p. 721.
[58] Dijon, Arch. dép., Côte d'Or, B 11926; B.-A. Poquet du Haut-Jussé, 'La Renaissance littéraire autour de Henri V, roi d'Angleterre', *Revue Historique*, 224 (1960), 329–38.

aim or policy as one of method or approach. For the Prince, the best way of achieving his objective was to support the Burgundian party in the increasingly bitter civil conflict in France. Furthermore, since 1411 the prospect of marriage had evidently become an important issue, and this, for the heir to the throne of England about to reach his twenty-sixth birthday, was a factor which must have loomed large in his life.

For the moment the Prince had little choice but to dissociate himself from the implications of the agreement recently reached with the Armagnacs, although secretly he may have hoped that the under-taking made by them, to help towards the recovery of Aquitaine, would bear fruit. In not giving open support to his father's plans, however, he risked being misunderstood. The resentment which this may have caused at court is most clearly seen in the decision, probably taken early in May even before the treaty with the Armagnacs had been sealed, that Thomas should lead the English force into France; in his creation as duke of Clarence on 9 July; and in his appointment, a few days later, as royal lieutenant in Aquitaine, perhaps 'a deliberate slight to the Prince'[59] who had held the title of duke of Aquitaine almost since the time of his father's coronation nearly thirteen years earlier.

The terms of the treaty were such to encourage the king to act quickly. Events were bringing matters in France to a head: reconcili-ation was in the air. On 21 July, in order to ensure that his opponents made no use of English help (that help had landed in Normandy ten days earlier and was slowly making its way southward), Burgundy issued a letter in the name of Charles VI (whose person he controlled) obliging all French princes, including himself, to declare invalid any agreements which they had made with the king of England. While Burgundy had relatively little to lose by such action, his opponents had. However, they could not ignore an order issued in their king's name. On 22 July the dukes of Berry, Orléans and Bourbon, together with the Lord of Albret, and Burgundy, wrote to the king of England and to his sons to announce the unilateral breaking of any undertaking made between them, and releasing the English from any obligations towards them.[60]

Clarence's reply to their letter, dated 16 September, and sent from near Blois, the point which the English had reached, has survived. By the time that he wrote it, Clarence would have heard that, on 22

[59] McNiven, 'Political crisis of 1412', 15.
[60] *Royal and Historical Letters*, ii, 322-5; *Lettres de rois, reines et autres personnages des cours de France et d'Angleterre*, ed. J.J. Champollion-Figeac (2 vols, Paris, 1839-47), ii, 328-30.

August, the warring parties in France had made peace with one another. The implications of the peace, and the dukes' denunciation of agreements or understandings reached with the English which followed logically from it, would have been evident to Clarence: he was no longer needed in France. For this reason, what he had hoped to get out of the arrangement, recognition of the English king's right to Aquitaine and help to achieve effective control of it, would no longer be on offer. His anger and frustration at having been made a fool of were evident in the defiant letter he wrote to the dukes of Berry, Orléans and Bourbon refusing to accept their unilateral disavowal of an undertaking solemnly made, and demanding that they honour it as they should. At the end (a sure sign that he regretted having followed what was a false trail) he said he understood that the duke of Burgundy had written similar letters of disavowal, something which greatly surprised him since the English had refused all alliances with him in favour of links with his rivals. Had they known that events would turn out in this way, they would have entered into a firm relationship with him from the start. It was an admission that, in lending aid to the Armagnac party, the king and his army had backed the wrong horse.[61] After a winter spent in Aquitaine, Clarence returned home in the spring of 1413.[62]

Although the leaders of the expedition may have reaped personal benefit, much effort had led to no real political or military advantage, other than the useful knowledge that the French leaders were bitterly divided among themselves. The Prince doubtless took this lesson to heart: he would have learned it without having had to take part in an expedition which had brought England so little immediate benefit. For the moment he stood vindicated over a difference among the leading members of the royal family that had become public knowledge. The inclusion in the St Albans chronicle of a letter of justification issued by the Prince at Coventry on 17 June proves this.[63] In this text we see him, as he was so often to do later, appealing to public opinion; we also see the course of events through his eyes, and gain an insight into what the issues were. It becomes clear that the past months had seen the court, or at least some of its members, turn against the heir to the throne. Did they see him as a threat to his father's throne? According to the justification, there were those 'sons

[61] *Royal and Historical Letters*, ii, 328–32; *Lettres de rois*, ii, 330–32.

[62] At Buzançais, on 14 November 1412, Clarence reached a financial settlement with the French involving 210,000 gold *écus*, 176,800 of which were for Clarence himself. As security Berry handed over gems and precious artefacts, while Orléans committed his younger brother, John of Angoulême, into English care (AN, K 57, no.28).

[63] *St Albans Chronicle*, pp. 65–7; McNiven, 'Political crisis of 1412', 7 seq.

of iniquity' who were intent upon depicting the Prince as such. Were there those who felt that he was not helping the effort to regain Aquitaine? Let him repudiate this by saying that none would desire the achievement of this end more than he. He was, and would remain, loyal to his father and to the crown.

A fortnight later, the Prince, 'with much people of lords and gentles', 'in numbers such as has not been in those days',[64] was in London taking up residence in the inn (or town house) of his old ally, Thomas Langley, bishop of Durham. The number and quality of his followers have intrigued historians. Was this an attempt to stage a coup d'état, to bring about his father's enforced abdication? Almost certainly not, particularly when considered in the light of the loyal sentiments expressed scarcely two weeks earlier in Coventry. Moreover, it is unlikely that many of those who accompanied the Prince were armed, for his aim was not one which depended upon armed force. Rather, it was to demonstrate his popular standing in the country and perhaps to remind the king and the council (who were meeting at that time in London) that many Englishmen had been surprised by the rapidity and completeness of the volte-face of English policy towards France. At the same time he demanded that those who had spoken or fomented trouble against him should be dismissed and punished. In reply, the king promised that, in parliament and in due time, action would be taken.[65] In the end, however, nothing was done. Rather the contrary, for the Prince's brother, Thomas, of whom he may have had his suspicions, was created duke of Clarence a few days later, the promotion scarcely suggesting that the king had lost confidence in him. The Prince, one historian has claimed, had been outmanoeuvred.[66]

Complaints about the Prince may have continued to circulate at court. This time it was said that, as captain of Calais, he had misappropriated the wages of the garrison. At the end of September he returned to London, once again accompanied by 'a huge people' of supporters. The account of what happened was put down a century later, although it was based on contemporary reporting. The Prince, having confessed himself and received communion, and wishing to have matters out with the king, attended upon him at Westminster Hall, where he lay ill. Having approached his father and demanded a personal interview, at which he spoke at length, he then offered the king a dagger, and asked that he should kill him. The king, unable to do this, burst into tears, threw away the dagger, and forgave his

---

[64] St Albans Chronicle, p. 67; McFarlane, Lancastrian Kings, p. 110.
[65] St Albans Chronicle, pp. 65, 68.
[66] McFarlane, Lancastrian Kings, p. 110.

son. A month later, after some account rolls had been audited, the Prince was exonerated from all accusations of malpractice as captain of Calais.[67]

For the Prince, Henry IV's reign was none the less in danger of ending on a note of bitterness and division. There may have been anger on the Prince's part at the tortuous policy which his father and brother had pursued in regard to France. He does appear to have had his critics at court; it may have been they who were responsible for the brief imprisonment of his treasurer in the Tower at this time, and it is evident that there were suspicions about his use of funds provided for Calais. Two well-known stories have assumed legendary character.[68] The first concerns the Prince's alleged imprisonment for contempt of court when he tried to defy the Chief Justice, William Gascoigne, who was trying one of his servants after an affray. The second alleges that the Prince, who was accustomed to keeping the company of men well below his rank, used to attack the receivers of other lords and, indeed, one day attacked his own. In later years the Burgundian chronicler, Monstrelet, recorded the further story of how the Prince, thinking that his father was dead, took up the crown which lay on a cushion by his bedside. At that moment the king, far from dead, awoke to observe what his son was doing.[69] The tale, which was taken up first by the Tudor writers Holinshed and Hall, and then by Shakespeare,[70] may have had an element of truth in it. What it and the others suggest is that in the last year or so of his father's reign the Prince had become disillusioned and frustrated at the way public affairs were being conducted. His father's ill-health and apparent irresolution; his lack of evident success in France; his own patent inability to influence or direct policy; the 'sniping' at both himself and members of his household by people at court, all combined to create tensions within the royal family and among those who served them. It was, in every sense, an act of providence when, on 20 March 1413, the feast of St Cuthbert, Henry IV died in the Jerusalem Chamber at Westminster Abbey. To the best of our knowledge he was at peace with all his sons, including his eldest who shared his name and now finally succeeded him as king of England.

[67] *PPC*, ii, 34-5, 37; PRO, E 404/26/175.
[68] F.S. Flood, 'The story of Prince Henry of Monmouth and Chief-Justice Gascoign', *TRHistS*, 3 (1886), 47-152; Kingsford, *Henry V*, pp. 87-91.
[69] Kirby, *Henry IV*, p. 248.
[70] *Henry IV, Part II*, IV, 3.

PART II

The Soldier and his Career

Chapter 4

HARFLEUR

The new king was a man of above medium height, with a strong and well co-ordinated body which, if not outwardly muscular, enabled him to run very fast, a characteristic useful in hunting, a sport which he loved. His neck was said to have been long; on the evidence of the surviving portrait of him later in life, his face was lean, his nose also long. On the same evidence, his hair was brown and straight. Of good complexion, the king was clean-shaven, although it is possible that he grew a beard in his later years. His eyes, brown too, were reported to be gentle, but they quickly lighted up when he was angry. What impressed contemporaries was Henry's stately bearing and fine manner. A Frenchman who met him in 1415 thought that he looked more like a priest than a soldier, a fact which may have deceived the French court into thinking that they could ignore the man who, persisting in his demands for territorial concessions, threatened war. Outwardly, the king may have seemed reserved, indeed stern, the kind who kept his counsel to himself. Inwardly, he was a man who already knew how to lead, who had confidence in his ability, and was motivated to fulfil what he saw as the main tasks of kingship.

Henry was about to rule over some two million people, unevenly distributed over the country. England's wealth, which bore the rapidly increasing costs of government, came in large measure from its foreign trade, still dominated, although less so than in years past, by the commerce in wool and cloth. For the good of both Henry's subjects and the balance at his exchequer, the king would have to give trade every encouragement at a time when war and serious bullion shortages were causing great difficulties to those engaged in trade, especially that undertaken overseas.

Henry's England was also part of the wide community of western Christendom, with the pope at its head. At the end of the fourteenth century, however, Christian unity was under severe strain. Since 1378 the headship of the visible Church, the papacy, had been divided between two claimants, causing a schism which only aggravated the already existing divisions in political society, those separating England and France being the most notorious. In addition England was experiencing the growth of heterodox belief and practice: Lollardy,

there can be little doubt, was a divisive factor in English society at
this time. No king as pious or orthodox as Henry, nor one bent upon
healing the divisions in his country, could ignore the spiritual dissensions around him.

As king, Henry was the leading member of the aristocracy which
dominated English society. Richard II had failed to understand the
role played by this group, which had been one of the factors in his
fall in 1399. His successor, Henry IV, although himself a member of
the highest aristocracy, had chosen to rely much on men of lesser rank
to assist him in government. By 1413 his son had already shown a
clear preference for closer contacts with the aristocracy; by emphasizing war, he was to appeal precisely to that class brought up to regard
warfare as its natural contribution to the wider society. Henry's
reliance upon the military aristocracy, based in many cases on
common experiences and friendships shared with soldiers, suggests
that the new king would be no great innovator in his vision of his
kingly role.

Perhaps this was just as well. No new king in 1413 could ignore the
long-standing conflict with France, semi-quiescent at that moment
but, like a volcano, ready to erupt again if one or other side chose to
cause it to do so. For over a century, since the time of Edward I,
English kings had been resisting French attempts either to win political and legal control over lands in France which the English regarded,
historically, as theirs, or to expel them altogether from that country.
In certain respects the English could be regarded as fighting a defensive war. In others, however, theirs was a war of aggression aimed,
since the 1330s, at securing the crown of France claimed by descendants of Isabella, Edward II's French wife, who ruled as kings of
England. The methods they employed, although typical of the time,
were not likely to bring success. The characteristic form of military
activity in the fourteenth century was the raid (or *chevauchée*), which
might last a few weeks or a few months. Its aim was to destroy, to
demoralize, to reduce the enemy's ability or willingness to resist. It
was a slow and (at least for those who suffered materially from it)
painful way of making war. While it minimized the risk of loss of life
for the soldier (battles were few and far between), it was generally
unsuccessful in bringing the enemy to the point of surrender. Would
this traditional method of waging war be sufficiently effective to fulfil
the new king's political ambitions in France? Or would the policy of
raids have to give way to that of vigorously contested conquest,
achieved by a nation united behind its king? Now that England was
'under new management', was the character of the conflict with
France about to change?

*

Custom had it that kings should be anointed and crowned on Sundays. The day chosen for Henry's coronation was Passion Sunday, which fell on 9 April, some three weeks after his father's death. Events in the intervening period were to give rise to the origins of one of the best-known stories concerning the new king: his 'conversion' from a seemingly irresponsible youth into a serious and highly responsible ruler. Whether they did so soon after the event or years later, all those who wrote of the new king in 1413 were anxious to show that his accession was a decisive moment, a time of expectation in English history. The author known as the Pseudo-Elmham, writing over a quarter of a century after the event, could record Henry's visit to a recluse at Westminster whose advice he sought and to whom he confessed all the sins of his past life.[1] In his work, the *Vita et Gesta*, the anonymous author emphasized how the new king threw himself upon the mercy of God (which could mean not only that he saw himself as a sinner but also that, in true humility, he was recognizing his inadequacy for the tasks ahead which could only be completed successfully with divine help), and how this had caused him to become a different man. The early sixteenth-century tradition, expressed in the so-called *First English Life*, which relied heavily upon Tito Livio, whose work on Henry was written in 1437–38, took the same view: Henry had gone through a moral and spiritual conversion.[2]

Such views were not simply those of later ages intent upon creating a legend about Henry. Thomas Walsingham, monk and chronicler of St Albans, whose last years coincided with the reign and whose writings about it were, generally, very favourable, left a brief account of the feeling of popular opinion regarding the new king as he took up his responsibilities. Good Englishman that he was, the monk commented on the snowy weather which the people of London experienced on that Passion Sunday, enough, it might be thought, to dampen the celebrations customarily associated with a coronation. Some people, he recorded, interpreted the snow as a sign of austerity to come. Others (more sensibly, he added) saw the signs in a favourable light: the cold and the snow would bring an end to difficult times and usher in the good, for winter he claimed, citing the Song of Songs, was now past, the rain over and gone.[3] This was more than a literary

---

[1] *Thomae de Elmham, Vita et Gesta Henrici Quinti, Anglorum Regis*, ed. T. Hearne (Oxford, 1727), pp. 13–15.

[2] *First English Life*, pp. 17–19.

[3] *St Albans Chronicle*, p. 69, citing Cant. Cant., 2, 11; *Chronicon Adae de Usk*, pp. 120, 299. The same line from the Song of Songs was to be cited to convey a similar idea of England 'revived' by a 'devoted chaplain' (perhaps bishop Henry Beaufort?) when writing to Henry V after the battle of Agincourt (*Letters of queen Margaret of Anjou and bishop Beckington and others, written in the reigns of Henry V and Henry VI*, ed. C. Monro

device (although Walsingham was fond of these): it represented an attempt to convey something of the expectation and hope of good rule which was brought by the accession of the twenty-six-year-old Henry, known already for his experience of government (the anonymous author of the *Gesta* significantly referred to him as being 'young in years but old in experience' at this time). [4] Henry's coronation, in the eyes of many, marked a real beginning.

The heightened sense of expectancy is also conveyed in another episode recounted by both Livio and the Pseudo-Elmham, namely that, only three days after his father's death, Henry received the oaths of allegiance of the nobility (parliament, in session at the time of Henry IV's death, had been dissolved, but the lords would still have been in London), something said to be without precedent, and intended to emphasize the expectation which the nobility had of the reign which was on the point of beginning. On this occasion Henry promised to rule for the good of the country; if he failed, he said that he would prefer to die and be buried. [5] Optimism was in the air. Here was a man who was taking his responsibilities seriously. The story recorded in the *Brut*, and which may date from twenty years later, regarding the new king's dismissal of his dissolute friends and the promotion of those few who had earlier dared to criticize his way of life was yet another way of showing that Henry's accession marked a break with the past. [6] People now looked hopefully to the future.

Of the ceremonies which accompanied Henry V's coronation (unlike that of a number of other kings), relatively little is known. [7] Two days before, on 7 April, Henry arrived in London, where he was met by many lords and knights, as well as clergy and citizens, in procession. At the Tower some fifty or so young men, all of them hoping to receive knighthood at the hands of the new king, awaited

(C.S., London, 1863), p. 2). Strecche also emphasized the bad weather ('The Chronicle of John Strecche for the Reign of Henry V (1414–1422)', ed. F. Taylor, *BJRL*, 16 (1932), 146–7). John Capgrave wrote of the fires which occurred that summer, and that they presaged a warlike king (J. Capgrave, *The Book of the Illustrious Henries*, trans. F.C. Hingeston (RS, London, 1858), p. 125).

[4] *Gesta Henrici Quinti – The Deeds of Henry the Fifth*, ed. & trans. F. Taylor and J.S. Roskell (Oxford, 1975), p. 3.

[5] *Vita Henrici Quinti*, p. 5; *Vita et Gesta*, p. 16; *First English Life*, p. 18.

[6] *Brut*, ii, 594–5; see also *First English Life*, p. 19. This, or a similar incident, would form the basis for Shakespeare's version: 'I know thee not, old man . . . Presume not that I am the thing I was . . . I have turn'd away my former self; So will I those that kept me company' (*King Henry IV, part II*, V, v). Shakespeare told the story of one man's conversion. He could not convey that it was popular because it symbolized the change which Henry's contemporaries hoped would come about under the rule of a new king.

[7] *Vita et Gesta*, p. 17 seq.

him; they served at the tables when a feast was held that evening. The following morning, having attended Mass, they rode, in splendid array, to the royal lodgings where, accompanied by their sponsors, they waited upon the king who dubbed them knights.[8] Later that day they accompanied the king through London as he rode to Westminster, where he was received in procession at his palace where he intended to spend the night, in prayer, in readiness for his anointing on the following day.

The ceremony does not appear to have been in any way out of the ordinary – except for one factor, the possible use of the miraculous oil of Thomas Becket in the ceremony of anointing.[9] According to tradition, the Virgin had appeared to Becket in a vision in which she had offered him an eagle-shaped vessel containing a stone flask filled with oil which, she said, should be used to anoint future kings of England. The French had a similar vessel, the *sainte ampoule*, which was said to have come down from heaven when St Remigius had crowned Clovis at the end of the fifth century; it, or something like it, had been used to signify divine approval of French kings ever since. That English kings might benefit from such approbation was clearly understood by Edward II and Richard II. Hoping to fulfil the prophecy that the king who carried the eagle about with him would achieve victory over his enemies and bring prosperity to his kingdom, Richard kept it by him. It was from him that it was taken in August 1399, and it is clear that Henry IV was anointed with the oil at his coronation later that year, thus helping to bolster his claim to the throne. Whether the oil was used to anoint Henry V in April 1413 is uncertain; only one reference to its use was specifically made.[10] However, the fact that both his father and his son were anointed with it makes it likely that Henry was, too. The tradition that the Virgin had informed Becket that kings thus anointed would recover lands lost by their predecessors, and that the first would regain Normandy and Aquitaine, must have been an added incentive to receive anointing with the sacred oil.

[8] The names of some of those knighted are recorded in BL, Stowe Ms 440, fos 86v–7; J. Anstis, *Observations introductory to an historical Essay upon the knighthood of the Bath* (London, 1725), p.[25].

[9] On this, see T.A. Sandquist, 'The Holy Oil of St Thomas of Canterbury', *Essays in Medieval History presented to Bertie Wilkinson*, ed. T.A. Sandquist and M.R. Powicke (Toronto, 1969), pp. 330–44.

[10] 'Unccione coelica' (*Vita et Gesta*, p. 21); *Liber Regie Capelle*, ed. W. Ullmann (Henry Bradshaw Soc., 92, London, 1961), p. 90 and n.3. The evidence of Oxford, Bodleian Library, Bodley Ms 117, fo.68v, is that the oil was used, and that there was a picture of the Virgin on the ampulla.

The conflict with France provides a thread with which to follow
Henry's entire career as king. The events of 1411 and 1412 had shown
that, far from being dead, English interest in French affairs was still
very much alive. Differences of method there had been, but both
Henry V and his father had shared a common aim, to make a reality
of the terms of the 'great peace' of Brétigny of 1360. While Henry
IV had hoped to achieve his end by lending English support to the
Armagnac party, support which had seemed to reap its reward in the
terms granted by the French princes at Bourges in 1412, his eldest
son had favoured a rapprochement with John, duke of Burgundy.
From the very first days of the new reign to its very last, English
policy towards France would have to take into account what the two
political camps which dominated French politics might allow the king
of England to achieve.

At the beginning of his reign, two factors would have influenced
Henry in his ambition in France: his personal interest in and responsibility for Aquitaine, of which he had been created duke late in 1399,
and above all else, his overwhelming desire to see justice, as he saw
it, done. Both these aims might be achieved if the French could be
brought to honour, in full, the terms of the treaty of Brétigny which,
for the past generation and more, had been at the centre of English
demands. If the terms could be fulfilled, they would bring to the king
of England two much sought after advantages: the restitution under
a legal status favourable to England of lands at present held by the
French; and the payment of that part of the ransom of King John II
of France which had not yet been paid to the English but which, by
treaty, they could justly regard as theirs. In addition, as a factor to
seal the settlement of the claim, the matter of a marriage between
Henry and Katharine, daughter of Charles VI, was placed high on
the diplomatic agenda.

Perhaps in the hope of allying himself to duke John, certainly with
the intention of furthering, to his own advantage, the political and
military divisions of France, Henry encouraged the continuation of
the relationship between England and Burgundy which had led to
English participation in the military events of late 1411. Such an
alliance seemed to be dictated by mutual interest. The year 1413
witnessed, in August, John's banishment from Paris and his exclusion
from power. A weak central government, now in the hands of his
Armagnac rivals, would suit both him and his English ally. An alliance with England, therefore, made sense in more than one respect.
It could be used as a possible military threat against the government
in power in Paris, while at an altogether different level, that of commerce between England and those areas of the Low Countries under
Burgundian rule, a peaceful relationship could bring material advan-

tage to both sides. A gauge of the warmth of that relationship was to be found in Calais, of which Henry had been captain since 1410. When there was hostility, both during these years and later, Calais was always liable to attack from its hinterland: in times of understanding between England and Burgundy, Calais prospered.

An understanding, better still an alliance, between England and Burgundy appeared to be much in England's interest as Henry began his reign. If relations had not always prospered under Henry IV, this had been largely the fault of a mutual failure to provide the peaceful conditions required for fruitful commercial relations between ports bordering the narrow sea, and because Henry IV preferred an alliance with the Armagnacs. From its beginnings the reign of Henry IV had been characterized by piracy and other illegal and provocative acts carried out at sea against the maritime and commercial communities. For more than a decade one of the chief concerns of Anglo-Burgundian diplomacy had been the settlement of disputes and claims for damages and reparation issued by both king and duke in the name of aggrieved subjects. The same kind of trouble had governed Anglo-French relations in the first decade of the century, in spite of the official state of truce which existed between the two countries. Nor was it only English trade in the Channel which had suffered. The French had used the ports of northern France, in particular Harfleur at the mouth of the river Seine, as naval bases from which to despatch troops to help Glyn Dŵr's rebels in south Wales, as well as the Scots in their incursions across the northern border.[11]

On the evidence of the Rolls of Parliament, the re-establishment of order at sea was one of Henry's main priorities when he became king. The legislation passed to achieve it did not, however, fulfil its desired end: Harfleur and Dieppe remained as thorns in the sides of England's sailors, and it would soon become evident that further action was needed if English commerce in the Channel was to be adequately protected. There can be little doubt that the choice of Harfleur as the first place to be taken by the king and his army in 1415 was influenced by the need to prevent the French using it as a place from which to harass English shipping and launch attacks upon the coast of southern England.

The diplomacy of the first months of the new reign showed what Henry felt needed doing. Almost immediately negotiations were opened with the court of Aragon;[12] and a few weeks later, in mid-July 1413, Henry Chichele, bishop of St David's, and Richard Beauchamp,

[11] C.J. Ford, 'Piracy or Policy: the Crisis in the Channel, 1400–1403', *TRHistS*, 5th series, 29 (1979), 63–78.
[12] *DKR*, 44, p. 545.

earl of Warwick, both of whom had served on the council in the previous reign, were empowered to treat for perpetual friendship with Burgundy, as well as to make a truce with France,[13] signifying that Henry was hoping for an alliance with Burgundy but was only seeking to avoid conflict with France. The truce was concluded at Leulinghem on 23 September, to be renewed in January 1414, January 1415[14] and again, as Henry actively prepared for war, in April and June of that year.[15] Behind this screen of truce renewals, English envoys were busy trying to extract concessions from the French. In March 1414 they were in Paris negotiating 'on the matter of justice',[16] by which they meant the cession of French lands to Henry, and reminding the French of the 1,600,000 *écus* of ransom still owed.[17]

The other way that might lead to a more lasting peace was through a marriage between the king and princess Katharine, a matter discussed between the parties in November 1413 and again later.[18] At the end of January 1414 Henry undertook to marry no other than Katharine until 1 May following,[19] using the threat of a possible contract with an Aragonese princess to show the French that he meant business. In June the pressure on the French was stepped up further when Henry Scrope, Hugh Mortimer, Thomas Chaucer, Philip Morgan and John Hovyngham, all trusted by the king, were appointed to negotiate the king's marriage with a daughter of the duke of Burgundy.[20] A month later envoys were named again to negotiate with France regarding the terms of a marriage for the king, while on 18 June the undertaking not to marry other than into the French royal family was renewed for a further six weeks, to be renewed yet again by John Prophet, Keeper of the Privy Seal, on 18 October.[21]

While all this was going on and the French king was being encouraged to place (even to increase) his deposit upon Henry as a future son-in-law, negotiations of a seemingly more significant kind were being conducted between England and Burgundy. When Burgundian envoys came to Henry during the parliament held at Leicester in the spring of 1414, a number of problems were discussed with them. It was agreed that, in view of the king's age, it would be better if he

[13] *Chronique d'Enguerran de Monstrelet*, ed. L. Douët d'Arcq (6 vols, SHF, Paris, 1857–62), ii, 391.

[14] PRO, E 30/380, 1575.

[15] PRO, E 30/389.

[16] '. . . in materia justicie' (AN, J 646, no.10).

[17] Ibid., no.10 bis.

[18] Ibid., no.14.

[19] *DKR*, 44, p. 551; *Foedera*, IV, ii, 66–7.

[20] *DKR*, 44, p. 554; Arch. dép. Côte d'Or, B 296 and B 11926.

[21] *DKR*, 44, pp. 553–4, 555, 557; *Foedera*, IV, ii, 81, 90–1, 96–7.

married Catherine, the elder of the duke's two daughters by two years.[22] The English record of the occasion went on that Burgundian envoys had introduced the matter of their duke giving allegiance to Henry in return for military help, limited to three months, to be rendered in France. On the crucial matter of Burgundian help to be given in the event of Henry invading France, the Burgundians replied that their lord would provide it in person to win back lands which the dukes of Orléans, Bourbon and Alençon held, at the moment, but that he was unwilling to act against the duke of Berry. Both sides promised not to ally themselves with any of these without the other's consent.[23] In August 1414 the process of consultation with Burgundy was taken one step further at Ypres when English envoys treated, in the presence of the duke himself, concerning the military help which he might give to Henry, and how that help might be paid for. Almost more important, however, was the fact that the matter of the homage which duke John might give to Henry, already discussed at Leicester, was now raised again, as well as the recognition of Henry's claim to Aquitaine which, it was admitted, went back to the time of Edward III.[24] Duke John was, in effect, going back to the position which he, and the other dukes, had publicly stated but had been obliged to retract by royal edict in July 1412.[25]

The year 1414 was spent by Henry testing the political and military waters. In January he had made a truce, to last ten years, with Brittany, a territory whose sailors had often shown their hostility to English traders and seamen. Not only would such an agreement stabilize English commerce, it would also help to detach the duke of Brittany from the king of France in the event of an English invasion of that country. On France's eastern border, Henry pursued his diplomatic initiative in July 1414 by appointing ambassadors, including Sir Walter Hungerford and John Waterton, to treat for a league with the emperor-elect, Sigismund.[26] Together with his approaches to the court of Aragon, and his very active negotiations with that of Burgundy, these constituted an attempt to rally some of France's closest allies to himself should he ever choose to attack that country.

Not the least of Henry's problems in trying to create this broad network of relationships with other European rulers was how far they could be certain of dancing to the English tune. The Bretons would not prove to be the most reliable of allies; nor would Sigismund. In the

[22] *Foedera*, IV, ii, 79–80.
[23] Dijon, Arch. dép., Côte d'Or, B 296; PRO, E 30/1531.
[24] Dijon, Arch. dép., Côte d'Or, B 11926.
[25] See *Cotton Manuscrit Galba B I*, pp. 329–31.
[26] *DKR*, 44, p. 554; *Foedera*, IV, ii, 86, 91. Henry had been in contact with Sigismund since at least 1411.

case of Burgundy, the question which has always puzzled historians is
who was leading whom? Duke John was one of the most important
Frenchmen of his day: he owed that position to his blood links to the
royal family of France. It should be recalled, too, that his quarrel
within France was not waged against the king, the unhappy Charles
VI, but against those dukes who were his rivals for power within that
country. John of Burgundy was an ambitious man whose policy and
public conduct were dictated more by a desire to achieve control of
the reins and sources of French power, which might be used to further
the wealth and status of his own duchy, than by almost anything else.
Would he, could he, give whole-hearted support to the English king
in fulfilling his ambition in France? Without too many adverse consequences, in the hope that he might help fulfil Henry's limited ambition
there and thus prevent him from developing others on a wider scale,
duke John could quietly admit the legality of Henry's claim to Aquitaine, which lay well away from his own lands on the other side of
France. But if English ambition were to develop into something
greater, or if it were to look like winning more power within France,
then the limits of the help which duke John might give to Henry
would need to be severely curtailed.

Like both his predecessor and his successor, John would find that,
in the conflict between the king of France and his counterpart in
England, he had to tread with the greatest care. A Frenchman with
ever-increasing interests on the borders of, and even outside, the kingdom, many of which could be furthered by a policy of co-operation
(such as trade) with England, yet a Frenchman at odds with others
at home over the exercise of power at a time when the king himself
was incapable of wielding it, John had a difficult task of balancing
duty, honour and self-interest without bringing disaster upon himself.
Regarded as one to whom the satisfaction of private ambition came
before the search for the public good, hated by many Frenchmen (he
had openly admitted to having organized the murder of duke Louis
of Orléans in Paris in 1407), and mistrusted by them as the man who
would bring the English into France and by the English as a typical
French double-dealer, duke John could do no right.[27] In allying himself to Burgundy, was Henry V allowing himself to be led by the nose?
Time might tell.

In the meantime, through talks with both the Burgundians and the
Armagnacs, Henry tried to wrest concessions from the French through
diplomacy. Discussions with the Burgundians went on through 1413
and 1414. At the same time, using a truce negotiated early in 1414 as
a basis of peace, he sent Thomas Montagu, earl of Salisbury, together

[27] *Brut*, ii, 424; *Gesta*, p. 175.

with bishops Richard Courtenay of Norwich and Thomas Langley of Durham to see the Armagnac leadership in Paris in July 1414, the aim being a general settlement between England and France. English demands were again both territorial and financial, the cession of the suzerainty of Normandy, Touraine, Maine, Anjou and the old Aquitaine, and the payment of the remainder of king John's ransom, matters which they insisted on linking with the negotiations for a royal marriage, something which the French wanted to keep separate, not least because a very large dowry might be involved. Although the proposals were discussed seriously, this embassy achieved little, but in February 1415 it was to be followed by another, consisting of the same two bishops, Henry's secretary, Richard Holme, and Thomas Beaufort, taking the place of Salisbury. It was clearly intended to impress the Parisians, who must have enjoyed seeing the arrival of the 600 or so Englishmen on horseback, as well as the jousting and feasting with which they were officially received.[28] Once again, however, the embassy was to return home empty-handed, although the French appeared ready to make some concessions. The English had also been ready to make concessions on the matters of the king's marriage and its financial conditions as well as on the territorial question, but found that they lacked sufficient authority to accept such concessions as the French were prepared to sanction.

From the chronicles we can detect the growing sense of mistrust of, and resentment against, the French developing at the English court at this time. These were to be fuelled by one of the most famous stories of Henry's reign, known to many through Shakespeare, the episode of the tennis balls. It is too easy to dismiss this tale as pure legend, although it is doubtful whether the balls were ever sent to the English court whence, as the writer of the *Brut* later recorded, they were returned as the hard gunstones which, some months afterwards, helped to batter down the walls of Harfleur.[29] The most telling and most contemporary account, that of John Strecche, canon of Kenilworth, written probably soon after Henry's death, records the Frenchmen's pride and arrogance, and, as an illustration of this, that they would send Henry balls with which to play and cushions upon which to lie, the implication clearly being that the king was too much inclined to love his creature comforts and too inexperienced in war to do any harm. The story, in all likelihood based upon a chance remark perhaps overheard by one of the English ambassadors sent to the French court, may have been reported at Kenilworth and, in this way,

[28] Monstrelet, iii, 59–60.
[29] *Brut*, ii, 374–6.

through the writings of John Strecche, entered the nation's mythology.[30] None the less, it may well reflect the mood of the king in the spring of 1415. He had twice sent embassies to Paris in a period of less than eight months, but on neither occasion had he got anything of what he wanted.[31]

The chroniclers tell us that, having heard the ambassador's report, Henry decided that the only way he might achieve his purpose was through war and invasion. John Strecche recounts, somewhat over-dramatically but none the less in a way which recaptures something of the feverish energy of those who sought to fulfil the king's instructions, how orders were given for a search for arms to be carried out in every castle and for all kinds of weapons, useful for both offensive and defensive war, including cannon, large gunstones and gunpowder, to be prepared.[32] Very early in 1415 men from several ports such as Sandwich, Winchelsea, Bristol and Hull were summoned to the king's presence at Kennington to discuss matters which would be explained to them; it is likely that this concerned the shipping and transportation of an army over the sea. And although the earliest indentures for service on this expedition into France (the documents were no more explicit than this, probably to prevent the enemy learning of Henry's intentions regarding a landing place) appear to have been sealed on 29 April, preparations for summoning a large army must have begun many months earlier.[33]

The long and meticulous preparations tell us something about Henry. They reflect his growing impatience with the French, who must have appeared to be fobbing him off with empty answers while preparing themselves to mount an effective resistance to any invasion which he might undertake. Time was not necessarily on his side. While he must avoid an unprovoked attack upon France (contemporary opinion would have condemned him had he launched his effort against France without good reason, as his great council of nobles reminded him in 1414), he badly needed to carry out his attack by the summer of 1415 (or else lose almost a year before a suitable time presented itself again). This required a firm decision to be made by March or April of that year, at the very latest. The failure of the February mission to Paris gave him the chance to act within the same year, and to present its failure as offering him the go-ahead for war.

---

[30] 'Chronicle of John Strecche', 150. John Capgrave was one of those who later reported the incident (*Book of the Illustrious Henries*, pp. 129–30). See also E.F. Jacob, *Henry V and the Invasion of France* (London, 1947), pp. 71–3.

[31] Monstrelet, iii, 70.

[32] 'Chronicle of John Strecche', 150–1; PRO, E 403/619, m.2.

[33] Orders to make tents went out early in February (*Foedera*, IV, ii, 103).

The French knew that plans were being formed,[34] and as part of their
defensive reaction they despatched an embassy, under archbishop
Boisratier of Bourges, to try to stave off the impending invasion and,
if possible, to find out where it was likely to land. Its members reached
the capital only to find that the king, having ridden through London
and formally taken his leave of the mayor and sheriffs on 15 June,
was already on his way to the south coast. It finally caught up with
the royal party at Winchester, where, in the episcopal palace, it met
Henry and his three brothers. In a speech of an eloquence which
impressed all who heard it, the archbishop offered major concessions
of land and money and more acceptable terms regarding the projected
marriage between Henry and the princess Katharine – all on condition that the king disband his army and abandon his intention of
invading France.

Proudly as their leader may have spoken, the French were in a very
weak position. Their hope at this time (it was now the beginning of
July) must have been to try to delay the departure of the expedition
long enough to make it too late for it to sail that year. Henry quickly
saw through this tactic and, with archbishop Chichele as his spokes-
man, made his final demand for the territories which he wanted,
Normandy, Aquitaine, Anjou, Touraine, Maine, Poitou, Ponthieu
and other lands, as well as a satisfactory settlement for a marriage
between himself and Katharine. If these conditions were not met he
would, with God's help, achieve them by the sword.[35] Seeking leave
to reply, Boisratier asked whether Henry would unjustly try to unseat
the legitimate king of France: if he did, he would surely fail. Henry,
handing over a formal, written refusal of the terms which he had been
offered, sent the French envoys home, causing them to delay their
departure so that they should not be able to report what they had
seen of the English preparations for war until it was too late for such
to have any practical effect upon French measures for defence.[36]

One thing remained to be done, to justify the decision which Henry
had reached to seek his right through war. As this and ample other

---

[34] Monstrelet, ii, 71.

[35] Ibid., ii, 73–5.

[36] Henry was very spy-conscious at this time. On 7 August, in one of his last acts
before sailing for France, he ordered all sheriffs to proclaim that a special watch be
kept at night, and that innkeepers might ask strangers why they were travelling:
those refused an answer were to send for a bailiff or constable to arrest the stranger
(*CCR, 1413–1419*, p. 278). On the matter of spies at the English and French courts
during this year, see L. Mirot, 'Le Procès de Maître Jean Fusoris, chanoine de
Notre-Dame de Paris (1415–1416). Épisode des négotiations franco-anglaises durant
la guerre de Cent Ans', *Mémoires de la Société de l'Histoire de Paris et de l'Ile de France*,
27 (1900), 140–72.

evidence makes clear, the king had a highly developed sense of the need to keep the world around him aware of what he was doing, and why. While at Titchfield Abbey, near Southampton, he ordered that officially authenticated copies of the treaty of Bourges made between his father and the French princes, in which they recognized the right of the king of England to territory in south-western France, should be made and sent to the General Council of the Church (then in session at Constance), to the emperor Sigismund, and to other rulers, so that the duplicity of the French should be exposed and the consistency with which the English had pursued their just claim should be widely recognized.[37] Having appointed John Waterton and John Kemp to seek an alliance with Aragon, and a marriage between himself and the princess Mary of that country[38] (had the king given up hope of a French marriage, or was the move intended to bring yet more pressure on the enemy?), Henry looked ready to sail.

But appearances could be deceptive. At the end of July a plot, seemingly to kill the king, was betrayed by Edmund Mortimer, earl of March, who revealed that Richard, earl of Cambridge, brother of the duke of York, Henry, Lord Scrope of Masham (once treasurer of England), and Sir Thomas Grey of Heton, in Northumberland, had hatched a conspiracy against the king. What kind of plot it was intended to be, what it aimed to do, and what brought the plotters to this point of seeming desperation has long puzzled historians. Was it a dynastic plot, centring on Edmund Mortimer? Possibly, but unlikely, since it was Mortimer himself who revealed the conspiracy. Or was it a revival, a kind of 're-run' of 1405, of the Mortimer-Glyn Dŵr-Percy alliance which had led to the planned tripartite division of England and Wales in that year? This was a possibility, for Grey might represent the dissatisfied Percy element just at the very moment when king Henry was securing the return to the English fold and to his earldom of Northumberland of Henry Percy, who had lived in Scotland since his father's death at Shrewsbury a dozen years earlier. Did Grey represent, too, the dissatisfaction of the northern shires with Lancastrian rule? Was it, as some contemporary writers presented it, a betrayal of the king's military interest in France, paid for by the French as a last-ditch attempt to prevent the invasion of their country, a conspiracy which followed the very recent visit to Winchester of the French king's ambassadors? Was it largely a plan which arose out of the kinship network which characterized the close family relationships between noble families at this time? Finally, was it part of a Lollard plot, involving the arch-heretic, Sir John Oldcastle, to deprive the

---

[37] PRO, E 30/1695; *Gesta*, pp. 17–19.
[38] *Foedera*, IV, ii, 140; BL, Cotton Ms Vespasian C xii, fos 147–147v.

king of his life, a repeat, in this case, of the conspiracy in London at the beginning of January 1414?[39]

As in a modern thriller, all the conspirators had reasons for bearing grudges against the intended victim, the king, or for seeing him out of the way. Mortimer, brother-in-law to Cambridge, had been fined 10,000 marks (£6666 13s. 4d.) by Henry for failing to secure royal permission to marry: the sum was undoubtedly a very large one, and must have caused resentment in Mortimer's mind. But there is little evidence that he was brought in to the conspiracy until fairly near the end, and none, certainly, that he was a prime mover in it, which would suggest that the creation of his and his family's political fortune was probably not the aim of the plotters, a view which the honourable treatment accorded to him by the king, and the way in which he loyally served his royal master in the coming years, would tend to support. Grey, too, probably joined the plot fairly late, brought in, perhaps, through the family connection fairly recently established with Cambridge, whose daughter, Isabel, was married to Grey's son. What may have been his motive? Perhaps the full restoration of the Percy heir, into whose family Grey, a man of standing in his border county, had married.

What may have turned Henry, Lord Scrope, into a conspirator? The answer is far from simple. That he had long had the confidence of the king and of his father is clear; it was, indeed, this fact which turned his participation in these events, in the eyes of Thomas Walsingham, into a particulary heinous crime. Had he expressed reservations about the expedition to the king (as an ex-treasurer, he might have thought it his duty to do so)? Was he in any way out of favour? Certainly this had not prevented him from planning to accompany the king with a very sizeable retinue on the expedition which was about to set out.[40] Were there remnants in him of the motives of the conspiracy of his uncle, Richard Scrope, archbishop of York, executed by Henry IV in 1405? The fact that he was linked with Cambridge, whose stepmother, Joan Holland, he had married, a marriage which also gave him family connections with the Mortimers, may have encouraged him to condone the plot. Even if he had had second thoughts, Scrope was not likely to betray Mortimer, who owed him large sums of money which he would never see again were he to reveal

[39] T.B. Pugh, *Henry V and the Southampton Plot of 1415* (Southampton Record Series, 30, 1988), presents the latest view of the events surrounding this conspiracy. His ideas are resumed in his article, 'The Southampton Plot of 1415', *Kings and Nobles in the late Middle Ages. A Tribute to Charles Ross*, ed. R.A. Griffiths and J. Sherborne (Gloucester/New York, 1986), pp. 62–89.

[40] PRO, E 404/31/168; E 101/69/384, 400.

the plot which would lead to Mortimer's execution.[41] If not an active conspirator, circumstances compelled him to keep his mouth closed regarding what he knew.

There can be little doubt that the original and most important plotter was Richard, earl of Cambridge. Through his first marriage to Edmund Mortimer's sister, Anne, he had become closely linked with that family; through his second marriage (about 1414) to Maud Clifford, he had established links with the Percies. It can be argued that he would certainly have been advanced had Mortimer become king, an argument further enhanced by the fact that the son, Richard, whom he had by Anne Mortimer, was Mortimer's heir. It is likely that Cambridge, perhaps a man of ambition, may have thought that he deserved more from the world. Created earl at the Leicester parliament in May 1414, he was already heir to his brother's duchy of York. But his own advancement to the high peerage had not been supported by sufficient royal endowment (as was the custom) to satisfy the demands likely to be made of a man in his new position. Cambridge, although the recipient of a 'signal mark of royal favour',[42] could not live up to his new status because he lacked the thousand marks of revenue which it demanded. It was, perhaps, the resentment of being 'merely a titular earl' with a 'courtesy title' which made him into a conspirator. The king had failed to realize that it was not sufficient to raise a man to one of the highest social ranks in the country: he had also to receive the endowments, as others had, of his newly won position. Without them, his advancement was little more than a mockery.

The plan was really too complicated, and depended upon too many uncertain factors, to succeed. Mortimer was to retreat to the nearby New Forest and, having proclaimed a general uprising, which, it was hoped, would make a substantial part of the army desert (thereby putting paid to the king's planned descent upon France), he would escape to Wales, there to await the arrival of the Scots, Henry Percy and the allegedly still-living pseudo-Richard II; the rising would also receive the support of the Lollard leader, Sir John Oldcastle, probably in hiding in the border counties of Wales at this time. Mortimer was to be crowned king, and, when challenged by Henry's military might, it was hoped that the Lancastrian usurper would be killed in battle. If Mortimer himself were to die, he would be followed by his young heir, Richard, son of the fellow conspirator, Cambridge, whose desire for position and wealth would thus be satisfied.

Once the plot had been revealed, Henry acted swiftly. It was prob-

[41] Pugh, 'Southampton plot', p. 84.
[42] Ibid., p. 74.

ably on 31 July that he learned of the danger to his person, and the conspirators were arrested at Porchester, near Southampton. On 2 August Grey, who had confessed, was executed in spite of pathetic pleas for mercy.[43] Three days later, on 5 August, the two peers were brought before a tribunal of their fellow peers (who included among their number Edmund Mortimer, the man who had revealed the conspiracy) presided over by the duke of Clarence, acting, not as the Tudors thought, as steward of the kingdom, but as the royal lieutenant and vice-regent. The indictment was a double one: the first accusation was that they had taken part in a conspiracy to kill the king, his brothers and others (which was how the chroniclers, in the main hostile to Scrope, reported it), and that they had urged Mortimer to desert and rise in revolt. Like Grey, Cambridge confessed: with Grey's confession to hand, it would have been difficult for him to do otherwise. Scrope, on the contrary, denied the first charge of conspiracy, although admitting that he knew about it. In his case, as has been pointed out,[44] the judges went against the provisions of the statute of treasons of 1352 by declaring that knowledge of treason merited the same penalty as treason itself, something on which parliament had not pronounced.

On being found guilty, both men were condemned to death. The sentences were carried out immediately. Cambridge was taken from Southampton castle to the place of execution at the Bargate, while Scrope went the painful way, being drawn there on a hurdle. Instead of allowing Scrope's wish, expressed in his will, that he should be buried near other members of his family in York Minster, the king ordered that his head be sent to York for public display on Micklegate Bar, that of Grey being despatched to Newcastle-upon-Tyne for the same purpose. Only Cambridge was allowed to have his head interred with his body in God's House in Southampton. The harsh treatment meted out to Scrope continued even after his death. While the lands and possessions of both Grey and Cambridge, although forfeited by them as traitors, were kept within their family circles, those of Scrope were subject to confiscation and almost indecently hasty seizure[45] before being redistributed in a manner which made it not unlikely that, in so acting, Henry went beyond the law. That he may have had later regrets of his treatment of the man who, until so recently, had been one of his most trusted helpers and lieutenants,[46] does not alter

43 DKR, 43, pp. 582, 587-8.
44 Pugh, 'Southampton plot', pp. 68–9.
45 *Historical papers and letters from the northern registers*, ed. J. Raine (RS, London, 1873), pp. 432–6.
46 '. . . quem dictus dominus rex plus aliis diligebat' (ibid., p. 432).

the fact that Scrope, a Knight of the Garter who had betrayed his trust and allegiance, had been treated both differently and more harshly both in life and in death by his sovereign lord, the king.[47]

It was not until almost a week after the executions that an observer would have seen Henry's fleet of some 1500 or so vessels, which included the royal flagship, the *Trinity Royal* (540 tons), sail down the Solent to the open sea and then in the direction of France.[48] The departure of the expedition, as we know from studies of such ventures in the reign of Edward III, was but the culmination of a colossal exercise of preparation which had been going on for months.[49] At the centre of it all had been the king, who had supervised both the general preparation and much of the detail. But Henry knew well that he could only succeed if he took others into his trust and delegated responsibility. The working breakfast is no modern invention. One day in April 1415 the king sat down to breakfast ('jantaculum') with his brother, Clarence, and other lords, and together they discussed and gave their advice on the forthcoming expedition to France.[50] Gathering together an army was one thing, transporting it in safety across the Channel was another. In May orders had gone out to the men of the Cinque Ports to go to sea to resist French attacks and doubtless keep the sea lanes clear.[51] In the same month the admirals were ordered to arrest all ships from different parts of the coast, together with their masters and crews, and to ensure that these should meet at Southampton as soon as possible.[52]

The need for ships was overriding; it cannot have been a popular one, for this was just the season when the fishing community would have been at its busiest, reluctant, therefore, to surrender use of its vessels for purposes of war. It was apparent, too, that England on her own could not provide sufficient ships for the size of the army being taken to France. Help would need to be sought outside the country. In April Richard Clitherowe and Reginald Curteys had been sent to Holland and Zeeland to see whether ships could be hired from those

---

[47] Pugh, 'Southampton plot', pp. 62–3.

[48] The figure of 1500 is the one generally accepted. In Venice, Antonio Morosini heard the number 1400 reported (*Chronique d'Antonio Morosini. Extraits relatifs à l'histoire de France*, ed. G. Lefèvre-Pontalis and L. Dorez (SHF, Paris, 1899, ii, 45)), while the 'Northern Chronicle' referred to 1600. (C.L. Kingsford, *English historical literature in the fifteenth century* (Oxford, 1913), p. 285.)

[49] H.J. Hewitt, *The organization of war under Edward III, 1338–62* (Manchester/New York, 1966), chs 2–4.

[50] PRO, E 403/621, m.2.

[51] Ibid., m.2. The ports were Dover, Hastings, Hythe, Romsey, Rye, Sandwich and Winchelsea.

[52] Ibid., m.4.

provinces.[53] On 25 April these two 'ingelssche' and ten other persons were granted permission to travel round the county of Holland on their business.[54] Their success can be measured by the fact that by mid-May 1415 ships, together with masters and crews, were already arriving at Dover from Holland and Zeeland.[55]

The place for which Henry's armada was sailing, accompanied as it left by a group of swans (taken as a good omen),[56] was Harfleur, the greatest and, strategically, the most important port of Normandy, the key to the capture of the duchy.[57] Situated on the north bank of the river Seine, the river upon which Rouen, the Norman capital, and, higher up, Paris, the French capital, lay, its position at the mouth of the wide Seine estuary gave it its strength. Furthermore, its well-defended walls presented a major problem to any invader hoping to use the river as a means of penetrating the interior of the duchy. Harfleur simply could not be bypassed or ignored. Nor was it an easy place to capture, for if threatened the citizens could flood the low ground which surrounded them. When Henry's fleet arrived off the westernmost point of land, known as the Chef de Caux (or Kydicaus, in the spelling of the time), on 13 August, it faced a difficult task. Part of it could be used from the seaward side to further any siege which might be undertaken, but the land forces coming up against the walls, ditches, dykes and bulwarks defending the town would encounter grave problems. From the reports of ambassadors and others who had passed through Harfleur, Henry knew that its capture was unlikely to be a formality. It is true that he had the advantage of surprise, for he had been careful to reveal to none what his objective in France would be, for fear that the possession of such information might enable the French to adopt defensive measures. If, sailing from Southampton, it was unlikely that Calais would be his point of landing, a spot in Picardy, perhaps at the mouth of the Somme, was not out of the question, in view of his relationship with the duke of Burgundy. Equally, a favourite landing place for English armies in the fourteenth century, one used by Clarence in 1412, had been St Vaast La Hougue, on the eastern side of the Cherbourg peninsula. It was even conceivable, if unlikely, that the large fleet might have been intended for Aquitaine. At all costs, the enemy must be kept guessing. The result

[53] Ibid., mm.3, 5; E 364/66, m.1d.
[54] The Hague, Algemeen Rijksarchief, Archief Graven van Holland, inv. nr 205, fos 156v, 172v. These references have come to me through the kindness of Yvonne Bos-Rops.
[55] PRO, E 403/621, m.6.
[56] *Gesta*, p. 21. Is it a coincidence that reference should be made to the bird which was the badge of the Bohun family and of the king himself?
[57] '. . . le souverain port de toute la duchié de Normendie' (Monstrelet, iii, 83, 86).

was that, although well guarded, Harfleur was not over-ready to resist the English invader.

Within two days of landing a few miles away, Henry had his army in position around the town's walls, with ships blocking access and egress from the sea.[58] The siege, which was to last some five weeks, showed at an early stage the king's strong determination to achieve his aim even when faced by stiff opposition and well-constructed defences. From the very first his experience of war in France was the continuation of one of his last personal actions in the long campaigns against the Welsh rebels, the siege of Aberystwyth. Henry had appreciated that this would be the kind of opposition he would meet. Not surprisingly, then, it is the care which he took in providing his army with the equipment needed for sieges which was emphasized by the writers of the chronicles: not merely cannon and gunpowder, but also scaling ladders, crossbows and tools for mining under walls, all of which (and others) would be of value to a besieging army. The clerical author of the *Gesta Henrici Quinti*, who was present as a member of the king's household, recorded the devastating effect achieved by the use of a number of bombards, or heavy guns, as well as lighter pieces against the town. Not only did they help to bring down the wall and destroy buildings; their effect as a psychological weapon, largely through the noise which both cannon and projectiles together could make, was also considerable among a largely civilian population which had refused to answer the king's call to surrender.[59]

If there was a certain inevitability about the fall of Harfleur, those within its walls, under the leadership of Raoul de Gaucourt, certainly did their best to avert it. But disease struck, and many of the inhabitants soon died. The English army, too, was to be severely affected by disease caught, it was said, by men eating unripe fruit.[60] Many died, including Richard Courtenay, bishop of Norwich, and Thomas, earl of Arundel, both known as friends of the king from the time of his father's rule. Others, including Henry's brother, Clarence, had to be sent home early in the hope of achieving restoration to health.[61]

[58] The best account by an eyewitness is in *Gesta*, chs 3–8.

[59] The influence of artillery upon the outcome of wars at this period, put in doubt by some historians, has been reasserted by M.G.A Vale (*War and Chivalry. Warfare and aristocratic culture in England, France and Burgundy at the end of the Middle Ages* (London, 1981), pp. 129–32).

[60] '. . . specialiter fluxus ventris et sanguinis nostros homines afflixit' (Kingsford, *English historical literature*, p. 285). The author of this chronicle claimed that almost 5000 Englishmen were struck by disease. See a list of sick in BL, Add. Ms 24512, fo. 146.

[61] 'Le roy veult et donne congie a tous lez personnes dont lez noms sont specifiez en une cedule a ceste bille annexee daler en Engleterre sanz empeschement. Et en tesmoign de ce le roy a fait mettre a ceste bille son signet par lez chamberlain et

But in spite of this, the initiative lay very much with the English. In mid-September, having twice called upon the town to surrender, Henry allowed a representative to leave to seek help from the French. As a guarantee, twenty-four hostages were handed over into English custody. A week later the envoy returned, empty-handed; nothing could now prevent capture by the English.

On 22 September a procession of leading figures emerged from within the walls and made its way to a spot where, on a prominence in the ground, Henry sat under a dais, dressed in majesty, surrounded by members of his nobility like stars around a sun. The formal ceremony of handing over of keys was thus carried out with ostentation to show who was master. With his well-developed sense of ceremony, of the impression which it could make on both bystander and participant, and of the submission which (in this case) it could be made to symbolize, Henry insisted that the formal surrender of the first place to fall to his army should be carried out with due ceremony.[62] Here was the reception of the rebels by their rightful lord: they must be made to recognize who, in this case, was master. On the following day Henry entered the town, and immediately went to the church of St Martin to give thanks for the deliverance of the place.

This done, the proper re-establishment of authority and order was completed by the appointment of the king's uncle, Thomas Beaufort, earl of Dorset, as captain of the town, with a garrison of some 2000 men under him. The king appears to have treated the people with respect: orders were issued that they should not be molested or maltreated. In so doing Henry was showing that an army need not always be feared; he was, at the same time, imposing discipline and efficiency upon his own troops. But the orders were also the product of another problem which dogged Henry throughout his military career in France. He could not claim to be king of France if he allowed his soldiers to treat Frenchmen as if they were the enemy. For better or worse his field of action was now curtailed, as it was to be again later in this matter. While he expelled a couple of thousand or so of the inhabitants, mostly women and children, he dealt with them fairly humanely, giving them an escort as they retreated in the direction of Rouen.[63] But his attitude towards them was clear. In resisting him they had rebelled, and while he was willing to take under his protection and restore the property of those who agreed to recognize the

seneschal de son houstel, le quint jour doctobre [1415]' (text of permission to return home: PRO, E 101/45/14). See photograph in frontispiece to J. Otway-Ruthven, *The King's Secretary and the Signet Office in the XVth century* (Cambridge, 1939).

[62] *Gesta*, p. 53; *Memorials of London and London life in the XIIIth, XIVth, and XVth centuries*, ed. H.T. Riley (London, 1868), pp. 619–20.

[63] *Gesta*, p. 55; *Brut*, ii, 377.

legality of his rule, those who would not must expect to suffer confiscation of their properties and expulsion from their homes. By such acts, and through their justification, which he knew would be reported elsewhere, Henry hoped to weaken resistance to him in the future. If he claimed territory in France through justice, he must act with justice; this meant acting consistently, taking a firm hand with his soldiers, too, so that people knew where they stood in relation both to him and to the army.

We have already seen something of the strategic and military importance of Harfleur, both to the defender and to the invader. In Henry's plan for the future, it had two further points of significance which should be noted here. First, it was to be for him not only a point of access into France, a second Calais or a second Cherbourg (handed back to the French [Charles of Navarre] by Richard II in 1394), but a place, too, which would act as a base for stores and equipment required by armies which might be active further inland, a task which its place at the mouth of the Seine admirably enabled it to fulfil. Secondly, it was to be the first example of Henry's new policy of colonization in Normandy, a development which changed the character of the war being fought in France, and which marked off the new phase of the conflict with France from that of the fourteenth century, characterized as that had been by a military policy of raids and, not infrequently, physical destruction. Henry was doing something significant. Within a week or two of the fall of Harfleur, he was to invite merchants and those, such as victuallers, whose presence had a military justification, to come to the town, where they would be given houses to live in and outlets for their trade in return for undertakings to set up permanent residence.[64] Harfleur was too important to remain a dead town. A substantial English presence would help revive its fortunes, assure its permanent defence, provide the English with the rapid and regular supply of their military needs on campaign, and help bring about the establishment of an English settlement in Normandy which, as the future would show, was to be the hallmark of the history of the duchy for the coming thirty-five years or so.

[64] *Calendar of Letter-Books preserved among the Archives of the Corporation of the City of London at the Guildhall, Letter-Book I, c. A.D. 1400–1422*, ed. R.R. Sharpe (London, 1909), p. 159.

Chapter 5

AGINCOURT

There were now important decisions to be taken. Of these, the most far-reaching in its implications was 'Where now?'. By the time that Henry was in a position to ponder this question closely, it was the last week in September. Valuable time, perhaps a fortnight or more (a factor of particular importance in view of the approaching autumn), had been lost. The events at Southampton had held him up a few days (the army had been mustered and ready to sail in the last days in July), and it is likely that the siege of Harfleur had taken longer than the king had hoped or expected. What would he do now? His opponents may have expected him to make for Rouen, the Norman capital, some fifty miles up the Seine and, like Harfleur, on the river's right bank: their forces and command centre were in and around the city. Such a plan presupposed that Henry's likely intention was to strike at Paris, as Edward III had tried to do once or twice in the previous century, to capture the capital and, with it, the political control of all, or at least of much, of France. Or was it, rather, the king's intention to emulate his brother Clarence's expedition into France in 1412 and make his way to Aquitaine, even, perhaps, to accept a large sum of money, as Clarence had done, to leave the country as soon as possible? Or did Henry have it in mind to copy his predecessors and use France as a military playground from which he, his captains and his soldiers could derive the maximum of personal profit to the material detriment of France, and principally at the expense of her civilian population? These were all possibilities.

What Henry had so far achieved, and his manner of achieving it, does not, however, suggest that he had any of these possibilities in mind. In spite of, or rather because of, the very elaborate preparations made for the expedition of 1415, it is unlikely that it was intended to be much more than an attempt to establish a firm base on the coast of Normandy. The capture of Harfleur gave the English a door into France and, at the same time, prevented the French from using it as a place from which to launch attacks upon English shipping and the southern coast of England. The elaborate preparations for the siege reflect both Henry's determination to capture Harfleur and his appreciation that technological development (particularly in the form of cannon) could be used to his advantage. Since nothing, however, was more cumbersome than the artillery of this age, Henry was faced with the almost inevitable consequence of having a large artillery train: he must either leave it at Harfleur or ship it back to England. With as yet so flimsy a base behind him and with the unreliable weather of autumn soon to come, he could hardly set out on an expedition further into France and take his cannon with him.

It is unlikely that he was planning to go much further than Harfleur in 1415. If not, what then? One possibility was to return home the way he had come; that, however, might have appeared too much like a retreat, allowed to the sick but not to those in good health. Nor can we be sure that the transport fleet was still available. A second possibility, the likeliest in the circumstances, was to return to England by another route which would take him to that other English bastion on the French mainland, Calais. The author of the *Gesta* tells us that Henry called together a council of his principal commanders and asked for their advice. Significantly (was it that they recognized the parlous condition of Henry's army better than did the king himself?) they advised him by a large majority to retire to England by the direct sea crossing.[1] Having heard them, however, Henry made up his own mind. His decision was that he, and those in the army who did not have leave to return to England by sea, should set out for Calais.

Implied in the chronicler's account is that the decision was Henry's, and Henry's alone. Was it a spirit of daring, temerity or folly which led him to make up his mind in this way? Commentators have taken different views. How well informed was he, on the one hand, of the geographical conditions and physical hazards which he and his army must encounter, and, on the other hand, of the likely presence of the enemy in the areas through which he was about to pass? At the best estimate and in the most favourable circumstances the ground which the English would have to traverse amounted to some 120 miles: it would take them about eight days.[2] Nor were the circumstances in any sense ordinary. The ford at Blanchetaque, not far from the mouth of the river Somme (where Edward III had successfully negotiated the crossing in 1346), was a likely place for the English to meet opposition, which might be effected by a relatively small number of men. Supposing that the English stumbled upon or were to be challenged by a much larger force, what might then happen? We cannot know the extent of Henry's information regarding French troop move-

[1] *Gesta*, p. 61.
[2] Ibid., p. 61.

ments in eastern Normandy and Picardy at this time.[3] It is possible that he may have been lulled into a false sense of security by the failure of the French to respond to the call for military help sent out by the men of Harfleur only a fortnight or so earlier.

Certainly Henry was not the first English leader to find himself in France some distance from a safe port of embarkation, and with a hostile enemy army somewhere not far away anxious to catch and punish him in formal battle. Edward III had been in a not dissimilar position, and in much the same area of France, in 1346; and his son, Edward, the Black Prince, had been returning to Bordeaux from a successful expedition into central France in 1356 when the French king, John II, had caught him up with an army. On neither occasion had the English been seeking battle: the initiative had come from the French, and on both occasions, at Crécy and later at Poitiers, they had been soundly defeated. These historic precedents, which would have been well known to the king, may have encouraged him. He cannot have been unaware that there was some risk; but that would not have worried Henry. The question was, how great was it? One may think that John Hardyng, who was on the march to Calais and later compiled a chronicle, understood all sides of the problem when he wrote that Henry 'homeward went through Fraunce like a man'.[4]

The march which began at the end of the first week of October was chronicled in detail by one of the king's chaplains, the anonymous compiler of the *Gesta*.[5] Henry may have been at the head of some 6000 fighting men, together with an unknown number of others in supporting roles. The march began with an air of confidence: it had been anticipated that it would take some eight days, and much opposition was clearly not expected. For the first days, although the English were shadowed by a force under Marshal Boucicaut and others, all seemed to go well; one or two towns such as Arques and Eu even offered to provide the army with food and drink on condition that they should not be subject to attack or their lands destroyed by fire.[6] It was only on 12 October that, through the report of some French prisoners, it was learned that the ford at Blanchetaque was in fact held by the French, who had effectively destroyed the causeway and

[3] When writing to the duke of Bedford on 7 October, William Bardolf, lieutenant of Calais, announced that a battle between Henry and the French was likely in the coming fortnight, as the enemy were intent upon barring his way to Calais. As it was, the battle took place almost three weeks later (*Foedera*, IV, ii, 147–8).

[4] *The Chronicle of John Hardyng*, ed. H. Ellis (London, 1812), p. 375.

[5] *Gesta*, p. 61 seq.

[6] This is clearly what the French, from the experience of earlier years, feared would happen to them.

erected stakes, a party of men sent from Calais having been too small
to be able to secure the crossing for Henry.

The psychological blow, already considerable, was made worse
when it was learned that a French army was patrolling the right bank
of the Somme, waiting for the English to cross. The anticipated eight
days had now almost passed; Calais was still a long way away, and
it was clear that a major detour would have to be made so that the
Somme might be crossed in safety. In fact the English were led by
their king for several days up the river's left bank, past Airaines,
Amiens and further south-east. It was not until 19 October that they
found themselves able to cut across the inside of a long bend in the
Somme west and south of Péronne, where a French army was waiting,
before discovering a place not properly guarded at which, although
not without some difficulty, they were able to cross the river. The
French, at least one contemporary was to write a little later, had
fluffed their chance.[7] Now that the river had been crossed, the English had overcome one of the main obstacles which lay between them
and Calais. On the other hand, they could scarcely avoid a confrontation with the enemy which, the 'bailli' of Hainault wrote to the
municipality of Mons on about 23 October, was planned for the following Friday.[8]

The *Gesta* presents evidence of an English army, now a fortnight's
march away from Harfleur, exhausted both physically and morally,
supporting a number of men who had not recovered sufficiently from
the illness contracted at the siege and who were now in a state of
physical collapse, men who were hungry and apprehensive of the
future. On 20 October, the day after the crossing of the Somme,
French heralds approached to announce that the dukes of Orléans
and Bourbon and the constable, Albret, had decided that the English
army should be challenged in the field. Henry replied that he would
march on, and that they could find him wherever he happened to be.
Such news can only have lowered his men's morale even further,
although the nadir must have been reached at the point when, as
recounted dramatically in the *Gesta*, the English saw in the road traces
of a large French army which had passed that way not long before.[9]
The king was going to need all his skill both as a reviver of spirits
and morale and as a soldier if he was to make an effective fighting
force out of the men whom he had brought thus far.

[7] 'Livre des trahisons', p. 128.
[8] *Cartulaire des comtes de Hainaut*, ed. L. Devillers (Brussels, 1889), pp. 46–7. Some
days earlier he had noted the very large number of French and English soldiers in
the area (ibid., p. 46).
[9] *Gesta*, p. 77.

For four days after the receipt of the French challenge, Henry and his army, the men-at-arms now wearing at least part of their armour in case of sudden attack, moved north-westward towards Calais, perhaps unaware that the French who had been at Péronne had joined up with a much larger army near Bapaume, and were now advancing only a little ahead of them. On 24 October, having crossed the small river Ternoise, the English caught their first sight of the French army, as large as a swarm of locusts, as the author of the *Gesta* put it.[10] For both king and army, this was the moment of truth. None would reach Calais without confronting the French in battle. The odds looked forbidding and, as the same text records, the priests in the English army were kept busy hearing confessions and granting absolution. For a while the two armies manoeuvred their positions, but by the end of the afternoon it was too late to begin a battle. That would be fought the next day. It was probably at this moment, in response to a comment by Sir Walter Hungerford that he wished the king had 10,000 more archers under his command, that Henry made the well-known statement that since God would be there to protect his people, they would make do with those they had.[11] In the meantime, however, Henry released all the French prisoners whom he held, on condition that if they were to be on the winning side they could regard themselves as free men, but if they were not, they were to return to captivity. It is likely that this was done to ensure that the English should not be attacked from the rear, as well as to make the maximum number of Englishmen available for the coming battle.

On strict orders from the king, the night was spent in complete silence in the orchards, fields and barns of the neighbouring village of Maisoncelle.[12] So quiet were the English that the French were not sure whether they had broken camp and slipped away. Henry wanted his men to get what sleep they could for they had marched about 250 miles in seventeen days and had enjoyed only a single day of rest. However, rain which fell in the long hours of darkness must have caused great discomfort and cold to the English. By contrast the French, whose camp lay not far away, could be heard making merry like an army confident of victory on the morrow. While the scene is

[10] Ibid., p. 77.

[11] Ibid., p. 79. The story reappears in Shakespeare's *Henry V* (IV, 3, ll.16–18).

[12] The main contemporary or near contemporary accounts are those of eyewitnesses: *Gesta*, pp. 79–93; J. de Waurin, *Recueil des croniques et anchiennes istories de la Grant Bretaigne, a present nomme Engleterre, 1399–1422*, ed. W. Hardy (RS, London, 1868), pp. 201–18; *Chronique de Jean le Fèvre, seigneur de Saint-Remy*, ed. F. Morand (2 vols, SHF, Paris, 1876, 1881), i, 243–69. See also J. Keegan, *The Face of Battle* (Harmondsworth, 1978), pp. 78–116; C. Phillpotts, 'The French plan of battle during the Agincourt campaign', *EHR*, 99 (1984), 59–66.

described in this way to convey a moral sense to the turn of events (the small army with the cards stacked against it emerging triumphant against a larger one too confident of itself), one cannot doubt that the French were justifiably hopeful that the next day would see them victors against the English.

Very early on the next day, Friday, 25 October, the king, fully armed except for his headgear, heard three Masses. Then, having donned a splendid basinet upon which had been fixed a rich golden crown (so that he would be recognizable from afar?), he mounted a small grey horse and, giving orders for the baggage to be guarded, he ordered the army to position itself in the field. This was an area of open ground, recently ploughed and sown, about 1000 yards long and 800–900 yards wide, bound on the left (as the English saw it from the village of Maisoncelle) by a wood in which lay the village of Agincourt and, on the right, a further wood surrounding the village of Tramecourt, the field being rather narrower at the end occupied by the English than it was where the French army was stationed. Anxious to prevent attacks upon his rear, Henry had to place his force in such a way that, as far as possible, it stretched across the whole width of the open ground between the woods: inevitably, with only an estimated 6000 or so men available to him (about 1000 men-at-arms and some 5000 archers dismounted for the battle), the line of men-at-arms (in contrast with the French) would be a thin one. It was done by ordering the army in an unbroken line of battle across the field, the king himself (surrounded by the banners of the Trinity, the Virgin, St George, St Edward and, finally, his own) occupying the centre of the field, with Edward, duke of York, in command of the van (the position of honour) on his right, the rear (on the king's left) being in the charge of Thomas, Lord Camoys.[13] While it is possible that there were groups, or wedges, of archers between the three sections, it is clear that the large majority of them were placed on the wings, looking slightly obliquely towards the centre of the French army which opposed them.

It is difficult to describe the French numbers and formations with precision. The call to arms appears to have evoked a very considerable and positive reaction, so that there can be no doubt that the army assembled under the banner of the constable, acting on this occasion in place of his absent monarch, was a large one, probably some three or four times the size of that commanded by Henry, who may have faced a fighting force of 20,000 men or more. In addition to its great size, what made it stand out from the English army was its very different composition. It had archers and crossbowmen, but in

[13] *Gesta*, p. 83.

numbers so small as to make no impression upon the battle, and some pieces of small artillery, of which the English probably had none. On the other hand the French had a very large number of men-at-arms, dressed in heavy armour of steel which went down to below their knees, their legs and arms being well protected, as were their heads and shoulders.[14] This army, which may be readily understood as having put fear and despair into the minds of most Englishmen who saw it, was drawn up in three great 'battles', reflecting not only the military might of a much larger kingdom, but an attitude to war which represented the collective responsibility of the nobility to defend the public good and a desire of men of that class to win glory in battle.

The French army was in large measure dismounted. Of the three 'battles' which stood one behind another, only the third included cavalry, although there were mounted soldiers on either wing, whose task it was to fall upon the English archers. If the English were thinly strung across the field, the two 'battles' of men-at-arms on foot were to come together presumably to cause the English line to collapse against such weight of numbers. In the centre, and to the front, were concentrated members of the highest nobility and office-holders; behind them, also on foot, were the other French 'battles'. It was at this stage that a group of eighteen French men-at-arms, fighting under the banner of the lord of Croy, planned to attack the person of Henry who, as we have noted, was not afraid to draw attention to himself through the use of banners and the wearing of a crown. It is likely indeed that Henry, with his sense of chivalry and understanding the mind of his opponents, deliberately acted in this way to draw the enemy towards him, aware that the vital work of his archers in the wings would be facilitated if this could be done. He may, indeed, have offered himself as a form of 'bait' to the enemy. Jean le Fèvre and Jean de Waurin, on whose eyewitness accounts we are obliged to cast much reliance, inform us that the group of eighteen notable French 'gentilz hommes', led by the lord of Croy, swore that when the two armies met they would strive to knock the crown from upon Henry's head, or die in the attempt. One of their number got close enough to the king to deliver a hefty blow to his basinet and in so doing to make a hole in it and break off part of the crown, before, like the others of his group, meeting his death in the battle. The action, none the less, had greatly impressed those who witnessed it: had all the French fought in the same way, it was said, the outcome would have been very different.[15]

---

[14] P. Contamine, *Guerre, état et société à la fin du moyen âge. Études sur les armeés des rois de France, 1337–1494* (Paris/The Hague, 1972), p. 226.

[15] Le Fèvre, p. 250; Waurin, p. 207.

To discuss the events of 25 October 1415, the feast of Sts Crispin and Crispinian, is to ask why it was that the seemingly likely outcome of events did not occur. The decision to challenge the English had been taken at a meeting of the French king's council held at Rouen on 12 October. But it had not been a unanimous decision. Although the young princes of the blood, most notably the dukes of Orléans, Bourbon and Alençon (all of whom had joined in the alliance with Henry IV in 1412), were in favour of positive action against the English, the two main military officers of the kingdom, the constable, Charles d'Albret, and the marshal, Boucicaut, both older men, favoured letting Henry and his army go and concentrating the main effort upon the recapture of Harfleur only recently lost to the English. Their advice, however, was to be overruled. Such division of opinion was to be aggravated by a factor of even greater significance: division of leadership or, indeed, no real leadership at all. The king himself, it was said, wanted to lead his army, but he was clearly unfit to do so, and leadership of the French army thus devolved upon others. The duke of Burgundy had been pointedly ordered by his sovereign not to claim the exercise of what might have been his natural right to assume command of the army, and in his absence a form of collective leadership, consisting of princes of the blood and royal officers, took charge. What was lacking was one man of natural authority and personal prestige to lead the large French army drawn from many parts of France. It was at this moment that France missed the presence and personal leadership of an inspiring king. The English, on the other hand, had both.

In this respect, the contrast between the French and English armies could not have been greater. If the French leadership was unsure about its aims and unclear about its chain of command (Pierre de Fenin recorded that all the French leaders placed themselves in the van of the army, whole units being left leaderless),[16] on the English side the king stood out as the undisputed leader of the army. As we have seen, the decision to march from Harfleur to Calais had been his. All the way, he had taken personal charge, and it had been his encouragement which the soldiers had received when things had appeared to be going badly. When, on the morning of the battle, Henry had addressed his men, the words which he uttered were the words of a soldier who appreciated full well the strains, both physical and psychological, which they were experiencing, and who knew how to lift them out of the trough of despondency, even despair, into which many had fallen. Agincourt was to show that, in Henry, England had

---

[16] *Mémoires de Pierre de Fenin*, ed. Mlle. Dupont (SHF, Paris, 1837), pp. 62, 64.

a leader who could animate an army even in apparently hopeless circumstances.

Raising spirits was one matter. As the military writers of classical times had often pointed out, leadership also consisted of making the most of opportunities presented on the day of battle. Henry was able and ready to take advantage of anything which might turn the course of events in his direction. One such factor was that heavy rain had fallen on the night of 24 October. When the armies came face to face by about nine o'clock on the following day, they did so across ground which was muddy and slippery, providing poor fighting conditions for both men-at-arms in heavy armour and, in particular, for cavalry. The rain which would have caused the English soldiery such discomfort in the hours of darkness might perhaps be turned to their advantage. For some three hours, between nine o'clock and midday, the opposing armies faced each other, hoping that the ground might dry a bit, and that the enemy might be prevailed upon to make the first move across the mud. The French may have thought it likely that, in their straitened circumstances, the English would move first, while the English hope was that the French cavalry and men-at-arms on foot would engage themselves in the hazardous conditions prevalent that day.

What could save the long, thin English line? It faced a much larger army with a majority of men-at-arms fighting on foot, only a relatively small force being mounted. Since the English, too, fought mainly on foot, the outcome was likely to be decided by what the dismounted soldier did. The difference between the armies was that while the French men-at-arms might have to cross muddy ground in order to fight the English, these, with their archers, could inflict damage, perhaps terrible damage, from a distance of some 200 yards. In the circumstances, that advantage was potentially decisive.

Given the character of each army, the condition of the ground assumed great importance. No wonder each waited to see what the other would do. In the end it was Henry who broke the deadlock. Realizing that the wait was having an adverse effect upon his men, he decided to move. 'Nowe is gode tyme, for alle Engelond prayeth for us; and therefore be of gode chere, and lette us go to our iorney.' Then he added, with a shout: 'In the name of Almyghti God and Saynt George, avaunt banerer! and Saynte George, this day thyn help!'[17] Slowly the army advanced the better part of 700 yards, stopping some 200 or so yards short of the enemy, now within range of English arrows. There the archers drove into the ground the stakes which each had been ordered to cut some days before, in such a way

---

[17] *Brut*, ii, 378 BL, Harley Ms 565, fo.110 has 'Felas, lets go'.

as to make it dangerous for horses and difficult for men-at-arms to attack them.

It was from this second position that the English were to fight the battle. The king's aim was still to make the French move towards him, bring them within range of his archers, who would make the enemy feel the full impact of their arrows, and then to allow those same archers, as lightly armed men, to attack the French with other weapons which they had to hand. At a range of some 200 yards, the English began to rain arrows (at something like the rate of ten per man per minute) upon the French men-at-arms, both mounted and on foot who had divided themselves into three 'battles'. The provocation was almost immediately successful in bringing about a cavalry charge upon the archers, who may have stood their ground until the last instant before seeking a measure of safety behind the stakes which had been driven into the earth, 'hedgehog-like', all around them. Some horses impaled themselves upon the stakes, their riders becoming easy victims of the English. Others, seeing the danger, tried to turn back against the forward-moving cavalry movement, and brought chaos to their own ranks. Others, still, forced their way between the archers on the wings and the wood, managing to reach the English line and push it back. That line, however, held.

Then there came the advance of the men-at-arms on foot, the bulk of the French army, which now set out to make contact with the English, probably some 300 yards away. As they advanced, there came from the wings some of those horses terrified by what they had just experienced and, in many cases, no longer controlled by their riders. Their ranks broken by the fleeing horses and with lances shortened (the idea was to give the lance greater strength), the men-at-arms advanced upon the thin English line which met them, to its undoubted advantage, with lances of normal length. In the circumstances it needed little to bring disaster upon the French army. It should be remembered that the English front was narrower than that of the French. Thus as they advanced, doubtless at no great speed, across the soft ground, the heavily armed French foot soldiers were gradually forced more closely together from the sides by the available ground, and from behind as rank upon rank advanced upon the English, who met them standing still, with the advantage of full-length lances as well as with the backing of archers who could aim their arrows either at the side of the advancing French or into them. Given the numbers of the enemy involved, arrows were likely to find a target.

Thus the mêlée, the meeting of the French and English men-at-arms, went very much the way of the English in spite of the superior French numbers. It was, indeed, this numerical superiority which contributed directly to the defeat of the French. For whereas they had hoped to crush the English in the narrow confines of the field by Agincourt,[18] those confines inhibited the proper use of weapons by the French men-at-arms, caused them to jostle and knock one another, and, as they came up against the English, to slip and fall and thus create the piles of bodies so vividly described by the chroniclers. Aided by the archers who, having used up all their arrows, joined in a form of counter-attack with knives, daggers and other weapons (including stakes), the English men-at-arms soon made it clear that the battle could have only one outcome. As more and more French, realizing this, turned to flee and ran into their fellows still advancing from behind, so the extent of the massacre broadened. Within an hour or so it must have been evident that, barring an extraordinary reversal of fortune, the English had won.

At the end of that time, in spite of the near-death of Humphrey of Gloucester, Henry must have been confident. Two French 'battles' of men-at-arms had been destroyed or scattered, their members dead, captured or fled. A third, however, remained. Nor could Henry fail to be aware that, not far off, stood a large number of prisoners, unarmed but still in their armour, guarded by the few men who could be spared. At this point, it seems, a break occurred: it was the moment when, if Henry were not careful, what looked like victory could be turned into defeat.

What happened in the next minutes has been the cause of much controversy and of the only 'black mark' against the king which has had any real chance of sticking. The late arrival and charge of Antony, duke of Brabant, brother of John, duke of Burgundy, had been absorbed: it had been ill prepared and presented no real threat. The same might not be said, however, of the preparations going on for an attack by the third French 'battle' which had so far taken no part in the proceedings. Led by the counts of Marle and Fauquembergue, it was seen to be preparing to enter the conflict. At the rear of the English army were the prisoners, loosely guarded. Might it not happen that, even in the moment of victory, the English could be denied the success which they had won for themselves? The predicament was a considerable one for Henry and those English leaders who may have been close to him at that moment. Both Christian teaching and the practices of chivalry emphasized that the unarmed man must not be cut down in cold blood and that the prisoner should be treated according to well-known conventions.[19] The live prisoner also had a market

---

[18] '. . . qui trop estoit estroicte pour combatre tant de gens' (*Guillaume Gruel, Chronique d'Arthur de Richemont*, ed. A. le Vavasseur (SHF, Paris, 1890), p. 17.

[19] One near-contemporary legal view can be found in *The Tree of Battles of Honoré Bonet*, trans. G.W. Coopland (Liverpool, 1949), p. 152 (ch.xlvi).

value: he might be ransomed. Once dead, his potential was immediately lost. Thoughts based on these factors must have passed through
Henry's mind as he decided how to counter the threat of the third
French mounted 'battle' looming over himself and his army. It is
likely that the threat was a very considerable one, perhaps greater
than most chronicle accounts are able to convey. For reasons which
are not clear, we must assume that, at the moment when the attack
from the French 'battle' threatened, the balance between victory and
defeat was still a fine one. It is likely that, even at this stage, Henry
felt victory could go either way.

It was this appreciation of the situation (and, in the circumstances,
a decision had to be taken very quickly) which led Henry to issue the
order that the prisoners taken in battle should be killed. At once, we are
told, he met resistance and refusal. For religious or moral reasons?
Quite possibly. For material reasons? Most likely. A man-at-arms, having got the better of one similarly armed in battle, would be unlikely to
relish killing him in cold blood: such action went against the ethical
and social code in which such men had been brought up. All the while,
valuable time was being lost: Henry finally met the refusal to carry out
his instructions by ordering a force of some 200 archers, led by an
esquire, to carry out the grisly task. How many were then killed is not
known. The chronicles reveal nothing specific on the matter of
numbers. The author of the *Vita* wrote of many being killed, all of them
nobles.[20] The version offered by the *First English Life*, compiled a century later, stated that the English killed 'manie of there saide enemies
prisoners, both Noble men and rich men', because they feared the prisoners who outnumbered them, but adding the statement,[21] taken from
Tito Livio, that the French were warned by the king's heralds that any
of them captured in the planned attack would be put to the sword without mercy, and that a similar fate awaited those who did not leave the
field at once.[22] On seeing that Henry was not uttering idle threats, they
immediately withdrew.[23] It is notable that, while regretting the loss
of noble prisoners, no contemporary French chronicler criticized the
morality of Henry's action. Was this because the French had unfurled
the 'oriflamme', or special, red war banner, taken as a sign of 'guerre
mortelle' during which no quarter was to be granted, and that this convention was used by Henry to justify the death of the prisoners taken by
the English on this occasion?[24]

[20] *Vita Henrici Quinti*, p. 68.
[21] *First English Life*, p. 61.
[22] *Vita Henrici Quinti*, p. 68.
[23] *Brut*, ii, 557, 597.
[24] See M.H. Keen, *The Laws of War in the late Middle Ages* (London/ Toronto, 1965),
pp. 104–6; Vale, *War and Chivalry*, p. 157.

Whether there was any real intention in the king's mind to pursue his instruction through to the bitter end has, in recent times, been put in serious doubt.[25] Henry, it is argued, came back to England with well over 1000 prisoners, perhaps more, men who may be regarded as the survivors of the massacre, for relatively few prisoners would have been taken after that time. In addition to these men, many others were left behind in Calais, some of them having already changed hands as a result of cash transactions. It is likely, then, that at the moment when Henry gave the order for the prisoners to be killed, they numbered 2000 or more men, mostly well armoured although by then without weapons or head-piece. How could the king ever expect such numbers to be killed in the brief time which would elapse before the anticipated charge took place? Would such a large number of men meekly submit to being put to death? Who was to carry out these 'executions'? At the best of times it would need a large number of men to do this, and the king, as we have seen, met refusal to carry out his orders. Even if those originally ordered to kill the prisoners had done so, the outcome of the victory would have been greatly put at risk by the attention which the men-at-arms would have been paying to the killings rather than to the threatened attack by the remaining French 'battle', which, had it taken place, could certainly not have been successfully met by the archers alone, granted that they had probably but few if any arrows left by this late stage. The order to kill the prisoners makes little sense in these circumstances. Rather, it is more likely that it was an attempt to frighten them into submission, and to cause them to allow themselves to be herded off the field by the archers, who were precisely the men whom Henry could, with least adverse effect, spare in view of the threatened charge by the French men-at-arms. If many were killed in the process, this was no deliberate wholesale massacre. It was, moreover, a 'massacre' which was brought to an end immediately it was recognized that the threat from the French men-at-arms was not going to materialize, in other words when they showed that they would withdraw and leave the English the victors on the field. Those prisoners who reached Calais and, finally, England, were the survivors of a tragic event whose extent has none the less probably been exaggerated.

With the failure of the third French 'battle' to make any impression upon the English, Henry, who now held the field, called to him the heralds who, in their role of observers, had been watching the conflict from the wings. From Montjoie, the French herald, he obtained a recognition that victory was his and, on being told that the name of the nearest village was Agincourt, he decided that the battle should

[25] Keegan, *Face of Battle*, pp. 108–12.

be named after it. At this stage men were sent round to find the wounded among the large number of dead lying on the field. Among the most notable of those 1600 knights and esquires who, according to Le Fèvre, were taken prisoner were Charles, duke of Orléans; the duke of Bourbon; the count of Vendôme; the count of Richemont, brother to the duke of Brittany; the count of Eu; and Boucicaut, the marshal. The list of the dead was a long and doleful one: Albret, the constable; Jacques de Chatillon, the admiral; the duke of Alençon; the duke of Brabant, and the count of Nevers, both brothers to the duke of Burgundy; the duke of Bar and his brother, and countless others. In all the chronicles, English as well as French, the lists of the dead and the captured were included as a reminder of the courage shown by large numbers who came to support their king against the foreign invader.

In the evening, the king retired to the nearby village of Maison-celle, where he had spent the previous night, and where he now entertained some of his most illustrious prisoners, notably the duke of Orléans, to dinner. No doubt much body-stripping must have been taking place while it was still light: Henry felt obliged to remind his men that they were not yet completely out of danger, and that no man was to take more than he needed to fit himself out. On the king's orders the remainder of the equipment was piled into a barn which was then set on fire, thereby effectively depriving the enemy of its use in the future.

Early next day, after preparations had been set in motion for the burial of many of the dead on the site of the battle (they were buried in large pits on ground specially consecrated by Louis of Luxembourg, bishop of Thérouanne, in whose see the field of battle lay) and steps had been taken to bring home the remains of the duke of York, who, along with Michael de la Pole, earl of Suffolk, was the leading English-man to meet death at this battle, the king set out for Calais, which was reached, without further incident, on 29 October. The arrival of the army and its prisoners was, however, scarcely welcome. The English had had little to eat for several days and were very hungry; nor were the French, after their defeat, in a good state, either. It needed Henry's organizational skills to see that the shorter the time they stayed in Calais, the better, and he arranged for his army and its prisoners to be shipped over to England, some landing at Dover, others at Sandwich, whence each soldier made his own way home.

The king, however, remained in Calais for some days. During his stay he was joined by the prisoners from Harfleur who, as they had undertaken, had made their own way there. Then, leaving France, Henry set sail for England where, after a very rough crossing, he landed at Dover, probably on 15 November. After a day's rest, the king made his way to Canterbury,[26] where he was met by archbishop Chichele and gave thanks at the cathedral. Then passing through Rochester, he travelled towards London, and took up residence in the royal manor of Eltham, south-east of the capital, there to await the formal royal reception which was to come.

The account of this event found in the *Gesta* is significant for a number of reasons.[27] The first is the stress and importance which it places upon the relationship which Henry had with the city of London.[28] The popularity which he had enjoyed in the capital in the days when he was still Prince continued during the remainder of his life. It was to the corporation of London that Henry had appealed for money early in 1415 when he was still seeking financial backing for his plans to go on expedition to France, an appeal which had led to a loan of 10,000 marks (£6666 13s. 4d.) and a number of smaller, private loans towards the war.[29] It was to London, too, that he had written on 22 September to announce the fall of Harfleur to his army.[30] Then a long period of silence had ensued, during which men came to fear that disaster might have struck the king and his army.[31] But on Tuesday, 29 October, the news of victory won at Agincourt reached London; church bells were rung and the people went in procession to Westminster as an expression of communal joy, relief and thanksgiving.[32] Preparations must have immediately begun to ensure that a welcome fitting for the man whom the mayor was to term 'thou conquerour'[33] was on hand when he arrived, preparations to which the city's guilds made contributions of various kinds.

On 23 November, a Saturday, the great reception took place.[34] Leaving Eltham, Henry came to Blackheath where he was met by the mayor, the twenty-four aldermen and a huge concourse of people, many wearing the colours of their guilds. They proceeded towards London, Henry accompanied by a number of the most important prisoners taken at Agincourt, to be met in Southwark by the clergy of London. When London Bridge was reached it was seen to have two giant figures, one a man, the other a woman, above the tower at its entrance, figures said to be extending a welcome to their

[26] PRO, E 101/45/7; Canterbury Cathedral Archives, J/B/A/1, no.46.
[27] *Gesta*, pp. 101–13.
[28] See below, ch.19.
[29] *Memorials of London*, pp. 613–14.
[30] Ibid., pp. 619–20.
[31] Ibid., pp. 621–2.
[32] *Letter-Book I*, p. 144. Bishop Beaufort made the announcement at St Paul's cathedral.
[33] BL, Harley Ms 565, fo.112.
[34] *Gesta*, pp. 101–13; *Chronicon Adae de Usk*, pp. 128, 311–12.

triumphant lord with, all around, staffs bearing the royal arms. Going further forward the king would have seen the figure of an antelope[35] with the royal arms hanging round its neck, and that of a lion holding in its right paw a staff with a royal standard unfurled, and then a large figure of St George in armour. In Cornhill could be seen the arms of St George, St Edward, St Edmund and of England, together with those of the dynasty, while at the entrance to Cheapside were the figures of the Twelve Apostles, together with twelve English kings, and saints.

On the cross at Cheapside, over which a wooden structure resembling a castle had been built, was the line 'Glorious things have been recounted about thee, city of God'. High above the gate were the arms of St George, with those of the king on one side and those of the emperor, Sigismund, on the other, together with those of other members of the royal house and the leading nobility on the lower turrets. On the drawbridge leading into the 'castle' a group of young women came forward to meet the king, all of them singing a welcome (they were compared by the author of the account to the maidens who had welcomed David after he had slain Goliath); while from all over the 'castle' came the voices of a large number of young boys singing the Church's great hymn of praise and thanksgiving, 'Te Deum laudamus'. Further along, on the way to St Paul's cathedral, was another scene with a canopy (regarded as a mark of honour) upheld by angelic figures, under which a figure of majesty in the form of a sun emitting dazzling rays could be seen, and to which the culmination of praise, 'Deo gracias', was being offered.

To the visual effects specially constructed for the occasion could be added the crowds of spectators who thronged the streets to see the king and his prisoners who, almost more than anyone, were the living signs of the victory so recently achieved. The king himself, if he came in triumph, did not come in pride. What struck the contemporary mind was the contrast between the outward signs of victory and the king's sober dress and demeanour on this occasion, the like of which had never been seen before by the Londoners. What impressed the author of the *Gesta* was the fact that Henry wore only a simple gown of purple and, instead of being surrounded by an escort of his knights, he chose to be accompanied by a small group of men from his household, the king riding at a gentle pace and seemingly more concerned with giving thanks to God than with seeking the glory which, not inappropriately, he might have claimed. In this way he proceeded to St Paul's, where he was met by a number of prelates who led him to the high altar where he gave thanks and made an offering, doing the

[35] The antelope was Henry's badge.

same at the shrine of St Erkenwald, a late seventh-century bishop of London. This done, he rode to Westminster Abbey, where he was met by the abbot and monks and a very considerable crowd, and where he left an offering at the shrine of St Edward the Confessor, founder of the abbey and a much favoured patron saint. From the abbey, he went to the palace of Westminster where, on the morrow, he received the mayor and another large group of citizens who gave him £1000 in two gold basins. Then, on the king's orders, a solemn funeral service for the dead of both sides was celebrated at St Paul's by the bishops who were in London for the convocation (or clerical assembly) of the ecclesiastical province of Canterbury.[36] The first expedition was now over.

What had been achieved? To attempt to answer this question is not to ask whether Henry thought that he had successfully completed the task which he had set himself: we cannot be sure what that task, in its entirety, really was. None the less, one major military objective had been achieved: Harfleur, described by bishop Beaufort in the speech which he made to parliament on 4 November as 'the king's lieges' greatest enemy', had been conquered.[37] The effects of this would be to give English merchant men a degree of safety at sea which they had not enjoyed for many years. The significance of this success was recognized on both sides of the Channel. The effort of the English to maintain their control of it; the attempts, in the coming months, of the French to wrest it back from the English; the offer, made by the emperor, Sigismund, to mediate between the parties regarding its future, all underline the significance which the capture of Harfleur was having – and would continue to have – at both military and diplomatic level.

Less easily measurable in its effects was the victory won at Agincourt. By emerging as victors from the battle, Henry and his army were able to reach their objective, Calais, from where they returned home. But the extent of their victory, and the manner in which it had been won, were to have effects which would be felt both immediately and in the future, effects which would not be limited to the kingdoms of England and France. The unlikely – or at least the unexpected – victor of any contest often emerges with the benefit of some form of charisma attached to him. The English may have been correct in thinking that the victory would cause fear among their enemies, a fear which would undoubtedly help in the future if Henry chose to face the enemy again. The respect which the French would show English

---

[36] *Chronicon Adae de Usk*, pp. 129, 312–13; *Register of Henry Chichele*, iii, 6–7.
[37] '. . . le pluis grande enemy as Lieges du roy' (*RP*, iv, 62).

military might would be made all the more necessary by the fact that France had suffered a grievous blow to her leadership, both military and political, with the death of over 600 knights and members of the nobility, including some of the very highest, a loss of leadership which affected, above all others, northern parts of the French kingdom, which had seen all its 'baillis', or senior royal officers in the localities, killed while leading their soldiers in the action. It is likely that the effects of the defeat at Agincourt were to be felt for some time, in particular in the lack of opposition to Henry's attempt at conquest which would begin two years later.[38] For the French, their losses were compounded by the many prisoners taken by the English. Of these, the most famous was Charles, duke of Orléans, destined to remain a captive in England until 1440, a political pawn of importance, as Henry understood when, on his deathbed, he ordered that Orléans should not be released until the new English king came of an age to know what the implications to England of such a decision might be.

The victory won at Agincourt represented not only power, but the recognition that one man, at the very least, knew how to use it. By increasing his reputation in countries other than France and England, strength was given to Henry's diplomacy. This helped in two ways in particular: it encouraged the king to seek alliances with other countries in his attempt to achieve his aims in France; and it gave his diplomacy at the council of Constance greater influence and weight.[39] In terms of England's standing, the victory had done nothing but good.

At home, as the reception given to Henry's army showed, a sense of triumphalism prevailed, carefully encouraged to create a 'spirit of Agincourt' but not so much that God's role was forgotten. The victory was undoubtedly used to help create a feeling of unity within the nation: Englishmen could now hold their heads high.[40] The audacious and ironic annexation of two French saints, Crispin and Crispinian, the cobblers from Soissons martyred for their Christian beliefs late in the third century, reflects the growing confidence of Englishmen. The battle of Agincourt had been fought on their feast day (Shakespeare was to make much of this) and yet they appeared to have supported the 'wrong' side with their intercessions. Was it that they were having their revenge on the Armagnacs who had fairly recently sacked their

---

[38] For the military effects, see F. Autrand, *Charles VI* (Paris, 1986), p. 537; J.B. Henneman, 'The military class and the French monarchy in the late middle ages', *AHR*, 83 (1978), 953–4, 963–4. The moral effects are well reflected in Alain Chartier's 'Le Livre des Quatre Dames' (*The poetical works of Alain Chartier*, ed. J.C. Laidlaw (Cambridge, 1974), pp. 198–304).

[39] See below, ch.11.

[40] See below, ch.19.

home town? Or, perhaps, did they recognize the justice of Henry's claims to France? In any event, they were to receive their reward in England when, late in 1416, archbishop Chichele ordered that, in future, the feast day of these two French saints, to whom the English people owed so much, was to be celebrated with increased reverence, with nine lessons in all, three for Crispin and Crispinian, three for the translation of St John of Beverley whose feast it also was, and three for the other martyrs.[41] It was through measures such as this, and the king's commemoration of the anniversary of the battle on 25 October 1416,[42] that the memory of Agincourt, and what it had done for England, was kept alive.

[41] *Register of Henry Chichele*, iii, 29. After Agincourt, Henry had the saints commemorated at one of his daily Masses for the rest of his life (*Vita et Gesta*, p. 68).

[42] *Gesta*, p. 179.

Chapter 6

FRANCE, 1416–19

Although lacking the high drama of 1415, the year 1416 was to be far from uneventful. The importance of the siege of Harfleur and of the battle of Agincourt, two successes achieved during an extraordinarily successful three-month period, came to be felt in the following year, which witnessed an attempt to appreciate what had happened and what the consequences might be. It was a year of significance, too, for the king himself.

Even before the French had lost so many of their nobility, either dead or captured, at Agincourt, the fall of Harfleur had been a blow both to national prestige and to security along the northern coast. On the death at Agincourt of Charles d'Albret, constable of France, his position had been given to Bernard d'Armagnac, a bitter and long-standing enemy of the duke of Burgundy and a leader of those who believed in pursuing a vigorous policy of war against England. To Armagnac and his supporters, English control of Harfleur could be neither condoned nor ignored. By their measures, the French put Harfleur where they felt it must belong, in the very centre of the military map. On 23 January 1416 Charles VI asked for an *aide*, the proceeds of which would be spent on an attempt to recover the town.

The French were not slow in putting the military pressure where they knew the English might be vulnerable, directly on Harfleur itself. Just as Henry had been able to use his fleet to prevent reinforcements from reaching the garrison when he had besieged it in the previous year, so the French now used their own ships, together with others supplied by their Genoese allies, to achieve a blockade which was to be completed by a French army closing access to Harfleur from the landward side. By February 1416 the position of the English garrison of some 1420 men led by Thomas Beaufort, earl of Dorset, was becoming very difficult, [1] if not desperate, although one ship had got through with its cargo of corn by flying the French flag with the white cross. In the following month Dorset decided to lead a large foraging expedition from Harfleur into the surrounding countryside in search of badly needed provisions. It was while they were near the village of

---

[1] Payment to this number in January 1416 (PRO, E 404/31/585).

Valmont, some twenty miles to the north-east, that they were confronted by a superior French force led by Armagnac himself. The accounts of John Strecche and the author of the *Gesta* are very favourable to the English point of view. When called upon to surrender, Dorset allegedly replied that it was not the English custom to give in without a fight, and that he would prefer to die than to surrender. The ensuing encounter, which took place in the late afternoon, appears to have cost many lives on both sides. [2]

That evening Dorset, on the advice of Thomas, Lord Carew (who had fought with the Prince in Wales in the previous reign), and the Gascon, Jenico d'Artas, decided that they might, with honour, return to Harfleur. This they did under cover of darkness by making their way down to the sea shore and walking along the sand in the direction of the Chef de Caux and Harfleur. At dawn a day or two later the French, who had followed along the cliff tops, decided to attack before the English reached Harfleur, when it would be too late. Coming down the cliffs in large numbers, but constrained by the narrowness of the paths, they attacked the English who, it was reported, killed a large number of them, the noise of the battle being heard some distance away in Harfleur. Members of the garrison who had been left behind then rode out and helped to put the enemy to flight, many French being either captured or killed.

While the events of March 1416 could be presented in the most favourable light, and French pressure upon Harfleur was undoubtedly relieved for the moment, the English quickly came to appreciate that it was a place whose garrison would be in almost constant danger and which, unless steps were taken to improve the situation, would remain at the mercy of the enemy. The problem was essentially that of supplies, and how to get these to the garrison (and to the small trading community) without trouble. As early as October 1415 Henry had ordered the fishermen of the Cinque Ports to sail to the coast of Normandy to fish with a view to providing the garrison with fish, [3] while in the following month beer was taken to Harfleur on the vessel the *Katherine de Bayonne* [4] and, in January 1416, cannon and other military equipment from the Tower of London were delivered in *La Trinité de la Tour*. [5] A month or so after Valmont, on 14 April 1416, Dorset wrote to the council in London urging its members, as they held dear the safety of the town, the advantage of the king and the

---

[2] 'Chronicle of John Strecche', 156; *Gesta*, pp. 115–21. Strecche claimed that while the English suffered no casualties, 2000 French were killed.

[3] PRO, E 403/622, m.1.

[4] Ibid., m.3.

[5] PRO, E 101/44/24.

wellbeing of the garrison and its inhabitants, to provide meat, flour and drink in large quantities, as well as weapons for the defence of the place.[6]

The arrest, in the spring, of more ships from ports north and west of the Thames[7] was probably concerned with the need to provide vessels for an expedition to Harfleur where the naval pressure, provided by ships from Genoa[8] as well as from Castile, was beginning to mount. In March messengers had been sent to different parts of the kingdom requiring knights and esquires in the king's retinue to prepare themselves for service, and in May they were ordered to assemble at Southampton on 22 June, ready to serve for three months in France.[9] It seems clear than an expedition, led by the king himself, was being prepared. In addition to 800 archers from Lancashire and Cheshire,[10] and the men of some fifty or more retinues,[11] Henry was thought to have sought soldiers from Ireland,[12] Gascony and Friesland, as well as other places, not forgetting a considerable number (one text refers to over 800) from Holland and Zeeland.[13]

In the spring of 1416, however, Henry had more to think about than war: he was soon to welcome a distinguished visitor. On 1 March 1416 the emperor-elect, Sigismund, whose most important contribution to the history of his time had been to convene the council of the Church currently meeting at Constance, and who aimed at securing peace between England and France, arrived in Paris to discuss the issues with the French king's council. His visit was not an unqualified success. His hosts found him both tactless and happy to spend more money than he had on reckless entertainment,[14] while he found them divided in their approaches to the conflict with the English and out of sympathy with his views, which they felt, not without justification, favoured the English cause. Realizing that a prolongation of his stay was likely to achieve little, Sigismund and his following moved north from Paris towards the end of April. Welcomed at Calais by Richard Beauchamp, earl of Warwick, the emperor took ship for Dover on

[6] BL, Cotton Ms Caligula D iii, fo.174.

[7] PRO, E 403/622, m.13.

[8] Perhaps in answer to the request for such aid reported by Morosini (*Chronique*, p. 89).

[9] PRO, E 403/622, m.12; 624, m.3; R.A. Newhall, *The English Conquest of Normandy, 1416–1424. A study in fifteenth-century warfare* (Yale, 1924), p. 31.

[10] PRO, E 403/624, m.3.

[11] PRO, E 101/328/6; E 101/69/532–550; 70/551–569.

[12] *Livre des trahisons*, p. 130; *Chronique normande de Pierre Cochon*, ed. C. de Robillard de Beaurepaire (Rouen, 1870), p. 277.

[13] *Livre des trahisons*, p. 130. This is confirmed by PRO, E 403/624, mm.3–4, 6.

[14] Morosini (*Chronique*, p. 95) reported that Sigismund's visit to Paris had been costly.

1 May. On landing, so a tradition in the Butler family was to maintain, he was greeted by Humphrey of Gloucester, Henry's youngest brother, constable of Dover and warden of the Cinque Ports, who, bearing a sword, waded into the water announcing that he was ready to deny him entry into England if he planned to exercise imperial authority there.[15] His status and motives thus established, Sigismund, accompanied by about 1000 men on horseback, travelled to London through Canterbury (where he was greeted by archbishop Chichele), Rochester (where Bedford met him), Dartford (where Clarence was awaiting him) and Blackheath (where a concourse of London citizens welcomed him), before reaching the capital, from which Henry came out to meet him as he approached,[16] before accompanying him, with Chichele, into the city. Henry lodged his guest in his palace at Westminster, he himself moving over the river Thames to stay at the archbishop of Canterbury's palace at Lambeth, refurbished for his own reception.

The imperial visit to England was to last just four months, and more than one contemporary writer commented on its cost to the English exchequer.[17] The king had gone out of his way to impress his visitor. Ships had been provided at the king's expense for the imperial entourage.[18] When Sigismund's visit had been announced, the sheriff of Kent had immediately been ordered to lay in supplies of provisions for the large imperial party in all the towns through which it would pass, Henry's intention being that none of the visitors should have to bear any expenses, which would be settled by his own officers.[19] And, in addition to having distinguished persons meet the emperor at every stopping place on the way from Dover to London, the king had instructed the sheriffs of England to order all the knights and esquires of their counties to be in London by 16 April in order, seemingly, to be in the party which would be around the king when he welcomed the emperor to the capital.[20]

[15] *First English Life*, pp. 67–8; C.L. Kingsford, 'A legend of Sigismund's visit to England', *EHR*, 26 (1911).

[16] Sigismund's visit to Canterbury is recorded in Canterbury Cathedral Archives, J/B/A/1, no.13. Some 20,000 were said to be waiting with Henry (*Gesta*, pp. 129–31; Kingsford, *English historical literature*, p. 287).

[17] Morosini, *Chronique*, p. 95; *St Albans Chronicle*, pp. 101–2.

[18] PRO, E 403/622, m.13.

[19] 5000 marks (£3333 6s. 8d.) were made available in March (PRO, E 403/622, m.13).

[20] *CCR, 1413–1419*, pp. 302, 303, 350–1; *Foedera*, IV, ii, 157. The king had already summoned all lords, knights, and esquires 'de retinencia regis' to London (PRO, E 403/622, m.13). In a sermon preached on 4 May to further the canonization of Osmund, nephew of William the Conqueror and bishop of Sarum, Richard Ullerstone asked for prayers for Sigismund, 'another Maccabeus who acts with all possible zeal

Henry was probably right in judging that his guest enjoyed the trappings of power and the outward signs of honour. Parliament, which had met in March, was prorogued over the Easter period to give Sigismund a chance of seeing it in session. On 24 May he was taken to Windsor for the specially postponed St George's day service of the Order of the Garter, to which, after a fine procession, he was admitted as a knight,[21] as well as receiving the SS collar of the Lancastrian dynasty which, to the annoyance of the French, he wore in future on specially formal occasions. It is legitimate to wonder whether he properly understood the implications of his admission to the greatest of the contemporary orders of chivalry, as perceived, at least, by the order's sovereign, the king of England. Did Sigismund appreciate that this was no empty honour, carried out simply to tickle his pride, but the forming of a personal bond between Henry and himself which, it was the king's hope, would lead to political and military advantages for England? At the same time, Sigismund tried to please his host. If the St Albans chronicler could poke gentle fun at the quality of the picture or ikon presented by the emperor to Henry,[22] the king would have been pleased to be the recipient of a very special gift, what was purported to be the heart of St George, no ordinary present, and one particularly welcome to Henry who had a special devotion to this saint.[23]

At the end of May William, count of Holland, Zeeland and Hainault, came to England to join in the discussions about peace; he was to stay nearly a month, lodging at the bishop of Ely's house near Holborn. As brother-in-law of John of Burgundy and father-in-law of John, duke of Touraine, who would become dauphin on the death of his elder brother, Louis, in December 1416, he was a man who, through family ties, might easily have played a significant role in the peace-making process. Indeed, he, John of Burgundy and the dauphin had recently met at Biervliet in Zeeland. However, created a Knight of the Garter by Richard II, count William's sympathies probably lay with England; he had, shortly before, allowed sailors and ships from his duchy to be used against the French. Yet he and Sigismund proposed at least a temporary settlement which involved taking Harfleur into their control pending something more lasting, a proposal which was to fail for lack of support from either the French or English

---

["stat zelatissime"] on behalf of the Church' (*The canonization of Saint Osmund*, ed. A.R. Malden (Wiltshire Rec. Soc., Salisbury, 1901), p. 238).
[21] '. . . at his desyre, as sayth the chronicler' (*Chronicle of John Hardyng*, p. 376).
[22] *St Albans Chronicle*, p. 100.
[23] Wylie and Waugh, *Henry the Fifth*, iii, 12–14.

side, and which may have been the cause of the count's withdrawal.[24]
The most that could be done was to persuade Henry to postpone his
expedition against Harfleur until he felt that continued inaction would
lead to its capture by the French.

By the end of June, in spite of the presence of his guests, the king
decided to go to Southampton to oversee the preparation of an
expedition intended to relieve enemy naval pressure against Harfleur.
In spite of what he saw as provocative action by the French, who sent
the archbishop of Bourges to London to negotiate while they were
strengthening their blockade on the port, Henry hung back from
taking military action, notwithstanding the large sums already paid
out for the provision of ships, soldiers, gunners, carpenters and others
from a host of trades who would be employed in the refurbishment of
Harfleur's defences once English control, as it was hoped, had been
properly and firmly established.[25] With his country in the process of
mobilization, and at a time when he must have felt reluctant to abandon practical command, Henry decided, probably about 22 July, that
he must return to the task of looking after his illustrious guest who,
still wishing to mediate between England and France, and probably
opposed to the English use of force, was now residing at Leeds castle,
near Maidstone.[26] In his place Henry left his brother, John, duke of
Bedford, who had indented to serve with 200 men-at-arms and 400
archers, for which, on 6 June, he had received an advance payment
of £1944 7s. 4d.[27] It was not merely as the king's brother but as
the leader of the largest retinue that Bedford took Henry's place in
command of the expedition which finally set sail from Southampton
and other ports on the south coast some time at the beginning of
August 1416,[28] the intention being to cut the Gordian knot which, in
spite of Sigismund's honest efforts, had been created by the diplomacy
of a deeply divided enemy.[29]

The battle which took place off Harfleur on 15 August, the feast of
the Virgin's Assumption, was, in its effects, the most telling of the few
naval battles of the Hundred Years' War. It was fought between two
quite large fleets, each comprising a variety of vessels, the French
relying heavily upon the high-sided carracks of their Genoese allies,
the Castilians having decided not to take part. The accounts stress

---

[24] *Gesta*, p.xlvi. In a letter of 13 June addressed to all sheriffs, Henry had insisted
that it was the French, not he, who had put paid to the proposal (*CCR, 1413–1419*,
p. 353). This view is confirmed by *St Albans Chronicle*, p. 100.

[25] See payments in PRO, E 403/624, mm.9, 11.

[26] £500 were paid towards Sigismund's expenses at Leeds (PRO, E 403/624, m.6).

[27] PRO, E 101/70/554; E 101/328/6.

[28] '. . . a lentree daoust' (BN, Ms fr.5028, fo.136).

[29] See Morosini (*Chronique*, pp. 99–103) on this matter.

the length of the battle (perhaps some seven hours) and the high casualties in vessels and men on both sides.[30] The English had much to fear from the carracks, who could use their superior height to advantage, but in the relatively shallow waters of the Seine estuary, with its many sandbanks, manoeuvrability was more important than mass or height. Whether through sheer hard work and acts of courage, or through the intercession of the Virgin to whom all Englishmen addressed their prayers, victory came to the English, who captured three Genoese carracks and other vessels including a number of balingers, and were later to see another large carrack run on to a sandbank before it broke up. While half the surviving English fleet entered Harfleur, the other half sailed back home with Bedford, who had been wounded in the battle. When he heard the news, Henry was at Smallhythe, near Rye, inspecting the building of a ship: he immediately went to Canterbury where, in the company of Sigismund, he ordered a 'Te Deum' to be sung in the cathedral in thanksgiving for the victory.[31] By 16 September the news of the English success had reached Venice.[32]

The victory brought much needed relief to the garrison at Harfleur, whose commander, Thomas Beaufort, emerged with an enhanced reputation. It also helped to achieve the virtual mastery of the sea which the English were to enjoy over the next few years. Since the victory had been won on a major feast of the Virgin, it must also have seemed to the king a powerful justification of divine approval of the policy of toughness which, in his pursuit of justice, he wanted to follow towards the French. He had a further reason for satisfaction. On the very day that his brother had been locked in combat off Harfleur, Henry and Sigismund sealed a treaty at Canterbury, proof that the king had formally persuaded the emperor that the French cause was unjust and that the cause of Christendom would be best served by a formal agreement between the two men.[33]

The treaty of Canterbury, as it came to be known, was a statement of perpetual alliance between the emperor and the king (or his brothers) which gave the subjects of each right of access to the lands of the other and, most important of all, recognized the other's use of all means to pursue claims to rights and lands at present withheld by the French. To Henry this implied not only that Sigismund approved of his war, but also that the English would receive imperial assistance

[30] Many bodies floated in the sea, providing food for the fish (*Gesta*, p. 145). Hardyng (*Chronicle*, p. 377) reported that some were still there at Christmas time.
[31] *Gesta*, p. 151; *St Albans Chronicle*, pp. 100–1.
[32] Morosini, *Chronique*, pp. 103–15.
[33] *Foedera*, IV, ii, 171–3.

in pursuing their claim in 1417. There can be little doubt that, in English eyes, the recent months of diplomatic bargaining involving Henry, Sigismund, William of Holland and French envoys had finally confirmed Sigismund in his unfavourable impression of French motives and intentions. Moreover, it appeared that Henry had used these months well, indeed cleverly. He had spent much money in an effort to please his visitor and had seemed to persuade him that the French could not be trusted. Although it came too late to influence the issue materially, the naval victory off Harfleur must have seemed to Henry total justification for his stand, as well as a sign of divine approval of the treaty sealed with the emperor.

The latter's reaction is not recorded, but it is evident that he left England satisfied and on the best personal terms with the king. The author of the *Gesta*, and others, recorded how members of the imperial entourage let drop from their horses copies of verses praising England and her king: 'O, thou happy England . . .' Henry accompanied his guest to Sandwich, and not long afterwards followed him on the crossing to Calais.[34]

In spite of the naval victory and the treaty with Sigismund, Henry had not yet got all that he wanted. The key to the future still lay in establishing a firm relationship with Burgundy. Henry allowed himself no respite in his search to achieve this. Contact had been maintained with duke John throughout the spring and early summer months of 1416; truces had been renewed and prolonged, and in mid-July Henry had made an undertaking to John that he would not break the truces by making an agreement or peace with any of his rivals in France.[35] On landing at Calais, the king met the emperor and at once set about trying to persuade duke John to come to join them for discussions. Emperor and duke had had a difference twenty years earlier and Henry had good political reasons for desiring their reconciliation. John proved difficult to convince. In the light of recent events and developments he may not have wished to be associated too openly in negotiation with, of all people, the emperor and the king of England. It is possible that he feared some sort of plot. As a security he demanded that Humphrey of Gloucester should go as a hostage into Burgundian jurisdiction while he, John, was taken up in discussion and negotiation. The request was granted. On 1 October Sigismund signed and sealed a safe conduct for duke John and 800 people to come to Calais to make peace.[36] On the same day Henry

[34] *Gesta*, p. 157.
[35] Lille, Arch. dép., Nord, B 564/15315, 15316, 15320[1,3–5]; BL, Add. Ch.55499.
[36] Lille, Arch. dép., Nord, B 565/15333[1]. Sigismund used his Luxembourg seal, as he did not have his great seal with him.

issued a safe conduct for the same purpose.[37] Two days later Gloucester published an undertaking that neither he, nor any of the 200
persons with him, would leave Gravelines, some ten miles to the east
of Calais, while the talks were going on.[38]

In all, they lasted some ten days, until 13 October.[39] Of what was
said or done, of what was the mood of the meeting and the discussions,
scarcely anything is known. Henry, who had a considerable number
of his own retinue with him, had also brought a team of men experienced in the problems raised by the diplomacy of war; whether he
consulted them, we cannot tell. Almost our sole information is a list
of articles, in the form of an undertaking which the English hoped
would be made (the future tense, 'promettra', is used) by duke John
to Henry. At least three drafts of this document have survived in
different stages of preparation.[40] Although the language is French, the
fact that all three are among English records suggests that the drafting
and inspiration were likely to have been English. Having placed the
blame for the war firmly on the French, Henry stated that he must
undertake a campaign to secure his right, since God was now the only
sovereign from whom he could seek justice. Duke John, now better
informed and recognizing Henry's right in France, a right confirmed
by God through the victories accorded to him and his predecessors,
then undertook to write letters in his own hand and sealed with his
own privy seal stating his support for Henry and his heirs as real and
legitimate kings of France. Furthermore, once Henry, with the help
of God, the Virgin and St George, had conquered a sizeable part of
France,[41] John would recognize him as sovereign lord and king by
giving him liege homage and the oath of fealty. To help bring this
about, as long as Henry made active war in France, John undertook
to help him in secret ways to achieve his conquest, and to win control
over those who opposed him. However, if in future the duke were to
make an exception of this in the case of the king of France or his son,
this was not to be construed as acting against the interests of the king
of England. Finally, in order that all should know that the duke
intended to keep the terms of this undertaking, he gave his oath on
the faith and loyalty of his body and on his word as a prince.[42]

What did this form of words turn out to mean in practice? Those
outside the immediate entourage of the king knew nothing of what

[37] Ibid., no.15333[2]; see also PRO, E 30/1761.
[38] Ibid., no.15333[3].
[39] Expenses were recorded in PRO, E 403/624, mm.2, 4, 6, 10.
[40] PRO, E 30/1609, 1068, 1273.
[41] '. . . une notable partie dudit royaulme de France.'
[42] '. . . par la foy et loiaute de notre corps et en parole de prince' (nos 1609 and
1068). The third text (no.1273) substitutes the phrase 'sans fraude ou malengin'.

had been discussed or decided.[43] But the wording of this text would have worried those who learned about it. How could the king rely upon an ally who, in spite of promising his support for a war which found its justification in the claim, recognized by the ally, that Henry was truly king of France, none the less refused to act against the present king, Charles VI, and his son? One cannot believe that Henry had not appreciated the difficulty. Did he, however, know things which were not openly stated? Was the clause inserted simply to protect Burgundy against claims of having committed treason against his king? Or was John to give military help only after it seemed as if Henry, having already won control of 'a sizeable part of the kingdom of France', was likely to win the rest, in which case Burgundy would then only be giving assistance to one already reasonably sure of total victory? Or was the clause declaring that duke John would not take action against his sovereign and his heir to be taken very literally, so that it would allow him to support the English if they appeared to be engaged in war against the leaders of the other factions, who were Burgundy's own sworn enemies? Such an interpretation may be allowed, all the more so as it was a way, in practice, of getting England to help Burgundy advance his interests in what was, in other respects, a rather one-sided agreement in favour of England.

The view taken of this document must influence opinion of Henry at this time. Having failed, although not necessarily through his own fault, to make a political settlement directly with the French, he had no choice (since the Bretons had little influence in France at this time) but to approach the matter through the Burgundians, a policy well in accord with the friendly contacts he had maintained with duke John from the time he was Prince. This placed a measure of initiative in the hands of duke John, who probably needed Henry less than Henry needed him, thus limiting what John could be persuaded to do. Proof of this lies in the wording of the text, which is far from being the whole-hearted commitment which Henry was probably hoping for, and in the vague undertaking made by John that he might, at some future time, make his declaration in favour of England. It can be argued that, in his need to secure an ally in France, Henry appeared as too keen a suitor of Burgundy. None the less it is unlikely that Henry made any political or military concession to duke John, although we do not know whether they discussed future military strategy or not. However, the king's chaplain expressed what may have been a common view when he reported that since he was French, duke John must have been taking part in double dealing, an opinion reflected

[43] See *Gesta*, pp. 173–5.

by the writer of the 'Northern Chronicle' that, in the end, the king
had achieved little or nothing.[44]

Whatever misgivings he, or others, may have had about the benefits
of the meeting at Calais, Henry was now set on an invasion of France
in the following year. From the moment of his return to England, he
worked relentlessly to prepare for it. First parliament, then the clerical
convocation, voted him large sums of money, some £136,000 for the
war. Diplomacy was used to make allies and isolate the French. Contact was maintained with Sigismund and other German princes;[45] an
embassy was sent to the king of Castile to remind him of the alliance
made between Henry III and Alphonso, and their heirs (copies of
this alliance were in the public records of each kingdom if proof were
needed) and to persuade him to abandon alliances which he may have
had with the enemies of the king of England, most notably France.[46]

Some time before Christmas Henry, who had been staying at the
royal manor of Mortlake, up the river Thames from London, moved
to Kenilworth, in Warwickshire, one of his favourite residences, to
spend the season of festivities there.[47] But there was probably not
much sense of relaxation in the king's mind. In January the long
process of building up an army, and the fleet needed to convey it to
France, was begun in earnest, the first indentures for one year's military service being sealed at the end of January and beginning of
February;[48] ships of twenty tons and over were to be arrested in the

[44] Ibid., p. 175; 'tractatus ille nichil seu modicum profecit' (Kingsford, *English
historical literature*, p. 287); M.H. Keen, *England in the later Middle Ages* (London, 1973),
pp. 364–5. Historians are far from unanimous in their views regarding this meeting
and its outcome. It is unlikely that any formal agreement between Henry and duke
John was ever made, although Henry may have been left hoping for Burgundian
support in the future. While John, as a French prince, could not openly make a treaty
against his own king, we should recall that his real enemy was the Armagnac party,
against whom he might be able to use the English. The Armagnacs certainly thought
that some sort of deal had been struck at Calais (P. Bonenfant, *Du meurtre de Montereau
au traité de Troyes* (Brussels, 1958), pp. 187, 200). The manner in which John made
so little effort to prevent the English conquest of Normandy between 1417 and 1419
or, seen from a different standpoint, the way he took advantage of Henry's invasion
to secure Paris from the Armagnacs in the spring of 1418 could be construed as
suggesting that John was ready to help the English cause, by following a policy of
non-intervention in Normandy, if it helped his own. According to the *Brut* (ii, 424)
the dauphin said to duke John at Montereau 'like as he had brought, he should
brynge hem oute', suggesting that as John had let the English into France, he should
now rid her of them. See below, n.63.

[45] PRO, E 404/32/267; Wylie and Waugh, *Henry the Fifth*, iii, 32.

[46] PRO, E 404/32/283, 286; instructions in BL, Cotton Ms Vespasian C xii, fos 150–
150v. See also PRO, E 101/328/6.

[47] PRO, E 403/629, m.4; *St Albans Chronicle*, p. 103.

[48] PRO, E 101/70/572 seq.

ports (particularly in those of the south-western coast); all the shires were visited by royal messengers bearing orders that those retained by the king for the expedition to France should prepare themselves for one year's service, and be ready for muster when called upon.[49] By the beginning of March John Waterton, master of the horse, had been to London, Reading and Abingdon, as well as several other places, to organize the raising and collecting of equipment.[50] In the same month the king called a meeting of the lords spiritual and temporal to assemble at Reading to discuss, among other matters, the coming expedition to France, for which a further call for ships, to assemble at Southampton as soon as possible, was also made.[51]

The early summer saw the preparations advancing rapidly. Only one real threat remained, the presence of a small flotilla of ships, mostly Genoese, off Honfleur, a port on the left bank of the Seine, near its mouth and almost opposite Harfleur. The flotilla needed to be moved, preferably destroyed, before Henry's invasion fleet might sail. In June the king despatched the earl of Huntingdon at the head of a task force to seek action with the enemy. On 29 June the English fought and defeated the Genoese, capturing four of their biggest carracks, as well as the enemy admiral, the son of the duke of Bourbon, 'with all his tresure that he shuld have waged [t]hem for half a yere',[52] an unexpected bonus which must have been the cause for considerable satisfaction on the English side. Yet again the importance of the ability of the English to keep the sea lanes to France open had been demonstrated.

By the last days of July everything seemed to be as ready as it could ever be. Henry and his army, with its 10,000 or so men probably a little smaller as a fighting force than that of 1415, were prepared for the second expedition in two years into France. Henry sailed in a great new clinker-built ship of 1000 tons, the *Jesus*, only recently completed at Winchelsea and representing something of an experiment in ship building.[53] The crossing was none the less made without trouble, and on 1 August, Lammas Day, the English landed near the small coastal castle of Touques (which promptly surrendered when

[49] PRO, E 403/629, mm.7, 10.

[50] PRO, E 404/32/287.

[51] PRO, E 403/629, m.15.

[52] BL, Cotton Ms Vitellius A xvi, fo.46, printed as *Chronicle of London*, ed. Nicolas and Tyrrell, p. 106. See also *Chronicles of London*, ed. C.L. Kingsford (Oxford, 1905), p. 71; Kingsford, *English historical literature*, p. 307. Another contemporary text refers to 'la gracious bataille de Kaie Cauxi' (PRO, E 28/33/68).

[53] B. Carpenter Turner, 'Southampton as a naval centre', *Collected essays on Southampton*, ed. J.B. Morgan and P. Peberdy (Southampton, 1958), p. 41.

threatened with the force of the entire English army), a day which came to be known in the coming years as 'la journée de Touques'.

On landing, Henry sent out an act of defiance to Charles VI. Having done his best, he claimed, to open up ways of establishing a relation based on faith rather than deceit (this being the characteristic most frequently attributed to the French in these years), he claimed that divine help and favour were behind him, and demanded that the French should restore to him 'de facto et realiter' the rights which were his, so that the peace of Christ should rest upon them all.[54] There was nothing new in this formal challenge to the king of France: it was, in many ways, simply one of the courtesies of war. Yet the day was to mark a new beginning. The expedition of 1417 was undertaken with a very different intention to that of 1415. Henry now knew that if he wanted to gain the throne of France, he would have, initially at least, to use force to do it. Under the agreement made with John of Burgundy the previous October, Henry could expect no help from him until he had shown what he himself was capable of doing. The theme of his second expedition could be simply stated: conquest. Those who came in his army, therefore, had to be prepared to serve for a year at least: their first engagement, through their indentures, was for that period of time.

Henry had also well understood the nature of French political geography, according to which an area of open country (the 'plat pays') was dependent upon a fortified town or castle as its local centre, from which protection, justice and fiscal authority were exercised, and which also acted as a centre for trade and other commercial activities. The relationship between the town/castle and the countryside being a close one, it was essential, in order to exercise effective control over the rural areas, to hold the towns and castles first. Once this was done, political and economic control (not least the ability to raise local taxes) might be achieved. However, nothing lasting could be done if castles and towns were bypassed and left untaken: this would only serve to encourage military activity behind an advancing force, which risked being stabbed in the back. Advance, to be thorough and effective, would not be speedy, so that every means possible (putting the fear of God into a population or offering material inducements to it to surrender – the twin policy of the stick and the carrot) would be needed to hasten the process of conquest. It was unlikely, however, that the campaigns would be anything but slow.

Where was Henry to go? Few would have been surprised if he had employed his control of Harfleur to land his army there. Perhaps it was too obvious. The next main point up the Seine, Rouen, was ready

[54] *Foedera*, IV, iii, 12.

for him, prepared to defend both itself and the road and waterway to Paris which lay beyond. Henry may have known that this was likely to happen. He chose, therefore, a less well-defended flank, and within a short time he had established himself on the left bank of the Seine at a spot which was none the less within the range of his garrison at Harfleur on the other side of the estuary.

There were advantages about trying to establish himself in that 'lower' part of Normandy. Since conquest would take time, and the attacker or besieger was, in such circumstances, vulnerable to attention from relieving forces, Henry wanted to experiment with his first efforts at conquest in an area of Normandy in which he would be relatively free from outside military interference. The Seine would act as an effective line of demarcation between himself and his Burgundian ally (if ally he was), while by initially moving westwards, Henry was concentrating his effort well away from both the Burgundians and the Armagnacs, who controlled Paris.[55] The likelihood that those who defended the towns and castles which he needed to capture would be able to secure help from the capital was, therefore, small. By placing his army, and the area which it might control, between these places and Paris he made it unlikely that any effective succour would ever reach them. They were virtually on their own.

None the less, it was not always going to be easy for Henry, for he had several lines of resistance to break down. Three-quarters of a century earlier, Edward III, whose claim Henry was now pursuing, had faced relatively little difficulty in attacking the towns of Normandy. The third quarter of the fourteenth century, however, had witnessed the carrying out of a huge programme of urban defence in many parts of France, of which Normandy was one. At both Caen and Rouen Henry would face problems on a scale which would not have been encountered by an attacker two or three generations earlier. His experience at Harfleur in 1415, therefore, was to prove to have been an invaluable one, for Henry would have learned many useful lessons about the art of siege warfare which could be put into practice on his second campaign.

The English would meet not only the innate resistance of walls; they were also to meet the resistance of soldiers and citizens who manned the gates and walls, drew crossbows, and fired cannon against them. Most of the towns and castles which Henry wished to capture enjoyed the protection of soldiers, mostly paid by the French crown, the number forming a garrison varying from a mere handful to several hundred men, according to the size and importance of the place to be

---

[55] The map in Vaughan, *John the Fearless*, p. 217, shows how the Burgundians were active around Paris in the summer and autumn of 1417.

guarded. It should not be supposed, however, that a large garrison necessarily ensured a greater degree of security. The example of Rouen was one day to show that the presence of the soldier might be the cause of discord within a community, whose civil element would consequently be more prepared to come to terms with the invading English.

Equally, however, the spirit and determination of a town's population might be almost as effective in defence as a wall and a well-disciplined garrison. Henry had already shown himself to be keenly aware of the need to establish a good relationship between himself and his army, on the one hand, and the local population on the other. At Harfleur, in 1415, he had shown respect for the women and children, and his military ordinances, which were reissued more than once during these campaigns, showed a regard for the rights of non-combatants under the military code. By appearing as a man whose word could be trusted, Henry hoped to influence the way in which the people of Normandy would come to see him. His claim to be the rightful ruler of the duchy carried with it the implication that the population was subject to him and could not be treated in the way that an enemy population might be. Henry also tried to win over people to the legality and justice of his claims in France, by stressing the need for good rule, whether in the form of taxes voted in assemblies or the reforming of the system of weights and measures, which would override the chaos stemming from the use of a number of local ones. Finally, we may see Henry trying to persuade Normans to accept English rule by the way that he returned con-fiscated properties to those who came forward to make formal acknowledgement of his conquest. While he was more than ready to use the heavy hand of force against 'rebels' who stood out against him (and he used the threat of this to break down the resis-tance of a number of places), he preferred to reward those who accepted him. On the whole, the double formula of stick and/or carrot achieved some success.

Immediately on landing, Henry moved west towards Caen, some thirty miles to the south-west, last visited by an English king in 1346. The town, second in the duchy in both size and importance, would constitute a centre from which Henry could administer a 'bailliage' and, by taking over a working fiscal and judicial system, impose some element of law without which his claim to provide good government would soon wear thin and the practical, everyday government of the area would collapse. Caen had a further advantage which Englishmen of earlier years had discovered: although it was ten miles or so to the sea, it lay on a river, the Orne, which would allow vessels to come up to the quays from the sea. The river was to prove a further direct link for maritime traffic, both civil and military, between Caen, its hinterland, and England.

The siege of Caen lasted some two weeks. The walls of the town took a considerable battering, and the population showed a strong spirit of resistance. The monks of St Etienne (now known as the Abbaye aux Hommes), founded by William the Conqueror and the resting place of his remains, planned to destroy their monastery in an attempt to impede the English. The St Albans chronicler, Thomas Walsingham, recounted how a monk, hoping to save the place, came out in search of the duke of Clarence, whom he found lying in full armour in a garden, his head on a stone, asleep. Awaking the duke, he impressed upon him the need to act quickly in order to save the abbey founded by his ancestor.[56] Clarence's action was commendably swift: he personally led an attack on part of the town's walls, and the place fell to the English before any major act of destruction could take place, the castle, outside the town wall, surrendering a few days later.

As at Harfleur two years earlier, Henry expelled part of the population which would not accept him, the women, although supposed to take next to nothing with them, leaving (it was reported) with their jewellery concealed in their skirts.[57] Although he may appear to have been acting harshly in driving out part of the population, Henry can be said to have acted sensibly and, indeed, quite legally. No conqueror would wish to have known dissidents within a town which had formally opposed him and which was to become the centre for the region around. Furthermore, it was necessary for the king to make an example of the first place which fell into his hands. The lesson must be that while acceptance of Henry's rule would be rewarded, opposition would be punished, both by expulsion (many of those who left Caen went to live in Brittany) and by the loss of property, confiscated for rebellion against him. Yet Henry was also acting with mercy. By the law of arms (in effect the conventions of war) towns and castles which refused to surrender when summoned to do so by a besieger were liable to the most stringent and extreme punishments if later captured. Caen had refused to surrender, and its population was liable to such penalties. By the custom of his day Henry was acting with considerable restraint in expelling only part of the population from the recently captured town.

In the case of Caen there may have been an additional factor in the minds of the king and those who advised him. The town had seen better days: her trade was in decline. Furthermore, the destruction recently caused at the time of the siege would have encouraged Henry

[56] *St Albans Chronicle*, pp. 111–12.
[57] Ibid., p. 113.

to try to restore some prosperity to the place.[58] Within a few days of
its surrender on 4 September (the feast of St Cuthbert, as the king
noted in his letter written the following day to the city of London),[59]
the duke of Clarence was requesting the mayor and corporation of
London to announce the good news of the town's capture, and asking
that merchants ready to settle and to accept the responsibility of
taking on properties, such as confiscated houses and shops which
might be given to them, should make themselves known.[60] This, to
some extent a copy of what had been done at Harfleur, and certainly
inspired by it, was to lay the foundation of a sizeable English community which settled in Caen and in places round about in the coming
years.[61]

With Caen in his hands, what was Henry to do and what place
would he aim at now? Nearly 150 miles away, in Orléans on the banks
of the river Loire, that question was also being asked. So important
was it that the answer should be known, that a spy was sent northwards to Falaise and then on to Caen itself to find out what direction
the English king intended to take next. If the spy found out what he
wanted to know (which he probably did), the answer cannot have
altogether comforted him or those who sent him.[62]

For Henry had decided to move south. He would have been aware
that just at the moment he was landing and about to besiege Caen,
John of Burgundy, whose aim was the capture of Paris and the defeat
of his Armagnac rivals, was beginning a military operation that
would, in the months of September and October 1417, make him
master of a number of towns forming a belt of pro-Burgundian centres
to the north and west of Paris. Burgundy now stood firmly between
Henry and Paris. At the same time this had the advantage that he
also stood between Paris and Henry, so that the English had few fears
of attack from an easterly direction, either from the Armagnacs, or
from the Burgundians, who were happy to let Henry carry on with
his conquest.[63] With his south-western flank reasonably well protected

[58] Some fifteen years later the English founded a university which flourishes to this
day (C.T. Allmand, *Lancastrian Normandy, 1415–1450. The history of a medieval occupation*
(Oxford, 1983), pp. 105–21).

[59] *Memorials of London*, p. 657.

[60] *Collection générale des documents français qui se trouvent en Angleterre*, ed. J. Delpit (Paris,
1847), pp. 220–1.

[61] Allmand, *Lancastrian Normandy*, ch.4.

[62] The man was away from 7–16 September 'pour savoir que[l] chemin le roy
d'Angleterre vouloit tenir' (Orléans, Arch. comm., CC 546, fo.20v).

[63] The pro-English sympathies of John of Burgundy were expressed in this way by
one French writer: 'Et pour appercevoir la faveur que le duc de Bourgogne avait aux
anglois, en ce meisme temps que le roy d'Angleterre descendit a Touques, ledit duc
de Bourgogne se mit sur les champs, et s'en vint a Paris sans faire guerre audit roy
d'Angleterre, mais sembloit mieulx qu'il fust de sa partie.' (BN, Ms fr.5028, fo.138).

by an understanding with Brittany,[64] Henry's only exposed flank was the southern frontier of the duchy. This he had to secure through forceful action. Some five weeks or so after the capture of Caen English troops were already fifty miles south, outside the gates of Alençon, which they took, before moving eastwards to Mortagne and Bellême, each town only about forty miles from Chartres, now in Burgundian hands. A truce with Anjou, Brittany and Maine won Henry what he needed. With winter approaching, the military map stabilized itself as it was.

All except for one place: Falaise. As Henry had advanced southwards, the birthplace of William the Conqueror had been deliberately passed by. Now with much of the surrounding countryside in English hands, Falaise was completely isolated, ready for taking. However, with its castle perched on a rock overlooking the walled town, it presented the besieger with a formidable task. With no little effort, the challenge was finally met, the town suffering considerable destruction, particularly to its walls, which the defenders were ordered to rebuild at their own expense for having resisted their proper lord, the king of England. Most significant of all was the time which the siege took. Begun late in the year, it did not end until the middle of February 1418. It was thus a long siege (of two and a half months) and one which kept Henry and his army in their tents almost right through the winter.[65] Henry was learning how to keep an army together in the most trying and difficult of conditions.

With the capture of Falaise, a firm wedge had been driven on the north-south axis right through Normandy, which Henry had now managed to divide into two. The Issue Rolls, which record many of the payments made for war, bear witness of provisions and equipment being sent from England to Normandy in these months: beer and other necessities to the king at Caen;[66] and bows and arrows, guns, saltpetre and powder in considerable quantities, as well as horses and carts.[67] By March 1418 Thomas Beaufort, who had been promoted duke of Exeter for his long and loyal service to the crown, was actively preparing an expedition in support of the king, and ships were being supplied by London and other ports, in addition to three royal carracks provided by the king himself, to convey Exeter, Clarence, Edward Holland, earl of Mortain, Henry FitzHugh (Henry's chamberlain) and Gilbert Umfraville, together with their 2000 men, to

[64] G.A. Knowlson, *Jean V, duc de Bretagne, et l'Angleterre (1399–1442)* (Cambridge/ Rennes, 1964), p. 102 seq.
[65] *St Albans Chronicle*, p. 116.
[66] PRO, E 403/633, m.11.
[67] Ibid., m.1; 636, m.4; *Calendar of signet letters of Henry IV and Henry V*, ed. J.L. Kirby (London, 1978), no.810.

France, where they were to serve for a year. In May the huge sum of £26,000 was taken by cart from London to Southampton, whence it was shipped over to France 'for the king's use'.[68] Pay day had come.

Henry spent Easter 1418 at Caen, and, almost provocatively, the feast of St George was solemnly celebrated in the castle there with the dubbing of new knights.[69] Several things were now going on at the same time. The king, wishing to establish at least a minimum level of normality in the administration of those parts of Normandy now under his control, was busy overseeing the work of those, some of them English, whose task it was to provide for everyday local government. He was also much occupied, in these spring months, in organizing the distribution of lands and estates, confiscated from 'rebels', among his English supporters and those Normans who were willing to help him. This was a vital aspect of his work of conquest, and one to which he devoted much time at this moment.[70]

All the while, the process of extending the conquest was going on. Part of the army was sent to establish more secure control of the rather vague southern frontier, much to the apprehension of the people of Orléans and other places, such as Meung on the line of the Loire, fearful of a sudden advance in that direction.[71] Having led the initial attack upon Normandy and upon Caen, Henry was now prepared to leave some of the implementation of his plans and strategies to others. Western Normandy was cut off from all hope of rescue, which might only come to it by sea; in view of the effectiveness of English control of the coastal waters, this was unlikely to happen. Between March and August 1418 the whole of the western part of the duchy came under English military and civil control. The only place to give trouble was Cherbourg, because of its location a difficult nut to crack. Besieged by Gloucester, it took him some five months, and the use of much artillery, to bring about its fall (September 1418), an exploit for which he rightly received much credit.

Important as was this part of the campaign, more significant events were taking place elsewhere. There was a risk that, if the English did not press ahead quickly with their military advance, towns in the eastern part of Lower Normandy, principally on the left bank of the Seine, might come under Burgundian control. The months of April, May and June 1418 were spent bringing this area largely under English control, so that by mid-summer almost the whole of Normandy on the left bank of the Seine was in Henry's hands.

[68] PRO, E 403/633, mm.15, 16.
[69] St Albans Chronicle, p. 118.
[70] See below, ch.9.
[71] BL, Add. Chs 3489, 3490, 3503; Orléans, Arch. comm., CC 546, fos 37, 37v, 48v.

It was at this time that an event of great importance to both French and English occurred. John of Burgundy had been increasing his stranglehold upon Paris for much of the past year, and at the end of May 1418 he managed to regain control of Paris. On 29 May the Burgundian forces broke into the capital, and set off a series of bloody massacres of those known to have Armagnac sympathies, the constable, the count of Armagnac himself, being one of the victims, although the dauphin, Charles, managed to escape. The result of this horrific episode was to make John of Burgundy effective ruler of France, a role which he would play for a little more than a year. It obliged him to become, at least for the moment, the continuator, if not the convinced exponent, of a military policy whose aim it was to stem the English advance and, ultimately, keep them away from Paris itself.

By 5 June, scarcely a week after the coup in Paris, Burgundians and Armagnacs along the line of the Seine came together in an attempt to withstand English military pressure. It was certainly badly needed, since the English, with Henry leading and his brother, Clarence, playing an important role, had approached the Seine from the south, taking in the great abbey of Le Bec (near which Clarence had been nearly killed while visiting a local church in the fulfilment of his Easter devotions),[72] the castle of Harcourt and the strategic town of Louviers (where one day, Henry, too, was almost killed by a missile which hit the central post of the tent in which he was).[73] At the end of June the king and his army approached the well-fortified town of Pont-de-l'Arche, situated on the left bank of the Seine close to where the river Eure, flowing northwards, joins the Seine. Robert Pollet, the priest to whom the city of Orléans paid £2 10s. in June for having gone to Normandy to discover what the English army was doing, would have been glad to report that the thrust of the English advance was now generally northwards rather than towards the south – and Orléans.[74]

The Seine was in more senses than one a real challenge, on an altogether different scale from that which Henry had faced when trying to cross the Somme in October 1415. It presented him with a complex, practical problem, granted the width of the river, the power of the current and the fact that the English were not unopposed. Delay, too, could only be of advantage to the enemy. The town and castle of Pont-de-l'Arche were eventually taken on 20 July, after a siege of more than three weeks, but the problem of how to cross the

[72] 'Chronicle of John Strecche', 162.
[73] Ibid., 163.
[74] BL, Add. Ch.3502; Orléans, Arch. comm., CC 546, fo.52.

Seine still remained. It was finally resolved by a ruse in which the English built a bridge of boats, thus enabling the army to cross, an exploit which won an expensive wager, in the form of a fine horse, for Sir John Cornwall from the Sire de Graville, captain of Pont-de-l'Arche.[75]

The crossing proved to be decisive. It had shown that Henry and his army could overcome major physical obstacles, something which the king's meticulous preparation had made possible and which was bound to raise the morale of his men. The English army now stood on the same bank of the Seine as did Rouen, and, because of its position, it could now control the river traffic between Rouen and Paris. It was to a city largely cut off from sources of help from the east that Henry sent a reconnaissance party, under Exeter, to spy out the land. On 30 July or 1 August, duly informed, Henry ordered the siege of the Norman capital to begin.

Destined to last until the middle of January, the siege was one of the major events of the time, whose outcome came to be reported as far afield as Venice.[76] Its outline was described by an English soldier, John Page, in terms which showed both admiration for the king and sympathy for the physical suffering and destruction which war brought upon the besieged and their city.[77] It was clearly understood by all that this city, with its Burgundian captain, Guy le Bouteiller, was a prize of such importance that Henry was determined to win it at all costs. As the capital of Normandy, with a castle the possessor of whose keep was traditionally entitled to regard himself as duke of Normandy, its capture would prove the culmination of one, major part of Henry's work. Nor was that all. In practice its 'bailli' was regarded as the senior 'bailli' of the duchy, much of whose administration, particularly the exercise of justice, was centred here. Rouen was also a focal point of financial administration, with its own mint, as well as being the seat of the metropolitical authority of the archbishop which extended right across Normandy, the other six sees of the ecclesiastical province being suffragans of Rouen. Most recently, particularly in the past eighty years or so, Rouen had become an important naval centre, its Clos des Galées on the left bank, almost opposite the city itself, being a dockyard of significance which had done much to provide and sustain the French with the ships with which they had maintained pressure on English trade and ports over

[75] 'Chronicle of John Strecche', 163–7.

[76] Morosini, *Chronique*, pp. 175–81.

[77] *Brut*, ii, 404–22; *The historical collections of a Citizen of London in the fifteenth century*, ed. J. Gairdner (C.S., London, 1876), pp. 1–46.

the past four generations or so.[78] It was a city which had to be taken.

When it was first seen by Exeter in the last day of July, Rouen had already prepared itself for what was to be a desperate defence of its integrity: Monstrelet was to write that, anticipating the siege, the citizens of Rouen had tried to get in food for ten months.[79] As a practical step towards denying the English houses in which to accommodate themselves, and to prevent them using suburban buildings as cover from which to fire upon the walls (mostly built in the second half of the previous century), the inhabitants had destroyed the wooden houses and even some churches which lay outside their well-defended walls. Such action should have suggested to Exeter that a long resistance was planned, and this was confirmed in no uncertain terms by the inhabitants themselves when the English sent messengers to enquire what their intentions were. Henry would have no option but to maintain a siege so tightly that the inhabitants would see that surrender was the only way out.

The English set up their tents all around the city, these being more numerous near the five gates (from which the inhabitants frequently tried to sally out), where the main leaders, Clarence, Gloucester (fresh from his success at Cherbourg), Exeter, Huntingdon, Warwick and others, had established themselves with members of their retinues encamped around them.[80] The king was lodged in what may have been the slightly greater, but none the less austere comfort of the Charterhouse to the east of the city,[81] in the direction of the Mont-Sainte-Katherine, from the top of which he was said to have been able to see over the city's walls and observe what was going on inside.[82] Every day, it was reported, some of the allegedly 400,000 people in the city (it contained large numbers who, having fled before the English army, would today be classed as refugees) tried to break out, and there were fights with English soldiers. Partly to keep such people in, partly to protect his army from sudden attack, Henry ordered a ditch and bank to be built all around the city, and stakes to be placed in it to prevent horses being used against him. The people might hope for relief from the duke of Burgundy (one day, to raise their hopes, Henry organized a 'phoney' battle between some of his men wearing the red cross of England and others bearing the white

[78] *Documents relatifs au clos des galées de Rouen*, ed. A. Merlin-Chazelas (2 vols, Paris, 1977–78).
[79] Monstrelet, iii, 282.
[80] *Brut*, ii, 387–8, 395–6; *Citizen of London*, pp. 6–10.
[81] *Brut*, ii, 387, 395. Henry was a keen supporter of the Carthusian order: see below, ch.12. Builders and workmen were sent from Evreux to re-roof the chapel and refurbish the royal lodgings (BL, Add. Ch.11449).
[82] 'Livre des trahisons', p. 140.

cross of France, at which point the bells of Rouen began to ring in anticipation of the hoped for relief of the siege), but in the end it never came. Rouen stood on its own.[83]

The city's position on the Seine gave easy access to its walls by river, which the English effectively controlled. By driving piles into the water from which an iron chain was suspended, Henry was able to exclude fluvial traffic which might come from Paris and other places upstream.[84] Not content with denying the enemy use of the river, Henry was able to take very positive advantage of it for the English. Although denied use of the Clos des Galées, like the suburbs destroyed by the people of Rouen before the beginning of the siege,[85] the king used the river as a means of bringing in provisions and equipment for the siege from Harfleur. When, on 9 September 1418, the earl of Warwick forced the garrison at Caudebec, 'a strong town standyng by the river of Seyne'[86] some twenty miles or so downstream, to agree to surrender if Rouen did, he also obliged the captain not to interfere with English shipping coming up the river in the meantime.[87] This enabled the king to make full use of the Seine for a long period of time, use which was greatly to facilitate the English effort at Rouen, for by using barges on the river, the cargoes of drink, food, powder, sulphur, bows and arrows sent from England to Harfleur (whose importance, in such a situation, was thus greatly enhanced) could be conveyed both cheaply and relatively safely to the quayside at Rouen, the point at which they would be used.[88] What might have been a serious problem of supply was thus fairly easily resolved.

Sealed inside the walls, the people of Rouen, those who had found a temporary refuge there and the soldiery, suffered the effects of the English action. Late summer turned to autumn, and then to winter. As food became more scarce, many died. Yet they did not die fast enough, and some of the old and infirm were pushed out of the gates and into ditches in the hope that food might thus be saved and the English feel morally bound to feed them. Such a tactic, Page wrote, greatly angered the king, who was dismayed at such an act of in-humanity. Yet those in Rouen who had thought that Henry would feel obliged to feed those expelled (and perhaps others to whom the

---

[83] See the details in *Brut*, ii, 387–91, 394–422.

[84] Ibid., ii, 388, 396; *Citizen of London*, p. 10. See the payments made for forging an iron chain 'ad custodiendam aquam de Secan' (BL, Add. Ms 24513, fo.66).

[85] '. . . et les clos aux gallees furent arses et destruictes; meisme les gallees qui flotoient en leaue de Saine furent arses' (BN, Ms fr.5028, fo.142).

[86] BL, Cotton Ms Caligula D v, fo.55.

[87] 'Chronicle of John Strecche', 169; *Brut*, ii, 388–9, 396; *Citizen of London*, p. 10.

[88] One ship was so large that it was said to have taken up the entire river (BN, Ms fr.5028, fo.142v).

same treatment might be meted out in future) found that they had miscalculated. In time of war, when so much was at stake, Henry could harden his heart. Except at Christmas time, when recognition of the feast of divine love demanded a positive reaction, he refused to accept responsibility for the men and women in the ditch: 'I put [t]hem not there,' he replied, when confronted with the facts.[89] His logic was inexorable. The people of Rouen should not oppose his acquisition of lordship over them, which was justly his. If they did, he would not be responsible for the consequences of their actions.

The time must have come (at what moment, we have no means of telling) when the people of Rouen realized that, in spite of promises, help would not come from either the duke of Burgundy or from his rival, the dauphin. As provisions grew more scarce, and the physical condition of the besieged deteriorated, many turned to eating vermin and scraps, and what their money could buy at utterly exorbitant prices, which, although the rates vary from chronicle to chronicle, convey to the reader something of the horror of what such a desperate situation could be like.[90]

By the end of December it was recognized within Rouen that some-thing had to be done. One night a group of citizens, having tried in vain to make contact with the besieging army from their position high up on the walls, finally won the attention of a knight, Sir Gilbert Umfraville from Northumberland, whose ancestors, it turned out, had come from Normandy.[91] At their request, a petition was presented to the king, who agreed to see a delegation of twelve men, four knights, four clergy and four burgesses. Their attempts to win Henry's sym-pathy proved unsuccessful. Although he met them at the Charter-house as he emerged from hearing Mass, the king was in no mood to grant mercy; his royal bearing impressed the petitioners, but his unsmiling countenance told them all they needed to know. The choice, they reported back, lay between death and surrender, a choice of options which appeared too stark to some of the richer citizens, who were accused of being ready to continue their resistance at the expense of their poorer, weaker fellows. However, such opposition was soon overcome. On Henry's insistence that those negotiating should have proper powers to treat, a meeting took place on 4 January in the 'manoir de la ville' at which a large number of citizens were present. By common agreement twenty-five persons, comprising the abbots of two abbeys, two canons of the cathedral and another member of the clergy, three knights, three esquires and fourteen others, were selected,

---

[89] *Brut*, ii, 410; *Citizen of London*, p. 30.
[90] See, for example, *St Albans Chronicle*, p. 122; *Brut*, ii, 400–1.
[91] *Brut*, ii, 404; *Citizen of London*, p. 23; 'Chronicle of John Strecche', 171.

of whom any number between twenty-three and eighteen were given full powers to negotiate with the English.[92] In the first week of the new year 1419 the two sides met in a large tent in the presence of archbishop Henry Chichele. After a first attempt at negotiation had failed, a second succeeded, and on 13 January terms for surrender, which were to take effect six days later unless help was forthcoming, were agreed.

The conditions negotiated, although hard, could have been harder, and while showing Henry's displeasure and his determination that none should resist him again in this way, did have their reasonable and positive aspects.[93] They were simple enough. Eighty hostages, twenty of them knights or esquires, were to be handed over to the English; a large fine of 300,000 crowns (the equivalent of £50,000) was to be paid in two instalments in the coming months; Normans in the garrison (regarded as 'rebels') were to be kept as prisoners; the citizens were to build what was evidently intended to be a new ducal palace on a site at the lower end of the town, within the wall (they were to lose land for this purpose) by the river; in the meantime the king would restore property to all those willing to do him homage, who would thus retain their possessions within the duchy of Normandy; and the commercial advantages of citizenship were also to be applied in the markets of the city. Men may not have been far wrong if, reading between the lines, they detected an attempt by Henry to impose neither the authority of the king of England nor that of the king of France. It was the mark of the duke of Normandy which Henry was trying to reintroduce into the old ducal capital which, having come under the sway of the king of France in 1204, he had now regained.

Surrender finally came on 19 January 1419, the feast day of St Wulfstan, as John Strecche, in a touch of national pride and interest in England's old saints, added in his text.[94] As Henry had sent the duke of Exeter ahead to reconnoitre the condition of the city in the previous July, so again he sent him ahead to take possession of the city in his name. Exeter entered with due ceremony, and rode to the castle, which he occupied in his master's name. On the following day, with greater outward ceremony, Henry entered his newly conquered capital. The crowds came out to meet him in, if we are to accept an English eyewitness's account, a mood of relief if not of rejoicing, in which they tried to explain to the king why, as subjects of the French

[92] BL, Cotton Ms Tiberius B vi, fos 96v–97v.
[93] See a copy of the terms in BL, Harley Ms 4763, fos 123–123v.
[94] 'Chronicle of John Strecche', 174–5. Caen was recorded as having surrendered on the feast day of another early English saint, Cuthbert: see above, p. 118.

king, they had felt obliged to oppose him. Banners bearing the arms of England and France (a sign of ambition as yet unfulfilled?), and of the Virgin and of St George flew at the gates. The ecclesiastical leadership – or much of it – including high clergy and abbots came out to greet the conqueror and lead him to the cathedral of Notre-Dame, where he gave thanks for all that had happened. Only then did he go to the castle to enjoy the significance of its possession. At the king's express wish, the citizens were able to have what, for most of them, may have been the first full meal they would have had for many long and painful weeks.[95]

[95] *Brut*, ii, 419–22; *Citizen of London*, pp. 42–5; 'Chronicle of John Strecche', 175. At Winchester the fall of Rouen was celebrated with processions in the streets (J.S. Furley, *City government of Winchester from the records of the XIV and XV centuries* (Oxford, 1923), pp. 144–5).

Chapter 7

FRANCE, 1419–20

The fall of Rouen was a further step in Henry's military career and in his search for justice in France. While it must have satisfied the king's ambition and resolved many problems for him, it created others. Henry had to be careful, for instance, not so to concentrate his troops around Rouen that he would leave Normandy's southern frontier inadequately guarded. This was vulnerable to attack from the dauphinists who, since their expulsion from Paris in May 1418, had come to concentrate their power in the valley of the Loire, where military reinforcements from Scotland were on the point of joining them. [1] Control of strongholds on that border was essential to Henry, and he made great efforts to maintain them.

In the east of Normandy he had got where he was through skill and judgement, but also not without a small amount of luck. Two factors might have stopped him. After the dauphin's flight from Paris in May 1418, his party (as we may now call the Armagnacs whose leader was now dead) lacked the strength to deal with Henry alone. [2] Combined with the Burgundians, however, something might be achieved, and it was with the purpose of acting together against the common English enemy that the two made terms at Saint-Maur-des-Fossés in mid-September 1418. The 'union' was soon to fail, partly because the parties were irreconcilable enemies, partly because Henry found it easy to drive a wedge between them by following his policy of offering to talk to one party at a time rather than to both together. The other factor which might effectively have stopped Henry was the possibility (an unlikely one) that John of Burgundy would make a determined bid to prevent him coming any nearer to Paris. In fact, he did nothing. For a whole month or more, from the end of November 1418 to the beginning of January 1419, at the height of the siege of Rouen, duke John remained fifty miles away at Pontoise with Charles VI.

When the people of Amiens decided, on 11 January 1419, to send

---

[1] B. Chevalier, 'Les Ecossais dans les armées de Charles VII jusqu'à la bataille de Verneuil', *Jeanne d'Arc. Une époque, un rayonnement* (Paris, 1982), pp. 85–93.

[2] The dauphin since April 1417 was Charles, later to become Charles VII.

men-at-arms and archers to Rouen for the siege, they did not know
that on that very day negotiations between besieger and besieged were
already being held.[3] In February 1419 Henry Glomyng, a haber-
dasher who had been at the siege of Rouen, somewhat cantankerously
stated his opinion (for the expression of which he saw the inside of
the Fleet prison in London) that 'y were there with iij M [3000] men
of armys, y wolde breke his Sege, and make [t]hem of Roon dokke
hys tale'. 'And fordermore he sayde that he [Henry V] were not able
to abyde there [Rouen], were hit that the Duk of Borgoyne kepte his
enemyes fro[m] hym'.[4] Duke John, indeed, was very conscious of the
results of his inactivity. Not surprisingly the people of Paris, whose
security and trade were likely to come under threat from the capture
of Rouen by the English, were critical of the duke, who for a while
left Paris for Lagny and then Provins, to the east and south-east of
the capital, taking the king and the court with him, and leaving a kind
of 'provisional government' to take charge in Paris, thereby ensuring a
division in the royal camp between those who followed the court and
those who lived in Paris. Meanwhile the people of Amiens felt certain
that the rumours circulating about the likelihood of the English
coming to attack them were to be taken sufficiently seriously for them
to purchase provisions and arms for defence.[5] The excuses made on
Burgundy's behalf in a letter sent by Charles VI on 19 January (the
very day of the surrender of Rouen) that he had not been able to
rescue the city because of difficulties placed in his way by supporters
of the dauphinist side may have been true, but they lacked conviction.
The simple fact was that Henry was master of the situation.

Or that was how it seemed to the Burgundian chronicler, Enguerrand de Monstrelet, with whom many would have agreed that there
was a widespread fear of Henry after the successful outcome of his
siege of Rouen.[6] How far was it justified? It is noticeable that already
in 1418 Henry was instructing his ambassadors to 'dryve' the other
side to the 'utmost profre' in their negotiations with the French parties.[7] Too much should not be read into this: it was a natural instruction to issue. Nevertheless, it suggests that the king was hoping to win
as much as he could by negotiation, and to do so within the shortest
possible time. Was this simply the attitude of an ambitious man in
a hurry? Probably not. Other factors had a bearing on the king's

[3] Amiens, Arch. mun., BB2, fo.136 (11 January 1419).
[4] *Original letters illustrative of English history*, ed. H. Ellis, 2nd series (London, 1827),
i, pp. 78–9. The letter was written in 1419, not in 1420.
[5] Amiens, Arch. mun., BB2, fo.137 (30 January 1419).
[6] Monstrelet, iii, 308.
[7] J.H. Ramsay, *Lancaster and York: a century of English history (A.D. 1399–1485)* (2
vols, Oxford, 1892), i, 263.

thinking and on the need to win prizes as quickly and cheaply as possible.

Speed and cost were related factors which were probably giving Henry increasing concern. Parliamentary support for his military needs had not lacked implied criticism of the costs of war; it is notable that the year 1419 witnessed the departure of no large retinues for France, which meant that Henry was having to make do with those already available. The cost of the war was clearly beginning to concern the king, too. As he reminded his council at home, he was having to pay his soldiers, and was having to be adamant, in order to maintain discipline and avoid antagonizing the population whom he regarded as his own subjects, that soldiers should pay for whatever provisions they bought. Moreover, in spite of every attempt to win over the population, few men of rank or standing had yet come into his obedience, which was another way of saying that he had so far failed to find acceptance among the people who counted and who might have influence upon others. Furthermore, no army, however successful, can be totally satisfied all the time. When John Feelde wrote home to Robert Frye, clerk of the council, in March 1419, complaining about the lack of peace, the deceitfulness of the French ('they ben yncongrue, that is to say in oolde maner of speche yn England they ben double and fals') and expressing the wish that his friends 'prey for us that we may come sone oute of thys unlusty soundyours [soldiers'] lyf yn to the lyf of Englond',[8] he had not only been away for longer than was good for him but was also reflecting a weariness and 'a general grouching'[9] about the war which he was likely to have shared with others.

These were Henry's problems, perhaps not appreciated by the French, who must not be allowed to learn about them. At no cost should he do the enemy's work for him.[10] Having come this far, Henry could not afford to show any chink in his armour: he could only go forward with all outward confidence. In the course of the coming months the remainder of Normandy, including the whole of the Caux region to the north of Rouen, was taken, although Château Gaillard, built by Richard I to guard the Seine above the Norman capital, did not fall until December 1419, after a siege of over a year.

The change in Henry's circumstances brought about by the success achieved at Rouen affected his diplomacy, which was to be his dominating activity in 1419. In November 1418 his envoys, sent to negotiate with those of the dauphin at Alençon, had been instructed to stress

[8] *Original letters*, pp. 77–8.
[9] BL, Cotton Ms Caligula D v, fo.36.
[10] Ibid., fo.37.

the marriage demand, as well as the implementation of the terms ceded by the French in 1360, the main emphasis being on the restoration and future status of lands in the south-west of the country. Henry was in no mood to discuss the future of lands recently conquered by him: they were his. These talks failed, and a meeting between Henry and the dauphin, arranged for mid-Lent 1419 at Evreux, never took place. But by this time Henry, the conqueror of Rouen, was being sought by the other, Burgundian, party. The policy of playing off one enemy party against the other (for that was the policy) gave Henry the chance of pressing further demands. Within a short time he had met Burgundian envoys, receiving from them the impression that if he pressed his demands upon the duke, they would be conceded. In this flush of optimism a meeting, to be attended by Henry, Burgundy, Charles VI, his queen, Isabeau, and their daughter, Katharine, was arranged. Expectations of a successful outcome were rising.

The original meeting was fixed for 15 May, but on 6 May it was agreed to postpone it until the end of the month; Henry, not wanting to be caught out again (as he had been at Evreux), demanded a written undertaking from the French that they would appear.[11] On 7 May, at Vernon, he issued powers to Sir Walter Hungerford and Sir Gilbert Umfraville to negotiate a marriage between himself and the princess Katharine. At the same time Hungerford and Lord FitzHugh, the king's chamberlain, were named with full powers to negotiate the terms of a final peace between the kingdoms. The arrangements were complex. It was clearly intended that, while the negotiators carried out their business, there was to be a more formal side to the proceedings, which might, after all, lead to peace and betrothal between Henry and Katharine. A field was chosen in advance, great care being taken to delineate exactly which part of it was for the English, which part for the French, and which part was to be common ground on which the negotiating pavilion was to be pitched. Security was tight: agreement was reached beforehand as to when and from which direction (that of Meulan) Henry would approach, while the French undertook to come to the convention from the opposite direction, that of Pontoise, which was their base on this occasion. Both sides agreed to abide strictly by the regulations established for the meeting.[12]

Henry clearly set much store by this meeting, and he must have feared that the French might not appear. But at three o'clock on the stated day they did so, although the king, said to be ill, was not among

[11] BL, Cotton Ms Tiberius B xii, fos 97–8; Harley Ms 4763, fos 128–129v; *Foedera*, IV, iii, 114.
[12] BL, Cotton Ms. Tiberius B xii, fo.99; Harley Ms. 4763, fos 130v, 131.

their party. Katharine, however, was, and Henry appears to have been easily won over to the role of the willing suitor on this, their first meeting. The negotiations, however, went rather less happily. The English declared that they sought nothing more than peace, but that this could not be achieved if they were not given their rights, which included the implementation of the terms of Brétigny, of which they submitted a copy in writing to the French, and the whole of the duchy of Normandy and other places outside its boundaries which had recently been taken, all such territories to devolve upon Henry, his heirs and their successors. The French, unhappy about this, then proposed that Henry should renounce his claim to the throne of France, something which he was willing to do 'saving the superiority of all lands to be granted by the present treaty', by which he meant sovereignty. In discussion on this vital matter the French urged that Henry should accept an enlarged Aquitaine in return for abandoning his claim to Anjou, Brittany, Flanders, Maine and Touraine, something which the king refused to do. On the grounds that the dowry given to Isabelle, Richard II's wife, had never been returned on his death, they asked that the one which might be paid for Katharine should be proportionately reduced, from 800,000 to 200,000 crowns. The omens for a happy outcome and a lasting settlement were not good.[13]

They had not been good from the beginning. As at the meeting between Henry and John held at Calais in October 1416, suspicion was in the air. Why was there a postponement in bringing the convention together? Was Charles VI really ill? Did the French feel that, in his absence, only concessions of less than fundamental importance could be made? Or was it that Burgundy was moving towards an agreement with his rival, the dauphin, and had at first wondered whether there was much point in negotiating with the English? Surely, in the circumstances, there was, for although he could not be the one who would make fundamental concessions to the English by negotiating with them, he was appearing as the defender of French interests (something which after Rouen he badly needed to do) and putting the pressure on the dauphin to meet his terms for an alliance.

Accordingly, duke John, by failing to appear at a meeting arranged for 3 July, effectively drew the Meulan negotiations to a close. Later, Henry learned from queen Isabeau that these had been abandoned because of a fear that if terms so favourable to the English (the cession to them of Aquitaine and Normandy in full sovereignty was on the agenda) were to be granted, Burgundian sympathizers would go over to the dauphinists, 'whence even greater war would have arisen'.[14]

[13] Vaughan, *John the Fearless*, pp. 270–2.
[14] M. Keen, 'Diplomacy', *Henry V. The practice of kingship*, ed. G.L. Harriss (Oxford, 1985), pp. 189, 191.

Another victim of this serious breakdown was a commercial treaty
with England whose negotiation the duke had authorized at Pontoise
on 14 June: a month later, the parties agreed to postpone further
business between them until October.[15] Notwithstanding a truce on
land between England and Burgundy, due to last until 29 July, duke
John almost immediately made an alliance with his rival, the dauphin,
whom he met on a causeway at Pouilly-le-Fort, near Melun, on the
Seine above Paris. There, on 11 July, the two parties went through a
form of public reconciliation. Recognizing that more and more of
the kingdom was being brought under English rule because of their
divisions, and urged by Alan, bishop of Léon, who had been sent by
the Pope, to make peace so as to save the poor from greater oppres-
sions, they agreed to ignore all unfavourable things said about the
other, to forget the past and to sink their differences: acting together,
they promised to expel the English.[16] How this was to be achieved
was not made clear. Nor was it stated explicitly that the two 'parties'
would not go, as before, along their separate roads. Apart from an
undertaking given by each not to make a treaty with the English
without the leave of the other, very little seemed to have changed.

In theory (and Henry was justified in treating it in this way) the
treaty of Pouilly posed a very considerable threat to the English.
Henry now knew that he could trust neither leader in France, and
that there was only one way of enforcing his will upon the development
of events. He must show who was master and, above all, who was
militarily superior to the others. His plan, aimed principally at the
duke of Burgundy, involved action intended to make a quick impression. On 29 July the truce made two months earlier expired, and on
the following day a state of hostilities was declared. That night two
groups, one led by the Gascon, Gaston de Foix, the other by the earl
of Huntingdon, set off from the English camp for Pontoise, a dozen
or so miles away. Huntingdon's party got lost. That led by Foix,
carrying scaling ladders, attacked the wall of Pontoise just between
the change of the night and day watches. The action was not decided
in a moment, and was, indeed, nearly lost, but the commando-style
nature of the raid gave the advantage of surprise to the attackers.
Fearing that the English were more numerous than they really were,
a number of the inhabitants prepared to flee out of the main gate,
only to be met not far off by Huntingdon and his force who arrived

[15] PRO, E 30/1069, 404.
[16] Lille, Arch. dép., Nord, B 313/15414bis; BL, Cotton Ms Tiberius B xii, fos
141v-143; Harley Ms 4763, fos 172v-174v; Vaughan, *John the Fearless*, p. 273. To the
Parisians the prospect brought cause for rejoicing (*Journal d'un bourgeois de Paris 1405-
1449*, ed. A. Tuetey (Paris, 1881), p. 126; ibid., ed. C. Beaune (Paris, 1990), pp. 143-
4; *A Parisian journal*, trans. J. Shirley (Oxford, 1968), p. 139).

in the nick of time.[17] The French court and some of the dauphin's envoys had recently been in the town, which was therefore still full of provisions and items of wealth, which fell into English hands. More significant was the fact that Pontoise, only a few miles up the river Oise from where it joined the Seine, was a well-defended town of importance, straddling the road from Rouen to Paris.

Henry now found himself master of the Vexin, the area between the Epte and the Oise, the buffer between Normandy and the area to the north-east of Paris which looked in the direction of the capital. More significant still was the sharp lesson which Henry hoped to have taught the Burgundians: they could not trifle with the king of England. The point was underlined by the anonymous Parisian 'Bourgeois', who described how, in the afternoon of the day that Pontoise fell to the English, large numbers of refugees from the town, many in a state of shock and disbelief at what had happened, began to arrive in Paris, spreading news of the events of that day. The unwillingness of the duke of Burgundy who, with Charles VI, was at Saint-Denis, a few miles away, to do anything by way of retaliation when the English attacked was said to have shocked everybody.[18] The English had the psychological upper hand. Two days later Clarence appeared under the walls of Saint-Denis, only six miles from Paris, and, a week later, on 10 August, the English were seen at the very gates of the capital itself.[19] Terrified, Charles, his queen and Katharine left Saint-Denis to go and set up their court at Troyes. The tightening of the screw on Paris was being increasingly felt.

Ever since he had taken Rouen at the beginning of the year, Henry must have realized that, if he could control the capital, he would be able to resolve many political problems in his favour. In economic terms, Paris might be a declining centre,[20] but in political terms it remained the effective centre from which power was exercised and patronage dispensed. The capture of Harfleur in 1415 had given Henry control of the mouth of the river Seine; the fall of Rouen in 1419 had shown the king working his way up its valley, while the capture of Meulan, Poissy and Saint-Germain-en-Laye later in the year brought English control of the waterway to within a few miles of Paris itself. When Clarence looked up at the walls of Saint-Denis,

[17] *St Albans Chronicle*, pp. 122–3. For Strecche's strange adaptation of this episode and editorial comment, see 'Chronicle of John Strecche', 143, 179–80.

[18] *Bourgeois de Paris*, ed. Tuetey, pp. 126–8; ibid., ed. Beaune, pp. 144–6; *Parisian journal*, p. 141.

[19] *Journal de Clement de Fauquembergue, greffier du Parlement de Paris, 1417–1435*, ed. A. Tuetey (3 vols, SHF, Paris, 1903–15), i, 311–12.

[20] J. Favier, 'Une ville entre deux vocations: la place d'affaires de Paris au XVe siècle', *Annales ESC*, 28 (1973), 1248–50.

the English had almost made it. Conversely, the Parisians, under Burgundian control since May 1418, regarded the advance of the English army with a mixture of fear and admiration, fear of what the English might do, admiration of Henry as a man who knew what he wanted and got it done, duke John being only too well known for his wavering nature and the dauphin as a sower of discord. The evidence of events provided by the anonymous 'Bourgeois' of Paris shows clearly that, while the king of England was seen as an enemy, he was an enemy with some control of things. That sort of characteristic the Parisians were ready, in the final analysis, to accept.[21]

Henry was soon to be regarded by the Parisians as a saviour. The treaty of Pouilly-le-Fort had stipulated that the dauphin and the duke of Burgundy should meet in the foreseeable future to make arrangements for their joint action against the English. The place chosen for their discussions was Montereau, some fifty miles south-east of Paris, where the river Yonne joins the Seine; the day was to be 10 September. Arrangements were elaborate. The meeting was to take place within a fenced-in area on the bridge; only the principals and their immediate and known advisers and household members were to be admitted on to that area, which was to be sealed off at both ends once the participants had arrived. At the appointed time, about five o'clock, the two allies came to the bridge, one from each end. They met in the middle and the duke of Burgundy was just rising from having bent the knee before the dauphin when he was struck down and killed by one of the dauphin's attendants. In the confusion which ensued a few more from his side were either wounded or met their deaths. A tragic and treacherous crime had just been committed, which, in the climate of distrust which existed among the leaders of France at this time, was to have far-reaching political and military effects. There is some doubt if, indeed, it was a plot: it was claimed that, as he rose before the dauphin, duke John put his hand on the handle of his sword which had got in the way, and that this act caused instant reaction on the part of men standing there. But whether or not involved in a plot, the dauphin, who was said to have been deeply affected by the assassination carried out in front of him, was naturally held responsible for what had happened, a fact which his rivals for power, whether Burgundian or English, were unlikely to let him forget. The consequences would be far-reaching.[22]

---

[21] 'S'il est le plus fort, eh bien! qu'il soit notre maître, pourvu que nous puissions vivre au sein de la paix, du repos, et de l'aisance' (cited from the Religieux de Saint-Denis by G. Ascoli, *La Grande-Bretagne devant l'opinion française depuis la guerre de Cent Ans jusqu'à la fin du XVIe siècle* (Paris, 1927), p. 12).

[22] The episode is discussed by Vaughan, *John the Fearless*, ch.10.

The news reached both Troyes and Paris on the following day, 11 September, and caused consternation to a population to whom the peace of Pouilly had brought hope of future political stability. At Troyes there was immediate fear of an attack by the dauphinists seeking to regain control of the person of the king. The queen very soon emerged as a figure who urged the continuation of the alliance between the court and Philip, the new duke of Burgundy. On 24 September the mayor of the Calais 'staple', anxious to know what effect the death of duke John might have on the renewal of a truce between England and Flanders which was soon due, wrote to the new duke regretting his father's death and asking what his attitude would be.[23] The sudden death of the man who effectively ruled France in the name of the king of France had caused consternation all round.

The opportunities which death so often brings were also to be seized upon by the two other main protagonists in these developments. On 15 September, only five days after the murder, the dauphin wrote from Nemours to duke Philip. Far from expressing any regret or remorse at what had occurred, his letter, apart from a paragraph on the peace of Pouilly, was consistently critical of what he saw as the late duke's tendency to favour the English (said to have dated from the meeting at Calais in October 1416), his willingness to alienate the heritage of the crown of France (in particular since 1416), and his failure to maintain the agreement made at Pouilly two months earlier. The general tone of the letter cannot have won the dauphin many friends precisely at that place, the ducal court, where he most needed them.

The approach of Henry V to the new turn of events was totally different. At Meulan, in June, he had agreed that, on the granting to him of certain conditions regarding the lands which he would hold in France, he would renounce his claim to the throne of France. Three months had changed that picture considerably, and the murder at Montereau was to change it yet further. Henry was now reviewing a situation in which three men felt they had a claim to power and, ultimately, to the throne of France: duke Philip, too young and lacking in experience, a candidate only in his own eyes, if a candidate at all; the dauphin, now morally excluded by the horrendous nature of his crime; and Henry, supported by an age-old claim and everyday master of a greater part of the kingdom of France, the best of the three. The events of early September had disposed of one rival whose heir had yet to make a name for himself; and they had completely disgraced another. With none to compete with him in reputation, military power or political astuteness, it was time for Henry, who had

[23] Lille, Arch. dép., Nord, B 569/15415[3].

not recently pressed his claim to the crown of France, to stake that claim once again. If he acted boldly, he might well transform a claim into a reality.

On 27 September, little more than two weeks after the murder at Montereau, and in response to an approach made to him recently from Paris itself, Henry, through his ambassadors, declared his intentions before the French king's council in Paris. It was, they reported, no longer their lord's intention to be satisfied with Normandy alone, but to work for the crown and the kingdom of France as well. Then with terms which were to find more than an echo in the treaty of Troyes, they proposed that, although they would have the same king, the kingdoms would none the less go their separate ways, and be free of each other. In addition, Henry again proposed to marry Katharine and, pursuing the logic of the earlier part of his statement, said he would do so without the expense of a dowry having to be found by friends, subjects or parents. Later, in discussion, the ambassadors were told that their king's demands had undergone major changes, and that the new duke of Burgundy could not stand by and see the powers of the French crown thus diminished. Replying to such observations, the English said times and conditions had changed, but emphasized that if their proposals were accepted, it would not mean the French king would be relieved of his throne. Indeed their master's intention was not to diminish the power of the French crown, but to maintain and strengthen it. Furthermore, Henry was the man who could most effectively bring unity, rather than division, to France.

The dauphin having excluded himself by the murder at Montereau, the ambassadors could allay Burgundian fears that, were Henry to marry Katharine and assume the throne himself, he would hand over effective rule of the kingdom to his brother-in-law, the dauphin. For good measure, supporters of the duke of Burgundy would be allowed to occupy again benefices which they had enjoyed but had been forced to abandon by the events of the last two years. At the end of their discussions, the English envoys reiterated the main points of their embassy. Then, in the hope of influencing events in their favour, they stated Henry's willingness to join with duke Philip in avenging the death of his father; they offered to arrange a marriage between one of the king's unmarried brothers (Bedford or Gloucester) or his uncle, the duke of Exeter, and a Burgundian lady; and they assured the duke that he would be allowed to hold lands in the kingdom of France.[24]

The English proposals had been skilfully expressed. Henry had been firm; he had also made it clear that he had a far better claim to the throne of France than did the young duke, Philip. At the same

[24] Bonenfant, *Du meurtre de Montereau*, pp. 191–5.

time he had been sympathetic and positive: it would suit both men to weaken the prestige of the dauphin and to be seen to be doing it in the name of vengeance, not personal ambition. Henry had also offered Philip some material reward in France in what was plainly intended to be an appeal for his help. To this, Philip's first pronouncement may have come as a disappointment. Probably influenced by his late father's supporters in Paris, and clearly hoping to gain time, his main concern appears to have been the protection of the capital by means of truces which Henry was proving reluctant to give him. He therefore ordered his ambassadors to be ready to make small territorial concessions if they deemed these to be necessary; but on the main issue, that of the throne of France, they were to turn down any proposal from England, and offer an alliance instead. What was meant by this was to be explained more privately to Henry. The example of the murder at Montereau was a terrible one which, if followed elsewhere, would mean that no person of authority would be safe from attack. Henry was then to be asked if he would join in seeking vengeance for the murder of Burgundy's father by making war on the dauphin. Meanwhile, duke Philip hoped for good relations at sea between England and his lands in the Low Countries.[25]

Henry was experienced enough to recognize that, although he might have wished for a more positive answer from the new duke, the one given him was the best which could be expected in the circumstances. Far from having slammed the door in Henry's face, he had expressed a wish to accommodate him: it could hardly have been Henry's expectation that Philip would be able to grant him all his demands in his first formal letter to him. Henry would have known that a young prince, in particular one new to his position, would take advice, which, in the circumstances, was unlikely to be unanimous. He would have known, too, how great a threat he and his army were to the Parisians, although he would probably not have known of the embassy sent from Paris, on 22 October, to tell the duke of Burgundy of the capital's worsening plight. It was an appeal to save the city. The shortage of provisions, in large measure the result of English control of the Seine almost up to Paris, had to be remedied. The autumn of 1419 was a very difficult time for the capital. Prices were high, money of little value; the weather was wet and very cold. Wood for burning was hard to find, action being needed to control its sale.[26] The evidence makes it clear that Paris was in a state of crisis during these months. The people, who wanted to live in peace, might seek that peace by letting

[25] Ibid., pp. 196–9.
[26] *Bourgeois de Paris*, ed. Tuetey, p. 135; ibid., ed. Beaune, p. 154; *Parisian journal*, pp. 142–4; Fauquemberg, *Journal*, i, 320, 322 and n.1.

in the enemy, and Burgundian power would thus be lost. At the same time Burgundy could save Paris; yet help had to come soon and it had to be considerable, for one was no good without the other. If the duke did not come quickly, and in person, Paris might be lost to him. He was urged to make an accord with the English, as the king's council and the Parisians would wish him to do.[27]

Paris was describing its own plight, seeking a remedy, and informing the duke of Burgundy that if he did not act, its inhabitants might change their allegiance. Pressure was also coming from the English side. At a meeting between Henry's representatives, those coming from Paris, and ducal envoys, held at Mantes at the end of October, Henry reiterated the proposals which he had put forward a month earlier for the resolution of the current impasse. Two further factors were stressed. The king wished it to be understood that he would not support Burgundy if he had ambitions for the crown, and would even go as far as making a treaty with the dauphinists, or others, to stop him achieving that ambition. Henry was beginning to show his impatience in public.[28]

The pressure on duke Philip and his council was mounting fast. We cannot be certain, but it is likely that the Burgundian embassy sent to Mantes had returned to Arras by the time a meeting, convened there to decide upon these questions, met at the end of October. Henry's shadow hung over the entire proceedings: if nothing were decided, then he would act, perhaps by making an alliance with the dauphinists. Both Henry and his ambassadors had made it clear that either by consent or by the use of force he would recover the crown of France. Although he hoped to avoid the second means, he was prepared to use it. It was made plain that he would make no further concessions in the future.[29]

The ducal council heard arguments on both sides. It would be wrong to give in to the king of England's moral pressure, a cause for perpetual reproach. As it befitted the first peer of the realm, the duke should defend the crown of France with force if necessary, or risk paying the penalty of such disloyalty. No man could regard defence of his sovereign as optional: he who failed might make enemies for himself within the kingdom, and, as all would have known, the duke did not need to have more enemies than he already had. However, non-intervention would have the advantage of avoiding the destruction, death and deprivation which would follow from a war with the English. Peace, too, would mean that the unity of the kingdom could

[27] Bonenfant, *Du meurtre de Montereau*, pp. 206–9.
[28] Ibid., pp. 212–15.
[29] Ibid., pp. 216–21.

be preserved. If, on the other hand, peace were to be refused, so too would the possibility of a marriage between one of the duke's sisters and a brother of the king of England. Furthermore, certain towns which were already in the English allegiance would be irretrievably lost: the duke must follow their example, or risk being lost himself. It should also be remembered that if the duke sought the crown of France, he would be opposed by Henry V, who might secure it, not for the dauphin, but for a member of the house of Orléans or Anjou. As it was, the king of England asked no money from France to marry Katharine, and the future of the king of France and his queen was assured. If Henry was obliged to take the crown by force, the king and queen of France would be lost, and many of the nobility slain. Out of loyalty to their persons, the duke must accept the English proposals. If the dauphin were to become king, duke Philip would have his mortal enemy on the throne, and there would need to be war with him. It was better to accept what the English king had got to offer.

Narrow principle ceded to a mixture of worldly wisdom, self-interest and fear. The decision, subject to the agreement of the French king, was taken probably during the final week of October and the news was conveyed to Henry.[30] During that week ducal envoys whose task it was to negotiate a renewal of a truce at sea with England were very uncertain how to handle the negotiations, since their master's attitude towards the English was undecided. On 7 November, however, as a sign of the positive decision taken by the ducal council, the negotiators were given full powers to treat as they wished with Henry's representatives.[31] Probably on the same day, and additionally, powers were issued to Burgundian envoys to begin negotiating an alliance with the English, an alliance which was the subject of discussion at a meeting of the ducal council held at Arras at the end of the month attended by a number, such as Louis of Luxembourg (bishop of Thérouanne), Philippe de Morvilliers (first president of the Parlement of Paris), Jean de Mailly (later to be bishop of Noyon), all later to serve Henry or his brother, Bedford, on the royal council in Paris.[32]

On 2 December duke Philip issued letters at Arras in which he recognized that peace was to be made between Henry and Charles VI, king of France, a peace which he undertook to support. By its terms, Henry was to marry Katharine, and their children were to succeed

[30] Ibid., p. 70.
[31] Lille, Arch. dép., Nord, B 569/15418².
[32] Bonenfant, *Du meurtre de Montereau*, pp. 221–7; B.J.H. Rowe, 'The *Grand Conseil* under the duke of Bedford, 1422–35', *Essays in medieval history presented to H.E. Salter* (Oxford, 1934), pp. 207–14.

to the throne of France; Katharine would be accepted without any dowry whatever; and Philip was not to prevent Henry from enjoying the royal dignity in France, or any benefits thereof. Once Charles VI had died, the crown of France would immediately devolve upon Henry and to his heirs for ever: all would give him the oath of fealty as true king of France, would allow him to rule, and would obey him. Anyone who opposed or diminished his authority in any way was to be denounced. Wishing to end the war and the many conflicts which had arisen, the duke promised to support the conditions which had been worked out to achieve the final peace.[33] The earl of Warwick and other English envoys who had arrived at Arras on 30 November would have been satisfied that the fundamental decision of principle had been taken.[34]

The principle, however, needed to be expressed in more permanent form. The English could never be sure of its legal validity until they had it under seal, while the Burgundians were probably hoping to obtain military aid (which they got) from Henry as soon as possible. They may, too, have been concerned by the distinct lack of enthusiasm, if not outright opposition, with which the decision to make the alliance with the English had been met both at the court at Troyes, at that time not always at one with duke Philip, and in some Parisian circles. It was for purposes of settling matters that a large embassy, including a number of men who would later serve the English cause, left Arras for Rouen, where Henry was now residing and occupying himself principally with matters of administration and reform in Normandy. Together they worked hard. On 24 December a general truce on land between England and France was made public. Its terms included the lifting of the economic blockade imposed upon Paris in June which was to lead to the reopening of trade with the capital, much of that trade coming by river now that the English had control of its whole length from Paris to the sea; it was a step likely to revive the economic prosperity of Rouen as well.[35] On Christmas Day 1419 Henry issued letters patent, sealed with his great seal, in which, in agreeing formally to the concessions made by duke Philip and his council at Arras on 2 December, he reiterated his desire for peace to be achieved through his marriage to Katharine and a marriage between one of his brothers and one of the duke's sisters; he further

[33] PRO, E 30/402; Lille, Arch. dép., Nord, B 295/15419bis; *Foedera*, IV, iii, 140–1. The document, with its 'per dominum ducem in suo magno consilio', had the approval of his council which, after the debate which had taken place within that body at the end of October, was hardly surprising.

[34] Monstrelet, iii, 363; Dijon, Arch. dép., Côte d'Or, B 1612, fo.62v. They had come 'pour traicter de paix et accord en ce royaume'.

[35] Bonenfant, *Du meurtre de Montereau*, p. 113 and n.2.

promised to support the duke's rights in France. The duke, on his part, agreed to help Henry pursue his claims in France. Both would strive for the punishment of the dauphin, Henry agreeing not to ransom him or any of his accomplices without the knowledge of duke Philip. Finally, Henry undertook to help the duke to secure the rights and interests of his wife, Michelle, daughter of Charles VI and sister of the dauphin.[36]

A vital constitutional and political step still needed to be taken. So far the main negotiations had been carried out between Henry and Philip of Burgundy. It was with the intention of obtaining the approval of the French court, resident at Troyes, that Henry sent Louis Robesart, a trusted follower of Hainault origin, to fulfil the delicate task of securing approval from the royal council for all that had so far been arranged and agreed. Little is known of this embassy: Robesart had few persons to accompany him, and the records contain no references to his journey. It is not unlikely that Henry, thinking there might be objections to what was being done, and fearing that the French court might turn to the dauphin, preferred to work without the publicity normally associated with an embassy. Yet Robesart must have done his work well. In February duke Philip, in the company of a group of English ambassadors and of Robesart himself, left his own territories to move slowly to Troyes, where he arrived on 23 March. Some days later an assembly of interests in the kingdom, but lacking the lawyers of the Parlement of Paris, debated the issues raised by the Anglo-Burgundian agreements. By 9 April, in spite of some objections, a text commanding support was ready,[37] and, while Robesart remained in Troyes, the English embassy returned to Henry, soon followed by a French one, bearing the text of the articles agreed on 9 April to the English king, now at Pontoise. After some discussion, during which some terms not acceptable to Henry were removed or altered,[38] a final text, which was to form that of the treaty of Troyes, was agreed on 5 May.[39] An English embassy set out ahead to fix the place where Charles VI and Henry would meet for the solemn sealing of the document. A few days later, on 8 May, Henry himself began the journey.

On 9 April Charles VI had undertaken to remain in Troyes until such time as Henry decided whether he would come in person to seal the treaty. He was also to make arrangements for a number of places,

[36] BN, Collection Moreau, 1425, no.92 (with seal and illumination); copy in Dijon, Arch. dép., Côte d'Or, B 11926; *Foedera*, IV, iii, 144.
[37] The agreement (of Charles VI) 'per regem in suo consilio' is in PRO, E 30/408; that of queen Isabeau and duke Philip in E 30/409.
[38] According to Monstrelet (iii, 388–90) the text 'fut lors corrigé à sa volonté'.
[39] Henry now had 'la plus grant partie de son intencion' (ibid., iii, 380).

Pont de Charenton, Lagny-sur-Marne, Provins and Nogent-sur-Seine, to be made available to Henry and his followers on their way to Troyes.[40] Leaving Pontoise on 8 May, Henry went that night to Saint-Denis, where he prayed and left an offering at the abbey which was named after the patron saint of the country whose rule he was about to assume, and which housed the burial place of the kings of France whom he was now likely to succeed. Although Paris was only some six miles away, he bypassed the capital, watched by some of the inhabitants from the walls, and rested at Charenton, leaving soldiers to guard the Marne. As he went, he left a contingent at each bridge which he passed. By 14 May he was at Provins, where he informed Charles VI of his impending arrival. On Monday, 20 May, he reached Troyes.

According to Georges Chastellain, who was but a boy when these events took place, and who had no great love of the English (although he admired some of Henry's characteristics), duke Philip met Henry some way from Troyes, and greeted him from a horse with discreet courtesy.[41] This was their first meeting, but Chastellain wrote that they got on well. The party then entered Troyes, at which point queen Isabeau and Katharine, who had been lodged at the sign of 'La Couronne' in the market place, moved out to a nearby Franciscan convent to make place for Henry and those with him,[42] his soldiers finding lodgings in the surrounding villages. Soon after his arrival, Henry went to pay a visit on the king, the queen and Katharine; Chastellain adds that, as he approached her, 'he bowed very low, and then kissed her with great joy'.[43] Then, after they had talked briefly together, he returned to his lodgings.

It had originally been suggested by the French that the convention might take place at a mutually agreed spot between Troyes and Nogent, and that each side might come with 2500 men (who might be armed or not, as they pleased), the ground to be carefully marked out beforehand; the arrangements resembled those made for the meeting near Meulan a year earlier.[44] In the end it was decided (perhaps without the consent of Henry) that the formal ceremony of ratifying the treaty should be carried out in the cathedral of St Peter at Troyes. On the next day, 21 May, that ceremony took place. On the French side, the king was not fit enough to attend, and two days before queen

---

[40] PRO, E 30/408.

[41] '... assez révéremment, ny trop, ny peu' (*Oeuvres de Georges Chastellain. I. Chronique, 1419–1422*, ed. K. de Lettenhove (Brussels, 1863), p. 131. The account of events in these days is printed on pp. 130–8). Thomas Walsingham (ii, 334) recorded a much larger reception committee.

[42] 'Livre des trahisons', p. 152.

[43] '... s'inclina bien bas et la baisa a grand joye' (*Chronique*, p. 133).

[44] PRO, E 30/409.

Isabeau and duke Philip had been granted powers to ratify the treaty and to see to the marriage of Katharine. Both sides had some 400 followers present, on the English side there being, in addition to the king, his brother Clarence and his wife, the duke of Exeter, the earls of Warwick and Huntingdon, and Sir Gilbert Umfraville, among others. A notable absentee was Henry Beaufort, who failed to appear although specifically asked to do so.[45] Henry and Isabeau entered the cathedral, met in the centre, and advanced side by side to the high altar. The articles of the treaty were then read and, consent having been given, the texts were sealed with the seals of both kings, Henry (with a nice ironic touch) using the seal employed by Edward III at the negotiations for the treaty of Brétigny. Then each party swore to maintain peace without discord.

This done, Henry and Katharine were solemnly betrothed in a ceremony presided over by Henri de Savoisy, archbishop of Sens, a strong Burgundian supporter.[46] Later, those present, including Clarence and duke Philip, swore to keep the terms of the treaty, to remain obedient to Henry while he was regent of France and to become his liegemen once he had assumed the crown. Peace was then formally proclaimed, first in French to the French there present, then in English to the English. Finally, letters of Charles VI, ordering his subjects to give the same oath as duke Philip and other notable persons had given, were read; the terms of the peace were then made public both in the city and in the English army.[47] The following day, in the church of St Paul at Troyes, with notaries present, Philippe de Morvilliers, first president of the Parlement of Paris, the bishop of Troyes, the 'baillis' of the region and others, lay and ecclesiastical, including some 1500 inhabitants of the town, came to swear to observe the peace as it was read to them and explained word by word,[48] and their names were thereupon written in a register.

On Saturday, 1 June, Henry came to visit the French royal family at their lodgings in Troyes, and together they attended vespers, duke Philip being present, dressed in black. On the following day, Trinity Sunday, the marriage between Henry and Katharine took place in the church of St John, a large number of musicians, all paid one recently minted salut d'or, playing, and many English lords and knights, richly dressed, being in attendance. On the French side, in addition to duke Philip, were a number of councillors and captains.

---

[45] K.B. McFarlane, 'Henry V, bishop Beaufort and the Red Hat, 1417–1421', *EHR*, 60 (1945), 343; reprinted in his *England in the Fifteenth Century* (London, 1981), p. 104.

[46] The betrothal was done 'de laice usque ad tempora ad hoc de iure ordinata iuxta observacionem ecclesie' (AN, X^{1a} 1480, fo.215).

[47] Walsingham, ii, 334.

[48] '. . . de mot a mot' (BL, Cotton Ms Tiberius B xii, fo.119v).

But, we are told, not many people attended the church for the ceremony.[49] Was this because many may have seen it as a 'political'
wedding ('the bond of matrymonie maid for the good of peas')[50]
arranged in unusual circumstances, the bride's father being too ill to
attend? Was it because it seems to have been very much a soldier's
wedding, the marriage of a military man attended by other military
men? What Katharine's thoughts may have been, we are left to
wonder. As Thomas Walsingham reported, the new queen-to-be of
England was given a new household, composed almost entirely of
English personnel. There remained close to her no one who was
French other than three noble ladies-in-waiting and two maid-
servants, the only ones known to the queen as she left her parents to
go with her new husband. She was not yet nineteen years old.

Along with the treaty of Brétigny (1360), the treaty of Troyes was the
most momentous of the long Anglo-French conflict. But it was a very
different kind of treaty from that made sixty years earlier, being born
of different aims and very different circumstances. In 1360 the intention had been to regulate a feudal dispute, chiefly as it concerned
territory in the south-west of France: the matter of the English claims
to the French throne had been put on one side. At Troyes, that view
of things had been turned on its head. What emerged was a dynastic
settlement, generally in keeping with Henry's ambition and made
possible by the turn of events, most notably by the murder of John of
Burgundy in September 1419. In 1360 neither side had imposed its
terms upon the other; in 1420 the English side did. In a real sense,
the treaty of Troyes was a logical outcome of the divisions which
had allowed (indeed encouraged) Henry to invade five years earlier.
France could not stand up to the enemy, who finally dictated terms
more far-reaching in their implication than anything envisaged before.
They were the conditions of a man who, through skill and persever-
ance, and a large measure of good luck which he turned to his advantage, had won sufficient political power to impose terms both on those
who governed from Paris and on the areas which they controlled.

Although largely dictated by Henry, the terms were issued as letters
published by the king of France, Charles VI. They were simple
enough. The first clauses concerned the marriage of Henry to Katharine (which would soon take place), and the disinheritance of the
dauphin, Charles, in favour of Henry, who, while Charles VI still
lived, would act as regent in his name with right of succession for
himself and his heirs when the crown of France fell vacant. There

[49] 'Livre des trahisons', pp. 155–6.
[50] BL, Harley Ms 861, fo. 123v.

followed details of how Henry saw his position as regent: he would rule for his father-in-law, but no changes in administrative structures, law or legal institutions would be introduced. Henry was taking over France as it was, and this was to include Normandy, recently conquered, which would be restored to the French crown when Henry became king. A number of clauses dealt with problems regarding land-holding which were largely the outcome of the recent hostilities. What was essential, now, was to end war and restore peace and good government, for which Henry would effectively be responsible. All Frenchmen were to contribute to that peace by taking an oath of acceptance of this treaty's terms, in practice of Henry's claim to rule France and to bring about a union of the crowns, but not the kingdoms, of England and France.

The solution to the long-standing dispute over the French crown was a novel one. Very much the result of the events of the past five years, it nevertheless reflected the divisions in France which went back further, to the beginning of the century, and to the polarization of political loyalties which had resulted from both those divisions and the English invasions, and how men had reacted to them. The emphasis on the need for peace contained in the treaty's text was more than pious phrasing. The desire for peace was now a political factor which, linked to Henry's reputation as an effective ruler, worked in his favour. Few Frenchmen would have regarded the political settlement envisaged in the treaty as ideal. Supporters of the dauphin (who had played no part in the negotiations) saw their prince disinherited: would they stick by him? To Burgundians, it was better than having dauphinists in power: the lesser of two evils.[51] In such a situation, what future did the treaty have?

To the Parisians, the treaty came as a great relief. Not only was their political master, the duke of Burgundy, on the 'winning' side, but the treaty meant that their economic lifeline, the Seine, could now be used again for commercial purposes. Paris, as the centre of great national institutions, must have felt reassured by the treaty's terms. In spite of its earlier reluctance to be involved in the negotiation of those terms, the Parlement and its officers were willing to give their accord to an agreement which would bring the sweetness of peace to a kingdom which had suffered for so long. Like the Parlement, the chapter of Notre Dame and the university were institutions of Burgundian sympathy. So, although the bishop strongly opposed the treaty, most of the city's leaders were in favour of acceptance. On 2 June 1420 the Parisians wrote to Henry approving the recent turn of events, including his marriage, urging him to keep their city and its

---

[51] Keen, 'Diplomacy', p. 197, citing Bonenfant, *Du meurtre de Montereau*, p. 218.

interests in mind. But they had to wait until 1 December before, accompanied by his queen and her parents, he came to visit them. On that day he was received with as much honour as could be mustered by a population whose number and wealth had been greatly diminished by war and mortality.[52] The Parisians were joyful to see their king once again, and, as Monstrelet reported, there was greater support for the peace which had been agreed upon than words could properly express.[53] The fact that, since the summer, Henry had broken the control exerted over the traffic on the Seine by the dauphinist garrisons at Montereau and Melun underlined the reasons for their favourable view of him. More than many, the Parisians were affected by factors of geography and tended to trim their political sails accordingly.

No capital is ever typical of the country of which it is the chief city. Paris supported the treaty. Abbeville agreed to observe its terms on 28 November; Montreuil-sur-Mer took the same decision two days later.[54] Both decisions accord with what one might expect of towns within the Burgundian sphere of influence.[55] Yet it would not be all plain sailing. Only an hour's ride from 'Burgundian' Paris lay Saint-Denis, in whose abbey French kings were buried. It came under Lancastrian rule as a result of the treaty of Troyes, but would be a reluctant subject of the new order, as events in the coming years were to prove.[56] We may note, too, that the town of Tournai, in the heartland of Burgundian influence, at first declined to accept the terms of the treaty and maintained relations with the dauphinists for several more months. Dijon, one of the ducal capitals, had· to be specially visited by the duke himself to persuade it to swear the oath to the treaty; while in Troyes, the very place in which the treaty had been sealed and the royal marriage had taken place, a certain equivocal attitude was to introduce itself, with opposition to the English led, as in Paris, by the bishop, Etienne de Givry.[57]

---

[52] AN, X¹ᵃ 1480, fo. 224; Fauquembergue, *Journal*, i, 389; *Bourgeois de Paris*, ed. Tuetey, pp. 144–5; ibid., ed. Beaune, pp. 162–3; *Parisian journal*, pp. 153–4.

[53] '. . . plus que la langue ne pourroit raconter' (Monstrelet, iv, 15–17).

[54] AN, J 646, nos 18, 17.

[55] Other places in that 'sphere' were Amiens, Lille, Douai and Arras (Monstrelet, iv, 204).

[56] On this, see G. Thompson, '"Monseigneur Saint Denis", his abbey, and his town, under the English occupation, 1420–1436', *Power, culture, and religion in France, c.1350-c.1550*, ed. C. Allmand (Woodbridge/Wolfeboro, 1989), p. 15 seq.

[57] Bonenfant, *Du meurtre de Montereau*, p. 172, n.3 (Tournai); A. Leguai, 'The relations between the towns of Burgundy and the French crown in the fifteenth century', *The crown and local communities in England and France in the fifteenth century*, ed. J.R.L. Highfield and R. Jeffs (Gloucester, 1981), p. 135 (Dijon); M. D'Arbois de Jubainville, *Inventaire-sommaire des archives départementales de l'Aube. Archives ecclésiastiques. Série G*, i, pp.viii–ix (Troyes); PRO, E 30/1634 (Langres).

Corporations were one matter, men another. It is hard to tell what caused doubt in the minds of certain individuals, particularly those who had close Burgundian connections. Philippe de Brabant, count of Saint-Pol, had been Burgundian captain of Paris for Charles VI during the months preceding the treaty. It was a worried royal officer (perhaps Ralph Cromwell) who wrote to Henry from Pontoise on 3 June 1420 to report the failure of Saint-Pol to take the oath, the reason given being that although he approved of the peace, he was resisting the oath 'because hym thoghte no blode riall shulde be comprehendet in no generalti'.[58] Not surprisingly, he was soon replaced as captain of Paris. In the same way, and perhaps for the same reason, his brother, Louis, bishop of Thérouanne, later to become a strong supporter of the English who greatly furthered his career, also showed a marked reluctance to submit. Both had to be ordered to give their assent by duke Philip. Guy de la Trémoille, count of Joigny, who had not wanted to take part in the formal ceremonies at Troyes, also refused at first, only to benefit later from English favours; while the Prince of Orange, although present at Henry's marriage, preferred to safeguard his independence by not taking the oath to the treaty of Troyes.[59]

Others reacted to different aspects of what they saw as the new situation. Some regarded the events of 1419–20 as a challenge to national identity, fearing that the kingdom of France, as it existed and had existed for centuries, would be subsumed into something greater, a kind of mega-kingdom ruled over by the king of England and his heirs, in which the existing France would lose her identity. Such people had to be reassured (as Englishmen were to need reassuring for much the same reason in the following year) that the concept of the 'double monarchy' was one which united crowns, not kingdoms, which would continue to exist with their laws, languages and institutions intact.[60] This had been made plain by Henry to the Burgundian envoys who had come to see him at Mantes in October 1419. That Henry should have been willing to make these concessions would have surprised none who knew what he had already done in Normandy, where revival of local custom and administrative practice had been an important aspect of his rule.[61]

[58] BL, Cotton Ms Caligula D v, fo.75.

[59] Bonenfant, *Du meurtre de Montereau*, p. 172, n. 4.

[60] See the text of the treaty of Troyes, clauses 7–11 (*Les grands traités de la guerre de cent ans*, ed. E. Cosneau (Paris, 1889)).

[61] W.T. Waugh, 'The administration of Normandy, 1420–22', *Essays in medieval history presented to T.F. Tout*, ed. A.G. Little and F.M. Powicke (Manchester, 1925), pp. 349–59; R.A. Newhall, 'Henry V's policy of conciliation in Normandy, 1417–1422', *Anniversary essays in medieval history of students of C.H. Haskins*, ed. C.H. Taylor (Boston, 1929), pp. 205–29.

Those, or some of those, who were flatly opposed to the terms of the treaty of Troyes, and to everything that it stood for, used tracts and sermons to publicize their views.[62] One such was Gerard de Montagu, bishop of Paris, who placed before his people a stark choice: they could either stand behind their king, whose sole heir was the dauphin, or place themselves in the hands of the English, the kingdom's old enemies who constantly sought to seduce the people of Paris. Neither the language nor the arguments used by Montagu to prevent the acceptance of the treaty suffered from overmuch subtlety. His was a straightforward appeal, reflecting the polarization of society already mentioned, to what he regarded as a necessity: that the public good could best be served by a return to the acceptance of Charles VI as undoubted king of France. If people wanted to see what life was like under the English, let them turn to Rouen or other places which had submitted to their rule. He was ready to work against the proposals, and he hoped that others would join him in opposing them.[63]

More interesting were the discourses made by a French speaker, the abbot of Beaubec, and the reply made by an unknown Englishman, before the Pope, Martin V, at the papal court. The abbot was much concerned with fictions and deceits. It had to be asserted that the dauphin was his father's true heir, and that only force had robbed him of his right. For this reason the peace thus established was a false peace, invalid because the use of the seals had been controlled by the duke of Burgundy, the dauphin's enemy. Peace could not come from the English, because their king claimed the throne through Isabella, sister of the last Capetian kings of France and wife of Edward II. Women, as he reminded his listeners, were excluded from the succession, but a son could never be so.

In reply, the Englishman took another approach. The French, he said, had claimed that the treaty was invalid because the king was not lucid, and the proper seal of France was not used. This was certainly not true, since the king knew full well what was being done, the royal council had agreed, and the proper seal, in the keeping of the duke of Burgundy, was used. The validity of the treaty, the speaker reminded his audience, sprang from the agreement given it by the people of Paris (in whose city the seal was kept) and by those of Burgundy, Normandy, Picardy, Artois, Champagne and other parts

[62] N. Pons, 'La guerre de cent ans vue par quelques polémistes français du XVe siècle', *Guerre et société en France, en Angleterre et en Bourgogne: XIVe – XVe siècle*, ed. P. Contamine, C. Giry-Deloison and M.H. Keen (Lille, 1991), pp. 143–69: '*L'honneur de la couronne de France'. Quatre libelles contre les Anglais (v.1418- v.1429)*, ed. N. Pons (SHF, Paris, 1990).

[63] PRO, E 30/1746, fos 1–iv: E. Déprez, 'Un essai d'union nationale à la veille du traité de Troyes (1419)', *BEC*, 99 (1938), 343–53.

of France. Failing to see that those territories (all in the north and north-east of the country) scarcely provided a convincing geographical basis for his opinion, he returned briefly to his opponent's argument by stressing that since the male Capetians had no heirs, the succession had devolved to Isabella and her heirs. The English claim was, therefore, a valid one. As if for good measure, he finished by stressing that the dauphin was guilty of *lèse-majesté*, or treason, for assisting at the murder of the duke of Burgundy, thus earning exclusion from the throne.[64]

Another writer felt compelled to offer what he termed 'observations' on the betrayal of the 'fleur de lys'.[65] This had been done under cover of peace and a marriage with France's mortal enemies, who used Latin as a subterfuge, since the king, the queen, Katharine and many nobles, among others, could not understand it; an allusion, perhaps, to the English insistence that Latin be used in diplomatic documents and proceedings to avoid misunderstandings. It was certain, the writer argued, that a free king would not have made this 'unnatural treaty' which placed the young and innocent Katharine in the power of the enemy and distanced her from the crown of France. None, least of all a king and queen in captivity, had the right to alter the natural succession. Since the dauphin had already acted as regent for the king, who was 'incapable of acting' (a reference, doubtless, to the dauphin Charles' assumption of the title late in 1418), how could he be disinherited?

Turning to the fear that the crown might pass out of French hands, the writer argued that since the youngest of Katharine's brothers (the dauphin, Charles) and two of her elder sisters were still alive, how could it be claimed that any right of succession to the French crown could be passed on through her? And, 'grand horreur', what would occur if Katharine were to die without children? All the English king's heirs, referred to in the treaty, would have a right to the crown of France. The peace had ignored those whom it most concerned, the people of France, and was bound to lead to more divisions than existed already. It did not even lead to good government: see the way the English governed in Normandy, and what their king's father had done with Richard II and his wife, daughter of the king of France (and, he might have added, sister of Katharine). What sort of peace was this which appealed to disloyalty, to force and violence, and to betrayal? 'Dieu, quel traité, quelle paix, quel acord, quelle franchise.'

[64] BL, Tiberius B xii, fos 124–125v.
[65] AN, PP 2298, p. 645 seq.

Chapter 8

FRANCE, 1420–22

News of the treaty which, Monstrelet was to write, greatly pleased Henry as giving him most of what he hoped to achieve, reached Venice on 9 July.[1] By that time the king was once again fully engaged on campaign, something in which he had not been properly involved for at least a year, the intervening months having been spent largely in diplomacy and administration. At some time, probably before too long, he would have to take his queen back to England for her coronation. In the autumn, in anticipation of the visit, repairs were carried out at Eltham and at other royal manors.[2] For the time being, the king and his household remained in France, supplied with what were probably items of luxury food, such as salmon and sturgeon, as well as with large supplies of oats for the horses, from England.[3]

Well before the news of the treaty and the marriage had reached Venice, Henry had embarked upon a policy of conquest required of him as a party to the treaty (the terms of which had demanded that those areas remaining faithful to the dauphin should be reconquered); required, too, by anyone trying to follow a logical policy of winning places then held by the enemy. The truth of the matter was that while Englishmen were in control to the north-west of Paris, and Burgundians were in charge of areas both to the south-west of the capital and in many (but not all) areas to the north of it, the dauphinists held sway to the south and, most important, to the east of Paris, particularly in the crucial area of the Seine valley below Troyes, where Henry had just been married. Two days after the ceremony, Henry forwent the chance of a tournament planned to celebrate the occasion in favour of some real fighting where men might show what they were worth and those who harmed the poor might reap their just deserts: accompanied by Katharine, the duke of Burgundy and his father-in-law, Charles VI, he set out in a south-westerly direction to lay siege to Sens, which lay on the river Yonne above the point where, at Montereau, it joins the Seine.[4]

[1] Morosini, *Chronique*, i, 189–91.
[2] PRO, E 403/645, m.13; 646, m.1.
[3] PRO, E 403/645, mm.8, 10; 646, mm.4, 5.
[4] *Bourgeois de Paris*, ed. Tuetey, p. 140; ibid., ed. Beaune, p. 159; *Parisian journal*, p. 151.

Sens gave Henry little trouble. On 10 June the town's inhabitants, perhaps in doubt whom they ought to obey, decided to surrender, some wearing the red cross (of England) hoping to curry favour in this way.[5] Montereau itself, however, proved more difficult. Summoned to surrender by the king of France, its liege lord, the garrison refused to do so, whereupon Henry turned his artillery on the walls.

The siege was to last some time. Only after a number of notable exploits both on and under the walls (where mines had been dug) and the public execution by hanging in full view of the defenders of some eighteen prisoners, a deed said to be an act of vengeance for an English knight who had been killed by a varlet, did the town surrender.[6] The occasion gave Philip of Burgundy the opportunity to visit the spot where his father had been hastily buried after his murder. The grave was respectfully covered with black cloth, and candles were lighted. On the next day, the body, fully dressed and the wounds still looking fresh, was exhumed amidst much lamentation, to be taken away to Dijon for honourable burial.

As he had done earlier at Rouen, which had been approached from the south-east to cut off relief by water from Paris, so, two years later, Henry attacked the remaining dauphinist garrisons on the reaches of the Seine to the south-east above Paris to counter their threat to the capital's trade. Once Montereau had fallen on 1 July, Henry moved down the Seine to Melun, the next stage on this systematic reduction of enemy-held towns. The place, well fortified,[7] 'was on[e] of the werste that evere he leyde sege to'.[8] Henry had with him Burgundy, his brothers, Clarence and Bedford, their brother-in-law, Louis of Bavaria, and a notable prisoner, James I, king of Scots; meanwhile Katharine and her parents were more comfortably established some distance away, at Corbeil. The siege was to be a long one, noted for its use of heavy cannon which forced the people to their cellars, and for Henry's realization, as Chastellain was to put it, that if he could not capture the town by going through its walls, he would have to make progress underneath them. As at Montereau, considerable mining operations took place, and in one encounter Henry met the captain of the town, the lord of Barbazan. Otherwise, as Chastellain recorded, the soldiers played cards and 'paume' (tennis?) to pass the time. Henry, in fact, went off (as modern man might go off for the weekend) to see his wife and her parents at Corbeil, returning with the king who, he hoped, would be instrumental in calling his subjects to

[5] Chastellain, *Chronique*, pp. 139–41.
[6] Ibid., pp. 142–7; Monstrelet, iii, 405–6; BN, Ms fr.5028, fo.148.
[7] '. . . une forte et maistraisse clef' (Chastellain, *Chronique*, p. 152).
[8] *Chronicle of London*, ed. Nicolas and Tyrrell, p. 108.

surrender.⁹ This they refused to do. Nor did some Scottish soldiers inside the town heed a similar call from their king, James, brought to the scene of the siege to help achieve an early conclusion. Henry, however, was nothing if not confident. On one occasion he is alleged to have told some local people that since he intended to have the whole French kingdom, they would soon become English; on another, he is reported to have gone to Saint-Fiacre-en-Brie in order to take the body of the saint, a seventh-century Irish hermit who had settled locally, for despatch back to his native country. Such behaviour on the part of a conqueror met with scant sympathy. Henry is said to have become ill as the result of this act, and to have been obliged to order the restoration of the relics to their historic resting place.¹⁰

The siege continued well into November, although news had been brought to Paris almost a month earlier that most of Melun had fallen, and prisoners could be expected.¹¹ In the end, as one chronicle records, it was famine which decided the issue, in addition to the effects of sickness, lack of sleep, the noise of cannon and general demoralization upon the minds and bodies of the besieged.¹² At one point, Flemish reinforcements who had come on the orders of the duke of Burgundy were mistaken by the besieged as a relieving force, and the town's church bells were rung, but, as on a not dissimilar occasion in 1418 when the inhabitants of Rouen had been deceived into thinking that help had arrived, so the people of Melun had to face the hard realities of life. By the terms negotiated with the earl of Warwick, some 500 men-at-arms, including Barbazan, were taken as prisoners to Paris, and then elsewhere (Barbazan was held in Château-Gaillard for seven years), and a number of persons were executed, in spite of pleading by Clarence for the life of one of them, Bertrand de Caumont, a Gascon, a pleading said to have elicited the reply that had Clarence been guilty of the same crime (of treason), he would have suffered a similar penalty. 'We will have no traitors around us,' Henry is reported to have said.¹³

As already remarked,¹⁴ the entry of Henry and the two royal families into Paris on 1 December was an occasion for considerable rejoicings among the people of the capital. Of the processional entry of Charles VI, Henry, Philip of Burgundy, Clarence and Bedford, the

⁹ Chastellain, *Chronique*, pp. 156-8.
¹⁰ Alain Bouchart, *Grandes Croniques de Bretaigne*, ed. H. Le Meignen, (Rennes, 1886), p. 179d.
¹¹ AN, X¹ᵃ 4792, fo.254v (20 October 1420).
¹² Chastellain, *Chronique*, pp. 177-8.
¹³ '. . . nous ne voulons, ny n'aurons, si Dieu plaist, nuls traistres emprès nous' (ibid., pp. 184-5).
¹⁴ See above, p. 147.

'Bourgeois' wrote: 'No princes were ever welcomed more joyfully than these; in every street they met processions of priests in copes and surplices carrying reliquaries and singing *Te Deum laudamus* and *Benedictus qui venit*.' In spite of the general distress caused by food shortages, the Parisians did their best, a splendid mystery or representation of Christ's Passion making a fine impression. On the following day it was the turn of queen Isabeau, Katharine, Henry's queen, and the duchess of Clarence. They, too, were received as warmly as the men had been the previous day.[15] Characteristically, Henry made a special point of visiting Notre-Dame to offer thanks for his successes, while an English chronicle reports that Charles, at that time lucid of mind, expressed his approval of the treaty of Troyes, saying that his heirs and successors would observe its terms.[16] Both the Bastille and the royal castle at Vincennes, to the south-east of Paris, now received English captains,[17] but the duke of Burgundy was asked to appoint a captain at the Louvre, a tactful move on Henry's part.

On 6 December the estates general of France (that part of France willing to accept the outcome of recent military and political events) met in Paris and some days later, having heard Charles VI in person urge its acceptance, the assembly ratified the treaty of Troyes, before accepting the need for currency reform and fiscal provision for the continuation of the war. On 23 December, at a solemn 'lit de justice' held in the presence of the two kings, the dauphin, Charles, was summoned to answer charges arising out of the murder of John of Burgundy at Montereau. Not surprisingly he did not appear, but the request of duke Philip and his family for justice was to some extent met by the general condemnation of the late duke's assassins and the declaration, along with the sentence of banishment, that the dauphin was incapable of succeeding to the French throne. It was another way of adding a judicial decision (soon to be ratified by the Parlement) to the terms of the treaty of Troyes.

Christmas 1420, according to the 'Bourgeois', was a time when the Parisians suffered from the cold weather, months of deprivation and prices much affected by a currency of wildly fluctuating value. They gave presents to the English royal family, but it was a rather pitiful French royal family which spent the festive period in the Hotel Saint-Pol, while the English were probably at the royal castle of the Louvre, surrounded by signs of regality, the young queen, Katharine, having

---

[15] *Bourgeois de Paris*, ed. Tuetey, p. 144; ibid., ed. Beaune, pp. 162–3; *Parisian journal*, pp. 153–4; Fauquembergue, *Journal*, i, 388–9; Chastellain, *Chronique*, pp. 187–9.

[16] *Henrici Quinti Angliae regis gesta*, ed. B. Williams (London, 1850), p. 146.

[17] BN, Ms fr.5028, fo.148v.

with her a number of English ladies of the court circle, including the duchess of Clarence and the countess of March.[18] Monstrelet was to refer to the strange turn of fortune which had brought the French crown so low while raising that of the ancient enemy so high, while later Chastellain, not a known anglophile, could comment on English arrogance and the sad sight of so few people visiting Charles VI, their natural lord.[19]

Henry had decided that he must soon return to England, which he had left in August 1417, to see and to be seen. There was work to be done, and Katharine would have to be crowned. On 27 December the queen bade farewell to her parents, and within a short time the English court was on the first step of its journey to England. Henry was intent upon visiting Rouen, which he had left the previous May to go to Troyes, and the Norman capital was reached in time for the Epiphany celebrations, Katharine being well received by the people of the city who gave her several valuable presents.[20] In the coming days Henry met the estates of Normandy and the 'Conquest', lands outside the duchy, including some lands very close to Paris[21] and part of the county of Maine, which had been 'conquered' from the French crown before the treaty of Troyes. As in Paris a month earlier, regulations for the coinage were issued, taxes to the value of 400,000 *livres tournois* were voted for the war, and matters concerning the government of the duchy were discussed. This visit also gave Henry the chance to receive homages, including those of his senior commander, Thomas, earl of Salisbury, for the county of Perche, and from Arthur of Brittany, technically his prisoner, for the county of Ivry, homages which were rendered in the hall of the castle, symbol of ducal authority.[22]

Some time in the second half of January Henry and his queen, together with Bedford, the earls of March and Warwick, and accompanied by a large force of soldiers, left Rouen. They may have gone to Beauvais for the solemn entry into his see of Pierre Cauchon, the staunch Burgundian who was ten years later to play so important a role in the trial of Joan of Arc. They then went to Amiens (where they stayed with the 'bailli', Robert le Jeune); then, passing probably not far from Agincourt, to Thérouanne (whose bishop, Louis of Luxembourg, another pro-Burgundian, would, in spite of having entertained doubts about the treaty of Troyes, become chancellor of France for

[18] London, College of Arms, Arundel Ms 48, fo.264.
[19] Monstrelet, iv, 22–3; Chastellain, *Chronique*, pp. 200–1.
[20] *Chronique normande de Pierre Cochon*, p. 285; BN, Ms fr.5028, fo.149.
[21] Mantes sent representatives to this meeting (Mantes, Arch. comm., BB 3, fo.78).
[22] BN, Ms fr.5028. fo.149v; *Henrici quinti . . . gesta*, ed. Williams, pp. 204, 256–7.

Henry VI in 1425); and finally on to Calais where, again, rich presents were received from the merchants and townspeople, and where a few days were spent resting before the crossing to England was made.[23] On 1 February the royal couple received an enthusiastic reception at Dover.

The arrival of Henry and his queen was to be commemorated in style, if not in quite the same style as on the return of 1415. None the less, minstrels went to meet them at Blackheath,[24] and while his queen stayed at Eltham, Henry went on into London to supervise preparations for the coronation.[25] The giant's head made for London Bridge took two days' work to make, and two men to guard it.[26] Henry was out to impress his wife and his people,[27] who welcomed him joyfully in large crowds. Teams of workmen were hired for the week to help in preparing for the royal arrival, and some of these were said to have worked day and night, 'steynours' (painters) receiving 9d. or 10d. a day, 'kervers' (carpenters) 9d. a day, and 'joiners' 7d. or 8d. As had been the case in the great reception of 1415, much painting was done with the intention of deliberately deceiving the eye, so that the mayor, sheriffs, aldermen[28] and members of guilds[29] who were present on these occasions must have had a show of considerable imagination before them.

Katharine arrived in London on 21 February, to be met by the corporation and members of the guilds, wearing white gowns and red hoods, each craft being distinguished from the others by an embroidery.[30] On the following day she left the Tower, where she had been lodged, and, accompanied by, among others, members of the Grocers' guild,[31] she was taken to Westminster, passing near London Bridge where she could have heard eight pairs of singing angels, and observed an image of St Petronella, an early Roman martyr, tactfully chosen for her long association with the crown and kingdom of France.[32]

[23] Chastellain, *Chronique*, pp. 204–6.
[24] London, Guildhall Library, Ms 11570 (Ordinances, remembrances and Wardens' accounts of the Company of Grocers, 1345–1463), p. 138.
[25] The recluse at Westminster Abbey benefited from the royal charity at this time (PRO, E 403/646, m.13).
[26] Corporation of London R.O., Bridge House accounts I (1404–1420), pp. 457, 462.
[27] Much work was carried out on the king's instructions, 'per dicta ordinata regis' (ibid., p. 458).
[28] Ibid., pp. 460, 461, 464.
[29] London, Mercers' Company, Wardens' accounts, 1344, 1347–1464, fo.76.
[30] Guildhall Library, Ms 11570, p. 136.
[31] Ibid., p. 138; Ms 5440 (Brewers' accounts, 1418–1440), fos 46, 46v.
[32] Corporation of London R.O., Bridge House accounts I, p. 480; C.M. Barron, 'The government of London and its relations with the crown, 1410–1450' (Univ. of London Ph.D. thesis, 1970), p. 471.

Then, next day, 23 February, the third Sunday in Lent, wearing a fine apparel and in the presence of many nobles drawn from all the country (doubtless those to whom royal messengers had been sent the previous month inviting them to attend the solemn occasion), she was crowned queen of England by archbishop Chichele at Westminster Abbey.[33] Henry exercised his right, given in the order of service, not to be present, or at least not to take part in the ceremony. There is no record of him having participated in his queen's 'big day'.[34]

Had Henry taken part in the ensuing banquet held at Westminster Hall, his presence would have been recorded. The account which we have makes no mention of him. Instead, Katharine was given pride of place at a feast attended by the king of Scots, a number of great lords and office-holders, and, naturally enough in the circumstances, their wives, along with a fair number of bishops, judges and representatives of the corporation of London. Since the season was lenten, the food was almost entirely fish, served in many forms over three courses. The menu was incorporated into the *Brut* and other chronicles of the time. Was it as unusual to persons of that time as it would be to those of today?[35]

Once Katharine had been crowned, Henry could turn his mind to some of the business which he had come to England to do. Although he had kept up with what had been going on in his absence, and had often been responsible for directing policy or settling such matters as the council had not felt competent to deal with, his long absence had necessarily put him somewhat out of touch with both events and the everyday requirements of government. He needed to see for himself what the mood of the country was. He needed, too, to be seen by his people, as the chancellor had said in his address to the parliament which had met in the previous December, when it was still hoped that Henry would be in England.[36] His most tangible gain, his new queen, had also to be shown to her subjects, while some problems arising out of an apparent misunderstanding of certain clauses of the treaty of Troyes had to be resolved.

The needs of government, whose burdens he had reassumed on his landing at Dover, had to be seen to first. On 18 February, scarcely back in London, Henry had a meeting with the chancellor, bishop Langley, archbishop Chichele, the bishop of Norwich and others, and it may have been on that occasion that the decision was taken to

---

[33] PRO, E 403/646, m.12.
[34] *Liber regie capelle*, p. 107. The service of coronation for a queen alone is on pp. 107–10.
[35] *Brut*, ii, 445–7; *Citizen of London*, pp. 138–41.
[36] *RP*, iv, 123.

summon another parliament for 2 May, writs being authorized by the
king himself at Westminster on 26 February. Henry then set out on a
tour of the country, during which he visited the shrines of Bridlington,
Beverley and Walsingham. But it was also a tour which, since its
intention was to bring him into contact with his subjects, could best
be satisfied by visits to towns. Setting out with a few attendants, and
leaving Katharine at Westminster, he first went west, to Bristol, and
then up the Welsh march through Hereford to Shrewsbury. Here he
was in the area which had given him so much trouble in his days as
Prince; yet it was an area, too, which had contributed substantially
in manpower and leadership towards the making of his army, and
from which he might secure support for continuation of the war. As
he went round, Henry had meetings with local gentry and sought
their help. The number of loans made in the coming months suggests
that he had not been entirely unsuccessful.

While in Shrewsbury in the first half of March, Henry received and
answered many petitions.[37] He also visited Weobley, his favourite
castle of Kenilworth, Coventry and Leicester, the town where his
mother lay buried and one closely associated with the dynasty of
Lancaster. Here he awaited the arrival of Katharine, who, travelling
through Hertford, Bedford and Northampton, arrived on the eve of
Palm Sunday.[38] While here, Henry distributed the royal maundy
money to the poor and here, too, Easter was celebrated with full
solemnity. After the festivities, the royal couple went on to Nottingham, then to Pontefract, and then York where they were very well
received and had gifts pressed upon them.[39] It was at this moment that
Henry made pilgrimages to the shrines at Beverley and Bridlington,
travelling on his own, the queen, now pregnant, remaining in York.

Events, however, were destined to take a sudden turn in an
unexpected direction. On 1 April a messenger left London for Yorkshire with important news touching the king intimately.[40] The messenger, who caught up with Henry soon after he had left Beverley, had
tragic, indeed devastating news to convey: Thomas of Clarence,
Henry's brother and heir to the throne since their father's death in
1413, had been killed on 22 March, the eve of Easter, in an encounter
with a Franco-Scottish force at Baugé, in Anjou. While on a raid into
this frontier territory, Clarence had heard from captured prisoners
that the enemy were not far away. Hitherto unaware of their presence

---

[37] '. . . pauperum querelas exaudiens, opprimentibus et oppressis justitiae com-
plementum ministravit' (*Henrici quinti . . . gesta*, ed. Williams, p. 148). On Henry and
justice, see below, ch. 14.
[38] 'Die parassenes' (PRO, E 403/646, m. 13).
[39] Kingsford, *English historical literature*, p. 290.
[40] 'intime' (PRO, E 403/646, m. 1).

and ill-informed about their number, Clarence decided to seek out and attack them in spite of a warning given to him not to do so. Disregarding advice to wait until his own force, which included archers, could be got ready, he advanced on horseback with insufficient support. Meeting at first only token resistance from men who may have been surprised to see him, he soon came upon the enemy's full force, which heavily outnumbered him. The lie of the land, with a stream and a bridge defended by the French, was also against him. In the confused fighting which followed, Clarence, lord Roos and the Northumbrian, Gilbert Umfraville, earl of Kyme, a firm favourite of Henry and the man to whom, John Hardyng reported, Clarence had confessed that he felt obliged to fight since he had not yet won honour in battle,[41] were killed, while the earl of Huntingdon and John Beaufort were among the distinguished prisoners.[42] 'The Scots, indeed, are the remedy against the English', pope Martin V was reported as having said when told the news,[43] and, in gratitude, the dauphin created the earl of Buchan marshal of France as a reward for his success.

In the absence of the king, the English had lost a battle in France. The death of his brother was one which Henry would have felt very keenly,[44] as indeed it was felt by the country as a whole, although the recorders of opinion did not hide the fact that they thought that Clarence had bungled the day, and had brought defeat upon himself and his fellow Englishmen by his lack of foresight and caution.[45] What the defeat could mean to men of the time it is hard to say.[46] For Henry, the event could not have happened at a more inopportune moment, so far away was he from the action. Happily for him, the French missed the chance which, had they taken it, might have led to disaster for the English. To an outstanding leader, a quick dash to Paris might have been appealing. Such an unlikely event as an English defeat opened up all kinds of possibilities, and Exeter felt obliged to

[41] *Chronicle of John Hardyng*, p. 384.

[42] Guillaume Cousinot asserted that the French would have much preferred to take Clarence alive, to exchange him for the duke of Orléans, captured at Agincourt (*Chronique de la Pucelle et chronique de Cousinot, suivie de la chronique normande de P. Cochon*, ed. V. de Viriville (Paris, 1859), p. 180). The possibility of exchanging prisoners taken at Baugé was raised in April and May 1421 (BL, Add. Chs 3549, 3551, 3552).

[43] Cited by Ramsay, *Lancaster and York*, i, 292, n.2.

[44] '. . . vehementissime doluit' (Kingsford, *English historical literature*, p. 290); '. . . valde contristatus' ('Chronicle of John Strecche', 185).

[45] The *Brut* (ii, 447–8) asserted he had been killed 'be-cause he wold not be gouerned and have take hys [h]ost with hym'.

[46] R. Planchenault, 'La bataille de Baugé (22 mars 1421)', *Mémoires de la société nationale d'agriculture, sciences et arts d'Angers*, 5e série, 28 (1925), 5–30; 'Les suites de la bataille de Baugé (1421)', ibid., 6e série, 5 (1930), 90–107.

get the Parisians to renew their commitment to the treaty of Troyes.[47] In Venice, rumour in April had it that the dauphin was in Paris and that, as a result, peace might now be made.[48] The English were also fortunate in one further respect. Serving under Clarence was the earl of Salisbury, a commander of great worth and experience. It was he who prevented a rout and extricated the English from the dangerous military situation in which they found themselves. Henry owed much to Salisbury for his efforts that day.

Typically, to give himself time to decide on his own what needed doing, and thereby to preserve the initiative for himself, Henry waited for a day before breaking the news of what had happened to those who were with him. Clearly, the military requirements of men and money had become more urgent than ever. It was either a measure of the confidence which he had in Salisbury as a commander, or his own recognition of what could, in practice, be done even in these critical days (he could not, for example, afford to miss another meeting of parliament, particularly in the new conditions which now prevailed) that Henry refused to be panicked by the recent turn of events. Rejoining his wife at Pontefract and travelling through Howden and Newark, he was at Lincoln on 15 April to see Richard Flemming enthroned as bishop, and to assist at the arbitration in a long-standing dispute between the dean, John Mackworth, and members of the chapter over rights of visitation,[49] after which he visited King's Lynn, Walsingham and Norwich. Then, returning to London, Henry set about raising his army, a task which had now assumed prime importance.

Commissioners were sent round the southern counties seeking what help might be given to the king in defence of his conquest in France, while all those in the king's retinue were ordered to come to London to discuss the forthcoming expedition.[50] In Lincolnshire, the king, perhaps anticipating a certain lukewarm manner, ordered that those who refused to help should have their names taken and sent to him,[51] while in Yorkshire, the response to the appeal was less than total.[52]

[47] Newhall, *English conquest*, pp. 276–7.

[48] Morosini, *Chronique*, i, 199–205.

[49] Kingsford, *English historical literature*, p. 290; Lincoln, Lincolnshire Archives Office, A/2/30. A modern stained-glass window in the chapter house depicts the king's action on this visit.

[50] PRO, E 403/649, m.2.

[51] 'Litera domini regis pro chevisancia' (Lincolnshire Archives Office, Reg[ister] 16, fo.240v).

[52] PRO, E 101/55/13; A.E. Goodman, 'Response to requests in Yorkshire for military service under Henry V', *Northern History*, 17 (1981), 240–52. Norfolk, although visited by Henry, produced no response (*PPC*, ii, 246–8).

At the same time, there were signs that preparations were moving actively forward. Enquiries were instigated in Essex and Kent regarding the availability of merchant ships which might be used on the expedition; on the south-west coast ships were arrested; saltpetre was purchased from a Catalonian merchant (a sure sign that strong action was planned);[53] while the chamberlain of Chester was able to recruit the 200 archers from Cheshire and Hawarden which had been demanded of him on 13 May, and four knights and 400 archers from Lancashire also promised to serve.[54]

Parliament met at the beginning of May to be told by the chancellor, Langley, that the king's patience in times of difficulty was no less than that of Job, a reference to Henry's acceptance of the death of Clarence and others at Baugé, as well as a clear attempt to restore confidence which might have been shaken by the defeat. Parliament had been called, Langley went on, to see to the maintenance of justice and order within the kingdom, and to ensure that those who had served in the war (and who were now returning home) should not be disadvantaged by the law because of their absence abroad. The treaty of Troyes was explained; the fear that, in the new order of things, England might be subject to Henry as king of France was dispelled, and the treaty's terms, as required, were ratified.[55]

Finally, there was the financial crisis which Henry faced at this time. In part, it was an aspect of a greater crisis which affected much of north-western Europe in these years. At the same time, it was the creation of the demands of war which, in the final analysis, caused the major deficit from which Henry suffered in his last years. In May 1421 it was anticipated that, by the end of the coming financial year in September, Henry would have about £3507 with which to pay for the essential expenses of daily government, not to speak of the high costs of maintaining war in France and defence in England, as well as the payment of royal debts, many of which went back to the last reign, 'a pitiless catalogue [which] shows on how small a margin Henry was conducting the war'.[56] The solution – or part of it – might have been found in a parliamentary grant, but Henry knew better than to ask for one at this moment, although the Canterbury convocation, meeting at the same time, voted a tenth, half to be collected by September, the other half a year later. In its place, he had to resort to loans: a huge one totalling £17,666 13s. 4d. which came from bishop Beaufort, down to the very small ones offered by individuals who, in

53 PRO, E 403/649, mm.2–5.
54 PRO, CHES 2/93, m.7; E 403/649, m.7; E 28/34.
55 *RP*, iv, 129, 135. On this matter, see below, p. 363, and n.59.
56 Jacob, *Fifteenth century*, p. 195; Wylie and Waugh, *Henry the Fifth*, iii, 274.

making these sacrifices, registered not necessarily their approval of what was being done but their regard for the king who was doing it.[57]

Early in June Henry set out from London for France. On 6 and 7 June he was at Canterbury; two days later he was at Dover with his council, waiting to cross the sea, during which time he made his will.[58] On this occasion he was accompanied by Gloucester and the earls of March and Warwick, and, in case his services were needed again, by king James of Scotland. Bedford remained behind to manage English affairs, including the organization of repairs at Windsor Castle in anticipation of the birth of the royal couple's first child.[59] On 10 June, once arrived at Calais at the head of some 4–5000 men,[60] Henry marched southwards, meeting the duke of Burgundy at Montreuil and learning from him that there was still considerable dauphinist resistance in Artois and Picardy. It had been his intention to deal with this, but on hearing that the enemy were undertaking the siege of Chartres, he decided to hasten southwards as quickly as he could, hoping that his personal reputation would make the enemy lift the siege.[61] Crossing the Somme at Abbeville, Henry advanced through Beauvais to Gisors and then to the important bridgehead across the Seine at Mantes, where he was greeted with the ringing of bells, wine and a procession for peace.[62] Leaving his army under Gloucester's command at Pontoise, Mantes, Meulan and Vernon, and accompanied by only a small force of archers and men-at-arms, Henry went up to Paris, where he arrived, almost unannounced, on 4 July; his intention was partly to reassure king Charles VI and the city that action was being taken, partly to consult with the duke of Exeter, whom he had left there in charge of the person of Charles on his departure six months earlier.[63] Henry needed up-to-date information on the military and political situation in France, notably on the progress made by the dauphinists both on the ground (they had captured Gallardon and secured Nogent-le-Roi by treaty) and on the

[57] G.L. Harriss, *Cardinal Beaufort. A study of Lancastrian ascendancy and decline* (Oxford, 1988), pp. 106–9, 401–2. The next largest lender was London, with £2000 (A. Steel, *The Receipt of the Exchequer, 1377–1485* (Cambridge, 1954), p. 163). The names of lenders are recorded in PRO, E 403/649, mm.5–7.

[58] P. & F. Strong, 'The last will and codicils of Henry V', *EHR*, 96 (1981), 89–98.

[59] PRO, E 404/37/116.

[60] Newhall, *English conquest*, p. 281.

[61] 'Chronique de Gilles de Roy' (*Chroniques relatives à l'histoire de la Belgique sous la domination des ducs de Bourgogne*, ed. K. de Lettenhove (Brussels, 1870)), i, 183, states that they did so when they heard that Henry was coming.

[62] Mantes, Arch. comm., CC 19, fo.30v, referring to the king of Scots, Gloucester and Warwick.

[63] AN, X^{1a} 1480, fo.236; *Henrici quinti . . . gesta*, ed. Williams, pp. 146–7.

diplomatic front. He had to recognize that the recent defeat at Baugé had persuaded the duke of Brittany that his destiny did not lie with the English: at Sablé, early in May, he had agreed to renounce his treaties with the English in favour of helping the dauphin. Henry could no longer feel free on his south-western flank.

After further consultations, it was decided that Philip of Burgundy would turn his attention to the pacification of Picardy, while Henry would assume military responsibility in the south. The town of Dreux, due west of Paris and for long a dauphinist outpost, was besieged and subjected to a considerable bombardment. Within a month it had surrendered and had an English garrison imposed upon it. Henry's campaign, it seemed, had got off to an auspicious start. However, the unwillingness of the enemy to confront him directly meant that he could not avenge Clarence's death (as Monstrelet claimed he wished to do)[64] nor could he inflict an important military defeat upon them.

The events of the coming weeks were to show two things. First, that at this stage the French army had neither the ability nor the will to stand up to a properly organized enemy, in particular one led by Henry himself. Secondly, the river Loire was a boundary difficult to cross. Having taken Dreux and cleared the surrounding area, Henry advanced southwards, through Chartres, without meeting opposition. At Beaugency, where the dauphinist garrison held the castle, he failed to cross the Loire.[65] So, some four years after the city had started to send out spies to discover what Henry's army was up to, the king brought his force as far as Orléans. There he found that its arrival had been anticipated, and that he could do little towards capturing either the place or its bridge. After two or three days Henry withdrew, and the city records could only refer to the day on which the English came before the city.[66] By now, Henry may have been suffering from a lack of provisions and sickness in the army; furthermore, his lines of communication were becoming increasingly long, and he was losing not only men, but also horses, carts, baggage and equipment. Assuring himself that the enemy would not fight, Henry rode north-eastwards through the Gâtinais, gaining the dauphinist stronghold of Villeneuve-sur-Yonne on the way.[67] Then he came again to Paris, where he received an honourable welcome from his father-in-law, the king, and from the Parisians.[68]

---

[64] Monstrelet, iv, 70.

[65] On 8 September Henry still found time to write to Louis Robesart (*CPR, 1416-1422*, p. 409).

[66] '. . . le jour que les Anglès vindrent devant la dicte ville' (Orléans, Arch. comm., CC 548, fos 13v, 19). See also fos 11, 12v, 14, 16, 22.

[67] Taken on 27 September, after a brief siege (Fauquembergue, *Journal*, ii, 27).

[68] *Bourgeois de Paris*, ed. Tuetey, p. 154; ibid., ed. Beaune, p. 173; *Parisian journal*, p. 163.

There remained one major fortified town which stood out as a bastion of opposition, and which had to be reduced. Meaux lay some thirty miles almost due east of Paris, on a horseshoe bend in the river Marne; the river in effect divided it into two, the town being on the northern side and the 'Marché', heavily fortified and protected by the river and a canal which had been cut through the peninsula, lying to the south. For the besieger the situation presented exceptional problems, and the determination of the garrison, of which the leading figure was the Bastard of Vaurus, a man of great ferocity and little scruple, with an unenviable reputation for acts of brutality, was likely to make the siege a lengthy one. Of the importance of this dauphinist outpost, so close to Paris and controlling the lower reaches of the Marne above the point where it flowed into the Seine, there could be no doubt. The logic of the policy of securing the upper Seine, begun by Henry immediately after his marriage but abandoned after the fall of Melun and Henry's return to England, had now to be pursued. If successful, it would enhance his reputation, make Paris into a safer place and be a considerable step forward in reducing the power of the dauphinists which the treaty of Troyes required.

A lengthy siege would also be a winter one. Henry was accustomed to this, having spent two of the last four winters (that of 1417–18 outside Falaise and the following one, 1418–19, outside Rouen) in these uncomfortable conditions. The siege of Meaux was begun about 6 October, with perhaps some 2500 English soldiers and a few French ones,[69] the sections of the army under Exeter, Warwick and March keeping in touch with one another by means of a bridge of boats across the Marne. Artillery was brought up in considerable quantity, and every effort was made to force a surrender.[70] But physical conditions deteriorated.[71] First rain made life very difficult for the besiegers, and then, in December, the Marne flooded, making it an exceptionally hard task to conduct a siege in an organized way. Matters were not helped by the presence in the surrounding districts of enemy cavalry, which made the work of foraging and victualling unusually difficult. The result was that rations had to be cut, and morale began to sink.

The king would have liked to end this siege as soon as possible, but his terms met with no response either among the townsmen, who felt that, in the circumstances, they might last out, or among the soldiers, whose numbers included some Scots who, together with English and

[69] Wylie and Waugh, *Henry the Fifth*, iii, 339.
[70] Some pieces of that artillery may be seen at the Musée de l'Armée in Paris.
[71] *Bourgeois de Paris*, ed. Tuetey, p. 160; ibid., ed. Beaune, p. 175; *Parisian journal*, pp. 164–5.

Irish deserters, could expect little mercy if they surrendered. The need to house part of his household near him had led Henry to take lodgings at Rutel, near Meaux, and then at the abbey of Saint-Pharon, nearby. From here (he had likewise conducted the siege of Rouen from his lodgings in the Charterhouse) he could direct the siege and, as far as he chose so to do, play his role as king in the affairs of both France and England. A number of letters which Henry wrote during these months have survived.[72] It was to the siege of Meaux that the people of Mantes sent a messenger in January 1422 to seek permission from the king to work on their defences, while in the following month the chancellor and treasurer of Normandy passed through Mantes, presumably on their way back to Rouen, after having been to consult him at Meaux.[73]

It was at this time, late in December 1421, while 'in the camp at Meaux', that Henry drew up his instructions for Richard Flemming, bishop of Lincoln, whose enthronement he had attended earlier that year, and Sir William Coggeshall, whom he was sending as his ambassadors to the emperor Sigismund, the archbishop of Trier and his brother-in-law, Louis of Bavaria.[74] The instructions, drawn up in English, are of interest for what they reveal of Henry's vision of the future and its problems. At the forefront was the war, which was not making the progress he would have liked. While his ambassadors were to show appreciation to Louis for his presence at the siege of Melun, they were to say that although their master was 'now in the point and conclusion of his labour', he none the less needed more help to bring the war to an end. Henry clearly saw the capture of Meaux as an achievement which would close a chapter in the conflict with the dauphinists. However, this was more easily achieved in the mind than on the ground, and the instructions reflect a strong note of realism in the king's make-up. They emphasized two factors. First, that although peace had been made in 1420, it had not yet won general acceptance: the dauphin had his supporters and was being helped by the practical assistance of allies, that of the Scots on land and the Castilians at sea. Secondly, Henry, too, badly needed military help, in the form of manpower, with an implication that more of this could come from Burgundy and that money to pay for assistance would be found if it were offered. The appeal to Sigismund must have been intended to revive memories of the obligation entered into in the treaty

---

[72] *CPR, 1416–1422*, p. 403; *Signet letters*, ed. Kirby, nos 911–17, 979. The law case between Guillaume Rose and Richard Handford arose out of the circumstances of this siege (*English suits before the Parlement of Paris, 1420–1436*, ed. C.T. Allmand and C.A.J. Armstrong (Camden, 4th series, 26, RHistS., London, 1982), pp. 75–85).

[73] Mantes, Arch. comm., CC 20, fos 11, 15.

[74] PRO, C 47/30/9, no.12; *Foedera*, IV, iv, 45–6.

of Canterbury, while the attempt to obtain help from the archbishop of Trier was based upon the fees of retainer which Henry had paid him in the past. There seems little doubt that the king felt let down by some of those from whom he thought, rightly or wrongly, that he could expect more. The delicate embassy upon which Flemming and Coggeshall were being sent, part of a wider diplomatic offensive, can be seen as an attempt to revive obligations among German-speaking allies which appeared to have fallen dormant.

There may have been considerable truth in what Henry had written. There may have been doubts even among those who were serving in his army. At Meaux, Sir John Cornwall's son, a promising and much-liked young man, was killed one day by a cannon shot while standing next to his father, who was wounded. According to Jouvenel des Ursins, this tragedy caused the bereaved parent to cry out that they had come only to conquer Normandy but now, against all reason and conscience, they were attempting to deprive the dauphin of that crown which was his by right. Soon afterwards, having sworn never to fight again, he retired from the war.[75] In England enthusiasm for, and commitment to, the war were probably declining. Recruitment was less easy, and it was becoming harder to pay those who were recruited. Nor was Henry's fear of the physical and, by implication, the moral support enjoyed by the dauphin a figment of his imagination. The defeat at Baugé had shown that the English were no longer invincible, especially without their king. The need for Charles VI to remind certain towns that the peace settlement made at Troyes would be defended reflected an unease felt by many, which mirrored a sense of uncertainty caused by the change in the French succession. What was worse was that that uncertainty was to be found among the Burgundians, from whom Henry could have been expected to draw his strongest supporters. Did the king expect too much of Philip of Burgundy himself? Could the duke be his own man while, at the same time, having to serve the new heir to the French throne, whom he had recognized in taking the oath to the treaty of Troyes? Philip did not visit Henry until early February 1422, and when they met it was not at Meaux but some miles away, at Lagny-sur-Marne.[76] Was their meeting away from the scene of the siege a sign of an unwillingness on the part of Philip to get involved in the conflict against the

[75] *Histoire de Charles VI, roy de France, par Jean Juvenal des Ursins* (Choix de chroniques et mémoires sur l'histoire de France, ed. J.A.C. Buchon (Paris, 1841)), p. 566. Cited by T. Goodwin, *The history of the reign of Henry the Fifth, King of England* (London, 1704), p. 321; *Henry quinti . . . gesta*, p. 155, n.2.

[76] The 'Bourgeois' reported that Philip was in Paris in January, his people doing nothing but harm to the surrounding district (*Bourgeois de Paris*, ed. Tuetey, p. 163; ibid., ed. Beaune, pp. 177–8; *Parisian journal*, pp. 166–7).

dauphinists? Furthermore, Philip brought few members of his nobility with him, for, as Monstrelet reported, they did not want to give the oath to the peace settlement as one of their number, the lord of Saint-George, had been asked to do when he had met Henry.[77]

The king must also have wondered what he had achieved militarily since his return to France in June 1421. His march to Orléans had shown that the French tactics of not meeting him face to face (tactics successfully pursued by them forty or fifty years earlier) were making it impossible for the English to achieve the political results they sought from a major military victory. How far, too, could Henry hope to advance into France? One crossing, or more, of the Loire would need to be taken and defended. Even if this were successfully achieved, could ever-lengthening lines of communication be adequately pro- tected? The further south the English advanced, the nearer they approached the heartland of dauphinist support. At this moment of truth, however, occurred the event which Henry would have been anticipating for some time, the birth of his child by Katharine.

The news that the queen had given birth to a boy at Windsor on 6 December was brought to Henry at Meaux, and was the cause of much rejoicing at a time when morale was in need of boosting.[78] Hardyng was to claim that the birth, which made the succession to the French crown clearer than before, helped to decide the loyalty of waverers, and that a number of towns now decided to give Henry their support.[79] In England, too, the event would have been a crucial factor in establishing the continuity of Lancastrian rule, for Henry was already thirty-five years old and his life style was one which caused him to face frequent danger.[80] His previous heir, Clarence, had only recently been killed at Baugé, and while two other brothers survived, the elder of whom, Bedford, was at present acting as lieuten- ant in England, the succession was better passed on to a direct than to a collateral descendant. Besides, Bedford himself was not married, and in an age of such uncertainty the birth of an heir, who, through his parents, would later be a figure uniting the royal families of both England and France, was an event much to be desired.

The king would have been heartened by the news from England, even though he was not present in person at his son's christening; Henry Beaufort and John, duke of Bedford, were the boy's godfathers,

[77] Monstrelet, iv, 78–9. Chastellain (*Chronique*, p. 292) refers this story specifically to the Prince of Orange.

[78] *Bourgeois de Paris*, ed. Tuetey, p. 163: ibid., ed. Beaune, p. 177; *Parisian journal*, p. 166; *Brut*, ii, 448.

[79] *Chronicle of John Hardyng*, p. 386.

[80] His wills were made as he left on his expeditions to France, in 1415, 1417 and 1421 (Strong, 'Last will', 80–1).

and Jacqueline, countess of Hainault, his godmother.[81] The longer
the commitment to capture Meaux grew, the more determined would
Henry have become to see it through to the end. Difficulties brought
out the spirit of determination in him, and his gifts of leadership were
seldom seen to better effect than at this siege where, unlike at Rouen
three years earlier, events conspired to deny him the troops which he
felt he required.[82] Yet, with every day that passed, events moved
inexorably in his favour. In March the town of Meaux fell: the
defenders, now confined to the nearby 'Marché', by the same token,
were running out of hope. They hung on with increasing desperation,
dysentery taking its considerable toll on both sides. The English
cannon finally did the work of destruction required of it, and the
decision to negotiate had to be taken.

The terms which Exeter and Warwick brought were hard. If not
relieved, the besieged would have to yield on 10 May: they would
surrender all the leaders, all deserters, all who had taken part in the
murder of John of Burgundy, and all who had sworn to keep the terms
of the treaty of Troyes, not forgetting the man who had brayed with
a trumpet at the king during the course of the siege[83] – all were to be
at the victor's mercy provided that other places held by or on behalf
of anyone in the 'Marché' were surrendered to the king. Four men,
including the Bastard of Vaurus, were told that nothing would save
them. There being no alternative, the terms were accepted. The four
and the foolish trumpeter were executed; the others, some technically
guilty of treason, were spared.[84] The haul of prisoners was very large.
They were taken to Paris, by boat down the Seine to Caudebec and
Harfleur, over the Channel to Portsmouth, and then to London.[85]
From there they were distributed for safe-keeping among the castles
of England and Wales: Harlech (30), Nottingham (24), Caernarfon
(20), Chirk and Holt (15 each), Conwy (12) and Flint (8).[86] Finally,
as an important source of compensation, there were the riches of
Meaux which came into English hands. All chroniclers are agreed
that the town, and in particular the 'Marché', contained very great
wealth, underlining the material advantages which could accrue to
the besieger once his labours were over.[87]

[81] *Brut*, ii, 427.
[82] Yet, 'as an example of scientific siege warfare, the leaguer of Meaux was probably Henry's masterpiece' (Wylie and Waugh, *Henry the Fifth*, iii, 338).
[83] '. . . ung qui a corne ung cor durant le siege que len dit estre nomme Grace'
(BN, Ms fr.1278, fo.87v).
[84] A fact stressed in Walsingham, ii, 343.
[85] PRO, E 403/656, m.12; *Brut*, ii, 428–9.
[86] PRO, E 403/656, mm.1, 2, 3d.
[87] '. . . moult de richesses' (BN, Ms fr.5028, fo.151); '. . . diviciis infinitis repleta'
(Kingsford, *English historical literature*, p. 290).

The exceptional difficulties faced by the English at Meaux (physical conditions, time, sickness, reluctant allies) must have been daunting. While the outcome had been successful, Henry may have been wondering whether the military task he had undertaken was beyond him. The problems which he faced at Meaux were so fundamental to the success or failure of the wider venture that they must have worried him deeply. There was, in addition, the matter of his health. It is possible that it may have been affected before manifestations of what was to prove to be a fatal illness appeared in June 1422; others, who had to live in less sanitary conditions than did the king, and who may not have been so well fed, died during the siege itself. The author of the 'Northern Chronicle' recalled that Henry was to die of a fatal weariness or apathy ('languorem exicialem').[88] If true, this may have had some effect upon the way he reacted at the end of the siege of Meaux, when, although the vulgar trumpeter was executed, others against whom there was a much better legal case were granted mercy. Was he beginning to lose some of the vigour which was normally so characteristic a part of his personality?

In this respect, the evidence of the terms granted at Compiègne on 16 May, a fortnight after the surrender of Meaux, is of significance. While requiring that those abandoning the town should leave their weapons behind, and that all Welsh, Irish and Gascons, as well as those who had previously sworn to accept the terms of Troyes, should be handed over, he allowed a safe conduct to be given to any who might wish to leave in order to live among the supporters of the so-called dauphin beyond the river Seine.[89] It was by no means the first time that he had given people the opportunity of choosing to live in the 'other' obedience: he had often done this since his first landing in Harfleur almost seven years earlier. In this last case, however, was he coming to the conclusion that his policy was unattainable, and that a divided France was all that might be hoped for? He would have known that the dauphinists had been virtually driven out of Picardy, while in June Warwick was to take St Valery on the Somme. As Monstrelet put it, only two places, Le Crotoy and Guise, stood between Paris and the sea.[90] May Henry's state of health have driven him to conclude that, since the unwillingness of the dauphinists to face his army meant that he could not deliver them another devastating blow, and granted the political and physical geography of France, it was better to settle and consolidate? His recent success had been

[88] Kingsford, ibid., p. 290.
[89] BN, Ms fr.1278, fo.113.
[90] Monstrelet, iv, 101—3.

bought at a considerable cost of life, time and money. Could he go on, seemingly indefinitely, in the same way?

At just the moment at which the terms for the surrender of Meaux were being agreed, Katharine and her brother-in-law, Bedford, who had with him about 1000 extra men, were about to set out from Southampton for France, Gloucester taking Bedford's place as lieutenant of England. As she travelled between Rouen and Paris, the queen, suitably accompanied by two widows and a number of 'damoiselles', most of them, judging by their names,[91] English, was received with the ringing of bells at Mantes, whose loyal population had very recently sent two of its members to Paris to buy silver cups to present to her, a gift which cost so much that the sum raised as a *taille* was not sufficient and an added fiscal burden had to be imposed upon those who had already contributed up to five *écus* each.[92] On 29 May Katharine, well escorted and with two ermine cloaks carried before her litter (how these should be interpreted caused considerable discussion: as a sign that she was queen of France and England?), entered Paris where, the next day, the citizens tactfully laid on a performance of the mystery of the Passion of St George for the benefit of the English.[93]

Henry and his wife (who had not brought her six-month-old son with her) celebrated Whitsun in proper style in Paris, but probably stayed at Vincennes. Even the moderate Monstrelet felt obliged to record the changes which he saw happening during those days. In addition to noting the different styles of living in the court of Henry and that of his father-in-law, Charles, he stressed the lack of generosity on the English side, a way of life which, to him, seemed to have given way to an emphasis on power and pomp. Many Frenchmen, he noted, deeply regretted how the French king was being overruled, and appeared to be without effective authority. Furthermore, the decision to raise taxes produced much murmuring, but no rebellion, since Henry was a man whom people feared.[94]

On 12 June, the day after Corpus Christi, the two courts moved out from Paris to the small cathedral town of Senlis, some twenty-five miles to the north-east.[95] It was there that the seriousness of Henry's sickness, presumably the result of unhealthy conditions at the siege of Meaux, became apparent. In response to a request from Philip of Burgundy for help in relieving the town of Cosne, only thirty-five

[91] PRO, E 404/38/2.

[92] Mantes, Arch. comm., CC 20, fo.25; BB 3, fos 110, 111, 111v, 113.

[93] *Bourgeois de Paris*, ed. Tuetey, p. 174; ibid., ed. Beaune, pp. 188–9; *Parisian journal*, p. 176.

[94] Monstrelet, iv, 98–101.

[95] See his signet letter from there, dated 18 June (*Signet letters*, ed. Kirby, no. 918).

miles from Bourges where the dauphin had established his centre, and almost as far south-east as he had ever been, Henry, never one to refuse a challenge, and probably preferring the life of the camp to the domestic existence of the court, set off to help. But he soon became too ill to ride, and was taken on a litter to Corbeil, south of Paris, Bedford and Warwick being sent on to Cosne. The seriousness of the situation which resulted from the king's fever and great weakness soon became apparent, as the king's physicians dared not give him medicine to be taken internally. On the king's own orders another physician, John Swanwich, was sent for from England, and in July the people of Mantes, on hearing the news, organized a procession to the church of the Celestines, attended by the mayor and others, to pray to God for the king.[96] Little, however, could be done. Henry, resting at Corbeil, was still playing a part in government as late as 6 August, when he issued instructions for a treaty with the bishop of Liège.[97] Soon afterwards he was moved by boat down the Seine to Charenton, but then, being unable to ride, he had to be carried to Vincennes.

He must have recognized that, barring an extraordinary development, death would soon take him. All his life he had prepared for events well in advance: this characteristic orderliness had been one of the factors behind his successes, particularly in war. Now, in his last days, he made a codicil to the will which he had drawn up at Dover some fourteen months previously, not, as he stressed in the short preamble, to make changes to the earlier document, but to add to it and to make its meaning clearer. It was the last expression of a man to whom order, in every sense, was of paramount importance.

The will of 1421 (he had made one in 1415 before leaving for France and two years later had drawn up a form of codicil intended to help those who might administer it) was still the basic declaration of his last wishes at the moment at which he prepared himself for death.[98] For us, it is an important window into Henry's mind and soul. Taken with the codicil, which is dated 26 August 1422, it is also a practical document. Lucid as he was until the very end, Henry would have recognized that the likely place of his death would create problems for those whom he would leave behind.[99] He was going to die abroad,

[96] Mantes, Arch. comm., CC 20, fo.30v. They also organized processions and rang the bells when news of the happy outcome at Cosne reached them in the following month (ibid., fo.32).

[97] Ramsay, *Lancaster and York*, i, 302, n.6.

[98] Will of 1421 in *EHR*, 96 (1981), 89–98 (see above, n.80); that of 1415 in *Foedera*, IV, ii, 138–9; the codicil of 1417 in *A collection of all the wills now known to be extant of the kings and queens of England*, ed. J. Nichols (London, 1780) pp. 236–43.

[99] The consequences of Henry's unexpected death abroad are described in R.A. Griffiths, *The reign of King Henry VI* (London, 1981), ch.1.

without having the advantage of the company of a number of official figures who might normally be at a king's side when he died at home. While he had with him Bedford, the elder of his two surviving brothers, and a substantial number of the greater nobility, his other brother, Gloucester, his former chancellor, Henry Beaufort, and his current chancellor, Thomas Langley, all three men of experience and authority, were in England. For his English kingdom, his death outside the country (the first since that of Richard I in 1199) was to present difficulties. It was necessary, in the absence of his 'English team', to spell out a little how he saw the future, particularly in terms of the education and upbringing of his son. Yet his hands were tied. In June 1421 he had had no heir, and the will of that time was silent about the future. Now, in August 1422, he had an eight-month-old son who would succeed him as king, but in whose formation he would have little or no say. No king, the lords were to claim in 1427, could dictate to the future. All that was open to him was to set out, in somewhat bland language that was both technical and not a little ambiguous, how his son's education might be conducted, and by whom.[100]

So it was that Gloucester was given the oversight of the protection and guard of his baby nephew, a natural appointment in keeping with his royal dignity. To Thomas Beaufort, duke of Exeter, a popular man of proven ability and loyalty, were committed the upbringing and education of the boy, as was the choice of servants and persons who would be in close contact with him.[101] Finally, possibly to act as a counterbalance to Exeter, the dying king appointed two stalwart friends, Henry, Lord FitzHugh, and Sir Walter Hungerford, both long-standing and important members of his household, to be around his person, one of them always to be present. If these were matters which he could neither practically nor legally dictate to the future, Henry could at least see that his young son was in the hands of men like himself, men whom he (and others) could trust.

His views on how his funeral should be organized had been set out in the will of 1421, and were allowed to stand as he dictated the codicil at Vincennes in the following year. His executors were to be given discretion in how it should be managed: all that he desired was for the royal dignity to be preserved and the excesses common to such occasions avoided,[102] although he described in some detail the way

---

[100] Strong, 'Last will', 84, 99–100; B.P. Wolffe, *Henry VI* (London, 1981), p. 28 seq.

[101] The *Brut* (ii, 429–30) claimed that both Thomas and Henry Beaufort were to see to the boy's 'good governaunce and kepyng in his tendir age'.

[102] Strong, 'Last will', 91.

the candles on the hearse should be set out, as well as their weight and number. His burial place at Westminster Abbey, whose building programme he had encouraged and to which he left many legacies as well as demands for spiritual services, was to be the usual one for kings: among kings and near the relics of saints who would intercede for him and for them. He had caused Richard II to be reburied in this church, and it seems likely that he saw his own burial there as part of the honour and respect due to the royal dignity. Westminster was already the last resting place of a number of kings of England (although his father had not been buried there).[103] Since he had been there, he knew that kings of France were laid to rest in the abbey at Saint-Denis; he would want to be buried in a similar mausoleum, close to Edward the Confessor, virtual founder of the abbey and the king-saint whom he had regarded as one of his special protectors throughout his reign.

What he died of we cannot be certain. Whatever it was, it took its time, sapping the strength and energy of a man normally well endowed with both. Contemporary statements suggest that it may well have been a chronic intestinal condition. His mind remained active to the end: he was fit enough to have thought about and dictated the codicil of his will only five days before he died. Furthermore, the accounts of his death suggest it was that of a man who had long suspected it was coming and gave himself plenty of time to prepare for it. It is possible that he died of fluid loss or imbalance. It was a hot summer, and his thirst would have been slaked with ale or wine; but a lack of salt in both would not have sufficiently accounted for the loss which he was said to have suffered from the flux which afflicted him. Those who saw him in his last moments may have been looking at a man of hollow eyes and sunken cheeks, a shadow of his former self.

In the end, Henry probably died fairly quickly. To the last, he showed concern for the needs of the future: for the education of his baby son upon whom the hopes of the dynasty hung; for the government of England in what would be a long minority; for the continuation of his work in France.[104] The Beauforts, Henry and Thomas, were given special care of the baby king; Gloucester was given authority, ambiguously expressed authority, in England; while in France rule was entrusted to Philip of Burgundy or, should he refuse it, to Bedford.[105]

---

[103] Henry III, Edward I, Edward III and Richard II were buried at Westminster, Henry IV at Canterbury.

[104] *Brut*, ii, 429–30.

[105] Ibid., ii, 493, 496.

Not unjustifiably, Henry may have had fears for the future, and in particular that divisions would appear among those to whom he left uncompleted work. It is likely that he saw his work in France as his main contribution to the future. Did he have fears that it could not be completed, or that others would not be as committed to it as he was? His request that certain prisoners should not be released or ransomed until his son, having come of age, was able to make his own decisions is in that respect significant. It was a request which his youngest brother, Humphrey of Gloucester, would take very much to heart and make much of in years to come.

Henry's death was pious, as had been much of his life. Prayers for the dying were recited to him, and one of his last statements is said to have been that, once his work in France had been completed, he would have wished to rebuild the walls of Jerusalem. He had founded a monastery to which he had given the name of Syon. The name was to be with him as, in the company of his soldier friends, the chamberlain of his household and his chaplain, he breathed his last. It was 31 August 1422.

Henry's body (the organs having been removed and buried in the church of Saint-Maur-des-Fossés)[106] was embalmed[107] and put in a wooden coffin which was then placed in a larger one of lead. It was not until 14 or 15 September that, bypassing Paris,[108] it was taken to Saint-Denis where, the next day, a form of service for the dead was held, a procession of princes and members of the royal household accompanying the coffin.[109] Over it lay a representation of the late king's body, made of boiled leather, royally dressed, with a crown on its head, a sceptre in its right hand and a golden orb in its left, over which, when the procession came into a town, a canopy of silk was carried as in a Corpus Christi procession.[110]

At Saint-Denis the cortège took to the water, proceeding down the Seine to Mantes where, on 9 September, the town's council had decided that a service of vigil would be said on the following day and Masses for the dead king on the day after that, at which special

---

[106] In the summer of 1978 a team of archaeologists unearthed a round, lead pot at Saint-Maur which, it was thought, might contain the viscera of the king. The discovery made news in the papers (see *The Times*, 8 June 1978) and on radio, but it was soon recognized that the finders were almost certainly on to a false trail.

[107] PRO, E 36/266, fo.7v; *Brut*, ii, 493; *Vita et gesta*, p. 336.

[108] *Bourgeois de Paris*, ed. Tuetey, p. 176, and n.6; ibid., ed. Beaune, p. 191; *Parisian journal*, p. 178.

[109] Others, such as the compiler of BN, Ms fr.5028 (fo.151v) and the *First English Life* (p. 183), recorded that it went through Paris.

[110] *Brut*, ii, 493; Waurin, p. 426.

candles would be burned and the church bells tolled. All the clergy were asked to be present. When Henry's body duly arrived, it was met in procession, with candles burning, and was placed in a 'chapel' (a wooden structure bearing candles placed above the coffin) which had been refurbished for the occasion. Mass was celebrated by the abbot of the Benedictine house at Neaufle, in the presence of the mayor and a congregation of townspeople, and the coffin was accompanied by forty torches as it left Mantes.[111]

At Rouen, on 19 September, ceremonial was organized for the reception of the funeral procession.[112] Pierre Cochon described the funeral car on which the figure of the king had been placed as being richly decorated, covered with a cloth and surmounted by a crown as was appropriate for a king. Before it walked eighty Englishmen, formally dressed in black, each holding a large torch, followed by royal chaplains singing dirges. Together with twenty of the leading citizens of Rouen, each bearing a large torch, the procession entered the cathedral of Notre-Dame (which the king had already entered in triumph in January 1419), accompanied by 200 more bourgeois, all dressed in black, each holding a torch. All the while the church bells, which had been heard since the king's body had approached Rouen, continued to toll: this went on until nightfall. During the night the body remained in the cathedral, while monks from the neighbouring Benedictine monastery of St Ouen, and friars from all four orders, recited the psalms associated with the Office of the Dead through the hours of darkness. The following day, after the service, the bier was put on its funeral car to be pulled by members of the nobility up to the castle. Before it were carried two banners, one of the Trinity, the other of the Virgin, together with Henry's own standard; behind it was borne a banner of St George, together with one bearing the arms of England and France. It was accompanied by many persons bearing torches. On the following Thursday, 24 September, queen Katharine, accompanied by Bedford, arrived, along with eighteen carts carrying the dead king's possessions and four carrying her own, all draped in black. The mourners remained in Rouen until 5 October,[113] when the procession set out for Calais, passing through Abbeville, Hesdin and Montreuil on the way, Masses being celebrated every day in the churches where the cortège stopped. All the while, the clergy recited

[111] Arch. comm., Mantes, BB 3, fo.121v; CC 20, fo.32v. The townspeople took advantage of Bedford's presence to tell him that they hoped he would not impose a tax on wine in the coming year. On 24 September it was decided to give him twenty pipes of wine, as well as four to his officers, in the hope of influencing his decision (ibid., BB 3, fo.124; CC 20, fo.32v).

[112] *Vita et gesta*, p. 337.

[113] *Chronique normande de Pierre Cochon*, pp. 288–90.

the Office of the Dead, the procession being accompanied by mourners, some dressed in white and bearing candles, members of the royal household and, some way back, the young widow with a great company of people.

By the time the procession reached Calais, ships from ports on England's south-east coast, specially arrested for the purpose, were there to convey it to England. On or about 31 October the small fleet landed at Dover, where it was met by the first of the 'herceis' specially authorized by the royal council, the stopping points of the procession being Canterbury, Ospring, Rochester, Dartford, St Paul's cathedral in London, and then Westminster, which was to be the place of burial.[114]

In London, the mayor and aldermen had made elaborate preparations for the reception of the king's body and the procession accompanying it. When it arrived at one o'clock on Thursday, 5 November, the streets of Southwark had been cleaned, and it was met by the city's leading personalities, all on foot and dressed in black, as well as by a number of bishops, mitred abbots and other clergy, chanting the Office of the Dead. Headed by an escort provided by thirty-one guilds, all its members clothed in white gowns given by the city chamberlain,[115] and carrying between them 211 torches (of which the Mercers[116] and four other guilds provided twelve each, and the Brewers eight),[117] the cortège advanced over London Bridge (the scene of earlier triumphal entries), with men from the neighbouring wards standing at the crossroads at Eastcheap, and the clergy of the nearby churches, in their finest vestments, censing the body as it passed them, the hymn *Venite* being sung all the while. In this way, the procession went from the corner of Eastcheap to Cornhill, then to the Stocks, on to the Great Conduit and, finally, to the west door of St Paul's.[118]

On the morning of Friday, 6 November, when Masses of Requiem had been sung 'with the grete solempnite of bisshoppes and other worthi lordes spirituel and temporell', and refreshment had been consumed,[119] the procession left for Westminster, with every house which

---

[114] This paragraph is based on PRO, E 403/656 (penultimate membrane; not numbered). See also *CPR, 1422–1429*, pp. 35–6; *Foedera*, IV, iv, 81.

[115] Guildhall Library, Ms 5440, fo.71v; *A book of London English, 1384–1425*, ed. R.W. Chambers and M. Daunt (Oxford, 1961), p. 145.

[116] Mercers' Company, Wardens' accounts, fo.83. It cost them £5 0s. 10d. They also contributed to payments for the mayor's barge and refreshments for the torchbearers.

[117] The cost of torches carried by the Grocers amounted to £1 19s. 6d. (Guildhall Library, Ms 11570, p. 149).

[118] Guildhall Library, Ms 5440, fo.71v; *First English Life*, pp. 184–5.

[119] '. . . after mete' (*Brut*, ii, 530); '. . . whanne the lordes hadde eten' (*Book of London English*, p. 145).

it passed supposed to have a torch held before it as the cortège went by.[120] The coffin, already covered in black velvet, with a cross of white satin and cloth of gold upon it, was borne by eight chamber knights, with four earls holding a corner of the cloth of gold and four knights bearing a canopy above it, to a waiting funeral car, uniformly black all over, covered on top but open on all sides. In this was laid the coffin, and upon it, covered with a cloth of majesty embroidered with an image of Christ in judgement, a figure of the king lying, sceptre in right hand, orb in left, and a crown upon the head, which lay upon a cushion of cloth of gold. At both head and feet torches burned, while on the figure's right side hung a banner of the Trinity, on its left one of St George, and at its feet one of the Virgin. The car was drawn by five fine horses draped with arms, two those of England, the others those of St George, St Edmund and St Edward. In front of the car walked yeomen and poor people bearing torches; behind rode pages and knights, their horses draped in black, bearing the shields of England and France and the king's helm, one carrying a battle-axe point down. With them were many lords and knights, and a large number of clergy, bishops, members of the chapel royal, as well as secular priests, monks, friars and other members of the late king's household. Behind the car came the mourners, and behind them councillors, riding horses draped in black, accompanied by other men who had served the king in a personal capacity. For these members of the household this was a poignant day, more the end of an era than it was for the bystanders who watched the procession go by.[121]

Among the bystanders were the lord mayor and aldermen and the representatives of the guilds who 'stode in good order' while the cortège filed by and then, as had been decided weeks earlier, took to the river,[122] their barges draped in black, no music 'or eny other solempnite', being permitted, the members of the guilds 'being of power' wearing either black or russet gowns and black hoods.[123] In attendance (although it is not clear how they got to Westminster) was a group of notable people, members of the royal entourage, who had come to pay their last respects to a man whom most had served for a number of years: the duke of Exeter; the earls of March, Warwick and Stafford; the young Edmund Beaufort; Lord FitzHugh, the royal chamberlain; Sir William Philip, Henry's treasurer; Sir William Porter, his carver and an executor of his will; as well as others, includ-

[120] Guildhall Library, Ms 5440, fos 71v-72; *Book of London English*, p. 146.
[121] W.H. St John Hope, 'The funeral, monument and chantry chapel of Henry V', *Archaeologia*, 65 (1913–14), 133–5.
[122] Use of barges is referred to in *Brut*, ii, 449.
[123] Guildhall Library, Ms 5440, fos 71–2.

ing Sir Walter Hungerford. They were mostly men who had served in an administrative or military capacity, or in both, some of whom still had notable careers in France before them.[124] At Westminster, where those who had come by river had disembarked at the pier ('pere'), the body, accompanied by lords, passed through the ranks of torch-bearers into the precinct of the abbey. Then it was taken into the abbatial church where, before the high altar, it was railed in and many large candles lighted. Then the *Dirige*, or short service for the dead, was recited, and the bier, to which offerings of cloth of gold had already been brought,[125] was left for the night in the care of monks and others for whom refreshment of beer, bread and fish had been provided.[126]

On the following day, Saturday, 7 November, after Requiem Mass had been celebrated, the king was 'beried with grete solempnite'. Thomas Walsingham reported that three dextriers and their riders were led up to the abbey's high altar, and there stripped of their arms and armour, a formal ceremony rich in symbolism.[127] Contrary to the statement of one historian of these days' events that no evidence confirms the story,[128] the Brewers' accounts[129] recorded that, at the Mass of Requiem, 'there were offred up atte high awter of Westmynster chirche iiij stedes ytrapped rially, with a knyght full and hool armed with the kinges cote armour and a croune upon his hede sitting upon on[e] of the said stedes, rially'. If the number of horses does not tally exactly with Walsingham's version, the two accounts are none the less recalling the same event which, in Walsingham's report, is described as being customary.[130] Henry was not only king, but God's knight and defender of His values. Before being laid to rest, he had to be divested of the armour which he had required in this world, but which he no longer needed. That done, he could be buried properly and honourably, among kings of England, his predecessors, between the shrine of St Edward and the chapel of the Virgin where the relics of the saints were kept, just as he had requested in his will should be done on his death.[131]

Henry had made two wills: one on 24 July 1415, the second (which

---

[124] Among them the earl of Warwick, Edmund Beaufort and Sir Walter Hungerford.

[125] Listed in WAM, Ms 19663. See also PRO, E 404/39/145, 146.

[126] St John Hope, 'Funeral', 138–9.

[127] Ibid., 135, citing Walsingham, ii, 345–6, and printed as appendix B.

[128] St John Hope, 'Funeral', 135.

[129] Guildhall Library, Ms 5440, fo.72; *Book of London English*, p. 146.

[130] 'ut moris est' (Walsingham, ii, 346).

[131] '. . . inter sepulturas regum in loco in quo modo continentur reliquie sanctorum' (Strong, 'Last will', 91).

has only fairly recently come to light) on 9 June 1421; and on 26 August 1422 he had added a codicil.[132] Together, they tell us a certain amount about the king. As might be expected from such documents, they reflect his piety, in Henry's case his love of the saints, in particular those of England, and his hope that the country could be kept free of heresy. He was also concerned with the arrangements for his funeral: how many Masses should be said for his soul (Masses in honour of the Trinity, the Virgin and the saints were given prominence), as well as the need to have the forgiveness of any he might have wronged. Legacies were numerous: money to the Bridgettines at Syon to enable them to build in 'bryk'; to the Carthusians at Sheen; to Saint-Denis, near Paris, for his memory to be preserved, as well as to the recluse at Westminster. He left gifts of books to Syon and Sheen, to Christ Church, Canterbury, as well as to the university of Oxford; jewels, ornaments and domestic goods to the queen, whose dower was to be paid from the revenues of the duchy of Lancaster and lands in France; vestments to the clergy who were close to him, Henry Chichele and Henry Beaufort; a missal to Thomas Langley; money and a bed to Exeter; horses to Bedford and Gloucester. To his successor, Henry bequeathed his armour, the remainder of his books, the apparatus of his chapel and, at first, his ships, although he was later to order these to be sold to pay his debts.[133]

The executors of his will were appointed from among the leaders of society, from his own household and from the administrators of the duchy of Lancaster, three groups with which he had had close ties in his lifetime, and whose support he was to seek in winding up his very complicated financial legacy. All were men whom he had known for years, men, therefore, whom he could trust. Overall responsibility ('tutela')[134] for the baby king was placed in the hands of Henry's brother, Gloucester, while his upbringing was made the task of the duke of Exeter, who was to decide with whom he might consort, work in which he was to be helped by Lord FitzHugh and Sir Walter Hungerford. The child's mother, Katharine, was expected to remain with him. To help pay off the royal debts, now so considerable that in 1421 he bequeathed his household only £4000 in contrast to the £10,000 he had allowed it in 1415, Henry gave instructions that jewellery, as well as ships, should be sold. The task of regulating his debts was to prove a formidable one; he had inherited a number from his

---

[132] *Foedera*, IV, ii, 138–9; Strong, 'Last will', 89–100. On 21 July 1417 he made arrangements for the administration of enfeoffed lands; this document is not a proper will. See Nichols, *Collection of wills*, pp. 236–42.

[133] Strong, 'Last will', 89–100.

[134] Ibid., 99.

father, and there were now many outstanding ones to be settled, some going back to 1415.[135] Progress was slow. It was to take Henry Beaufort, who gradually came to assume a pre-eminent position among those responsible for the work, some twenty years to satisfy both the wishes of the late king and to unravel the many difficulties which his will caused his executors.[136]

It was the responsibility of the executors, too, to see to the construction of Henry's earthly monument. The king had left detailed instructions concerning the place of his interment, which was to be at the east end of the Confessor's chapel.[137] These instructions involved certain structural alterations to the chapel. Stone was immediately brought over from Caen,[138] and work on the tomb was already under way by the time that the funeral ceremony took place nearly nine weeks after Henry's death. The tomb itself was to be of Purbeck marble.[139] On it was to lie a bed of wood, but the figure of the king, in a gown and holding two sceptres, was not of cast metal or alabaster but was made of a wooden core, plated with silver gilt, angels being placed at the head, beasts at the feet. The work, said to have been done 'at the cost of Quene Katerine',[140] took some years, and was probably completed about 1431.

The large chantry chapel itself,[141] planned by the king and described in his will of 1415, was not begun until 1438, and may be seen almost as a memorial erected by Henry Beaufort, who took on the main responsibility for building it.[142] Through its statuary, it was to reflect the late king's devotion to the Trinity,[143] to the Virgin (the

[135] One example, among many, is Exeter's claim for money owed for service in 1415 (*PPC*, iii, 101–2); another that of the executors of Sir John Harrington (ibid., iii, 128–9).

[136] J.S. Roskell, *The Commons in the parliament of 1422. English society and parliamentary representation under the Lancastrians* (Manchester, 1954), pp. 113–20; Strong, 'Last will', 82–3, 86–8; Harriss, *Cardinal Beaufort*, p. 127.

[137] *Foedera*, IV, ii, 138; Strong, 'Last will', 89–90.

[138] PRO, E 403/656 (penultimate membrane).

[139] St John Hope, 'Funeral', 145–53; *King's Works; Middle Ages*, i, 488–9.

[140] *Brut*, ii, 494. Parts of the effigy were soon to be stolen. In 1971 the work of attaching a new head and hands (long lost), made of polyester resin, was completed (*The Times*, 7 July 1971).

[141] St John Hope, 'Funeral', 153–83, with illustrations.

[142] Harriss, *Cardinal Beaufort*, pp. 324–5.

[143] It may be noted that Henry built a ship called *The Trinity*; that he was married on Trinity Sunday, 1420; and that a banner of the Trinity was carried before his funeral car in France. Henry's devotion to the Virgin Mary, in whom he had placed all his hope (Strong, 'Last will', 91 (vi)), is also well known, as was his regard for the saints referred to here: banners of St Edward, St Edmund and St George covered his hearse in London (Oxford, Bodleian Library, Ashmole Ms 1109, fo.148; *Foedera*, IV, iv, 81–2).

altar was to be dedicated to the Annunciation and all the saints), to the English royal saints, Edward and Edmund, as well as St Denis (the French connection) and St George. Antelopes (Henry's badge)[144] and swans (that of Bohun) were carved in the vault and cornices, while the decoration of an iron gate included both lions and fleurs-de-lis. The outer side of the chantry bore images of Henry's coronation, in which he wore an arched, or imperial, crown. Completed about 1450, it reflected both Henry's religious sense and his feeling for the dignity of the office which he had held. The size and site of the monument ensured that the man whom it commemorated would not be quickly forgotten.

Henry had always emphasized the need for prayer, both of intercession and thanksgiving. The help of the heavenly body was to be sought in the search for personal salvation. Acts of piety, supported by the prayers of holy monks and poor men, would help to that end. In his will of 1421 Henry set out in detail the number and size of candles that were to burn for him at his funeral and later; the number of Masses to be said for the repose of his soul; the legacies which were to be made to the abbey at Westminster, and how, each year, at a special Mass of Requiem to be said on the anniversary of his death, twenty-four poor men were to be paid 10d. each to hold candles at this service, and £20 of English money was to be paid over to the general benefit of the poor.[145] In addition to the £100 to be paid annually to the abbey (from duchy of Lancaster lands),[146] the abbey was to administer substantial sums of money to be distributed for charitable purposes on the king's anniversary. In 1445 Henry VI granted to the abbey lands in Berkshire and Huntingdonshire to provide money for its monks 'ther perpetuelly to synge and pray for the soule of the most noble prince your honorable fader, king Harre the Ve, whom God assoille, and also for to holde and kepe his obite with certeins distribucions to poure peple . . .'.[147]

Among the surviving records at Westminster are the accounts of the warden ('custos') of the manors of Henry's anniversary foundation: these begin in 1437 and, with a few gaps, continue to 1534.[148] They show that the occasion was used not only for prayer and recollection, but as an opportunity for the abbey to entertain notable persons from outside, when sweet red wine, bread and fish were bought for

---

[144] The trappings of the horses bringing Henry's body from France were 'brawdered with antilopps' (Liverpool Cathedral, Radcliffe Ms 26, fo.14v).
[145] Strong, 'Last will', 90–1; WAM, Ms 3803.
[146] See WAM, Ms 24127.
[147] WAM, Mss 3798, 3803; *RP*, v, 303.
[148] WAM, Mss 24122–24225.

the reception of the aldermen and citizens of London,[149] as well as of leading ecclesiastics. The accounts of one city company, that of the Mercers, contain regular references to payments being made for the expenses of its members travelling to Westminster (and back) 'pur lannyversaire le roy' or 'pour le obite du roy Henry le Ve', sometimes in the company of the mayor, such entries lasting from the very early years of Henry VI's reign until almost its end.[150] The late king had successfully made sure that, even in death, he should be remembered.

[149] WAM, Ms 24133.
[150] Mercers' Company, Wardens' accounts, fos 88, 93, 97 etc.

PART III

The Exercise of Kingship

Chapter 9

NORMANDY

The military events of Henry's conquest of the duchy of Normandy have already been outlined. How did the new 'conqueror' act in the duchy, and what factors influenced him to act as he did? In all his dealings with France, the king claimed to be influenced by the dictates of justice, with that term's implied reference to rights inherited from the past. Justice could – and did – mean the application of Edward III's claims to France and the fulfilment of the terms of the treaty of Brétigny. But it meant more than that. Henry's sense of justice stemmed from even deeper historical roots. Kings of England were numbered from the conquest of England by William I, duke of Normandy, from whom Henry V was descended. King John may have lost Normandy, and his son, Henry III, may have forsaken all right to it by the treaty of Paris of 1259, but Edward III had staked an active claim to the duchy, and Henry V would now do the same.

As the anonymous author of the *Brut* wrote of the king's meeting with his nobility in 1414, Normandy, along with Gascony and Guyenne, were wrongfully withheld by the French, even though these lands had been claimed by 'trewe titill of conquest & right heritage' by Edward III and his ancestors before him. [1] The author of the *Gesta* put it even more precisely when he wrote of the duchy of Normandy, 'which belongs to him entirely by a right dating from the time of William the first, the Conqueror, even though now, as for a long time past, it is thus withheld, against God and all justice, by the violence of the French'. [2] The historical link between the kings of the eleventh and the fifteenth centuries was also stressed by Thomas Walsingham, who, in his account of the siege of Caen in 1417, had a monk of the abbey of St Etienne impress upon the duke of Clarence his obligation to protect the abbey since he was descended from the line of kings responsible for its foundation, building and endowment. [3] The same approach was reinforced when, a few days later, Henry pardoned the monks of the abbey which, the text points out, had been

[1] *Brut*, ii, 374.
[2] *Gesta*, p. 17.
[3] *St Albans Chronicle*, pp. 111–12.

founded by William, king of England and duke of Normandy, his ancestor.[4]

Henry's attitude to the duchy was at once historical and proprietorial. As a successor to William I on the throne of England, he was his natural heir as duke of Normandy. He would also have been aware of the sense of separatism which had surfaced within the duchy in the previous hundred years: at the time of the granting of the famous 'Charte aux Normands' in 1315 (which all French kings since that time had renewed), and more recently, at the time when the dauphin, Charles, and Charles of Navarre had encouraged the development of a spirit of independence in the late 1350s. That separatism had been partly assuaged by the creation of the dauphin as duke of Normandy in 1355. Yet, since 1364, when the dauphin had become king as Charles V, there had been no duke to represent Norman interests, only complaints that the duchy, the richest province of France, was being subjected to too much attention from Paris. In 1380 Charles VI had confirmed the 'Charte', but this had not prevented a revolt (the 'Harelle') from taking place in Rouen two years later. In 1416, almost as Henry was preparing his second invasion, a further rising took place in Rouen which led to the murder of the 'bailli', the chief royal officer in the area, and to the expulsion of many working for the French crown.

It was into this situation that Henry sailed on 1 August 1417. In some measure, at least, history held him under its powerful influence. It was an influence which Henry might turn to his advantage to justify his intervention in the duchy. He could appeal to the sense of distrust of Paris, and he could also emphasize his sympathy for Norman separatism by stressing the continuity between himself and the dukes of former times, underlining this through an appeal for the revival of 'historic' institutions which predated those introduced as a result of the duchy's conquest by the French crown in 1204.

First, however, there was the matter of his own position and authority within the duchy. Henry might claim Normandy by right, but he could only exercise that right through conquest. The success of his invasion demonstrated that he had earned the right to rule the duchy 'as a conque[r]oure yn his right'[5] and, according to contemporary thinking, that God had approved his cause by allowing events to run in his favour. By 15 December 1417, while engaged in the siege of Falaise whose capitulation was to be negotiated only a few days later, Henry styled himself in a letter not only as 'roy de France et

[4] C. Hippeau, *L'abbaye de Saint-Etienne de Caen, 1066–1790* (Caen, 1855), pp. 129–30.
[5] *Brut*, ii, 421.

d'Angleterre, seigneur de Hirlande' but also as 'duc de Normandie',[6] a title which he used again in the following February. The capture of Rouen, the old ducal capital, saw Henry come into his own, with John Page's poem recalling that the people of the city came out to greet him with cries of 'welcome, oure lord / welcome into thyn owne right / as it is the wille of God Almyght!'[7] Having entered the city, Henry went to the cathedral to give thanks for his success, after which he proceeded to the castle, the possessor of whose keep (or 'donjon'), according to tradition, could be looked upon as the legitimate ruler of Normandy.[8] The fact that he would very soon control every corner of the duchy lent practical weight to the claim. Once Rouen was in his hands, Henry could take a very much more vigorous attitude towards ruling Normandy. On Candlemas day, 2 February 1419, scarcely a fortnight after he had entered the city, Henry formally wore his ducal robes, visual confirmation of his de facto right to rule.[9]

However, although controlling the instruments of political power, he still had to win acceptance from his people. Aware of this, he made no attempt to impose English-style institutions upon the duchy; nor, for that matter, did he at any time in the future try to 'anglicize' institutions in France, preferring to accept what he found as an integral part of his inheritance.[10] Although the 'baillis' whom he appointed were English, very few Englishmen received other, lesser administrative functions under the king/duke. Henry doubtless felt that his closest associates and immediate deputies in government should be English, but he had no wish to antagonize the population unduly by appointing Englishmen to the lower echelons of administration,[11] which normally and regularly came into contact with the local population, whose support he badly needed.

With the need to organize government in a way which would appeal to the people of his newly won duchy, Henry deliberately turned to the historic past to emphasize that sense of continuity between those whose heir he claimed to be and his new subjects. His revival of ancient institutions is an example of this. Under the Plantagenets,

[6] BN, Ms fr.26042, no.5249.
[7] *Brut*, ii, 421–2.
[8] Allmand, *Lancastrian Normandy*, p. 125.
[9] 'Et porta robe de duc, comme duc de Normandie' ('Chronique de Normandie', *Henrici Quinti gesta*, ed. Williams, p. 192); Waugh, 'Administration of Normandy', pp. 353–4. In a charter sealed on 24 March 1420, Henry referred to himself and his heirs as dukes of Normandy ('nos aut heredes seu successores nostros duces Normannie . . .') ('Cartulaire de la chapelle du château de Rouen', ed. le Comte Robert de Germiny (*Mélanges*, 9e sér., SHN, Rouen/Paris, 1925) no.21).
[10] Such was the attitude which led to clauses in the treaty of Troyes affirming the need to preserve existing institutions in France. See above, ch.7.
[11] Wylie and Waugh, *Henry the Fifth*, iii, 251.

the duchy's most powerful official had been the seneschal, an office abolished by the French crown in 1204 but now deliberately revived and filled first by Sir Hugh Lutterell and later by Richard Wydeville.[12] The revival had a twofold importance, one symbolic, the other practical. It served as a sign that Henry wished to emphasize the links with the past implied in his claim to rule the duchy.[13] At the same time, since the seneschal's work had been principally that of inspection, it stressed (as did the creation of special commissioners for overseeing garrisons) that Henry wished to appear to be taking the perennial problem of controlling abuses by his officers very seriously indeed. The independence and self-sufficiency of the duchy's finances were underlined by the creation of a treasury, itself subject to a 'Chambre des Comptes', both based on Caen, which remained the financial centre of the English administration until the beginning of his son's reign.[14] In the age of the dukes, the finances had traditionally been centred upon Caen, which was now having its ancient role in Norman government restored to it.

To organize justice, Henry appointed Philip Morgan as ducal chancellor in April 1418; on 3 December 1419 he would be consecrated bishop of Worcester in Rouen cathedral. During the period of conquest, this judicial function of government must have been difficult to fulfil, and it would only have been after the capture of Rouen, in January 1419, that a return to anything like normality can have been achieved. Even in this matter, Henry was not afraid to go along with Norman susceptibilities. While the duchy's finances were organized in Caen, justice would be centred upon the capital, Rouen. It is unlikely that the Norman 'Echiquier', the highest court in the ducal legal system, was restored. Yet Henry was aware of the need to provide a place where important cases, including those arising out of the advent of a large number of Englishmen into Normandy, might be heard, in the last resort, within the duchy itself. The body which could do this best was the king's ducal council, under his ducal chancellor, which, transforming itself into a judicial body, could settle cases that had worked their way up through the courts or, as probably also happened, were brought to it in the first instance. In this way there emerged a judicial body, the 'cour du conseil', which, from very early on in the reign of Henry VI, was to stand for Norman separatism

[12] Newhall, *English conquest*, pp. 244–6.
[13] When, at the feast of the Ascension, 1420, the 'bailli' of Rouen, Walter Beauchamp, refused the people of Rouen the right to exercise an ancient privilege (of freeing a prisoner) associated with St Romain, the king wrote to him from Mantes ordering that it be properly observed (A. Floquet, *Histoire du privilège de Saint Romain* (Rouen, 1833), i, 116).
[14] Waugh, 'Administration of Normandy', pp. 354–5.

in matters of law and could challenge the sovereign claims of France's highest court, the Parlement of Paris.[15]

It was, furthermore, the putting into effect of Henry's historic claim to Normandy which, in large measure, was responsible for his attitude towards the land and its people. While there can be no doubt that the conflict which Henry waged (or, as he would have put it, was obliged to wage) caused considerable destruction, contemporaries generally acknowledged that Henry was intent upon reducing the ravages of war to their minimum. In every way this made sense. English armies in the fourteenth century had been hated and feared in France because of their many acts of wanton destruction. But it was not in Henry's military or political interests to be the cause of fear or resentment in Normandy. His aim was rather to win over the sympathies of the people, something best done and most easily achieved by the pursuit of a policy which one historian has labelled as that of 'conciliation'.[16]

As already noted, one aspect of that policy was the encouragement given to local institutions, whether historic or existing, and the sense that the new ruler wanted Normandy to have a political, financial and judicial existence of its own which these would help to create. But Henry's policy of conciliation went deeper than that. While it was found necessary on occasions to expel whole sections of the populations of captured towns (as Henry did at both Harfleur in 1415 and at Caen two years later), he ensured, as far as he could, that the vulnerable, in particular women, were not molested by his soldiers. Thomas Walsingham reported that the clergy and ecclesiastical property were given the benefit of Henry's special protection, so much so that many men took to shaving part of their heads so that these 'tonsures' and the 'clerical' dress which they wore would provide them with adequate outward sign of their status and the special immunity that now went with it.[17] As Henry was reported as having said to a vagrant monk brought before him, he had not come to Normandy to seize ecclesiastical property, but rather, as a king should, to prevent it from being despoiled.[18]

Henry's assumption that he was the legitimate ruler of Normandy lay behind his demands for loyalty from, and implied recognition by, all classes in the duchy. From the very beginning of the second expedition in 1417, the policy won at least some response. By 21

[15] Allmand, *Lancastrian Normandy*, ch.5: *English suits before the Parlement of Paris*, index, 'Normandy'.
[16] Newhall, 'Henry V's policy of conciliation', passim.
[17] *St Albans Chronicle*, pp. 110–11.
[18] Ibid., p. 110.

September, 483 Norman parishes had already submitted to him in return for the promise of the royal protection,[19] the people having been assured that their legal rights would be recognized and wholesale changes would not occur if they submitted and returned to their homes. This proclamation suggested an important development: that the population of at least parts of Normandy had already pulled up its roots and fled, with all the social and economic disruption that this would have brought to a largely rural society in the last weeks of summer. Henry was himself partly responsible for this; when Caen was captured in September 1417, the town was ransacked, and a substantial part of the population departed.[20] Yet, at first, Henry made no real effort to discourage or prevent people from leaving. At this early stage he may not yet have appreciated the scale of the movement and disruption of population. More likely, he may have felt that he would be able to rule with greater effectiveness if those who had opposed him, and who then still preferred to emigrate, were allowed to do so.

What led to this considerable emigration from the duchy? Fear was probably the main motive. By 1417, with the assault and capture of Harfleur, as well as the victory at Agincourt, behind them, the English king and his army must have inspired considerable trepidation among the people of Normandy. Henry's army (and that part of it which was left to garrison towns and castles as these fell to the English) was only the latest in a line of armies which had left their mark on Normandy during the past seven decades or so. It was scarcely surprising that people should have been afraid of the English.

A second factor to have encouraged emigration was loyalty to the crown of France and a basic but growing sense of patriotism. Because it is so emotive, discussion of this subject is difficult; even today, it can lead to sharp but generally rather futile verbal battles. What is indisputable is that, for all his claim to be regarded as duke of Normandy, Henry V was a foreign king, who spoke a foreign tongue and who used foreign soldiers to make Normans submit to his rule. In 1417 and in the years immediately following, the French crown proved itself weak, vacillating and incapable of defending its subjects, as the defeat at Agincourt and the failure to succour Rouen had shown. Yet it could still appeal to the loyalty of its people, and to many there was only one way of expressing that loyalty, by flight, even if this meant sacrificing estates, homes, commercial interests or ecclesiastical benefices.

In spite of the lure of a pardon and readmission to the enjoyment

[19] Newhall, 'Henry V's policy of conciliation', p. 207, n.11.
[20] *Brut*, ii, 384; *St Albans Chronicle*, p. 113.

of property and the security of the king's peace, many who had left chose not to return.[21] Their reasons for doing so varied. Some fled to earn their livings and preferred the place where they had settled; others chose flight to escape the debts which they owed.[22] To many, a lack of security and, in some ways stemming from it, an insecure economic future must have acted as deterrents. Many members of the nobility who had served the French crown in the duchy remained loyal to it, and left; others, out of necessity concerned for the welfare of their lands, preferred to remain under English rule. A large proportion of the higher clergy accepted Henry, who provided the many graduates among them with benefices through the patronage which became available to him; at the parish level, too, the clergy appear to have been largely ready to accept the new order of things. It is difficult to impose any satisfactory pattern, whether of social rank or of geographical origin, which will help us determine who left (whether temporarily or permanently) and who stayed. The English invasion certainly split loyalties, and, in so doing, it split families, too. The effects of this would be seen a generation later.

The economic disruption resulting from war would also have encouraged people to leave the duchy. This, it should be emphasized, cannot be blamed entirely upon Henry's invasion, significant as its effects were. Caen, for instance, suffered considerably from the siege of 1417, which led to the departure of many of its citizens. However, Caen's economy had not been flourishing for some years: both its port and its manufacturing industries were in decline, so that, for many, the destruction caused by the siege was the last straw, making some of its citizens, at least, think that they might do better elsewhere, for example in lands controlled by the duke of Brittany, where many emigrés went. At the same time, the effects of some two years of war upon the economy of Normandy cannot be doubted: destruction or shortage of crops (with the consequence that seed might not be available for the following year); inability, in time of an uncertain political future, to procure capital to rebuild houses and farms, as well as to replace agricultural tools, destroyed or damaged in war; loss of personnel to carry out trade or work on the land (the effects of depopulation); the problems of travel and, consequently, the dangers of commerce carried out over anything more than the shortest distance. All of these difficulties contributed to a decline in the economic prosperity of a normally rich duchy, and to the creation of a feeling that greater security and wealth might be found elsewhere.[23]

---

[21] Allmand, *Lancastrian Normandy*, ch.8.
[22] Ibid., pp. 214–15 and n.9.
[23] On the economic background to the English invasion, see ibid., pp. 153–9.

So people emigrated.[24] Others remained behind in Normandy to oppose from within. While they were to be found in every part of the duchy, these opponents of the English came largely from the lower orders of society. To latter-day French historians, they have appeared and acted as heroes, a minority of men who took to the woods for safety while waging a form of guerrilla warfare against the invader and usurper, for which, if they were caught, they often paid the ultimate penalty.[25] What did such people represent? To some they can be regarded as martyrs ready to die for France and its crown, to others they were the product not merely of the English invasion and occupation but, since both their activities and the name of 'brigand' given to them were well known before that invasion, of economic and social conditions which existed before the English came to Normandy and which their arrival only served to aggravate. While they represented a 'nationalist' opposition to the English, the 'brigands' also reflected a situation which predated the English invasion.

Was Henry so blinkered by what he regarded as the justice of his conquest of Normandy that he failed to appreciate the measure and significance of the opposition which he encountered and, above all, the importance of the emigration which his invasion provoked? Those who fled might rid him of an opposition movement which he could well do without. In economic terms, however, their departure would have very serious consequences. The loss of such people could have only an adverse effect upon the duchy (modern research has emphasized the disastrous local results of depopulation), which, in its turn, would deter others from returning. The levels of taxation it would be possible to collect would also be threatened by such large-scale departures. Furthermore, the prolonged absence of part of the population was a challenge to the legality of Henry's rule, an insult to his claim to be the legitimate ruler of Normandy. He had to stop emigration and encourage the return of those who had left. First he needed to reconcile the soldier and the civilian. The problem was partly a historical one. Bad memories of how fourteenth-century armies had treated civilian populations lingered on. Henry would have been aware of this as he took measures to control his men, measures which would also increase the efficiency of his army.[26]

[24] L. Puiseux, *L'émigration normande et la colonisation anglaise en Normandie au XVe siècle* (Caen/Paris, 1866): G. Bois, *The crisis of feudalism. Economy and society in eastern Normandy, c.1300–1550* (Cambridge/Paris, 1984), pp. 65, 316–27.

[25] See R. Jouet, *La résistance à l'occupation anglaise en Basse-Normandie (1418–1450)* (Caen, 1969), passim.

[26] After Henry's death, Bedford, his successor in France, pursued a similar policy. See B.J.H. Rowe, 'Discipline in the Norman garrisons under Bedford, 1422–35', *EHR*, 46 (1931), 194–208.

It soon became clear, however, that problems remained. By 1418, the number of references to deserters in the Norman Rolls had increased; soldiers were not acting under their captains, which made it necessary to appoint Hugh Lutterell, lieutenant of Harfleur, to ensure that the laws of military discipline were being generally applied, power being given him to hang those found absent without leave.[27] Some months later, in November 1418, Henry decided to mete out strong punishment, as allowed by the laws of the duchy of Normandy and military regulations, upon all 'brigands' imprisoned at Falaise, a further sign of the problem which he faced and of his determination to resolve it.[28] On 8 December of the same year, when still before Rouen, the king showed how seriously he regarded relations between the civilian and the army by ordering the 'vicomte' of Caen to proclaim that all who had suffered injury at the hands of a member of the garrison should come before him to seek redress.[29] Practical measures too, it was hoped, would help restore order at those points where soldier and civilian met, Henry insisting in an order issued on 10 April 1419 that soldiers should not antagonize local people by refusing to pay for goods (such as food) which they bought from them.[30]

If, later in the reign, less is heard of violence towards the citizen (perhaps because of these measures?), the number of deserters referred to in the rolls for the summer of 1419 nevertheless suggests an army disaffected by bad pay and conditions or, as was the case in that year, by not being sufficiently involved in war.[31] The second half of 1418 had been spent before the walls of Rouen. In 1419, as the diplomatic pace quickened, that of military activity slackened further still. Likewise, the process of conquest had led to a need to man the garrisons of towns, castles and other strongholds. Those who formed these garrisons might have relatively little to do, being denied access to the activities (and gains) of war available to any field army on active service. Paradoxically, it was lack of action which placed the civilian population most at risk and which constituted a threat to the king's peace. Henry, we may be sure, was aware of this.

By improving conditions in Normandy, Henry could make it a better place to return to. On this matter, too, his attitude changed. Whereas those who had either left Normandy or refused to take the oath of fealty had been denied access to, or use of, their lands within

[27] *DKR*, 41, p. 716.
[28] Ibid., 41, p. 719.
[29] Ibid., 41, p. 720.
[30] BN, Ms fr.26042, no.5345.
[31] *DKR*, 42, pp. 321, 323, 325, 328.

the duchy (a move likely to win the king few friends), Henry now made a conscious attempt to win their allegiance and residence. On 4 February 1418 it was proclaimed that all wishing to do him homage could have a safe-conduct to enable them to do this.[32] The measure was not entirely successful, and the period within which submissions were to be given had to be extended. Yet Henry's purpose is clear. Taking the oath of allegiance meant a declaration of faith in and recognition of the legitimacy of English rule which, if broken by opposition within the duchy or by desertion to dauphinist France, rendered the rebel liable to the most severe penalties. From now on, those who broke their oath of allegiance could expect to be regarded as traitors.

As the conquest of the whole of Normandy progressed, so further appeals to those who wished to enjoy the benefits of allegiance were issued. To these, Henry was willing (if not always able) to extend his protection, and for the consideration of 10 *deniers* (later 4 *sous*, a sign of inflation?) those who had formally recorded their allegiance to him could receive a 'bullette', or pass, demanding that the royal protection be accorded to them. Allegiance, or the achievement of the status of a 'juratus', also formally restored the right to property. On 6 May 1419, at the request of Robert de Corday, esquire, said to be a 'juratus', and by virtue of his royal authority, Henry confirmed Corday in the enjoyment of all the lands which he had held within Normandy on 1 August 1417, on the same terms and conditions which had applied at that date. Corday was to hold these lands according to the custom of the duchy, and he was to fulfil his obligations as before. The text emphasizes not only that the initiative for this action had come from the 'juratus' himself, but also that Henry had confirmed him as the legal possessor of estates on 1 August 1417 (the 'journée de Touques' as it soon came to be known), the day on which Henry had landed to stake his claim to Normandy.[33] References to the 'journée' were a means of dating by reference to an event remembered by all. They were also a way of marking the demise of the old, Valois order and the beginning of the new, achieved without a break. In brief, the confirmation granted to Corday and to many others marked 'no change'. It was as the representative of 'no change' that Henry sought to win acceptance.

Henry had never wanted large-scale emigration. From an early date he had made it known by public proclamation to those living long distances from Normandy (some had gone as far south as Poitou in central western France)[34] that he would like them to return. Some did

[32] Newhall, 'Henry V's policy of conciliation', p. 212 seq.
[33] BL, Add. Ch.1412. For a similar confirmation, see Add. Ch.3509.
[34] R.G. Little, *The Parlement of Poitiers. War, government and politics in France, 1418–1436* (London, 1984), p. 9.

so; others hung back, reluctant to decide, so that the deadlines for the receipt of the oath of allegiance were postponed several times. Yet, once Henry had brought the siege of Rouen to a successful conclusion (with all that this meant to his ability to rule the duchy effectively), he began to act with increasing firmness. He needed to impose himself upon his subjects, to show who was master. He was anxious to re-allocate lands, partly to reward and encourage those who served him faithfully, partly to ensure the proper exploitation of land for the general welfare. He needed to know who his subjects were, and whether they lived within his obedience. Were people for him – or not?

The picture which emerges of Henry aiming to maintain the old order as far as possible is broadly confirmed by his relationship with the churchmen of the duchy. Within five weeks of the landing at Touques, clergy were coming to the king to give the oath of allegiance expected of them. To such, Henry immediately (and doubtless grate-fully) ordered the return of their temporalities; it was not his intention, he wrote to John Ashton, seneschal of Bayeux, on 4 December 1417, that the divine service should in any way be affected or diminished by the lack of material support, and those who recognized him should hold freely such lands and properties as they had held before.[35] Such decisions, coupled with another made later, in January 1420, granting ecclesiastics throughout the duchy exemption from taxation on food and drink,[36] indicate the goodwill of their new ruler towards the Nor-man clergy, 'a class whose interests were notoriously well cared for by the invader'.[37]

Henry treated churchmen well because it was his instinct to do so, even though ecclesiastics and their property were conventionally among those granted special protection from the attention of the sol-diery. Yet he did it, too, because he needed all the help which the Church and its clergy could give him. In a predominantly rural society, the influence of the priest could be a powerful one, and few sights can have been more gratifying to Henry than that of the people, led by their clergy, coming to give their allegiance to him. What Henry wanted was to make use of the political influence of the clergy, and through them to win a measure of control over the people.

This may be seen in a number of ways. The Norman Rolls contain many presentations to ecclesiastical benefices in the first two years or so of the occupation. In some cases Henry may have been exercising what was normally episcopal patronage; in other cases it was probably

[35] *Foedera*, IV, iii, 28.
[36] Rouen, Arch. dép., Seine-Maritime, G 3681.
[37] Wylie and Waugh, *Henry the Fifth*, iii, 55.

that of the crown; in yet other instances it would have been lay patronage not exercised because of the absence (for whatever reason) of the patron. Henry made good use of these opportunities, and in so doing was able to appoint clergy who had given the oath of allegiance and who owed their position to him; their loyalty, as well as that which they might encourage from the pulpit, would be of great value to him.

Just as, properly controlled and rewarded, the clergy were a group who would give Henry their support, so, equally, they could act to undermine his claims and position. A cure of souls whose pastor had deserted as a sign of opposition was a continuous reminder that not all had accepted the English, and it was a contagion which could spread. Yet there was a limit to what Henry could do before the capture of Rouen in January 1419. Once this had been achieved, and the authority of the absentee archbishop could be exercised, he soon set to work. Within a week the chapter of Coutances cathedral, said to have been electing absentees to canonries and prebends, was ordered not to elect a bishop or dispose of vacant benefices without a royal licence:[38] Henry was determined to exercise at least a measure of control over the promotion of 'acceptable' clergy. In the next month the attempt to make absenteeism a political crime was extended when letters in the same vein were sent to the chapters of four other Norman cathedrals, those of Rouen, Avranches, Evreux and Lisieux, likewise forbidding them to elect or appoint to any ecclesiastical position without the king's special leave.[39] At the same time, just as attempts were made to persuade lay landowners to return, so endeavours were to be made to entice back those clergy who 'support the party opposed to our lord the king, by advising, aiding and abetting brigands and opponents of the king'.[40] The moral authority of the clergy was something to be won.

Whether the church authorities lacked the power or the will to enforce residence, by early February 1420 Henry had come to recognize that the previous methods had not worked. He now felt obliged to call upon his financial officers to act by seizing the benefices of those clergy who were absent.[41] Even this measure was to prove insufficient. If the absentees would recognize no order written in his name, Henry would have to try other means. In March 1421 the council in

[38] *Foedera*, IV, iii, 83.

[39] 'Roles normands et français et autres pièces tirées des archives de Londres par Bréquigny en 1764, 1765 et 1766', *Mémoires de la Société des Antiquaires de Normandie*, 3e sér., 23 (1858), no.1453.

[40] '. . . tiennent le party contraire de monseigneur le roy, en conseillant et confortant et aidans les brigans et adversaires de mondit seigneur le roy' (BN, Ms fr.26042, nos 5325, 5365; Newhall, 'Henry V's policy of conciliation', p. 221).

[41] BN, Ms fr.26043, nos 5476, 5478.

Rouen commanded that those who did not reside would now face not only penalties imposed by the king (deprivation of temporalities) but the canonical sanctions of the church itself (deprivation of office).[42] On 14 July 1421, two and a half years after gaining control of Rouen, Henry finally announced that, in view of the archbishop's continued absence and persistent refusal to give the oath of allegiance, he would now enforce his 'regalian' right of appointment to benefices during what would, in effect, be regarded as an episcopal vacancy.[43] This was followed a few days later by orders from the absent archbishop's vicars that some twenty-five of the cathedral clergy were also being deprived of their benefices for non-residence and for having lived in the obedience of the dauphin. The date by which they should have submitted had been extended four times; their cures had no pastors, and for the people's sake this situation could not be allowed to continue indefinitely.[44]

Henry was not having it all his own way. That the clergy should return of their own free will must have been what he desired above all. When they did not, he had to be patient and, in the end, he only took action against them step by step, each more severe than the last. It is clear that he wanted to promote the service of God. But he also wanted, indeed he needed, a clergy whom he could trust, and in his position he could trust none who consistently refused to give him the oath of allegiance. A rather similar set of conditions was to help dictate Henry's relationship with the holders of Normandy's seven bishoprics which, together, formed the ecclesiastical province of Rouen. Of the seven bishops, four fled the duchy before the English army and were never seen again, three of them (Coutances, Evreux and Lisieux) being victims of the massacre of Armagnacs carried out by Burgundian supporters in Paris in May 1418, the fourth (Rouen) 'retiring' to Poitou. Of the remaining three, one (Séez) gave his oath to Henry in the spring of 1418, another (Bayeux) died in Rome in the following year, while the bishop of Avranches was absent for part of the time.

Replacing the bishops was a slow process, not helped by the determination of pope Martin V to see that his own nominees received promotion. Such a situation may not have troubled Henry all that much, and in the absence of bishops he appears to have been able to deal firmly, but amicably, with their vicars-general or the chapters of their cathedral churches, to whom most of his correspondence was

[42] *Foedera*, IV, iv, 15.
[43] Ibid., IV, iv, 38.
[44] Arch. dép., Seine-Maritime, G 1202 (printed in *Rouen au temps de Jeanne d'Arc et pendant l'occupation anglaise (1419–1449)*, ed. P. le Cacheux (Rouen/Paris, 1931), pp. 27–34); G 2123, fos 3, 3v.

directed. In the absence of bishops, Henry was also able to exercise
the regalian rights normally claimed by the king in time of vacancy.
This gave him the double benefit of the revenues of the sees of Normandy (which contributed substantially to the royal revenues in 1419
and 1420) and control over the bishop's patronage, a vital factor in
the situation, as we have already seen. No wonder that Henry does
not appear to have been in any great hurry to have the vacant bishoprics of Normandy filled. Without the bishops, he enjoyed greater
benefit from his control over the church in the duchy than with them
installed in office.

In one matter Henry, generally conservative in the policies he pursued in Normandy, went far beyond what his predecessors had ever
done. By granting confiscated estates and properties, both within the
duchy and, by 1419, outside it, to new landowners, both English and
Norman, he hoped to secure and reward their support, and thus, by
giving them a stake in the success of their common enterprise, to make
the conquest permanent. There is nothing to indicate that Henry
envisaged a Norman Conquest in reverse,[45] or that he had made
public beforehand plans to make land in France available on a considerable scale to those who served him. Yet, in the event, both his
de facto conquest of the duchy, as well as the confiscation of lands
from those who, either by open resistance or by leaving Normandy,
opposed what he regarded as the legitimacy of his rule, conferred
upon Henry rights and titles to lands which, taken into his hands,
could in turn be conferred upon those who supported him.

Events, rather than policy, had placed the sources of considerable
wealth under Henry's control.[46] Confiscated land and property could
be used to reward past services, and to encourage men to help in the
future.[47] They could also be used as incentive to personal settlement
in Normandy. Merchants, for example, were offered the chance of
establishing themselves in Harfleur and Caen in the hope of providing
stimulus for the economies of these two towns, in particular the

[45] Seward, *Henry V*, title to ch.11.
[46] The subject is dealt with generally in the compass of an article by C.T. Allmand,
'The Lancastrian land settlement in Normandy, 1417–50', *EconHR*, 2nd series, 21
(1968), 461–79, and Allmand, *Lancastrian Normandy*, ch.3. It is treated more completely in R.A. Massey, 'The Lancastrian land settlement in Normandy and northern
France, 1417–1450' (Univ. of Liverpool Ph.D. thesis, 1987); his main conclusions
are in R. Massey, 'The land settlement in Lancastrian Normandy', *Property and politics.
Essays in later medieval English history*, ed. A.J. Pollard (Gloucester/New York, 1984),
pp. 76–96.
[47] References to the 'commissaires sur le fait des confiscations' (BN, Ms fr.21226,
fos 2–3v) strongly suggest that Henry had set up an organization to deal with the
whole matter of confiscated lands and the revenues which, albeit temporarily, they
would bring to the crown.

second.[48] Such actions remind us that Henry was also intent upon restoring the regional economy, deeply affected as it was by war. By 1417 Harfleur was firmly in English hands and was likely to remain so. Although, because of its strategic position, it took on an important role as a military base, the English doubtless hoped to recreate its trade as well. The same must have been planned in the case of the declining economy of Caen. The grant of rural estates and lordships was likewise seen as a first step towards restoring, then maintaining, an economy and social structure adversely affected by war, by flight (of lord, or of tenant, or of both) or by other economic disruption. Economic historians have underlined the adverse effects of war upon parts of Normandy in these years.[49] An active policy of making grants might be a means of bringing that decline to a halt. The obligations and conditions imposed upon some recipients of land strongly suggest that they were expected to make their newly acquired estates pay — or at least halt a decline resulting from the negligence and destruction brought about by war. The economy of the duchy in general, and the amount of money coming into the king's exchequer through taxation in particular, both stood to benefit from estates restored to at least a respectable level of production.

Whatever Henry's motives and intentions were in different cases, he acted with caution and restraint. Both Harfleur and Caen, taken by storm, became the property of their conqueror. Henry acted with responsibility, showing that he saw the possible settlement of Englishmen in Caen not simply in terms of the profit which it might bring them as individuals, but also for the advantage they might bring to Caen. The letter written by Clarence, whom Henry had appointed captain, to the corporation of London on 11 September 1417, asking for merchants willing to settle in Caen, emphasized two factors.[50] One was the need to repopulate the town after the destruction caused by the siege and the departure of a sizeable proportion of its population; the other was to provide for the requirements of its defence, above all when soldiers, badly needed in the field, could not be spared for garrison duty. The king had both the present and the longer-term interests of Caen firmly in his mind.

Caen fell in September 1417, and in the coming eighteen months the conquest of almost the whole of Normandy was achieved. During that period and the months which followed it, Henry slowly developed a conscious policy of granting his supporters lands which had come into his hand by confiscation or death, ultimately by conquest. This

---

[48] For Caen, see Allmand, *Lancastrian Normandy*, ch.4(i).
[49] E.g. Bois, *Crisis of feudalism*, cited n.24 above.
[50] Delpit, *Collection générale*, pp. 220–1.

policy was considered, patiently executed, and had more than the
interests of the persons to whom grants were made in mind. If it was
slow at first in development,[51] this reflects Henry's sense of responsibility, for it was necessary, as far as possible, to establish existing
ownership of land and to find out where owners' loyalties lay. Along
with an understandable desire to reward those who worked for him,
it should be recalled that Henry wanted to entice men who had fled
back to Normandy. They were less likely to return if they knew that
their confiscated estates had already been given away, perhaps to an
Englishman. Care was needed. We see that care in action in the fact
that the first grant recorded in the Norman Rolls, made to Thomas,
earl of Salisbury, was dated 25 September 1417, after which the process almost stopped, to be taken up again in March and April 1418,
only to cease almost totally between June 1418 and the early weeks
of 1419.

The reasons for this policy of 'stop:go' are clear. In the winter of
1417–18 Henry was occupied with his conquest: the siege of Falaise
held his attention. That over, he felt more confident; he had time for
administration, which he carried out from Caen and Bayeux where he
spent much of the spring. In short, a measure of order was returning to
those parts of the duchy which the English controlled, and the
machinery required for the making of grants (the 'Chambre des Com-
putes' in Caen acted as a form of land registry) was at hand and
functioning again. Not surprisingly, this was a period of considerable
grant-making, but one which ended once Henry had set out on campaign, not to function again until well after the fall of Rouen early in
1419.[52] There now began a period of considerable activity. During
this time not only did Henry gain control of the whole duchy, he
must, by now, have also become aware of those likely to refuse the
oath of allegiance and whose lands, therefore, would become subject
to confiscation and thence available for redistribution. The period
was to last about four months, coming to an end in June 1419 at
about the time that Henry began to advance up the Seine valley
towards Paris.[53]

Henry had been engaged in pursuing sieges during two consecutive
winters: that of 1417–18 before Falaise, that of 1418–19 before Rouen.
Summers were spent on campaign. So it is that we may locate the
two main spells of grant-making to the seasons of spring of 1418 and

[51] Massey, 'Lancastrian land settlement', pp. 23–4, 374, 181.
[52] Only ten grants are recorded between June 1418 and January 1419, a period
which corresponds fairly closely to the months taken up with the siege of Rouen
(ibid., p. 23).
[53] Ibid., pp. 26, 374–5.

1419, the periods between the sieges and the campaigns in the field. This strongly suggests that Henry completed his administrative tasks in the relative peace of those months, which enabled him to act with care and consideration. There was nothing rushed about the way the king set about rewarding his supporters: like so much of what he did, this was done in a deliberate way. This argument is supported by further factors. Grants, normally conceded in response to a request or petition, were made not in haphazard fashion, but strictly in accordance with the needs – and above all the military needs – of the moment, and also as to whether it was thought that the recipient had the means (which often meant social rank) to meet those needs. Several factors point to this. The first grants, made in the spring of 1418, were of lands in the 'bailliage' of Caen (at that time the centre of English power in Normandy) which, if pinpointed on a map, would create a form of buffer around this zone of influence.[54] This makes even more sense when it is realized that many recipients were given lands on essentially feudal conditions, often including some form of military obligation such as the provision of a man or men to guard a town or castle (as was expected of the merchants settled in Caen)[55] or, in the case of larger lordships, the provision of soldiers to fight in the king's army, thereby involving Normans in the defence of their duchy and even, possibly, in English military involvement outside it.[56] The recipient of the king's favour might thus have serious and even costly responsibilities thrust upon him.

As the conquest developed, so another factor came into consideration as lands were distributed by the king. A captain might receive land near to, or in the general area of, the town or castle of which he had charge,[57] just as civil administrators, such as those who served in the 'Chambre des Comptes', were given houses to occupy in Caen. Once again, such a policy bore the marks of thought on somebody's part, probably Henry himself. Similarly, the way in which the size of grants corresponded to the social status or wealth of recipients reflected the degree of involvement in war expected of them. The great estates went to those from whom much might be asked, the smaller ones to those from whom much less could be expected.[58]

[54] Ibid., pp. 9–11.
[55] The obligation was known as 'guet et garde'.
[56] Massey, 'Lancastrian land settlement', pp. 16, 246; A.E. Curry, 'The first English standing army? – Military organisation in Lancastrian Normandy, 1420–1450', *Patronage, pedigree and power in later medieval England*, ed. C. Ross (Gloucester/Totowa, 1979), p. 199, emphasizes the drawbacks of this system.
[57] See the evidence presented in Massey, 'Lancastrian land settlement', pp. 34–53, 197–9.
[58] Ibid., p. 248, table 1.

Some towns had resisted the English. The way in which their resistance had been dealt with had made most realize that surrender
brought less trouble than did opposition to the English army.[59] Towns
thus came to form an important element in the English rule of Normandy. What had held up the invader – their defences – could now
be used in their favour, and the fortified towns of the duchy were to
assume a significant role as strongly defended administrative centres
as well as, in the case of some, commercial centres of importance. It
was from a number of such towns, Rouen, Caen, Cherbourg, Falaise,
Alençon among them, that the duchy's administrative and judicial
system was made to work. It was from these places and, most important, because of their strategic position on the Seine, from Harfleur
and Honfleur, that the military organization functioned; while it was
from Rouen that the economic vitality of the duchy stemmed. In all
these towns (and others) Henry made grants to Englishmen.[60] Of
these places, Rouen was the most significant and it was here that
administrators, merchants and a few clergy were given houses or
canonries in the cathedral which entitled them to lodging in the city.

Such grants, by comparison with those made in rural areas, came
comparatively late in the day. Very few were made in Rouen until
about December 1419 (by which time the city had been in English
hands for almost a year), the period of grant-making lasting until
April 1420, to be followed by another in January 1421. Such evidence
reinforces a point made above. Although Henry was probably in
Rouen in the spring of 1419, the situation was not yet sufficiently
settled, nor was his knowledge of existing property-holding sufficiently
detailed for him to make grants within the city without the risk of
creating problems for the future. Then, in the summer and autumn
of 1419 he was away advancing English fortunes in the Seine valley;
he returned to Rouen in time for Christmas, and it was then, enquiries
having been made in the meantime, that he felt ready to grant property in the Norman capital to his fellow Englishmen and others who
had supported him. This went on until his departure for Troyes in
May 1420, and would be resumed when Henry visited Rouen, in the
company of queen Katharine, on his way to England in January 1421.

The distribution of land in Normandy, land which was part of the
demesne and of which the king was feudal lord, was controlled with
the greatest of care by Henry himself. What did such grants mean to

[59] A.E. Curry, 'Towns at war: relations between the towns of Normandy and their
English rulers, 1417–1450', *Towns and townspeople in the fifteenth century*, ed. J.A.F.
Thomson (Gloucester, 1988), p. 158.
[60] Massey, 'Lancastrian land settlement', pp. 179–201 (for Henry V and the
towns).

their English recipients who, by the end of the reign, probably numbered some hundreds, drawn from all ranks of society?[61] To the highest nobility they were a source of involvement, pride and, to a certain
extent – depending upon their exact location in the duchy – revenue
for the recipient (lands in the north were less liable to attack than
those on the southern frontier). We may be sure that Salisbury
received his estates as a measure of gratitude for the military services
which he had rendered Henry, just as Clarence did. However, we
would be hard put to attribute the financial motive as the only one.
Although Harfleur, for instance, was to attract settlers who reaped
the profits of rents from multiple grants of houses in the town (Henry
wanted a large English 'presence' in this port whose location and
recent history underlined what a risk to English security it was), we
have so little evidence of the type of 'settler estate accounts' that it is
difficult to reach firm conclusions about the drawing power of the
financial and economic incentive.[62] But one factor is clear. Harfleur
apart, Henry had no wish or intention of substituting an English
population for a Norman one.[63] While it is true that in some towns,
such as Caen, Englishmen might live in close proximity to other
Englishmen, the aim of Henry's policy (after an initial moment of
doubt when garrisons were not permitted to live in the towns which
they guarded) was essentially that of integration, a process in which
marriages, allowed by Henry from the beginning, were intended to
play a part.[64] The close link between the location of grants and the
garrison in which the recipient of the grant was serving underlines
the very deliberate nature of the settlement planned by Henry V.

A final point may serve to support this observation. Although
administrative errors were made (certain lands were granted to two
beneficiaries, one of whom then pointed out the mistake), there is no
doubt that the king was largely personally responsible for the land
settlement in Normandy during his lifetime[65] (grants of land not made
by him directly required his personal ratification).[66] While most
grants were made in tail-male – that is, they were made to be inherited
with a long-term perspective in view – Henry also made them at

[61] Massey (ibid., p. 376) has a total of 358 grants to settlers between September
1417 and June 1422. Almost exactly two-thirds of these (241) were made in the
calendar year 1419.

[62] Ibid., p. 333.

[63] Ibid., p. 201.

[64] Allmand, *Lancastrian Normandy*, ch.4 (i).

[65] '. . . the hand of Henry V did much to shape the substance and the form of the
early settlement' (Massey, 'Lancastrian land settlement', p. 250).

[66] A grant made by his brother, Clarence, to William Alyngton was later confirmed
by the king himself (*DKR*, 42, p. 400).

pleasure or for life, giving him the option of revoking them. His clear wish to control the holding of land by English and French recipients of his favour is shown in his decision, made public at Moronval, near Dreux, in August 1421, that Englishmen could only dispose of lands given to them by the king to other Englishmen, while Frenchmen could dispose either to Englishmen or to Frenchmen.[67] Two closely related conclusions may be drawn from this. First, that lands given to Englishmen probably had either greater financial or, more likely, greater strategic value than those given to the French; secondly, that because of these factors, it was intended that such lands, deliberately given to Englishmen, should as far as possible remain in English hands. To ensure that, in cases of dispute between recipients, this should be done, all suits arising from grants made by the king were to be heard by the council in Rouen. It was the most effective way of ensuring that the land settlement continued to fulfil the intentions of the man who had been responsible for its creation.

[67] Massey, 'Lancastrian land settlement', p. 273. Lands given to Clarence and others killed at Baugé on 22 March 1421 were taken back into the king's hands by an order issued at Rouen on 3 April ('Roles normands et français', no.981). Since Henry was in England at the time, it is likely that its contents reflected a decision to keep lands in English hands already taken before the king's departure for England two months earlier. For a case brought before the Parlement in 1426 arising out of Henry's 'ordonnance . . . que les maisons et heritages par lui donnéz aux Anglois ne seroient point venduz aux Normans', see *English suits before the Parlement of Paris*, pp. 154–68.

Chapter 10

ARMY AND NAVY

THE ARMY

Henry is rightly thought of as a soldier-king. He had been gaining experience in war ever since he was a young man, and he felt at ease among soldiers. Command and decisive leadership came naturally to him. It was the army which enabled him to win the respect due to a conqueror, and it was his conquests which primarily gave his brief reign its particular flavour and characteristics. What kind of army did he lead to these successes?

That which Henry took to France in 1415 had, as its leaders, the traditional fighting class, the nobility, who turned out in large numbers, although, because there had been relative peace since the mid-1390s, many must have had little or no practical experience of war.[1] The participation of this group, dukes, earls and barons, supported by knights in large numbers, provides ample evidence of the wide involvement of the community in the king's enterprise, an involvement underlined by the fact that the dukes and earls were responsible for recruiting about half the army which embarked at Southampton in August 1415. The presence of a number of men who were, or had recently been, MPs is a further indicator of the active involvement in a national enterprise of persons of reputation and standing among the broad English community.[2]

By 1417, however, there were hints that change was beginning to occur. In June the king wrote from Salisbury to the sheriffs of Southampton, Wiltshire, Sussex and Dorset. It had come to his attention, he told them, that men of little standing were assuming coats of arms, or 'cotearmures', to which they had no claim. This meant that some were being given consideration which they did not merit, and

[1] M.R. Powicke, 'Lancastrian captains', *Essays in medieval history presented to Bertie Wilkinson*, ed. T.A. Sandquist and M.R. Powicke (Toronto, 1969), pp. 371–82; M.H. Keen, 'English military experience and the court of chivalry: the case of Grey v. Hastings', *Guerre et société en France, en Angleterre et en Bourgogne, XIVe–XVe siècle*, ed. P. Contamine, C. Giry-Deloison and M.H. Keen (Lille, 1991), p. 135.
[2] Powicke, 'Lancastrian captains', pp. 371–7.

the king had to say that measures would be taken to ensure that all should have to prove their status or risk losing their position in the army. The only exception to this which would be recognized would be men who had fought at Agincourt.[3] Henry was drawing attention both to a social phenomenon (to be observed a few years later by another commentator)[4] and to a factor which could affect the leadership of his army.

Very late in 1419 or early in 1420 justices and sheriffs received orders from the king to locate knights and esquires 'qui portent armes d'auncestrie' who might serve with him in France. The returns from some thirty counties survive. These provide information of the number of men who might come into consideration; in a few cases, the numbers who had been approached; the reason why not all those considered were suitable; and, in the case of Warwickshire, the excuses offered 'quas nescimus determinare'. From these returns, it becomes clear how important 'esquiers pluis hablez et sufficeantz portauntz armes dauncestrie' were becoming in Henry's army. We now witness an increasing number of esquires as the leaders of retinues, and the introduction into the record of the phrase 'de nom et d'armes' opposite a man's name as a means of maintaining the outward signs of social status among those who acted as 'men-at-arms' or 'speres'.[5] Such a development suggests that esquires who had previously provided many of the men-at-arms were now being recruited and promoted to positions of greater responsibility and command, their credentials as the legitimate bearers in arms having been accepted. There are also indications that, when he called for men to serve in France in the summer of 1421, Henry wanted archers who were not only experienced in their art but who also came from gentle or yeoman stock;[6] at the same time, while dukes and earls continued to serve, the same could not be said of barons and knights. Were they finding it too expensive to take an active part in war over a prolonged period of years? Were there problems for those with estates which they did not want to leave for too long? It is not unlikely that the reasons behind this change were economic in nature.

The army's command structure depended upon the indenture which bound the king to his captains, and these to the men whom they brought with them. Captains contracted to appear at a certain place and time with an agreed number of men (their retinues), who

    [3] *CCR, 1413–1419*, p. 433.
    [4] N. Upton, *De studio militari*, ed. E. Bysshe (London, 1654), pp. 257–8.
    [5] See PRO, E 28/97/2A-35B (32B for Warwickshire), and E 404/35 (indentures of February 1420).
    [6] '. . . de progenie generosa', *CPR, 1416–1422*, p. 341.

might total five or 500, largely depending on the status of the captain. The king himself had men who were bound either to perform military service themselves or provide others to do it for them. The knights who were members of the king's household, called, since Richard II's time, king's knights, were important recruiters of men, mainly from the localities from which they came.[7] There were also annuitants, such as those of his duchies of Cornwall and Lancaster, who helped provide the core of the contribution made by the royal household to the formation of the army, besides acting, on occasion, as leaders of groups of archers from their area of origin. Such personal retainers of the crown did not necessarily reside with the king or even at the court, but they were among those specially summoned in 1415, 1416, 1417 and 1421 to come to the king at Westminster to give him their advice and, if necessary, to serve.[8] Otherwise, as happened in the summer of 1416, general proclamations would be made that those who were able to serve should be in a state of readiness to do so.[9]

This preliminary was followed by two main forms of recruitment which must have taken place simultaneously. Those who sealed indentures with the king tried to raise the number of soldiers, men-at-arms and archers (some mounted, others not) whom they had undertaken to provide. Those with large estates might recruit from these, and it seems probable that they were helped in this task by the local officers who acted as their agents in this important work; in 1415 Thomas, earl of Arundel, used his estates on the Welsh march as a recruiting ground.[10] Those with lesser estates, but with a measure of local standing and influence often came at the head of men many of whose names suggest that their origins were to be found within the boundaries of one or two counties. A local base could provide a valuable background for drawing men into military service, so that some captains appeared at the post of embarkation with more men in their retinue than they had undertaken to provide.[11] Some, although they lacked a formal indenture, none the less turned up at Southampton with a retinue, ready to serve.[12]

[7] C. Given-Wilson, *The royal household and the king's affinity. Service, politics, and finance in England, 1360–1413* (New Haven/London, 1986), pp. 211, 221–3.
[8] *CCR, 1413–1419*, pp. 270, 352; PRO, E 403/622, m.12; 629, m.10; 649, m.2. Annuitants of the duchy of Lancaster who failed to accompany the king to Calais in September 1416 were not to have their annuities paid to them (PRO, DL 42/17, fo.120v).
[9] PRO, E 403/624, m.14.
[10] PRO, E 403/621, m.4.
[11] Sir Thomas Erpingham, for example, came with too many in July 1415 (PRO, E 101/44/30/3).
[12] See the king's signet letter of 17 July 1415 in which he ordered Nicholas Longford to be paid for himself and his retinue of twenty-four men, even though he had no indenture (PRO, E 101/46/3). The letter is not calendared in *Signet letters*, ed. Kirby.

The possibility of this happening was the result of the recruiting effort carried out by a number of royal officers and agents in different parts of the country. In the spring of 1415, for instance, royal messengers were despatched to the sheriffs and to many town authorities requiring that they raise men to join the king's forthcoming expedition to France.[13] In this way, both rural and urban areas became potential sources of manpower. It was through such an application of this system that, in 1415, John Merbury, chamberlain of South Wales, was able to make an indenture with the king for the provision of several hundred archers (predominantly foot archers) who may either have remained together as a contingent or have been absorbed into the retinues of some of the captains who had made agreements with the king.[14] In the same year Richard Urswick, sheriff of Lancashire, paid for 500 archers, presumably drawn from the fertile recruiting ground of Lancashire, who entered in equal numbers the retinues of eight knights and two esquires who had sealed indentures to serve the king in his wars.[15]

The king also employed commissioners to raise troops in other ways. In 1420 Robert Waterton was sent in this capacity to Yorkshire to exhort the gentlemen of York to join the army in France. He was, as he wrote to the king, to 'exyte and stirre sych as bene able gentilmen wythin the shyre and the contree . . . to kome ovyr to yowe at your wage, armyd and arayde as langys [is appropriate] to thaire astate to do yowe servyce'. He would, he assured the king, 'speke with many of the gentyls' at the next Session of the Peace which would take place in York a few days later, and then let him know what success he had had.[16] But as he and his colleague, Anthony St Quentin, found when performing the same task in the same county a year later, recruiting men, even those suitably qualified in terms of wealth (the qualification 'ryght suffisaunt of lyvelode' suggests that those chosen would incur some expenses) and training, was not always easy. Excuse was piled on excuse. One knight said he had acted as sheriff, another that he had been a collector of the fifteenth, the lay subsidy: both clearly felt that they had already made their contribution to the general welfare. Some claimed poor or bad health: one feared to go abroad 'for fear of seknese'. Several claimed that war, both in France and against the Scots, had already cost them a good deal, with the implication that

[13] PRO, E 403/621, m.4.
[14] PRO, E 101/46/20.
[15] PRO, E 101/46/35; copy in BL, Add. Ms 24512, fos 149–50. See also, for example, E 403/624, m.3; 629, m.12 (Cheshire and Lancashire); 649, m.7 (Cheshire only); SC6/776, mm.2d-3d (lists of knights and esquires from these counties in 1415).
[16] BL, Cotton Ms Vespasian F xiii, no.74; *Original letters*, ed. Ellis, 1st series, i, 6–7.

they would not contribute any more; one insisted that it would cost him too much to buy horse or arms. Of William Thomlynson it was noted that he was 'abull of persone [but] sais he is no gentilman'.[17] There seemed to be no way round that problem.

In Lincolnshire the problem was tackled a little differently. On 15 April 1421 the king, who was in Lincoln at the time, wrote to the bishop, Lord Willoughby, Lord de la Ware, the dean of the cathedral and Sir Ralph Rocheford asking them to arrange a meeting between themselves and the abbots, priors, knights and esquires and other people of substance from within the county to discuss who, being suitable, might be approached with a view to carrying out military service in France for the king, and at his wages. Those who agreed were to come to Westminster on 12 May, where they would be given their instructions. Probably as a means of reassuring them, they were told that steps would be taken for them to receive payment from subsidies collected locally.[18]

Henry drew his men from all over the country, many of them from towns. Some came from Ireland. The prior of Kilmain, with 200 horsemen and 300 men on foot, passed through Southampton before crossing over to serve the king at the siege of Rouen in the autumn of 1418; they were to be remembered for their rather wild behaviour as well as their outlandish clothing habits.[19] Others came from Wales, both north and south;[20] yet the large majority were English. As the Black Prince had found in the previous century, the north-western counties provided a very substantial proportion of those who came to fight for the king.[21] In the case of Henry, he was not only king but duke of Lancaster and earl of Chester as well. During the Welsh revolt of his father's reign he had found how being earl of Chester could

---

[17] PRO, E 101/55/13; discussed by A.E. Goodman, 'Responses to requests in Yorkshire for military service under Henry V', *Northern History*, 17 (1981), 240–52. Only about one in six approached agreed to serve (E. Powell, *Kingship, law and society. Criminal justice in the reign of Henry V* (Oxford, 1989), p. 233, n.14), while in Norfolk the royal commissioners received no positive response (*PPC*, ii, 246–8).

[18] Lincoln, Lincolnshire Archives Office, Reg.16, fos 240v-241.

[19] *An anthology of chancery English*, ed. J.H. Fisher, M. Richardson and J.L. Fisher (Knoxville, 1984), p. 98; *Signet letters*, ed. Kirby, no.830; *Issues of the Exchequer*, ed. F. Devon (London, 1837), p. 356; *Brut*, ii, 397–8.

[20] E.g., PRO, E 403/645, m.6.

[21] P. Morgan, *War and society in medieval Cheshire, 1277–1403* (Chetham Soc., Manchester, 1987); M.J. Bennett, *Community, class and careerism. Cheshire and Lancashire society in the age of Sir Gawain and the Green Knight* (Cambridge, 1983), ch.9. Henry was able to offer the inducement of a pardon to many in return for an undertaking to serve in the war. A number of notable soldiers who went to France had had brushes with the law (Powell, *Kingship, law and society*, pp. 232–40). The author of the *Gesta* commented (p. 55) on the presence of thieves among those serving in the royal army in 1415.

help in providing both soldiers and money. Now, as king, he had the duchy of Lancaster lands as well as those of Cornwall. Of these, the two northern counties proved to be good recruiting grounds, both in terms of knights and of ordinary soldiers.

From indentures, accounts and chronicles it is possible to gain a reasonable idea of what the army under Henry V consisted of, and what was expected of it. Indentures, for instance, list the numbers and ranks of those above the rank of esquire, with a few 'gentilmen' added,[22] the position of members of the king's household being sometimes stated. The higher the rank of the captain, the higher, too, the rank (and, by implication, the skill and experience) of those who accompanied him. In 1415 Clarence agreed to serve with 240 men-at-arms, which included himself, one earl, two bannerets, fourteen knights and 222 esquires, together with 720 mounted archers;[23] Gloucester was to have 200 men-at-arms, comprising himself, six knights and 193 esquires, in addition to 600 mounted archers;[24] Edward, duke of York,[25] Thomas, earl of Dorset,[26] and Thomas, earl of Arundel,[27] each contracted to bring 100 men-at-arms (of whom, in each case, well over ninety per cent were esquires) and 300 mounted archers. By comparison with most, these were very large retinues; even the earl of Salisbury could undertake to bring only 120 men in all.[28] Lesser lords might agree to bring men-at-arms of unspecified rank, while men of lower social rank came at the head of a tiny handful of men-at-arms (or none at all) and a small group of foot archers. Retinues varied very much in size, a factor which emphasizes to us how widely the responsibility for getting Henry's army together had been spread.

The army which Henry took to France in 1415 may have numbered some 10,500 fighting men, of whom (in broad figures) forty per cent were mounted archers, thirty-five per cent foot archers and twenty-five per cent men-at-arms, usually mounted. This meant that sixty-five per cent of the army had one or more mounts. The composition of the fighting force tells us something of what Henry may have been planning to do. The presence of so many mounted soldiers on a campaign dominated at first by a major siege suggests that the king may have had more in mind than simply capturing Harfleur, for which

[22] E.g., John de Wynyngton in 1415 (PRO, CHES 2/88, m.5); John Ferrour and Richard Harewood in 1421–22 (E 101/407/7); Everard Dygby in 1422 (*CCR, 1419–1422*, p. 186).
[23] PRO, E 404/31/155.
[24] Ibid., no.250.
[25] Ibid., no.184; E 101/69/389.
[26] E 404/31/238.
[27] Ibid., no.149.
[28] Ibid., no.174.

purpose a smaller mounted force might have been sufficient. So many mounted archers indicates that, had the siege been completed more quickly, Henry might have advanced into France rather further than he did. Their presence, however, made more feasible the march to Calais which, with the confidence reflected in the *Gesta*, could be carried out in a few days.

The indentures for 1415 also underline Henry's determination to capture Harfleur, whatever the effort might take. Crossbowmen (with a weapon more effective against immobile targets, such as are more likely to be found at a siege) were brought in from Gascony;[29] 120 miners, who may have come from the Forest of Dean area (six of them receiving the wages of esquires, the remainder those of archers), remind us that much effort was likely to be spent in trying to bring about the collapse of the walls and bastions of Harfleur.[30] A variety of labourers, armourers (several, judging by their names, not English),[31] pavilion and tent-makers,[32] and cordwainers[33] to make shoes suggest that a siege-situation was envisaged, one which would not be over all that quickly.

The evidence of accounts makes it amply clear that the neat divisions of retinues, each listed with the name of its leader, which may have sailed together soon began to break up. Many men, we know from the chronicles, died at the siege, most from sickness; others became ill, had to be granted certificates allowing them to leave, and were then taken home by ship.[34] Lists which are probably incomplete suggest that at least 1687 men were officially regarded as unfit for service. They include a wide cross-section of people: Clarence; the earl marshal; knights such as John Fastolf; Thomas Rodborne, the king's confessor; the crews of a number of ships; three minstrels accompanying the earl of Arundel, saddlers, smiths, stablemen, labourers and three hangmen.[35]

It is likely that sickness accounted for some fifteen per cent of the total English manpower at Harfleur, and perhaps more. Sickness, we may recall, also raged inside the walls, and may have had its effects on those who came into the town after its capture, their symptoms developing only on the march to Calais: the army which arrived at Agincourt was numerically smaller than the one which had left

[29] Ibid., no.315.
[30] Ibid., no.386. They were led by the Herefordshire veteran, Sir John Greyndore, an old comrade-in-arms of the king.
[31] Ibid., no.437. They included one Nichol de Hongery.
[32] Ibid., no.416.
[33] Ibid., no.409.
[34] 'Infirmitates' (PRO, E 101/45/14/1, 2); *Gesta*, p. 59.
[35] PRO, E 101/44/30/1; 45/1.

Harfleur a fortnight or so earlier.[36] Death and sickness, therefore, were significant factors in changing the face of the English army between August and October 1415. Other factors played their part, too. Some men were killed at Harfleur; others remained behind in the composite garrison which was created and left under the charge of the earl of Dorset.[37] A number were captured on the way to Agincourt, some only the day before the battle,[38] others still during the battle itself. Some died on the field, one killed 'cum uno gune'.[39] Some were to die at Calais, from wounds, sickness, exhaustion? We know not.

The effect on retinues must have varied considerably. Sir Rowland Leynthale left England with a retinue of forty-eight persons, including himself. Of these, three men-at-arms were sent home sick, and two archers were killed at Harfleur, while the remaining forty-three persons, having survived the battle of Agincourt, returned safely to England.[40] Sir Richard de Kyghley left Lancashire at the head of two groups. One consisted of fifty archers whom he had contracted to bring to the king at Southampton.[41] Of these, ten (or twenty per cent) became ill and were sent home before the fall of Harfleur; six (twelve per cent) died there; eight (sixteen per cent) were left as members of the garrison; seven more (fourteen per cent), having survived the march to Agincourt, were captured on the eve of the battle: only nineteen (thirty-eight per cent) of the original group made their way home in November.[42] The second group consisted of Kyghley's retinue of six men-at-arms and eighteen archers which, including himself, made up twenty-five men. Of these, two archers (eight per cent) fell ill and returned to England; one man-at-arms (four per cent) died at Harfleur, as did three more men-at-arms, including Kyghley himself (twelve per cent) at the battle of Agincourt, where four archers (sixteen per cent) were also killed. Fifteen (sixty per cent) returned home.[43] This meant that one third of Kyghley's retinue (eight out of twenty-five) died while serving the king; that half the dead were men-at-arms; and that over half the men-at-arms (four out of seven) who left England never returned; while Harfleur claimed three victims from the original twenty-five arrivals. Such figures were not typical, but they cause us to modify the statements put about by the chroniclers that few Englishmen died at Agincourt. Only by contrast with

[36] BL, Add. Ms 24513, fo.23.
[37] Sir Thomas Erpingham, for instance, stayed at Harfleur (ibid., fo.21).
[38] '. . . le iour prochain devant la bataille' (PRO, E 101/44/29).
[39] Ibid., 47/32.
[40] Ibid., 46/13.
[41] Ibid., 46/35; BL, Add. Ms 24512, fo.149.
[42] PRO, E 101/44/29.
[43] PRO, E 101/46/5; 69/386; E 404/31/252.

the number of French killed can this claim be said to have any meaning. Nearly thirty per cent of Kyghley's original force did not survive the battle: of those who got there, an even higher proportion did not leave the field alive.[44]

The principle of recruitment by indenture remained the standard practice through the reign. The army of 1417 numbered just over 10,000, but of that number the ratio of archers had gone up from about 1:3 to 1:3.5, a small but interesting change, important as emphasizing the more significant fall in men-at-arms of about eight per cent, as well as a decline in the number of knights who served as captains or in the retinues of those of higher rank. A reinforcement of some 2000 men in 1418 brought the number of fighting men available to Henry to a figure in the order of 12–13,000, a total which was maintained into 1420, when some 1200 crossed over to France in the retinue of the duke of Bedford.

By this time the military needs of the English had changed. It is clear why, in both 1415 and 1417, major efforts at providing 10,000 or more fighting men should have become necessary. Thereafter, requirements were different. It is significant that, after the fall of Rouen early in 1419, Henry should have appealed for more men to join him from England; very few did so, and he managed to do without them. The reason for his ability to do so is clear. The conquest was being advanced almost as much by diplomacy as by war, and more and more men could now be made to fulfil the task which followed logically upon earlier military successes: manning the garrisons of castles and towns now in English control.[45] Furthermore, as the conquest moved further away from the Channel coast, so the needs of Harfleur became less demanding.

R.A. Newhall calculated how the garrisoning obligations of the English changed between 1416 and 1420, years which saw a developing commitment of English arms in Normandy. Early in 1416 the garrison at Harfleur had numbered some 1420 men;[46] by 1417 it was about 590, but had risen to over 700 by the year 1418. By March 1419, with the war moving away, it was down to 311; by November 1419 a mere 221 kept watch on the place. By contrast, however, garrison commitments elsewhere rose as the successes of 1418 multiplied, so that by the end of that year a force of at least 3000 – probably

[44] Jacob (*Henry V*, p. 106) accepted a figure of some 400–500 English dead. Later (*Fifteenth century*, p. 156) he preferred a figure of 'below 300'. This seems the more likely.

[45] It is possible that the limited military activity which gave way to diplomacy in 1419 was a result of the poor response to Henry's appeal and to a growing sense of restlessness among the soldiery.

[46] PRO, E 404/31/585.

more than a quarter of the total English force in Normandy – was occupied in garrison duties. By 1419 that figure had risen by another thousand (found, probably, from among Henry's army, which did little fighting in that year, and, significantly, from the feudal service which Henry was beginning to demand from those to whom he was granting lands within the duchy); in 1420 the garrison army was 4000-strong.[47]

As would be expected, Henry's army did not consist solely of fighting men. Attention has already been drawn to a number of different occupations found among the sick sent home from Harfleur. An army was accompanied by a good deal of equipment, so that a number of trades provided men whose work would be partly that of maintenance and repair, partly that of making from new. Carpenters and wheelwrights would be required for the vital task of keeping the army on the move; food had to be cooked, and coopers were needed in the kitchens to see that the supply of beer or wine was properly stored and made available when required. The presence of fletchers indicates that although large numbers of arrows were sent from England, the need to provide more on the spot had been foreseen, while the makers of various forms of armour (including mail) were brought over to pursue their occupations and keep the soldiers properly armed.

The army also had its small medical corps. Master Nicholas Colnet, described as 'physician', served on the expedition of 1415, and was given three archers for his protection.[48] Thomas Morstede and William Bradwardyn, 'noz surgeons', appear to have acted as a team. In April 1415 both agreed to serve the king abroad for one year. Like Colnet, they were to have a guard of archers, who were very certainly needed, since they were each to be accompanied by nine surgeons, making a team of twenty in all. On the expedition of 1415 they were paid from the day they mustered at Southampton on 8 July until their return to England on 24 November, a total of one quarter and 49 days, the cost to the country of their wages and 'regards' (financial benefits) being £230 11s. 8d.[49] Perhaps they were luckier than most to have survived the sickness which afflicted so many at Harfleur and the battle of Agincourt, at which they were present.

Moving an army was, in a very real sense, to move the court, too, as the evidence of 1415 shows. Indentures make it abundantly clear that many of those who accompanied the army, but who had no fighting role, were members of the king's normal entourage, present to perform the many daily tasks which would have been carried out

[47] Figures are mostly taken from Newhall, *English conquest*, ch.5.
[48] PRO, E 404/31/359; E 101/69/381.
[49] PRO, E 101/48/1/1–5, 8.

had the king been in England. The household maintained its rightful place around the king even when he was on campaign. Members of the 'esculerie', the 'chambre', a whole staff of persons to set up and look after the king's tents and pavilions, a group of heralds ready to bear his messages, minstrels to play music, as well as William Kynwolmersh, the cofferer of the household, were in attendance.[50] Most notable – because least expected – was the presence not merely of two clerks of the chapel, but of the dean, Edmund Lacy, one day to become bishop of Exeter, and of some thirty or so other members of the king's spiritual staff.[51] Proof of the king's piety, it is also interesting evidence of the way in which the daily routine, war or no war, was pursued by the king and his household.

Providing an army with its requirements in horses and weapons was a major undertaking which, if not properly carried out, would have led to disaster. Horses were an important consideration, especially in an army which included, as that of 1415 in particular did, many men of high rank and social standing: dukes might have fifty horses, earls twenty-four, barons sixteen, men-at-arms four, and mounted archers one.[52] For the first expedition of 1415 this could have meant something in the order of 15,000 horses; in 1417 Henry's army would also have included a similar number,[53] while in April 1420 some 5000 horses are recorded as having been transported from Southampton to France.[54] The supply of oats shipped from Kent and Essex during these years suggests that England was being drawn upon as a source of food for these animals.[55]

Apart from the bow at Agincourt, the weapon which made the biggest impact on the war was the cannon. Henry had the good fortune to live at the moment in the development of this weapon when its effectiveness, which had been a factor of increasing importance during the past half century, was advancing quite rapidly, and when the counter-measures, which would be found in architecture, had not yet emerged. Henry, as the aggressor, had the full weight of cannon behind him, and both he and his brother, Gloucester, were to use it to good effect. Because of the very complexity of its structure, it would be some time before the English could manufacture artillery in France, although the quarries around Caen (which were used to provide stone for building in England and, indeed, for Henry's own chantry chapel

[50] PRO, E 404/31/408, 412, 416, 427, 401; BL, Add. Ms 24513, fo.6ov.
[51] PRO, E 404/31/411, 444.
[52] Newhall, *English conquest*, p. 194, n.27.
[53] Ibid., pp. 194, 191, n.7.
[54] PRO, E 403/645, mm.2–3, 6.
[55] Faversham to Rouen (ibid., m.6); Leigh and Maldon to Rouen (ibid., mm.6, 14).

at Westminster Abbey) were to supply stone for cannon shot, Caen being used as a form of ordnance depot during these years, artillery being taken to sieges by boat whenever possible.[56]

The preparation of cannon began early in the reign. At the Tower of London, the country's main armoury, smiths were at work in late 1413 and early 1414 for the king's secret needs,[57] while at the end of 1414 Nicholas Merbury, keeper of the Wardrobe which was responsible for the organization which lay behind the preparation for war, was already beginning to collect gunpowder.[58] The chroniclers leave us in no doubt that the artillery barrage played a significant part in bringing about the surrender of Harfleur. By 1416 the needs of war were on the increase: records of the purchase of iron cannon, iron for the making of 'machines', together with powder and stones,[59] emphasize the use being made of artillery of various kinds, a point which is reinforced by the presence of eighteen gunners in the garrison at Harfleur in that year.[60]

The records continue to refer to the preparation of weapons at home for transportation to France. In April 1418 a great gun was being made on Tower Hill ('apud Tourchill') in London, and coal, saltpetre and gunpowder were being purchased at the same time.[61] In October 1420 payment was made for 1600lb of gunpowder, while in May 1421 saltpetre was bought from a merchant from Catalonia.[62] The records also leave evidence of the wholesale provision of other, more traditional weapons, all extensively used: lances ('hastae'), bows,[63] arrows and strings were bought and then shipped in huge quantities. Bows and arrows made of ash were the best,[64] and in 1416 parliament had to take steps to stop this wood being used for other purposes, notably the making of clogs, which may have been the cause of the observations made by the king that the price of arrows was rising rather steeply.[65] It has been calculated that between 1418 and 1421 about 1,350,000 arrows may have been bought for the king and that between 1418 and 1422 £2457 2s. 6d. was spent by the English exchequer on bows and arrows alone.[66]

---

[56] BN, Ms fr.26043/5439; *Signet letters*, ed. Kirby, no.972.
[57] PRO, E 403/614, m.2.
[58] Ibid., 619, m.2.
[59] Ibid., 624, mm.7–8.
[60] Ibid., 624, m.11; E 404/31/585.
[61] PRO, E 403/636, m.1.
[62] Ibid., 646, m.1; 649, m.5.
[63] Ibid., 621, mm.4, 5; 646, m.10.
[64] See the reference to a cedar fletcher (1421) (ibid., 646, m.10).
[65] *RP*, iv, 103, cited by Newhall, *English conquest*, p. 259.
[66] Based on Newhall, *English conquest*, pp. 260–1 and n.66. On 16 July 1421 the treasurer ordered 1,190,000 wing feathers of geese to be raised from twenty-eight counties and brought to London before 15 August (*CCR, 1419–1422*, p. 166).

The acquisition of a regular supply of food was a constant problem which faced all those in charge of military units, of whatever size. On the sealing of indentures of service with the crown, a captain received a quarter's wage in advance, and a further quarter in advance when his retinue arrived at the meeting point (often a port) to be mustered there. Thereafter, the captain was paid by the quarter in arrears, so that his third payment was not received until the end of the ninth month. He was, however, expected to do a number of things with the money which he had received in advance: one was to ensure that he and his retinue had sufficient food with them to last two months.[67] Provided that there was no long delay before sailing, this meant that an army arriving on French soil should have had no worries about where its next meal would come from for at least some weeks. The advantages of this were considerable: the army had time to settle to new conditions after landing and, most important in Henry's mind, sufficiency of provisions meant that it was easier to keep discipline over his men, with fewer disputes between soldiers and civilians likely to arise.

The army could find its food in a number of ways. Provisions could come from England, as much of them did, particularly in the early part of the reign. Harfleur, with its large garrison, needed large stocks of food; it was the ability of the French both to prevent these coming from England and to stop the army from using the surrounding region as an area from which supplies could be obtained which led Thomas Beaufort to go on a foraging expedition which led to the near-disastrous skirmish at Valmont in March 1416.[68] Indeed the skirmish may serve as a reminder of the supreme importance of keeping castle garrisons well supplied, and what might happen if they were not. But even the field armies needed food to be provided for them. Until the army was well established in Normandy, much of its food came from England, some of it going directly (by sea and river) to the king at Caen late in 1417,[69] some passing through the hands of Reginald Curteys, the victualler at Harfleur.[70] His stock would have included corn, oats, beans and peas; meat in the form of beef and bacon; fish, some fresh, some dried; honey for sweetening; wine and beer.[71] While the siege of Rouen was taking place in 1418–19, large quantities of

[67] Sometimes it was much longer – six months, according to one royal order of 1417 (*CCR, 1413–1419*, p. 380).
[68] *Gesta*, p. 115.
[69] PRO, E 403/633, m.11; *CCR, 1413–1419*, pp. 438–9.
[70] In November 1415 exports of grain other than to Calais and Harfleur were forbidden (*CCR, 1413–1419*, p. 236).
[71] All were included in the Harfleur diet of 1416 (PRO, E 404/32/87).

fish were sent there by boat,[72] together with beer, flour, vinegar and mustard seed, while the king's household had its wheat sent directly by boat from Chichester to Rouen.[73] From early on London was a great provider, and it was to the capital that Henry wrote at the time of the siege of Rouen to ask for provisions, in particular for beer.[74]

Food continued to come from England even in 1418 when the supply lines in Normandy had become fairly well established. The king, anxious to maintain good relations with the local population, tried to ensure that as little demand as possible was made of it by the soldiers. In its place, a system of purveyance, with a 'victualler royal' and at least one subordinate, largely dependent upon Breton, English and Norman merchants, helped to provide the field army and the garrisons with what they required through markets which supplied the needs of the soldiers. One thing which might have been attempted was to pay soldiers in kind in lieu of wages. This does not appear to have been tried.[75]

The military 'machine' available to Henry had to be run efficiently to make it successful. War could only be won if it were waged in an orderly fashion. Matters of importance, such as the preparation of a campaign, could not be left to chance; the detail of preparation was of significance, and emphasis on such detail was typical of Henry's approach to so much of what he did. Henry liked to be in full command of what he was doing. He liked, too, to be in command of his soldiers: an army had to be an ordered force, well disciplined, kept in check. Contemporaries recognized Henry's ability to control his armies and, by implication, pointed to what was one of the basic causes of his success. They admired his sense of order, hardly typical of so many of the military commanders of the past two or three generations. Disorder in the army, which would have done his cause in Normandy such harm and earned him antagonism rather than acceptance from the people of the duchy (his subjects, as he saw them), was something which he had to stamp out. The problem had surfaced in the previous century to become a subject much discussed among contemporary commentators, and had caused Richard II to issue ordinances of war in 1385 in an attempt to restore his authority over the army.[76] It was an example which Henry was, in due course, to follow.

[72] PRO, E 403/639, mm.6, 15.

[73] Ibid., 644, m.16. It also enjoyed stockfish and salmon in July 1420 (ibid., 645, m.10).

[74] Ibid., 640, mm.4, 8; *Memorials of London*, pp. 664–5.

[75] On this point, however, see p. 397, below.

[76] *The Black Book of the Admiralty*, ed. T. Twiss (4 vols, RS, London, 1871–76), i, 453–8.

He made his point early on, at the fall of Harfleur in 1415. Henry's priorities were to establish rights for the civilian population of the town, including old men, women and children, and what might and might not be done to them.[77] At Caen, in 1417, he issued rules about the treatment of the population of a town which, according to the generally accepted and legally enforced military laws of the day, had forfeited every right to mercy as a result of its refusal to surrender when called upon to do so.[78] If, in this case (as in that of Harfleur), Henry's practical intention had been to prevent scenes of disorder all too often associated with the capture of a town which had resisted, the emphasis which he appears to have placed on his regulations was not so much the negative one that soldiers should commit no outrage against the civilian population, but the positive assertion that the population (if it did not oppose the English with force) and churches deserved to have their rights respected. Restrained behaviour was therefore expected, and infractions of the rule would be severely punished. That the king meant business was made plain by those chroniclers who recounted the story of the soldier who, not long afterwards on the march to Calais, thought that he had the chance of paying his way by stealing a sacred vessel (a pyx) from a church which the army was passing. His immediate execution by hanging, on the king's orders, for what was a flagrant disregard of the regulations may have come at a good moment for Henry, perhaps in need of re-establishing his authority over his army; but, as told by the chroniclers, the incident was proof to them that the king was a man who, recognizing the need for discipline, had taken steps to enforce it, and had punished the offender who had chosen to challenge him.[79]

It was at Mantes, some time during 1419, that Henry issued his main war ordinances.[80] Essentially their character was twofold. In the first place they tried to set out that all military activity should be carried out in an orderly fashion, the pattern of which should be made known to all, not with the intention of stifling initiative but in the hope that the army would become an efficient, and therefore effective, instrument of war. It was to be an army under command (the king was the supreme commander), with the legal and disciplinary authority of the captains emphasized. These were now given an enhanced

[77] *Gesta*, pp. 26, n.1, 27, 61.

[78] *Brut*, ii, 384.

[79] *Gesta*, p. 69; *First English Life*, pp. 44-5.

[80] N.H. Nicolas, *History of the battle of Agincourt* (2nd edn, London, 1832), appendix 8, pp. 31-40; *Black Book*, i, 459-72; *The essential portions of Nicholas Upton's De Studio Militari, before 1446*, ed. F.P. Barnard (Oxford, 1931), pp. 33-48; *Excerpta Historica, or Illustrations of English History*, ed. S. Bentley (London, 1833), pp. 30-40; see also BL, Add. Ms 38525, fos 111-19.

authority; at the same time, their responsibilities to the king for their soldiers were increased, and the full power of the indenture as a contract of service to which men could be held (indiscipline would soon come to be seen as a breaking of a contract) was beginning to emerge.

At the same time, implicitly in several of the clauses, more explicitly in others, the obligation not to molest those who did not stand in the army's way (a member of the clergy, if armed, could be taken) and the right of the ploughman or the merchant going about his work to be left unhindered were emphasized. Pillaging after peace or truce had been declared was forbidden; children under fourteen years of age were not to be taken prisoner, and captives were to be handed over to authority. The tone of the text is conciliatory: there was to be no wanton destruction of property; the authority of those in charge within the army itself was to be respected. And in case any should claim that he did not know what the new rules of the game were, captains had instructions to proclaim them aloud to all their soldiers.

It would be absurd to try to claim that Henry's attempt to impose strict order upon his army was wholly successful. The courts of Normandy, as well as the court of the constable (an office held by Clarence), in effect a military tribunal, had many cases heard before them in the years of Henry's reign and later.[81] But a less than one hundred per cent success story should not prevent us from appreciating the importance of what Henry was trying to do, both in terms of the long-term problem of the establishment of effective authority over the soldier (to which Henry's reign is a contribution) and of the short-term advantages which there were in it both for the success of the English army in France and for the wellbeing of the native population of that country.[82]

THE NAVY

The successes won by Henry and his army on land should not allow us to ignore the importance of the role played by naval forces in the successful pursuit of the war. No study of Henry V can leave this aspect of war undiscussed, for two reasons. The first is the growing appreciation in this reign of the role which the sea, seamen and ships should have in any prolonged conflict with France. The second is the personal interest which Henry showed in matters naval and his

---

[81] R.A. Newhall, 'Discipline in an English army of the fifteenth century', *The military historian and economist*, 2 (1917), 141–51.

[82] For the regulations issued by Henry on 6 September 1419 regarding the authority given to his captains, see 'Rôles normands et français', no.653.

understanding of how an active naval policy could further England's war aims. Henry V was not the founder of the English navy, a role which may be claimed with greater justice by Henry VIII. Yet his fleet was 'the finest task force ever seen in England' before the age of the Tudors, and fifteen years after the king's death the author of the *Libelle of Englyshe Polycye*, advocating a strong English presence at sea, could look back on the previous reign as a time when English maritime strength had existed for all to see.[83] How far was that opinion justified?

An aspect of that strength was closely connected to the crown's policy of maintaining order upon the sea, so that commercial traffic could circulate freely and in safety, all this being part of the 'bon governaunce' promised by Henry. As the parliamentary evidence makes clear, the threat to orderly trade at sea had become a major problem during the early years of the century. The point was raised by Henry Beaufort on more than one occasion in the addresses which, as chancellor, he made at the beginning of parliamentary sessions. In 1414 an attempt was made to increase the authority of royal agents by the passing of legislation known as the Statute of Truces, by which conservators of truces would have power to enforce strict measures against those who flouted the law either by acts of violence at sea without royal approval or in contravention of safe-conducts properly issued, acts said to be 'to the great dishonour of the king and contrary to his dignity'.[84]

Such legislation reflected the fact that, early in his career, Henry had come to appreciate the wider significance of the sea. He understood the dangers risked by Englishmen who ventured on to it, in particular by those who lived in the coastal areas, all liable to attack from Frenchmen, especially from those based at Harfleur. There can be little doubt that, as Prince, Henry would have watched with increasing anxiety and irritation the activity of French naval forces based there, backed by the services offered by the 'Clos des Galées' or shipyard, in Rouen. It would have brought home to him the importance of achieving a high level of naval power both to protect English maritime interests in the widest sense and, should there be war, to support military endeavour on land. It would be one thing to wrest control of Harfleur from the enemy; quite another to maintain English power there in the years to follow. Henry's experience in the war against the Welsh had shown him the value of being able to besiege places on the coast of the principality through the use of naval power.

[83] C.F. Richmond, 'Royal administration and the keeping of the seas, 1422–1485' (Univ. of Oxford D.Phil thesis, 1963), p. 26; *The Libelle of Englyshe Polycye*, ed. G. Warner (Oxford, 1926), pp. 51–3.
[84] *Black Book*, i, 414. See ch.14 for the Statute of Truces.

It is no coincidence that the number of ships owned by Henry IV increased very considerably (from two to seven, or possibly eight) in the year 1410,[85] the very year that Henry, then Prince, took control of the council. The likelihood is that the increase was due to a conscious decision taken by him, probably with encouragement and support from Henry and Thomas Beaufort, both known to have had an interest in guarding the sea. If this was so, it appears that Henry had already understood the importance of having rapid and easy access to ships, particularly in periods of emergency.

It was the war against France which demanded the encouragement, at the highest level, of English naval potential. It is to Henry's credit, and an essential, if insufficiently well-appreciated element of his grasp of military affairs, that he made full use of that potential. The notable victory won by Bedford off Harfleur on 15 August 1416 rightly brought recognition both to him and to those whom he led. At the same time, however, it was made possible by the planning and organization which had been taking place for a period of some two years, and which was characteristic of the king's ability as a leader in war, as well as of his understanding of the potential which England might call upon to defend her interests and achieve her ends.

The Channel was both a barrier and a road. As a barrier it separated the island kingdom from the continental mainland, principally from France. As a road, it was the way which any force, large or small, wishing to attack the other had to travel. The sea, therefore, was certain to be an area of contention, control of which, at crucial times, was bound to be important. How far did control, either as a concept or as a reality, have any real meaning in the context of the fifteenth century? Given the paucity of ships of war and the relatively primitive state of weapons used in battle at sea (which, to have any effect, needed to be used at close range), the extent of physical control to be won by direct confrontation was bound to be limited. The only sense in which the concept was at all meaningful was in terms of deterrence, by showing the enemy that his plans and intentions were known in advance (hence the significance of the growing use of espionage), and by effectively getting to the scene of any possible action before him. Control implied readiness, not merely in port (although that was to be of great importance), but upon the very sea itself, first of all to deter the enemy from venturing out and, if that failed, to be in place and fully prepared to give chase with the intention of destroying or, better still, of capturing his vessels, so making the sea safe for trade or for the transport of armies.[86] The aim was to convey

[85] I owe this information to Dr Ian Friel.
[86] It is surely no coincidence that ch.24 of the *Gesta* is largely concerned with naval affairs in the Channel.

the message 'Hands off . . . or else . . .'. If the enemy ventured out, he did so at his own risk, for 'with a fleet at sea the initiative had been won'.[87] In a very practical sense 'control of the sea' could be effectively achieved by the squadron or flotilla on patrol.

It is noticeable, then, that as Henry's plans for invasion developed, late in 1414 and early in 1415, so the records of expenses involving service at sea begin to multiply: the building of the 'great ship', *The Trinity*, at Greenwich and the *Grace Dieu* (a little later) at South-ampton;[88] consultations held at the royal manor of Kennington, to the south of London, between the king and men from the ports of Sandwich, Winchelsea, Bristol, Hull and Newcastle-upon-Tyne at which we may reasonably suppose that plans for the expedition to France, and its naval requirements, were discussed; the further attempt, by the king, to build up the number of ships available to him by the purchase of a 'barge', the *Katherine de Gerand*, from Brit-tany;[89] and the appointment of Thomas, Lord Carew (who had served the Prince well in Wales some years earlier), to serve at sea for fifty days on patrol.[90] In March 1415 Dorset, who was admiral, received orders to arrest, as a matter of urgency, all vessels of twenty tons and over, and have them sent to Southampton by the beginning of May, no doubt for refitting in anticipation of a later departure. No ship, of whatever nationality, was to be allowed to leave port without special command of the king.[91] By April Henry was requiring the Cinque Ports to send ships to sea to resist the French, while his representatives were in Holland and Zeeland raising vessels for the expedition which he was personally planning to lead to France.[92] The need to provide transports, and to ensure that they reached their destinations with the least loss and trouble, was already coming to preoccupy the king.

By early 1415 an increasing number of men were being recruited and ships impressed for patrolling the sea. This needed to be done with two purposes in mind. The southern coastline and its ports had to be guarded against threats from attack by the French and their allies, notably the Castilians; and, secondly, steps had to be taken to

[87] C.F. Richmond, 'English naval power in the fifteenth century', *History*, 52 (1967), 3.

[88] PRO, E 403/619, m.3; 629, m.13.

[89] Ibid., 619, m.10.

[90] PRO, E 101/48/9/6.

[91] *CCR, 1413–1419*, p. 162.

[92] PRO, E 403/621, mm.2, 3 and 5. Henry employed ships and sailors from the Low Countries for much of his reign (E 101/48/15, 21, 22; E 364/57, m.4d; E 403/624, m.6; 645, m.8), just as he hired men with knowledge of artillery from those parts. Expenses for ships from those parts were still being settled in 1433 (Richmond, 'Royal administration', p. 50, n.1).

create favourable conditions for the enterprise to be undertaken in the summer. The scale and importance of what was done can, in some sense, be measured by the reaction of ship-owners, who organized a petition to the king in the parliament of 1415 for the restoration of the old rate of payment of 3s. 4d. a ton per quarter for vessels impressed for royal service.[93] In the following year, with Harfleur besieged by the French, and the need to get supplies and armaments to the beleaguered garrison now increasingly urgent, the tasks of escorting ships carrying reinforcements to Harfleur and of meeting any attack from the French or their allies coming from the west were given to the earl of Huntingdon who had, as his immediate subordinates, Sir Edward Courtenay and John, Lord Clifford.[94] In 1417 the unglamorous task of keeping the Channel free of hostile shipping was largely in the capable hands of Lord Carew,[95] although it was Edmund, earl of March (all doubts which may have existed at the time of the Southampton plot behind him, and now again in royal favour), who stole the chronicler's headlines when he 'skimmed the see' in the summer of that year, while at the end of June Huntingdon defeated a squadron of Genoese carracks off the Chef de Caux at the mouth of the Seine.[96] By 1418, with Henry now well in control in Normandy (Cherbourg had fallen in September), the threat to the Channel was beginning to recede, although Sir John Arundel served for six months at sea,[97] a duty in which Hugh Courtenay, second son of the earl of Devon, succeeded him in the following year and again in 1420.[98]

Signs that the enemy had been effectively chased or warned off the sea by the summer of 1417 are strongly suggested by two factors. The invasion fleet of 1417 appears to have had little trouble in getting itself to Normandy, and scarcely anything is heard of English losses at sea resulting from direct enemy action. The enemy's tactic now seems to have been to attack the ports and coastline of southern England, to prevent fleets from sailing or finding practical support at home. It was this policy which led to raids on Southampton and Portland in 1416.[99] In November 1417 Richard Spicer agreed to serve

[93] *RP*, iv, 79. See the payment made to the owner of the barge, the *Mary of Bridgwater*, for six weeks service in the summer of 1415 (PRO, E 404/31/532). Payment could be made indirectly, by exempting cargoes from custom dues at the moment of arrival in port prior to arrest for royal service (PRO, E 364/50, m.3).

[94] PRO, E 403/624, m.1; Devon, *Issues of the Exchequer*, p. 346.

[95] PRO, E 101/70/572; E 404/32/274; Newhall, *English conquest*, p. 196.

[96] *Brut*, ii, 383; *Chronicles of London*, ed. Kingsford, p. 71.

[97] PRO, E 403/633, m.16.

[98] PRO, E 101/70/640; Newhall, *English conquest*, pp. 198-9.

[99] *Gesta*, pp. 135-7; *Signet letters*, ed. Kirby, no.856; *Anthology of Chancery English*, no.51.

for three months at sea with forty archers to guard the ships at South-ampton.[100] The following year witnessed a scare that a Castilian fleet might attack the naval bases on the south coast; lest it should give the slip to Sir John Arundel and his fifteen vessels, the king gave orders that defences should be built at Portsmouth, to include a tower which would enable the king's ships, the town and the country round about to be defended.[101]

The evidence strongly suggests that, between 1415 and 1418, the English established an effective control over the Channel, although they could not prevent the Scots shipping soldiers to France to help the dauphin. None the less, ships sailing from England to Normandy, whether they carried men, animals, weapons, food or the money with which to pay the king's army, needed some form of protection, and the provision of escorts made fairly constant demands for ships, crews and money. What was available to the king and to those who helped him organize the war effort? Like all his predecessors, Henry depended very largely upon the traditional right of the crown to sum-mon ship-owners to give him the use of their vessels in time of war. Every merchant ship was a potential fighting ship, once essential alterations had been carried out to the structure: largely the building of castles fore and aft in the case of a ship destined for fighting,[102] or the building of stalls in one intended to convey horses over the sea. Given time, patience and money, it was open to the king to secure for himself quite a large fleet in this way. But the procedures were slow, the delays frequent. Months before he knew that he would require a transport fleet, the king had to order the arrest of merchant ships, together with their masters and sailors, through the services of local port officials, admirals, the warden of the Cinque Ports, or special commissioners whose task it was to secure the use of all vessels, usually over twenty tons,[103] the masters being ordered to bring their ships to some suitable meeting point which, in this reign, was often South-ampton.[104] For such service, the owner received a small payment, the master and crew being paid regular wages of 6d. for the master, half that amount for sailors, according to the terms contained in the formal indentures.[105]

There were occasions, however, when the requirements could not

[100] PRO, E 404/33/202.
[101] PRO, E 403/636, m.13 (1418); 639, m.2 (1418); 644, m.5 (1419); Signet letters, ed. Kirby, no.809; Anthology of Chancery English, no.3.
[102] I. Friel, 'The documentary evidence for maritime technology in later medieval England and Wales' (Univ. of Keele Ph.D. thesis, 1990), p. 112.
[103] PRO, E 403/622, m.13; 629, mm.7, 11.
[104] E.g., PRO, E 403/621, m.3 (1415); 629, m.13 (1417).
[105] Newhall, English conquest, p. 195, n.32.

be met. In 1415 the king had to obtain assistance from the Low Countries, a fact which helps in understanding his policy of trying to come to, and remain on, good terms with duke John of Burgundy and William, count of Holland, whose acquiescence would be needed before vessels, intended for purposes of war, might be raised in those parts. In 1416 ships from Dordrecht were employed by Henry,[106] probably in anticipation of his expedition to relieve the hard-pressed port of Harfleur, while in the following year, that of the second invasion of Normandy, Dutch, Venetian and Genoese vessels were taken compulsorily into English service.[107]

The ways of securing ships and crews were traditional. What constituted the difference between the reign of Henry V and those of his predecessors was the involvement of the king himself in the work,[108] the scale of the enterprise being undertaken, and the response with which its requirements were met. Henry not only needed more ships (the way he had sought foreign vessels showed that), he also needed to control them himself. It was not an innovation for the crown to own ships; the novelty, which reflected both Henry's needs and his determination to meet them, lay in the number of ships actually belonging to the king himself which came to be used 'on his majesty's service'. Henry's father had never owned more than six ships (in 1401–02), but that figure had sunk to two in 1409. By contrast, his son already owned eight, three inherited from his father, only four months after his accession in 1413, while by July 1418 the figure was to rise to thirty-nine, never falling to less than thirty-two after 1417. It is not until the time of Henry VIII that we again find royal ships in such numbers.

While we should not be too readily influenced by such a contrasting set of figures (it is as well to recall that, in all probability, not every one of Henry's ships would have been in service at the same moment, since some, at least, would have been in yards for repairs), they do indicate that a development of considerable importance was taking place. Henry was having 'great ships' built for war;[109] he had one in 1415, but five years later the number had risen to four, one of which, the *Grace Dieu*, would prove to be but a stunning failure, while others, the *Trinity Royal* (built at Greenwich), the *Jesus* (from Winchelsea), the *Holy Ghost of the Tower* (a Spanish ship won through piracy,

[106] See above, n.92; PRO, E 403/624, m.6.
[107] Newhall, *English conquest*, p. 195. In 1417 at least one of Carew's vessels was a Venetian carrack (PRO, E 101/48/14).
[108] Henry is recorded as having visited the shipyard at Smallhythe in August 1416 (*Gesta*, p. 151).
[109] Much of this information was supplied by Dr Friel. See also Richmond, 'Royal administration', pp. 29–31.

and completely rebuilt at Southampton, to include elaborate decor-
ations of antelopes and swans, and the arms of St George, all closely
associated with the king), were to see active service at sea, either in
naval operations or transporting personnel to and from France.[110]
Together with eight balingers or barges, these appear to have been
the only vessels specially built for Henry.

It was the state of war, however, which gave the king his greatest
opportunity to secure vessels by legitimate capture at sea. The chronicles tell us of such occasions, the most notable being the battle won
by Bedford on 15 August 1416 and that achieved, off the Caux, by
the earl of Huntingdon on 29 June 1417. Both produced a crop of
vessels, including three Genoese carracks taken on the first occasion
and four on the second, which might be refitted or repaired before
entering the king's service, a total of nineteen in all for the reign. Of
these, the 'naves', or ships, were the most useful for the transportation
of goods, balingers (which the French used predominantly for war)
being employed for naval operations by the English, although they
also served a useful purpose as transporters of personnel and stores
in time of war.

As in the case of soldiers, much of our knowledge of the conditions
regulating those who served at sea comes from indentures. In terms
of nominal authority, the most important commander was Thomas
Beaufort, from 1416 duke of Exeter, one of the most able of the crown's
servants during this reign. As admiral, he had both social position
and practical power, and Henry was fortunate to have a supporter
both so capable and so close to him as the leading figure in the navy.
Under him there served a group of men, who included the earls of
Devon, Huntingdon and March, and Thomas, Lord Carew, who, like
Exeter, enjoyed high social position while at the same time proving
to be good and experienced commanders of the country's naval forces.
Leadership, under Henry V, was still in the hands of men of the
highest standing. At the same time he wished to make the best captains available for service to the crown and, probably, thereby to
make ships ready at short notice. Early in August 1417 Henry decided
to grant annuities to 'certein maistres for owr owne grete shippes,
carrakes, barges and balyngers'.[111] As was the case of other annuitants, he now placed these sea captains in a position of obligation to
him, so that he could call on them to give immediate service in time
of need. The king wanted to make his ships both quickly available
and efficient – this was one way of doing it.

The length of service contracted for varied considerably. Normally

[110] Carpenter-Turner, 'Southampton as a naval centre', pp. 41–2.
[111] *Signet letters*, ed. Kirby, no.808; *Anthology of Chancery English*, no.2.

not less than eighty days, it was often three months, sometimes four, and, in the case of Sir John Arundel who deputized for Dorset in 1418, six months. The vessels and crews were normally provided by the maritime community or its members (the Cinque Ports still owed service to the crown on certain occasions), the soldiers who joined them normally being recruited separately. Once again the terms of service were set out formally in the indenture. When Hugh Courtenay agreed to serve at sea 'en deffense du roiaume' for three months beginning on 1 May 1419, it was agreed that he should have the use of four carracks, one 'grande nief . . . La Marie', and other ships (niefs) to be assigned to him at Southampton. His indenture was also specific regarding certain important aspects of his service. He was to stay at sea for the entire period of three months, and was to come into port only to take on fresh water or in the case of bad weather at sea; he was to patrol chiefly between Dieppe and Cherbourg, and in particular in the Seine estuary, unless chasing enemy ships, in which case some of his own ships must be left to guard the mouth of the strategic river; and, in a condition reminiscent of the troubles at the beginning of the reign, he was to respect truces.[112] In the precise instructions, and in particular the need to observe truces, the hand of the king may be detectable.

Ships which left port ready to fight were manned by proper crews, who thus formed one element of a ship's company. The other consisted of those whose task it was to fight, men who might be lords, bannerets, knights, esquires (listed as men-at-arms) or archers. Whereas in a land army the ratio of men-at-arms to archers was usually 1:3, when recruiting forces to fight at sea the ratio of 1:2 was normally used. Figures which can be culled from indentures give some idea of the numbers involved. In January 1415 Sir Gilbert Talbot indented for fifty days' service at sea with 120 men-at-arms and 240 archers, undertaking not to come ashore for longer than one day and one night, unless forced to do so by the weather.[113] In 1416 Huntingdon was to lead 350 men-at-arms and 700 archers, while John, Lord Clifford, had a force of 200 men-at-arms and 400 archers, making a total of 550 and 1100. Since there was a time gap of more than two months

---

[112] PRO, E 101/70/640; E 404/34/274. The area to be patrolled included the coast of Normandy to which fishermen of the Cinque Ports went to fish (E 403/622, m.1). There may have been an element of fishery protection in what Courtenay was ordered to do. These instructions, and those given to John Cole and Thomas Treverak in 1418, to prevent harm being done to faithful lieges off the Norman coast, recall the disciplinary measures ordered by Henry to protect the material interests of his new subjects in Normandy. All reflect the king's respect for order, and his determination to achieve it.

[113] PRO, E 101/69/356.

between the indentures, those who served Clifford may already have served under Huntingdon.[114] In 1417 the numbers rose, 616 men-at-arms and 1232 archers serving under separate contracts made with Thomas, Lord Carew, Sir John Mortimer and Pons de Castelhon; in this case, since the forces mustered in different places (Carew at Dartmouth, the others at Winchelsea), we may be sure that each man had only been estimated once.[115]

The year 1418 may have seen a slight fall in numbers: Sir John Arundel, acting as deputy for Exeter, had charge of 365 men-at-arms (including those knights and himself) and 776 archers; Sir Richard Le Scrope led 120 men-at-arms and 240 archers, based on Kingston-upon-Hull, to counter Scottish threats by sea;[116] while John Cole and Thomas Treverak served at sea in the south and west with 60 men-at-arms and 120 archers, totalling 545 and 1136 for the year.[117] By 1419, to all appearances, the needs for armed service at sea had greatly diminished. Hugh Courtenay indented with 380 men-at-arms and 780 archers, while in the following year he did so again with 500 men-at-arms and 1000 archers for a period of seven months.[118] By 1421 the need to raise forces to patrol the Channel had further declined, although Sir William Bardolf was given charge of a fleet sent to sea in the spring.[119] The fifteen days' free service which the king demanded from the Cinque Ports, through Gloucester, their warden, in the spring of that same year, was probably only intended to supplement the fleet assembling to take his third expedition to France; little more than escort duty was being asked of them.[120]

The army of more than 7000 fighting men which, on the king's orders, was raised in the spring of 1416, and which the king intended to lead in person to relieve the worsening situation at Harfleur, besieged and blockaded by the French and their Genoese allies, was regarded as a naval task force: the ratio of two archers (not three) to every man-at-arms shows this to have been the case.[121] The list of advance payments suggests that while lords and knights were reasonably well represented, the large majority, something in the order of

[114] PRO, E 404/32/12, 136.
[115] PRO, E 101/48/14; E 404/32/274-5, 277; *CPR, 1416-1422*, p. 141; Newhall, *English conquest*, pp. 196-7.
[116] PRO, C 81/1542/17.
[117] PRO, E 404/33/215; 34/128; E 403/633, m.16.
[118] PRO, E 101/70/640; E 404/34/274.
[119] *CPR, 1416-1422*, p. 329.
[120] *CCR, 1419-1422*, pp. 141-2.
[121] PRO, E 101/69/532-569; Newhall, *English conquest*, p. 32 and n.159. Wylie (*Henry the Fifth*, ii, 353) suggested a figure of some 10,000 men.

two-thirds of those classed as men-at-arms, were esquires.[122] The reasons for this are not clear. Was there a feeling among the knighthood of England that fighting at sea was not the thing to do? Or was it further evidence that, as in the army, the esquire appeared to be taking over from the knight and the lord? Neither of the indentures sealed by Huntingdon or Clifford for service at sea in this year suggests much active participation by the knights: of Huntingdon's 350 men-at-arms, only he and nine others were to be knights (less than three per cent), while in Clifford's case only he and four others, out of a total of 200 men-at-arms (two and a half per cent) had to be knights.[123]

Contemporaries and their immediate followers realized that Henry's reign had witnessed a considerable development in the use of naval power and in the role which it would play in the war. The king's appreciation of the importance of the sea had grown while he was still Prince, born of his recognition, impressed upon him by his Beaufort uncles, of the need to keep the peace at sea for England's commercial advantage. From that, he had learned that he must provide a reasonable degree of safety at sea for those engaged in his military enterprise and for the merchants whom he installed in Harfleur and Caen. He had to be ready to provide a squadron to 'skim' – or patrol – the sea, to frighten the enemy off, or confront it with force if the need arose; the activities of the earls of March and Huntingdon show how this was done. It required a far greater degree of preparation than the system had hitherto allowed. For this, there is credit to be given, as Sir John Fortescue recognized a generation or more later.[124] Trade could not be protected adequately unless a few ships, at least, were on 'stand-by' to meet emergencies. What Henry did was to create for himself a much larger flotilla of 'king's ships' than had existed before. This process began while he was still Prince, and it went on until well into his reign to the time, about 1419 or 1420, when the enemy, deprived of access to ports along France's northern shore, was almost forced off the sea.

Nor was Henry's understanding of the importance of the sea reflected simply in the provision of more ships to defend English military and commercial activity at sea. He appreciated the advantages to be gained from exploiting the relationship between the sea and the rivers which served as the arteries of Normandy. We have already observed how, having captured Harfleur, the English were able to use the river Seine as a means of access to Rouen, thus enabling

[122] PRO, E 101/328/6.

[123] PRO, E 404/32/12, 136.

[124] Sir John Fortescue, *The governance of England*, ed. C. Plummer (Oxford, 1885), p. 123.

Henry to ship provisions and weapons directly to the quayside there. The method had already been used at the siege of Caen in August 1417, when ships were employed to bring support up the river Orne to the town (artillery is specifically referred to) as well as to ensure that no relief came from the sea to the aid of the besieged population. Having achieved virtual control of the Channel by 1419 (loss of ports had effectively denied the French access to it), Henry was able to make use of sailors in the war on land, particularly at the sieges of Falaise and Rouen.[125] In these circumstances, the ports on both sides of the Channel came to assume great importance, which was reflected in the efforts made to defend and maintain them. Much attention was given to, and much money spent on, Harfleur. It is significant, too, that in 1421 William de la Pole, earl of Suffolk, acting as admiral of Normandy, was reported as having seen to the repair of the duchy's harbours.[126] It is clear that the English appreciated the importance of port facilities as their control of the sea, and of Normandy itself, became increasingly effective.

Behind all this lay the need for essential organization and co-ordination to make the best use of what was available. The army was organized centrally; the navy must be, too. The events of 1378, when the London merchant, John Philpot, had organized privately a naval force to protect English interests at sea, must not be allowed to happen again. Such activity was a royal responsibility which Henry took seriously. First, under William Catton, who had been in his service as Prince, and who served the king as keeper of his ships between 1413 and 1420 (thus being in charge of the royal fleet during its busiest period), and thereafter under William Soper, Henry's reign was to witness a programme of ship-building (or rebuilding) of considerable dimensions.[127] It saw, too, the move of England's main naval centre from the docks adjoining the Tower of London to Southampton. It has already been emphasized how much of Henry's success as a soldier depended upon advanced and detailed planning for his army. His navy was also to receive the benefit of attention of this kind. It was part of the preparation which he saw as being necessary for the fulfil-ment of both military and commercial policy at sea. That policy, which, to be fully understood, should be seen as part of his wider military needs, was to be almost too successful. By the end of his reign, some of Henry's ships were already being laid up: they were

---

[125] PRO, E 364/54, m.2.

[126] *Grandes croniques de Bretaigne*, p. 179d.

[127] *The Navy of the Lancastrian kings. Accounts and inventories of William Soper, Keeper of the king's ships, 1422–1427*, ed. S. Rose (Navy Rec. Soc., London, 1982), pp. 232–3, 6–28.

no longer needed. Of the thirty-nine ships which he owned in 1418, only thirty-two remained on his death four years later.[128] The expenses of building, the costs and difficulties of maintenance, the rapid decline in demand were to lead to a reduction in the number of king's ships almost as rapid as had been its growth.

The reign was important in the longer-term history of English naval power. Not only did it witness a marked increase in royal patronage of ship-building, which corresponded to the development of royal control of the navy. It saw, too, significant developments in techniques, such as the setting up of a special forge at Southampton for the construction of royal ships, something very rare at that date.[129] The reign, too, saw support for the development of larger ships and the application to them of technology new for the age. New pumping systems, for instance, were being introduced during these years.[130] More important was the encouragement given to the building of multi-masted ships from about 1416 onwards, an advance made possible through the introduction of the mesan sail during the second decade of the century, and the improvement in the techniques of building strong masts, all this leading to the *Grace Dieu*, with its three masts, in 1420.[131] While such a vessel may be regarded today as something of a white elephant, as an unnecessary expense at a time of such financial stringency, its building has a significant lesson to teach. Like his brother, Humphrey, who was ready to use the technology associated with artillery to its best effect, Henry V was a man in sympathy with technological advance, ready to experiment with the new and the unusual. He was not going to be left behind by others.

[128] Friel, 'Documentary evidence', p. 5.
[129] Ibid., p. 35.
[130] Ibid., p. 339.
[131] Ibid., pp. 11, 127, 154, 209, 382, 385.

1 John of Gaunt, duke of Lancaster, Henry V's grandfather; from the Register of Benefactors of St Albans Abbey. (British Library, Cotton MS Nero D vii, fo.7)

2 The Great Tower of Monmouth castle. It was in this castle, part of the duchy of Lancaster estate, that Henry was born.

3 Kenilworth castle, Warwickshire. Also part of the estate of Lancaster, it was a favourite place of retreat for Henry as a young man.

4 Henry IV, Henry's father, from the Great Charter of the Duchy of Lancaster. (PRO, DL 42/1, fo.51)

6 Wooden effigy, perhaps modelled on that of Henry V, of Henry Beaufort
as a cardinal; from his chantry tomb in Winchester cathedral.

7 Decorated initial H from a letter dated 30 May 1412 from Prince Henry to John, duke of Burgundy. The bow of the H is formed by a swan, badge of the Bohun family; the mottoes on the upright – 'Une sanz plus' and 'soveraine' – were used respectively by Henry and his father. (Dijon, Arch. dép., Côte d'Or, B 11926)

8 Tomb effigy of Henry IV and Queen Joan, Henry's stepmother; erected in Canterbury cathedral after Joan's death in 1437.

9 One of the coronation groups on the outer sides of Henry's chantry chapel, Westminster Abbey. In this one, the king is seated, with archbishop Arundel on his right and the abbot of Westminster on his left; the antelope and swan at the top are both Henry's badges.

10 Jean de Galopes presents his French translation of Bonaventura's *Life of Christ* to Henry V, *c.*1421–22. (Corpus Christi College, Cambridge, MS 213, fo.1r)

11 Permit, given under the king's signet, to named soldiers who are sick ('infirmitates') to leave the siege of Harfleur and return home, 6 October 1415. (PRO, E 101/45/14)

12 The battle of Agincourt; a mid-fifteenth-century English illustration.
Note the French banner, with fleur-de-lis, lying on the ground,
as well as the misfortunes being experienced by soldiers of the white cross
(that of France). (Lambeth Palace Library, MS 6, fo.243)

13 French coin bearing Henry's title of heir of France, 1421.
The obverse reads H:REX:ANGLIE:Z:HERES:FRANCIE.
The reverse SIT:NOMEN:DOMINI:BENEDICTVM. (British Museum)

14 The imprisonment in the Tower of London of the duke of Orléans, captured at Agincourt. (British Library, Royal MS 16 F II, fo.73)

ES nouuelles Dalbyon
ſi vous en plaiſt eſcouter
mon frere z mon compaignio
Sachiez qua mon retorner
...y eſte ſera ſa mer...
E ceu a joyeuſe chiere

15 Part of a letter, traditionally thought to have been written by Henry himself, regarding the detention of the duke of Orléans and other French prisoners. (British Library, Cotton MS Vespasian F iii, fo.8)

16 Stained glass figure of Henry V, *c.*1440, with a new head
made in the nineteenth century; All Souls College, Oxford.

17 Reverse of Henry's Great Seal, showing the king
as a knight on horseback; Winchester College.

18 Decorated initial H from a letter of 19 October 1416 from Henry V to emperor Sigismund; note the lions and fleurs-de-lis on the upright and bow of the H, and the eagle under an imperial crown within the space of the letter. (PRO, E 30/391)

19 The Siege of Caen, 1417. The text stresses the military role of Richard, earl of Warwick, in the campaigns of these years. (British Library, Cotton MS Julius E iv, fo.19)

20 John, duke of Bedford, Henry's second brother, kneeling in an attitude of prayer before St George (who may have been intended to represent Henry V); from the Bedford Book of Hours. (British Library, Additional MS 18850, fo.256v)

21 Example of a signet letter written in English from Henry to Bedford, ordering him to act immediately against those who have attacked Breton interests. Bedford has failed to act swiftly upon previous orders; Henry does not wish to have to write again; 29 November 1418. (British Library, Cotton MS Julius B vi, fo.97, no.35)

22 The towers and walls of Falaise (birthplace of William the Conqueror), captured by Henry and his army in January 1418.

23 Alabaster effigy of Henry's first brother, Thomas, duke of Clarence, killed at Baugé in 1421, in full plate armour. As Margaret Holland's second husband, he lies on her right on their broad tomb chest; Canterbury cathedral, c.1440.

24 Crayon drawing of Henry's youngest brother, Humphrey, duke of Gloucester, made in the sixteenth century from a contemporary portrait. (Bodleian Library)

25 Brass in St Mary's Church, Ewelme, Oxfordshire, commemorating Thomas Chaucer, son of the poet, who worked with Henry as both prince and king.

26 Erpingham Gate, Norwich, 1420. At the top is the kneeling figure of Sir Thomas Erpingham, devoted servant of the house of Lancaster and of Henry V in particular.

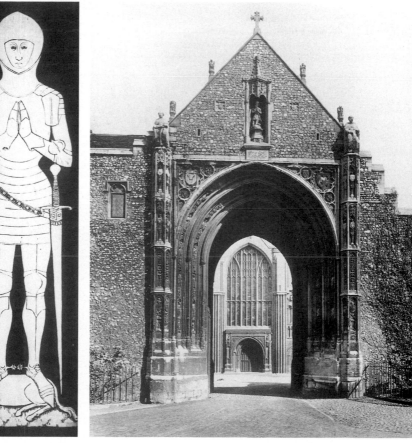

27 Memorandum ('Memoires') of tasks to be done
by the king, late 1420. The use of 'mon' and 'ma' suggests
dictation by Henry himself to a French secretary.
Note the two items in English at the end. (PRO, E 30/1619)

28 The keep of the royal castle at Vincennes, to the south-east of Paris.
It was here that Henry died in August 1422.

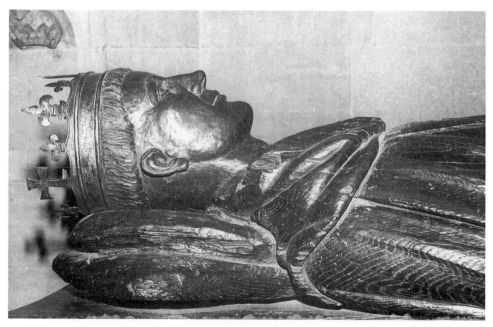

29 Henry V's effigy, Westminster Abbey; the modern (1971) head
was made to replace the one stolen centuries ago.

30 The west end of Henry's chantry chapel, Westminster Abbey.
The statue of the female saint on the outside of the north turret (to the
left) is of St Katharine. To her right is a cardinal, possibly Henry Beaufort,
who directed the building project.

Chapter 11

SIGISMUND AND THE
COUNCIL OF CONSTANCE

By no narrowness of imagination can the history of Henry V's life
and reign be confined to the island of Britain. The war against France,
one of the period's main themes, would be more than enough to prove
the opposite true. It can also be argued that England could not remain
untouched by another sequence of events, the so-called Great Schism,
begun in 1378 with the election of two popes, which troubled Christendom's conscience, as well as its system of political alliances, for a
period of some forty years. The crisis, one of unity which could only
be resolved by a single pope whose authority all Christians would
recognize, came to a head in Henry's reign. The king could not ignore
it. Far from standing aloof, he sought to help resolve it in a manner
which would bring the maximum benefit both to the Church and to
England.

The crisis had started soon after the beginning of Richard II's
reign. The papacy had just returned to Rome after a long exile of
some seventy years at Avignon. Already vulnerable, it suffered a terrible blow when, on the death of Gregory XI early in 1378, the
cardinals chose an Italian, Urban VI, whose election was soon followed by that of Clement VII by a group of those same cardinals
who felt dissatisfied by their original choice; it had been made, they
claimed, under pressure from a Roman crowd which had demanded
that an Italian occupy the chair of Peter. So began the Great Schism,
with its two popes, two administrations (Rome and Avignon) and its
two allegiances, which split Europe asunder, accentuating differences
and divisions such as those which already resulted from the long
Anglo-French conflict. It was soon to become clear that those differences could not easily be resolved. As successive popes died, so they
were replaced in elections carried out by those very cardinals whom
they had themselves created. So Urban VI was succeeded by
Boniface IX in 1389, by Innocent VII in 1404 and by Gregory XII
in 1406; while Clement VII had as his successor Benedict XIII,
elected in 1394. All Christendom faced a crisis which was at once
political, legal and moral: political, in that the division of allegiance
was accentuated and aggravated by existing political divisions, such

as those which made England and France supporters of rival popes
and thus unlikely to agree on how the crisis should be resolved; legal,
in that men had no practical experience of how to resolve such divisions within a legal framework; moral, in that the division within
that authority, which many were to regard as tantamount to heresy,
undermined papal leadership and, above all, the spiritual authority
of the Church over the faithful.

The last two decades of the fourteenth century saw the proposal
and discussion of two main plans for the ending of the crisis, plans
which were, in essence, the ideas of the academic community and,
above all, of the university of Paris which, throughout, was to play a
leading role in proposing and urging practical solutions to the schism.
One method suggested, the 'via cessionis', was the withdrawal of
obedience from both popes, in the hope that they would resign and a
fresh election, acceptable to all, could take place. In 1398 the French
withdrew their obedience from Benedict XIII, only to restore it some
five years later, thereby illustrating the practical problems caused by
such action if the pope thus forsaken refused to bow before this form
of pressure. Not surprisingly, in the light of the evident failure of such
a measure, more radical ideas which had been taking shape almost
since the beginning of the crisis now came to be seen as the only
effective way of resolving the situation. It was no longer enough to
threaten or carry out withdrawal of obedience, which the king of
France, taking up the lead offered him by the university of Paris,
proclaimed for the second time in the autumn of 1406. By 1407–08
what was being advocated was the condemnation and deposition of
popes no longer regarded as worthy of governing the faithful. The
method to be used to pursue this drastic step was one well known to
the Church, the 'via concilii', or the summoning of a council, the last
of which had met at Vienne, in France, in the early years of the
fourteenth century.

As for England, her attitude to the papacy since the outbreak of
the schism had largely been dictated by her attitude to France. Since
France was the national enemy, England would line up behind the
pope who opposed the one enjoying French support. The battle
between Rome and Avignon was a reflection of that between England
and France. Both Richard II and, for the first half of his reign,
Henry IV gave support, more or less willingly, to the 'Roman' popes,
whom they regarded as the legitimate successors of earlier pontiffs
whose claim to recognition had been unchallenged. A further factor
encouraged inactivity: other than in Richard II's reign, the two English universities were given relatively little opportunity to pronounce
upon the rights and wrongs of the argument, so that the English
academic contribution to the debate, compared to that of France and

Germany, for example, was small. Solutions to the crisis would not be found in England. [1]

So much was admitted by archbishop Thomas Arundel when, in 1408, he wrote that 'we in England have till now taken little pains to work for union, by reason of which our prestige is manifestly weakened'. [2] That year, however, was to witness the start of a decade of involvement, at times intense involvement, in the affairs of the Church which was to have significant repercussions not only upon the outcome of the schism but also upon English policy, in particular upon her relationship with the French and Sigismund, king of the Romans, or emperor, as he was more usually known.

The change was provoked by an earlier change of position on the part of certain cardinals, supporters of Gregory XII and Benedict XIII, who, coming together, decided that the calling of a general council, which might depose a pope before electing another, was the only way to proceed. Taking this task upon themselves, they summoned a council to meet at Pisa in March 1409. Cardinal Francesco Uguccione, archbishop of Bordeaux, an upholder of successive Roman popes and a man long known to the English, was sent to persuade both England and France to adhere to the council and to take part in its work. In an oration delivered before Henry IV, the Prince and an assembly of clergy at the end of October 1408, Uguccione explained why Gregory XII, whom the English supported as the heir of Urban VI, could not be trusted: contrary to an oath taken before his election, he had created several cardinals and was now wilfully prolonging schism by refusing to co-operate with the cardinals in calling a council, thus making it necessary for drastic action to be taken against him. [3]

On 12 November, although a late supporter of the conciliar cause, Henry IV took the decision to send to Pisa a royal embassy which would include Nicholas Rysshton, a former curial lawyer with much recent diplomatic practice who was to write a short work justifying the power of cardinals to call a council; Thomas Langley, bishop of Durham, who had already served as chancellor of England for almost two years and would do so again in the next reign; Robert Hallum, bishop of Salisbury, the most reform-minded member of the English hierarchy who would appear in a more important role a few years later; and Michael de la Pole, who also attended as a representative

---

[1]   M. Harvey, *Solutions to the Schism. A study of some English attitudes, 1378 to 1409* (Sankt Ottilien, 1983), p. 196.
[2]   Cited by E.F. Jacob, *Essays in the conciliar epoch* (2nd edn, Manchester, 1953), p. 57.
[3]   *St Albans Chronicle*, pp. 48–52; C.M.D. Crowder, *Unity, heresy and reform, 1378–1460* (London, 1977), pp. 47–51.

of the king.[4] In addition, the two convocations of Canterbury and York chose their own proctors, as did the universities and some of the religious orders. All in all, it has been calculated that about thirty-five Englishmen attended the council, many acting both in their own capacity and as representatives of other persons or corporations.

The council's main task was to judge and depose the two popes, Gregory XII and Benedict XIII, a task which was accomplished in June 1409, the month which witnessed the election of their successor, the pope intended to end the schism, Alexander V, his election being carried out by the cardinals but with the authority of the council. Other than this, the council of Pisa attempted little else. It was not its fault that, less than a year later, pope Alexander should die, there being chosen to succeed him the worldly figure of Baldassare Cossa, who took the name of John XXIII. At the same time, the two deposed popes still had their followings, and neither seemed willing to acknowledge the election of John XXIII. The attempt of this pope to call a further council at Rome in 1412–13 was not very successful. While the heretical teachings of the Englishman, John Wyclif, were condemned in February 1413, the failure to achieve reform and to deal firmly with heresy was all too evident. John XXIII's total lack of moral authority, coupled with the weakening of his position which stemmed from the failure of either Gregory or Benedict to surrender his position, in spite of the act of deposition of 1409, was beginning to make men ask whether stronger measures, promulgated in the name of the Church, were not required.

To one man, and to one group of men, action was certainly required. To Sigismund, two matters were of vital importance. Heir to the throne of Bohemia, he wanted strong measures to be taken by the Church against heresy. Furthermore, Sigismund was a genuine supporter of reform by methods which, since they would curtail the power of the papacy to grant exemptions to the canonical rules of the Church, were bound to appear as an attempt to limit the effectiveness of papal authority. While such steps, proposed on behalf of the man who was, in effect, Holy Roman Emperor, might be construed as an attempt to control the papacy, there can be little doubt concerning the sincerity of Sigismund's hopes for reform. Equally sincere, albeit similarly tinged with an element of self-interest, was the desire of the cardinals to bring about the election of an undisputed pope, but to do so in a way which left their right to choose the new pontiff unhindered by outside influences. It was, after all, the claim that undue pressure had been brought to bear upon the election of Urban VI in 1378 which had triggered off the schism in the first place. The cardi-

---

[4] Harvey, *Solutions*, pp. 144–5.

nals, forming a body which had seen its authority increase considerably in the fourteenth century, wanted independence of action in the crucial matter of the election which would end the schism.

It had been the cardinals who had summoned the council of Pisa; it was also the influence of some of them on both Sigismund and John XXIII which was to bring the council of Constance into being. But while John was made to act against his will, Sigismund was not. Since 1411 he had been in contact with the English court. In February an English embassy, consisting of Sir Hartung van Clux and John Stokes, had visited him to seek and to offer mutual aid, an attempt to achieve general, rather than specific, co-operation between Sigismund and the Prince, then in effective control of power in England. Once the Prince had assumed the crown in March 1413, Sigismund wrote to him expressing the hope that he would help in the work of achieving the general good of Christendom.[5] By this time the council of Rome had manifestly failed, and Sigismund may already have been planning to call another. By the autumn of 1413 he was ready. On 30 October Sigismund issued his summons for a new council to be held in the imperial city of Constance. Six weeks later John XXIII began to issue bulls of summons to the council, the one sent to the archbishop of Canterbury (who, from the spring of 1414, was to be Henry Chichele) being dated at Lodi 12 December 1413. The new council was to meet for the first time on 1 November, All Saints' Day, 1414.

By the time that the summons reached England, Henry V had been king for the better part of a year. What factors may have influenced his thinking on the matter of the council, the tasks to which it might address itself, and the implications of any successes which it might achieve? The question is put in this way because it is clear that although ecclesiastical representatives dealt with spiritual questions, the opinion of the crown was often looked to in matters concerning politics and the relationships between states. This had been the case with regard to the council of Pisa. It had been Henry IV who had heard Uguccione plead for the English to participate; the king could decide the number and status of his delegates; it was the king's government which had influenced policy towards the council.[6] It was now evident that the days when England had contributed but little to resolving the international discords of the schism were now past. Much was hoped for from England, as Sigismund's letter of March 1413 had indicated. By 1415, as the French cardinal, Guillaume Fillastre, wrote, England, along with France, was among those

---

[5] C.M.D. Crowder, 'Henry V, Sigismund and the Council of Constance', *Historical Studies*, 4 (1963), 96–8.

[6] Harvey, *Solutions*, pp. 150, 183, 193–4.

countries from which most was expected. In this matter, leadership
must come from the king himself.

Those who met at Constance faced three major problems: that of
seeking unity under one pope; that of extirpating heresy; and that of
promulgating reform. The act deposing Gregory XII and Benedict XIII, passed at Pisa, had been a failure: neither pope had
accepted deposition. Worse still, Alexander V, the pope elected at
Pisa, had been chosen for his probity and had won respect during his
brief pontificate; but his successor, John XXIII, was seen as a disastrous choice. The council of Constance, although summoned by bulls
issued in his name, had been called against his will, for the pope knew
well that there were those, notably the cardinals and even Sigismund
himself, who were intent upon forcing his abdication or, failing that,
securing his deposition. That drama was to occupy much of the council's attention and energies in its early months in the spring of 1415,
while the issue of the papal election would assume major proportions
at a later stage in the council's history.

Heresy, the second problem which concerned those assembled at
Constance, was a matter which touched England and her king very
closely. Many were aware of the close links between the teachings
of the English heresiarch, John Wyclif, who had died in 1384, and
those of the Bohemian, John Hus. Some of Wyclif's works had
been condemned in his own lifetime; more recently his books had
been burned at the council of Rome, only shortly before Henry
had ascended the throne. Although Wyclif was dead, his influence
was thought to live on, both in Bohemia and in England. While
he was Prince, Henry may have shown some ambivalence towards
the claims and ideals of the Lollards, as Englishmen who shared
some of Wyclif's views were known; but as king he had to take a
firm stand against heresy. The first nine months of his reign had
witnessed the condemnation of Sir John Oldcastle by a church
court, followed by the so-called 'Epiphany Rising' of 1414 against
the royal authority. When he came to sending his representatives
to Constance, and to giving them their instructions, the king could
not be 'soft' on the matter of heresy.

On reform, Henry's position is less clear and straightforward. How
far did he personally believe in or, more important, desire reform?
We know of his sympathies for some of the more rigorous religious
orders and his support for the Bridgettines and, by implication, for
the aims of their founder. We know, too, of his desire to 'shake up'
the English Benedictines, a process in which he was to play a personal
role in 1421.[7] More immediately, in 1414, his sympathies for the

[7] See below, ch.12.

reforming work of the council are to be seen in his appointment of the now highly experienced and well-regarded bishop of Salisbury, Robert Hallum, as leader of the English royal delegation. Hallum, as we have seen, had already been to the council of Pisa; more important, he was well known as a reforming bishop whose cathedral chapter numbered among its members some of the more progressive clergy of the day. [8] By allowing such a man to emerge as his leading representative, Henry was showing his sympathy for the aims of the council, as well as pleasing Sigismund who had the cause of reform close to his heart. If doubts remain about Henry's zeal for reform, they result from the attitude which he was bound to strike as king of England. As a private individual he may have wished for the advance of spiritual values; as king, he would have been forced to defend the interests and powers of the English crown in spiritual and ecclesiastical matters. It is diffi-cult to see Henry, or any other ruler of the time, encouraging or allowing blanket reform in matters which were opposed to the inter-ests of the state of which he was head.

Henry's view, then, is likely to have been that by participating in the council's activities Englishmen would help advance the good of the Church. He would also have appreciated that the council gave him excellent provision for furthering the interests of England, in particular in the conflict against France which, in the autumn of 1414, was seen as the pre-eminent factor on the diplomatic and military agenda. Participation at Constance could help in two ways. First, it could be used to further the English cause against France by making the most of the opportunities presented by a large international gath-ering (for a church council could be likened to a meeting of today's United Nations) to propagate English views regarding the legality and justice of Henry's cause against the king of France. One well-known example of this was Henry's decision to have copies of the treaty of May 1412, by which his claim to sovereignty over certain French lands was recognized by a number of leading French princes, sent to the council as he tried to demonstrate to the world the unreliability and lack of good faith of the French. [9] In so far as the war against France was a war of words, the prize being the support which might be won against the French, an active participation in the work of the council was a necessary step.

Secondly, and more important than securing the support of Euro-pean opinion, was the winning of practical, possibly military help

---

[8] *The Register of Robert Hallum, bishop of Salisbury, 1407–17*, ed. J.M. Horn (C&YS, 72, 1982), p. xiii and n.5; E.F. Jacob, 'The medieval chapter of Salisbury cathedral', *Wiltshire archaeological and natural history magazine*, 51 (1947), 479–95.

[9] *Gesta*, p. 17.

from Sigismund himself. As already noted, the king of the Romans had, as long ago as 1411, been the recipient of a general offer of co-operation from the Prince, while in 1413 Sigismund had expressed a similar wish, couched in terms of the help which could be given to Christendom, in a letter to the new king. In July 1414, at a time when he must have been thinking of the response which he would give to the papal and imperial summonses to attend the proposed council at Constance, Henry sent Sir Hartung van Clux, along with the trusted Walter Hungerford, to see Sigismund again. Were the king of England and the king of the Romans making plans together? It is likely that Sigismund was seeking reassurance of English co-operation in his attempt to bring about reform of the Church through the deposition of John XXIII. Since, traditionally, England was part of the German 'nation', or large geographical voting block, it was natural that the two leaders should co-operate. Did the same factors, however, motivate Henry's policy? Probably not. While Sigismund worked with high-minded idealism for the success of the council, Henry saw it as his chance to win over Sigismund to his side in the war against France which, in 1414, Henry knew would soon begin once more. For Henry the politician, anxious to find allies where he could for the coming conflict against the French, participation in the council presented an opportunity both to influence the outcome of ecclesiastical affairs and to win an important ally on France's eastern flank for the duration of the war.

Co-operation with Sigismund, then, was demanded on more than one count. By 1415, as John XXIII himself noted with a touch of bitterness, the Germans and the English spoke with one voice. Or so it appeared. In fact, their aims were not as close as they seemed, for while the Germans, under the lead of Sigismund, were primarily concerned with reform and the making of peace between France and England, the English had as one of their main aims the wooing of Sigismund precisely with the aim of waging war more effectively.

From the very beginning, the English approach to the council was a dual one. This was plain from the membership of the delegation which Henry nominated to represent him, for in addition to Hallum and a number of other clerics, he sent some important laymen who were close to him, notably Richard, earl of Warwick, and Sir Walter Hungerford, who had been sent to see Sigismund in the summer of 1414. As Henry had chosen an impressive embassy, so, too, he hoped that its arrival would make an impact. If so, he was not disappointed, for the local burgher, Ulrich Richental, from whom much information regarding the council has come to us, reported the arrival of the English embassy on 31 January 1415, with its seven wagons and several fine horses, his account stressing the pomp of the occasion.[10] Furthermore, the English claimed and, although somewhat reluctantly, were granted the right of 'nationhood', independent of the Germans.[11] Not only was this a symbol of national status (but one which was to be challenged in 1417); it also enabled the English to act and vote as Henry might order them to do without being unduly dependent upon the German nation and Sigismund. As for Sigismund, so long as the English voted with him, he could scarcely object for, if they did so, theirs was an extra vote, not part of the German one. In terms of votes, as in other ways, the English alliance could be of great value to Sigismund.

From the very origins of the council it appears that there were likely to be tensions between the German and the English nations as to where their priorities lay. The Italian curialist, Jacob Cerretano, reported that, early on in the proceedings, Sigismund showed that he wanted reform while Thomas Polton, on behalf of the English, allegedly asked for reform to be deferred so that John Hus could be condemned, together with Wyclif and his writings.[12] The early months of 1415 were spent mainly trying to persuade John XXIII to abdicate, an aim which the Germans and the English, as well as the French, had in common.[13] By the end of May that spirit of unity and of determination to get things done, a matter upon which Hallum had expressed himself with some force soon after the arrival of the English embassy the previous January, led to the deposition of John XXIII. The pressure was to be maintained. Now was the time to consider the fate of John Hus, with whom Wyclif could be associated. For the second time in little more than two years, forty-five theses of Wyclif, concerning, among other matters, his denial of transubstantiation, his doctrine that no bishop or priest in sin could administer the sacraments validly, and that dominion could not be exercised by any person in mortal sin, suffered condemnation.[14] His books were ordered to be burned and his mortal remains were to be ejected from consecrated ground.[15] All these injunctions were made at the eighth session early in May. At the fifteenth, two months later, as an almost inevitable

[10] *The Council of Constance: the unification of the Church*, ed. L.R. Loomis (New York, 1961), p. 104.

[11] Ibid., pp. 107–8.

[12] Ibid., pp. 474, 471.

[13] Ibid., p. 220 seq.

[14] E.C. Tatnall, 'The condemnation of John Wyclif at the Council of Constance', *Councils and Assemblies*, ed. G.J. Cuming and L.G.D. Baker (Cambridge, 1971), pp. 209–18.

[15] When bishop of Lincoln, Robert Flemming had Wyclif's bones dug up and burned at Lutterworth in 1428.

consequence of what had happened to Wyclif, Hus was condemned and burned. The council was taking strong action against those who propagated heresy or who, like John XXIII, were scandalous opponents of unity and reform.

In the fourteenth session, just before Hus's condemnation, good news had been brought to the council: Gregory XII, along with Benedict XIII the object of an act of deposition promulgated at Pisa in June 1409, had finally agreed to abdicate, his formal act being presented to the council by Carlo Malatesta. This meant that, within two months, two of the three men who had claimed to be pope at the time when the council had first convened little more than seven months earlier were no longer exercising the papal office. For Sigismund, whose stock in public opinion was rising steadily on account of these successes, the main task now was to try to secure the abdication of Benedict XIII, the Spaniard Pedro de Luna, whose persistence and obduracy had to be overcome before a new pope could be elected, and whose continued presence in northern Spain was effectively dividing Spanish opinion and preventing it being properly represented at the council. On 18 July 1415, only two days after the execution of Hus (and just at the moment when Henry V was assembling his army at Southampton prior to sailing to France), Sigismund departed from Constance for Narbonne and Perpignan where negotiations with Benedict were to take place, leaving Louis of Bavaria, Henry's brother-in-law, to act as the council's secular protector.[16] The discussions with Benedict were long, but he could not be persuaded to put the cause of Christendom first, so that his resignation was not brought about. His stance, however, lost him much support, and at the end of January 1416 it was announced that the kingdoms of Aragon and Castile would withdraw their obedience and would send their representatives to Constance, which they were to do in the autumn. Sigismund had recorded a partial, albeit important, success.

It was while these negotiations had been going on in the autumn of 1415 that Henry V had won his first success in France with the capture of Harfleur and then, a month or so later, had routed the French at Agincourt, so drastically altering the military balance between England and France. It is likely that, at this stage, Sigismund was still so committed to the ideal of peace between England and France, peace that would make the work of the council more likely to succeed, that he determined to turn his attention to resolving Anglo-French differences. Leaving the south of France, he first travelled to Perpignan to treat with Benedict, and then, by way of Lyon, to Paris, where he arrived on 1 March 1416. He received a cool reception from

---

[16] Loomis, *Council of Constance*, p. 55.

a French court rather suspicious of both his imperial pretensions and his apparent closeness (perhaps rather more imagined than real at this stage) to the English at the council. The visit could not be counted a success; Sigismund was suspicious of the French, and criticisms of his policy must have rankled with him as he and his large entourage made their way to England on their mission of peace.[17]

We have already seen something of the splendour of the reception which Henry accorded Sigismund, as well as the attention paid to him during the next three months, which was no mere outward show of friendship.[18] This was part of a concerted attempt by Henry to win an ally who might help the English cause forward both at the council and in the field of war. Henry's victory at Agincourt had made him realize that, with effort, he might make peace with France on his own terms, rather than on those which Sigismund might succeed in negotiating. His vision of peace was different from that of his guest. But that guest stayed with him because, on his part, he wanted Henry's support in the council, while he also realized that the English king, rather than he, was more likely to achieve Anglo-French peace, upon which, for the sake of Christendom and of the council, he had set his heart. As far as Sigismund was concerned, peace lay through sticking with Henry and England.

For Henry, an alliance with Sigismund, based upon the willingness of each to act for their mutual advantage (which had first been the subject of discussion five years earlier in 1411), was coming to assume crucial significance. As recently as April 1416 Henry had made an agreement with the archbishop of Cologne against the French. An alliance with Sigismund was the next major diplomatic step in the sequence, while the friendship of John of Burgundy, whom Henry (as Prince) had helped out in 1411 (now to be seen as a year of significance in the search for future allies), was also to be actively sought in an attempt to win alliances on France's eastern flank as Edward III had once done.

Henry's courting of Sigismund resulted in the treaty of Canterbury, sealed on 15 August 1416, a broad declaration of mutual aid which each would provide against the other's enemies if asked to do so; it was an agreement which was seen as a declaration of hostilities by Sigismund upon the kingdom of France. For Henry, the treaty was the culmination of much hard work, a considerable diplomatic triumph.[19] To all appearances he had won an ally, and an important one at that. Sigismund, too, must have been pleased. The Anglo-German

[17] Wylie and Waugh, *Henry the Fifth*, iii, 4–8.
[18] See above, ch.6.
[19] Wylie and Waugh, *Henry the Fifth*, iii, 19.

partnership at the council was strengthened, and the cause of reform within the Church advanced; furthermore, Sigismund, as heir to Bohemia, might have occasion to call upon military aid from England if the difficult situation within his own territories deteriorated. It looked as if the ringing of bells at Canterbury to mark the sealing of the treaty was justified.

Leaving Sigismund to make his way to Dover, an occasion which gave members of his entourage the opportunity to drop little leaflets bearing Latin verses in praise of England and her king,[20] Henry had time to savour the sweet taste of another success achieved on the same day as he had sealed the treaty with Sigismund: the victory at sea and the relief of Harfleur achieved by his brother John, duke of Bedford. Here was further evidence that if peace between England and France were to be achieved, it would come about largely through the military successes (in this case the third in less than ten months) won by English arms. When Henry sailed from Sandwich early in September to rejoin Sigismund in Calais, both men must have been confident that the treaty would help each of them to achieve their very different ambitions.

For Henry, the year 1416 was that in which he sought allies before returning to pursue by force his ambition in France. The meeting in Calais, which took place in the presence of Sigismund himself, was intended to see whether the French would concede some of Henry's demands, particularly in the light of the naval defeat which they had recently suffered. The attempt failed: led by the count of Armagnac, the French were in no mood to surrender. Nor can they have been impressed by the way in which Henry and Sigismund emphasized their newly formed alliance. Sigismund had by now lost all credibility in French eyes as a possible arbitrator with England. Henry hoped for yet more from this meeting. He wanted to cement an understanding with John, duke of Burgundy, for action against France, and to bring about a reconciliation between John and Sigismund, who, for a very long time, had been suspicious of each other, not least very recently when it was said that John XXIII, seeking refuge after his flight from the council of Constance, may have sought Burgundian help. For Henry, the task of reconciliation, which, at least outwardly, was effected, was a way of strengthening the alliance against France on her north-eastern border. It was into this diplomatic jigsaw that the understanding reached with the archbishop of Cologne eighteen months earlier fitted. The process of winning allies and isolating France was continuing.

Having been accompanied by Englishmen on the first part of his

---

[20] *Gesta*, p. 156 and n.2.

return journey to Constance, Sigismund re-entered the city of the council on 27 January 1417, after an absence of some eighteen months during which relatively little progress on the main issues had been achieved.[21] A few days after the event John Forester, who was at Constance, wrote to the king to report what had happened.[22] One is obliged to take into account the general tone of the letter, for the writer's intention was clearly to please Henry. None the less, what he wrote did not conflict fundamentally with the account which cardinal Fillastre included in his diary. When Sigismund returned he had been met by a crowd of cardinals and members of the council; what struck the king's correspondent was that he was wearing the insignia of the Order of the Garter, 'a glad syghte for alle your lyge men to se'. In the cathedral, bishop Hallum of Salisbury mounted the pulpit ahead of cardinal Pierre d'Ailly who 'had purposed to make the first address in the king's presence in honour of the French nation', and spoke in words which praised Sigismund's achievements. According to this account, Sigismund paid great attention to members of the English nation but to few others. The following day, he gave them audience, an occasion for both parties to speak words of fulsome praise regarding Henry and his kingdom, in particular of the way in which religion was practised in England. On the following Sunday Sigismund (whom the writer refers to twice as Henry's 'brother', as if he recognized the closeness of the relationship which bound the two men) 'publicly wore the robes of the Garter with your collar at High Mass',[23] insisting on joining Richard Clifford, bishop of London, and others at table afterwards. The feast, which 152 lords also enjoyed, consisted of three courses, each of eight dishes, with plays between them. It made a great impression.[24]

Sigismund's somewhat tactless acknowledgement of his close links with England, coming so soon after the alliance forged in the treaty of Canterbury, must have done harm to his position as the 'neutral' leader of the council, a position which, in the absence of a pope, would naturally have fallen to him. That he sent a gift of some special meats to Henry in February 1417, as well as a fine copper candlestick in the following month, was something not known to the burgher of Constance, Ulrich Richental, alone.[25] Sigismund's policy was still to pursue reform; his failure to persuade Benedict XIII to abdicate, as well as the fear that if an election took place soon, the members of the

[21] Loomis, *Council of Constance*, pp. 311–12.
[22] *Foedera*, IV, ii, 192–3.
[23] I.e., the Lancastrian 'SS' collar.
[24] Loomis, *Council of Constance*, pp. 311–12, 148–9; Crowder, *Unity, heresy and reform*, pp. 106–7.
[25] Loomis, *Council of Constance*, pp. 149–50.

council, for whom life in Constance was expensive, would immediately return home leaving the important work of reforming the Church incomplete, probably inclined him to stick to his early policy of placing reform, rather than election, high on his list of priorities. In this, if we may trust Forester's letter to the king, he had the support of two of the most influential members of the English embassy, Robert Hallum and, more surprisingly, John Catterick, bishop of Lichfield, who, along with the other English representatives, were 'fully disposed to forward reform in the Church, in head and in members';[26] they were determined, moreover, to do this with the advice of Sigismund who, Fillastre recorded in his diary, twice returned the compliment (in January and again in March) by defending the legal concept of the English 'nation' against those who attacked it.

Indeed, the weeks following Sigismund's return to Constance showed how much had happened to change attitudes since his departure in search of unity a year and a half earlier. The council was now markedly more divided than it had then been. Guillaume Fillastre, a French cardinal, wrote that, by February 1417, what had begun as a rumour of an Anglo-German alliance was now recognized as being a reality. Sigismund, he claimed, had drawn up a declaration of war against France, something which greatly perturbed the council, and it took considerable pressure, including that of the German 'nation', to persuade him not to send it, although he was said to have despatched a herald to deliver the text to Henry V, saying that his English ally should feel free to call upon his aid whenever it should be required.

Sigismund's problems did not end with the decline in the trust being placed in him. By March 1417 the kingdoms of Spain, Aragon and Castile, having withdrawn from the obedience of Benedict XIII, had sent delegations to the council, only to find that their position as a 'nation' had been taken from them by the English who, from the council's earliest days two years earlier, had claimed 'nationhood'. The quarrel which took place regarding this issue, and in which the French moved from de facto acceptance of the English 'nation' to a hostile attitude towards it, called forth some fascinating arguments and witnessed the expression of deeply held convictions on all sides.

Basic to the argument was the principle of each 'nation' having only one vote. When it came to voting, could a geographically small country with only two ecclesiastical provinces and a mere handful of bishoprics claim the same rights as a large country with more churches and a longer Christian past? By what right could England claim to exercise one fifth or, worse, one quarter of the votes upon issues affecting the whole of Christendom? The English might claim,

---

[26] Crowder, *Unity, heresy and reform*, p. 107.

as Thomas Polton did on their behalf, that their right to be regarded as a 'nation' was based upon historical as well as geographical factors.[27] What everyone knew was that the English had been permitted to assume the rights of a 'nation' in the absence of delegations from Spain (the Spanish had only themselves to blame for this), and had been encouraged to do so by Sigismund as a means of countering the influence of pro-papal Italians who attended the council in large numbers, but whose voting power (expressed in their nation's single vote) did not reflect their numbers. Moreover, Sigismund, as we have seen, would have preferred the English, as his allies, to have a separate vote which helped to counter the voting power of the Latin 'nations'.

None the less, it was now recognized that the Church was much nearer than it had been little more than a year earlier to the moment when its unity might be expressed in the election of a pope. This, with Sigismund's return, was coming to be seen as an essential part of the council's work, the details of which could now be discussed. Yet here again was a factor which caused division. There was no unanimity as to when the election might take place: was it to be before or after reform had been promulgated? Nor was there one view as to how it should take place. Were the cardinals, and they alone, to elect the new pope? Traditional practice was on their side. Yet it was recognized that it had been their failure in 1378 which had led to the election of two popes and to the outbreak of the schism. Two further factors had also to be considered. Those who believed in 'conciliar' authority, based on the words of the decree 'Haec Sancta', passed in April 1415, that a council 'represented the catholic church and held its authority directly from God', might justly press for wider representation upon the elective body. Furthermore, the realities of power, expressed in the national groupings, could not be ignored. Such was the argument favoured by the Germans and the English, who, in contrast to the other 'nations' and in particular to the Italians, had no cardinals who would enable them to have a say in the election which, in the eyes of many, could not be delayed much longer.

The spring and summer of 1417 were dominated by the growing prospects of a papal election, over which the second English invasion of Normandy, where Henry landed with his army on 1 August, cast its influential shadow. On 10 June Fillastre could record that there was fear of trouble between Sigismund and the French over the implications of his alliance with the English, while on 5 July he wrote that Sigismund 'treated the two nations of Germany and England as if

---

[27] J.-P. Genet, 'English nationalism: Thomas Polton at the Council of Constance', *Nottingham medieval studies*, 38 (1984), 60–78. See also below, ch.19.

they belonged to him and they did what he wanted', the other nations being divided among themselves.[28] Outwardly, at least, Sigismund still seemed to have control of the council.

By the summer of 1417, however, it is evident that that control was slipping out of his hands, mainly because of the deadlock which had been reached regarding election. The council was now firmly divided into two. Election was desired by the Latin group of 'nations', and in particular by the cardinals, who wanted to exercise their power to elect and doubtless to exert a measure of influence over the man whom they would choose as pope. Reform, as a precondition to all else, was the aim of Sigismund and, it seemed, of his English allies who, through the leadership of bishop Hallum, acted at his bidding – or so Fillastre thought. For Sigismund, there was an advantage in having no pope. His own position benefited from this situation; nor did he want an active papacy which might strive to work in its own interests (and how could it fail to do so after so many years of division and schism?) rather than in those of Christendom as a whole. Sigismund was not in favour of the plan (French in origin) produced on 29 May 1417 which would allow national representatives to take part in the election as long as the cardinals were not outnumbered and their historic position as electors protected.[29] Yet time was not on his side; rather, it favoured the other parties.

By 1417 the council's patience with Benedict XIII, who still steadfastly refused to abdicate, was coming to an end. At the end of July a crisis appears to have been reached. On 25 July Sigismund suddenly left Constance for an unknown destination:[30] Fillastre wondered whether he had gone with the aim of fighting on behalf of the English against the French. Three days later he reappeared. But in those three days the council had acted. On 26 July it had deposed Benedict XIII as 'a persistent violator of the one holy, catholic Church' for causing incorrigible scandal throughout Christianity and for 'continually nourishing and fostering the schism and division of God's Church', in spite of every effort to admonish him.[31] For the second time in his life, Benedict had suffered the ignominy of being deposed from the papal throne. The pressure to elect a pope of unity to take his place was now irresistible.

It lay in English power to decide whether the crisis would be resolved sooner rather than later. The key to our understanding of

[28] Loomis, *Council of Constance*, pp. 367, 382.

[29] C.M.D. Crowder, 'Some aspects of the English Nation at the Council of Constance', (Univ. of Oxford D.Phil. thesis, 1956), pp. 354, 364.

[30] Loomis, *Council of Constance*, p. 388.

[31] Crowder, *Unity, heresy and reform*, pp. 126–8.

English policy in 1417 lies in one word: France. In the previous year Henry had spent much effort and money in winning Sigismund over to his side; and he had finally achieved this end in the terms which he had agreed to with his visitor at Canterbury. His new ally probably desired an agreement with England more for the backing it would give him at the council (hence Sigismund's open flaunting of his membership of the Order of the Garter which had so surprised the members of the council) than for the military aid which he might expect from England. Henry, on the other hand, preferred to stress the political and military advantages which the treaty might bring him; he appeared less interested than Sigismund in reforming the Church. As early as October 1416, the diplomatic meeting at Calais scarcely over, Henry decided upon war for the following summer. While divisions broke out at Constance once Sigismund had returned there in January 1417, we must recall that Henry and his kingdom were preparing for the forthcoming invasion of France in which, in one way or another, it would be advantageous to involve as many allies as possible, whether directly or indirectly. By July 1417, when the invasion force was almost ready, Henry had to take some decisions which would affect England's policy towards the council, indeed, in all likelihood, the very future of the council itself. His aim was to precipitate a sequence of events which would free Sigismund from the work of the council and make him available to help Henry further his cause in France.

Henry was not the kind of man who would be held up by an apparent deadlock. He would doubtless have heard, in the course of the spring of 1417, that the council risked being forced into inaction. He would also have realized that his own representatives at Constance were probably not unanimous as how best to move forward. It is likely that bishop Hallum, influenced by his long-standing desire to reform the Church, would have used his influence as leader of the king's embassy to favour co-operation with Sigismund with the aim of reform in mind.[32] It was perhaps principally at Hallum that Henry's directive, reconstructed by historians and probably dated 18 July (a little less than a fortnight before he sailed for France), was aimed. In this the king ordered that all his ambassadors should hold to the instructions which he was issuing; penalties would be imposed upon those who did not. The language was firm, indeed tough. It suggests that those who had hitherto spoken for the king at Constance may have become too accustomed to expressing their own views rather than his. He was now asserting his authority over them. They must do as they were ordered. The reason is clear. Henry was preparing to

[32] Crowder, 'Aspects', p. 370 seq.

follow a new policy, and his envoys must be united in their presentation of it.

The change of policy (the need for the English ambassadors to speak with one voice shows that Henry recognized the importance of what he was doing) was nothing less than a reversal of priorities, with all that this entailed in terms of the council's future achievements and the future, too, of the Anglo-German alliance. We do not know exactly when the new instructions were received by the English ambassadors at Constance, probably some time in the second half of August, perhaps towards the end of the month, for they would almost certainly have been drawn up on or about 18 July, along with the order that the ambassadors should obey them. In August, however, before they arrived, there were still some English who agreed with the Germans that reform should have precedence over election.[33] But Henry was to be spared division or, worse, opposition to his new policy from within the ranks of the ambassadors themselves. On 4 September bishop Hallum, leader of the reform interest, died of dysentery, quickly and unexpectedly, at Gottlieben, about a mile outside Constance. News of his death reached Salisbury three weeks later, on 25 September.

Hallum may not always have been the soul of tact, and he doubtless crossed swords with many people during his two-and-a-half-year sojourn at Constance. But he had a considerable reputation as a man of spirituality who had the future of the Church very much at heart. When he died, this man who, but for the refusal of Henry IV to release him, would have become a curial cardinal, was given a burial worthy of his status and his contribution to the good of the Church, being laid to rest before the high altar of the cathedral at Constance on 9 September. The occasion was to be an important one, as the opportunity of preaching the oration in honour of the dead bishop gave Richard Flemming, who was not a royal envoy, the chance to reflect on the council, its work, and the delays which it was now enduring. In order to break the deadlock, he now proposed that the council should prepare itself for an election; the English, he added, doubtless to the surprise of many, would help to bring this process about. Not for the last time, a formal occasion had been used to announce a crucial change of policy with far-reaching implications.

It is obvious what this abrupt change of policy, almost certainly announced without prior warning being given to Sigismund, might do. Henry had to face the fact that his 'betrayal' of the emperor, who now risked political isolation, might have the opposite effect to the one which he desired, and that Sigismund, badly let down, might

[33] Ibid., p. 376.

refuse to co-operate with the English outside the council. They therefore did not move into active opposition; their aim could be presented
as an attempt to make compromise possible between increasingly
entrenched positions, and in so doing to enable the council to make
progress. After Hallum's death, Fillastre was to note, the English
asked the cardinals to join them in making peace with Sigismund by
mediation. A change of policy did not necessarily mean abandoning
the Germans. Indeed, the mediation worked.[34] On 19 September
Sigismund agreed in principle with the cardinals to bring forward the
election of a pope, promises that reform would be undertaken being
made in return.

By the end of September compromise was becoming an accepted
fact of the situation. It is important to recognize this in order to put
into perspective the next turn in the story. On 18 July bishop Henry
Beaufort had announced his intention of going on pilgrimage to the
Holy Land. The date is significant, it being that on which Henry had
written to his ambassadors in Constance telling them to obey the new
instructions which, as already noted, were sent either on that day or
very soon afterwards. Five days later, on 23 July, Beaufort resigned
the chancellorship which he had held since the first day of the reign,
bishop Langley being appointed in his place. Free of public office,
Beaufort set out on his pilgrimage. Early in September he was in
Bruges, and four weeks later at Ulm, some two days' journey from
Constance.[35] In all likelihood the English ambassadors at the council
knew that he was coming, and that he was close at hand. The cardinals were informed, and Beaufort was invited to come to Constance
to see whether he could encourage Sigismund further along the road
of compromise. Like a veritable *deus ex machina*, Beaufort allowed himself to be persuaded to undertake this work. To Thomas Walsingham,
he was so convincing that his personal intervention soon led to a
papal election.[36] It is probably nearer the truth to say that Beaufort
confirmed a compromise on procedure which had already been
reached. In other words, Beaufort pushed the parties down a road to
which they were already, if somewhat reluctantly, committed.

None the less, his sudden appearance at Ulm, supposedly on a
pilgrimage not normally taken at that time of year (but which he did
complete), the timing of his arrival, as well as speculation as to who
took the decision that he should travel to Jerusalem (might not the
king, about to leave the country for a campaign in France, have
preferred to leave a very experienced administrator-chancellor behind

[34] Ibid., pp. 387, 390.
[35] Ibid., p. 391.
[36] *St Albans Chronicle*, p. 107.

him in England?), have been questions which have teased historians
of the reign. It does appear that much of what happened had been,
to a certain extent, planned. The coincidence of the events of 18 July
is remarkable, and highly suggestive that some kind of sequence of
events had been foreseen. This would make sense both of Henry's
dramatic change of policy (the first stage) and of Beaufort's visit (the
second stage), needed perhaps to persuade Sigismund to accept as
the way forward the *modus vivendi* worked out in the intervening weeks
at the behest of the English ambassadors. By making himself available
at Ulm, Beaufort was furthering Henry's cause of making sure that
the process towards an election got under way, as well as acting as
Henry's personal messenger (and pacifier) to a man who may well
have felt strongly that the English had betrayed him. The whole
episode underlines yet again how important Henry regarded his
change of policy (it must not be allowed to fail for lack of supportive
effort) and how vital it was to him to preserve the friendship of Sigismund. If, as may have been suggested, there was some reward to be
won for Beaufort (the papacy itself?), then all well and good. What
seems likely is that Beaufort, like the English delegation at the council,
worked for an election 'at the command of the English king'.[37] It was
Henry himself who decided what English policy at the council should
be.

Arrangements to put decisions into effect were not all plain sailing:
the English were among those who opposed a German plan for election put forward during the month of October.[38] Eventually, however,
with the English acting as the middle men in the discussions on
election procedures, the French plan which allowed each of the five
nations to choose six representatives to enter the conclave with the
forty or so cardinals came to be accepted. Also accepted was that the
successful candidate should have two-thirds of the votes cast by
the cardinals and the same proportion of the votes cast by each delegation before he could be declared elected. As for the election itself,
it was to be held in the merchants' Great Hall in Constance and, in
view of claims of intimidation in 1378, its integrity was to be guaranteed by Sigismund himself.

In spite of its enormous significance in restoring the unity of the
Church under one head after a period of division which had lasted
all but forty years, the conclave itself proved uneventful.[39] Perhaps
because the likely candidates were already known and knew one
another from a more or less long acquaintance in the council, the

---

37 Loomis, *Council of Constance*, p. 406.
38 Ibid., p. 413.
39 Crowder, 'Henry V, Sigismund . . .', 106; *St Albans Chronicle*, pp. 107–9.

outcome was soon settled. Neither the English nor the Germans were likely to vote for a Frenchman. Neither the English nor the Germans had a cardinal. Consequently, while there may have been support for a Spaniard, the 'winner' of the election was likely to be an acceptable Italian, and a cardinal. According to Fillastre, the leader on the first ballot was cardinal Odo Colonna, for whom all the English electors voted, the only body to do so unanimously.[40] At the second ballot, he secured all the necessary majorities, and with these he became the choice of the Church as its leader, a choice to which the English cannot have objected. Having regard to the saint on whose feast day he had been elected, the new pope took the name Martin V.

What had been the extent of the role of Englishmen in Martin's election? It seems that whoever had been elected would have been indebted, in some measure, to English action. That the election took place when it did, rather than later, owed much to Henry's decision; but it had been a decision intended to bring advantage to Henry, as well as to the Church. Beaufort's intervention, which had almost certainly been planned, served to round off the work of convincing Sigismund that an election must come soon, thus complementing what had already been begun by the English ambassadors and the cardinals. As for the election itself, the unanimous vote of the six Englishmen in the conclave (all of them the king's official envoys at the council) played a not unimportant part. Their unanimity, which reflected the cohesion of the small royal embassy at Constance (a factor remarked upon with some envy by contemporary commentators) and which probably reflected the will of their royal master, was undoubtedly a factor in securing Martin's election. He was the candidate whom they wanted chosen; if they could remain unanimous in that choice, the rules according to which the election was conducted could prevent them from allowing any other candidate from securing the votes he would require from the electoral college.

Even if not decisive, the disciplined role played by the Englishmen may be said to have been of great importance in bringing about the unity of the Church through the election of Martin V. Once the result of the conclave reached England a fortnight later, the new pope was immediately acknowledged.[41] We may discount Thomas Walsingham's story that it was a change of mind by Richard Clifford, bishop of London, one of the six English electors who had been sent to Constance in the late summer of 1416 to add 'weight' to the body

[40] Crowder, 'Aspects', pp. 401–5.
[41] M. Harvey, 'Martin V and Henry V', *Archivum Historiae Pontificiae*, 24 (1986), 51.

of royal ambassadors, which secured Martin's election.[42] But the new pope fully recognized who were his friends; the French did not immediately acknowledge his election. So it was that Englishmen were to be among the first to receive recognition of the part which they had played.[43]

Clifford secured a bull from Martin regulating in his favour a dispute in which he had been involved with his cathedral chapter over the matter of the personal residence of canons in London, as well as a letter commending his services written in fulsome terms. Richard Flemming, who had announced the English decision to give precedence to the need to elect, returned to England early in 1418 as papal nuncio; late in the following year he would be provided to the see of Lincoln, and be consecrated by the pope himself in Florence in April 1420. Thomas Polton who, like Clifford, had taken part in Martin's election, had for long been a frequenter of the papal curia, or court; he, too, was appointed to a bishopric, that of Hereford, and he too, like Flemming, was consecrated at Florence.[44] The greatest reward of all was to be reserved for bishop Henry Beaufort. On 18 December 1417, little more than a month after his election, Martin announced the creation of his first group of cardinals, among whose names was that of Beaufort.[45] The fact that Henry did not allow his uncle to accept the red hat cannot obscure the fact that the new pope was not unappreciative of the efforts which Englishmen had made on his behalf.

The supreme irony of this lengthy episode in Henry V's reign is that, while some of those who spoke and acted on behalf of the king at Constance received recognition and reward, Henry himself failed to derive the military advantages of his alliance with Sigismund which had been the main motivating factor behind his decision to support those who thought that a papal election should come before reform. The decision must have been a difficult one to take, for it had involved withdrawing support for the ecclesiastical policy of the man whose military help Henry was seeking (and which he felt he was entitled

---

[42] *St Albans Chronicle*, p. 108. The role of Englishmen in the immediate aftermath of the election was stressed by Thomas Walsingham (ibid., pp. 108–9). See also Harvey, 'Martin V and Henry V', 50.

[43] Martin referred three times to abbot Spofford's role in the conclave which elected him (*The Register of Thomas Spofford, bishop of Hereford (1422–1448)*, ed. A.T. Bannister (C&YS, 1919), p.ii). The pope also rewarded Walter Medford, dean of Wells, with the office of papal collector in England in recognition of his services to the Church at the Council (*Letter-Book I*, p. 193).

[44] L.-R. Betcherman, 'The making of bishops in the Lancastrian period', *Speculum*, 41 (1966), 405–6.

[45] Harriss, *Cardinal Beaufort*, p. 94 seq. See also below, ch.12.

to have according to the terms of the treaty of Canterbury). Was it expecting too much that Sigismund would give support in war to the ally who, he must have felt, had let him down in the pursuit of his policy of reform in the Church?

Two matters may be raised in regard to this question. Did Henry really believe that, once Christendom had a head who would be generally recognized, Sigismund would then turn his attention to providing his English ally with the help he needed against the French? Is this not to argue that the process of reform, already begun before Martin V's election and an essential part of the agreement reached to make a papal election possible, would be put on one side? It is to misjudge Sigismund to think that his desire to achieve reform was only skin-deep. Secondly, did Henry make the error of thinking that his enthusiasm for the French war was shared by Sigismund? That possibility cannot be dismissed. Should we assume, however, that, deep down, Sigismund was anti-French? To cardinal Fillastre, he may at times have appeared so. But the fact remains that, although he allowed himself to be persuaded to enter into a general alliance to give his support to Henry against England's enemies (did he do this chiefly to secure English support at Constance?), he had, until his visit to England in the spring of 1416, seriously been trying to make peace between England and France. It needs to be emphasized that, once the council was nearing its close, Sigismund saw his role as a peacemaker, not as an abettor of war. It is in this light that we should see his insistence, expressed to the pope who had sent two cardinals, Fillastre and Orsini, to France to make peace, that he, too, desired to be involved in the business of making peace.[46]

Where did this land Henry, and what is to be our opinion of this episode in his life? We may, with justice, admire the king for the decision which he took in July 1417 to attempt to break the deadlock at Constance by seemingly siding with those who opposed Sigismund, thereby forcing his hand to concede that an election should take place. That aim was successful. But Henry derived no military advantage from his volte-face. Although Sigismund appears to have taken the treaty of Canterbury seriously (its terms had been presented to the Reichstag), he may have felt let down by the policy pursued by the English at Constance in the summer and autumn of 1417. Would he support an ally who treated him in this way? Furthermore, did Henry misjudge Sigismund's commitment to peace, seen in his desire to reconcile the differences between England and France? Did Henry seriously think he could get this man to help him against the French? Henry must have known, too, of Sigismund's other commitments,

[46] Harvey, 'Martin V and Henry V', 55; *Foedera*, IV, iii, 45.

notably his ambitions in that much divided country, Bohemia, whose king he was to be crowned in 1420.

There were many reasons why, in the end, Sigismund must have seemed to be an unreliable ally, and why, in the last year of his reign, Henry sent Richard Flemming (not the most tactful choice of envoy to send to Sigismund) to see if military help would be forthcoming. The answer was a negative one: Sigismund needed his army to fight a 'crusade' in Bohemia. The king would never have read Flemming's report, although he must have guessed what it would contain.[47] In the last resort the treaty of Canterbury had not given Henry what he wanted from it. The fault must, in part, lie with him. He had misjudged the man with whom he had sealed the treaty, which meant rather different things to those who had bound themselves to its very general terms. Fundamental differences of outlook, ambition, character and circumstance separated the two men. For Henry, this meant that the treaty would not turn out to be what he had planned it should be. It was not to be one of Henry's great successes.

[47] V. Mudroch, 'John Wycliff and Richard Flemming, bishop of Lincoln: gleanings from German sources', *BIHR*, 37 (1964), 239–45.

Chapter 12

PAPAL RELATIONS, REFORM AND FOUNDATION

One of a late medieval king's main tasks, for which, should he carry it out successfully, he deserved the greatest praise, was the defence of the Church in his lands.[1] In Henry V's reign that defence might take several forms. It could be furthered by helping to restore unity to Christendom as a whole; the English were to play a prominent role in securing the end of the schism through the election of Martin V in November 1417. Nearer home, it could be achieved through vigorous opposition to the heretical views of the Lollards, whose leader, Sir John Oldcastle, was finally captured, tried and executed at almost exactly the same moment as Martin was being elected pope in Constance. It might be furthered, as we shall see it was, through encouragement given to both the organization and the spiritual life of the Church in England through reform and innovation. It also meant establishing a good working relationship with the new pope as he struggled to restore unity to the Church and authority to his office after a period of division which had lasted some forty years.

From the deposition of John XXIII in May 1415 to the election of Martin V in November 1417 England had recognized no pope, so that Henry, through the bishops and, above all, through Henry Chichele, whom he had chosen to succeed Thomas Arundel at Canterbury in the spring of 1414, was effectively master of the Church in his kingdom.[2] Neither too forceful nor too independent, Chichele viewed religious matters in much the same way as did his royal patron: for its own good, the Church must be ruled in an orderly manner, and every encouragement must be given to growth and development. As archbishop and metropolitan, with charge over the majority of the sees

---

[1] Such was one of the themes of the *Gesta Henrici Quinti*. When, in 1414, proposals for reform were sent to Henry by the university of Oxford, they were addressed 'Christianissimo principi, catholicaeque fidei strenuissimo defensori Henrico . . .' (D. Wilkins, *Concilia Magnae Britanniae et Hiberniae ab anno MCCCL ad annum MDXLV* (4 vols, London, 1737), iii, 365.

[2] R.G. Davies, 'The episcopate in England and Wales, 1375–1443' (Univ. of Manchester Ph.D. thesis, 1974), i, 274–7.

of England which comprised the ecclesiastical province of Canterbury, Chichele possessed great spiritual authority. This, he knew, would not be challenged by the king. If a challenge were to come, it would be from the papacy, anxious to reassert its own influence over Christendom after so many years of division.

In practice, that could be done in two, very important, ways. One would be the reassertion of papal authority in England (and, for that matter, elsewhere) through direct intervention in the appointment of English bishops; the other would be to reactivate the papacy's right to tax the people of England and, above all, its clergy. The first was a claim of principle as much as one of history: the papacy asserted its right to nominate the pastors, or bishops, who would lead and direct the Church under the chief pastor, the pope. In the fourteenth century the papacy had asserted this claim with considerable success. Papal constitutions had 'reserved' to it the appointment to the most important (and often the richest) positions in the Church. The period of schism, however, had inevitably weakened the papacy and its ability to exercise to the full the claims which lay behind these constitutions, so that it was now to be the policy of Martin V, guided and encouraged by men who wished to perpetuate the system, to revert to those policies which had brought the papacy both power and wealth in the past. Its need to make money should not be underestimated. The schism had placed the popes in the debt of secular rulers from whom they had borrowed large sums, thus making them increasingly dependent upon the temporal powers. Papal policy would have as one of its aims that of freeing the popes from that dependence.[3]

Englishmen saw matters differently. The advance of papal claims to appoint to leading positions in the English church (and to charge those so appointed accordingly) was deeply resented, all the more so as the fourteenth-century papacy, settled between 1309 and 1378 at Avignon, appeared to be dominated by Frenchmen, men of the nation with whom England was at war. Although claiming to be defending the traditional rights of cathedral chapters to elect their own bishops, kings of England were in fact defending their de facto right to have men acceptable to them placed in the positions of highest responsibility within the church in England. Two pieces of legislation, the Statute of Provisors of 1351 and that of Praemunire of 1353, had enabled the crown to imprison those 'provided' by the papacy and, in certain conditions, to fill the vacancies itself, while forbidding any subject of the king to appeal to the papal court by taking a dispute (for example

---

[3]   E.F. Jacob, *Henry Chichele and the ecclesiastical politics of his age* (London, 1952), p. 6.

one concerning an ecclesiastical benefice or preferment) outside the country and therefore beyond the jurisdiction of the king's justices. [4] In 1393 another (the 'great') statute of Praemunire had been enacted. This time the intention had been to prevent the pope translating bishops at will, without informing either them or the king: it was now an offence to allow into England any papal document ordering such matters. A stand was being taken against the exercise of these particular papal pretensions in England.

For the first five years of his reign Henry had no trouble in getting the leaders of the church whom he wanted. He had been crowned only a few days when the see of Norwich became vacant on the death of bishop Alexander Tottington, and he was able to ensure that his close friend, Richard Courtenay, was provided to the bishopric. Once set in motion, the system looked after itself, and for the next five years men well known to the king, often through personal service to him, were named to rule English sees. Henry may well have heaved a sigh of relief when his old political opponent, Thomas Arundel, died in February 1414, leaving the primatial see of Canterbury vacant. Without doubt the most suitable candidate, the man with whom Henry saw that he could establish the all-important working relationship, was Henry Chichele, a man with a legal and diplomatic background, considerable sympathy for modest reform and useful links (through his family) with the city of London. [5] Once again, Henry's wish was met, Chichele being replaced as bishop of the Welsh see of St David's by John Catterick, an active diplomat with a legal training and a friend of bishop Henry Beaufort.

When Catterick was promoted to the see of Coventry and Lichfield in the following year the man chosen to follow him at St David's was Stephen Patrington, a Carmelite friar who was the king's confessor, and clearly his personal choice. A few months later, when bishop Courtenay died from disease contracted at the siege of Harfleur (he was granted the honour of being buried at Westminster Abbey), the choice of his successor fell upon John Wakering, whose appointment was confirmed by archbishop Chichele on royal orders, notwithstanding the rights of the papacy, then vacant. Wakering was a man well known to the king who, once again, was getting his own way in the matter of episcopal appointments. The same was to happen at Hereford early in 1417, when the choice fell upon Edmund Lacy, dean of the king's private chapel, and at Salisbury at the end of the year when there was no royal intervention against the choice of the dean, John

---

[4] W.A. Pantin, *The English church in the fourteenth century* (Cambridge, 1955), p. 92.
[5] Jacob, *Henry Chichele*, p. 4.

Chaundler, elected by the chapter as successor to Robert Hallum who had died at Constance in September.[6]

During these years Henry had been working in very exceptional circumstances, at least as far as his relations with the papal curia were concerned. His luck, if it is seen as that, could not hold. The final months of the year 1417 witnessed two events which were to have profound effects upon England's relationship with the papacy. The first was Henry's invasion of Normandy, where he landed on 1 August. From now on he would need friends, and in due course the papacy might become one of these, but only on terms for which some kind of price might be sought. The second event, Martin V's election as pope, came a few months later, on 11 November. The new pontiff, too, was going to need support in his search for ways by which to restore the authority of his office to its former level. One of those from whom support might be obtained, once again at a price, was the king of England.

Almost immediately Martin asserted the authority of his predecessors. It was the new pope who provided William Barrow, who had been at Constance, to the see of Bangor, vacant by translation, early in 1418. At Chichester, where the chapter had elected Henry Ware, a man well known to archbishop Chichele as he was to the king, early in the same year, Martin quashed the election and provided Ware to the see himself. Much the same was to happen in the other vacancies (at Rochester, Worcester, Carlisle and Exeter) which occurred in 1418 and 1419. The bishops provided to these sees were chosen in England but their appointments were officially made by the pope himself.

In the matter of episcopal appointments Martin was doing the best he could in the circumstances. Yet it was difficult, if not impossible, for him to reassert the effective power of his office very quickly. Furthermore, as he fully realized and was not afraid to admit, he owed his election in at least some measure to the policy of the king and to those Englishmen who had been members of the electoral college which had chosen him to be pope. None the less, only a month after his election, he set out to reassert his authority in England and, in so doing, to test Henry's will and determination to challenge him. On 18 December 1417 Martin created Henry Beaufort a cardinal and personal legate (*legatus a latere*) in England for life. A short while later, perhaps at the request of John Catterick, bishop of Lichfield, a close associate of Beaufort and one of the pope's electors,[7] Martin

---

[6]   Davies, 'Episcopate', i, 271–88. Henry was encouraged by certain cardinals at the council to lend his support to the election of Catterick at Salisbury (BL, Cotton Ms Cleopatra E.ii, fo.351).

[7]   *St Albans Chronicle*, pp. 107–8.

appointed Beaufort bishop of Winchester *in commendam*, thereby, as Chichele wrote to Henry, breaking the time-honoured convention that cardinals worked and lived at the papal curia and did not act as bishops in their own country. [8]

This startling development, a bold reassertion of papal authority in English ecclesiastical affairs, never made the chronicles. Only the discovery of a paper in the public records some years ago has revealed the details of the episode to us. [9] It is clear evidence that Martin, so recently elevated to the papacy, had totally misjudged the mood of the king and underestimated the fears of archbishop Chichele. As Gloucester was to put it many years later, in a bitter statement denouncing Beaufort, Henry 'had as leef sette his coroune biside hym as to se him were a cardinal's hatte'.[10] On 6 March 1418 Chichele wrote to Henry expressing his grave misgivings about the promotion of a man who, as bishop of Winchester, was one of his suffragans. How could he, as archbishop, allow his primatial authority to be undermined by the permanent legatine authority of one who was, on another plane, his inferior? History and the laws of the land were on his side. Chichele presented the dangers of the appointment to others than to himself: Beaufort would act as a kind of tax-gatherer extraordinary, and the king's subjects would suffer. The promotion could not be allowed to stand. Thus threatened, even by a man who was his uncle and had long been one of his closest advisers, Henry acted discreetly but firmly. Invoking the statute of Praemunire, he killed the project dead. Beaufort was forbidden to take up his new position, but was allowed to continue life as before, undisturbed by the law.

Martin was concerned not only with testing the English waters but with the peace-making process as well, work in which he was following the efforts of his predecessors. Early in 1418 he nominated two cardinals, Guillaume Fillastre and Giordano Orsini (the second of these more sympathetic than his French partner to the English point of view), to attempt to bring the Anglo-French war to a peaceable conclusion. Whether Henry welcomed such intervention at this stage when his conquest of Normandy was going forward satisfactorily is debatable. Although he could scarcely refuse to see a papal envoy sent specifically on such a mission, he could keep him waiting while the English consolidated their position. In June 1418 he finally met Orsini, who was to help persuade the duke of Burgundy, now master

[8] Harriss, *Cardinal Beaufort*, p. 94 seq.
[9] See McFarlane, 'Henry V, bishop Beaufort and the red hat', 316–48: reprinted in his *England in the fifteenth century*, pp. 79–113.
[10] *Letters and papers illustrative of the wars of the English in France during the reign of Henry the sixth, king of England*, ed. J. Stevenson (2 vols, RS, London, 1861–4), II, ii, 441.

of Paris, to negotiate with the English. However, the time for meaningful negotiation was not yet ripe, for although the English by now
controlled much of Normandy, the siege of the ducal capital, Rouen,
had not yet begun, and there was some way to go before, almost a
year later, Henry was to be master of the entire duchy. For the
moment little could be achieved.

In the meantime, however, Henry was following a policy towards
ecclesiastical appointments as much in keeping with the ambitions of
Martin V as the pope might reasonably hope. In France, the pope
faced a country divided on the way papal pretensions should be faced
and dealt with. On the one hand, the Armagnacs adopted a very
nationalist ('Gallican') stance, intended to protect the rights of local
patrons at the expense of the papacy. On the other, the Burgundians
favoured a relationship which gave something to all parties, both local
interests and papacy. In March 1418 the Armagnacs (the party then
in power in Paris), anxious to react to what was plainly seen as
an attempt by Martin to intervene in French ecclesiastical affairs,
published in the Parlement of Paris (a body which strongly supported
a 'Gallican' approach) an ordinance condemning all reservations and
papal exactions, and declaring that elections and presentations to
ecclesiastical offices should be carried out according to the dictates of
canon law. A month later a second ordinance forbade the export of
all monies to pay papal taxes without royal licence, papal collectors
being condemned for exacting wealth from the clergy under the guise
of elections, confirmations and presentations.[11]

The tone of these ordinances was stridently anti-papal. However,
by the time Martin negotiated an agreement, or concordat, with the
French, the colour of the government in Paris had changed completely. The document issued in May 1419 was an agreement which
reflected Burgundian, rather than Armagnac, attitudes. The pope was
to be given considerable freedom in the appointment not only to
bishoprics but also to a large group of senior benefices, using a system
of 'alternative' months to decide the matter of which patron, local or
papal, should present. The raising of certain papal taxes, notably
annates, although halved in value, was to be permitted. It was a
compromise which each party could accept.[12]

It was this system which the English inherited in Normandy. In
practice (the point is important as it indicates clearly that Henry was

[11] *Ordonnances des rois de France de la troisième race* (22 vols, Paris, 1723–1849), x,
445–9; C.T. Allmand, 'The relations between the English government, the higher
clergy, and the papacy in Normandy, 1417–1450' (Univ. of Oxford D.Phil. thesis,
1963), p. 179.
[12] Allmand, 'Relations', p. 180.

in no way anti-papal on principle) the pope did well in the appointment of Norman bishops in the next few years. In 1419 there were
sees to fill, and by virtually ignoring the terms of the concordat,
Martin was able to impose his own choices. He was helped by the
fact that Henry did not want to entrust a Norman see to a Frenchman
too soon after his conquest, thus making it relatively easy for Martin
to appoint outsiders. Henry had also made it known to the pope
that he would not apply the English legislation of Praemunire to his
Norman lands, thereby depriving himself of the possible use of
a weapon against Martin. The result of it all was predictable. At
Coutances, in late 1418, the pope provided an Italian, Pandulph di
Malatesta, one of his own electors, in place of a local man, Nicolas
Habart, who had the chapter's backing and even the king's approval.
At Lisieux, in 1420, the king wanted to have the Canterbury Benedictine, John Langton, as bishop, but in spite of much pleading at the
curia, the pope provided a cardinal, Branda da Castiglione, to the
see. The fact that Castiglione was friendly towards England and a
man of great influence at the curia would, doubtless, have helped to
sweeten the pill. At Evreux, although the chapter had secured leave
from Henry to elect, it was a papal candidate, another Italian, Paul
de Capranica, who obtained the see in the summer of 1420. At Bayeux,
the pope again ignored the choice of the chapter, the dean, Jean du
Homme; in his place (after du Homme had resigned his claim) Martin
appointed Nicolas Habart to take charge of the see.[13]

Whether we see it as a case of strong papal influence being exerted
or of a lack of determination to stand up to that influence (neither
interpretation on its own will do: it was unlike Henry to allow any
papal policy to which he objected to be put into effect), Martin was
having things much his own way in Normandy. This may have led
him to think that it was worth making a determined effort to regain
his full 'ecclesiastical liberties' in England,[14] by which euphemism
was meant the annulment of the statutes of Provisors and Praemunire.
By 1419, in response to what may have been an appeal from Henry
for help against the French, he may have felt that the repeal of the
anti-papal legislation was now something which might be brought
about.[15] What Henry was demanding, however, was more than
Martin could give. The pope was never convinced of the soundness
of the English case against France, and was never to condemn the
murder of John of Burgundy at Montereau by associates of the

[13] Ibid., pp. 219–25.
[14] Harvey, 'Martin V and Henry V', 58.
[15] McFarlane, 'Henry V, bishop Beaufort and the red hat', 339; reprinted in his
England in the fifteenth century, p. 103.

dauphin, Charles.[16] Nor, after the treaty of Troyes had been sealed, did he accept its terms or the new alignment of the French political scene which it had created. To Martin, Henry was never (in public, at least) regent of France or heir to the throne; nor for that matter, did he ever address Henry VI as king of France.[17] We must not doubt the sincerity of the pope's view. None the less, it must be stressed that by withholding support and sanction for the settlement agreed at Troyes, Martin was creating a negotiating position for himself: Henry could buy his support, but the price would be the repeal of the acts of 1351, 1353 and 1393.[18]

In 1421 Martin tightened the screw a little more. By this time the papal collector, Simon of Teramo, was in England working against the anti-papal legislation. In July 1421 Henry sent him back to Rome. Teramo was to stress to the pope that the legislation was not of Henry's making (although he was among those who benefited from it), and that in lands conquered in France he was acting in a manner which favoured papal claims and interests. However (in what may well have been an empty promise), Henry wanted the pope to know that he was willing to discuss the repeal of the offending legislation with parliament. Martin's reaction was to step into a confused and disputed succession to the see of London, made vacant by the death of Richard Clifford in August 1421, a dispute which ended with him imposing his own choice, John Kemp (whose third see in two years this was), upon the chapter. This would show who was master. If the king did not like it, he knew what he had to do to change matters.[19]

A year later Henry was dead, having made none of the concessions hoped of him. It is as well to be clear what kind of a relationship existed between England and the papacy in these years. No single word can characterize it either completely or accurately. While there were clear disagreements between Henry and England, on the one hand, and Martin V on the other, the relationship was certainly not one of confrontation. In the appointment of bishops Henry knew that there was generally a way of getting the men he wanted, and he was normally willing to allow the pope to exercise his now almost traditional rights of appointment. If the king, scarcely in England at all after 1417, was thus unable to exercise his will over episcopal appointments as strongly as a fully resident ruler might have done,[20] he had at the curia two men, Thomas Polton and John Catterick, well

[16]   Harvey, 'Martin V and Henry V', 61.
[17]   Ibid., 68–9.
[18]   Ibid., 51, 61–2.
[19]   Ibid., 64–6.
[20]   Davies, 'Episcopate', i, 301.

known to the pope (Polton, like Catterick, had been among Martin's electors)[21] and well versed in the affairs of the church in England, who were able to sustain and defend the English point of view. At home, Henry's long absence in France placed great responsibility for the everyday running of the church upon the shoulders of his loyal lieutenant, archbishop Chichele, whose plea in defence of his rights as primate and metropolitan against bishop Beaufort becomes all the more readily understandable in the absence of the king abroad.

Chichele's role in sustaining a balance between the affairs of the church and those of the state was crucial. Doubtless consulted on all important matters concerning the church, he was particularly influential in the king's absence as a leading member of the royal council,[22] always likely to be called away to deliberate with other members of that body even when parliament or, in particular, convocation (the clergy's assembly) was in session.[23] Much the same was true of some of the other bishops who, through membership of the royal council, 'became part of the governing mechanism of the country'.[24] If he had stopped to think, Martin V would have realized that his promotion of Beaufort was bound to impinge upon both the personal and the 'institutional' susceptibilities of archbishop Chichele. On the other hand, he may not have fully realized that, as a royal councillor, Chichele could not give his support to all papal actions and claims when these went contrary to English interests and English law. Thus, having already opposed Beaufort's promotion in 1418, Chichele's criticism of some aspects of papal policy regarding provisions was not understood for what it was: loyalty to his country and to his king.[25] In Chichele's view, the world would be a better place if the interests of both church and state, not simply one of them, were recognized and met.[26]

Those appointed to sees, two-thirds of which saw the nomination of a new bishop during Henry V's reign, constituted an interesting group of men, reflecting a considerable breadth of talent and experience. Eighteen in number (together they filled the twenty-five vacancies which occurred during the reign), nine were trained in canon and/or civil law, five in theology, while four are not known to have graduated.[27] A striking characteristic of many was that they must

---

[21] *St Albans Chronicle*, p. 108.
[22] See below, ch.16.
[23] Jacob, *Henry Chichele*, pp. 3, 24.
[24] Ibid., p. 3.
[25] Ibid., p. 13.
[26] E.F. Jacob, 'Two lives of archbishop Chichele', *BJRL*, 16 (1932), 464.
[27] The following bishops were graduates in law: Barrow, Catterick, Chichele, Courtenay, Kemp, Morgan, Nicholls, Polton, Ware (9). The theologians among them

have been very much aware of the world outside England. Almost
half (seven) had been at the council of Constance at one time or
other,[28] and Thomas Spofford had also been at Pisa; none, however,
enjoyed a reputation as reformer such as that bestowed upon their
senior, Robert Hallum. Many (again about half) had had diplomatic
experience either in the service of the English crown or of the restored
papacy of Martin V.[29] Chichele had played his role in the surrender
of Rouen, while Philip Morgan and John Kemp held office in Normandy. Lacy could count himself happy on more than one count: he
had been at the battle of Agincourt and lived to tell the tale. A small
number, including Polton and Catterick, knew the ways of the papal
curia and could brief the king on its thinking.[30] Both Thomas Polton
and Thomas Spofford, although not yet bishops when they had taken
part in the papal election in November 1417, were to receive their
mitres before Henry V's death, both being appointed successively as
bishop of Hereford in 1421.

The curial link, not surprisingly in the circumstances of the day,
was a powerful one when it came to choosing men to raise to
episcopal rank. So, too, was the friendship or approval of the king.
Stephen Patrington, one of Henry's confessors, and Edmund Lacy,
first dean of his chapel, were rewarded with sees, while Chichele,
Courtenay, Catterick, Ware and Kemp were all well known to the
king by the time they achieved their promotions. The bishops thus
formed a homogeneous group, most of them known personally to
either king or pope, and more important still, like so many of
Henry's military commanders, most known to one another. There
was greater unity among the bishops appointed during this reign
than may at first appear. It is therefore scarcely surprising that
the king should have used them much more than his father had
done in government, diplomacy and administration.[31] Neither he
nor they had cause to complain about the other. When the time
came to constitute the council of regency for Henry's heir in 1422
there were five bishops among its members, as good a sign as any
that they were not only spiritual leaders but trusted men, experienced in the affairs of this world.

*

were Flemming, Lacy, Langton, Patrington, Whelpdale (5). Bishops Chaundler,
Heyworth, Spofford and Wakering do not appear to have graduated, although Spof-
ford had been a student of theology.
    [28] Barrow, Bubwith, Catterick, Flemming, Polton, Spofford and Wakering were at
Constance.
    [29] Davies, 'Episcopate', ii, 501.
    [30] Ibid., ii, 499.
    [31] Ibid., ii, 639.

Reform in the Church, reform of the papacy, reform of the clergy at all levels had for long been a matter for debate – and for hope – among those who wanted the spiritual power to give the lead from which peace among nations would stem. The papacy of Avignon had had its critics, and since 1378, in particular, the crisis of the schism had put the broad matter of reform, however that was understood, near or very near the top of the ecclesiastical agenda. That it had never won universal support was the result of a number of factors. One was the great problem created by the schism, that of how to reunite the Church under one head, which appeared to be the main and most urgently pressing matter requiring resolution. Another was whether general agreement about what needed reforming could ever be reached. A further difficulty was that without a head to direct reform throughout the entire Church, general and meaningful renewal could never be achieved. Finally, could such a reformer ever be found, for even a pope would face such great pressures against him that he would never be able to battle successfully against them.

The difficulties were made manifest at both the councils of the Church which met in the first two decades of the fifteenth century. At Pisa, the main work was that of unity. Having dropped both men, Gregory XII and Benedict XIII, who claimed to be the Church's legitimate pilots, and taken on another, Alexander V, to act in their place, the members of the council went home, leaving the fundamental problems of reform 'in head and members' to be considered by the next council which would meet three years later. By the time that body met at Constance late in 1414, the most immediate and pressing issues to be dealt with were heresy, personified in John Hus, and what should be done about John XXIII who, elected to succeed Alexander V on his death in 1410, was causing scandal in the Church. It was not until John had been deposed in May 1415 that a properly constituted commission for reform was set up three months later, by which time the emperor Sigismund had departed on a tour which would take him to Spain, France and England, leaving behind him instructions that no fundamental reform was to be completed in his absence. By the time that he returned to Constance in January 1417 the pressure for election was beginning to mount, so that when a second commission was established, under the presidency of Nicholas Bubwith, bishop of Bath and Wells, in the summer of 1417, it was soon to be pushed into the background by the fast-moving events which led to the election of Martin V in November. Although it was not for lack of ideas or good intentions, reform had not succeeded in imposing itself properly upon the conciliar agenda.

What were the attitudes of Englishmen to reform? At the council of Pisa the ideas of Richard Ullerstone had made their mark,[32] as had those of bishop Hallum of Salisbury, a much respected figure at Constance whose cathedral chapter included some of the men most sympathetic to reform in the England of the time. Of those others who went to Constance, either as royal envoys or as proctors representing more local interests, one, Thomas Spofford, abbot of the Benedictine monastery of St Mary's, York, appointed a royal representative in October 1414, appears to have considered reform seriously, taking part in meetings of German members of his order aimed at bringing about reform in the administration and monastic discipline of the Benedictines of that country. It is noteworthy that while the English were, in a very real sense, responsible for delaying the election of Martin V through the long support which they gave to the German-backed call for reform, in the end they abandoned that position in favour of election. Such a decision, taken by Henry for what now appear to have been largely political reasons, hardly suggests strong attachment to the long-term cause of the reformers.

Yet was it really so? In common with the Germans, the English saw their needs best served by reforms which, although sanctioned at the highest level, would generally be decided upon locally, a view which, broadly speaking, worked against the Italian opinion that reform should be imposed upon the Church by an unreformed hierarchical structure dominated by Italian cardinals. It was this manner of seeing things, a way which was regarded as more likely to bring effective reform to bear upon the church in England, which had led the English and the Germans to act together against the interests of the more 'Latin' nations at the council.

It seems likely that the king, wishing to establish some form of effective control over the church in England, would favour reforms which applied locally rather than those which, however appropriate to English conditions, reflected the more 'universalist' claims of the papacy. That Henry was open to ideas of ecclesiastical renewal is, in itself, scarcely subject to doubt. The list of forty-six desirable reforms, submitted to him by the university of Oxford in 1414 in response to his request that they should discuss such matters, shows clearly that its members saw in the king a man who would encourage improvement among the clergy of England.[33] It is also interesting to note the basis upon which the proposed reforms were based. In trying

[32] See M.M. Harvey, 'English suggestions for the reforms to be undertaken by the general councils, 1400–1418' (Univ. of Oxford D.Phil. thesis, 1964), on Richard Ullerstone.

[33] 'Articuli concernentes reformationem universalis ecclesie' (E.F. Jacob, 'A note on the English concordat of 1418', *Medieval studies presented to Aubrey Gwynn, S.J,* (Dublin, 1961), p. 353).

to get the king, society's secular leader but one who had undergone coronation, to give his support, it was stressed that temporal peace depended upon spiritual wellbeing. Put a little differently, if the temporal and the spiritual powers could work together, society as a whole would benefit from this; it was a way of viewing the role of the spiritual in secular affairs which came close to Chichele's view that an archbishop of Canterbury, both spiritual leader and secular councillor, was acting for the good of society as a whole.

A consideration of the Oxford proposals supports this view. Although drawn up in the months following the dramatic events of the Lollard rising, the proposals make little direct reference to them. Only towards the end was there a call for secular royal officers to join with the bishops in arresting and punishing all heretics and Lollards, and in particular for action to be taken to confiscate books in English which might cause the simple to be deceived.[34] Almost all the other proposals arose out of long-standing practices, many of which were regarded as abuses. In some cases, it would seem, the king was being asked to ensure that certain papal practices be halted or, at least, curtailed. Heading the list was the bold statement that too many cardinals were being appointed (in 1414 England had no cardinal),[35] followed by the requests that papal indulgences should be curtailed,[36] as should the practice of translating bishops from one see to another (the implication being that they sought translation to richer sees) and demanding fees for the privilege.[37] The holding of sees *in commendam* (in effect in plurality) should be done away with, and all who held benefices should be able to speak the language of the country in which they were situated, a swipe at the granting of such benefices to foreigners.

A second group of requests sought to bring about an improvement in the personnel of the Church and in the ways it carried out its spiritual functions. Perhaps a little unfairly, those who drew up the proposals were deeply critical of the bishops, of their abilities, their administration and their practices on visitation. The effects of appointing young bishops were singled out for criticism.[38] It was argued that care, too, should be taken to guard against 'false' preachers.[39] Although the criticisms do not specifically mention the Lollard problem, it is none the less possible that what was being said could be interpreted as a failure on the part of ecclesiastical leaders

[34] Wilkins, *Concilia*, iii, 365, nos 43, 44.
[35] Ibid., 361, no.2.
[36] Ibid., no.6.
[37] Ibid., 361, nos 7, 8; 363, nos 24, 27.
[38] Ibid., 361–3, nos 9, 10, 15, 25.
[39] Ibid., 365, no.39.

to act against the heresy and those who propagated it. Had the English church been properly led, the recent troubles, it was implied, might never have happened. The way forward was to accept the help of the secular power to ensure that it did not happen again.

Reform could take forms other than an improvement of competence among the bishops. The clergy as a whole did not emerge unscathed from this document; many of them, it was said, were not being properly and sufficiently examined before ordination.[40] Very important and very English in their significance were the critical statements made about the appropriation of churches, a practice which, by allowing a religious house to take the revenues and appoint a vicar who would fulfil the spiritual obligations for a pittance, reduced the status of the benefice concerned. This practice, along with that of uniting one or more benefices into a single one, helped to bring about a serious contraction in the number of benefices available to clergy, and was strongly opposed, in particular by university graduates, many of whom depended upon ecclesiastical patronage for their livelihood.[41]

Graduates (not for the last time) were not always finding it easy to obtain benefices. In the fourteenth century the Avignonese papacy had encouraged universities to submit to it – on rolls – the names of their graduates who could be promoted to benefices as and when these became vacant. The system benefited the graduates of European universities, while the exercise of patronage helped to extend the practical authority of the popes. In England, however, these halcyon days had been brought to an end in 1393 by the passing of the statute of Praemunire, which forbade all papal influence and interference in the filling of ecclesiastical vacancies other than by specific permission of parliament. (In France, too, the passing of 'Gallican' legislation aimed at preserving the rights of local patrons at the expense of the papacy was to lead to something approaching the same result.) By the end of the fourteenth century the ability of graduates to obtain the best (which often meant the richest) benefices was being severely undermined. Nor did the conditions of the schism help them, either. The effect upon the clerical intelligentsia was to divide its loyalties. On the one hand, the system of papal provisions could be said to lead to abuses of non-residence and pluralism, abuses which were worthy of condemnation. On the other hand, however, those who might advocate reform were the main beneficiaries of such abuses for which many might argue economic justification in difficult times. Such men, whose number was on the increase, were caught in a dilemma.

---

[40] Ibid., 362, no.18; 364, nos 36, 38.
[41] R.N. Swanson, *Church and society in late medieval England* (Oxford, 1989), p. 44; Jacob, 'English concordat of 1418', pp. 355–7.

The issue demanded action. At the end of 1417 (the king being in Normandy with his army) Chichele summoned a meeting of the convocation of the province of Canterbury to see what could be done 'concerning the estate and utility of the English Church and the resplendent Universities of Oxford and Cambridge, and the profit of their graduates'. At a very early meeting a letter from Constance, addressed to the duke of Bedford, was read, announcing the election of Martin V as pope. During the next few days representatives of both Oxford and Cambridge addressed the assembled meeting, the representative from Cambridge, it was said, being outshone in eloquence by his counterpart from Oxford. Chichele replied that he and his fellow bishops were very sympathetic to the problems described and would work to have them resolved. By the end of the meeting, however, it had become clear that there was no unanimity as to what should be done, the regular clergy (monks, in particular, and friars) objecting to proposals, which led to a dissolution of the convocation with little achieved. When Chichele finally proposed that the universities should let him have the names of their graduates (just as they had done earlier by sending the rolls of their names to the popes) the plan was turned down. It was clearly going to be a difficult problem to resolve.

Little more was to be done about it until the king returned to England in the spring of 1421. Reform, if of a broader kind, was still in the air. At Constance, a third commission had been appointed after the papal election to assist Martin in this matter.[42] It worked slowly, but eventually it led to the making of a number of agreements, called concordats, with England, France and Germany. It is plain that the method of general reform had been abandoned in favour of national agreements reflecting the particular circumstances and conditions of the three countries. The French sought and obtained a more liberal regime of papal taxation;[43] the Germans better representation at the curia from which they felt excluded.[44] The concordat made 'for the reformation of the English church' was agreed to at Berne on 30 May 1418.[45] It contained no fireworks, and was described by a modern critic as rather timid.[46] However, seen in the context of the state of the Church in general and of the Oxford demands of 1414 in particular, this view cannot be sustained. The document was brief. It contained an undertaking, as the 1414 demands had sought and the

[42] Crowder, *Unity, heresy and reform*, p. 22.
[43] *Sacrorum conciliorum nova et amplissima collectio*, ed. J. Mansi, 27 (Venice, 1784), 1184–9.
[44] Crowder, *Unity, heresy and reform*, p. 23.
[45] 'Pro reformacione ecclesie Anglicane' (*Register of Henry Chichele*, iv, 202).
[46] *Cambridge Medieval History*, viii (Cambridge, 1936), 18.

legislation of the council of Constance had made explicit, that not too many cardinals would be appointed in future. It included, too, undertakings on indulgences, which were high on the list of Oxford demands. Most important, however, it dealt with dispensations, necessary for men who were prepared to spend time to achieve high academic qualifications, while also recognizing the problems created by appropriations and the union and consolidation of vicarages – in other words, the particular anxieties of graduates – which were to be investigated by the bishops to see what might be done.[47]

With her statute of Praemunire, England had little to fear from those who tried to obtain benefices by papal provision without the permission of parliament. The English concordat, in contrast with that of France, had nothing to say about ecclesiastical appointments made by papal authority. The emphasis was now on how to improve a system of appointment by local patrons.[48] In May 1421, at the Canterbury convocation, Chichele presented proposals which, after debate, were published in July. These included the important decision that spiritual patrons were to confer the first benefice falling vacant, and every third one occurring thereafter, upon a graduate.[49] It was a compromise system, but a modest way of demonstrating that, with the help of the pope, attempts were being made, in what were difficult times for the English universities and their graduates, to see that something was done to reconcile the care of souls with the reasonable material demands of those who took them into their care.

*

Reinvigoration of the monastic life, with the importance which it attached to prayer and to both spiritual and physical discipline, was another aspect of the religious history of this reign which owed much to the personal intervention and initiative of the king himself. One indication of this, noted by the majority of chroniclers of the period, was Henry's foundation of two religious houses on the river Thames above London, not to mention the plans which he had to establish a third, which never materialized. These foundations have earned for Henry the merit of being virtually the last royal founder of religious houses in England before these were dissolved at the time of the Reformation.

Henry's personal piety, his respect for the church's divine worship and for the men and women who chose to follow the religious life, cannot be in serious doubt. That he should have encouraged such

[47] *Register of Henry Chichele*, iv, 202–3; Jacob, 'English concordat of 1418', pp. 353–8.

[48] Jacob, 'English concordat of 1418', p. 352.

[49] *Register of Henry Chichele*, iii, 72–5; Wilkins, *Concilia*, iii, 401–2.

foundations is in no way surprising: from a wide variety of sources we know of the importance that Henry attached to prayer and intercession. A number of his pious endowments suggest this, and it should not appear strange to the modern mind that the king, so very much a soldier, should show great awareness of the reality of God and of life in the hereafter. As a soldier, Henry was one who diced with death: had he not been wounded at the battle of Shrewsbury in 1403? As important was the preoccupation which men of this time had with both physical death and the spiritual death caused by sin, which spared neither the soldier nor the man of rank and responsibility. The endowment of places of prayer by those who had worldly wealth to leave was characteristic of the age. A very notable soldier of the fourteenth century, Walter Manny, had founded a Charterhouse (or house of Carthusians, one of the more austere orders) by the terms of his will in 1371, while another Carthusian house, that of St Anne near Coventry, was founded a decade later by Lord Zouche, and had received the active support of Richard II, who had laid its foundation stone.

Tradition, in this case a reasonable tradition which can be neither proved nor disproved, has it that Henry decided upon the foundation of a monastery at Sheen, on the south bank of the Thames up river from London, to fulfil part of the penance imposed upon his father by Gregory XII in 1408 as an act of expiation for the judicial murder of archbishop Scrope of York three years earlier. Henry IV had not undertaken the work, and his successor felt obliged to carry it out. The site chosen by Henry was a warren close to the royal manor house (in what is today Old Deer Park, near Richmond) where Anne, Richard II's queen, had died in 1394, and which her distraught husband had ordered to be demolished.[50] It was this site which Henry determined to develop again and close to which, by virtue of the foundation charter sealed on 1 April 1415, he established the first of a cluster of monastic buildings for forty Carthusian monks to which was given the name of the House of Jesus of Bethlehem.

The monks, as those who asked to enter the order were reminded at their service of initiation, were to live a life of 'strictness and austoritie'. Their clothes were rough and simple; no linen, only 'shirte of heare' (hair) or 'wolen shirts'; they slept on a blanket upon a bed made of straw, and their diet was basic. They lived in silence, each monk inhabiting a small set of rooms which kept him apart from his

[50] D. Knowles, *The religious orders in England. ii: The end of the Middle Ages* (Cambridge, 1955), ch.13, especially p. 175; *VCH Middlesex*, iii, 96. I have to thank Dr Neil Beckett for allowing me to see the results of his work on Henry's monastic foundations while I was preparing this chapter.

companions, whom he met only in choir and in chapter. It was neither
an easy life nor a life of ease: the religious literature associated with
members of this order emphasizes the deep spirituality which characterized those who chose it. The House, which appears to have
accepted thirty rather than forty monks, was built of stone brought
from as far afield as Yorkshire and Caen, in Normandy, and of bricks
from Calais.[51] It was well endowed, largely with lands which had
been taken from the English estates and ecclesiastical patronage of
French monasteries. It is ironic that the system of appropriation of
benefices which, as seen above, was regarded as a critical issue at this
period, should have been encouraged by the king himself in order to
support the monasteries which he was founding.[52] Henry's personal
involvement in the venture is further witnessed to by the fact that, in
the first will which he made within months of sealing the foundation
charter, he bequeathed £1000 to his new religious house for its completion.[53] In addition, Henry granted the monastery the privilege of
exemption from all taxes and demands for secular service. He saw it,
as the charter emphasizes, as a place of prayer, where the monks
would intercede for him while he remained alive and for his soul once
he was dead, as well as for his relatives and all the dead. In addition,
they were to pray for the good of the kingdom.[54]

In founding the Carthusian house at Sheen, Henry was doing as
others had done before him. He was demonstrating his admiration
for the order's ideal, while underlining the fact that the life of austerity
was one which merited the admiration and support of lay people of
the time. His second foundation had more than a little of novelty
about it, reflecting the king's interest in recent developments in the
monastic life, this time in Scandinavia, where Queen Bridget of
Sweden had, in the last century, established a new order for both men
and women whose rule, however, had not yet received proper papal
approval. When Philippa, the younger of Henry's two sisters, had
married Eric, king of Denmark and Sweden in 1406, a granddaughter
of Bridget who had been appointed as head of her household had
taken her to visit the order's centre at Vadstena. It was here that Sir
Henry (later Lord) FitzHugh, who would one day become Henry's
chamberlain, promised to endow the order with lands which he held
at Cherry Hinton, near Cambridge. Although FitzHugh finally did
not fulfil this undertaking, it is not unlikely that he was instrumental

---

[51] R.A. Brown, H.M. Colvin and A.J. Taylor, *The History of the King's Works. i &*
ii: The Middle Ages (London, 1963), ii, 999.
[52] D.J.A. Matthew, *The Norman monasteries and their English possessions* (London,
1962), pp. 116, 127.
[53] *Foedera*, IV, ii, 138–9.
[54] *Monasticon Anglicanum*, ed. W. Dugdale (6 vols, London, 1817–30), vi, 31.

in influencing the new king towards establishing a house (the intention was, indeed, for more than one) of the order in 1415.

The religious house founded on rather marshy ground near the Thames at Isleworth, almost opposite the Carthusian monastery already discussed, had its foundation stone laid by the king himself, in the presence of Richard Clifford, bishop of London, on 22 February 1415.[55] As is made clear by its foundation charter, witnessed by a veritable galaxy of the kingdom's most important people gathered at Westminster on 3 March, the house was to be a house of prayer, where thanks could be rendered to God, and intercession made to the Trinity, the Virgin Mary and St Bridget for the good of the king and the kingdom. Peace, Henry stated, was what he sought, and it was as a true son of the God of peace that he was establishing a community of sixty nuns, under an abbess, and twenty-five men of religion, led by one of their number called a 'confessor'. The community (the total of eighty-five represented the thirteen apostles, to include Paul, and the seventy-two disciples) was to pray for Henry both in his lifetime and after his death; for his father Henry IV, and for 'our most dear mother', Mary; for his grandfather, John of Gaunt, and his wife, Blanche; for all the king's ancestors and all the faithful departed. Living under the rule of St Augustine, the male and female sections of the community were to live quite separately, although the nuns and priests appear to have shared a church, the nuns being upstairs, the men downstairs. The spiritual direction, however, was to be provided by the men, some of whom would have to be priests.[56]

The foundation, granted Martin V's bull of approval on 18 August 1418, was given appropriated churches as part of its endowment. In this, as in the legacy of £1000 granted to it by the king in his will of 1415, it was being treated in the same way as the neighbouring Carthusian house at Sheen. One may speculate about the name, Syon, given it by Henry. One of the hills of Jerusalem, Syon (or Zion) conjures up a vision, possibly of the house of God or of heaven as the final home of the believer. The foundation charter as good as tells us why Henry chose the name: Syon was a vision of peace chosen by 'a true son of the God of peace, who gave peace and taught peace and chose St Bridget as a lover of peace and tranquillity'. These facts should not go unnoticed. In 1414 Henry was negotiating with the French for his rights in their country; in 1415 he went to war to

[55] *The Incendium Amoris of Richard Rolle of Hampole*, ed. M. Deanesly (Manchester, 1915), p. 105.
[56] Dugdale, *Monasticon*, vi, 540–3. The terms of foundation made this almost a house of prayer for members of the house of Lancaster.

maintain the justice of that claim. Justice would bring peace, and Henry always maintained that he wanted no more than what was rightly his. The religious in the house which he was founding, partly dedicated to St Bridget, were also to pray to her for peace; they were to do so in a place which, by virtue of the name bestowed upon it, might be regarded as representing the actual attainment on this earth of the heavenly goal of peace. As we try to understand Henry's thinking not only about war but about peace in the early period of his reign, the name of Syon assumes some importance.

The abbess and confessor of the new foundation were soon appointed, and in May 1415 some nuns and another brother arrived from Sweden. However, probably because there were disagreements over the interpretation of Bridget's Rule, which was not yet, due to the years of schism, properly accepted by the Church, it was not until the summer of 1418, in answer to a request by Henry himself, that approval was obtained from Martin V. Before that not much could be done. But on 1 April 1420 (the king and founder being at that moment in France) thirty-seven men and women took their vows, and the monastery, destined to move its site a decade or so later, came properly into existence. On 5 May the first abbess and confessor were formally installed by the bishop of London.[57]

How, we may ask, did this new 'mixed' community appear to the world outside? The view of an outsider, himself a monk, is instructive. Writing about 1420, Thomas Walsingham, the Benedictine from St Albans, a man of mature years who had spent his life in an all-male monastic community with many contacts beyond the cloister, could give his not uncritical view of how he regarded this latest addition to the monastic community of his declining years. The facts which he gave suggest that he had, or had had, a copy of the foundation charter in his possession. He referred to their austerity: they used not linen, but wool; they had to estimate each year how much food they would consume during the next, and could therefore not afford to waste any; they were not allowed possessions, nor could any visitor enter their cloister. This was life according to the rule of Christ, which Walsingham briefly described ('before hurrying on to other affairs') with a mixture of awe and disbelief. How could men and women living in religion exist so closely together? He had to respect the way of life which they had chosen (after all, the house had been founded by a man whom he greatly admired) but one senses that it was all a little too novel and a bit beyond him.[58]

Although it failed – and failed quickly – the third of Henry's pro-

[57] BL, Cotton Ms Cleopatra E.ii, fo.374.
[58] *St Albans Chronicle*, pp. 82–3.

jected foundations must be mentioned, for once again it suggests to us that his choice of orders in some way reflected an important aspect of his character: austerity. Founded in Italy and named after Celestine V, the man who had resigned the papal office in 1294 after a brief pontificate of less than half a year, the Celestines had done well in France, and had an important house in Paris. Their rule was essentially Benedictine but, as Thomas Walsingham noted, they observed it to the letter, and in addition they cut themselves off from any contact with the world outside their walls.[59] What the fate of Henry's experiment was is not clear. It is known that before August 1414 Henry had already stated his intention of encouraging a foundation in England, and that at that time bishops Courtenay and Langley, while on embassy in Paris, visited the order's house there, whereupon three monks accompanied them back to England with the intention of establishing the monastery which Henry was planning to found at Sheen. But, probably because of war, the plan did not develop, and little else was heard of this project.[60]

Henry's personal encouragement of the active religious life was to take another direction, that of reform. In this, as in his choice of which religious orders to encourage, we see Henry motivated by two factors: his own desire that the monastic life, especially that of the Benedictines, should be led to the full; and the wider interest in reform which was part of informed opinion of the day. What spurred him into action in 1421 we do not know. Thomas Spofford, abbot of St Mary's, York, and royal ambassador to the council of Constance in 1414, had participated in the reform of the German Benedictines at Petershausen in 1417, and it is possible that Henry, who had had not a little to do with monasteries of the order in Normandy since that time, may have been contemplating action on his return to England. He was perhaps urged into action by the prior of Mount Grace, whose observance of the monastic rule was stricter than that of the Black Monks, as the Benedictines were known. There appears to have been some unease about the way the three presidents of the Benedictine order's chapter had been chosen in July 1420, and how this might affect the next meeting due to be held three years later.

It was while he was celebrating Easter at Leicester that Henry, having enquired from the abbot of Bury St Edmunds when the next

[59] Ibid., p. 82.
[60] *King's works: Middle Ages*, i, ch.9, especially 266. Like his immediate predecessors, Henry gave encouragement to the development of another Carthusian abbey, that of Mount Grace, near Thirsk, in Yorkshire. He also helped in the building of the College of St Mary in the Newarke at Leicester, another foundation very much associated with the family of Lancaster, since Henry's mother, Mary Bohun, had been interred there in 1394 (Knowles, *Religious orders*, ii, 137; *King's Works: Middle Ages*, i, 266–7).

chapter would be held and being informed that it lay with the presidents to take such action, none the less decided to initiate action himself. On 25 March 1421 he wrote to the presidents that, 'for certeyn matiers chargeable concernyng the worschipe of God as wel as the goode of youre ordre', he wanted a meeting of its members to be called at Westminster on 5 May.[61] It was probably two days later (parliament and the convocation of the ecclesiastical province of Canterbury were also in session) that Henry addressed the 360 or so monks who had come to the meeting. As the modern successor to men who had founded and endowed monasteries and encouraged the monastic way of life (a neat reference to his own efforts of earlier years), he was concerned that the rule was being ignored and that the original spirit which lay behind the monastic vocation was in danger. Just as, in founding his monasteries at Sheen and Isleworth, he had emphasized the importance he attached to prayer, so, in addressing the assembled Benedictine monks, he stressed how he had been encouraged that the country's monastic communities had been praying for him and his army as it prepared to face the French army at Agincourt.[62]

Henry, however, did more than exhort. In his name a document of thirteen proposals for the improvement of monastic life was put forward for discussion between his own representatives, Edmund Lacy, once dean of his chapel and now bishop of Exeter, his secretary (probably William Alnwick) and the prior of Mount Grace, and six monastic representatives, who included Thomas Spofford, who would soon become bishop of Hereford. The document was in no sense radical; rather it was an appeal for a stricter observance of existing rules, not a call for real change or reform. Henry was demonstrating the limits of his rather conservative vision of the religious life. But on one matter, prayer, he was insistent. His royal predecessors had been among the founders of the monasteries concerned: the monks had a duty to offer a quid pro quo of prayer for their benefactors. As in the case of his own foundations, he was only asking for what he felt was due: his emphasis on the efficacity of prayer was typical of the man. His other proposals, however, about monastic food, dress and accommodation, his 'call to regularity', met with little response. After discussion, much of it in committee, most of Henry's proposals were rejected. In their place, the monks were offered a set of seven proposals drawn up by

---

[61] *Documents illustrating the activities of the general and provincial chapters of the English Black Monks, 1215–1540*, ed. W.A. Pantin, ii (Camden 3rd series, RHistS, London, 1933), 105. The letters included in this collection (pp. 104–5) should be added to *Signet letters*, ed. Kirby.

[62] *Chapters of the English Black Monks*, ii, 99.

the abbot of St Albans, John Whethamstead, to which they were able to agree, and it is likely that these were accepted by the order's chapter when it met at Northampton in 1423.[63]

By that time Henry V was dead, but his short reign had none the less been, in the words of one modern critic, 'an epoch in English church history'.[64] At a national level it had witnessed the rebuff meted out to Lollardy which, after the revolt of 1414, was no longer the danger to English society which some contemporaries had considered it to be. It had also seen some attempt to bring a new sense of animation to the oldest monastic order, as well as the encouragement given to the more up-to-date expressions of the monastic ideal. Henry had continued the age-old tradition of the king, even, as in his case, a very militarily minded king, acting as the founder of monasteries, particularly of orders dedicated to a life of austere self-discipline, contemplation and prayer, characteristics which reflected both his strongly held belief in the power of intercession and a streak of the puritanical in his nature. Above all, perhaps, the reign had witnessed what were to be among the last attempts in the pre-Reformation world to influence the broader Christianity of Europe and to submit to ideas being introduced from outside England. The English contribution to the council of Constance cannot be ignored; nor can the introduction of ideals of reform and renewal which entered England during these years. Henry was a very 'English' king. It should not be forgotten, however, that in matters spiritual, both England and her king were part of a Christendom which transcended national boundaries. There is a case for seeing Henry not merely as king of England, but as a man with a wider vision, influenced by events which occurred, and by ideas which came from, outside his island kingdom.

[63] Ibid., ii, 99–100, 104–34.
[64] Knowles, *Religious orders*, ii, 175.

Chapter 13

LOLLARDY AND SEDITION

The clerical author of the *Gesta Henrici Quinti* saw the outstanding episodes of Henry's life as a series of trials by means of which God tested the constancy and determination of his elect. The first of these recorded was the rising which took place in London on 9 January 1414, when Henry had occupied the throne for less than a year. Contemporary or near-contemporary narrative was intended to leave the reader in no doubt that the events of that day, planned by the forces of evil, were intended as both an attack upon the king and his brothers (hence upon the throne itself) and an attempt to undermine the higher levels of the country's social order. In trying to stress the grave danger from which England was saved only by the king's prompt action, the chroniclers, notably Thomas Walsingham, emphasized the plotting and collusion which occurred between those who took part in the rising, as well as their large numbers. Since there had been some kind of conspiracy against the king, the Church and the law, then the most must be made of it. The difficulty experienced by later historians has been to disentangle fact from fiction, exaggeration from likely truth. In brief, what is felt to be lacking in contemporary accounts is a sense of proportion. It is the modern historian's task to try to introduce that vital element, an element of judgement, into the story.

On the last day of the year 1384, some two years before Henry V's birth and close on thirty years before the events which, for a few hours, appeared to threaten the throne, John Wyclif died at Lutterworth, in Leicestershire, where he was rector. His career, largely spent in the relative seclusion of the university of Oxford from which, however, he had sometimes emerged to help Edward III in his diplomatic dealings with the papacy, is an excellent example of the influence of the intellectual upon a much wider sphere of life than the subject of his attention, theology, might suggest. First employed by the king to justify a strong measure of local (hence royal rather than papal) control over appointments to ecclesiastical offices and benefices in England, the development of Wyclif's theological ideas was to have wider implications for contemporary religious thought and practice, as well as for certain aspects of social thought. His doctrine of dominion by grace (certainly not new, for he had inherited many of its ideas from the great archbishop of Armagh, Richard FitzRalph) had fundamental implications for how men should respond to authority. Wyclif came to teach that authority could only be truly exercised by a person in a state of grace, whose soul, in a word, was at peace with God. Only authority thus validly exercised had to be obeyed. But only God, not man, knew the state of the soul of a person in authority. The implications of that way of thinking were far-reaching. Any act of authority, indeed any authority, whether spiritual or temporal, could be defied, as no human could prove that another was in a state of grace, and therefore in a proper state to exercise authority.

Wyclif's influence did not stop there. By the end of his life he was denying that, in the Mass, the bread and wine used in the sacrament became the true body and blood of Christ at the moment when the words of consecration were uttered by the priest. To hold this view was not only to deny one of the central truths taught by the Church; it was also to undermine the power of the priesthood, for only the ordained priest had the power to perform this miraculous act. The process went further still. Under the influence of Wyclif other of the Church's sacraments – baptism, confession – came to be put in doubt, while a number of acts of piety, such as the use of images in churches or the practice of going on pilgrimage, came under attack.

Wyclif was also intimately linked with another development which was to have far-reaching effects: the translation of the Bible, now to be made available to an ever-widening circle of literate people and, through them, to others as well. For Wyclif and those who were inspired by him, the Bible became the central driving force of their lives, the source of inspiration of both their beliefs and, often, of their social attitudes. Such religious fundamentalism had far-reaching and drastic implications, for, once again, Wyclif was tending to undermine the traditionally accepted role of the priest as the interpreter of God's word. Some were to argue that each Christian, if he or she so chose, should be the judge of how the Bible spoke to him or to her, a view which soon came to be extended into an obligation imposed upon the individual to win others to Christ by bearing witness to him through preaching. The traditional priesthood (entirely male) was to be replaced by one consisting of those (both male and female) who felt inspired to bring God's word, contained in the Bible, to others. The Bible, then, must be translated and made available. It was the *sine qua non* of popular preaching.

We should not criticize the Church of Wyclif's day for having looked upon his teaching as subversive, even heretical, and his immediate disciples as a threat to itself and to contemporary society. Its reaction was a natural one, all the more so as England had been surprisingly free of heretical views in the past, and had no real experience of how to react to them. With hindsight, however, the historian, writing centuries later, may see things differently, for he is able to suggest a wider, European context in which the radical proposals put forward by Wyclif and his followers may be better appreciated. It is apparent that, within that context, those Englishmen who, knowingly or not, acknowledged Wyclif as their source of inspiration, were trying to bring back a greater spirituality and personal involvement into religious practice, factors which, over the past few centuries, had been lost in a Church increasingly legalistic in its attitudes and desirous of imposing theological definitions upon its members. In a Church governed too much by such a mentality, the position of the priest as teacher and interpreter had come to be over-stressed. Wyclif saw the vernacular Bible as a way of countering this, of making lay people, however untrained and unlearned, true and full members of a Church which he, along with many before him, regarded not as a body dominated by a hierarchical structure, but as a community of men and women chosen by God's grace. Such a view, then, sees the Wycliffite 'movement' not solely or primarily as a heretical 'movement', but more as one of 're-form', attempting not the destruction of the Church as it existed but its regeneration according to a different view of its origins and nature. As in some of the continental reform movements, the emphasis should be placed upon the positive aspects of what men were trying to achieve.

The movement towards this 're-form' reflected something else that was happening in the world of the late fourteenth century, namely the increasing awareness of lay people of their rightful place in society, a factor which owed much to the development and extension of educational possibilities and the accelerated growth (certainly true in England) of the vernacular language as a means of conveying ideas. In religious matters this could be seen in the fact that, in 1354, Henry of Grosmont, first duke of Lancaster, had written a work of piety entitled *Le Livre des Seyntz Medicines* (in which he described himself as 'a poor miserable sinner'), [1] while some forty-five years later Sir John Clanvowe, a knight from the Welsh marches, could compose another work of piety, *The Two Ways*, in which he showed how the soul who chose the 'way' of God should proceed. [2] Both are examples of the

---

[1] K.A. Fowler, *The king's lieutenant. Henry of Grosmont, first duke of Lancaster, 1310–1361* (London, 1969), p. 195.

[2] See *The works of Sir John Clanvowe*, ed. V.J. Scattergood (Cambridge/Ipswich, 1975).

lay piety which was sweeping across Europe at this time. The main distinction between them lies not so much in their content as in the languages in which they were written: Lancaster wrote in what was still the language of the nobility, Anglo-Norman; Clanvowe, on the other hand, used English. It is this change, as much as any, which needs emphasis, for his work represents an important development, the recognition that the educated (who need not have been the recipients of much formal education) had a part to play in both the formulation and the propagation of religious ideas expressed in the everyday language of their time. Yet, from the point of view of ecclesiastical authority, which regarded it as its duty to protect an unsuspecting laity from the snares and delusions of heretical doctrine, the development of the book written in English was something which presented a threat both to the Church's traditional teaching authority and to the eternal salvation of the souls under its care.

If the ideas developed by Wyclif and those who came after him may be explained, to a certain extent, by contemporary developments, it remains that their propagation owed much to the fact that, late in the fourteenth century, England had few means of countering such ideas, however subversive they might appear. Indeed, Wyclif received the support (if not the active protection) of John of Gaunt, duke of Lancaster, son-in-law of the author of *Le Livre des Seyntz Medicines*, and grandfather of Henry V. Whether Gaunt sympathized with Wyclif's ideas, it is difficult to tell. It seems clear, however, that such sympathy was no longer extended after Wyclif had been condemned by the clergy of the province of Canterbury, under archbishop Courtenay, in May 1382, at a meeting which defended the Church's teaching on the eucharist, on confession and on a subject of increasing controversy, the right of the clergy to own property, or temporalities, which had been vigorously attacked by Wyclif. The subversiveness of his ideas upon social thinking was now becoming increasingly apparent and had to be taken seriously.

Yet it took a while for this to happen. Among those who came and went from Richard II's court was a small handful of men of rank, known to history as the 'Lollard Knights', who appear to have enjoyed the king's favour as long as they did not publicize their unorthodox views too openly. With this they seemed content, and so kept their position at court. None the less their existence was well known to men such as Thomas Walsingham, whose task it was to record and comment upon the events of the time. Does this mean that Richard II himself may have sympathized with some of their ideas? Probably not. Yet Richard was a sensitive man who may have understood some of the less radical ideas of the movement. In any event, there seems to be little doubt that the taking of measures against heretics was left, for the present, entirely in the hands of the bishops. However, this could not last. Just as Wyclif himself had taught that the Church should be placed under the ultimate control of the secular ruler, so in 1388, under pressure from parliament, the king's council took it upon itself to ensure that heretical writings be seized. Church and secular power had now decided to act as one, each giving moral and practical support to the other.

Yet heretical ideas did not die that quickly. When archbishop William Courtenay was in Leicester on a metropolitical visitation in the autumn of 1389, several propounders of heterodox views were denounced to him; they were said to favour consubstantiation and preaching by the laity, and to oppose indulgences, the veneration of images and the unconditional payment of tithes to clergy who did not merit them. In the winter of 1392–93 nearby Northampton experienced a measure of social disorder provoked, in part, by the mayor, John Fox, and others who found themselves at odds with commissioners sent out by the bishop of Lincoln, in whose diocese the town lay.[3] Then, in January 1395, as parliament was in session, a Lollard bill, a form of manifesto of a dozen points, was affixed to Westminster Hall (where parliament was meeting) and to the doors of St Paul's cathedral. Transubstantiation was a 'feigned miracle'; the priesthood of today was not what Christ had ordained it should be, and it had no power to absolve; the practices of pilgrimages and of praying before crosses and images were idolatrous. War was condemned; many religious foundations should be abolished, and the rights of the Church to own land should be seriously considered.[4] As an appeal to the sympathies of a number who sat in parliament, the manifesto failed. Indeed, it provoked something of a reaction. Steps were taken to carry out a purge at Oxford: one such victim was to be a scholar named John Claydon. Two years later the bishops, now led by Thomas Arundel, who had succeeded Courtenay as archbishop of Canterbury in the autumn of 1396, asked in parliament that the death penalty be allowed as the ultimate sanction against heretics, thus bringing England into line with general practice on the European continent.

By the time that Henry's father seized the throne in the late summer of 1399 the law appeared to be taking a more serious view of the threat which Lollardy posed to society. One reason for this must have been that the ideas of some of its more extreme exponents were now

---

[3] K.B. McFarlane, *John Wycliffe and the beginnings of English nonconformity* (London, 1952), pp. 139–42.

[4] Ibid., p. 147; P.McNiven, *Heresy and politics in the reign of Henry IV. The burning of John Badby* (Woodbridge/Wolfeboro, 1987), p. 58.

being better understood and the positive threat which they might constitute more widely appreciated. It is important, too, that heresy should be viewed in the wide perspective of the new dynasty's problems: the plot by a number of earls, which threatened both the king's life and the succession early in 1400; the alleged survival of Richard II (which was to last well into his son's reign); and the outbreak of revolt in Wales late in 1400 (which was to constitute a difficulty for a decade and more). We may say, perhaps with a measure of justice, that Henry IV was paying the price paid by most usurpers, namely insecurity. It is clear that heresy was now seen not merely as a threat to ecclesiastical authority and discipline. In the minds of an increasing number of people, it was becoming a danger to secular authority, a step reflected in the growing involvement of the temporal power in the tracking down and punishing of heretics, which had been taking place since at least 1388.

The necessary legislation was passed by the parliament which met at the beginning of 1401. But even before that could be done William Sawtry, a Norfolk chaplain who had already been convicted of heresy in 1399, became the first victim (possibly ever) of anti-heretical sentiment in England. Sawtry had taught a mixture of heretical views: that after consecration the bread of the eucharist remained bread, and nothing more; that it was more important for a priest to preach than for him to say the set prayers of his office; that the bodies of saints were more worthy of honour than was the true cross, for only Christ, and not his cross, should receive that honour. On 26 February, having already been pronounced a lapsed heretic three days earlier, he was stripped of all priestly power and on the very same day, in a move that has reasonably been seen as prearranged, he was publicly burned in London, an example to others of what might be in store for them. [5]

It was only a while later that the clergy in convocation submitted a petition to the king in parliament asking for measures to be taken against what they regarded as the rising threat of heresy. Those who taught or even secretly believed anything contrary to the Church's teaching were to be punished by penalty to be fixed by parliament; all preachers were to have a licence from a bishop; while the writing or copying of heretical works featured prominently on the list of fears about the current situation expressed by the clergy. The statute which emerged from the petition, known as 'De Heretico Comburendo', [6] gave the clergy all that they wanted: bishops regained some of their power to imprison those convicted of errors; heretical writings were to be surrendered under pain of imprisonment or fine; and abjured

[5] *RP*, iii, 459; McNiven, *Heresy and politics*, pp. 81–92.
[6] *SR*, ii, 125–8 (2 HIV, c.15).

or relapsed heretics were to be burned in public. At the special request
of the clergy, the act was not to come into force until Pentecost, so
that its contents might be made known throughout the land, a decision
which seemed contrary to the spirit which had led to Sawtry being
executed by royal order even before the statute had been officially
petitioned for by the clergy.

The passing of the statute 'De Heretico Comburendo' meant that
those of Lollard sympathies had to be very careful what they said and
wrote. Whether Henry IV held strong views about orthodoxy is not
known. [7] He was on excellent terms with Sir John Cheyne, MP for
Gloucestershire, who, on the occasion of the first parliament of the
new reign, had been elected speaker only to be forced to resign by
archbishop Arundel when it was reported before a meeting of convocation, taking place at the same time, that he had long been an enemy
of the Church and held anti-clerical views. [8] This was not to harm the
relationship between the king and the ex-speaker, who soon became a
member of the royal council and served the crown in a number of
ways in the years to come. If there were Lollard knights in Henry's
court, as there had been in that of Richard II, they appear to have
been tolerated. At the parliament which met at Coventry in 1404 they
came out into the open. Thomas Walsingham was to report that on
this occasion archbishop Arundel complained to the king that he had
been deeply scandalized by some members of the royal entourage
who, by seemingly turning their backs, had failed to do honour to the
Host which was being carried in procession. [9] At the same parliament
(1404), too, it was proposed that the revenues from the temporalities
of the Church should be diverted, for a period of a year, into the royal
coffers, a move seen as one answer to the financial difficulties facing
the country at the time.[10] To the clergy, such a suggestion smacked
of the simmering debate on their rights to own sources of wealth,
anathema to many Lollards who regarded it as wrong that the true
imitator of Christ should own a surplus of this world's goods. Some
two years later during the long parliament of 1406 Arundel again had
to complain to the king, this time about one of his closest associates,
Robert Waterton, who had allegedly urged a servant to make an
unseemly gesture to a preacher as he defended the right of the Church
to own temporalities.[11] To Thomas Walsingham, it seemed that it was

[7]   Richard II was apparently uncertain regarding the degree of devotion to the
Church of the man who deposed him (A. Hudson, *The premature reformation* (Oxford,
1988), pp. 112–13).
[8]   Roskell, *Speakers*, pp. 136–7.
[9]   McNiven, *Heresy and politics*, p. 76.
[10]   Roskell, *Speakers*, p. 145; Wolffe, *Royal demesne*, pp. 76–82 and Appendix B.
[11]   *St Albans Chronicle*, pp. 1–2.

time for steps to be taken to counter such attacks upon the Church, her practices and her beliefs.

By the last days of 1406 the reactions of the Prince to heresy start to become apparent. Very late in the parliament which had witnessed the disrespectful gesture of Robert Waterton's servant, a petition was presented to the king by the speaker, John Tiptoft, in which the petitioners, headed by the Prince and including the lords spiritual and temporal of the realm, besought Henry to take firm action against those who aimed at undermining Church, faith and sacraments.[12] The Church, it was emphasized, had been endowed both by the king's predecessors and others with lands whose revenues enabled her to maintain the divine service, do acts of charity for the living, and pray for the souls of the dead. Recently, it was stressed (and the petition was probably referring to events which had occurred in the current parliament), some of the Church's enemies had tried to move men against her by denying her a right to hold land. Unless something were done quickly to prevent this, the next stage would be for such men to try to seize the lands of secular lords, an act which would undoubtedly lead to the final destruction of the kingdom. Furthermore, certain persons were trying to sow division by claiming that Richard II was still alive, while others still were adding lies and false prophecies in their attempt to destroy the power of the king, his heir and all his lords. The petitioners now humbly invoked the protection of the law; any man or woman preaching or inciting others against the Church, its teachings or its sacraments, who urged others to deprive it of its wealth, or who insisted that the 'fool' called Richard II was still alive, should be arrested and brought to answer for his crime before parliament. They urged that proclamation of this statute be made as widely and as soon as possible, and that it should take effect on the next feast of Epiphany, namely 6 January 1407.

What may be learned from this petition of the Prince's reaction to some of the main strands of Lollard thinking? We may first observe that he had allied himself with the leaders of both Church and secular society, with whom he was to be on good terms for the remainder of his life. There is no hint here of any concession on his part to the anti-clericalism which was found among some of the members of the parliament of 1406. Nor is there any doubt in his mind, nor (naturally) in the minds of the clerical lords, nor (significantly) in the minds of the secular lords that the Church's teaching authority or its doctrine regarding the sacraments should be put in doubt. The text suggests four-square support for opposition to radical ideas, from whose

[12] *RP*, iii, 583–4.

implementation the Prince, among others, would suffer. Finally, there is the urging given to the king that he should not tolerate the spreading of tales and rumours about the pseudo-Richard. Here we see the Prince and the lords spiritual and temporal taking a firm stand against disorder which might ensue in society if such tales came to be widely accepted. Not only would the future of the Lancastrian dynasty be at risk; the peace of the country would be, too. Surprisingly, nothing was said about such acts being regarded as treason: the attitude to be adopted to anyone accused of them was not harsh. Yet the fact remains that since such actions could lead to public 'commocion . . . et final destruction & subversion' of the kingdom, any man who pretended to be Richard II was being accused of treason in all but name.[13]

In framing this petition, the Prince and archbishop Arundel, soon to become chancellor of England, appear to have been at one in their opposition to some of the political implications of Lollard teaching.[14] Yet, just as Richard II and Henry IV could be accused of tolerating men of known heterodox opinions, so the Prince had friends whose orthodoxy could, or might, one day be put into question. There seems to be little doubt that the area of the Welsh marches was, perhaps on account of its relative remoteness from London, perhaps because of its accessibility to the mountains of Wales, a favourite area into which a number of men accused of Lollardy and threatened with the sanctions of the law had chosen to 'retire' or 'disappear' from the late 1380s onwards. One such was the well-known Midlands heretic, William Swynderby; another was Walter Brute. Along with Worcestershire and Gloucestershire (and nearby Bristol), which served as a preaching ground for William Taylor, this was the area which had become familiar to the Prince during the course of his wars against the Welsh. Not only that. He was on close terms with knights from this area who were thought or known to have Lollard sympathies: Sir John Greyndore (a servant of the duchy of Lancaster, a member of the Prince's household and a future justice itinerant in south Wales in the next reign); Sir Roger Acton (in the Prince's service in 1403); and, not least, a certain Sir John Oldcastle (close companion-in-arms in the Welsh wars) who, along with Acton, would die for his beliefs –

---

[13] McNiven, *Heresy and politics*, pp. 100–2.

[14] It is clear that the distinction between certain offences committed against the spiritual and the civil authorities was now likely to be abandoned and the two merged as treason, to be countered by powers given to both ecclesiastical and civil authorities together (see P.J. Horner, ' "The king taught us the lesson": Benedictine support for Henry V's suppression of the Lollards', *Mediaeval Studies*, 52 (1990), 199–200; G. Leff, *Heresy in the later middle ages. The relation of heterodoxy to dissent, c.1250–c.1450* (2 vols, Manchester, 1967), ii, 596).

and his treason – against Henry V.[15] We cannot make any real judgements from what little information we have; but it should be noted that the Prince numbered among his associates men who showed some – and in two cases much – sympathy for Lollard doctrines of a rather extreme kind.

While he exercised power as chancellor (a period which lasted from early 1407 to late 1409) Arundel took steps in his capacity as archbishop of Canterbury to try to flush out more Lollard sympathizers from Oxford and to exercise greater control over preaching in his province. In 1407 the provincial convocation was summoned to meet in Oxford, and the archbishop took the opportunity to issue a set of new constitutions intended to regulate both preaching and teaching at the university. Two years later, in June 1409, under some pressure, the university of Oxford was to condemn seven of Wyclif's works, a further step in the drive against heterodox teaching and the propagation of the Bible in English.

Arundel would doubtless have wished to do more. By Christmas 1409, however, he had resigned the chancellorship, and effective control of government came into the hands of the Prince and his allies, the Beauforts. Before long, things began to happen. It was probably at this parliament that a group of knights with Lollard sympathies presented a bill demanding what was, in effect, a systematic disendowment of the Church's lands in favour of the king, whose authority would benefit to the tune of £20,000 from the money thus made available, and the creation and endowment of fifteen new earls, 1500 knights, 6200 esquires, 100 extra almshouses and a number of new universities. The plan was costed and, in terms of what it would produce, appears reasonably accurate.[16]

Its ideas had been aired at the end of the fourteenth century; its present importance, however, lay in the fact that it was being put before parliament at a time when control of the council lay with the Prince. Did he have knowledge of it and, if so, did he have sympathies with its aims? It was, after all, presented while he was trying to regulate and bring under control the very great expenses of the crown; the implementation of the plan could have resolved his difficulties. One part of the Prince may have welcomed the proposal; another, that which had urged his father to act against Lollard plans at the end of 1406, would have been firmly against it. How he reacted, we cannot tell, for our knowledge of the whole episode comes not from the official parliamentary record in which, as one critic has noted,

[15] McNiven, *Heresy and politics*, p. 155.
[16] *Selections from English Wycliffite writings*, ed. A. Hudson (Cambridge, 1978), pp. 135–7, 203–7.

actions proposed against the Church were usually passed over in silence,[17] but from copies of the proposals which have been found elsewhere. While there is no record of the Prince's open opposition to it (was his attitude equivocal?), nevertheless one cannot imagine so radical a plan winning effective backing without some support from the Prince.[18] It is noteworthy that a further petition, intended to protect those arrested for Lollardy, was also rejected a short while later. One cannot believe that a far more radical proposal would have been accepted by the Prince if one of such lesser significance had been refused. The possibility is tempting, but the evidence is not convincing.

The episode was scarcely over when another, of greater significance, followed it.[19] On 5 March 1410 John Badby, an artisan from Worcestershire, was burned for heresy at Smithfield in London, the first man (as far as is known) since Sawtry in 1401 to suffer the extreme penalty for his beliefs. Like many others, he could not bring himself to accept the Church's teaching on transubstantiation, but by expressing it in the way he did, that 'John Rakyer of Bristol had the same power and the same authority to make the body of Christ as any priest', his words could be taken as an explicit attack upon sacerdotal power. Already declared a heretic by his own bishop in 1409, and detained in the episcopal prison, he was brought to London in February 1410 to face not only a daunting number of bishops, including Arundel, but a group of prominent laymen as well, including Edward, duke of York, and Thomas Beaufort, the recently appointed chancellor. The proceedings, it must be recalled, took place in the shadow of recent events in parliament, which had witnessed the attempt by Lollard sympathizers to deprive the Church of her temporal endowments. The trial, which can therefore be seen as a showdown between orthodoxy and heterodoxy, could have only one outcome. As it was, Badby did nothing to save himself: he would continue in his beliefs and, if necessary, pay the consequences. It was decided that he must die, and that he must do so immediately.

Badby's execution by burning was to be witnessed by an 'exalted company', including some of the bishops who had been present at his trial and condemnation. Also in attendance was the Prince, whose presence was recorded in the contemporary records, and whose motives have been the subject of close scrutiny in recent historical writing. Why was he there? What was his witness of Badby's last moments intended to signify? It must be recalled that this was only

[17] Kirby, *Henry IV*, p. 229.
[18] McNiven, *Heresy and politics*, p. 195.
[19] Ibid., ch. 11.

the second sentence of death for heresy to be carried out in England, and that, as a consequence, there was no real precedent as to who should witness it, especially as William Sawtry's execution (in 1401) had been carried out hurriedly before the passing of the legislation 'De Heretico Comburendo'. It is likely, then, that the Prince's presence was intended as an act of support for the Church in her determined fight against heresy, and that it should be seen in the light of his likely opposition to the Lollard-inspired plans for disendowment which had been debated only a few weeks earlier. His presence, too, was intended to show that the secular power was now assuming control in deciding who would be burned for heresy. In the particular circumstances of the day, an execution for heresy would show where the Prince stood in regard to the defence of traditional religion; it would also be seen as an act for which the secular power was ultimately responsible. In brief, it was an assertion of authority by the secular power over its spiritual counterpart.

The matter of the Prince's presence was one thing. How he reacted to the burning of Badby was another. The victim had been placed in a barrel and the fire lighted (heat and smoke would have rendered him unconscious very quickly) when the Prince suddenly ordered it to be put out: he wanted to talk to Badby. This he did, appealing to him to use this opportunity to save his life, and offering him a daily allowance of 3d. if he would do so. Badby spurned these offers; the barrel was replaced on the fire and the execution went forward to its predetermined end. What had the Prince been trying to do? Had he been trying to steal the limelight from Arundel, his political 'rival' whom he had replaced as the effective head of government only three months earlier? Was he hoping to persuade Badby to recant when Arundel had failed to do this? Either reason is possible; neither is likely. We cannot tell. However, one thing was evident. While the Prince was in charge of government, firm, indeed stern, action might be expected against those who dared to rock the ship of state, in particular if their crime were the 'spiritual' one of heresy. From now onwards, his position was clear.

This could be seen in the way that the Prince reacted to archbishop Arundel's attempts to purge the university of Oxford of what he saw as its remaining support of Wycliffite heresy. Fifteen years earlier, in 1395, the university had obtained a bull from the pope of the day, Boniface IX, granting it exemption from ecclesiastical jurisdiction. Two years later, with Arundel now at Canterbury, Richard II had agreed that the archbishop had a right to visit the university and, in spite of Boniface's bull, it was upon this that he acted. Autocratic by nature, Arundel saw it as his duty to root out the last defiant remains of heretical doctrine from the institution which had witnessed its birth.

In November 1407 Oxford had served as the scene for the publication of constitutions regulating preaching, and, with a view to expelling them, steps had been taken to make regular enquiries among the academic community about those who might hold corrupting opinions. Such steps appeared to be justified. In the previous year, probably at a moment when parliament was meeting in London, the principal of St Edmund Hall, William Taylor, had preached at St Paul's Cross in favour of Wyclif's views that the clergy should be denied the benefit of temporal possessions; while later in the same year Peter Payne, one of his successors as principal, had written a letter under the university's seal to the supporters of John Hus in Prague agreeing with their views, which, it was said, were approved of by Englishmen at Oxford and elsewhere.

It was the energy of Wyclif's last supporters which Arundel wanted to crush. In 1409 he issued further constitutions intended to curtail religious disputation, forbidding the translation of the Bible into English other than with episcopal approval. Trying to enforce these measures, he came up against Richard Courtenay, chancellor of the university and a firm friend of the Prince, to whom Courtenay appealed. Courtenay wanted to do his best for his university, and he did not make Arundel's task an easy one, on one occasion barring him and his followers from entering St Mary's church. The dispute had become rather more a matter of principle of the right of visitation than of cutting off heresy at its roots. It now went to a final judgement before the king who, in September 1411, came out in favour of Arundel. The archbishop's rights were recognized, Courtenay was deposed, and the university had to seek a formal pardon from the Church. Before long, however, Courtenay was restored: it is likely that the compromise was worked out with the help of the Prince,[20] who, in the spring of 1413, had him appointed to the vacant see of Norwich.

*

By that time the Prince had succeeded his father as king. As a means of assessing the situation, it is worth asking what problems Lollardy constituted for the new king. There was that of belief or doctrine or, as it was regarded by its opponents, heresy. Lollards, as we have seen, had no uniform set of beliefs: as individuals, they disagreed with particular parts of the Church's doctrine, much as their inclination took them. There were those (Sawtry and Badby had been tragic examples) who denied a central tenet of the Church's teaching, that of transubstantiation, an explicit attack on sacerdotal power, conferred upon a priest by a bishop. That was bad enough. What made

[20] Kirby, *Henry IV*, p. 236; *Snappe's Formulary and other records*, ed. H.E. Salter (Oxford Hist. Soc., 1924), p. 175.

it more dangerous was that, in the minds of men who agreed with John Badby, traditional priestly power was supplanted by another, that of the priesthood of all believers, teaching which not only challenged accepted doctrine but made a mockery of ecclesiastical discipline and, ultimately, of episcopal (even papal) power and authority. Outwardly, they argued, no man was better than the next; only God could distinguish between them as He alone could know whether they were in his grace or not. Authority was dealt a devastating blow.

To the guardian of the Church's traditional teaching (be he priest, bishop or king), heresy which concerned the rejection of one or more sacraments was the worst kind: it had implications in the after-world. To the layman, the social implications of such teaching were the most shocking and frightening. The attack on the Church's authority to define her beliefs and to defend them could be pressed further. As the petition presented to parliament in 1406 pointed out, an attack on clerical property would, if not halted, soon lead to a similar one on secular property. Too literal an interpretation of the Bible could lead to the acceptance of a spurious form of egalitarianism and the breakdown of the social order. It could also lead, as had already been seen, to an attack upon clerical property on the grounds that as Christ and his immediate followers had been poor men, so their successors should be poor as well, for none could serve two masters, God and mammon.

Upon whom did the sect (a word used at the time) depend? Originally academic, as we have seen, it came to be accepted by many with no academic ambitions or formal education of any kind (many Lollards were not even literate) largely through the efforts of preachers and teachers, many of whom sacrificed their careers and even put their lives at risk to bring the new doctrines to those who wished to hear them. In this they were greatly helped by members of the social group whom today's historians of the subject have identified as the vital force behind the spread of Lollardy: the gentry. Lollardy found little support among the high nobility; the secular nobility, let us recall, had joined the Prince and the spiritual lords in 1406 in seeking that firm steps be taken to contain the damage which could be done by Lollard-inspired proposals in parliament. Some gentry held anti-clerical views and sympathies together with Lollard ideas on disendowment, but such views hardly made them heretics. Few went so far as Sir Thomas Latimer, whose seat was at Braybrooke in Northamptonshire, who used his patronage of the parish church to install and protect priests whose views he shared, even if the bishop did not.[21] More typical of men known to have had Lollard sympathies were Sir Thomas Chaworth or Henry Booth, who both represented

[21] McFarlane, *John Wycliffe*, p. 146.

Derbyshire in parliament in the reigns of the first two Lancastrians, or Thomas Brooke, who sat for either Dorset or Somerset in Henry V's reign. Others still, such as the so-called 'Lollard knights' of Richard II's reign, had brought their sympathies to court; it is possible that they had successors there in the reign of Henry IV, and that the Prince himself may have known them.

Were these men determined heretics, bent upon self-immolation if need be? If so, only a tiny handful proved to be of that mettle. What they did represent, however, was a disillusionment with much of religion and many of the religious practices which existed at the end of the fourteenth and beginning of the fifteenth century, disillusionment sometimes reflected in the works of William Langland, Geoffrey Chaucer and John Gower.[22] By offering financial help towards the copying of sermon cycles (now recognized as a vital part of the propagation of Wycliffite ideas), such Lollard sympathizers helped to make heterodox views respectable in the country.[23] It was almost certainly the gentry who tried, on a number of occasions during the reign of Henry IV, to have some of the more radical Wycliffite proposals (social ones such as the disendowment of the Church) passed in parliament. Their attempts failed; but they probably had a good measure of support, underlining the importance of this social group in furthering 're-formist' ideas.

These points are confirmed by the career of the last of Lollardy's knightly standard bearers, Sir John Oldcastle, of Almeley in Herefordshire. Probably about ten years older than Henry V, he had served in the war against the Scots in 1400 and then, like so many with lands in the marches, for a number of years against the neighbouring Welsh under the command of the Prince, whose friend he had become. He does not appear to have been one of those Lollards who was opposed to war. A man of position in his county, he sat in parliament in 1404, acted as a justice of the peace in 1406 and as sheriff of his county two years later. Between 1410 and 1413 he was summoned to sit among the lords in parliament by virtue of his title of Lord Cobham, which he had acquired by marriage in 1408. In brief, Oldcastle was a man of action, accustomed to public service, the kind of person who might be said to make ideal Lollard 'material'.

What turned him into a heretic of firmly held views we do not know. It is likely that he knew William Swynderby[24] (who was opposed to war) and he probably had links with another Lollard preacher,

[22] Harriss, *Henry V: practice of kingship*, p. 24.
[23] A. Hudson, 'A Lollard sermon-cycle and its implications', *Medium Aevum*, 40 (1971), 146–52.
[24] McFarlane, *John Wycliffe*, p. 134.

Richard Wyche.[25] What is known is that in September 1410 both Oldcastle and Wyche wrote letters to Bohemia (rather as Payne had done in 1407) congratulating the Hussites on their successes and urging them on in their fight against the anti-Christ (the Pope).[26] A year later Oldcastle wrote to the Bohemian king, Wenceslaus, referring in his letter to the contact he had made with Hus. By this time, acting as if he were 'a recognized leader of the English sect',[27] his contacts were already known to the Church, although the knowledge does not appear to have been publicized and may not have been known to the Prince. Oldcastle even assisted the earl of Arundel in the expedition sent to help John of Burgundy against the Armagnacs in 1411, an expedition sanctioned by the Prince himself.[28]

The Prince, however, had no sooner become king than he must have been made aware that Oldcastle was already in trouble with the Church.[29] At first it had been a matter of housing a chaplain, named John, a man of unorthodox views, in his castle at Cooling, near Rochester. Before long, however, the extent of Oldcastle's involvement in heresy became apparent when he confessed, in the presence of the king, that some tracts of a heretical nature found in a shop in Paternoster Row in London were, indeed, his. Pressed on the matter, he admitted that the doctrines which they contained were worthy of condemnation, but that he had failed to understand their proper meaning. The king was deeply shocked by this revelation, while the clergy, probably more accustomed to such writings, prepared for further action against Oldcastle. In the meanwhile, it was agreed that the king, as his friend, should be asked to see what he could do.

The king soon found, however, that he could do nothing. By August 1413, when it was clear that he was making no progress, Henry gave archbishop Arundel leave to proceed against Oldcastle for heresy. Summoned to appear, Oldcastle locked himself into his castle at Cooling and refused contact with the outside world. Clearly, there was a limit to how long he could last out. By the end of September he was in custody in the Tower of London, and his trial was about to begin. The account drawn up by Arundel's registrar, copies of which were to be circulated later to the ecclesiastical authorities (thus making possible Thomas Walsingham's careful account of the proceedings

[25] M.H. Keen, 'The influence of Wyclif', *Wyclif in his times*, ed. A.J.P. Kenny (Oxford, 1986), p. 131.
[26] W.T. Waugh, 'Sir John Oldcastle', *EHR*, 20 (1905), 443; McFarlane, *John Wycliffe*, pp. 161–2.
[27] McFarlane, *John Wycliffe*, p. 162.
[28] *English Chronicle*, p. 36.
[29] It appears that he knew, and rejected, his friend's heretical views before he became king (*Vita et gesta*, p. 31).

incorporated into his chronicle), shows that Oldcastle was treated with consideration and fairness.[30] Like so many before and after him, he chose to use the occasion to publicize his views, little realizing that such an exposition of ideas helped to create a climate of opinion against him. What Arundel wanted was to press him on the vital question of the eucharist: did he or did he not believe in the Church's teaching on transubstantiation? Given two days to think the matter over (he was even given a copy of the Church's doctrine in English to ponder over) he failed to convince the court that his views were not heretical. In such circumstances, Arundel had no choice: Oldcastle was excommunicated and handed over to the secular power for punishment.

The ball was now firmly in Henry's court. The situation was not so very different from that which he had been faced with when Badby had been condemned in 1410. The king had it in his power to decide whether Oldcastle lived or died. Yet, in 1413, there were differences. Badby had had to die because of the perceived threat to the Church of the demands for its disendowment. Furthermore, Oldcastle was known as a friend of the king. Could these factors save him? Whether out of friendship's sake or because, as Walsingham wrote, he did not want a sinner lost without some effort being made on his behalf, Henry granted Oldcastle forty days to consider his position. It was as far as he could go. Meanwhile the excommunicated heretic was to be confined in the Tower of London.[31]

Oldcastle would not give in; he must have realized that Henry would not do so, either, and that consequently his fate was sealed. By 28 October he managed to escape from prison under cover of darkness and probably with the help of accomplices, one of whom, William Fisher, a parchment-maker of Lollard sympathies, hid him in his house near Smithfield, while the country hunted high and low to find him.[32] On that day Henry issued a proclamation urging that he be apprehended and returned into custody, a sizeable reward of 500 marks (£333 13s. 4d.) being offered to the man who arrested him, as well as fiscal privileges to the community within whose boundaries he would be taken.[33] The appeal failed to produce results. All the time the object of the hunt lay concealed, as Walsingham put it, plotting his revenge on the king. That he must have had some way of contacting the world outside is clear. For what Oldcastle was now plan-

[30] St Albans Chronicle, pp. 70–7; The episcopal register of bishop Robert Rede, Ordinis Predicatorum, lord bishop of Chichester, 1397–1415, ed. C. Deedes, Sussex Rec. Soc., 8 (1908), i, 151–9.

[31] St Albans Chronicle, p. 76.

[32] Letter-book I, p. 166, where he was condemned for treason.

[33] Ibid., pp. 119–22.

ning was a last, desperate throw, a plot to subvert the king and his brothers and, in the final analysis, to bring about a change in the social order similar, perhaps, to what was being done in Bohemia.[34] What it was that he had in mind we do not know. Did he plan to kill the king and his brothers, or simply capture them and, by holding them to ransom, force change upon them? The chroniclers of the time, almost at one in their dislike and fear of Oldcastle, accused him of trying to overthrow the secular order and destroy the spiritual one.

What is evident is that the intervention of laymen to bring about change over the past three decades had not achieved the desired results: attempts to do this, principally through parliament, had failed. The Church had hung on more successfully than its enemies had anticipated, while the accession to the throne of Henry V, the man of whom some Lollards may once have had some expectations, now dashed all their hopes. Was there, in Oldcastle's rebellion, an element of personal vendetta against the king who had not only allowed him to be judged by the Church, but had singularly failed to pursue the great aim of reform through disendowment? The aim of securing reform by legal means was being abandoned.[35] The events of early 1414 reflected the last gamble of a small but determined group of men to bring about the changes which they so desired; many of them were firm in their religious beliefs which they knew would bring them into confrontation with established authority. It was clearly now or never.

The plotters planned their action to take place in London, but for it to be a success they needed large numbers of supporters ready to turn out in one great, co-ordinated effort. To achieve this required the personal and active participation of their leader, Oldcastle, to help raise such a force. Secrecy was also needed. In effect, the plotters enjoyed neither advantage. It is likely that Oldcastle emerged from his hiding place only at the last minute; his personal intervention in raising his rebel force was, therefore, not available to the rebel leaders. Furthermore, secrecy was scarcely compatible with the participation of the large numbers which this desperate exercise demanded. In order to keep the venture secret, those who took part in it had to arrange to meet in the dark, in other words in a place whose location many who came from outside London did not know, and at a time when their presence, even in the most favourable and peaceful conditions, would have aroused suspicion.

[34] For his admiration for the reforming measures of king Wenceslaus in Bohemia, see Powell, *Kingship, law and society*, 146–7.
[35] Ibid., p. 156; McNiven, *Heresy and politics*, p. 225. Vengeance, Walsingham wrote, was a factor which motivated Oldcastle (*St Albans Chronicle*, p. 88).

Exactly when Henry got to know that something was afoot we cannot tell. But we do know that he had spies and informers in his pay, and that they did their work effectively. Henry and his brothers and some of their friends had spent Christmas 1413 at Eltham, a royal manor now in a suburb of south-east London and then out in the country, conveniently situated near the road to Canterbury and Dover. The new year was spent there, and it was intended to celebrate the Epiphany (Twelfth Night) there, too. At the last moment, however, someone involved in the conspiracy revealed to the king what was being planned. As a result of prompt action by the lord mayor, a few men were arrested in London on the evening of Twelfth Night before they could set out for Eltham, where, under the guise of acting plays before the court, they planned to take the king and those around him. The arrest of the actors took place on a Saturday night, but although it must have been known very soon by the other plotters, it did not make them change their minds. They still planned that their enterprise should take place on the night of the following Tuesday– Wednesday, 9–10 January, one reason being that those who intended taking part in it were, in many cases, already on their way, and it was almost impossible to countermand previous plans and intentions.

On the Monday Henry moved back to Westminster; at this stage he did nothing more, anxious as he was that the conspiracy be encouraged to reveal itself. But when, on the Tuesday night, men began to arrive at the appointed field, many were arrested by the waiting authorities. Others who realized that all was up, tried to flee, some being killed, some captured, others managing to get clean away in the confusion of the night.[36] Among those taken was the Shropshire knight, Sir Roger Acton, once in the Prince's service. One of those who eluded capture, however, was the plot's ringleader himself. Leaving his supporters to their fate, he disappeared. Nearly four years were to pass before he was finally captured.

The impression deliberately given by certain contemporary chroniclers, notably Thomas Walsingham, was that this was a conspiracy led by Oldcastle involving several thousand people from different parts of England. There was truth in the first part of the statement, although one may doubt how effective could be the leadership of a man who in all probability was in hiding in London until the last minute.[37] But there is very much less truth in the picture of a quite widely supported conspiracy involving very large numbers of people. Granted that some, arriving late, never got to London before turning

[36] See Walsingham's hostile and sarcastic account in *St Albans Chronicle*, pp. 78–9.
[37] PRO, E 403/614, m.13, for the search of the house in Smithfield where Oldcastle had recently been in hiding.

for home on the advice of those who were fleeing from the king's officers; granted that many managed to get away in the general confusion and darkness, we would still expect a fairly large number of persons to have been caught and tried or to have been accused of having taken part when the royal commissions of enquiry got down to work soon afterwards.

But the legal records tell an altogether different and much less dramatic story. Only one known rebel came from Kent (one of the main centres of the Peasants' Revolt of 1381 and of Cade's Rebellion in 1450) and none came from Oldcastle's land at Cooling; Essex, on the other hand, was the county of origin of a more sizeable number, as were Leicestershire,[38] Derbyshire (to be represented in the parliament of 1420 by Henry Booth who had been accused of sheltering a Lollard), Northamptonshire, Warwickshire, Bedfordshire, Hertfordshire and Buckinghamshire.[39] Perhaps the largest contingent from outside London came from Bristol: it numbered over forty persons, craftsmen and chaplains, two groups to whom the teachings of Lollardy appear to have had a special appeal. All in all, the call for numbers had provoked very little response. Those who appear in the records, for whatever reason, total but 300 or so at the most. No wonder that the late K.B. McFarlane, who did more than most to study this rising, felt obliged to write about 'the minute scale of the affair'.[40]

Henry reacted in the only way open to him. Of the eighty or more persons arrested during the rising, sixty-nine were condemned for treason on 12 January, probably by martial law or by a court in the city of London.[41] On 13 January thirty-eight of these were executed: seven were hanged and burned as both traitors and heretics, while thirty-one were hanged simply as traitors, indicating that less than one in five went to his fate for reasons which had to do with belief. On the contrary, far from being dominated by theological issues, the rising was taken over by social gamblers; it had become 'a treasonable scramble for property and preferment'.[42] Walsingham reported that Robert Morley, an ambitious brewer from Dunstable, hoped for the grant of the county of Hertfordshire, and that he was captured wearing spurs, the symbol of the knighthood to which he had pretensions. Others, Walsingham claimed, had taken part encouraged by promises of reward made to them by Oldcastle.[43]

[38] J. Crompton, 'Leicestershire Lollards', *Transactions of the Leicestershire Arch. and Hist. Soc.*, 44 (1968–9), 26.
[39] McFarlane, *John Wycliffe*, pp. 172–6.
[40] Ibid., p. 176; Powell, *Kingship, law and society*, pp. 149–61.
[41] J.A.F. Thomson, *The later Lollards, 1414–1520* (Oxford, 1965), pp. 6–7.
[42] M. Aston, 'Lollardy and sedition, 1381–1431', *Past and Present*, 17 (1960), 26.
[43] *St Albans Chronicle*, pp. 78–9; McFarlane, *John Wycliffe*, p. 177.

It is significant that all those condemned in the courts – these were secular courts – for their part in the events of early January 1414 were hanged. As we have seen, a small proportion were also burned for their heretical views; burning reflected the victim's heresy, hanging his treason. When, nearly a month after the rising, Sir Roger Acton was executed in St Giles's Field outside London, he was not burned but hanged, in spite of his known Lollard sympathies.[44] What the authorities wanted to stress was the dimension of treason in the activities of those who had taken part in the rising. Inspired it may have been by Lollards, Lollard ideas and by the social implications of those ideas. But by both those in authority and by the chroniclers (who reflected their views), the rising was an attempt to endanger the life of (if not to kill) the king and his brothers who were his heirs, and thereby to threaten the succession to the crown of England. This was treason, an open attack upon authority within the realm, and it had to be dealt with as such in ways that people of the time understood.

Even after the rising, William Sawtry and John Badby remained the only two men who had to face the ordeal of death by fire for the sake of their heretical opinions alone. A largely new image of the Lollard danger was now being conveyed to the public. It was portrayed neither merely nor principally as a threat to the Church, but as a threat to the crown and, therefore, as a danger to the very source of established order. That order, although briefly under attack, had never seemed vulnerable, and quickly reasserted itself. It did so with confidence. On 15 January Henry was present at a service at St Paul's, presided over by archbishop Arundel, at which litanies of intercession and prayers of thanksgiving were offered.[45] The king was already confident of victory, especially after four more of the condemned were executed on 19 January. A few days later, on 23 January, Henry began to issue pardons, first to individuals, then, less than a month later, to larger groups. On 28 March he offered a general pardon (a few in prison were excluded from its terms) to all those who would sue for it by 24 June.[46]

These were the acts of a man who felt in command of events, who could act without vindictiveness in the hope of restoring normality as soon as possible. When released, some of those accused of having supported the rising were handed over to their bishops, presumably to have enquiries made into their religious views.[47] But ecclesiastical

[44] McFarlane, *John Wycliffe*, pp. 172, 177.
[45] Wylie, *Henry the Fifth*, i, 276.
[46] *CCR, 1413–1419*, pp. 176–7; *Foedera*, IV, ii, 72.
[47] See, for example, the letter from the king to bishop Repingdon, dated 26 January 1415, in which it was reported that Thomas Noveray, from Leicestershire, had been questioned by royal commissioners regarding certain opinions which he held: 'est

sources fail to give any impression of 'witch hunting' on the part of the bishops. One reason may well have been that their leader, archbishop Arundel, died on 19 February, and that the death of this man, who had seen it as one of his main tasks to defend the doctrines of the Church against Wycliffite and Lollard attacks,[48] may have had an effect upon how ecclesiastical authorities followed up the counter-attack against the defeated and demoralized enemy. When, early in 1414, bishop Repingdon of Lincoln carried out a visitation of part of his diocese which lay in Leicestershire, near to where a visitation in May 1413 had revealed a number of men who held Wycliffite ideas, he was not minded to see them charged with treason.[49] Their religious ideas might be erroneous, but did that necessarily make them into traitors?

If anything, the reaction of the laity to the presence of persons sympathizing with, if not professing, Lollard views in the aftermath of the rising of 1414 seems to have been more hostile than that of either king or clergy. At Canterbury, the mystic, Margery Kempe, was threatened with fire as a 'false Lollard' by the people; while at Leicester, in 1417, the mayor, calling her 'a false strumpet, a false Lollard and a false deceiver of the people', ordered her to prison.[50] It was the bishop of Lincoln, Philip Repingdon, himself a former Lollard sympathizer, who secured her release.[51] In London, Thomas Fauconer, lord mayor in 1414–15, was to find himself committed to the Tower and fined £1000 for allegedly having ordered the execution of an old heretic, John Claydon, recently found guilty of heresy and relapse by the court of the new archbishop of Canterbury, Henry Chichele. More may lie behind this episode than meets the eye. While Claydon was probably quite legally executed, a little while after the event it was claimed that an associate, Richard Baker or Gurmyn, had been burned along with letters of pardon which the king had granted to him. If this was the case, mayor Fauconer could be said

Lollardus et sustinet oppiniones hereticas contra fidem catholicam', mainly about confession and pilgrimages (Lincolnshire Archives Office, Reg.15b, fo.18). See McFarlane, *John Wycliffe*, pp. 170, 174.

[48] Walsingham wrote with appreciation about his efforts to control heresy, efforts, he claimed, which would have been more successful if he had received more support from his suffragan bishops (*St Albans Chronicle*, p. 81).

[49] Crompton, 'Leicestershire Lollards', 30.

[50] *The book of Margery Kempe*. A modern version by W. Butler-Bowdon (Oxford, 1954), pp. 37, 145. Members of the laity were less convinced of Margery's beliefs than were the bishops (Hudson, *Premature reformation*, p. 435); J. Catto, 'Religious change under Henry V', Harriss, *Henry V: practice of kingship*, pp. 112–13; J.A.F. Thomson, 'Orthodox religion and the origins of Lollardy', *History*, 74 (1989), 50–1.

[51] *Book of Margery Kempe*, p. 155; McFarlane, *Lancastrian kings and Lollard knights*, pp. 217–18.

to have been acting in flagrant defiance of royal authority. Did his action perhaps reflect the personal hostility of the mayor to those associated with heresy? Or, further possibility, was it an attempt by Lollards to cause unrest and dissension within the city?[52]

In one sense, the action of the mayor of Leicester and the lord mayor of London were in keeping with legislation which was passed soon after the rising of January 1414. The decision of Henry to hold the coming parliament in Leicester was a bold gesture, the town being at the centre of an area which, as bishop Repingdon's visitations showed, was still a centre of heterodox thinking and practice. It also showed how confident the king was about the decline of the Lollard threat: for a brief while the men of Leicester could see many of the most important figures in the land walking in their streets. The meeting, originally planned for January 1414, finally took place at the end of April. The main message of chancellor Beaufort's speech was the lack of respect for the law and the accompanying disorder, troubles provoked by the Lollards.[53]

The legal remedy of this analysis soon followed. Steps had to be taken to prevent congregations and insurrections by Lollards against the king, the social order and the law. The king wanted to strengthen the law, to stop what had happened from occurring again, and to frighten Lollards into a state of inaction. A tightening of earlier legislation was to take place, obliging office holders, from the chancellor downwards, to swear to act against all Lollards, and to give the Church every assistance possible in locating them, justices of the peace being burdened with special responsibilities in this respect.[54] If we wish to see this legislation in its full context, we must observe that Henry was at the same time placing great stress on the work of the courts to restore justice in the north and west midlands. In other words, the king was strongly inclined to see the threat of Lollardy not so much in spiritual terms but rather as part of a wider threat to public order. By doing so, he could not only give it a high profile among the social problems to be faced; he could also exercise a strict control over the means used to combat it. In this way a considerable measure of royal control over the Church was being achieved and maintained.

What, in the meantime, had happened to Oldcastle? Summoned to appear before the Middlesex shire court, he failed to do so; on 14 June 1414 he was declared an outlaw. Later in the year the king tried to

[52] Thomson, *Later Lollards*, pp. 140–3.
[53] *RP*, iv, 15.
[54] Ibid., iv. 24–5; E. Powell, 'The restoration of law and order', Harriss, *Henry V: practice of kingship*, p. 63.

induce him to seek a pardon if he would only surrender. The attempt failed. According to Thomas Walsingham, Oldcastle remained a figure of darkness, lacking courage to emerge into the light.[55] Yet neither was he betrayed, in spite of offers of financial rewards to those who might reveal his presence. Until the autumn of 1417 Oldcastle remained at large. To be sure, sightings of him were reported. In the summer of 1415 he was almost captured near Malvern; in August that year he was known to have been in Warwickshire,[56] just at the moment when there was an 'outbreak' of Lollard bills urging revenge upon the king who was then in France.[57] Then, for some two years, Oldcastle disappeared, probably into Wales where he was in contact with Gruffydd, one of Glyn Dŵr's sons,[58] and where, probably in November 1417, he was finally arrested, not without difficulty, near Welshpool on lands belonging to Edward Charlton, Lord Powys.

This time Oldcastle was not allowed to escape. Wounded in the fight which led to his capture, he was conveyed, on a litter, to London under heavy guard, brought before parliament on 14 December, and confronted with the judgement which had declared him guilty of treason almost four years earlier. On being asked if he had anything to say, he stated that mercy was what became the true Christian: vengeance was for God. When it became evident that, as at the time of his condemnation by Arundel four years earlier, he would take the opportunity to ramble on and on, he was cut short by the chief justice, who told him to be brief. At this point he said that he would recognize none of those present as his judge, adding that his only proper judge, Richard II, was in Scotland. Condemned for treason out of his own mouth before the assembled parliament, he was at once sentenced to immediate execution. Taken to the Tower, he was laid on a hurdle and dragged, with an escort of eighty mounted men, to St Giles's Field where, before a large crowd which included the lieutenant, the duke of Bedford, he was hanged from a new gallows, the 'Lollard gallows' as they came to be called, while a fire was lighted beneath him. His last words, spoken to Sir Thomas Erpingham, were that he would rise on the third day. To the very end Oldcastle maintained his hostility to authority and to the Church of his time.[59] The fifty-six shillings which his execution cost must have seemed money well spent.[60]

[55] *St Albans Chronicle*, p. 89.

[56] McFarlane, *John Wycliffe*, p. 181.

[57] *St Albans Chronicle*, p. 88 (and p. 104); Thomson, *Later Lollards*, pp. 10–11; see above, n.35.

[58] H.G. Richardson, 'John Oldcastle in hiding, August-October, 1417', *EHR*, 55 (1940), 433.

[59] *St Albans Chronicle*, pp. 116–17; *RP*, iv, 107–10.

[60] PRO, E 364/52, m.1d.

The death of Oldcastle effectively signalled the end of the Lollard threat during Henry V's reign. There were signs of it, here and there, in the last years of the reign, such as perhaps the breaking of stained glass depicting the Virgin Mary at Exeter in 1421,[61] and some heresy at Tenterden in Kent (heresy which would reappear later) in 1422. It is likely, too, that the midlands, which had been one of the sect's main power bases for many years, continued to be a centre for heretical views, since these emerged again in the reign of Henry's son. But the worst was over. What had begun in Richard II's reign as a movement of re-form (one of a number with different emphases witnessed in Europe at this time) had led to the broad acceptance of some of its more moderate doctrines by a not unsubstantial group of gentry who, dissatisfied with much contemporary religious practice, saw, chiefly in some of the social implications of its teachings, ideas which they could support. That support had been given in parliament, the public forum where such persons could most effectively put forward their proposals. In the end, however, with the failure of the measure for disendowment of the Church proposed in 1410, this way of urging change was seen to have no future. If there was to be action, it would have to be taken in more drastic fashion, by men who would be willing to risk their lives in rebellion, for there to be any chance of success.

By the very last years of the fourteenth century, heresy was beginning to be regarded by some as a form of treason, a view which became more widely accepted in the early years of the fifteenth century, as not merely the theological teachings of the Lollards, but their social doctrines, too, were recognized as having serious social and political implications for the country as a whole. This meant (the consequence could scarcely be avoided) a greatly increased involvement of the secular power in what appeared to be the domain of the Church, as the secular authority and its representatives at first helped the Church defend itself and then, in the reigns of Henry IV and Henry V, began to exercise more effective control over what had been the concern of the spiritual power. When the Lollards called Henry 'the priests' king' ('princeps presbiterorum')[62] they meant it at least half mockingly. Henry had sprung to the defence of the clergy and what they represented, and was now their chief protector; Thomas Netter, the king's Carmelite confessor, had been given the role of chief exponent of what was orthodox. There was also irony in the use of the term when used by men who favoured a Church under secular authority. For the

[61]   R. Foreville, 'Manifestations de Lollardisme à Exeter en 1421?', *Le Moyen Age*, 69 (1963), 691–706; Thomson, *Later Lollards*, p. 173.
[62]   *St Albans Chronicle*, p. 88; *Letters of queen Margaret*, p. 6.

phrase 'the priests' king' could mean not only that Henry was the clergy's protector, but their master, too. In the view of one Benedictine preacher, as the man approved by God to steer the English ship of state, Henry also controlled the Church within it; in the words of another, having destroyed the Lollards' 'cursed temple', the king had built a new one with himself as the 'strong pillar in the middle' upon which the structure was to be founded. The re-formers had achieved something. Although Henry had saved the Church and the orthodox faith, he had done so at a price, an increase in the control exercised by the secular power over the spiritual. To all appearances defeated, the Lollard rebellion had, paradoxically, achieved something.[63]

---

[63] Horner, 'Benedictine support', 211, 214–15, 220; 'In all but name, more than a century before the title could be used, Henry V had begun to act as the supreme governor of the Church of England' (Catto, 'Religious change', Harriss, *Henry V: practice of kingship*, p. 115).

Chapter 14

ORDER

Early Lancastrian England was not a well-ordered society. The last years of the reign of Richard II had witnessed attempts to make the rule of law more effective, but the reign of the first Lancastrian king had only seen the situation deteriorate. The maintenance of social peace was becoming part of the 'bone et jouste Governance' which the Commons now sought and which Henry IV, in his very first parliament in 1399, promised to provide.[1] The twin themes of law-keeping and the administration of justice to all, both rich and poor, were to be found with regularity in the allocutions delivered by Henry IV's chancellors before the assembled parliaments, perhaps most notably and significantly in the address made by Henry Beaufort to the parliament of January 1410, at the very moment when the Prince had achieved control of the council.[2] At least six out of Henry IV's nine parliaments were to hear a chancellor make specific reference to the need for the law to be better observed, while the matter of law infringement was regularly the subject of petitions presented by those assemblies to the king. Under Henry V's rule, there was little change. In three parliaments, in particular those of May 1414, November 1417 and December 1421, the need to keep the law was stressed by bishops Beaufort and Langley. It should be recalled that both these men had acted as chancellor under Henry IV; Beaufort had delivered the allocution of 1410 already referred to, while Langley, as bishop of Durham, was only too well aware of the dangers presented by lawlessness in the area of his episcopal jurisdiction.[3] Both the parliament of 1414, and the events which surrounded it, were largely concerned with a drive towards the re-establishment of the law as a force to be observed and obeyed. It remains to be seen whether that effort was successful or not.

Few of the threats to public order, including that presented by heresy, experienced in Henry V's reign were entirely new. Ever since

[1] *RP*, iii, 415.
[2] Ibid., iii, 622.
[3] R.L. Storey, *Thomas Langley and the bishopric of Durham, 1406–1437* (London, 1961), ch.2.

the last years of the life of John Wyclif many had feared that the Lollards might attack the stability of society by undermining its two main props, the crown and the Church. The language used by those in authority to describe how they regarded the rising of January 1414 is instructive. The commission appointed on 10 January 1414 to enquire into events in London and Middlesex was given power to act against treasons, insurrection, rebellions and felonies committed by Lollards, who planned to set up Oldcastle as regent of the realm, to the ultimate destruction of the Church and the royal dignity; all this was to be accomplished by 20,000 men from various parts of the kingdom 'arrayed like traitors in warlike fashion in form of rebellion against their allegiances'.

Another commission appointed the following day to make similar enquiries in Essex was reminded that the king was taking action as any true Christian prince, bound by the oath he had given at his coronation, should do.[4] Henry, it was asserted, had a duty to maintain peace and the institutions of order so that religious and political society would function. When issuing a pardon to the London fuller, Henry Dene, on 23 January 1414 (scarcely a fortnight after the uprising), Henry underlined the same point. Dene, it was said, could not maintain the heretical opinions which he held as long as the royal power and the estate and office of prelacy (by which he meant episcopal authority) survived. It was for this reason that he had schemed against both king and Church, hoping at the same time to kill the royal brothers and turn men away from religion.

If this is what Dene – and many other Lollards – believed, then the ideas of the heretics might constitute a threat to the secular authority, for Lollards required the overthrow of the political order before their beliefs could be adopted. Such a threat demanded positive action on the part of the crown. The statute of Lollards, passed at the 'law and order' parliament held at Leicester in April-May 1414, reiterated the crown's point of view. Lollards, it claimed, were guilty of creating rumours and uncertainty in men's minds, since they spoke and acted against the law of God, the Church and all authority, including that of the king. What was more – and the accusation, in the light of other events of the day, was a significant one – they were forming congregations and insurrections which were a threat to order. As defender of both Church and realm, the king had a duty to act against them through the law, whose punishment they would come to fear. To make sure that the law was effectively imposed, parliament had requested that all officers with judicial power should take an oath to

---

[4] *CPR, 1413–16*, pp. 175, 177; *Select cases in the court of King's Bench, Henry V*, ed. G.O. Sayles (Selden Soc. 88, London, 1971), p. 218.

root out heresy within their jurisdictions, and all judges and justices were to make enquiries about Lollards and their abettors. When found, such men were to be arrested by the sheriffs and taken before the ecclesiastical authorities.[5]

This was for the future. By May 1414 it was felt, with some justification, that the main threat presented by Lollards could now be dealt with by the Church. In the more immediate aftermath of the January rising, the secular courts had been used to deal with those involved in it. Early in February Lollard sympathizers had been presented by juries before royal commissioners sitting at Loughborough in Leicestershire.[6] This traditional system, whereby the jury took the part of levelling accusations on behalf of society against an individual or a group, implied that the ideas of those indicted of holding and practising Lollard opinions were known to members of the society in which they lived. Thomas Noveray, who came from Illston near Leicester, was said to be a prominent speaker in unlawful places; doubtless his less than orthodox views on images, burial rites and pilgrimages were already known locally. Had he gone no further, he might have merited a warning, even a censure, from ecclesiastical authority. But the jury reported that he had sold his property before the rising, and had been up in arms in his village, against the king and in support of Oldcastle, on 4 January, well before the more dramatic events which were to take place in London nearly a week later. Noveray was finally pardoned and discharged, but not before he had been brought before the king at Shrewsbury in May, so as to underline the seriousness with which his crimes were regarded.[7]

It should be appreciated how, particularly early in his reign, Henry may have regarded the Lollards as a threat to the future of his dynasty. The danger was accentuated by disorder in the far north of England, and by attempts made to maintain that Richard II was still alive. Under Henry IV the two principal threats to the throne, associated with the Percy and Scrope families, had originated in that region, but had effectively ended with the victory won against Northumberland at Bramham Moor, between Wetherby and Tadcaster, in February 1408. The problems of relations with Scotland, however, refused to go away. Since 1406 England had held James, heir to the Scottish throne, in captivity, his country being ruled in his absence by Robert Stewart, duke of Albany. To increase the Lancastrians' difficulties, the Scots had lent their support to one Thomas Warde, of

[5] SR, ii, 181–3.
[6] Dr Powell (Kingship, law and society, p. 154) stresses the repetitive nature of the Lollard indictment, suggesting the existence of a central model.
[7] Sayles, Select cases, pp. 226–7.

Trumpington, said to resemble Richard II, thereby maintaining the sense of uncertainty which was politically damaging.

One allegedly taken in by these machinations was a certain John Whitelock, who, after lying low for a number of years, plotted against both Henry IV and his son 'by unceasing murmuring, rebellion and dissension', hoping to subvert the realm, although it was well known that Richard was dead, and that Henry V was to be honoured and obeyed by all 'by right and by the law of nature'.[8] Alleged to have affixed bills, in which he affirmed his belief that Warde was really Richard II, on the doors of the abbeys of Westminster and Bermondsey, Whitelock was in sanctuary (whence, it was said, he had scorned and defied the king) from the last days of Henry IV's reign until early June 1413; he was taken before Henry himself on 5 July, accused of inciting the people against their king, and urging the Scots and the Welsh to enter the kingdom for its destruction. Having fearlessly avowed responsibility for the declaration regarding Richard II, he was ordered for trial two days later. Sent for safe-keeping to the Tower, he managed to escape. Nothing more was to be heard of him.[9]

In 1415, according to an enquiry held in Yorkshire two years later, Henry Talbot of Easington-in-Craven had been involved in a further conspiracy, with Albany and other Scots, to seize Murdoch of Fife, Albany's son, an English prisoner since the battle of Homildon Hill in 1402, as he was being taken northwards prior to an exchange which had been arranged with Henry Percy, a virtual prisoner in Scotland since the battle of Shrewsbury in 1403. Although the plot succeeded, Murdoch was soon retaken.[10] However, the planned exchange had to be postponed for almost another year. In February 1417, it was alleged, Talbot was again involved with the Scots, inciting rebellion and claiming that Richard II was alive and ready to come into England. An enquiry held in Northumberland to coincide with the Yorkshire one revealed the same tale. Two years later, in the summer of 1419, it would again be claimed that Richard II was alive and about to enter England to plot rebellion.[11] His had been a difficult spirit to exorcize.

For reasons not difficult to discern, the government of the Lancastrians was seldom slow to point out links, real or imagined, between conspiracies and their perpetrators. What these contacts really were,

[8] '. . . de iure et naturaliter' (ibid., p. 212).

[9] Ibid., pp. 212–15. See Powell, *Kingship, law and society*, pp. 136–9, and p. 137, n.102 for one of Whitelock's original bills.

[10] P.J. Bradley, 'Henry V's Scottish policy: a study in realpolitik', *Documenting the past. Essays in medieval history presented to George Peddy Cuttino*, ed. J.S. Hamilton and P.J. Bradley (Wodbridge/Woolfeboro, 1989), p. 182.

[11] Sayles, *Select cases*, p. 249.

it is difficult, even impossible, to know. The three conspirators involved in the Southampton plot of July 1415, Richard, earl of Cambridge, Henry, Lord Scrope, and Sir Thomas Grey, in particular the last two, had close links with the north-east of England. It is possible that there were connections between them and those who, like Henry Talbot, had got involved to capture Murdoch. Once in their hands, Murdoch could be exchanged by them (rather than by the king) for Henry Percy and, possibly, for the 'pseudo-Richard'. At a stroke the plotters might gain the support of Percy (and of all that this meant in the north) and of the figure who might be passed off as Richard II, in the circumstances, a vital figurehead to control. Difficult as it is to unravel the complexities of the situation, the involvement of Cambridge as active leader, that of Edmund, earl of March, although only as a figurehead, as well as that of others in the broad conspiracy which, if successful, could only favour the house of York, suggests that something serious was afoot.

To contemporary writers such as the author of the *Gesta* and the compiler of the *Brut*, primarily concerned with the war against France, the Southampton plot was an act of treason involving French gold used to foment a rising against Henry to prevent or deter him from invading France.[12] The king's response was to draw up an indictment in such a way as to ensure that there would be no chance of acquittal: the charge was that the accused had plotted the death of the king, his three brothers and others. In fact, there appears to have been no such plot, only one of rebellion leading to usurpation in the name of the earl of March, helped along by an invasion of northern England by the Scots, by assistance from the Welsh and, possibly, by some kind of link with Lollards. None the less, the indictment, similar to the very general accusation levelled against the Lollard conspirators eighteen months earlier, was enough to ensure conviction. The plot, as it was intended it should, came to be regarded as a threat to the king and to his dynasty.

While there were threats against the throne in the early years of Henry's reign, the wider difficulties of social disorder presented those in authority with different and less tractable problems to resolve. Born of usurpation and an act of violence, Henry IV's reign had witnessed fairly constant demands in parliament that action be taken against evil-doers. In certain parts of the country the level of crime, much of it against the person, now reached high levels. While it is not always evident why there should have been considerable violence in counties and areas such as Derbyshire, Leicestershire and Lancashire, where

[12] *Gesta*, p. 19; *Brut*, ii, 375.

duchy of Lancaster influence was strong, the disorder not uncommon in border counties is more readily explained.

Northumberland, for example, was one such area where law and order – or the lack of it – was affected by long-standing border wars against the Scots, mainly aimed at the destruction of crops, the rustling of cattle, and the capture and consequent ransoming of individuals. Such activity, conducive to disorder and the use of violence, was bound to cause fear and uncertainty among the population. Other factors contributed to make this an area of England in which it would prove difficult to enforce order. One was the great influence of the Percy family, in practice more respected than were the officers of the king of England, but, since the battle of Shrewsbury in 1403, providing no leadership within the county. Another was the great distance from London (approaching 300 miles from the capital) which made it hard to administer justice effectively, thus leaving this aspect of social existence more and more in the hands of the local 'overlord', if there was one. Nor was it merely a question of distance. The palatinate of Durham, ruled by the prince-bishop, formed a separate jurisdiction which was, in all but a few matters, free of the authority of the king.[13] The law of England was no longer a proper force in regulating what was, even in good times, a troublesome society to rule.

It is not difficult to give the impression that a particular area was subject to excessive lawlessness. In the case of Northumberland, parliamentary records indicate clearly that there was fear that the law was losing control. As it was reported in 1410, the justices responsible for enquiring into disorders and bringing the culprits (said to be armed men and Scots) to justice were powerless to act for fear of the violence which might be used against them.[14] Parts of the Scottish border lands (and matters were not necessarily much better in Westmorland where, in 1405, it was said that the sheriff was involved in crimes of violence and menaces) had become 'no-go' areas to those appointed to uphold the law.[15] Even the appointment, in 1410, of a commission of oyer and terminer, normally a fairly effective weapon of law enforcement, appears to have had little effect.[16]

Much of the trouble in Northumberland in Henry IV's reign had resulted from the hostility shown by the earls of Northumberland to the royal authority. The involvement of Sir Thomas Grey in, and the suspected sympathy of others for, the Southampton plot showed how

[13] As was reported of Northumberland in Henry IV's last parliament 'le dit counte est si long de la ley' that it was suffering from the 'noun-venue de les Justices' (*RP*, iii, 662; Storey, *Thomas Langley*, p. 140).
[14] *RP*, iii, 629–30.
[15] Ibid., iii, 564.
[16] Ibid., iii, 624.

precarious was the hold of Henry V upon Northumbrian society. It was largely in order to install the true, surviving Percy heir to his dukedom that the king entered into negotiations with the Scots which finally led to Henry Percy's restoration and the rendering of his oath of fealty to Henry V. Improvements in the situation there were, but in 1421 strong complaints were again heard in parliament about crimes committed in Redesdale (where the king's writ did not run as the area was a franchise), and in the neighbouring counties of Northumberland, Cumberland and Westmorland. The point being underlined here had already been made and legislation passed at Leicester in April 1414: the franchise protected the criminal who lived within its jurisdiction wherever his crime was committed. Those who lived in areas where the king's writ did not run[17] (and Northumberland included two more such, Tyndale and Hexhamshire) were very difficult to bring to justice.

Similar conflicts of jurisdiction meant that it was no easier to pursue malefactors in the counties which marked the border with Wales, nor in the large area which constituted the lordships of the march. The effects of the Glyn Dŵr revolt upon the economies and state of order of these counties were considerable. In the parliament of 1407 complaints had been made of the impact which events of the past years had had upon Shrewsbury. Its people had been maltreated by the soldiers of Richard II in 1398; the town had been burned by Welsh rebels; its economic prosperity, which depended largely on farming, had greatly suffered from attacks; the effects of the battle of Shrewsbury of 1403 had been felt locally; while the costs of watching out for the Welsh, and of maintaining defences against them, had often been met by the citizens themselves.[18] From almost the beginning of Henry IV's reign, complaints had been lodged against Welshmen who crossed the border by both day and night to steal.[19]

Nor was Shrewsbury, and its county, Shropshire, alone in voicing such complaints. In 1407 Hereford, to the south, complained that those living in the march came into Herefordshire to seize cattle, and even people, who were then ransomed; instead of standing on the side of order, many men from marcher lordships gave help and encouragement to those engaged in such criminal activity, which the law officers were not seeking to stop.[20] As on the northern border, individuals, not merely movable property, were liable to be taken and ransomed. In 1416 some thirty persons were reported in parliament as having

---

[17] '. . . ou le brief le Roy ne court mye' (*RP*, iv, 21; *SR*, ii, 177–8).
[18] *RP*, iii, 618–19.
[19] Ibid., iii, 474.
[20] Ibid., iii, 615.

captured a group of local people in Hereford whom they threatened with death or with being taken away to Wales unless they undertook not to pursue them through the law for their actions. Although, by this time, the revolt was in effect over, its adverse economic effects on Wales, as well as a desire to avenge themselves upon those who had 'won' the war, were to encourage Welshmen to continue raiding the property of their generally more prosperous English neighbours.[21]

Local evidence, much of it taken from legal records, suggests that economic factors played their part in creating 'the disturbed conditions resulting from Glyn Dŵr's rebellion', both in the lordships of south Wales and in the English border counties.[22] While conditions of disorder were markedly worse in some than in others, none was exempt. The records reflect a certain 'overspill' of violence into Gloucestershire, doubtless that area of the county which lay to the west of the river Severn. In neighbouring Herefordshire, although little crime was recorded early in Henry V's reign, by 1417 matters were changing for the worse. While there were still raids from the direction of Wales carried out by men whom it was difficult to apprehend, more trouble appears to have been caused by members of the county's own gentry, who employed their tenants and servants (whom they hoped to protect from the law) in pursuit of their local quarrels.

The effects of such activities were not limited to the county in which the crimes took place. In 1416, when William Walwayn committed a murder in Herefordshire, he did so with the help of a gang of men, some of whose members came from nearby Worcestershire and Gloucestershire. When accused of murder in 1419, John Abrahall, another of the more disreputable members of Herefordshire society, threatened one of the chief witnesses against him, and gave help to John, Lord Talbot (who held land in Herefordshire), in Talbot's quarrel in his native Shropshire against the earl of Arundel.[23] Crime (and this was one of the chief problems faced by those whose task it was to track down evil-doers) knew no territorial boundaries. The effectiveness of the law, however, was restricted.

It is from the neighbouring counties of Shropshire and Staffordshire that the evidence of the highest level of violence comes. The parliamentary rolls for 1410 record petitions concerning trouble which had

[21] G. Williams, *Recovery, reorientation and reformation. Wales c. 1415–1642* (Oxford, 1987), p. 21; *SR*, ii, 171–2, 188–9.

[22] *The Marcher lordships of South Wales, 1415–1536. Select documents*, ed. T.B. Pugh (Cardiff, 1963), p. 7.

[23] A.E. Herbert, 'Public order and private violence in Herefordshire, 1413–61' (Univ. of Wales MA thesis, 1978), p. 51; 'Herefordshire, 1413–61: some aspects of society and public order', *Patronage, the crown and the provinces in later medieval England*, ed. R.A. Griffiths (Gloucester/Atlanta Highlands, 1981) p. 105.

recently taken place in Staffordshire.[24] These are supported by legal evidence which records much crime such as theft, killing animals, treading and cutting down hay, corn, scrub and trees, and chasing game from parks. However, further legal evidence for Shropshire, brought before the courts in the spring of 1414, told of much more serious offences, at which coroners' rolls had already hinted: large-scale larceny; a disturbing number of homicides and assaults; waylaying travellers and merchants on the highway; extortion (often by persons holding official positions), as well as cases of receiving or protecting felons known to be guilty of crime.

The disease was contagious. The links between Shropshire and Staffordshire, on the one hand, and Cheshire on the other, had always been close. From the reign of Henry IV into that of his son, men came out of Cheshire to commit crime in neighbouring counties. While the accusation brought against William Newhawe, parson of Tilleston in Cheshire and archdeacon of Chester, that he had been involved in theft carried out at night in Lichfield and that he had stolen a book worth £30 from the library of Lichfield cathedral, may appear as the peccadillo of a bibliomaniac (he was finally acquitted of the charge), men of Cheshire were notorious for the sorties which they carried out into neighbouring counties.[25] Derbyshire shared a border with Cheshire (as it did with Staffordshire). It was in the parliament of 1420 that a report was made that the sheriff of Derbyshire had made proclamation against John de Leigh of Bothes who, accompanied by a large group of armed men, was said to have attacked men in Derbyshire before escaping back into the relative safety of Cheshire, protected by its palatinate status.[26] All this could happen in spite of the fact that, in his first parliament in 1399, Henry IV had consented to a petition that men of Cheshire who committed felonies in counties other than their own should be punished there.[27] The privileges enjoyed by palatine counties were not popular outside their boundaries.

John de Leigh of Bothes had been sheriff of Cheshire in 1414. As a result he would have known a thing or two about the law and its management, and what it could and could not do. Furthermore, he belonged to that social group, the gentry, men of local standing and influence, upon whom so much of the administration of a shire depended and many of whom wished to advance their fortunes, and

[24] *RP*, iii, 630–2.
[25] B.H. Putnam, *Proceedings before the justices of the peace in the fourteenth and fifteenth centuries: Edward III to Richard III* (Cambridge, Mass., 1938), p. 323.
[26] *RP*, iv, 125.
[27] Ibid., iii, 440.

those of their families, within the society in which they lived. Some English counties had no leading or dominant family within their boundaries. Cheshire was one such county, neighbouring Staffordshire another. In Cheshire, under Henry V, the lord was the king, represented by an impersonal form of administration which gave no help or patronage to members of an ambitious family. Staffordshire was a county dominated by the duchy of Lancaster;[28] it was an area in which legitimate ambitions of alliance with the powerful could only be satisfied by joining the local 'establishment', or by reacting against it. In Derbyshire, too, a not dissimilar situation existed. Such examples suggest that the absence of a 'great lord', both to keep men in order and to provide them with 'lordship' (patronage, opportunity to improve 'standing' through the exercises of local office, money, all these were involved), encouraged men to take the law into their own hands if that were needed to secure their own advancement in what was, in effect, a political and social vacuum at local level waiting to be filled.

Where lordship was exercised, the symbol of its control was the retainer, who, often armed and perhaps wearing a distinctive livery, or uniform, sought to pursue the particular interest of his paymaster. This development in the social order, given the name 'bastard feudalism' a century or so ago,[29] was one which tended to encourage disorder whose dangers were well recognized, and which led to a flurry of legislation during these years. In Henry IV's first parliament legislation had been passed forbidding the giving of livery because its effects were not conducive to peace and order.[30] In the following year it had been laid down that only the king's livery could be worn, and then only in certain circumstances, the Prince having special permission to grant his 'liveree del Cigne' (the swan of Bohun) to his retainers.[31]

The legislation appears to have met with only limited success. In 1404 the Speaker asked in parliament that the statutes be properly observed at the very moment when it was admitted that the earl of Northumberland had broken them.[32] By 1407 it was said that groups of retainers consisting of 200–300 liveried men were not unknown, and that quarrels were sustained with their help. Parliament decided to impose fines of £5 upon the giver and £2 on the receiver of every set of livery, and men were encouraged to report those who acted against the statute with a promise that fines would be shared with

[28] See Powell, *Kingship, law and society*, pp. 208–16.
[29] K.B. McFarlane, ' "Bastard feudalism" ', *BIHR*, 20 (1945), 161.
[30] '. . . pur ouster meintenance & nurrir amour, paix & quiete de toutz partz parmy le Roialme' (*RP*, iii, 428; *SR*, ii, 113).
[31] *RP*, iii, 477–8; *SR*, ii, 129–30.
[32] *RP*, iii, 524.

them.[33] At Henry IV's last parliament, in 1411, further enforcement
was demanded. It was particularly requested that no pardons be
granted for this trespass, and that both justices and judges be encouraged to enquire how it was being observed, king's bench in London
to be informed of any known infringements. The petition was
approved: 'Le Roy le voet'. The statute was to record that the king
thought that its observance would be conducive to the achievement
of peace throughout the realm.[34]

Legal evidence about the activities of armed groups is plentiful; it
comes not merely from the west midlands and the borders with Wales
and Scotland, but from other parts, too. In Staffordshire, members of
the family of Erdswick, particularly Roger and Hugh, were notorious
for their lawless activities: the name of Hugh appeared with some
regularity in king's bench records from 1405 onwards, and later in
the formal parliamentary record. In Shropshire, where the Talbots
were trying to consolidate their rising power against the longer-
established influence of the earl of Arundel, securities had to be taken
from Arundel for the good behaviour of a number of his chief adher-
ents, some of whom, in the absence of their lord, had presumed to
take over his authority and were abusing their positions.[35] In Cornwall, another 'royal' county lacking a great landowner,[36] there is evidence of influence being exerted through grants of annuities and
appointments to lucrative offices. Early in Henry V's reign there were
complaints against Geoffrey St Aubyn and Ralph Vivian, who had
ambushed John Trewoyff, who asserted that they were 'great main-
tainers and ill doers and of such great alliance in the county that the
said petitioner can have no help of remedy by the common law'. A
few years later, in 1420, it was claimed that John Cook of Paderd was
'so gret of rule in hys contre and of grete fees with the grete of the
same contre and also iustice of the peace that the said beseecher may
have no recovere at Comune lawe'.[37]

To presenters of such petitions the most important aspect of these
affairs was their inability to secure justice from the law at a local
level. Since such statements had to be made to support a petition to
chancery, it is not easy for us to judge how accurate or justified they
really were. None the less they are significant evidence of a historical
phenomenon characteristic of this period: the need for those who

---

[33] *RP*, iii, 600; *SR*, ii, 155–6.

[34] 'molt profitable pour ease le quiete de luy et de tout son roialme' (*RP*, iii, 662;
SR, ii, 167).

[35] Powell, *Kingship, law and society*, p. 223.

[36] C.J. Tyldesley, 'The crown and the local communities in Devon and Cornwall
from 1377 to 1422' (Univ. of Exeter Ph.D. thesis, 1978), p. 16.

[37] Ibid., pp. 21, 22, 80.

sought to exercise power and influence to have the support of local gentry and of men holding offices of authority, perhaps as justices of the peace or as sheriffs, within the community. The illegal granting of cloths of livery, recorded on several occasions in the accusations presented against wrongdoers in Shropshire in 1414, was one such way for a lord, or even a prosperous member of the gentry, to impress his power upon a region.[38] That such liveries created divisions as well as bonds within a society, seems all too clear.

The apparent disregard for the law was to be found even among men who were in close contact with the crown. Between 1410 and 1412 Louis Robesart, an esquire of the Prince, was said to have been involved in supporting acts of piracy at sea.[39] In 1414, as we have seen, Thomas, earl of Arundel, a close associate of Henry, was among those obliged to take out recognizances to the total of 10,000 marks for the good behaviour of his people in Shropshire;[40] while in the following year the earl of Salisbury, a soldier destined to win himself a great military reputation, was fined for an assault in the parish of St Giles, outside the walls of London.[41] Such examples suggest that personal interest could rank higher in men's priorities than observance of the law. On the second day of the parliament of 1411 a petition was presented by William, Lord Roos, who complained that Robert Tirwhit, a justice of king's bench, had tried to intimidate Chief Justice Gascoigne, who was arbitrating in a dispute between them, by attending the meeting at the head of a large group of men, reportedly some 500 in number, armed and ready for war.[42] The complaints against disorder and the abuse of power made by Thomas Hoccleve were not based on the writer's imagination.[43]

Reference to the acts of piracy allegedly encouraged by Louis Robesart reminds us that some of the worst crime during these years was committed not on land, but at sea. The problem was not a new one, for acts of piracy (or of hijacking as we might regard them) had occurred since the development of international trade in the thirteenth century. The fourteenth century had seen a further increase in trade

[38] 'Extracts from the plea rolls of the reigns of Henry V and Henry VI', ed. G. Wrottesley, *Collections for a history of Staffordshire* (William Salt Archaeological Soc., 17, 1896), pp. 22, 27, 29, 30, 32 etc.

[39] *Select cases in chancery, 1364–1471*, ed. W.P. Baildon (Selden Soc., 10, London, 1896), pp. 99–100.

[40] E. Powell, 'Proceedings before the justices of the peace at Shrewsbury in 1414', *EHR*, 99 (1984), 539.

[41] Sayles, *Select cases*, pp. 231–3.

[42] *RP*, iii, 649; Powell, *Kingship, law and society*, pp. 122–3.

[43] 'On observing of the laws', *Hoccleve's Works. III. The Regement of Princes, A.D. 1411–12*, ed. F.J. Furnivall (EETS, London, 1897), pp. 100–8.

and even greater risks for those involved in it. To prevent goods falling into the hands of pirates, ship-owners took steps to protect themselves. The use of the convoy system, which gave a measure of safety to a number of vessels sailing together in formation, or the employment of armed men on board trading vessels, or of armed ships as escorts, was a recognition that safety at sea was a real problem and that appropriate measures had to be taken to ensure that vessels arrived safely at their ports of destination.

The problem was carried over into the fifteenth century, and became one for the new Lancastrian dynasty to face and resolve. To some, it was part of the growth of lawlessness, remedies against which were demanded in Henry IV's parliaments either under requests for sound rule or in more specific demands that the law be kept and justice be done to all who asked for it. To others, especially those who represented fishing or trading communities, the problem was one which concerned the survival of their prosperity. To others still, lack of order at sea was linked to the defence of the English shore, which the enemy might invade. In the parliament which assembled at Coventry late in 1404 the possibility that the French and the Bretons might land in England appeared to some to be very real. To Henry IV and his advisers, lack of order at sea may have had to be accepted out of necessity, although they would have been aware of the pressure upon them to restore it. At the best of times, this would have been difficult. What made the task harder was the political situation, the state of truce which dominated England's relations with France during much of Henry IV's reign. In practice, the truce was never fully observed, not least because France was anxious to cause difficulties for England by supporting hostile Scottish activity on the northern border, while it was part of English policy to ensure that this help never reached where it was intended to go. Piracy, therefore, might become policy, so that for the first five or six years of Henry IV's reign official steps to curb it were not pursued with too much vigour.[44]

With the increased participation of the Prince in government, however, things changed. Could he allow the law of the sea to be openly flouted, even if political and military considerations seemed to demand it? In his allocution to parliament in March 1406 bishop Langley re-emphasized the need for advice to be given to the king for the proper observance of his laws;[45] there could only be peace if the law were obeyed. In the following parliament, which met in October 1407, archbishop Arundel spoke of the need to observe the laws and to defend the kingdom, picking out for special mention the Welsh

[44] Ford, 'Piracy or Policy', 63–77.
[45] '. . . la bone Governance de ses Loies' (*RP*, iii, 567).

rebellion, the need to safeguard the sea and lands in France, and
requirements on the border with Scotland.[46] The emphasis towards
law keeping was to be most marked in January 1410, at the moment
when the Prince took charge of the royal council and bishop Beaufort,
as chancellor, addressed parliament.[47] The country, he stressed,
should see to it that the laws were kept and justice achieved, and he
emphasized in particular the need to keep the truces on the Scottish
border and to defend Calais (of which the Prince was captain) against
the threats of the duke of Burgundy. Seizing upon this, some presented
a petition demanding that 'bone et sage governance' be maintained
by the king and his council (this was for the Prince's hearing) 'for the
good and sure keeping of the sea all round about',[48] so that the malice
of enemies might be resisted, the defence of England and Wales
achieved, and the truces be observed, as merchants would be the first
to suffer if they were not.

The reply to the petition bore a clear message. The king wanted
the seas kept, and steps were to be taken to achieve this. As for the
truces, they, too, should be observed for the good of the kingdom, in
the manner his council was advising him.[49] Not surprisingly, Calais
was picked out for special treatment. In November 1411, in what was
to prove to be Henry IV's last parliament, and just at the moment
at which the Prince was being relieved of his responsibilities, Thomas
Beaufort, as chancellor, made a declaration which reflected the thinking of the Prince and the Beaufort family. Once again the stress was
on keeping the law: abuses must be quickly punished. In addition,
the sea must be defended, and money should be requested for the
special needs of its defence and safe-keeping.

Such statements bear the clear imprint of the Prince's influence, as
well as that of the Beauforts, two of whose members, John and
Thomas, had acted as admirals in recent years. The political and
diplomatic rapprochement with Burgundy which characterized the
new relationship developed during the period of the Prince's control
of the council (1410–11) required that peace and order be restored at
sea, for such a relationship had, as an essential characteristic, an
active policy of trade between England and lands under Burgundian
control. Conversely, there could be no long-lasting or effective peace
at sea unless it were negotiated with the duke. The Burgundian alliance which the Prince sought was intended not simply to achieve

[46] *RP*, iii, 608.
[47] Ibid., iii, 622.
[48] 'pur la bone & sure Garde de la Mere en toutz parties environ . . .' (ibid., iii, 625).
[49] Ibid., iii, 625.

political and military aims; it was, as the complex negotiations with the Low Countries show, essential for Henry if he was to succeed in restoring a measure of order at sea. He could not do it alone. Partnership with the authorities on the other side of the sea was a fundamental requirement of maritime peace.

Even the firmest of intentions, however, could not break what were, for some, habits of a lifetime. Legal evidence taken from cases heard in chancery or before the king's council, as well from Henry's parliaments, strongly suggests that many flouted the king's best intentions. In the far south-west (like Northumberland, an area far from the authority of Westminster) piracy could not be totally prevented. The activities of the two John Hawleys, first those of the father, who died in 1408, and then those of his son, were often beyond the control of local royal officials, who complained of intimidation on the part of Hawley supporters.[50] That such people existed and were employed by the Hawleys is made clear by the text of a petition, presented to archbishop Arundel, as chancellor, in 1412, in which redress was sought from John Hawley, junior, alleged to have seized a prize captured at sea from the French, with the support of 'a hundred men or more armed and arrayed in manner of war . . . to the great dismay of the persons aforesaid [the petitioners] and of all the country round, and to the damage of the said suppliants of £250 . . .' On this occasion Hawley appears to have had the backing of Thomas, Lord Carew (who was later to help Henry organize his war at sea).[51] As on land, waylaying at sea was carried out by well-connected persons who should have had a greater respect for the spirit of the law.

Economic crime is the final category to be considered. As such, it was a broad one. In 1414 the king was said to be worried by the charges imposed (and hence the profits made) by goldsmiths;[52] in 1420 it was action against the falsifiers of weights that was to be taken;[53] while in 1416 the bishops, in response to complaints, were to be asked to moderate the fees charged for granting the probate of wills,[54] and penalties invoked by statute 12 Richard II c.4 were to be imposed on those who accepted excessive wages.[55]

However, it was crime associated with the falsification of the country's coinage which was taken most seriously. The growing diffi-

[50] *A calendar of early chancery proceedings relating to west country shipping, 1389–1493*, ed. D.M. Gardiner (Devon & Cornwall Rec. Soc., new series 21, 1976), pp. 12–13.

[51] Baildon, *Select cases in chancery*, pp. 90–1.

[52] *SR*, ii, 188.

[53] Ibid., ii, 210.

[54] Ibid., ii, 195–6.

[55] Ibid., ii, 196–7; *The Shropshire peace roll, 1400–1414*, ed. E.G. Kimball (Shrewsbury, 1959), p. 48.

culties being experienced in maintaining a good standard of coinage were creating anxieties from the very beginning of the reign, and in particular from 1416 onwards. The need to exclude poor coinage, whether it came from Scotland or the Burgundian Low Countries, was very much at the forefront of the minds of those responsible for minting England's coinage and maintaining its standard.[56] A number of statutes of Henry IV's reign had concerned themselves with this matter, two at the end of the reign insisting particularly upon it. That the problems were not new when Henry V became king is made plain both by these statutes and by the report that the practice of clipping coin was already being practised and punished in his father's reign.[57] By the time that Henry had been king little more than a year the courts had brought before them men alleged to be 'common clippers of money, both gold and silver'.[58] One day in August 1416 magistrates in Essex were faced with one William Morton, a woolman from New-castle-upon-Tyne, accused of practising the doubtfully legal art of multiplication, contrary to statute 5 HIV c.4, which had condemned it as a felony.[59] Morton, it was said, made a powder called 'elixir' which when cast with reddish molten metal (copper or brass) turned its colour to gold; if cast with white metal (lead or tin) it looked like silver, as was proved when, foolishly, he demonstrated his skills before villagers of Hatfield Peveril in 1416.

Three years later the prior of Wenlock, in Shropshire, was said to have clipped coins and to have recast false ones according to the methods of the art of multiplication taught him by William Careswell of Witney, in Oxfordshire, who turned approver to save his own skin.[60] By this stage of the reign charges of counterfeiting, formerly a common law trespass but, since 1416, a treasonable offence, were being taken with far greater seriousness, since it was essential to preserve the value of the coinage which could greatly suffer from such illegal clipping, washing or filing.[61] In 1419 the step was taken of arraigning suspects without indictment. They could only secure their freedom if juries found them to be of good reputation. The measure underlines the seriousness with which the government regarded crimes involving England's coinage which, if it were to suffer further, might seriously

[56] See below, ch.18, pp. 385–6 for further reference to this matter.
[57] *CPR, 1413–16*, p. 151.
[58] '. . . sunt communes cissores monete, videlicet auri et argenti' (*Shropshire peace roll*, ed. Kimball, n.181).
[59] *SR*, ii, 144.
[60] Sayles, *Select cases*, pp. 242–6.
[61] 'Dialogus cum amico' (*Hoccleve's works. I. The minor poems*, ed. F.J. Furnivall (EETS, London, 1892), ll. 99–196).

damage the country's ability to continue the war against France.[62]

In the minds of those who drew up the statutes of 1406, observance of the law was crucial for 'peace within the realm [to] be holden and kept, so that all the king's liege people and subjects may from henceforth safely and peaceably go, come and abide, according to the laws and usages of the same realm'.[63] None was more aware of this ideal – as it was of the reality – than the Commons who sat in the parliaments of the first two Lancastrian kings, and who, through its petitions, was responsible for most of the legislation of these reigns;[64] the proportion of such petitions leading to statutes increased from some twenty-nine per cent under Richard II to thirty-three per cent under Henry IV and, finally, to some forty-five per cent under Henry V. Although the Commons protested in 1414 that the texts of petitions were being altered before being incorporated into statutes, such alterations were, on the whole, small (they concerned mainly penalties or exemptions) and did not change the spirit or substance of the petition which remained generally unaltered, much as had been the case before 1413.

What is apparent is that there were, in this reign, very few statutes which had been 'officially' sponsored (what might today be called a 'government bill'). The influence of the Commons on legislation was, therefore, correspondingly strong. This suggests that Henry, concerned as he was about the enforcement of the law, was not a major innovator (as Edward I had been) at least as far as most everyday law making was concerned.[65] In 1414, replying to a complaint about attacks on his subjects in Staffordshire, he stated that 'the law of the reign of Henry IV is sufficient against them',[66] while in 1417, reacting to another petition against those who infringed the peace and tranquillity of the realm, he replied simply that the existing statutes should be put into execution.[67]

He had reasonable cause for reacting in this way. The years following the Peasants' Revolt of 1381 had seen Richard II's government responding to crime with the statutes 15 RII c.2 and 17 RII c.8.[68]

[62] Powell, *Kingship, law and society*, pp. 258–61.

[63] *SR*, ii, 150.

[64] H.L. Gray, *The influence of the commons on early legislation. A study of the fourteenth and fifteenth centuries* (Cambridge, Mass./London, 1932), p. 258.

[65] The powers given by the Leicester parliament of 1414 to curb disorder (*SR*, ii, 184–7) were intended to grant greater authority to the statute of riots of 1411 (*SR*, ii, 169); but they scarcely deserve to be regarded as a 'major' innovation.

[66] 'Y ad sufficeant remedies ordeigne par estatut fait en le Parlement tenuz a Westm' l'an du regne le Roi Henry quarte puis le conqueste' (*RP*, iv, 32). Which year is not indicated.

[67] 'Soient les Estatutz ent faitz misez en execution' (ibid., iv, 114).

[68] *SR*, ii, 78, 89.

Commons' petitions for the reign of Henry IV, however, indicate quite clearly that crimes against both persons and property were still frequent.[69] These led to the statute 13 HIV c.7 which emphasized that the main problem was not insufficient legislation but the inability of law officers to enforce it by arresting malefactors and bringing them to court. Sheriffs and justices, unable to lay hands on criminals, could now gather information and, in the manner of a jury of presentment laying accusations, could place such information before the king's bench or the council. One of these bodies would decide the punishment to be imposed. If the accused did not appear, he would be convicted of riot after the third failure. As a sting in the tail, the statute ordered that a fine of up to £100 should be imposed upon any who failed to execute the statute's provision.[70]

The wording of 2 HV, st.1, c.8 shows how Henry was reacting to the problem of lawlessness, about which, it was said, many complaints had been lodged in the parliament which assembled at Leicester in April 1414.[71] The existing laws were not being put into proper execution, and justices were told to act with determination, with the help of a county's posse if necessary, against those who caused riots or otherwise broke the law. Sheriffs, too (shades of the act of 13 HIV), were to record allegations for use in court; juries might be asked to present evidence, so that such allegations could be reported to the king and his council. Failing such methods, special commissions were to be appointed under the great seal to make enquiries, and their findings were to be returned to chancery. Emphasis was placed not only upon evil-doers (for whom stiffer prison sentences were ordered) but also upon coroners and members of juries who failed in their duty by not attending the courts. They, too, were to pay the penalty of a fine were this to occur.

Such was the apparent lack of confidence in the system of catching and then convicting persons accused of crime that it was decided to place greater stress on the power of chancery to act effectively and decisively. The statute 2 HV, st.1, c.9, which was to stand in full force only until the end of the next parliament (indicating that it was hoped its powers might not always be required), gave chancery the authority to issue writs of *capias* to sheriffs to arrest felons and bring them before chancery.[72] The language of 1414 indicates clearly that Henry was determined that effective measures be taken against criminals. The reason why the law appeared to him to be held in such low regard was

---

[69] *RP*, iii, 497–8, 615; *SR*, ii, 134–5, 159.
[70] *SR*, ii, 169.
[71] Ibid., ii, 184–6.
[72] Ibid., ii, 186–7.

because the penalties which it threatened could so easily be ignored by those who broke it. Proper enforcement of existing law, rather than new statutes, was what was needed.

The system of law enforcement on which Henry was relying was essentially locally based, dependent upon persons from the county both to apprehend criminals and to judge them. As the statute 2 HV st.2, c.1 specified, justices of the peace were to be chosen from among the better off residing in the county.[73] Inevitably, in the less than peaceful conditions prevailing early in Henry's reign, this meant relying upon a group of persons who were, themselves, often involved in crimes, if not of violence, at least of intimidation or embezzlement, or who were susceptible to such pressures from others.[74] Much the same might be said of sheriffs. In his choice of sheriffs, however, Henry did show that he appreciated the danger of relying upon men with too many local interests. In Devon, for example, he followed his father's example of trying to reinforce the effectiveness of sheriffs with strong commitments outside the county. He did this largely by choosing men who were his retainers (hence bound to him in a formal manner), without interests in the county, and to whom he sometimes gave a second term when the normal legal limit of service was one year.[75] Such men, it was thought, were less susceptible to local influences, and the extension of their term enabled them to exercise their office with greater confidence and experience.

Countering social problems with new statutes was a way of reacting whose effectiveness depended to a large degree upon the personal commitment of the king to see it work. Before war began to take up much of his time and, after 1417, to demand his almost constant presence in France, Henry had discharged his responsibilities to the law and to his people with energy and conviction. In his fulfilment of that part of his coronation oath,[76] the year 1414 was of paramount importance. The Lollard rising in January, by focusing upon the risks of disorder in certain localities, was to prompt Henry into further action. When parliament met at Leicester at the end of April, members found the court of king's bench, which had not moved out of London in the previous reign, already in town, holding a 'superior eyre'. Prompted by this, members complained about lawlessness in different parts of England.[77] Henry, as usual sensitive to such opinions, now initiated the major visitation of the west-midland coun-

[73] Ibid., ii, 187; see also *RP*, iv, 51.
[74] Powell, 'Proceedings before the justices', 536.
[75] Tyldesley, 'Crown and local communities', p. 208.
[76] Powell, *Kingship, law and society*, pp. 127–30.
[77] *RP*, iv, 21, 24–8.

ties, which took place between May and the beginning of July, the court travelling from Leicester to Lichfield, then to Shrewsbury and finally to Wolverhampton before returning to London.[78]

The method used was intended to show the importance attached by the king to the need to do justice in areas where the application of the law had run into difficulties. The fact that the court was 'the most powerful agency of justice available to the Crown',[79] with jurisdiction in both civil and criminal cases, at whose appearance within a county all other forms of justice immediately ceased to function, may have made men appreciate how determined the king was to see the law, so easily flouted, obeyed. In some two and a half months, over an area comprising five counties, about 2000 summonses were issued, of which, it has been calculated, some thirty-seven per cent were answered, about fifty per cent in cases of fairly recent crime.[80] At every session, the coroners' rolls were sent for, and all cases not determined by the inferior, local courts were judged. Cases going back many years were considered, the exercise being an attempt, as far as was possible, not only to do justice and re-establish a proper regard for the law, but also to sweep up a large backlog of cases which had built up over the years in an area of now notorious lawlessness. All this time, the king kept at a discreet distance: early in June he was at Burton-on-Trent, where he dealt personally with John and William Mynors from Staffordshire, and considered irregularities in the administration of the abbey.[81] By the vigour of his actions he would have shown that he wanted social peace to be restored.

A further arm of central justice to be used by Henry was the commission of enquiry. This had several advantages. It was an exceptional, rather than a normal form of setting the judicial process in motion, and one whose very existence depended upon a decision taken at the highest level. The hand of the king himself could, therefore, be discerned in the appointment of such a commission. It had a further advantage. While nominations to membership might include local people (William Roos of Hamelak was on an enquiry about rebellions and insurrections in Nottinghamshire in 1413,[82] while Lord FitzHugh headed a commission which enquired into riots in Nottinghamshire and Derbyshire in 1414),[83] they also often included men well known

---

[78] Powell, *Kingship, law and society*, ch.7.

[79] Ibid., p. 177.

[80] Ibid., p. 177 seq.

[81] Ibid., pp. 213–14.

[82] *CPR, 1413–16*, p. 35.

[83] S.J. Payling, 'Law and arbitration in Nottinghamshire, 1399–1461', *People, politics and community in the later middle ages*, ed. J. Rosenthal and C. Richmond (Gloucester/New York, 1987), p. 142.

to the king, many of them lawyers. Furthermore, since the nomination lay in royal hands, the king could appoint men unknown in the area under investigation, as he did with the nomination of sheriffs in Devon. In November 1413, when a commission of oyer and terminer was appointed to do justice in Devon, it included only one local man, the remaining four being members of the king's close circle. When another commission of enquiry was named in July 1414, it consisted of a powerful body of men, none of whom, however, was local. This enquiry was particularly successful, a number of hundreds in Devon being fined for not sending juries of presentment to sit before it, and many individuals being accused of impeding the work of the earlier commission.[84] Such commissions of oyer and terminer were among the more effective ways of doing justice available at this time.

Henry used the council and chancery as yet another means of dealing with lawlessness, in particular when those accused of crime refused to appear in local courts to answer their accusers. The threat of a summons to appear before the council (a body very close to the king) could make wrongdoers think twice about refusing to do so, partly because the summons meant that their local law officer, in all probability the sheriff, had reported them, partly because the penalties meted out by the council were more severe than in lower courts.[85] As for the court of chancery, which, under the chancellor, held its formal cases in the Great Hall at Westminster, it based its methods more on the practices of equity than on trial by common law. In an age when justice was known to be slow and cumbersome, and when men known to be guilty escaped because of technicalities in the indictments presented against them, the proceedings of chancery were seen as a means whereby those without power or influence might see wrongs righted. During these years, because its procedures were comparatively simple and informal, and its examination of parties more effective than the methods used in the common law courts, this speedier form of justice found popularity as a means of suppressing disorder. Further encouraged by the suspension of the possessory assizes in 1415 and again between 1417 and 1421, a measure introduced to protect the interests of those serving in France, the court of chancery's business saw the beginning of a rapid development in the reign of Henry V.[86]

Recent research on the law and the maintenance of order has tended not to stress the weakness of royal and local institutions, but to see

[84] Tyldesley, 'Crown and local communities', pp. 217, 219; Powell, *Kingship, law and society*, pp. 201–8.

[85] *RP*, iv, 163–4.

[86] M.E. Avery, 'An evaluation of the effectiveness of the court of chancery under the Lancastrian kings', *LQR*, 86 (1970), 84–8; Powell, *Kingship, law and society*, p. 248 and n.6.

disorder more in terms of divided societies, and peace as being the product of a wish or determination not to allow such divisions to triumph. What, it may be asked, did society do on its own to regulate conflict within itself and to ensure peace in the future?[87] In cases of local disputes, over land, for instance, the most satisfactory arrangements were those agreed locally within a given society, a process in which the land-owning class took an increasingly active part through private arbitration. Attempts to contain such disputes were not always successful. That which sought to resolve a bitter quarrel between Hugh Erdswick and Edmund, Lord Ferrers, a quarrel which came to involve others, in Staffordshire in the autumn of 1413, was to fail, in spite of the local importance of the arbitrators who acted under Richard Beauchamp, earl of Warwick. No award had yet been made when the conflict it had been intended to end flared up again, and it required the departure of Ferrers in the army to France in 1415, following the visit of the king's bench in 1414, to bring the dispute to a conclusion.[88]

In another dispute, however, Warwick was more successful. At Easter time 1414 he arbitrated to settle criminal proceedings initiated by the prior of Worcester against Sir Thomas Burdett and his son, Nicholas, who were held responsible for the violent death of two of the cathedral's tenants at Shipston-on-Stour. The prior and Thomas Burdett were to agree to be friends, while Nicholas was to go to Worcester cathedral, offer a taper of wax weighing 5lb in reparation of the wrong done to God and the Virgin Mary, and then approach the prior and his fellow monks in the chapter house to ask their pardon, besides offering the sum of £5 to Thomas Compton of Shipston in compensation for his crime.[89] In another long dispute between Alexander Meering and John Tuxford regarding the ownership of part of the Nottinghamshire manor of Markham Clinton, originally referred to arbitration in 1411, supporters of the two sides raised sizeable bands which nearly led to outbreaks of violence. As a result, the criminal matters came before king's bench in June 1414; the underlying quarrel, however, was to be settled two years later by an equal division of the disputed lands between the parties.[90]

Henry was aware that arbitration had great advantages over the

---

[87] Payling, 'Law and arbitration', p. 140; Powell, *Kingship, law and society*, pp. 240–6.

[88] Powell, *Kingship, law and society*, pp. 240–2.

[89] *HMC Fifth Report*, p. 303; C.Rawcliffe, 'The great lord as peacemaker: arbitration by English noblemen and their councils in the later middle ages', *Law and social change in British history*, ed. J.A. Guy and H.G. Beale (London, 1984), p. 41.

[90] Payling, 'Law and arbitration', pp. 141–3, 147–8; Powell, *Kingship, law and society*, pp. 226–7.

imposition of the rigours of the law, which, in any case, could not always effectively be applied.[91] In this respect he was in keeping with the practice of the day; he was also, as his treatment of the descendants of his father's political opponents suggests, a reconciler, ready to apply the law leniently if political and social advantage could be gained. His treatment of the Staffordshire malcontents is a good example of his wish not to make matters worse, but rather to try to meet some of the troublemakers' ambitions and, in so doing, to show that he understood the social and economic forces which motivated them. The Mynors brothers, one already a member of Henry's household, the other appointed to office within the duchy of Lancaster in the county, were reconciled to the king and formally pardoned. William Mynors was to serve in Normandy in the years to come; his brother, John, was to pass on his office to his son.[92] Where Richard Beauchamp had failed, Henry now made peace between Edmund, Lord Ferrers, and Hugh Erdswick: Ferrers fought before Harfleur, at Agincourt and also before Rouen, staying in Normandy for some years;[93] Erdwick soon won the recognition he had been seeking, becoming first a justice of the peace in the county and then a regular office-holder there for at least a generation.[94]

Such evidence suggests that it is too simple to regard men such as Hugh Erdswick merely as high-class thugs.[95] The trouble which they undoubtedly gave to the law and to local society stemmed from social deficiencies within their localities, the most important of which was the absence of proper magnate influence within those societies. It was to Henry's credit that, in the period before he left for France in 1415 (and again, briefly, in 1421),[96] he took an active role in reconciling differences at a local level. The *Brut* recalled how 'in the first yere of his regne, ther were ij knyhtis at gret debate: the tone was of Lankestyr-shire, & the tothyr of York-shire; and they made them as stronge of peeple as they cowde, & scarmysshid togedyr; and men were slayne & hurte on bothe partyes'. The chronicle then recounted how both parties were summoned to Windsor and ordered by the king to settle their differences by 'that tyme that he had etyn his owystrys, [or] they shulde be hangyd bothe two [bef]or ever he sopyt'. We are not given the names of the men concerned, and there is an element of the legend in the way that the story is told. None the less, it sums up both how Henry showed his determination to bring local feuding

[91] Powell, *Kingship, law and society*, pp. 97–107.
[92] Ibid., pp. 213–14.
[93] Ibid., pp. 215, 241–2; *Brut*, ii, 388, 396.
[94] Ibid., p. 215.
[95] Ibid., p. 216.
[96] See above, ch.8, for Henry arbitrating at Lincoln in this year.

to an end, and how he actively used his own authority to force those who had been at odds to end their quarrels through reconciliation.[97]

The various and varied difficulties experienced by Henry in getting the law observed may have obliged him to use forms of legal practice which were not wholly in keeping with England's common law traditions. Ever since the reign of Edward I kings of England had toyed, more or less seriously, with the more arbitrary solutions presented by Roman law. In particular, the law of treason, expressed in new terms in the statute of that name promulgated by Edward III in 1352, came usefully to hand to help Henry face some of the difficulties of his reign. In 1415 the act was used as a basis for the accusations levelled against the Southampton conspirators: theirs was a plot against both king and the general good, whose existence Lord Scrope was accused of having kept concealed. If this was not active plotting on Scrope's part, it was the next best, 'misprision', passive agreement in a plot intended to lead to the king's death.[98] Although the idea was not entirely new, the term was; the concept was one borrowed from Roman law. Other crimes came to be treated in the same way. It became treason to allow a prisoner to escape from a royal prison.[99] In 1416 the state of the coinage was showing such deterioration that drastic measures were taken: clipping or sweating the king's coin moved up the scale of gravity of criminal offences from being a felony to becoming an act of treason.[100]

It was, however, in his response to the major problem of how to maintain order at sea, particularly in times of peace or under conditions of truce, that we observe Henry taking the most dramatic steps. This matter was one about which, as Prince, he had felt very strongly, as his reply, made to the parliament of 1410, promising action, had shown. It seems clear that Henry came to the throne committed to the absolute need to safeguard the sea, and that both Henry and Thomas Beaufort strongly supported him. Yet, by the time the Leicester parliament met in April 1414, it was evident that both Henry and his subjects were worried that the terms of truces were not being properly observed. Criminals, it was reported, were acting against them; persons were at risk at sea, and help and encouragement was being offered to those who committed such outrages. Something had to be done.[101]

The complaints voiced in the Commons led to legislation, the

[97] *Brut*, ii, 595.

[98] J.G. Bellamy, *The law of treason in England in the later middle ages* (Cambridge, 1970), p. 222.

[99] Ibid., p. 131.

[100] Ibid., pp. 130, 142.

[101] *RP*, iv, 15, 22.

so-called Statute of Truces of 1414, which, in its opening lines, briefly
set out the background for the action being proposed.[102] Attacks were
being made both at sea and in ports, to the loss of the king's honour
and dignity. At the Commons' request, such acts were now to be
regarded as treason. This was an important step to have taken; more
was to follow. In order to see that truces were properly kept, it was
now established that each port should have a 'conservator' of truces
(an office which derived its origins from ideas stemming from Roman
military law), to be drawn from those who owned land worth £40 per
annum or more, appointed by commission issued by the Admiral of
England, to enquire about all acts against truces perpetrated at sea
or abetted from the land. Assisted by two experts in the law, the
conservator was to have full right of enquiry both at sea and on land;
he could punish all indicted before him of infractions of the truce,
although the exercise of the death penalty was reserved for the
Admiral or his lieutenant.

The conservator's terms of appointment were important. He was
to receive at least £40 per annum (presumably to make him able to
resist corruption), and none was to seek favours from him: all
attempting to obtain these were to be fined. He was to reside in the
port of his appointment; on sailing from there, every ship's master (or
owner, if he were present) was to make an undertaking not to act
against the truces; furthermore the master's name, that of his ship
and the number of sailors aboard were to be recorded. If any prizes
were taken at sea, they had to be declared before being sold, a letter
confirming their declaration, and bearing his seal, being provided by
the conservator. All who disobeyed these laws were to forfeit their
ships and prizes to the king; masters (but not owners, unless they
were present) were to be put in prison until they had paid a fine. As
for the Cinque Ports, they, too, came under the jurisdiction of the
new conservators; only cases involving the death penalty were the
concern of the Warden, who, in such cases, was to receive all forfeited
property.[103]

It is a measure of the importance which Henry attached to the need
to defeat those who harassed trade and impeded the aims of the king's
diplomacy by attacking ships belonging to jurisdictions with which
truces had been arranged (it should be recalled that such truces were
arranged for the political as well as for the economic advantages which
they might bring) that he was willing to make such acts crimes against
crown and kingdom. Equally important, from the historical point of
view, was the appointment of special conservators with powers which

---

[102] This statute is referred to above, ch.10, p. 221.
[103] *SR*, ii, 178–81.

might easily come into conflict with privileges and the practices of common law, in particular when the conservator, an officer regarded with suspicion by those anxious to defend the common law and local privileges, claimed the right of jurisdiction on both sea and land.

The Statute of Truces, passed in May 1414, was a serious attempt to come to terms with piracy at sea. Its enactments were intended to lead to a reduction in the number of maritime 'incidents' which hindered both confidence and trade, as well as better relations with other countries, notably Burgundy. As such, they were also part of English diplomatic policy to win Burgundian help. In practice, however, the statute was to be the cause of difficulty, almost injustice. In the parliament of November 1415 it was argued that maritime communities from Orwell to Berwick were much affected by the trouble caused to them by the terms of the statute. For these people, many of them caught up in the almost perpetual state of conflict with the Scots, the causes of the difficulties were simple to perceive: they had been deprived of the right of retaliation against their rivals when redress could not be obtained for wrongs suffered on both land and sea. Placed at a grave disadvantage, since they were forbidden from seeking redress from those who attacked their trade, English merchants asked the duke of Bedford, as lieutenant, to repeal the act. All that he could do, however, was to promise some possible modification of it.[104] When parliament next met, in March 1416, this time in the king's presence, the whole matter was raised again. Englishmen, it was reported, could not take effective measures to defend their interests by direct action against enemies who, contrary to the truces, attacked them on land and at sea, killing or ransoming Englishmen and destroying their property. Henry was asked to grant letters of marque, authorizing retributive measures against fellow nationals said to have committed acts of violence against his subjects, whenever these were petitioned for.[105]

The petition, with which the king may have had much sympathy, none the less placed him in a difficulty. It had been part of Henry's policy since at least 1410 to encourage the development of stable conditions for trade at sea. Furthermore the good relationship which he wished to build up with Burgundy (he and duke John were to meet in Calais less than six months later) would depend in some measure upon a fruitful commercial link which, unless protected and encouraged by legislation, risked becoming a bone of contention between the parties. The measures authorized by Henry bore the mark of caution. Letters of marque might be issued, but only after complainants had

[104] *RP*, iv, 68.
[105] Ibid., iv, 105.

addressed themselves to the Keeper of the Privy Seal, who would seek
a remedy on their behalf. If none were made after a reasonable period,
the chancellor would have authority to issue letters under the great
seal. If the actions complained of took place within the jurisdiction of
the Scottish marches, the wardens should be requested to make calls
for restitution by public proclamation. Then, if nothing were done,
they might issue the complainant with the letters of marque which he
sought.[106]

To some the Statute of Truces was a cause of weakness to English
merchants in their everyday relations with foreigners. It forbade them,
they claimed, the use of the weapon of instant retaliation against those
who used force to disrupt their legitimate trade. In the view of others,
those charged with the enforcement of the statute were coming
dangerously close to undermining the delicate balance of local rights
based on custom and common law. In the parliament of 1415 the
people of Sandwich complained that in a case concerning the seizure,
by certain subjects of the king, of goods belonging to a Flemish widow,
goods which they claimed were worth about £40 but which the widow
said were worth twice as much, the constable of Dover castle,
responding to a royal commission, was acting against common law in
demanding the restitution of the higher valuation of the goods concerned, without giving the men of Sandwich the right of reply. Such
action, it was said, was against common law and the terms of Magna
Carta which stated that no man should be judged other than by
common law, as did other ancient statutes which protected men's
right to be judged by that law alone. Reacting to the petition that
the commission be withdrawn to enable the truth to be ascertained
according to common law principles, Bedford could only reply that
the chancellor would arrange for the matter to be settled according
to the terms of the truces established between England and Flanders.
The measures of the Statute of Truces had been challenged and,
seemingly, overridden.[107] Henry had had greater success with the law
elsewhere.

[106] *SR*, ii, 198–9.
[107] *RP*, iv, 67–8. The effectiveness of the new statute is put in doubt by Dr Powell,
who informs me that he has found no evidence that conservators of truces were ever
appointed.

Chapter 15

THE FAMILY CIRCLE

Although king, Henry V did not rule alone. It is easy to see him as a man closely involved in the affairs of ruling his kingdom, taking decisions, implementing them, in general stamping his personality upon events. Such an observation is generally well founded: Henry was very much a king who ruled. But it would be wrong to ignore the role played by others during his reign. In particular it is important to assess the contribution made by a small circle of men who, as descendants of John of Gaunt and, therefore, 'men of Lancaster', helped Henry as Prince and, later, as king to fulfil the tasks of government.

The eldest of a long line of six surviving children, four of them male and all born in legitimate wedlock, Henry had the good fortune to be closely associated with the wider 'Lancastrian' family, the three illegitimate male children of John of Gaunt by Katherine Swynford, all legitimated by pope Boniface IX in 1396 and given civil rights early in 1397. These rights were confirmed by Henry IV in 1406 at the cost of their exclusion from the succession to the English crown, an exclusion accepted and never challenged by them, although those whom it concerned were to live for years within the shadow of the throne. Loyalty to the common ancestry, and therefore to the dynasty of Lancaster, was a factor which Henry could always count upon. It formed a solid basis upon which to build a relationship between generations, a bond which united a handful of the most important, influential and able men in the kingdom around the king (placed in the position of highest responsibility by birth) in what was, in many respects, an exercise for the survival of the dynasty which had achieved power in 1399. If that dynasty collapsed, the descendants of Gaunt one and all risked the loss of position, power and wealth. They had an interest in acting and sticking together.

In approaching this subject we must recognize that we are dealing with the male members of the family. Neither of Henry's sisters played a part in his reign, since both were married to continental rulers and one, Blanche, died while Henry IV was still king.[1] Henry's world

---

[1] The Beauforts' sister, Joan, became countess of Westmorland by marriage. In his will, made in 1415, Henry V described her as 'our friend' ('amica nostra') (*Foedera*, IV, ii, 139).

was one very much dominated by the men of the family. John, the first of Gaunt's illegitimate children by Katherine Swynford, and one day to be earl of Somerset, was probably born in 1372. The second, Henry, born about 1375, was, as Cardinal Beaufort, destined to play a major role in history in the period during which the Lancastrians ruled England. The third, Thomas, born in 1377, was to play a role of importance in the reign of Henry IV and one of greater significance in the successes achieved by Henry V. Since they shared a father, John of Gaunt, these men were the half-brothers of Gaunt's legitimate heir, Henry, who won the throne in 1399. As such, they belonged both in time and in common ancestry to Henry IV's generation; some ten or fifteen years older than Henry V (their half-nephew) they represented a 'senior' branch of the family and, most important, they were consequently among the men from whom Henry, both as the young Prince and later as king, sought advice and help in matters of government and war.

The abilities and qualities which these three men brought to bear upon such practical matters were considerable. It was probably because he died in 1411, at the age of nearly forty, that John Beaufort appears to have made the least impression upon the growing Prince. Yet John was a man who, like his half-brother, Henry IV, had taken part in crusading warfare, had been involved in relations with France in the last decade or so of Richard II's reign, and served in Wales in 1403 and 1404, at that moment when the Prince was beginning to take up his Welsh responsibilities seriously. In brief, he appears to have been a man of action. Yet, although the Prince and he would have known each other, John's lack of active participation in the work of government during the first decade of the century, and his relatively early death, mean that there was probably not much contact between him and the Prince in the important, formative years.

Of Henry Beaufort, bishop of Lincoln in 1398 and of Winchester in 1404, very much more is known, and much has already been noted. [2] By virtue of his birth, he could have been a close companion to the Prince, to whom he may have acted as tutor. As chancellor of England between 1403 and 1405, he would have been in a position to help make policy, in particular in relation to the troubles in Wales, the increasing difficulties caused by France and the problems created by lack of security on the maritime trade routes, especially in the Channel. Was it, as has been suggested, the origins of his mother, who came from Hainault stock, that made Henry Beaufort appreciate the importance of maritime trade and the link with the dukes of

---

[2]   On Henry Beaufort, see Harriss, *Cardinal Beaufort*.

Burgundy,[3] and was it he who stressed these factors to the Prince as being of significance to the future peace and prosperity of England? Certainly Beaufort would have emphasized the importance of king and council working well together, and of the need for the relationship between king and parliament to be one of trust. The growth of the personal rapport between the Prince and the bishop of Winchester was an important development of these years. It is likely that it was the bishop who impressed upon the Prince the need for careful and controlled exercise of expenditure and financial management from 1407 onwards, and who stood by him in his differences with archbishop Arundel. Not surprisingly, on the very day on which he succeeded his father Henry appointed the bishop to the chancellorship, the second time that he had held the office, which was to remain his for more than four years, until his resignation in July 1417.

Thomas, the youngest of the three Beaufort brothers, was certainly a help to and an influence upon the Prince in his formative years. An excellent soldier with an ability to command, he served in Wales in 1405 under the Prince but, even more significantly, he acted as captain of Calais castle between 1408 and 1414. Admiral of the northern fleet in 1403 and of the western fleet in 1408 (both offices were held for life), his role as a naval leader helps us understand the importance which Henry, both as Prince and later as king, was to attach to peace at sea and a good understanding with Burgundy. The existence of a harmonious and trusting relationship between Thomas Beaufort and the Prince is further seen in the appointment of Beaufort as chancellor in the administration set up by the Prince early in 1410. What his role was, it is difficult to gauge. But his promotion to the earldom of Dorset in July 1411 (doubtless the Prince, at the head of the council, would have played a major role in that appointment) and his nomination as Clarence's lieutenant in Aquitaine in 1412 suggest that in Thomas Beaufort there was a man whom all could trust, whatever their personal and political differences. His ability to get on well with all parties seems to have been one of his main attributes, and it is likely that this personal quality greatly helped the establishment of good relationships between the leaders of English society during Henry V's reign.

By the time that he became king, Henry had won the friendship of the two surviving Beaufort sons, both loyal and senior members of the house of Lancaster, both experienced in a variety of affairs (including the chancellorship), neither afraid of work or of responsibility. His opinion regarding his brothers may have been more mixed. He can

3 Ibid., pp. 387–8.

have found little to criticize in the work of John, who had acted as Warden of the East March against Scotland since 1403, an important but thankless task for a young man, but one more than satisfactorily accomplished, John demonstrating his ability in both border warfare and administration.[4] Of the youngest brother, Humphrey, we know very little at this time: he came to the fore only on the accession of his brother to the throne.

It is in trying to understand Henry's relationship with the eldest of his brothers, Thomas, that the historian experiences the greatest difficulty. The two men appear to have taken different parts, and it is likely that they were very different personalities. But what divided them, if, indeed, they were divided? Were they both ambitious men, only one of whom (Henry) was able to satisfy his ambition? Was Thomas jealous of his position? There appears to have been a genuine disagreement in 1412 regarding the policy to follow in relation to France, and this led to a difference which involved their father, Henry IV.[5] Nor did their difference stop there. Henry recognized and rewarded loyalty and devotion to duty; it was this characteristic which he admired in both his brother John and in Thomas Beaufort. These qualities seemed to be lacking in his brother Thomas, who appeared to have taken his responsibilities as royal lieutenant in Ireland, a post to which he had been appointed at a salary of 12,000 marks a year in 1401, with less than serious intent. Admittedly, as Henry IV's financial difficulties had grown, so the sums paid to Thomas had diminished, £6000 in 1406, 7000 marks in 1408. In 1409 the Prince and the council had threatened to offer Thomas even less, as his personal commitment to his Irish responsibilities appeared so greatly diminished. He suffered what was, in effect, a severe reprimand for his inactivity, and it is notable that, on his father's death, he did not find himself reappointed to his position in Ireland.[6] What is likely is that his rather cavalier treatment of the post of royal lieutenant had angered not only the Prince but bishop Beaufort too, for both were anxious to see not only good rule, but rule which made proper use of the limited funds available. His career, up to 1413, may not have suggested either to Henry or to his increasingly influential adviser, bishop Beaufort, that Thomas, created duke of Clarence and earl of Aumale by his father in July 1412, was a man to be relied

    [4] E. Carleton Williams, *My lord of Bedford, 1389–1435* (London, 1963), chs 2 and 3; S.B. Chrimes, 'Some letters of John of Lancaster as Warden of the east marches towards Scotland', *Speculum*, 14 (1939), 3–27.
    [5] See above, ch.3: McNiven, 'Political crisis of 1412', 6–16.
    [6] E. Matthew, 'The financing of the lordship of Ireland under Henry V and Henry VI', *Property and politics: essays in later medieval English history*, ed. A.J. Pollard (Gloucester/New York, 1984), pp. 97–8; *PPC*, i, 320.

upon. Although a man of talent and undoubted military ability, Clarence's record in Ireland did not inspire trust. In future, he would be kept fairly close to the king who could thus supervise what his brother was doing.

By the time that he assumed power in 1413 Henry would have known where he stood in relation to his five male blood relatives. The Beauforts were able and could be counted on. What was more, they held views about the way that government should be managed and what importance should be given to certain policies which agreed with those of the new king. So close to the royal family and yet, because of their illegitimate birth, not quite part of it, they were of value to Henry for their age and experience, as well as for their social position. Treated with respect, they could – and would – serve him to mutual advantage. Of his brothers, it must have been clear that John would be an ideal foil to Henry himself, a man with the experience of taking decisions far away from the seat of power but content to work within a broad framework of policies worked out beforehand. Put very simply, John did not seek the limelight. As an admirer of his eldest brother, he appears to have been content to carry out the everyday tasks of government without complaint. Henry trusted him completely. The fact that he had experience of military organization and of war on the borders was an added, and important, bonus. Clarence, on the other hand, a man of restless energy and some ambition, but lacking the patience which made his brother John the ideal man to whom governmental responsibilities might be left in the king's absence, may have caused Henry some concern. Only slightly younger than Henry, whose heir as king he now became, he was well accustomed to command. In his future relationship with the new king, the matter of how each would react to the other would be very important, for the relationship was one which would be bound to have far-reaching repercussions within the royal family and, indeed, beyond. Very different in character, recently divided in public regarding which faction to support in France, Henry and Clarence always carried the possibility of further division. Of Humphrey of Gloucester, there is not much to say. By 1413 he had made little impression upon his contemporaries. It would be up to Henry to initiate him in matters of war and government.

The role of Henry's family in his nine-and-a-half-year reign was to be a crucial one. To his credit, the king built on the experience of his uncles and brothers. As the king's 'oldest and closest councillor', Henry Beaufort was given the post which most suited his position as a bishop and a man of the highest social rank: on the day of his accession, Henry restored his uncle to the position of chancellor, which he had held when the Prince had been in charge of the council in 1410 and 1411.[7] Here the bishop was at the centre of things, in close and frequent contact with Henry, a regular member of the royal council and in a position of both authority and influence when it came to dealing with parliament, at whose openings it was his responsibility to report on developments and needs, explain the king's policies and finally to ask for the funds required to put them into effect. In the early years of the reign it is likely that the bishop encouraged two policies in particular: the restoration of order at sea and a return to peaceful maritime trade with the lands of John, duke of Burgundy, with whom he favoured a close working relationship; and, secondly, the vigorous pursuit of a strong and determined policy towards France.[8]

In this, he would almost certainly have found the support of his brother, Thomas, who himself favoured an increased awareness of the importance of the sea and of the need to defend England's interests upon it, as well as the pursuit of a consistent policy towards France. Both did what they could to further these ends. For the chancellor, persuading parliament in 1414, 1415 and 1416 to vote money for war was a logical development of the policy which he had advocated in public.[9] For Dorset, both his negotiations with France in 1414 and his exercise of the role of admiral (certainly not the sinecure which it may appear to have been) were a commitment to vigorous action to restore England's power and prestige under the rule of their nephew.

Indeed, behind all this there lay a latent sense of growing national consciousness expressed and fostered, according to a recent argument, by bishop Beaufort himself. It is likely that it was he (calling himself 'the devoted chaplain') who wrote to the king a few days after Agincourt to congratulate him on the victory which, he was careful to point out, although won by the effectiveness of Henry's army, was due to God's power, in answer to the demands of justice and the prayers of the people of England.[10] From this, it is argued, was developed the idea that God favoured his people of England against the unjust French. Yet, although successful, the English must not rest upon their laurels. Looking back too much was reprehensible; only continued effort would bring success and, since effort required money, Beaufort could assure the king that both the clergy and the laity would willingly help in that way. In this letter, and in speeches made before parliament, bishop Beaufort was helping to create a sense of collective

[7] The reader is referred to Harriss, *Cardinal Beaufort*, ch.4.
[8] Ibid., p. 72.
[9] Ibid., pp. 79, 86–9.
[10] *Letters of queen Margaret*, pp. 2–6; G.L. Harriss, 'Henry Beaufort, "Cardinal of England" ', *England in the fifteenth century*, ed. D. Williams (Woodbridge, 1987), p. 112.

achievement (some prayed while others fought)[11] under the personal leadership of the king, the effort being blessed with victory by God who allowed those with the just cause to be vindicated.[12]

That the war had got off to a good start was in part due to other members of the family. Dorset, Clarence and Gloucester had all three taken part in the expedition which had set out from Southampton in August 1415. At Harfleur they had played an active military role, although Clarence had been one of those whom the king had sent home because of illness. Henry's trust in Dorset was to be shown in his appointment as captain of Harfleur, a considerable responsibility as matters turned out. Gloucester, the youngest and the least experienced of Henry's brothers, was present at the victory won at Agincourt, on which occasion it is reported that he was saved, when wounded, by the swift action of the king himself.

The year 1416 was to give others their chance. The early spring witnessed increasing military and naval pressure being applied by the French and their allies to the vital port of Harfleur. Early in March, Dorset had led a large foraging party out into the surrounding district in search of provisions, and on 11 March he encountered a French force which, in the fight which ensued between them, killed many Englishmen, although it failed to prevent them making their way back safely to Harfleur.[13] To English chroniclers, this was a victory which confirmed what had happened in the previous year at Agincourt. God was still on the English side, and Dorset was a hero. Later in the year, detained by the imminent departure of Sigismund from English soil, Henry had to despatch Bedford to take charge of the fleet with which it was intended to break the naval blockade imposed upon Harfleur. This was probably Bedford's greatest moment during his brother's reign: the news of the rout of the enemy, many of them Genoese, was greeted by the order that bells should be rung, as if a great victory had been won. At a personal level, Dorset was given good cause to celebrate his success when, on 18 November, he was created duke of Exeter for life in parliament, being given £40 a year from the issues of Devon and £1000 from the exchequer to sustain his rank and position. It is clear that Exeter was not only able, but well liked, too. Thomas Walsingham could report that many thought the sum accorded to him was an inadequate recognition of what the man had done for England.[14]

[11] Was Beaufort here expressing his support for the contemplative religious orders which, as intercessors, were encouraged by Henry?
[12] Harriss, *Cardinal Beaufort*, pp. 84–6.
[13] See above, ch.6.
[14] *St Albans Chronicle*, pp. 102–3.

If 1416 had seen members of the dynasty achieving successes – it was notable how Sigismund had been met by all three of Henry's brothers in their order of seniority as he progressed from Dover to London to meet the king himself when he arrived in May – the year 1417 provided the best example of how much Henry owed to his close male relatives, two of whom, Clarence and Gloucester, accompanied him on his second invasion of Normandy. His choice was interesting. Was it, as already suggested, because he wanted to act in close unison with him and to supervise his activities personally that Henry ordered Clarence to accompany him? And was it to give him further experience of war, in particular of siege warfare and of the use of the new artillery, that he chose Gloucester to take command of part of the army? In both cases, but for rather different reasons, Henry may have felt that he would prefer to have these two men under his orders.

Two things are notable. The first is that both men remained in Normandy under Henry for at least two years, each loyally committing his life at this time to the fulfilment of Henry's ambition, making it almost the ambition of the dynasty. The second is the extent to which these two men, in their contrasting military 'styles', assisted Henry in his conquest of Normandy. Clarence was the man of flamboyant action seen, for instance, in his scaling of the wall at Caen and his cry 'A Clarans, A Clarans' recorded by the chronicler, and in the manner in which he and a small force of men captured Pontoise in a daring dawn raid on 30 July 1419.[15] Such notable actions achieved success, and were duly recorded by the chroniclers who still wrote in a chivalric vein whenever the opportunity occurred. Those very same chroniclers were also interested in the relatively new techniques of war which developments in artillery presented. They thus admired Gloucester's contribution to the war, his rapid conquest of north-western Normandy in the spring of 1418 when towns and castles surrendered in quick succession to his army. Most of all, they noted his successful completion of the six-month siege of Cherbourg,[16] carried out by a man with relatively little practical experience of war behind him, but with an interest in siege warfare and in particular the advantages which the use of artillery was now giving the attacker. Nor should we think of Gloucester as a man who preferred to win success from the comparative safety of an artillery emplacement. Like all his brothers, he was no coward; the *Brut* records that, at the siege of Rouen to which he went after he had taken Cherbourg, Gloucester deliberately pitched his encampment closer to that city's wall – and

[15] *Brut*, ii, 384, 424; *St Albans Chronicle*, pp. 122–3.
[16] *Brut*, 385, 389, 397; K.H. Vickers, *Humphrey, duke of Gloucester* (London, 1907), pp. 60–9.

hence closer to danger – than did any other commander.[17] The important point to underline is that Clarence and Gloucester presented
Henry with useful contrasts in military style; one was ready for dramatic action when required, while the other preferred to use the new
weaponry to achieve less dramatic but equally lasting results.

In 1417 the important role of Cinderella was played, as it had
already been played in 1415, by Bedford, whose qualities as a reliable
administrator were well known to Henry. His position, however, was
no sinecure. As he had done in 1415, Henry again left an uncertain
situation on the Scottish border, an area with which Bedford was all
too familiar. Within a fortnight of Henry's sailing for Normandy,
Bedford, as lieutenant of England, had to issue a summons for military
service to resist the Scots. With the help of Exeter (also in England)
and Henry Bowet, archbishop of York, a sizeable army was raised,
and the Scots, caught unawares by the vigour and strength of the
English reaction, returned to their own country leaving behind the
engines with which they had besieged Berwick. Together, Bedford
and Exeter had won a success which allowed Thomas Walsingham
to sing the praises of the country which, in spite of its heavy commitment in Normandy, could find so many men and such fine leaders to
defend its northern border against an enemy who dared not await to
face the English army but rather, informed of its approach by spies,
turned tail as a group of women might have done.[18]

To complete the picture of activity in this *annus mirabilis* we must
retrace our steps briefly to the role played by bishop Henry Beaufort.
It was the year 1417 which witnessed the climax of activity at the
council of Constance which led to the election of Martin V as a pope
acceptable to all. As we have seen, bishop Beaufort acted as the
representative of the king, furthering a deliberate decision taken by
Henry that England should make an advance in the council's work
possible by siding with those who were urging that an election should
come before reform.[19] English contemporaries were not far wrong in
claiming that it was the personal intervention of the bishop which
broke the impasse, and made possible the election of the new pope.
As in so much else, Beaufort's role in the diplomatic field was a
considerable one.

He is also known, perhaps too well known, for another form of
contribution to the government of England, the loans which he made
to all the Lancastrian kings (including six to Henry V) and which
would total more than fifty in number when he made his last one in

---

[17] *Brut*, 389, 397.
[18] *St Albans Chronicle*, p. 114; Bradley, 'Henry V's Scottish policy', pp. 188–9.
[19] See above, ch.11.

1446, some months before his death.[20] Where the money came from is still a mystery. What his motives were, however, is now much clearer. A sound case can be made for seeing this financial support as part and parcel of his total commitment to the future of the house of Lancaster. He saw clearly where the future lay: he devoted his energy to preparing the diplomatic ground along lines, including a close alliance with Burgundy, which he thought vital for the further-ance of that future; and he devoted huge sums, totalling £35,630 in loans to the crown, to make possible the policies which he advocated.

And yet he did so, to a certain extent, under a cloud. His first three loans, one made in 1413, two in 1415, amounted to less than £4000. In 1417, however, he lent £14,000, and he was to do so again four years later. The first of these can be explained by its timing. Henry, about to set out on his second expedition to Normandy, was hard-pressed to find the financial support which he needed. Having advo-cated the war, Beaufort must have felt in duty bound to support it, although it was unlikely that he would get his money returned to him for several years. But on the second occasion, before which he had been to the council of Constance and on pilgrimage to the Holy Land, the circumstances were very different.

In 1419 he found himself in deep disgrace with the king, for in December 1417 the newly elected pope, Martin V, had named Beau-fort a cardinal and his personal legate *a latere*, at the same time allowing him to keep the bishopric of Winchester, which he was now to hold *in commendam* of the pope.[21] To Henry, it looked as if his uncle, hitherto his staunchest supporter, had completely deserted him to enter the papal service. To have an Englishman as a cardinal was flattering and useful; to have him reside in his diocese as the pope's personal representative and in an altogether higher position than his own metropolitan, Henry Chichele, archbishop of Canterbury, was quite another. Further still, for such an appointee to exercise episcopal jurisdiction in the wealthy diocese of Winchester by papal authority was unacceptable. When Beaufort met Henry in Rouen in March 1419 he was quietly told that the red hat and the legatine authority had been refused. His own position, vis à vis the king (and the law of England), was now very difficult.

Henry had a watch kept on his uncle, what he did and whom he met, a responsibility placed upon the shoulders of his first cousin, Thomas Chaucer, son of the poet, supporter of the Lancastrian family, member of parliament and former Speaker of the Commons. From

[20] See below, ch.18; Harriss, *Cardinal Beaufort*, appendix 3.
[21] The story is given in detail in McFarlane, 'Henry V, bishop Beaufort and the red hat'.

1419 to 1421, living in England, Beaufort did what he could to mend the fences between himself and the king. Henry, to his credit, was not bent on vengeance: contemporaries knew little more than that the offer of a red hat had been turned down. In May 1421 came Beaufort's chance to make amends. Henry was back in England to raise money to support the war, which could have taken a difficult turn after the death and defeat of Clarence at Baugé in March, and he badly needed all the financial support which he could muster. All classes of society were asked for loans, made all the more necessary by the unwillingness of the Commons to vote a tax. To give practical assistance, Beaufort offered a second huge loan of £14,000, equal to that which he had made in 1417, of which he had so far recovered about forty per cent. We may assume that this was done, if not under royal pressure, at least at the royal suggestion. Beaufort was buying his way back into favour, and he was buying it successfully.

Within a very short time he was back on the political scene which he had never really abandoned. When the king made his last will at Dover, only a few weeks later, he left his uncle a vestment and his breviary, or prayer book, in two volumes, which had belonged to Henry IV, his father and the bishop's half-brother. Beaufort was also named as an executor of the king's will,[22] as well as one of its administrators, Gloucester and Exeter, together with Thomas Langley, bishop of Durham and chancellor, being the other three. The fidelity with which, in the years ahead, he sought to execute his nephew's wishes and bring about the achievement of his policies strongly suggests that the episode of the red hat was the result of a wish to advance himself, not to betray the king. Both men emerged with credit out of the episode, which was the result more of ambition than of infidelity to a man or to a cause.[23]

The last three years of the reign show no departure from the basic pattern which has emerged, other than that Bedford was twice asked to cross to France – once for the ceremonies surrounding the sealing of the treaty of Troyes and Henry's marriage, and a second time to accompany queen Katharine to France in the summer of 1422, an occasion which enabled him to be present at Henry's deathbed on 31 August of that year. On both occasions, Bedford's English responsibilities were assumed by Gloucester, now much in Henry's favour after his successful and responsible performance in the war and upon whom the dying king placed the responsibility of seeing to the good of his baby son. Exeter, who may have been Henry's favourite captain both because of his loyalty and his high level of competence in any

[22] Strong, 'Last will and codicils of Henry V', 94, 97.
[23] Harriss, *Cardinal Beaufort*, ch.5.

task asked of him, followed the king on all his campaigns, accepting to the full every military and civil responsibility placed upon his shoulders.[24] To pursue Exeter's career in France in these years is really to follow the pattern of the conquest. Like Bedford, he was at Henry's deathbed, receiving the legacy of a tapestry (or 'arras') in the will made at Dover in June 1421, and having the heavy responsibility of the education of the king's heir, Henry VI, thrust upon his shoulders in the codicil drawn up at Vincennes a few days before Henry's death.[25]

As for Clarence, whose only period of responsibility in England had lasted some six weeks in September and October 1416 while Henry was in Calais to negotiate with John of Burgundy, he remained close to Henry on his second expedition until the king brought Katharine over to England at the beginning of 1421. At that point Clarence was left on his own, with full military powers in Normandy. By the end of March he had gone to his death, 'because', the *Brut* recorded, 'he would not be gouerned'.[26] Sadly, even at the age of about thirty-three, Clarence could not contain his energy and impose discipline upon himself. His impetuosity, which had been so useful to Henry on a number of occasions, and which the king had been able to control through his authority as commander of the English armies, finally got the better of him. Although it is likely that he was misled about the number of enemy present, in his desire to win a victory, but to do so without archers and with the help of mounted noblemen and gentry alone, he courted defeat and death, and met both. Until the birth of the baby, Henry VI to-be, at the beginning of the following December, Bedford was now heir presumptive to the throne of England and to the regency of France.

When Henry lay on his deathbed at Vincennes in August 1422 he gave the 'tutela', or control of his young heir's estate during his minority, to Gloucester, at that moment lieutenant of England.[27] The

---

[24] Ibid., p. 104.

[25] Strong, 'Last will', 99; *Brut*, ii, 429–30.

[26] *Brut*, ii, 447.

[27] This provision was to provoke a considerable legal and constitutional crisis after Henry's death. Gloucester claimed to be protector of the realm by right of kinship and the wish of the late king expressed in the codicil to his will, a claim recently confirmed by the discovery of the codicil to have been a fair one (Strong, 'Last will', 99). Bedford entered a counter claim on grounds of seniority. It was finally decided that Henry's will had no force; no king could say how the realm would be governed after his death. Bedford was to act as protector on his visits to England. Gloucester would exercise the powers of that office when his older brother was away, but with several restraints placed upon his authority (S.B. Chrimes, 'The pretensions of the duke of Gloucester in 1422', *EHR*, 45 (1930), 102; J.S. Roskell, 'The office and dignity of protector of England, with special reference to its origins', *EHR*, 68 (1953), 204.)

personal care of the child, with choice of his servants, was confided to Exeter, bishop Beaufort being associated in this appointment; while the most difficult task of all, that of acting as regent of France, was given to Bedford.[28] To the end, when the two members of his family circle to whom he felt closest, Exeter, his uncle, and Bedford, his brother, were present, as well as other friends and servants of long standing, Henry sought to keep authority and the exercise of power within the control of men of his own blood. It can be argued that he had no choice, that he had to look for assistance from those who had served under him during the past decade or so. Yet the fact remains that, even in death, he was able to influence the future through his choice of men who would hold responsibility for the welfare of both the country and its young king.

Both Exeter and Bedford were men of moderation; both were devoted to the dying king; both were intent upon trying to see his wishes and ambitions fulfilled. In all that they did, they were to have an ally in the person of bishop Beaufort who, as an executor of Henry's will, as well as the inspirer of much that he had sought to achieve, was there to help them. Even Gloucester, whose powers were much less clearly defined, was given authority. Whether it was in the dying king's powers so to do raised considerable questions. But of Henry's wish to leave the main positions of authority in the hands of members of his family there can be little doubt. It was his only way of ensuring that the path which he had mapped out with so much effort would be followed in the years to come. The participation of the four sons of Margaret Beaufort, sister-in-law of bishop Henry Beaufort and of Exeter, in the war in Normandy under Henry V and Clarence was a sign that the future of the Beaufort family, if it lay anywhere, lay in war, at least for the foreseeable future.[29]

Meanwhile, service to the king brought its rewards to members of his family. In the case of Clarence, it led to the 'confirmation' of his ducal title, originally conferred upon him by Henry IV in July 1412 on the eve of his departure for France, in the first parliament (that of Leicester) held after his return from France, an act which also 'confirmed' the grant of the earldom of Dorset upon Thomas Beaufort by Henry IV. The same parliament was to witness the creation of Henry's two youngest brothers, John and Humphrey, as duke of Bedford and earl of Kendal, and as duke of Gloucester and earl of Pembroke respectively; both were creations for life, both carried an allowance of £60 for the sustenance of these dignities.[30] Later in the

[28] *Brut*, ii, 429.
[29] Harriss, *Cardinal Beaufort*, p. 103.
[30] *RP*, iv, 17.

year, in the parliament held at Westminster in October 1414, Bedford also had the reversion of the earldom of Richmond, including its castles and honour, then in the hands of the earl of Westmorland, granted to him.[31]

There were to be limits to Henry's promotions to the nobility. Thomas Beaufort, earl of Dorset, was advanced to the dukedom of Exeter in the parliament held in the autumn of 1416, Henry granting him an annuity from the exchequer in addition to a sum from the receipts of Exeter.[32] No other peers, however, were created in this reign. In making promotions, Henry restricted himself to members of his own family. He did not create titles as Richard II, for example, had done; and when he did, he had parliamentary approval for his choices. As in the cases of restoration of heirs to their titles and inheritances, all was done openly. We may be confident that the decision to do so was deliberate.

In addition to titles in England, there were prospects in France, too. On 27 February 1418 the king gave his brother Clarence the 'vicomtés' of Auge, Orbec and Pont-Audemer for him to enjoy for life.[33] By July, now that he felt even more confident of the success of his enterprise, Henry awarded Exeter the 'comté' of Harcourt and the castle of Lillebonne, both in tail-male (succession limited to the male heir), the first specifically excluded from the grant made to Clarence five months earlier, the second not yet physically in English control. This serves as an example of the way a grant was sometimes intended to spur the recipient into military action; in this case, the capture of Lillebonne was to take place on 31 January 1419, scarcely a fortnight after the surrender of Rouen, of which Exeter had just been appointed captain.[34]

What can even a brief study of Henry's relations with members of his family tell us? There is little doubt that, collectively, they made a contribution of major significance to Henry's ability to rule and to any successes which may be attributed to him. They made it possible for him to leave England confident that the country would be well ruled in his absence by men whom he could trust. At one stage or other, each of Henry's brothers was left in charge of English affairs, Bedford for longer than the other two put together.[35] All three took

[31]   Ibid., iv, 40–1.
[32]   Ibid., iv, 96.
[33]   Wylie and Waugh, *Henry the Fifth*, iii, 111.
[34]   Massey, 'The land settlement in Lancastrian Normandy', p. 80.
[35]   The information on the English 'regency' contained in *Handbook of British Chronology*, ed. E.B. Fryde, D.E. Greenway, S. Porter and I. Roy (3rd edn, London, 1986), p. 41, is incorrect in this regard. Bedford did three spells in that office, not two, while Gloucester did two, not one.

part in negotiation and diplomacy: they helped as a family to greet and entertain Sigismund, England's most notable visitor of the reign. All three participated actively in the war, some for longer periods than others, and each used his abilities differently: Clarence, whose contribution would have been better appreciated in the chivalric ethos of the previous century and whose manner of dying has coloured men's view of him to his disadvantage, chiefly as a soldier; Gloucester as a soldier who, like his eldest brother, the king, understood the possibilities offered by the new artillery; Bedford as a leader who showed his mettle in the naval battle of the Seine and as a notable administrator.

It was a family of men of high ability which Henry had to lead. Their skills, their callings, their dispositions were each different, but all had an interest in the success of the king's enterprises, which would offset any possible threat to the throne. Together, they set an aristocratic stamp upon the leadership which Henry had at his disposal. That they managed to work together (so unlike the princely rivalries and squabbles which characterized the weak rule of Charles VI in France) was partly the result of their diverse characters, abilities and ambitions. It was also a result of Henry's skill as a leader of men that he could get the best out of them and weave them into a team, one, however, which broke up once his restraining hand had been removed by death. For the moment the fact that they were numerous helped: it increased the chance that at least one of Henry IV's sons would be ready to assume the unglamorous but vital role of lieutenant during his brothers' absences abroad. Having this group of blood relatives to help him (with one exception there is no hint of dissent on the part of any of them during the reign) meant that Henry could act with confidence. It was confidence which enabled him to deal so firmly with his uncle, bishop Beaufort, over the latter's elevation to the College of Cardinals. He knew, too, when Beaufort's punishment had reached its limit, when he could return to the royal confidence from which he had been temporarily excluded. It was qualities such as he showed on this occasion, qualities of controlled anger without vindictiveness, patience and firmness which helped to make Henry into a leader of men.

One last point may be noted. With the exception of Gloucester, who, as his modern biographer remarked,[36] took up his public duties fairly late in life, the Beaufort brothers, together with Henry's own, represent a strong and vital element of continuity with the past. From an early age Bedford had given himself to practical public service in the north; Clarence, too, although with conspicuously less success,

[36] Vickers, *Humphrey, duke of Gloucester*, p. 10.

had been involved in war and administration. Both the Beauforts had served as chancellor – as well as doing much else – in Henry I V's reign. It was at that time that they had got to know Henry and he had got to know them, each recognizing the other's abilities and devotion to the cause of country and family. When he finally became king in 1413, Henry knew whom he could rely on, because that reliance was largely mutual. It was a factor which would also help to build up the loyalty of those of less exalted blood who were to serve him, as both Prince and king.

Chapter 16

THE PERSONNEL OF GOVERNMENT

Henry was a man of such energy and achievements, and the tendency to concentrate upon the king is so strong, that we need to remind ourselves that Henry relied a great deal upon others to help him in his work. This ability to make others work for him was one of the outstanding characteristics of his powers of leadership. And while these men worked for him, they also worked with one another, thereby forming a special cohesion among those who administered the king's will. The reign was remarkably free of 'former' servants of the king: once appointed, people tended to stay. Does this show that Henry's choice of servants was a good one or, rather, that all were loyal to one other? In any event, these years bear little evidence of criticism of either the king's government or of those who acted on his behalf.

Government at this period was closely associated with the household, the group of perhaps 200 or so men who lived close to the king, and whose principal officers, mainly bearing titles with domestic connotations, were appointed by the king to help him in the daily tasks and routine of government.[1] Two related factors should be borne in mind. As kings changed, so did the personnel of the royal household, for the personnel reflected the choice of the head of household, the king himself. Secondly, it may be noted that the choice of the main members of the household depended not only on ability and political reliability. In selecting the personnel the king was, in effect, selecting his friends and companions, the men (and the point was particularly important in the case of a bachelor monarch) with whom he would work and take recreation.[2] In other words, it was of great importance that such men should be acceptable both to the king and to one another. Not surprisingly, the general character of the members of the household, the experiences which they may have had in common, and their attitude to the ruling house were vital in creating

---

[1] J. Catto, 'The King's servants', *Henry V: The practice of kingship*, ed. G.L. Harriss (Oxford, 1985), p. 84: Given-Wilson, *Royal household*, passim.
[2] A. Rogers, 'The royal household of Henry IV' (Univ. of Nottingham Ph.D. thesis, 1966), pp. 2, 9.

cohesion among themselves and ensuring their loyalty to the king, their master.

The household consisted of two groups of men who formed concentric circles around the king. Closest to him were the men of the chamber, the king's most intimate friends, who were under the control of the aptly named king's chamberlain. These men were responsible for seeing to the king's everyday requirements, and for the task of provisioning those who lived in close companionship with him. Control of the king's own private finances and of the material evidence of his wealth, notably his jewels and precious ornaments, was in the hands of the treasurer of the chamber who was also keeper of the jewels, this system undergoing some modification in 1415. A further department of the chamber – and one of great importance in Henry's reign – was the chapel royal, whose members, under their dean, were responsible for the liturgy and singing of the church services which Henry attended with great regularity.[3] To advise him on matters of spirituality and conscience, Henry had his confessor who, like the other members of the intimate circle, lived near the king[4] and owed his position to him. To protect the person of the king – and to do this they had to sleep in close proximity to him – was a small group of chamber knights who, working in rotation, ensured that there were always four of their number with the king. As was the case with their fellow members of the chamber, the squires of the body and yeomen of the chamber, these men were hand-picked, and in practice must have included the closest of the king's friends and confidants.[5] Their regular contact with the royal person makes it reasonable to assume that such was the case.

The outer circle of the household was formed by those who worked in the wardrobe, under the direction of the steward. A bigger organization than the chamber, the wardrobe received money from the exchequer (there were no financial dealings between the chamber and the exchequer, since the chamber drew on the king's 'private' revenue) and was, in effect, responsible for very much more than the running of the royal household. For while the cofferer was the 'real financial officer of the household',[6] the seemingly more important treasurer of the household became, in 1416, treasurer for war, enabling the conflict against France, fought by an army which was regarded as the king's household in arms reinforced by dependants of the greater nobility,

---

    [3] Ibid., p. 28 seq: E.H. de L. Fagan, 'Some aspects of the king's household in the reign of Henry V, 1413–22' (Univ. of London MA thesis, 1935), p. 36 seq.
    [4] '. . . en nostre houstell' (re Stephen Patrington, PRO, E 404/30/177).
    [5] Fagan, 'King's household', pp. 64–5, 77, 84.
    [6] Ibid., p. 176.

to be organized and financed by the wardrobe, which was part of the royal household. As Edward III had found, the system of paying the army through the services of an organization which accompanied the king had many advantages. [7] In addition to the treasurer and cofferer, the wardrobe also had a controller, whose task, particularly in time of war, was the provisioning and conveying of troops. This important, indeed vital, work was thus carried out by an office whose members worked in close co-operation with the treasurer for war with the aim of making the king's army into an efficient military machine, the privy wardrobe, based on the Tower of London, being responsible for the storing of weapons, in particular the pieces of ordnance which were now assuming greater and greater importance.

We may thus see that, in response to the rising demands of administration provoked by the needs of war, Henry was making the fullest use of the existing household organization in the administration of public affairs, and of war in particular. This adaptation of the machinery provided by the wardrobe was especially marked once the treasurer of the household had become the treasurer for war. Among its advantages, one, in particular, may be noted. The use of the royal household to organize the different aspects of the English war effort gave the king himself the chance not only to decide military policy but also to keep a close eye on how it was being carried out. The system was undoubtedly efficient. It also helped the king to stamp his own mark on the way that war was (to be) organized. [8]

This was equally true of the remaining office within the household to which reference must be made, the privy seal. In order that they should carry out the king's orders, both the chancery (which issued royal letters and charters under the great seal) and the exchequer (which paid out money in the king's name) had to receive warrants, or orders, under the privy seal before either could act. [9] As the practical intermediary between the king and the two great offices of state, the privy seal office had an important role to play, both in the fulfilment of this role and in the carrying out of an additional one which had been developing for some years but which, under Henry, was to be given greater significance: diplomacy. The office where the king's private correspondence was written had now become the office through which he could exercise personal control over diplomacy, particularly important in time of war, when relations with states and princes needed to reflect the interest and involvement of the king himself. [10]

[7] Ibid., pp. 225–6, 228.
[8] Ibid., p. 244.
[9] Catto, 'King's servants', pp. 79–80.
[10] Ibid., pp. 79–81.

Those who helped Henry to rule England and, to a certain extent, his lands overseas, did not constitute a large group. To a man, those who held influential positions were known (often well known) to the king himself. Their 'roots', the origins from which they sprang, gave them a sense of loyalty to the Lancastrian dynasty, to the king himself, and to one another. The family of Lancaster, we have been reminded, appreciated continuity of service.[11] From the time of Henry's great-grandfather, Henry of Grosmont, first duke of Lancaster, to the death of his own son, Henry VI, the family enjoyed well over a century of power at the very centre of government. The dynasty mattered, not least because it gave a sense of continuity to those who entered its service.[12] Henry, Lord FitzHugh, the Yorkshireman whom Henry appointed to be his chamberlain at the very beginning of his reign and who still held the post in 1422, came from such a background. His father had served in France under John of Gaunt, while he himself had shown interest in the crusade and had been retained as a king's knight by Henry IV, who had sent him as one of the party which accompanied his daughter, Philippa, to Denmark for her marriage to king Eric in 1406. FitzHugh, who for years would never for long be far away from Henry (and upon whom he appears to have had some influence), represented two considerations important to the new king: he and his father were staunch 'Lancastrians', while he himself, as a Knight of the Garter, represented a military tradition which was certain to have appealed to Henry.[13] Much the same might be said of others.

Before he became Henry V's steward of the household, an office which he held for the first two years or so of the reign, Sir Thomas Erpingham had acted in the same capacity for Henry IV, whose chamberlain he had also been for a while; he had been given these posts of responsibility not only as a servant who had risked all to put Henry IV on the throne in September 1399, but also as one who had served his father, John of Gaunt, before him.[14] As steward, Erpingham was succeeded by Sir Walter Hungerford, whose background fitted a similar pattern. The son of Sir Thomas Hungerford who, an intimate servant of Gaunt, had been Speaker in the parliament of 1377 at a time when Gaunt virtually controlled the government, Walter had been one of those knighted on the eve of Henry IV's coronation,

[11] Goodman, 'Gaunt: paradigm', 136.
[12] See Walker, *Lancastrian affinity*, passim.
[13] On FitzHugh, see Given-Wilson, *Royal household*, pp. 195–6, 229, 236, 245; A.C. Reeves, *Lancastrian Englishmen* (Washington, 1981), pp. 65–139.
[14] Given-Wilson, *Royal household*, p. 190; T. John, 'Sir Thomas Erpingham, East Anglian society and the dynastic revolution of 1399', *Norfolk Archaeology*, 35 (1970), 96–108.

and had been appointed chamberlain to the king's younger daughter, Philippa. A good pedigree of loyal service to the dynasty would have impressed Henry V. In Hungerford's case there was more that would appeal to the new king: Hungerford was a soldier (like FitzHugh and Erpingham, he was a Knight of the Garter), an able administrator, a man of culture and intelligence who would not shame his master as a royal ambassador at the council of Constance. It is not surprising that such a man should have found favour and achieved influence from the position which he exercised at the very centre of Henry's court.[15]

These men, and others, were drawn into the king's service through loyalty to his father and grandfather. We may also see early connections with the Prince, such as through service to the duchy of Cornwall, rewarded in later years. John Rothenhale was already the receiver of an annuity from the duchy when he became one of those knighted by Henry on the eve of his coronation.[16] Controller of the household from 1413 to 1416, he succeeded Roger Leche as keeper of the wardrobe in January 1416, confirmation of the recognition already given him by Henry when he had appointed Rothenhale an executor of the will he had made at Southampton the previous July as he prepared to sail for France. A second duchy of Cornwall servant was also to be advanced under Henry's rule. Like Rothenhale, John Waterton, one of a family which had stood high in Henry IV's esteem, and which included his brother Robert, who had served as master of the horse to Henry IV, was an annuitant of the duchy who was later to be sent on embassies to France, evidence that the royal confidence in him had been confirmed.[17] The further example of Thomas Carnika, receiver for Henry as Prince, who also had connections with Cornwall, and who became keeper of the great wardrobe and dean of Wells in 1413, shows how Henry, as king, continued to employ those who has served him reliably in earlier years.

The years of youthful experience in Wales were also to be reflected in a group of men who, having served the Prince in the Welsh campaigns, would serve him further once he had become king.[18] Hugh Mortimer had fought at Shrewsbury in 1403. He was already old enough to have represented Gloucestershire in parliament in 1397, and to have been the Prince's chamberlain from 1403 to 1411. During these years he went four times on embassies to France, as well as to

[15] Roskell, *Speakers*, p. 157.
[16] Wylie, *Henry the Fifth*, i, 3, n.10; BL, Stowe Ms 440, fos 86v–87. He was still receiving £5 from the duchy of Cornwall in 1419 (DCO, Rolls Series 95/203).
[17] DCO, Rolls Series 94/201, 202; BL, Harley Ms 4304, fos 20–20v. He had also served the Prince in Wales in 1403 (PRO, E 101/404/24, fo.5).
[18] Griffiths, 'Military career', ch.5.

Burgundy. One of a small group to whom Henry authorized a gift of wine in August 1413,[19] he had been named chamberlain of the duchy of Lancaster in April and served again on an embassy in 1414, before being appointed treasurer of the exchequer in 1416, shortly before his death.[20] Richard Beauchamp, earl of Warwick, owner of estates in the Welsh march, a loyal Lancastrian servant and a close personal friend of Henry, was present at Shrewsbury and was made Knight of the Garter on the following day, before serving in Wales in 1403–04 and again in 1407, becoming a paid member of the royal council under the Prince in 1410.[21] In the same way Thomas, earl of Arundel, another marcher lord, who was indentured for life to the Prince on 20 February 1408,[22] became a member of the royal council with Warwick, and was leader of the force sent to help the duke of Burgundy in 1411, before finally becoming treasurer of England in 1413.

The Welsh war was to serve as a training ground for the war later to be fought in France. It served, furthermore, to stamp a strongly military character upon those who worked in close proximity to Henry in the government of England. Warwick and Arundel were not the only ones to fight both in Wales and in France. Thomas Beaufort, Henry IV's half-brother, did likewise, as did Lord Grey of Codnor, who was later sometimes to be found at Henry V's court, and Thomas, Lord Carew, who served Henry in a number of different ways in both wars.[23] The border counties of Shropshire and Herefordshire were prominent at this period not merely through their close association with Lollardy and disorder. They also provided a number of soldiers who played a significant part in Henry's wars: John, Lord Furnival, later to become earl of Shrewsbury; Walter Devereux; John Scudamore; and Sir John Greyndore, a loyal duchy of Lancaster servant born in the year of the battle of Poitiers, who had seen much activity against the Welsh after 1401, before going to Harfleur in 1415 and probably dying there in the following year. In the years of peace in Wales which followed Glyn Dŵr's rebellion, soldiers with practical experience, known to Henry and to one another, were appointed to the main constableships of southern castles; once again, Herefordshire was the county from which most of them originated.[24] Not surprisingly

[19] PRO, E 101/406/7/3.
[20] Somerville, *Duchy of Lancaster*, i, 417; *Register of Henry Chichele*, i, 666.
[21] A.F.J. Sinclair, 'The Beauchamp earls of Warwick in the later middle ages' (Univ. of London Ph.D. thesis, 1987), ch.3.
[22] PRO, CHES, 2/79, m.3.
[23] *Register of Henry Chichele*, i, 644; PRO, C53/183, mm.1, 9, 14, 22, 40.
[24] R.A. Griffiths, 'Patronage, politics, and the principality of Wales, 1413–1461', *British government and administration*, ed. H. Hearder and H.R. Loyn (Cardiff, 1974), pp. 76–7.

this was the first area to which Henry came in 1421 when he wanted to raise more soldiers for the forthcoming campaign in France.

As in the case of Wales and Cornwall, the duchy and county palatine of Lancaster, which Henry V was the first to inherit with the crown of England, provided the background and experience for men who rose to serve him as king. Of those who occupied important positions within the royal household, Sir Walter Hungerford, Sir Robert Babthorpe and Sir Roger Leche were associated with the duchy. In addition, three of the duchy's four chancellors appointed between 1402 and 1413 were to receive later recognition: John Wakering, a lawyer, was named keeper of the privy seal in 1415 and bishop of Norwich in the following year; John Springthorpe was to be a receiver of petitions in most of the parliaments of the reign; while John Wodehouse, the Prince's steward at Castle Rising, who was to become one of the new king's esquires of the body, and to one of whose children (appropriately called Henry) the Prince had stood godfather in 1406, was appointed chamberlain of the exchequer for life in July 1415, as well as being named an executor and one of the two administrators of the will made by Henry at Southampton at the end of that month.[25]

Another duchy official favoured by Henry was John Leventhorpe. Already well known to Henry IV, an executor of whose will he was, he had been appointed receiver-general and attorney-general of the duchy in 1399; three times in parliament during Henry V's reign as a knight of the shire representing Hertfordshire (although exempted from taking knighthood in 1413), Leventhorpe became a feoffee of Henry V and, like Wodehouse, an executor of his will, sharing with bishop Langley the honour of fulfilling that role for both Henry IV and Henry V.[26] In south Wales the important office of chamberlain of duchy lands and chief justice was to be granted in 1421 to John Merbury; a king's esquire, he, too, had proved his worth as an able administrator and supporter of the house of Lancaster over a number of years before gaining recognition for his ability and loyalty.[27]

Such men owed their positions to their competence and experience in administration. They owed them, too, to the fact that, for a variety of reasons, they had come to the notice of Henry over a period of years. It was also important that they should have felt that they belonged to a 'team', and that they should have known one another. Time spent in the service of the crown and of the duchy of Lancaster, for example, would have helped to achieve this. Evidence taken from

[25] Somerville, *Duchy of Lancaster*, i, 177, 389; *Register of Henry Chichele*, i, 683–4.
[26] Somerville, *Duchy of Lancaster*, i, 397–8.
[27] Ibid., i, 639; Griffiths, 'Patronage, politics and the principality of Wales', p. 77.

their wills suggests that close bonds existed between a number of them
and the king, as well as between themselves as his servants. Hugh
Mortimer, for example, asked that Henry V himself, together with
Henry Chichele and Thomas Langley, should act as supervisors of
his will, while John Leventhorpe and John Wilcotes, an influential
man at court at this time, were among Mortimer's executors.[28] John
Springthorpe, one-time chancellor of the duchy of Lancaster and a
chancery clerk, bequeathed his Bible to John Wakering, his predecessor in the duchy, a belt to Thomas Langley, the former chancellor,
and a cup to another duchy servant, Henry Kays, who acted as a
supervisor of the will, as well as being appointed to act as an executor
in Wakering's own will, made a brief time later.[29]

Others, too, sought executors from among those with whom they
had worked. When William Kynwolmersh, the cofferer of Henry V
who had become treasurer of England, made his will in March 1421,
he left money for Masses to be said over the next ten years both for
himself and his benefactors, among whom he would have numbered
the king; while to John Wodehouse he bequeathed a silver drinking
cup, called a 'bolle' (given him by the countess of Hereford), appointing Wodehouse an executor and Thomas Langley as supervisor of his
will.[30] Marriages between families who served the crown are also
recorded. When Sir Hugh Waterton, employed by the duchy of Lancaster since 1386 and later as a member of Henry IV's council, died
in 1409, his widow married again. This time she took as her husband
another important supporter of the house of Lancaster, and of Henry
V in particular, Sir Roger Leche; treasurer of the royal household and
chief steward of the duchy's northern parts in 1413, Leche, as Hugh
Waterton himself had been some years earlier, was appointed chamberlain of the duchy in 1416, in which year he died while also fulfilling
the office of treasurer of England.[31] Sir Robert Babthorpe, yet another
duchy servant, rose to be steward of the royal household in 1421 and
was appointed as an executor and administrator of the will which
Henry made that year (John Leventhorpe, John Wodehouse and John
Wilcotes were also among the executors);[32] Babthorpe married John
Waterton's daughter, and acted as executor of the will of John's
brother, Robert.[33]

War, too, encouraged a certain cohesion among many who worked
closely with Henry. The king naturally chose to have about him men

[28] *Register of Henry Chichele*, ii, 87.
[29] Ibid., ii, 306–7, 314.
[30] Ibid., ii, 236.
[31] Somerville, *Duchy of Lancaster*, i, 417, 419.
[32] *RP*, iv, 399.
[33] Somerville, *Duchy of Lancaster*, i, 563.

who had shared his experiences and who may also be said to have shared his outlook on the world around them. A list of the household officers, headed by Henry, Lord FitzHugh, the royal chamberlain, shows a predominance of men who were military figures of experience, or who had taken part in a lesser way in one or more of the king's expeditions. All three stewards of the household, Thomas Erpingham, Walter Hungerford and Robert Babthorpe, were knights, as were four of the five treasurers of the household, Roger Leche, John Rothenhale, Walter Beauchamp and William Philip.[34] Since, particularly after 1416, these men became involved in the organization of war, it is not surprising that they should have come from the military class. As for the office of treasurer of England, this was held by two members of the nobility (the earl of Arundel and Lord FitzHugh), by two of Henry's old friends, both knights (Hugh Mortimer and Roger Leche), and, finally, by one clerk, William Kynwolmersh, who had been to France in 1415 in the royal retinue as 'cofferer of the household'.[35]

Although lay influence in the royal council appeared to be at its height in those very years, 1410 and 1411, when the Prince had been in control (Thomas Beaufort had been chancellor and the active participation of episcopal members of the council reached its lowest point in the reign at this time),[36] none the less both Henry V's chancellors, Henry Beaufort and Thomas Langley, were bishops and men of great experience. Their influence was extended to the keepership of the privy seal, an office exercised by five clerics, four of them with degrees in civil law.[37] The growing involvement of the privy seal office in diplomacy has already been noted. The activity of the keepers themselves reflected a considerable clerical influence in the team employed by the king as he sought to further England's interests abroad.

Both the war and the consequent need for Henry to be out of the country for long periods (Henry spent more than half his reign as king of England in France) meant that for much of this time those who served in his household were likely to be with him in France. As the war drew the military class across the Channel, so, under the guidance and supervision of one of Henry's brothers who remained behind, the everyday domestic government and administration of England was left in the hands of a small group of men dominated by clergy. Both Beaufort and Langley were regular attenders at the council, at which they were sometimes joined by archbishop Chichele,

[34] The exception was Thomas More, an experienced clerk who held the position briefly at the beginning of the reign (*Register of Henry Chichele*, ii, 665).
[35] *Handbook of British chronology*, 106.
[36] See Kirby, 'Councils and councillors', appendix, for names.
[37] E.F. Jacob, *Archbishop Henry Chichele* (London, 1967), pp. 101–2.

particularly in the last year or so of the reign. Of the five keepers of
the privy seal, four were regularly at the post in London. The exception was John Kemp, who spent much of his time in office occupying
another, that of chancellor of Normandy, his chief task being negotiation with the French.

In the king's absence from England, his place was taken by his
brothers, each of whom, at one time or another, acted as *custos* (vari-
ously translated as guardian, keeper or warden; more simply as lieutenant) in his absence. In no other single way can Henry's good
fortune in having three brothers upon whom he could rely be made
so evident. In France, in Henry's own lifetime, the presence of royal
brothers and uncles around the king, and the struggle for power and
influence to which this led, showed how a weak king's rule might be
made even weaker by ambitious members of his own family. Henry,
however, made good use of his kinsfolk, his three brothers and his
Beaufort uncles, without whose loyal assistance his prolonged absence
in France between August 1417 and February 1421, and all that this
meant in terms of his ability to apply his attention to the war, would
have been impossible.

On each of his four departures from England, for Normandy in
1415, for Calais (briefly) in 1416, for Normandy again in 1417 and,
finally, for France in 1421, Henry left behind a lieutenant to act for
him during his absence. The powers granted to them were established
in those given to Bedford at Portsmouth on 11 August 1415 as Henry
was about to set sail for Normandy.[38] In general terms, the need to
keep the peace within the kingdom was underlined, as was the obligation of the king to see that justice was accorded to all. All were
enjoined to obey the lieutenant whom the king was leaving to act on
his behalf. A second document set out the powers which were being
granted. These were narrow and limited, and allowed for little personal initiative on the part of the royal lieutenant; they were certainly
not the powers which, it might be thought, would be accorded to
a regent who would be exercising them for a considerable period.
Independence of action was severely restricted by the requirement
that the lieutenant should only make decisions 'after discussion and
with the approval of the council, and not otherwise', the council to
consist of nine persons. While he could call parliament through writs
issued in the king's name, and could negotiate with it, the lieutenant
could not act with the same authority as the king. He could authorize
ecclesiastical elections, and confirm certain of them; those of importance, however, had to be referred to the king. Likewise he could

---

[38] *Foedera*, IV, ii, 112, 144; A.L. Brown, 'The privy seal in the early fifteenth
century' (Univ. of Oxford D.Phil. thesis, 1954), pp. 96–7.

receive oaths of fealty from persons entering into new inheritances; homage, however, was to be reserved for the king alone once he had returned to England. In brief, the powers of those acting on the king's behalf were subject to considerable limitations, evidence that it was Henry's firm intention to maintain personal control over the making of important, sometimes even routine, decisions in English affairs, even when he was out of the country.[39]

While, exceptionally, Bedford and Exeter could be called upon to take military action (such as the repulsion of the so-called 'Foul Raid' mounted by the Scots in the autumn of 1417), such powers as Henry's lieutenants might exercise in England during his absences were essentially administrative. In practice, moreover, those who exercised them were not the lieutenants but the full-time administrators, a small handful of men most of whom came from outside the household, which remained with the king. Of these men, by far the most important were the two chancellors, of whom, since his period of office coincided with that of the king's absence after the summer of 1417, Thomas Langley must be accorded the more important place. Like Henry Beaufort, his predecessor, Langley, who originated from near Manchester, was a staunch Lancastrian who served John of Gaunt and all three Lancastrian kings with devotion and loyalty. Keeper of the privy seal and chancellor under Henry IV, he came in addition to be an expert in diplomacy, gaining much experience in that field between 1407 and 1415. When he became chancellor (for the second time) on 23 July 1417,[40] he brought to the post a high degree of professional and administrative ability, enhanced by a decade of experience as bishop of Durham. His orations made to the last five parliaments of the reign clearly show him to have had a firm commitment to the aims and person of the king.

He appears to have worked well with Bedford and Gloucester, who acted as lieutenants for much of the reign after 1417. Bedford in particular was a good administrator, and would have shared with Langley a common experience of first-hand knowledge of the difficulties of defending the Scottish march. There can be little doubt that much of the administrative routine was left to Langley, aided by the treasurer, William Kynwolmersh, and, for the last year of the reign, the keeper of the privy seal, John Stafford.[41] And behind them all, on the king's specific orders, there was the council. Even while he was in England, the king himself appears to have made but infrequent

[39] Jacob, *Fifteenth century*, pp. 430–1.
[40] He had already served between 1405 and 1407.
[41] Storey, *Thomas Langley*, pp. 38–41.

appearances at the royal council.[42] When the council met at the royal manor of Mortlake on 2 May 1417, the king was present,[43] but we have no such assurance for the large majority of meetings which took place in or nearer London, at Blackfriars, the house of the Dominican friars, at the Tower of London or even at the royal palace of Westminster itself. Attendances seldom seem to have exceeded ten or so persons, and meetings often consisted of the chancellor, the treasurer and the keeper of the privy seal, afforced, perhaps, by one or two other members or even, possibly, non-members brought in so that their specialist knowledge might be put to good use. One thing is clear. Whatever the theory about the council's 'permanent' membership, permanence or regularity of attendance was almost inconceivable for a man such as Richard, earl of Warwick, reappointed to the council at 200 marks per annum in April 1413.[44] In his case, his involvement in both diplomacy and war meant long and frequent absences from the country which precluded his regular participation in the council's work.

Once assembled, how did the council despatch its business, and what did it consist of? Much of its discussion must have been routine, and could easily have been carried out by a handful of men. On other occasions, such as on 27 May 1415 when it met in the Tower, the council decided to split itself up into small committees to review what may have been an accumulation of work. At this moment the king was actively preparing for his first invasion of France and with one exception, that of Lollardy, all the items to be discussed were related, in most cases directly, to the war. So it was that instructions to be given to an embassy being sent to the duke of Burgundy were considered by four men much experienced in the matter, archbishop Chichele, Hugh Mortimer, Philip Morgan and John Hovyngham, the last three not normally found at council meetings; loans secured on the royal jewellery were discussed by Bedford, Henry Beaufort, the chancellor, and by Richard Courtenay, bishop of Norwich and keeper of the jewels; the terms under which Sir John Tiptoft was to be sent to rule in Guyenne were considered by Gloucester, Thomas Beaufort (who had recent experience of this matter) and John Prophet, soon to retire as keeper of the privy seal; while other measures, such as the provisioning of the army and Calais, and the paying of sailors, were discussed by the treasurer, Sir John Rothenhale, the admiral, Thomas Beaufort, the controller of the household, and Sir Roger Salvayn,

[42] Jacob, *Fifteenth century*, p. 427.
[43] *PPC*, ii, 231–2.
[44] PRO, E 404/30/110.

treasurer of Calais.[45] The method used suggests not only efficiency, but also the recognition that, outside the formal membership of the council, there existed persons with specialized knowledge and practical experience which could be used with advantage. The fact that the chancellor, Henry Beaufort, was a member of three such committees underlines his own importance as the council's leading member. It was, in fact, true that none, except perhaps Henry himself, had greater experience of the practices of government at this time than did the bishop of Winchester, upon whom the king placed so much reliance.

It is reasonably clear that Henry was present at a meeting of the council which took place on 25 February 1416, for the agenda reveals that there was to be discussion with him regarding instructions to be given to English ambassadors, a discussion which Philip Morgan and John Hovyngham, two of the three 'experts' noticed above, were to attend. In addition to this, messengers and others who were to carry letters to a number of European princes in what was a major diplomatic initiative were chosen, the king deciding that his herald, Aquitaine King of Arms, should take the letters destined for the emperor, the general council and other princes of the empire.[46] Until July 1417 the council was regularly concerned with aspects of war: diplomacy; defence; raising money, soldiers and weapons for the conflict with France; dealing with the safeguard of important prisoners taken at Harfleur and Agincourt; excusing royal annuitants who pleaded that they were not fit or able to fight for the king, as their obligation demanded.[47] Henry's departure for what was to be an absence of about three and a half years marked a change. One has a distinct impression that something of the spirit of the English council left it with the king's second expedition into France.

Henry's long absence abroad, and his wish to establish a legitimate system of government in Normandy, led to the creation of a second administration, this time outside England. Normandy was given its own chancellor, and from his chancery were to emerge the so-called 'Norman Rolls' which are of such value to historians today.[48] Furthermore, Henry had with him a second privy seal, together with a small staff of clerks brought over from England. It was natural that the keeper of the privy seal, John Kemp, appointed in October 1418, should have remained near the king, since the seal was the one used by Henry to authorize indentures, grants of land, and the payment of

---

[45] *PPC*, ii, 167–9, cited by Catto, 'King's servants', pp. 82–3.
[46] *PPC*, ii, 191–2.
[47] Ibid., ii, 153–5, 165, 184–5, 171.
[48] See above, ch.9.

wages to captains and soldiers in Normandy itself.[49] Moreover, when
Henry needed to deal with the exchequer in England, work normally
done by his lieutenant and the council whom he had left behind, he
wrote to that body using the second privy seal as the exchequer would
not accept warrants issued under another seal.[50] However, when writing to the chancellor and, more particularly in the years of his absence,
to his lieutenant or to the council in England, Henry made use of the
smaller, more private seal, the signet. This administrative development recognized that while the privy seal had been (and was still
regarded as being) a household office, over the years it had moved
away from the king and the court to a more permanent base in
London, leaving the signet, kept by the royal secretary and normally
immediately available to the king, as the chief means of authenticating
the royal will.

The use of the signet, a source of dispute in Richard II's time,
came to be limited to uncontentious matters, but its place in the
administrative history of the early fifteenth century is now generally
recognized.[51] Letters issued under the signet represented the personal
will of the king and, as such, they were his way of setting in motion the
legal and administrative, if not the financial, machine which depended
upon him. Written according to a well-established formula by the
king's secretary or one of his small staff,[52] they were often dictated by
Henry himself in a style which, in its brevity and lack of verbal
ornamentation (one is tempted to call it 'telegraphic'), reflects a man
of decisive mind, who, in discussion or conversation, would have been
accustomed to come straight to the point. Written in French until
August 1417, and thereafter only in English, these signet letters, 'the
voice of the king',[53] constitute 'the direct exercise of his authority',[54]
the chief means by which he communicated his orders to his administration in England. Of the 110 or so of Henry's surviving signet letters
written after August 1417, only seven were sent while the king was
in England in 1421.[55] The other hundred are evidence of his active
intervention in English affairs even in his absence in France.

Under Henry IV a sizeable proportion of the surviving signet letters
had been addressed to the keepers of the privy seal. Under his son,

---

[49]   Brown, 'Privy seal', pp. 99–100; Otway-Ruthven, *King's secretary*, p. 52 and n.6.
[50]   Brown, 'Privy seal', p. 101; *Signet letters*, ed. Kirby, p. 3.
[51]   *Signet letters*, pp. 1–3.
[52]   Ibid., pp. 6–8.
[53]   M. Richardson, 'Henry V, the English chancery, and chancery English', *Speculum*
55 (1980), 731.
[54]   Otway-Ruthven, *King's secretary*, p. 19.
[55]   Five are calendared in *Signet letters*, nos 902–6: texts in *Anthology of Chancery
English*, nos 90–4.

things were to change. Since Henry had taken a second privy seal to France in 1417, the correspondence which normally went through that office, such as that directed to the exchequer, could be dealt with in France. A look at the recipients of Henry's signet letters shows that some seventy per cent of those which have survived[56] were intended for the chancellor, reflecting the importance of that officer (rather than that of the king's lieutenant) as the practical head of the administration in England, as well as his position as the kingdom's chief law officer. Those recipients making up the difference were the two lieutenants (Bedford and Gloucester), the council as a body, the lieutenant and the council jointly, while others included the administration in Calais, Bordeaux and Normandy, a number being destined for the city of London.

Consideration of the content of Henry's signet letters underlines how uncontroversial they were, and that the signet letter was now an administrative device, not a political one as it had been under Richard II. Henry Beaufort would have been sympathetic to the king's order, sent in August 1414, that steps be taken against abuses perpetrated at sea upon merchants from Holland, for such acts prevented them from coming to trade at Calais, 'to the great loss of the king and his customs'.[57] The letters include petitions seeking the redress of injustice, these being forwarded by the king to his chancellor with orders to act.[58] Others concerned men serving Henry in France who complained that, because of their absence from England, they were finding it difficult to secure justice at home.[59] The king seemed particularly anxious to ensure that men in this position should not suffer injustice for that reason. Yet others concerned difficulties experienced by those who did not receive their annuities, which, in some cases, were nearly six years overdue.[60] Evidence suggests that, in many cases, redress of legitimate grievances was achieved.

While the royal lieutenant could issue writs ordering episcopal elections, power to confirm these and to authorize the restoration of the new bishops' temporal revenue lay with the king alone. When John Chaundler was elected to the see of Salisbury late in 1417, both the lieutenant (Bedford) and the new chancellor (Langley) received signet letters from the king, then besieging Falaise, on the matter,[61] as did the chancellor in the cases of Henry Ware, elected to Chichester in

[56] 125 out of 175 listed in *Signet letters*.
[57] *Signet letters*, no.778.
[58] *Signet letters*, nos 784, 796, 870–1, 897–8; *Anthology*, nos 65–6, 84–5.
[59] *Signet letters*, nos 886, 902, 908; *Anthology*, nos 73, 89, 95. On action taken on this matter in parliament in 1421, see above, p. 161, and n.55.
[60] *Signet letters*, no.888 (see also nos 771, 840); *Anthology*, nos 75, 34.
[61] *Signet letters*, nos 815–16: *Anthology*, nos 9–10.

July 1418, Philip Morgan, consecrated as bishop of Worcester at Rouen on 3 December 1419, and Edmund Lacy, once dean of the royal chapel, who was translated from the bishopric of Hereford to that of Exeter in 1420.[62] It is evident that the king was anxious to preserve firm control over the granting of temporalities to new bishops whose appointments he had helped to arrange.

By contrast with the large number of signet letters received by the chancellor (and in particular by bishop Langley, Henry's second chancellor) only a small number were sent to the king's lieutenants or to the royal council, and only a few of these are of particular interest. In one, sent from Vernon (on the Seine between Rouen and Paris) on 28 April 1419, the king told Bedford that the Flemings had asked for an extension of provisions for trade which had recently expired. Bedford and Langley were to appoint envoys to negotiate, but the terms which they were to arrange were set out by Henry himself.[63] Almost a year later, on 30 March 1420, Henry wrote to Gloucester and to the council in England regarding recommendations made by Sir John Tiptoft, seneschal of Guyenne, about the government of that area, and the reactions to these made by those around the king. Ordered to put the recommendations quickly into effect, the council in London was not apparently given any opportunity to comment upon the proposals, which had by now assumed the status of being the royal will.[64] In another letter, sent from the siege of Rouen on 29 November 1418, Henry reprimanded his brother Bedford for not acting upon repeated instructions made to him that breaches of the truce with Brittany be seen to, since the Bretons were still lodging their complaints. The chancellor was told to take immediate steps to ensure that those whose names appeared on the petition of complaint should be sent to the king forthwith, the letter ending with a curt expression of hope that this sort of thing would not happen again.[65]

The interpretation of such letters can be difficult. Their directness has appeal, for the formulas of so much medieval (and later) letter writing are wearisome and uninspiring. On the other hand there is an apparent lack of consideration of persons, in this case that of Henry's own brother whom, it is clear, he normally respected. In the letter to Bedford, we gain a sense of the king's exasperation at the failure of his lieutenant to get his, the king's, orders put into practice, and of his annoyance at those who did not live up to his exacting standards. From a narrowly English point of view, Henry's apparently

[62] *Signet letters*, nos 841, 892, 901: *Anthology*, nos 35, 79, 88.
[63] *Signet letters*, no.862; *Anthology*, no.57, *PPC*, ii, 250.
[64] *Signet letters*, no.890; *Anthology*, no.77.
[65] *Signet letters*, no.851; *Anthology*, no.46; *PPC*, ii, 243–4.

cavalier treatment of his lieutenants and the council in England, left with few important political decisions to make and reduced to carrying out orders based on decisions taken elsewhere, is open to criticism, a criticism which may reflect the feeling of some Englishmen of the time that the king was abandoning them in favour of France. On the other hand, it was Henry's great virtue to have been able to give a sense of united leadership to an enterprise which meant ruling both England and a growing part of France at the same time, an enterprise which not merely required, but demanded, decision-making by one man who, in this case, could only be the king. In a state of war, at a time when a delicate balance of alliances had to be achieved and maintained, the great enterprise needed a man (a conductor, perhaps) to see that all the sections of the orchestra were playing together. Henry's note to chancellor Langley that he should see to the alleged extortions practised by a Leicester notary upon Marjory Deye and her husband, and that a remedy be quickly provided 'consideryng the pourete of the saide Margerye',[66] suggests that even from a distance the king could take active steps to ensure a merciful application of the law, so that justice should be both done and seen to be done.

---

[66] *Signet letters*, no.905 (text, p. 19); *Anthology*, no.92.

Chapter 17

PARLIAMENT

Unlike the relationship which had existed between Henry IV and his parliaments, that between Henry V and the parliaments elected during his short reign was generally cordial and based on mutual understanding.[1] As Prince, Henry had attended a number of parliaments, and would have observed at close quarters the problems created by his father's policies (in particular his failure to understand the unfavourable reaction provoked by his inability to live within his means) and his way of handling the country's representative assembly. There are indications that the parliaments of 1410 and 1411, called while the Prince was in charge of the council, included a number of men elected through the efforts of bishop Beaufort, Thomas Chaucer and others who were sympathetic to what he was trying to achieve. By the time that he became king, Henry already appreciated the importance of the political role which parliament could play as a national body and as a source of influence in local political and social life, and he understood both the need to manage it carefully and the advantages which such management could bring to him as king.

On what was only the second day of his reign, Henry issued the writs of summons to his first parliament, an indication that he wanted to establish quickly a working relationship with it in what he saw as being, in many respects, a joint enterprise in government. Parliament was to be called eleven times during the reign, meeting every year except 1418 and 1422 (the parliament of that year, which assembled in November, was to be the first in his son's reign), sometimes, as in 1414, 1416 and 1421, twice a year. Henry was personally present at only six of these meetings, and after October 1416 he attended only the parliament of May 1421, Bedford presiding over four and Gloucester over one. Was this a devaluation of the importance of the institution? Certainly, it could appear that way, for there are indi-

[1] I am much indebted to the trustees of the History of Parliament Trust, and in particular to Dr Carole Rawcliffe and Dr Linda Clark, for allowing me access to unpublished biographical and other material concerning MPs, to be published in the forthcoming *The Commons, 1386–1421* (4 vols), under the general editorship of Professor J.S. Roskell. On the whole subject, see Harriss, 'The management of Parliament', *Henry V: practice of kingship*, ed. Harriss, ch.7.

cations that membership of parliament became a less sought-after honour in this reign than it had once been. On the other hand, there is nothing to suggest that the king deliberately snubbed the institution. The plain fact was that Henry's absence was the direct result of the role which he had chosen for himself, that of military leader, active in war and conquest. He knew full well that he had in his two youngest brothers men upon whose ability to deal with parliament he could count.

The official record, contained in the *Rotuli Parliamentorum*, tells us relatively little about the day-to-day discussions of issues and events as these must have taken place. Yet, if close attention is paid to the rather sparse record, it is possible to appreciate something of what went on in parliament and how the assembly was used as an instrument of government by Henry and his advisers. Every parliament, as it met, was addressed by the chancellor in terms not unlike those used today in the address from the throne. These statements, even in the brief form in which we have them, are of the greatest importance, for although they were delivered in the presence of the king or of his representative, and the text would have been agreed beforehand, they represent the considered views of two men, Henry Beaufort and Thomas Langley, both wielders of great personal influence at the court, who were able to project to their audience in parliament and beyond a consistent image of the king and of what he was attempting to do.

The addresses given before the first six parliaments of the reign (up to 1416) were the work of Henry Beaufort. Taken together, they show how, over a period of some four years, the king's most senior and (at this stage) probably most trusted and influential adviser saw Henry's role as king of England. One recurring theme is the fulfilment of the royal office. Henry, Beaufort told parliament in May 1413, must keep the oath he had sworn at his coronation: to do right, to administer justice and to seek 'bon governance'. A year later, at the parliament which met at Leicester, Henry was told that, as king, he should ensure that the law was observed, whether it was the law of the land, the law of religion (a reference to the recent rising of the Lollards) or the law at sea which protected England's trade. By late 1414 and for the coming two years Beaufort insisted on action. He applauded the king's decision to take vigorous measures against the French, demanded that the country support him and, after Agincourt, emphasized that the victory had been won with divine help, proof that the promise made by Henry in 1413 had been fulfilled by a man who placed his trust in God. [2]

[2] *RP*, iv, 3, 15–16, 34, 62.

There can be little doubt that Beaufort was deliberately trying to
convey as favourable an impression as he could of a king with a
programme approved by God. In so doing, he can be said to have
succeeded admirably, so that the five addresses made by Thomas
Langley, his successor as chancellor, between 1417 and 1421, carry
an air of *déjà vu* about them. None the less, this was the period of
fulfilment. In November 1417 Langley (who, on this occasion, had no
king present listening to him) could tell parliament that Henry had
gone to win his right in France; in 1419 he could praise him for having,
with the country's help, fulfilled the task (that of making war) which
had been forced upon him; while in 1421, with the king sitting next
to him, he was to emphasize that England's endeavours in France,
now crowned with success, were really the work of God. [3]

It seems likely that these addresses (at times so moral in content
that one is inclined to call them sermons) were part of a concerted
and deliberate effort to create an image of Henry as a man who
fulfilled the concept of kingship in every way. Taken as a whole, they
depict him as one who saw that the law was observed (this would
bring peace), who defended the rights and institutions of the Church
(the Christian king) and who adopted a firm attitude towards the
country's traditional enemy when it denied him his just claims. Such
an image bore a close resemblance to the portrait of the king conveyed
by the anonymous author of the *Gesta Henrici Quinti*, written before
the autumn of 1417 by a chaplain who was a member of the king's
court. [4] It is not unreasonable to claim that the view of Henry as the
just king supported by God, portrayed in the addresses of his two
chancellors as well as in the *Gesta*, bears every mark of court influence,
and that of Henry Beaufort in particular.

The *Rotuli Parliamentorum* thus constitute important contemporary
evidence of the effort to create an image of Henry which, with a work
such as the *Gesta*, was to lay the foundations of the inspired and
divinely protected ruler of later legend. But as a source they go further
than this. By reporting the subjects referred to by the chancellors and
recording some of the decisions taken, as well as the main petitions
put forward in each parliament, the rolls have much to tell us about
the mood and concerns of members at specific moments, and also
about the issues which troubled contemporaries. By providing us with
windows into the public soul, we may learn how, together, king and
subjects considered the measures needed to ensure the good government of the country.

As the legislation of the time indicates, physical threats to 'bon

[3] Ibid., iv, 106, 116, 129.
[4] See *Gesta*, p. 3; Harriss, *Cardinal Beaufort*, pp. 84–5.

governance' in the first two years of the reign came principally from Lollardy and local disorder, which were experienced chiefly in the marcher counties between England and Wales, as well as in the border counties of the north. The time which it took to capture Oldcastle after the Lollard rising of January 1414 (he was finally taken only in the autumn of 1417) and the place of his capture, in Wales itself, are both significant: no one had chosen to betray him to the authorities during that period of nearly four years, while the marcher counties, recovering from the effects of Glyn Dŵr's revolt, were not among the most peaceful in the country. The complaints of disorder in areas of England (such as Staffordshire and Cheshire) which touched on the march, as well as the activities of felons in Northumberland, demanded attention, which was provided by the parliament which met at Leicester in April 1414. Yet the firm action taken by the king in the early summer of that year by no means led to a restoration of social peace. When Thomas Langley addressed parliament in November 1417, both persons and property were still under threat (Lollards were regarded as the causers of this kind of trouble), while in both 1419 and 1420 complaints were made in parliament regarding troubles in Lancashire and, in 1421, similar disturbances in Cheshire. The fact that riots and social troubles were referred to specifically in the records of seven out of eleven parliaments indicates clearly how important the matter of 'law and order' was during this reign. [5]

Lack of order at sea was a matter with which Henry had already been associated while he was Prince. It was doubtless a desire to ensure continuity of what was clearly regarded as good policy which prompted Henry Beaufort, while chancellor, to give prominence in parliament to this important subject. In the first two parliaments of the reign Beaufort, encouraged no doubt both by the king and the interests of the city of London, advocated firm action against those responsible for disorder at sea. Parliament responded in April 1414 with the vote of tonnage and poundage, a tax on wool, wine, hides and other goods to be used for the defence of English maritime interests. [6] It also enacted legislation, the Statute of Truces, to help the English merchant community in its ongoing struggle with marauders at sea. [7] The seriousness with which the protection of maritime trade was regarded by all parties is revealed by its regular reappearance as a theme in the parliamentary record, which suggests that measures being taken were not always fully successful. In the parliament which met in November 1414 subsidies were voted for the defence of the

[5] See above, ch.14, and Powell, *Kingship, law and society*.
[6] *RP*, iv, 16.
[7] *SR*, ii, 178–81.

realm and, more specifically, for the safe-keeping of the sea.[8] A year later, in the euphoria which followed the victory won at Agincourt, parliament granted the king 'tunnage and poundage' for life, a step which, it was stated with emphasis, was not to be regarded as a precedent by English kings.[9]

Yet whether the voting of these taxes, generous as it might seem, was likely to lead to the provision of adequate protection of trade is to be doubted. The parliament of March 1416 was treated to an account of the difficulties experienced by the owners of the *Christopher of Hull* before acts of piracy,[10] while merchants from York and Bristol, Dartmouth and Lynn complained of the activities of Bretons at sea.[11] Six months later, in the following parliament, further complaints were lodged against Bretons, while criticism was made of the evident inadequacies of the Leicester statute of 1414 against the breaking of truces.[12] In 1421 the whole, broad issue was raised again, this time in relation to life on the Scottish border, also ruled by the terms of the Statute of Truces.[13] On this occasion, demands were made for the statute's repeal, so grave were the difficulties experienced by Englishmen in those parts required to observe its terms, while Scots and others were not. These were times, it was implied, when 'bon governance' could not be achieved by the enactment of statutes, however well intentioned these had originally been.

Henry used parliament as a body whose approval he sought in the promotion of men to places of honour in the peerage, or in the restoration to his grace of those whose fathers had, in years past, fallen foul of his own father's anger. In his second parliament, in May 1414,[14] Henry created his two younger brothers, John and Humphrey, dukes of Bedford and Gloucester respectively, while Edward of York was formally restored to his duchy and Richard, his brother, was created earl of Cambridge. On the same day Henry 'confirmed' his own brother, Thomas, as duke of Clarence, doing the same for Thomas Beaufort as earl of Dorset. The promotions of Bedford and Gloucester were natural; in the case of Bedford in particular it was a well-deserved reward for years of service on the Scottish border. The decision to 'confirm' the titles already conferred by Henry IV on Thomas Beaufort in 1411 and on his own son, Thomas, in 1412 may

  [8] *RP*, iv, 35.
  [9] '. . . et que ceste graunte ne soit pris en ensample as Roys d'Engleterre en temps a venir (*RP*, iv, 64).
  [10] *RP*, iv, 85–6.
  [11] Ibid., iv, 88–9.
  [12] Ibid., iv, 103–5.
  [13] Ibid., iv, 143. See above, pp. 330–2.
  [14] Ibid., iv, 17.

have sprung from the fact that, although valid, these creations had not been made in parliament, and it may have been felt that to do so would strengthen the claims of their holders to them. Such a 'confirmation' may be regarded as a gesture of friendship towards Clarence, who had not always seen eye to eye with the Prince, but with whom an open form of reconciliation was now felt to have value. The restoration of Edward, duke of York, to the duchy which he had inherited in 1402 may have been part of an agreement involving his resignation of the earldom of Cambridge in favour of his brother, Richard; it was almost certainly, too, a way of rewarding Edward for his long services to Henry IV and the Prince in the wars in Wales and Aquitaine.

Recompense was associated with reconciliation. One of Henry's tasks was to bring to an end, as publicly as possible, divisions which might remain as the result of his father's usurpation and the opposition shown to him at different times during his reign. It was one of the ways used by Henry to mark a break with the past. By the spring of 1414 he felt strong enough to encourage such moves, intended to reconcile to himself members of the nobility whose continued resentment might be the cause of trouble at a time when their energies and leadership could be put to better use in the forthcoming war against France.

By 1414, then, steps were already in train to restore to Henry's favour the heirs of certain of his father's enemies. In April Thomas Montagu, earl of Salisbury, petitioned parliament that the judgement of treason made against his father, murdered by a mob in Cirencester in 1400 before he could be formally tried for rebellion against Henry IV, should be reversed. In this case it took seven years for the process to be completed, but in the end Salisbury got his way. His restoration to favour may be seen as a reward for his contribution to the successful war in France. At the same time the benefit which such an act brought to the king should not be ignored: Henry had made a loyal friend, who was one of the finest English soldiers of his time.[15] In November 1414 the young Henry Percy, victim of the revolt of 1403 which had led to the death of his father, Hotspur, at the battle of Shrewsbury and to his own exile in Scotland, sought the regrant of the entailed lands of the earldom of Northumberland, a petition which was to lead to his creation as the new earl in parliament in March 1416, and to him doing homage to the king, also in parliament, soon afterwards.[16]

[15] Ibid., iv, 17–19, 35–6, 141–2. He had recently played a crucial role in saving the English army after the death of the duke of Clarence at Baugé.
[16] Ibid., iv, 37, 71.

It may have been the influence of the important events of the summer of 1416 which enabled the supplication of John Holland to be
restored to the titles and estates of the earldom of Huntingdon, confiscated from his father in 1400, to be answered very quickly. By
October 1416 Holland had received an affirmative response made,
significantly, 'by the king our sovereign lord and the lords of parliament'.[17] The king was well repaid by the service given by Huntingdon
in the years to come.

The importance of these decisions should not be lost on us. The
permission granted to the Welshman, Griffith Don, to buy and hold
land in England contrary to statute,[18] and the settlement made in the
parliament of May 1421 of the king's suit with Anne, countess of
Stafford, over the Bohun estate, are clear evidence of the king's wish
that petitions for exemption from statute should pass through parliament, as was his desire that his long-standing claim to his mother's
inheritance should likewise receive the formal and weighty stamp of
parliamentary approval.[19] These cases constitute important evidence
that, when it was in his interest, Henry was willing to soften his
attitude in order to forgive and forget, and to restore men, whose
services he wanted and would use, to their ancestral estates and titles.
Although normally regarded as a punctilious observer of the demands
of justice, Henry was also influenced by a deeply ingrained sense of
mercy. As the handbooks on kingship taught, mercy, as much as
justice, was one of the hallmarks of the Christian king.

One of parliament's main functions was to provide a way for
decisions taken centrally to be conveyed to different parts of the kingdom; another was to serve as a means by which the attention of the
king could be drawn to the requirements of his people, be they a social
group, or the people of a particular locality, or even individuals who,
for example, might find themselves victims of an injustice or malfunc-
tioning of the law, for which reform might be demanded. Under
Henry IV petitions had come to be presented in larger numbers by the
Commons, the proportion of those which led to enactments likewise
increasing. The same was true of his son's reign; very few of the
statutes passed during Henry V's reign had their origin or inspiration
other than in a petition presented to parliament. All ten statutes which
emerged from the parliament of 1413 originated in petitions presented
before that assembly.[20] Yet, probably because about two-thirds of

---

[17] '. . . par le roy notre soverain seigneur et les seigneurs du Parlement' (ibid., iv,
100–1, 110).
[18] Ibid., iv, 130–1.
[19] Ibid., iv, 135–40.
[20] Gray, *Influence of the commons*, pp. 259, 286–7.

them had their wording (and thereby perhaps their intention) changed between petition and statute (three out of ten had few or no changes made), the parliament of April-May 1414 requested (the petition is recorded in English) that, since it was 'as well assentirs as peticioners', no petition should henceforth be amended in a negative way 'that sholde chaunge the sentence and the entente axked by the spekeres mouthe, or the petitions biforesaid yeven up yn writyng . . . withoute assent of the forsaid Commune'. This petition, the nearest to one of 'constitutional' significance found for the entire reign, provoked a positive answer from the king. Care would be taken, it was said, to ensure that no text would be engrossed as a statute contrary to the Commons' petition; the king none the less emphasized his prerogative 'to graunte and denye what him lust of their petitions and askynges', thus reserving his right to refuse petitions if he so chose.[21]

What the causes and outcome of this petition were is not clear. Was it something of a possible crisis which led to the presence of the unusually large number of twenty-four triers of petitions being present in the parliament of May 1414, whereas the number in attendance at the meetings of 1419 and December 1421 was to be only six?[22] Was there opposition to the king on account of changes made to seven of the ten petitions presented in the previous parliament before these became statutes? If so, this may have been because a larger than average number had experienced changes in their texts than had been usual in the past few years.[23] In May 1414 every effort appears to have been made to observe the letter of the king's agreement; by the time that parliament met in November, however, modifications and amendments (such as the duration of the statute's life) were being reintroduced, but in no way which contradicted the spirit and substance, if not strictly the letter, of the petition.[24] In effect, things were going to be done in much the same way as they had been done before 1413.

From the beginning Henry chose to involve his subjects closely with him as he faced the prospect of war. By emphasizing that the conflict with France was being forced upon England by the refusal of the French to return to him what was his due in France (the war, therefore, was one which England and her king were being obliged to fight in the name of justice), a chord of sympathy between ruler and ruled

[21] *RP*, iv, 22: *Select documents of English constitutional history, 1307–1485*, ed. S.B. Chrimes and A.L. Brown (London, 1961), pp. 237–8.
[22] A.R. Myers, 'Parliamentary petitions in the fifteenth century', *EHR*, 52, (1937), 394.
[23] Gray, *Influence of the commons*, pp. 271–2.
[24] Ibid., p. 278.

had been struck. This did not mean that Henry had things all his own way. In 1414 he had been advised to achieve his ends through negotiation rather than through war, and he had heeded that advice. But the failure of negotiation in 1414–15 had led to the expedition of 1415, while it was on his return from an unsuccessful attempt to make peace at Calais in September-October 1416 that Henry had announced his intention of invading France again in the following year. In all these enterprises he received the strong support of parliament, in particular in the five-year period from early 1415 to the beginning of 1420,[25] during which time some eighty per cent of the money voted by parliament for the requirements of war was actually collected.

A sign of the trust put in Henry can be seen in the subsidy on wool and woolfells voted for four years in 1413, along with 'tunnage and poundage' for one year. This grant, which surpassed any made to Henry IV, was improved in 1414 by the grant of 'tunnage and poundage' for three further years, to bring it into line with the wool subsidy. Henry was now in a position to plan ahead. By the end of that year, with an expedition to France now becoming more likely, two full subsidies (each calculated to bring in some £37,000) were voted for the defence of the kingdom and the defence of the sea, the first to be raised by February 1415, the second a whole year later. This was generous provision, which had the further and important advantage of enabling Henry to plan ahead right through the following year and, if necessary, to request that the collection of the second levy should be brought forward, or accelerated. Perhaps, too, Henry, with his mind on the possible turn of events in 1415, did not want a meeting of parliament to interfere with preparations and departure for France. By obtaining the vote of a double subsidy, he may have been hoping to avoid summoning a parliament in 1415. In the end, he could not do so, and it was left to Bedford, acting as lieutenant, to call a meeting planned for late October. Seeing the country's money well spent in the capture of Harfleur and the great victory of Agincourt, parliament now not only made the grant of 'tunnage and poundage' into a grant for life, but it also agreed to accelerate the collection of the subsidy due in February 1416 to mid-December 1415, a new subsidy agreed originally for collection in February 1417 being brought forward to November 1416.[26]

When parliament met in March 1416, steps were already actively under way to prepare for an expedition to relieve Harfleur: once again, agreement for the acceleration of a grant due in November to June

25 Harriss, *Henry V: practice of kingship*, p. 145.
26 *RP*, iv, 63; Roskell, *Speakers*, p. 161.

was achieved, although no new subsidy was voted.[27] Probably to remedy this, and to do so while the memory of the success won at the naval battle of the Seine in August was still fresh and the most could be made of the anti-French sentiment which the court was helping to generate, parliament was called again in October 1416. This time, however, while generous enough to vote two whole subsidies, one and a half of which were to be raised by February 1417, the remainder in November, parliament did so only on condition that no other taxes be levied and that no agreed date for collection be brought forward. The shoe was now clearly beginning to pinch. If the king needed more money, he could borrow it, approval being given both in the permission that the half subsidy to be raised in November 1417 might be used by the king to repay debts, and in the guarantees made to parliament by Clarence, Bedford and Gloucester that they would assure repayment of loans in the event of the king's death.[28]

In November 1417, with the initial successes of Henry's second expedition into Normandy already known (he and Clarence had written from Caen to the city of London to report on the outcome of events and to ask for men ready to settle in Normandy), and urged on by chancellor Langley's words that both king and country would reap honours from work well done, parliament voted its third but last double subsidy, half to be raised in February 1418, the other a whole year later, a condition being that the collection of these grants should not be accelerated.[29] Why there was no parliament in 1418 (the only year in the reign, apart from 1422, which was to be that of the king's death) is not clear. By now Henry was finding it increasingly difficult to finance the war, which, after the summer of 1418 and the beginning of the siege of Rouen, must have appeared to those in England to be progressing rather slowly and without any very evident major gains. Was it an idle threat of Langley's to hint, just as Henry was about to begin to negotiate the terms later agreed at Troyes, that the whole enterprise might have to be abandoned if help, in the form of money and men, were not forthcoming?[30] The effect, after an interval of two years during which no tax had been voted but the two subsidies granted in November 1417 had been collected, was to persuade parliament to vote a whole subsidy and a third, one subsidy to be levied in February 1420, the remaining third, intended for the repayment of loans mainly from civil and ecclesiastical corporations, to be raised in the following November.[31]

[27] *RP*, iv, 71.
[28] Ibid., iv, 95–6.
[29] Ibid., iv, 107.
[30] Ibid., iv, 116.
[31] Ibid., iv, 117.

The period of intense taxation was now over. With the sealing of the treaty of Troyes in May 1420, England was no longer technically at war with France, whose affairs many came to regard as the concern of that country alone. Henry's English subjects, therefore, could feel that their responsibilities for war (at least against France) were over. The mood in England was changing. Members of parliament could no longer be counted upon, as they had been in the past, to finance the war. Besides, they wanted their king back in England, as they made clear in the parliament of December presided over by Henry's brother, Humphrey. The reactions to the terms of the treaty of Troyes were very mixed. While these meant a welcome end to the legal obligation to provide finance for the war, fear was expressed that Englishmen would be subject to Henry as regent and, ultimately, as king of France; there was fear, too, that Henry would become over-engrossed with the affairs of his French kingdom.[32]

Members of parliament cannot have been reassured by the answer given them that, even after a continuous absence of well over three years, Henry was still too busy with affairs in France to return to England; nor by the statement, made by the chancellor, Langley, that in future Henry would spend some time in England, some time in France, the details to be left to the king himself. Meanwhile, it was possible that he might return in the lifetime of the present parliament which he had himself summoned; were that to happen, Humphrey's powers would cease. In that event, too, parliament should not be dissolved, but would continue, a manner of proceeding which would be followed in future if parliament were to be summoned by the king while he was abroad.

Parliament could do little about what some members may have regarded as an unsatisfactory position (the king had not attended a session of parliament for four years). Its reaction none the less suggests that members felt some resentment at the way their institution and the kingdom as a whole appeared to be treated. It responded sharply to the proposal that petitions should, if necessary, be sent abroad to receive the royal approval; the lieutenant should be empowered to do this himself within the life of the parliament; otherwise petitions should at once become 'voides et de nul effect'.[33] There was an implication here that, in future, the king should attend all parliaments in person.

By such action parliament was showing its criticism of Henry's long absence and what, to some, may have seemed his increasingly cavalier attitude towards the problems of his English kingdom, which he

[32] Ibid., iv, 127.
[33] Ibid., iv, 124, 128; *SR*, ii, 203.

appeared inclined to leave to the care of his lieutenants. Not surprisingly, parliament was not asked to vote a subsidy in December 1420. Nor could Henry, back in England at the beginning of February 1421, expect much from the parliament which he called for May. In spite of the king being present, there is no record of a subsidy being sought, although soundings had been taken about the possibility of seeking one.[34] But, in the circumstances, both the parliamentary mood and the general economic situation in the country would have been against it. For the moment, Henry could not count on general support in parliament to provide him with the financial backing which he still badly needed. He had to rely on individuals and corporations to give him what they could.

He achieved some success with the tour of the country which he undertook in March and April, and Henry Beaufort, although still owed £8336, agreed to a loan of £14,000, this good example of public spirit being formally recorded in the parliamentary roll.[35] It was not until December 1421, with the king now back in France and having begun what was to prove his last siege (at Meaux), that Bedford and Langley persuaded parliament to vote a subsidy. Was the cause behind their successful pleading the very recent birth of a son and heir to Henry and his queen? In all events, Henry was voted a subsidy for the war. It was to be the last accorded him, and the last such formal contribution made by parliament to the war effort for the next seven years.[36]

The reign of Henry V was no revolutionary period in the history of parliament. Indeed, the proceedings had been much livelier during parts of the previous reign. Some might say that in this decade parliament had become docile. This can be taken as a sign that the policies pursued by the king had the approval of the community's representatives (thereby creating harmony not dissension) and that, at least until the very end of the reign, the policies appeared to work. Behind everything lay the trust in which the king was held by parliament. In his very first parliament as king Henry had been reminded that while there had been promises of improvement, particularly in financial management, during his father's time, such promises had largely not been kept; members would, however, have been aware of the Prince's attempts to reform the country's finances after 1406 and, in particular, during his period as head of the council in 1410 and 1411.

Trust there certainly was. Yet it was not won without work and

[34] Harriss, *Henry V: practice of kingship*, pp. 150–1.
[35] Harriss, *Cardinal Beaufort*, p. 401.
[36] Harriss, *Henry V: practice of kingship*, p. 151.

effort. If the policy of war appealed, and the aim of restoring peace at home and at least a measure of order at sea found much support, it was not only because war appealed to the military class and peaceful trade would bring advantages to the maritime community, both of whom were well represented in parliament; it was also because Henry's publicizing of his thoughts and intentions, through the mouths of his two chancellors, met with a positive response. This can be judged in two ways. After 1406 Henry IV had summoned parliament on only four occasions in some six years. By contrast it became his son's habit to call parliament much more frequently. Henry did so eleven times in a reign which lasted barely nine and a half years; the first six meetings took place in a period of only three and a half years, between May 1413 and October 1416; and in the eleven months between November 1415 and October 1416 parliament met three times.

Yet the returns of members show that, in spite of the frequency of meetings, many were willing to return several times during the reign; a number had experience of parliament going back beyond the previous reign to that of Richard II. As far as is known, Roger Hunt, elected Speaker in 1420, sat in eight parliaments; Roger Flore, also a Speaker, sat seven times; John Wilcotes represented Oxfordshire six times and Kent once between 1413 and 1421; while John Russell, the unsuccessful candidate in a contested election for the Speakership in 1420, represented Herefordshire on six occasions, as many times as Robert Cary sat for Devon during Henry's reign. Much the same story could be told of the burgesses, many of whom, like William Wood who represented Winchester eight times between 1413 and 1423, were returned to several parliaments during the reign. Of the members who attended the first parliament of Henry VI's reign, called when Henry V had been dead only a few weeks, 'at least two out of every three . . . had previously sat in parliaments', only a quarter of the 'knights' at that meeting attending for the first time.[37] Re-election, even if not consecutive, suggests a measure of continuity. Does it also suggest a measure of approval of the measures being pursued by the king? This may have been so.

A look at the membership of those elected to the Commons during this reign gives the clear impression that many may have been chosen through the local influence of the crown or that of members of the

---

[37] J.S. Roskell, 'The social composition of the commons in a fifteenth-century parliament', *BIHR*, 24 (1951), 155. The text (*RP*, iv, 151) states that the subsidy was made 'pur defense du dit roialme d'Engleterre en especial', probably to make it clear that the money was not intended to be spent on the war in France other, perhaps, than in Gascony.

local nobility or gentry favourable to the crown. Such a statement conjures up visions of corruption and influence. We should beware of accepting this conclusion too readily. At the same time, however, social, political and financial factors could easily help to create friendships, groups, even interests, none of which can be ignored. The study of what can be learned of the careers and connections of parliament's personnel can only yield instructive information. While the Speakers, the first of whom had been elected in 1376, were the spokesmen of the Commons rather than representatives of the crown (as Sir William Stourton found to his cost in 1413 when he was effectively disavowed by the Commons for agreeing to put into writing certain specific complaints which the Commons preferred to have expressed in general terms), they were clearly men who could dictate both the course and, to a certain extent, the content of debate.[38] Although chosen by the Commons rather than by the king, most of them must have been elected in the knowledge that a Speaker known to the king and trusted both by him and by the Commons was more likely to assist the passage of debate and any consequent bargaining which might take place.

Nine men occupied the Speaker's chair during the reign, Thomas Chaucer doing so twice, Roger Flore three times.[39] Most of them had some connection with the king, which may have gone back to the previous reign, or with men of influence around him. William Stourton had been in Henry's service as Prince of Wales and as duke of Cornwall.[40] Thomas Chaucer, son of the poet and a first cousin of both Henry and Thomas Beaufort, had worked closely with the Prince in earlier parliaments and had been reappointed to the office of chief butler by the new king on the second day of his reign; by 1421 he had experienced his fifth period as Speaker, having held that office three times in Henry IV's reign.[41] Roger Flore was appointed chief steward of the northern parts of the duchy of Lancaster only a few weeks after being elected to the Speakership in October 1416; this appointment, and the fact that he was chosen to preside in the two following parliaments of 1417 and 1419, suggests that he was acceptable to all parties. Having a man of experience, trusted by both king and Commons, in charge of proceedings was of great importance in securing a smooth relationship in the working of this vital institution.[42]

But having men who might be biddable to the king's point of view

[38] Harriss, *Henry V: practice of kingship*, pp. 144, 157.
[39] Parliament met eleven times; the first meeting had two Speakers.
[40] Roskell, *Speakers*, pp. 154–5.
[41] Ibid., pp. 149–53, 171–4.
[42] He was to be elected to the Speaker's chair in the parliament which met on 8 November 1422, the day after Henry V's funeral.

could not depend on the Speakers alone. Elections were important, and in that vital process influences of one kind or another could play a crucial part. Some men, such as John Wilcotes (well known to Thomas Chaucer since they both represented Oxfordshire), a member of the council in Henry V's absence in Normandy and a man who had for long been associated with service in the royal estates in Cornwall, would have helped to make Henry's views known in parliament. Others, such as John Golafre and John Leventhorpe (the latter an executor of the will of both Henry IV and Henry V), were in receipt of annuities from the king, while others still, Sir Walter de la Pole and Sir William Lisle, went on diplomatic missions for him. The war against the Welsh produced a crop of men, such as Sir Thomas de la Haye and Sir John Scudamore, who sat for Herefordshire in 1413 and 1414, or Sir William Porter, the friend of the Prince who sat for Cambridge in 1413, and John St John who was a member for Northamptonshire four times between 1410 and 1421. A substantial number, nearly fifty per cent of the 'knights', had some experience of the war in France before the end of the reign.[43] Three Yorkshire knights, Sir Robert Plumpton, twice MP (once for Yorkshire, once for Nottinghamshire), Sir William Gascoigne and Sir Brian Stapleton, were all to be killed in France, while five out of thirteen 'knights' from Lancashire served there under Henry V.

Local influences were equally important. Duchy of Lancaster officials or annuitants were to be found among the representatives of several counties, in particular Derbyshire, Leicestershire, Nottinghamshire and Norfolk, while many of those who represented the county of Cornwall were bound to the king either as annuitants or as officers of the duchy. Links with members of the nobility who strongly supported the crown were also very important. Some of those who represented the border counties of Shropshire were associated with the Arundel and Talbot families, both strong upholders of the Lancastrian house; in Devon the same could be said of the retainers of the Courtenay earls of Devon; in Warwickshire and Worcestershire men such as John Throckmorton, tenant and retainer of the Beauchamp earls of Warwick, were returned to parliament;[44] while in Hampshire, Berkshire and Oxfordshire, men known to Henry Beaufort and Thomas Chaucer found themselves elected.

It has to be stressed that links of this kind did not mean unquestioning obedience to the interests of the patron: changes of patron were not infrequent. The fact remains, however, that if the patron remained

---

[43] This figure is offered by Roskell, 'Social composition of the commons', 171, and *Parliament of 1422* (Manchester, 1954), p. 94.

[44] Roskell (*Parliament of 1422*, p. 70) stresses Beauchamp influence.

on good terms with the king and his star appeared to be high, it was often to the retainer's interests to remain in his master's service. One important factor was to encourage this. While in Richard II's reign the so-called shire 'knights' had been largely true, belted knights, the first years of Lancastrian rule had witnessed a marked change which led to the election of men who, while possessing the financial qualification to be knighted, had chosen not to be so.

This change was far from uniform over the country. It could have been observed as early as 1397 in Berkshire (which returned only one true knight out of eighteen known returns of 'knights', two for each of nine parliaments, for Henry V's reign), or from 1399 in Buckinghamshire and Norfolk (the first, like Berkshire, returning only one knight, the second electing four during Henry's reign). The change becomes more marked towards the end of Henry IV's reign in Hampshire (two out of twenty), Devon (three out of eighteen) and Sussex (one out of twenty), and continued into the reign of his son. During these years only one out of twenty was elected in the counties of Bedfordshire and Shropshire and, possibly, Westmorland, while no knight was elected in Surrey in the parliaments for which we have returns. In a few places the situation was different: Derbyshire elected eleven knights, Cumberland twelve, Nottinghamshire thirteen, while in Yorkshire seventeen knights occupied the eighteen positions for which returns survive.

How is this information to be interpreted? There seems to be little doubt that the outward distinctions between 'knights of the shire' and 'burgesses', distinctions such as social rank or wealth, were disappearing, and that persons of broadly comparable rank, most of whom came from the county community and were office-holders, men thus well versed in local affairs, were being elected.[45] What did this reflect? Was it, as could be thought, disenchantment with parliament, particularly at a time when the king was out of the country for long periods? Certainly, the numbers present at elections appear to have diminished quite considerably in some counties during this period, evidence which could suggest that elections were not worth attending, perhaps because the results were predictable? In some shires the reign witnessed the election of many new, relatively inexperienced members,[46] while in others it was rare for two men of experience to be elected together.

Does all this explain why Henry V seldom met much opposition,

[45] Many MPs had been, or were to be, JPs, escheators or sheriffs of their counties (ibid., pp. 85–8).
[46] Cambridgeshire eighteen out of twenty-two, Kent fourteen out of sixteen. In both cases, information is about known MPs.

other than a certain 'grouching' about his rule in the last year or so
of his reign? Did the apparent willingness of Henry V's parliaments
to meet his demands result from the decline in numbers of major
county figures and their supplanting by men of lesser position who
owed their elections to persons or institutions ready to lend their
support to the king and his policies? In the final analysis, although
the background of members of the Commons, as well as the intentions
of men helping to secure their elections, should be taken into account,
this does not wholly explain the success which Henry had in dealing
with parliament, which may be contrasted with his father's relative
failure to get it to do his will.

While royal influence among members must have been valuable in
securing the support which the king needed, it was his ability to
advocate policies which met the mood and needs of the day (war with
France, protection of trade at sea, the provision of wool to Flanders)
which won him support. If Henry came to enjoy rather less parliamentary support in his last years, this may have been because, in the
circumstances, shire 'knights' without experience of war were present
in greater numbers, in the place of those away. In 1421 he may have
been encouraged by the fact that parliament included a substantial
number of members with French experience who had returned to
England with him, and upon whose support he might count. If so, he
was to be disappointed. In 1421 Englishmen assumed that, since the
treaty of Troyes, the costs of war would now be borne by French
sources. Henry was advised that a demand for a subsidy would probably meet with a refusal; this made him realize that he could only
obtain the money by bypassing the normal parliamentary channels
and having recourse to loans raised from individuals and corporations,
loans which parliament would be ready to guarantee.

In this, individual members of parliament came to Henry's help.
Some who represented London, for instance, offered the king personal
loans to supplement the advances for the campaigns against France
made by the corporation and guilds.[47] Even more significant is the
substantial list of members of the Commons known to have been
active in the raising of loans in England between 1419 and 1422, the
very time that the king was facing his most acute shortage of money
due to parliament not voting subsidies for the war. Some, such as
Nicholas Merbury, who sat twice for Northamptonshire, or John
Uvedale, who did the same for Hampshire, helped to raise loans once,
in 1421 and 1419 respectively. Others, such as Richard Whittington,
first elected to represent Gloucestershire in 1384 and who had last sat

[47] Robert Chichele; William Cromer, Thomas Fauconer, Thomas Knolles, Nicholas Wooton (*Letter-Book I*, pp. 202–3).

in parliament in 1414, assisted twice, in 1419 and 1420. John Golafre, who represented Berkshire, John Wilcotes and his fellow Oxfordshire 'knight', Thomas Chaucer, all three of whom sat in one or other of the two parliaments of 1421, helped to raise loans in those counties in that year. In Norfolk, where duchy of Lancaster influence was strong, John Lancaster and Oliver Groos, both 'knights' of the county in 1419, and John Wodehouse, Edmund Wynter and John Lancaster (again), who represented the county in 1421, all helped in the same way. The residence qualification, required by an act of 1413, could have some effect in enabling MPs to wield influence on behalf of the crown in the counties which they represented.

Support for Henry's military undertakings might be expressed in other practical ways. A number of members of parliament acted as commissioners of array, mustering troops before they left for the war in France. John Mitchel, one of London's representatives in 1420, was on a commission to hire and requisition ships to convey provisions over the sea; Richard Hankford, son of the lord chief justice, who had represented Devon in 1414 and 1416, was providing anchors and cables for ships two years later; while Oliver Groos, member for Norfolk in 1419, organized the shipping of soldiers from Norfolk and Suffolk in the following year. Groos was an old annuitant of the house of Lancaster who had seen service in Spain with John of Gaunt as long ago as 1386. With him, as with others, the tradition of military service was strong.

Royal annuitants, if they could not serve in person, helped or encouraged others to do so. Even the less young, such as Sir Robert Laurence, born about 1371 and member for Lancashire in 1414 before being knighted on campaign in the following year, fulfilled his obligation as an annuitant by recruiting archers in 1421, while another annuitant, Simon Camp, who had sat for Middlesex in 1414 and 1415, indented with the king in February 1422 to provide one mounted archer whom he, Camp, would pay for nine months. There may be significance in the decision of William Cheyne, who had sat only once for Kent (in 1416), to organize loans in that county in 1421. In 1416 his fellow 'knight' had been John Wilcotes, who in 1421 was seeking financial support for the king in Oxfordshire and Berkshire. Had these two men kept in touch with each other? Certainly they were of one mind in this matter, equally determined to raise money to further the king's cause. In these simple facts we have evidence of the loyalty which Henry could arouse, and upon which much of his appeal and his success as king can be seen to have depended.

Chapter 18

FINANCE

Proper financial management had been promised by Henry to the Commons when they had sought 'bon governance' in 1413. It would be one of the ways by which the new king would be judged. If not found wanting, it was likely to give them confidence in him, to encourage them to support his policies, particularly his wars, with welcome financial aid. How they did this was likely to become a yardstick according to which the people's support for their king could be measured.

Successful financial management was a prime way of distancing the king from his father's rule. Henry IV had been short on both financial sense and money, lack of which had been an almost constant irritant in his relationship with parliament. Among those who provided, confidence in the crown's ability to rule had been shaken. Since Henry IV's financial needs were not only considerable but 'recurrent and concurrent', his inability to satisfy them contributed substantially to his difficulties as king. In this respect three matters stood out: the war against the Welsh; the king's need to win support at home through the 'purchase' of men's loyalty by means of large-scale grants of annuities; and the payments due to the sizeable royal household.

The Welsh rebellion had begun at about the time of the first anniversary of Henry IV's accession to the throne, when he had already involved himself in a pointless and costly expedition against the Scots. Fated to last about a decade, the crushing of the rebellion needed to be properly justified before the Commons. Who was financially responsible for it? Was it a 'foreign' war which could be presented as a threat to the country's security, and for which help from the people could be demanded? Or was it an 'internal' conflict, a rebellion whose suppression should be financed mainly out of the king's ordinary revenue, and that of the principality of Wales, aided by the great border lords of whom the Prince, as earl of Chester, could be regarded as the leader? While there was a case, frequently resisted by the Commons, that Glyn Dŵr's revolt was a threat to national security, it was clear that Henry IV's other financial problems were largely of his own making, and that he should not expect aid from his subjects in resolving them. Consequently, in his search for political support, the king was obliged to alienate portions of the royal estates, a policy which diminished the sources of revenues available to him, so that, before long, he was obliged to seek parliamentary support to carry out those functions of government which he was normally expected to finance from his own resources. The other twin problems, that of the high number of annuitants (a characteristic of European courtly societies at this time, as well as a legacy of Richard II and of Lancastrian family tradition), together with what contemporaries were to term the outrageously high expenses of the royal household, were to help cause serious difficulties to those responsible for the expenditure of the king's ordinary revenue.

Instead of being on the increase, that revenue was actually in decline. The resources of Wales were the first to suffer from the violence and destruction of war. Nor were the revenues from the duchy of Lancaster, now (since 1399) part of the new king's resources, as productive as Henry V was later to make them. Similarly, the crown's revenue from the customs charged to foreign trade, principally on wool and cloth, was going through a period of temporary decline, yields being considerably reduced. Not surprisingly, Henry IV found himself obliged to borrow the money which his extravagant way of ruling required.

It was not only these factors, crucial as they were, which caused difficulties. The reigns of the first two Lancastrians were caught up in a period of bullion shortage which, from the declining years of the fourteenth century to the end of Henry V's reign, was to affect the economy of much of western Europe. The fundamental problem was a lack of specie – money which could be handled – which resulted from two factors. The first was a decline at this period in European mining activity (much of it in Bohemia, a country experiencing social revolution and civil war in these years), which led to a decrease in the amount of silver generally available for coining. The second, like the first European in scale, was the widespread increase in war in these years, war which greatly encouraged the demand for coin in which soldiers, supplies, weapons and the costs of transport would be paid.[1] Every country, therefore, tried to maintain and improve its stock of silver and gold, a game which not all could win at the same time.

Continental practice was for the ruler to debase his territory's coinage (technically, it was his to do what he liked with) through recoining, a practice which, from his point of view, had the advantage of enabling him to pocket what was known as a seigniorage, a percentage

---

[1] On this, see the thesis presented by H.A. Miskimin, *Money and power in fifteenth-century France* (New Haven/London, 1984).

of the value of money brought in for this process. Although practised
in France and in the duchy of Burgundy, recoining was scarcely
known in England. True, Edward III had attempted a debasement
in 1351, but he had been obliged to renounce the practice in the
following year, so that English coinage, while in short supply, was
generally of a quality which compared well with that of other countries, whose inferior currency, when found in England, was sent to
the London mint for recoining according to English standards. [2] In
order to preserve sufficient stock of metal in England, it had been
decided in 1386 that alien merchants should spend half their takings
within the country before leaving it, while after 1401 they were only
permitted to take away the remaining half by special licence, a concession which was to be revoked two years later. [3] Such coinage as
could be obtained from foreign merchants trading at Calais was also
to be reminted there before being returned to England. The significance of this continental outpost in the money war was considerable.

Whether the bullionist policy, hotly contested by the Burgundians
who controlled England's principal trading partners in the Low Countries, was a success or not, the reign of Henry IV saw a marked
decline in the quality of newly minted money available for circulation.
This unsatisfactory situation affected both trade (deterred by the
requirements that money coined in England must be spent there, too)
and wages paid to soldiers fighting in Wales. The policy of control
and budgeting introduced by the Prince, a policy inspired by decisions
such as that of Henry Beaufort (in 1403) to stop all annuities payable
by the Hanaper (the department of chancery which received fees for
the sealing of documents) and all exemptions granted for the use of the
great seal (controlled by Beaufort as chancellor) was not immediately
appreciated. [4] In the parliament which met in November 1411, just
as the Prince and his 'ministry' were about to be dismissed, requests
were made 'because of the severe shortage of money at present experienced in the kingdom' for a reduction in the standard weight of coins,
although their quality was to remain untouched. The gold noble was
reduced in value by one tenth, the silver shilling by one sixth, the
change to take effect from Easter 1412. [5] It is likely that the reduction
was equal to something like the actual deficiency found in the average
coin of the day, which was liable to cutting and washing, so that the

[2] J.L. Bolton, *The medieval English economy, 1150–1500* (London, 1980), pp. 297–8.
[3] J. Craig, *The Mint. A history of the London mint from A.D. 287 to 1948* (Cambridge, 1953), p. 81.
[4] N. Pronay, 'The hanaper under the Lancastrian kings', *Proceedings of the Leeds philosophical and literary society (Literary and historical section)*, 12 (1967), pt 3, 80.
[5] 'Item, pur la graunde Escarcete de Monoye q'y ad a present deins le Roialme d'Engleterre . . .' (*RP*, iii, 658–9).

change, the first since that ordered sixty years earlier by Edward III, may have been but a recognition of the real value of England's coinage rather than a deliberate attempt to get rich quickly through debasement.

Henry IV's financial difficulties had helped to create one notable constitutional issue, 'the use to which parliamentary taxation was to be put'. Should the 'ordinary' costs of government be paid out of subsidies, which were generally regarded as covering only its 'extra-ordinary' costs, such as those of war? The appointment, at the Commons' insistence, of Sir John Tiptoft as treasurer of the king's household in 1406 has come to be seen as a political act, aimed at achieving a measure of control over the king's expenditure. There is significance in the fact that, in the first year of the Prince's administration (1410), no lay subsidy was collected, while in the second year, when it was collected, no financial advances, or assignments, were made from money taken from it towards the expenses of the king's household.[6] In so acting the Prince was demonstrating his sympathy for those who thought that the country should not be obliged to support the royal household through parliamentary subsidies. The king should live within his means: subsidies were to be applied only to the expenses of foreign war.

It was this kind of 'abuse' which Henry hoped to avoid on becoming king. He was greatly helped by the success of the recoinage begun a year earlier. More silver coin, supplemented by large amounts of gold coin, was minted between 1412 and 1416 than at any time in the previous fifty or so years. Yet it was not a particular measure but rather a firm attitude towards the proper use of available resources which distinguished Henry's approach to government finance from that of his father. Henry understood well how Henry IV had created financial problems both for himself and for others. As Prince, he had already shown that he understood the difficulties, and had considered possible remedies. His sense of responsibility led him to appreciate that a king must do all in his power to live off his own.

In the first parliament of the new reign, Henry agreed that the payment of annuities, by means of which political and military support was won and maintained, should be reduced by the value of £10,000:[7] it is notable that with bishops Beaufort and Langley as his chancellors, only two annuities were paid out by the Hanaper during the reign.[8] Such savings were practically useful. They also showed

[6] A. Rogers, 'Henry IV, the Commons and taxation', *Medieval studies*, 31 (1969), 66–7. A few crept back in 1412–13, once the Prince was out of favour.

[7] *RP*, iv, 5; Wolffe, *Royal demesne*, p. 87.

[8] Pronay, 'Hanaper', 81.

the importance which Henry attached to such financial strategy, and must have won him much approval. In his desire to live within his means, Henry could – and did – go much further. Like his father, he could reap the financial advantages of being duke of Lancaster, whose estates, covering much of the country, provided valuable resources of supplementary revenue. Happily for Henry, the duchy's lands brought in more in the second decade of the century than they had done in the first, mainly because peace in Wales brought stability to those parts. [9]

It was not simply the end of the revolt, however, which lay behind the dramatic improvement in Lancastrian revenues from Welsh sources. Much depended upon the determination of the king – as duke – to root out dishonesty and inefficiency among his officials (many being replaced by others known to him personally), and to follow a persistent policy of seeking out arrears which were owed, while realizing that it was better to settle for a fine in cases in which it would cost more than would be gained if this policy were taken too far. All this bore the mark of directives given by a man who knew what he wanted – that the duchy's lands should yield as much as they could – and who insisted on a firm, but not necessarily heartless, policy of efficiency to translate this aim into reality. Mindful of criticisms levelled at his father, Henry cut the number of annuities paid out of the duchy's revenue by more than a third; he could make good use of the savings thus achieved. His personal involvement in improving the duchy's financial contribution to the crown's income is seen in the meeting of its council which the king attended in London in February 1417, when reforms aimed at increasing revenue were put into effect, and in the way that the council held over decision-making on important matters until he could be consulted. Not surprisingly, the reign witnessed a very substantial rise in the 'clear yield', from about £2500 under Henry IV to some £6400 in 1419. [10]

Henry made use of other estate revenues which had not been available to his father. The recovery of the principality of Wales from the rebellion was encouraged by the king's policy of moderation towards it, [11] which signalled a return to a higher level of revenue than had been obtained in the last decade or more. Whereas north Wales and

[9] Somerville, *Duchy of Lancaster*, i, 161, 187.
[10] This paragraph owes much to R.R. Davies, 'Baronial accounts, incomes, and arrears in the later middle ages', *EconHR*, 2nd ser., 21 (1968), 219–29; Harriss, 'Financial policy', *Henry V: practice of kingship*, pp. 169–70; Somerville, *Duchy of Lancaster*, i, 187, 189.
[11] R.A. Griffiths, 'The Glyndŵr rebellion in north Wales through the eyes of an Englishman', *BBCS*, 22 (1967); W.R.M. Griffiths, 'Patronage, politics and the principality of Wales', p. 76.

south Wales had brought in about £1000 at the turn of the century, the average for the period 1409–20, at £3100, showed a 'spectacular' improvement, which made up for the rather paltry £250 which the principality contributed to the royal coffers.[12] The duchy of Cornwall, unlike many parts of the country, was going through a period of prosperity which coincided with the period of Henry's rule. It had already provided him with much of his revenue when he was Prince. Now, as king, he was able to benefit from the high level of production in the Cornish tin mines, from a developing textile manufacture, and, best indicator of all, from increasing accession, or inheritance fines which, raised in 1406, were raised yet again in 1413 and 1420, a date which also saw wages for labourers, both skilled and semi-skilled, begin to rise.[13] The earldom of Chester was a further, albeit much less profitable, source of revenue to the crown. The Prince had already used revenue from the county to help pay for the force sent to support the Burgundians in the late autumn of 1411. Although payments to the royal exchequer were only made after 1417 (and consisted largely of the mises, or taxes, raised in the county), the local exchequer was used as a spending department through which a number of royal annuitants received their fees. With the ending of the Welsh war, and therefore the reason for the earldom's separate existence, Cheshire revenues were slowly integrated into those of the crown. They had made a very useful, if unspectacular, contribution to the royal finances.[14]

Revenue from land was one thing; revenue from fees or charges was another. Henry set out to make the most of this. Exemptions from the paying of fees to the Hanaper had been virtually abolished in the previous reign. Henry made the most of the crown's right to grant pardons, not usually for major crimes, but rather for technical misdemeanours which had been committed. In 1414 Edmund, earl of March, was fined the huge sum of 10,000 marks (£6666 13s. 4d.) for having married without royal permission,[15] while in 1413 Henry sought sureties, together totalling 80,000 marks, from three earls and seven lords, as part of an attempt to secure order and good behaviour from them.[16] The payment of increments on sums rendered for the

[12] Harriss, 'Financial policy', p. 169, n.10.
[13] J. Hatcher, *Rural economy and society in the duchy of Cornwall, 1300–1500* (Cambridge, 1970), pp. 149–56.
[14] See Curry, 'Cheshire and the royal demesne', 113–31, and, for further detail, A.E. Curry, 'The demesne of the county palatine of Chester in the early fifteenth century' (Univ. of Manchester MA thesis, 1977), upon which the article is based.
[15] It is likely, however, that he never paid the sum during this reign. See P.A. Johnson, *Duke Richard of York, 1411–1460* (Oxford, 1988), pp. 8–9.
[16] Harriss, 'The king and his magnates', *Henry V: practice of kingship*, p. 46. Once again, we cannot be certain that the money was actually paid over.

rent of lands held by the crown or for the farm of the ulnage (fees paid for the inspection or measurement of cloth) is a marked characteristic of many entries in the Fine Rolls for the first year or two of the reign. On such occasions Henry exercised his fiscal rights to the full. Sometimes, such as when he charged King's Lynn £100 for the renewal of its charter (in the past, it was said, £10 or ten marks had been demanded), this caused resentment.[17] Such steps may not have brought in a great deal, but they showed Henry determined to make his royal rights pay. When considered alongside the exercise of his rights over the marriage of wards, or over the temporalities of major churches at times of vacancy, the revenue from such sources can be shown to have increased by nearly fifty per cent (£10,260 to £15,210) between 1406–07 and 1420–21, a significant increase by any standard.

There is no doubt that Henry attributed very great importance to the revenue which came to him from the customs and subsidies on trade, particularly on wool and cloth. The great days of the wool trade were by now part of history, but since the middle of the fourteenth century the manufacture and export of cloth had gone some way towards making up the shortfall. Trade, which piracy had done much to dislocate, needed to be encouraged and protected. The active policy followed at the behest of parliament and encouraged by his chancellor, Beaufort, of protecting commerce at sea, particularly in the reign's early years, would have had as its aim the attempt to make trade with foreign partners as lucrative as possible. The imposition of legislation to protect commercial activity at sea, and the use of diplomacy to make treaties and truces, to protect trade, was one way of proceeding.[18] Another was to see that the customs due to the king were properly collected. It was typical of Henry that, within a few days of becoming king, he should have ensured that all ports through which wool might pass should be provided with a proper customs house.[19] As in much else, Henry was not an innovator; he was simply intent that the existing system should be made to work efficiently for the crown's and, ultimately, the country's benefit.[20]

---

[17] Harriss, 'Financial policy', pp. 170–2. In December 1414, Kingston-upon-Hull paid only 20 marks (£13 6s. 8d.) for its charter, a more reasonable sum. (*Charters and letters patent granted to Kingston-upon-Hull*, trans. J.R. Boyle (Hull, 1945), p. 30, a reference which I owe to Elizabeth Danbury.)

[18] Truces at sea were proclaimed in London when they were made or renewed (e.g. *Letter-book I*, pp. 123, 163).

[19] Harriss, 'Financial policy', p. 173.

[20] Professor R.R. Davies ('Baronial accounts', 228) has stressed that making the existing system work properly, not the creation of innovation, was characteristic of the way estates were managed at this period.

Although, by the fifteenth century, 'the king was granted the customs as a matter of course',[21] such a grant was made by special grace and depended upon the goodwill of the Commons. This was underlined when, in the parliament which met in November 1415, immediately after the victory won at Agincourt, the Commons voted the subsidy on wools, hides and wine, 'for the life of our said sovereign lord the king for him to dispose of the proceeds at his gracious will and discretion',[22] the only known precedent for such an act being a similar grant made to Richard II in 1398 under very different circumstances. The concession was not only a way of recompensing the king for his achievements. More significantly, it constituted a major vote of confidence in Henry, not least in the manner in which he was organizing his finances. The contrast between the increasingly stringent criticism levelled at Henry IV in the first seven years or so of his reign, and the grant of subsidies for life to his son, for him to do what he wanted with, could not have been more striking.

What did the customs, 'the bedrock of royal finance', contribute to Henry's wealth? The average number of sacks of wool exported annually during the reign was about 13,800, but in three years the figure was not reached (in 1421–22 by a very large margin). The export of cloth during Henry's reign averaged some 27,900 broadcloths annually, a figure not achieved in four years, two of these (1415–16 and 1419–20) being years during which wool exports also failed to come up to average.[23] In all, the gross yield was probably between £48,000 and £49,000, a little better, but not much, than had been achieved in the second half of the previous reign. In view of the fact that the increase was largely due to the activities of denizen merchants (that of aliens being in decline), it was an achievement of some importance.

A consideration of parliamentary and clerical taxation brings us up against extraordinary taxation, namely that which was voted not, as Henry insisted, for him to spend as he wished, but only for certain tasks, the most important of which was the defence of the realm's interests. Parliamentary subsidies, ten and a third of which, each valued nominally at about £37,000, were accorded to Henry during his reign, were closely linked with the war against France. In the relatively brief five-year period between November 1414, when the king had all but decided to go to war, and the autumn of 1419, when the conquest of Normandy was complete, Henry was granted eight

---

[21] Jacob, *Fifteenth century*, p. 78.
[22] '. . . a tout la vie notre dit soverain Seigneur le Roy, pur ent despoiser & ordeiner a sez tres gracious volunte & discretione . . .' (*RP*, iv, 64).
[23] Figures are based on E.M. Carus-Wilson and O. Coleman (eds), *England's export trade, 1275–1547* (Oxford, 1963), pp. 56–7, 91–2.

and a third subsidies (eighty per cent of the parliamentary subsidy)
for the purposes of war, a very high rate of taxation applied over a
relatively brief period of time. The point is made only a little differently when it is noted that subsidies were voted at only seven of the
parliaments which met during the reign. At the other four, subsidies
were not asked for.[24] On the other hand, at three of the parliaments,
a double subsidy was agreed,[25] while in October 1419 the king was
granted an extra third above the normal subsidy, specifically for the
repayment of those who had lent money to the crown.[26]

It is worth drawing attention again to two further factors which
show how intensely Henry was pursuing his quest of collecting money
for the war, and of doing so as quickly as he could. One was the
bringing forward, or acceleration, of parliamentary subsidies from the
date agreed for their collection to another time, to the benefit of
the king and the disadvantage of his subjects. In October 1415, and
again in the parliament which met over Easter 1416, the collection of
parts of subsidies was accelerated, the first by a mere two months,
the second, however, by nearly half a year.[27]

In the spring and early summer of 1416, Henry needed money
badly. The defence of Harfleur was proving costly, while the visit of
Sigismund and his court which, along with that of the count of Holland, was 'alle at the Kinges cost',[28] was turning out to be very
expensive. At the same time, the assembling of a fleet to relieve Harfleur was a further drain upon already severely strained resources. In
the circumstances, Henry's methods of raising money, in particular
what may have been regarded as a growing propensity to seek the
acceleration of subsidies, were to meet opposition. This was made
clear in the parliament which met in October 1416 when, while voting
two subsidies for collection in 1417, the Commons demanded that
acceleration should cease, and that loans should be sought if the king
required money quickly. The point was underlined a year later,[29] and
it is notable that this was the last occasion in which the matter was
raised during the reign.

The sense of urgency felt by Henry in the years 1415 and 1416 is
further seen in the way that the church came to be involved in the
process of raising money for the war. Ecclesiastics formed an important group for whose financial support Henry could feel much gratitude since they contributed very substantially to the costs of the war.

[24] Those of April 1414, March 1416, December 1420 and May 1421.
[25] Those of November 1414, October 1416 and November 1417.
[26] *RP*, iv, 117. The sum was to be raised by November 1420.
[27] See above, ch.17.
[28] *Brut*, ii, 381.
[29] *RP*, iv, 107.

In all, the southern province of Canterbury raised eight and a half tenths, the northern one of York seven and a half, on clerical benefices whose real value was generally regarded as being more than £10 a year. The southern province was not only bigger, it was also richer, and produced markedly more than did its northern counterpart. Both, however, were affected by the devastation of war: clerical revenues in Wales (which was in the southern province) would have been reduced by the effects of the Glyn Dŵr revolt, while the northern province which, at this time, consisted of the sees of York, Durham and Carlisle had experienced the ravages of war waged by the Scots. Pleas for exemption, not all genuine, were therefore often heard. None the less, the church made a very sizeable contribution to the moneys being raised for war, probably a good third of the value of a secular subsidy, raised on a minority of the people, although one whose members, especially the monasteries, were not necessarily among society's poor.

The northern province met in York, the southern one in London. For that reason, if for no other, pressure could more easily be applied on the southern body to meet royal demands. Such pressures were not unlike those imposed on parliaments, both in their nature and in their timing. The southern convocation, meeting in December 1417, received a visit from the chancellor, Thomas Langley, the duke of Exeter and the earls of Northumberland and Westmorland, sent by the lieutenant, Bedford, to explain the king's needs for the war; the result was the vote of a double tenth.[30] Two years later the king ordered the southern convocation to convene at the end of October, an exceptional step as far as this assembly was concerned, but, as Henry wrote to archbishop Chichele, he was incurring expenses in his war which his subjects must be called upon to pay.[31] Further pressure was sometimes exerted by arranging the meetings of the convocations to coincide with those of parliament, thereby exerting influence on one body to follow the example of the others. Between November 1414 and January 1415, for example, parliament and both convocations met: all voted either a double subsidy or a double tenth. Three years later, in November 1417, both parliament and the southern convocation allowed the king a double subsidy or tenth; on this occasion, however, the northern convocation did not vote more than a single tenth. Like the laity, the clergy were persuaded by the urgency of the situation to accelerate tenths voted by them at an earlier date. In the spring of 1416, with preparations for the expedition to relieve Harfleur under way, the southern clergy brought forward to June a tenth payable in November (in the end it does not appear to have been

[30] *Register of Henry Chichele*, iii, 32.
[31] Ibid., iii, 51; *CCR, 1419–1422*, p. 51.

paid until February 1420),[32] while in January 1417 the convocation of
the northern province agreed to accelerate by two months a tenth due
in June, and voted another to be collected in November.

The convocations showed their practical support for Henry not only
through the sums which they voted, but also by making those votes
coincide with the times he needed them most. The timing of a subsidy
was almost as important as the willingness to make it. Between
October 1414 and January 1416 the convocations voted seven tenths
(four from the south, three from the north). This was almost half their
contribution for the entire reign (sixteen tenths in all) voted within
the space of some fifteen months which coincided with the period of
intense taxation allowed by parliament. Moreover the church might
be relied upon to provide at those moments when others were less
willing to do so. Through its votes at the southern convocations which
met in October 1419 and May 1421, and at the northern meetings
of January 1420 and September 1421, the clergy contributed in a
substantial way towards the costs of war at the very time that parliamentary support was at a low level.

The sums voted by parliament and the convocations came in cash,
a point of importance to a king using this revenue for war. Yet the
subsidies, together with the 'ordinary' revenue of the crown (the
sources of which were now being exploited as well as they could be),
were still insufficient to pay for the high expenditure of war. In order
to raise more money, Henry was obliged to turn elsewhere and to use
other methods in his attempt to make up the shortfall. To achieve
this, he had to borrow, and to do so on a scale greater than ever
before. Loans raised in the three financial years between 1414 and
1417 showed what could be done. The response to the personal effort
which Henry, on his visit to England in 1421, put into raising funds
for the war was likewise a sign of what a king might achieve if he
appealed directly and persuasively to his people.[33] By the same token,
the lack of success in raising a loan in 1419 (which can be linked to
the reluctance shown by parliament before it finally voted its subsidy
in that year) may very well be attributed, in some degree, to the king's
absence from England at that time.

What was the king appealing to when he asked for loans? Certainly,
it was to personal loyalty, to recognition of his achievement, to future
participation in what he wished to be regarded as a communal enterprise against the enemy. On two occasions, in 1416 and again in 1419,
he sought loans to be raised with explicit parliamentary approval.
This gave both Henry and those who lent money the moral and

[32] *Register of Henry Chichele*, iii, 19–21.
[33] See above, ch.17.

practical support of parliamentary assurance or guarantee given in the king's presence (and, in 1416, further guaranteed personally by Clarence, Bedford and Gloucester that these commitments would be honoured were Henry to die) that the loans would be safeguarded by specific subsidies, both lay and clerical, parts of which would be used to repay them.[34] Furthermore, in the parliament of May 1421 Henry was permitted by parliamentary authority to raise loans for the coming campaign on terms arranged by his council. If parliament would not vote a subsidy, it would do the next best thing and formally approve a loan, giving support to anything that the king and the council were to arrange in this matter.[35] Such evidence suggests that loans were not raised by an irresponsible king acting on impulse, but that the financial implications had been thought out by those concerned.

It may be recalled that loans were regarded as a vestige of the obligation of subjects to help their king in time of necessity.[36] Yet they did not constitute a tax in the strict sense, but were a means of raising money quickly from persons of property, men of importance in their localities, and royal annuitants, all of whom would expect the sums lent to be repaid from the next available tax, such as a clerical or parliamentary grant. A loan was evidence of the king's personal standing, support for his policy and recognition of the crown's political and financial authority and good faith, a test of a subject's loyalty to the crown. In a word, it was a test of unity.

Henry began to test that unity early in his reign. He had been king only four months when the first references appear to loans, received from individual merchants (one of them, Richard Whittington, lent £2,000), from the city of London, as well as from bishops and abbots, while in 1414 he had to borrow a further £2000 and another sum from the great London draper, John Hende.[37] Both an active policy aimed at doing away with piracy at sea, and diplomatic initiatives intended to establish acceptable trading terms with the duke of Burgundy, would have constituted the kinds of step for which loans from London, either from individual merchants or from the city corporately, would have been provided. In the spring of 1415, when Henry realized that he had insufficient cash to pay the army which he planned to lead to France later in the year, it was to London, among other places, that he turned.

[34] *RP*, iv, 95–6, 117–19.
[35] Ibid., iv, 130.
[36] On this, see K.B. McFarlane, 'Loans to the Lancastrian kings: the problem of inducement', *Cambridge Historical Journal*, 9 (1947); G.L. Harriss, 'Aids, loans and benevolences', *Historical Journal*, 6 (1963).
[37] Steel, *Receipt of the Exchequer*, pp. 149–51; Jacob, *Fifteenth century*, p. 136.

On 10 March the mayor, aldermen and others were summoned to the Tower to be informed by the king of his plans and, doubtless, of the shortfall in his finances. Four days later a second meeting was held at the Guildhall, attended by archbishop Chichele, who had powerful family connections in the city, Henry Beaufort, the king's brothers, Bedford and Gloucester, and Edward, duke of York, at which, under the mayor's chairmanship, it was agreed that the king should receive a corporate loan of 10,000 marks (£6666 13s. 4d.) on the security of a great collar of gold, composed of crown and antelopes richly enamelled and bejewelled, the formal indenture being sealed on 16 June.[38] In addition to this, many individual loans were made, more or less willingly. Bishop Beaufort lent £1983 in June, followed by a further 1000 marks in November.[39] The county of Norfolk, on the other hand, did so with much less good grace,[40] while a group of northern Italian merchants only contributed after they had been threatened with imprisonment by Beaufort, acting in his capacity as chancellor, sitting with a small committee of the king's council.[41]

Cash loans in the financial year 1414–15 amounted to some £27,000, over a fifth of the £131,000 made available that year,[42] money which, paid through the exchequer to the wardrobe, was thereafter used for purposes of war.[43] Henry was now well launched on a policy which was to make his reign the 'peak period of borrowing by the crown'.[44] In the year 1416–17, an accounting period which finished soon after Henry's departure on his second, and longest, expedition into France, he did even better, raising loans valued at £51,000, this figure approaching a third of the larger total of £161,000 raised in cash that year. The huge sum, a mark of singular confidence in Henry, his aims and his ability to fulfil them, drew upon every known device to bring money in. Once again, in March 1417, the city of London made a corporate loan of £3333 6s. 8d.[45] (half of what had been offered two years earlier) guaranteed by part of the subsidy on wool to be collected in the port of London. Later, in June, forty-three citizens lent £2160 in separate amounts ranging from 500 marks to £10, for which the king pledged them a Spanish sword mounted in gold and enriched with stones and pearls valued at £2000.[46] Such

---

[38] *Memorials of London*, pp. 603–5; *Letter-book I*, p. 143.
[39] Harriss, *Cardinal Beaufort*, p. 401.
[40] H.J. Hillen, *History of the borough of King's Lynn* (Norwich, 1907), i, 161–3.
[41] *PPC*, ii, 165–6.
[42] Harriss, 'Financial policy', p. 164.
[43] Steel, *Receipt of the Exchequer*, p. 181.
[44] Ibid., p. 180.
[45] Ibid., p. 155.
[46] *Letter-book I*, pp. 203–4, 214.

guarantees were necessary: the demands of war upon the crown's finances had not permitted the discharge of certain large debts already contracted, for which items of royal jewellery still stood surety. Once again, too, Henry Beaufort showed his loyalty to the house of Lancaster and to its leader's policies by supporting him with a loan of £14,000.[47] Of significance, too, because of their political implications, were the many small loans made in the year by individuals. Now that the crown was finding it less easy to raise corporate loans, it was having to turn to both the very big lender (Beaufort) and to many small ones to satisfy its needs.[48]

The cash flow was beginning to dry up.[49] Perhaps men were reluctant to lend without sufficient guarantees; perhaps there was a growing doubt about how far men should become involved in what the king was trying to achieve. More likely, however, it was a growing shortage of cash, to which several chroniclers refer, and a fear that the export of bullion to pay soldiers in France was doing the economy of England no good. Certainly, the output of both gold and silver coinage declined in the years 1417 to 1419. Significantly, when Henry asked the city of London for help in August 1418, he asked not for money but for provisions, a measure which involved no export of coinage.[50] Yet when he sought loans in 1419 and 1420, Henry won some support from a number of individual members of parliament who acted as commissioners in the counties which they represented in either one or, in some cases, both years.[51] None the less, the result of their efforts, particularly in 1420, was disappointing.[52]

However, when Henry tried again in 1421, the results were more satisfactory. This time the king was in England, and on 6 May, after his travels around the country in search of support for the war, he

---

[47] Harriss, *Cardinal Beaufort*, p. 401.

[48] Steel, *Receipt of the exchequer*, pp. 154–8. Bristol lent 1000 marks (£666 13s. 4d.) in July 1417 (*CPR, 1416–1422*, p. 111).

[49] J.L. Kirby, 'Henry V and the city of London', *History Today*, 26 (1976), 227.

[50] Ibid., 228.

[51] See above, ch.17.

[52] R.A. Newhall, 'The war finances of Henry V and the duke of Bedford', *EHR*, 36 (1921), 173. By the autumn of 1419 Henry's need for cash was so great that, through the council, he ordered the arrest of his stepmother, Joan, on charges of sorcery. These were never pressed, but they gave Henry the excuse to seize her dowry, worth £666 13s. 4d. a year, and other revenue for his own advantage. At a stroke, this increased, by some ten per cent, the revenue of a government which, after June 1420, would have owed the new queen, Katharine, a dowry of the same value. At the end of his life the king ordered that Joan should have both her liberty and her money restored to her. (A.R. Myers, 'The captivity of a royal witch: the household accounts of queen Joan of Navarre, 1419–21', *BJRL*, 24 (1940), 262–84.)

was at Lambeth, where he received a report that ordinary revenue in the past year had been £55,700, of which indirect taxation yielded £40,600 (some £26,000 of which came from wool), the remaining £15,100 being derived from payments by sheriffs and feudal incidents.[53] If the war were to be pursued as it should be, Henry needed money, plenty of it, and quickly. Beaufort at once lent £17,666, of which £14,000 were secured on customs' receipts from Southampton.[54] The remainder came from a variety of other sources: towns,[55] many of them ports, contributed, as did churchmen, including a number of bishops, deans and chapters, and abbots. While few of the nobility or knightly class subscribed (in the circumstances this was hardly surprising), many gentry and yeomen did so.

The reaction of the counties was variable. It is possible to see the personal influence of the king in this matter. The people of Lancashire responded well. Men of the counties through which Henry passed were, on the whole, more generous: Hertfordshire and, more notably, Yorkshire (where he stayed some while and where the loan was more acceptable to the gentry than was active military service) and Lincolnshire (where, near the end of his tour, Henry demanded to have the names of those who would not serve). It is notable, in addition, that Bedfordshire and Northamptonshire, through which queen Katharine travelled on her way to join Henry at Leicester, also contributed well, as did Kent and Sussex, Devon and Somerset.[56] Perhaps much depended on the effectiveness locally of those who helped to raise the loans. As in 1419 and 1420, some members of parliament gave assistance in the shires which they represented. Although such figures are, in all likelihood, only approximate, they none the less make it clear that, by the end of his reign, Henry was having to appeal not only to traditional lenders (including churchmen) but also to a broad section of society which, while not properly noble, was still willing to assume certain responsibilities which the higher ranks, more and more directly involved in the war through service in the army, could no longer accept.

The deliberate policy of seeking loans was forced upon Henry at an early stage of his reign. By the end, it had become a means of raising money in which he outdid his immediate predecessors. It might be supposed that, after sealing the agreement at Troyes in May 1420, Henry would have transferred financial responsibility for paying

[53] Wylie and Waugh, *Henry the Fifth*, iii, 273–5.

[54] Harriss, *Cardinal Beaufort*, pp. 401–2.

[55] At the request of the king, twelve persons from the city of Hereford and its neighbourhood (including the mayor) contributed £40, the sum asked for (PRO, E 28/33). See also E 403/649 for further evidence of loans made in May 1421.

[56] Details in PRO, E 403/649, m.5.

for the war to his French lands and subjects. Parliament certainly reacted as if he had done this. Was Henry, in his last years, able to alter the balance of providing payment for the war from England to France, as historians have claimed?[57]

The answer must be that for the two years or so which separated the treaty of Troyes (with its commitment to further conquest) from his death, Henry faced very grave financial difficulties in France which he could only resolve, in the absence of parliamentary subsidy, by seeking loans in coinage of good value from his English subjects. Henry was thus recognizing what, for him and most Englishmen, must have been the unpalatable fact that, in spite of having successfully established a financial administration in the wake of his conquest, his French possessions were experiencing very serious economic and financial problems. These were having adverse effects upon the king's ability to raise the revenue which he needed to further his war aims in the ways he would have wished.

By 1420 the conquest had left its mark on most of the well-defended urban centres, Caen, Cherbourg, Falaise and, most notably, Rouen experiencing physical damage to walls and amenities which it took time and money to restore. Trade, both internal and external, had been disrupted. Partly because of the flight of substantial sections of the population, the rural economy suffered and the cost of food rose sharply; nor did the English always find it easy to reverse the process of migration from the countryside. Important, too, were the climatic conditions which prevented the rapid return of the duchy to a state of economic normality. In 1420 a bad summer, experienced by much of Europe, brought adverse effects to the economy. Hot weather in both 1418 and 1421 left epidemics in its wake, while the cold weather of 1420–21 lasted until the end of May, resulting in the starvation of many and the upsetting of the normal cycle of production. In brief, Henry's military activity was being carried out under conditions which were bound to have unfavourable effects upon his ability to get Normandy to pay for it.[58]

These conditions were compounded by others which, although aggravated by war, were born out of something other than the English conquest. France already faced a growing economic and financial crisis of some dimension by the time that the English invaded. By 1419, with the invasion in full swing, a currency crisis was being felt both in Paris and in the areas overrun by the occupying army. In certain respects, the problem which Henry faced was one familiar to

[57] E.g. Newhall, *English conquest*, pp. 150–1.
[58] Allmand, *Lancastrian Normandy*, pp. 154–7. The siege of Rouen had also brought an epidemic to the city in 1419 (Arch. dép., Seine-Maritime, G 9195).

his administrators at Calais and certain English ports who had already had to confront attempts to bring foreign currencies of poor quality into England. In Normandy, where coinage from a number of different parts of France circulated, the effect was bound to be adverse, since the English coinage was the only one not to have suffered recent debasement. The general effect upon all sections of society was disastrous.[59] Those, such as the farmers of the king's taxes, who had to pay the crown in good coin found themselves in great hardship, as did the crown which thus faced increasing difficulties in persuading people to farm taxes. As was said in March 1422, it was hard to force people whose revenues had been diminished by war to pay their taxes in any currency other than the poor one which they had at that moment.[60]

In its simplest terms, Henry's problem was to restore the value of the currency used in his French lands. From his experience as king of England, he already knew of the debasements which the dukes of Burgundy favoured. With both parties courting popularity, the civil conflict in France had led first the Burgundians in January 1418 and, later in the year, the Armagnacs to announce the abolition of the *aide* which, because it brought in so little, could be deftly replaced by a debasement in the value of the currency.[61] It is to Henry's credit that, faced with this situation, he chose to counter it by deliberately sticking to the principle of taxation and to his attempt to rebuild the value of the coinage.[62] By August 1419, with the consent of his council, the king ordered the by now traditional 'quatrième' on drink and a five per cent tax on other goods to be levied in Normandy, as had been the practice prior to the English descent upon the duchy.[63] Later, on 12 January 1420, noting that much inferior coinage was entering Normandy from France, Henry ordered money to be coined at the mint at Rouen, the designs and weights of the new currency being set out in detail.[64]

In December 1420, on his first visit to Paris, Henry won the agreement of the estates of France that strong bullionist measures should be taken, the estates voting a double subsidy, payable in unminted metal, intended to provide the new coinage.[65] In an ordinance dated

[59] Allmand, *Lancastrian Normandy*, pp. 157–8.
[60] AN, KK 323.
[61] J. Favier, *Les contribuables parisiens à la fin de la guerre de cent ans. Les rôles d'impôt de 1421, 1423 et 1438* (Geneva, 1970), p. 4; *Ordonnances des rois de France*, x, 429, 450, 455.
[62] G. Ll. Thompson, 'The Anglo-Burgundian régime in Paris, 1420–1436' (Univ. of Oxford D.Phil. thesis, 1984), pp. 42–4.
[63] BN, Ms fr.26043, no.5409.
[64] Ibid., 26043, no.5464.
[65] *Contribuables parisiens*, p. 4.

19 December 1420, Henry set out the context for his reform.[66] The country required proper administration, based on justice, order and the ability to fight a war. Nothing could be achieved without extra financial help, for, as was well known, the royal domain was of little value. From 1 February 1421 not only would the 'gabelle' (salt tax) and the 'quatrième' still be collected: a levy of five per cent would be imposed on the sale of cloth of gold, wool and silk. All basic cereal foods, however, would remain exempt. These taxes, to be raised more from the sale of luxuries than necessities, from the better-off rather than from the poor, would be used for the good of the entire community.

The high level of taxation was certainly required to cover the costs of war and administration. It was also deliberately used to flush out good money (which men might be hoarding) for reminting. As such, taxation was employed as a means of enforcing the first priority, reform of the currency. What Henry needed was to bring good coinage and sound metal into open circulation for purposes of reminting at a good standard. On 18 January 1421 Henry met the estates of Normandy at Rouen.[67] He obtained from them their agreement to raise 400,000 *l.t.* (*livre tournois*) a quarter of which (in practice 85,000 *l.t.*) was to be in royal hands by the beginning of March, and a further 55,000 *l.t.* in good money by May. The tax only came in slowly: it was still being collected in 1422, by which time Henry had received between 250,000 and 300,000 *l.t.* of the sum originally voted. Along with this tax, Henry also demanded that those with an income of more than 100 *l.t.* should surrender one silver mark, for which they were to receive a coin of inferior value in return.[68] The policy of making sound metal available for the public good was being fiercely pursued.

The sacrifices, which affected the rich as well as the poor, were considerable. On 4 July 1421 (by which time Henry had returned to France for the last time) the value of the *gros*, hitherto the equivalent of 20 *deniers*, was suddenly reduced to five.[69] Such a step, however, was not drastic enough. In September it was noted in Paris that good money was still lacking, so that on 3 November the value of the *gros* was further reduced to two *deniers*.[70] In Normandy, so Pierre Cochon reported,[71] there was opposition to the payment of taxation in good

---

[66] *Ordonnances des rois de France*, xi, 109–11.

[67] H. Prentout, *Les états provinciaux de Normandie* (3 vols, Caen, 1925–27), i, 145; iii, 9; *Chronique normande de Pierre Cochon*, p. 343; BL, Add. Ch.507.

[68] 'Roles normands et français', no.937.

[69] BN, Ms lat. 5932A, fo.24; Ms fr.26043, no.5464.

[70] AN, X^{1a} 4793, fo.107v.

[71] *Chronique normande de Pierre Cochon*, p. 343. Opposition to the tax is recorded in BN, Ms fr.26044, no.5634.

money, which, since it cost the clergy dear, some refused to pay, while confiscated fiefs put out to farm in July and September 1421 attracted little bidding.[72] Improvement came, but it did so only slowly, and involved bringing silver from England. None the less, by November 1421 sufficient good money was being collected to keep the mints, now established in Rouen and St Lô, in business, new coins being sent to Caen castle for safe-keeping.[73]

Henry, however, did not immediately order this sound coin to be put into circulation. On 30 November, in a further ordinance on the coinage, he emphasized that an essential element of a stable society was a stable currency.[74] While claiming credit for having prepared new coinage, he stressed that the dauphin had been infiltrating Normandy with an inferior currency resembling the one which Henry had minted in the hope of attracting the latter into his own jurisdiction. As an act of retaliation, Henry had decided to put poor coinage into circulation. Now, however, he planned to issue the good one, including gold nobles made in England. No steps should be taken which might jeopardize the success of this policy. A fine summer in 1422, bringing with it an abundant harvest, was a great help in re-establishing economic order.

It would be wrong to give Henry more credit than he deserves over the matter of monetary reform and stabilization. The fact remains that he had arrived in France at the moment at which a crisis, already developing for some time, was coming to a head. The economic difficulties which he faced constituted an important and integral part of the war which he was waging against the dauphin. It was a challenge which Henry faced and took up. He had no choice but to do so, for the area of France which he claimed to rule, as well as the wider kingdom, was in the grip of difficulties from which England itself was not exempt. It was because he could not expect instant results to the measures which he had initiated in 1420 and in the first days of 1421 that Henry had come to seek loans from corporations and institutions in England to tide him over his immediate difficulties. In France he had had to act boldly, taking steps which might win him no political popularity, and which might not even provide the remedies which he sought. According to Pierre Cochon, the year 1421 was the worst man had ever known: in a state of general shortage, commissioners sought out those who charged excessively high prices.[75] Yet, by the end of the year, the value of money was returning to a realistic level. The

[72] BL., Add. Chs 3554, 302.
[73] *DKR*, 42, p. 429.
[74] 'Roles normands et français', no.1058.
[75] *Chronique normande de Pierre Cochon*, pp. 344–6.

troubles over the state of the currency, begun in 1415 and aggravated by the English invasion, were ending. Some kind of normality was returning. From 1423 until 1428 Normandy enjoyed a brief period of relative economic stability. Not without justice historians have praised Henry for this particular achievement.[76] He took on the dauphin in a war over monetary stability, a war with wide implications for his conquest. It was an aspect of their struggle in which, although he did not live to enjoy the benefits, he may be said to have been the victor – on points, at least.

[76] Allmand, *Lancastrian Normandy*, p. 158.

Chapter 19

CROWN, UNITY AND NATIONHOOD

A poem, composed in English to commemorate Henry's coronation in April 1413, indicated the way in which its anonymous author saw the future. England could be successful if she were at peace with herself, and if her people would 'stande with the kyng [and] mayntene the crown'. 'What doth a kynges crowne signyfye', he went on, 'whan stones & floures on sercle is bent?' His answer was more metaphysical. The crown, he suggested, consisted of 'Lordis, comouns & clergye / To be all at on[e] assent', while 'The leste lyge-man, with body & rent, / He is a parcel of the crowne.' The crown symbolized the visible unity of a country's people, a 'sercle' which the king could wear on his helm in battle. The stones set in the crown represented the king's subjects who, together, existed to defend its interests. From another point of view the stones could be taken to signify the wealth and power of the kingdom, notably its possessions abroad. These represented strength, but a strength which needed to be expressed in unity, for otherwise the country's enemies would triumph, and 'froo the right heire wolde take the crowne'. For that reason, the king had an obligation to rule well; if he failed, the unity thus visibly represented would be broken. England must be a kingdom of truth, justice and respect for the law; in this way the hearts of her people would be won. Together, the king and the Commons could bring greatness to the country. 'God, kepe in thy governance / Oure comely kyng, and save the crowne.'[1]

The theme of unity was further emphasized in a series of sermons preached during the reign by a man (probably a Benedictine monk) 'particularly partial to the allegory of war', whose choice of language reflected a marked military influence.[2] England, he argued, had experienced many difficulties over recent years. Yet the appearance

---

[1] 'God, save the kyng, and kepe the crown', *Twenty-six political and other poems*, ed. J. Kail (EETS, London, 1904), pp. 50–5, ll.8–12, 15–16, 40, 151–2. Text reprinted in *Historical poems of the XIVth and XVth centuries*, ed. R.H. Robbins (New York, 1959), pp. 45–9.

[2] R.M. Haines, 'Church, society and politics in the early fifteenth century, as viewed from an English pulpit', *Church, society and politics* (*Studies in Church History, 12*), ed. L. G. D. Baker (Oxford, 1975), p. 145.

of Henry V, 'the celestial knight',[3] was to bring hope and change, and the wheel of fortune, recently on the down turn, would begin to curve upwards again. In one sermon, the preacher used the imagery of the ship to demonstrate the country's unity.[4] The people were the hull; the clergy and nobility represented the great fore- and aft-castles; the saints, whose intercessions were always being sought, were the top-castle. Commands were given by the 'maistur mariner, oure worthi prince', Henry V himself, who had his hand on the rudder of the 'faire schippe'. The vessel was propelled by the power of oars, which the author likened to the prayers and litanies of those at home and the processions in which they took part. 'Let us alle row to gedir,' he exhorted his listeners, a statement reflecting both a desire for the country to act as one in the war against France and a confidence in the effectiveness of prayer shared by the king himself. Prayer was not only a supplication for divine aid; it was also a bond created between those who prayed for a particular cause.[5]

The crucial importance of the part to be played by the king himself in bringing about unity was well understood. How he ruled was a matter of public concern, and writers were not afraid to offer him advice which, in general, depicted how contemporaries saw a king fulfilling his functions, in particular how he dealt with problems peculiar to his time.[6] In his last years as Prince and at the start of his reign, Henry was subjected to much such advice on how best to fulfil his role as king, advice which took as its starting point the need for him to rule for the good of all his people. The urge to offer counsel, in itself a sign of the times, arose out of the fact that neither Richard II, regarded as having ruled deviously and arbitrarily, nor Henry IV, seen as lacking competence and political sense rather than honesty, had made a favourable impression as king. When Henry succeeded his father, Englishmen had lacked positive leadership from the crown for well nigh half a century.

As in France, where monarchy was also facing considerable, if different, problems, this had led men to speculate about authority and how it should be exercised. It was a fruitful field for exploitation by anyone with views to express on how best to resolve the crisis in the relationship between king and subject which had grown since the declining years of England's last popular king, Edward III.

---

[3] '. . . iste celestis miles' (ibid., p. 150, n.54); '. . . qui digne portat gladium Domini' (Oxford, All Souls College, Ms 42, fo.308, kindly shown me by Mr P.S. Lewis).

[4] Text in R.M. Haines, ' "Our master mariner, our sovereign lord": a contemporary preacher's view of King Henry V', *Medieval studies*, 38 (1976), 87–96.

[5] See Henry V's exhortation at Agincourt: 'nowe is gode tyme, for alle Engelond prayeth for vs' (*Brut*, ii, 378); see also *Gesta*, pp. 85–7.

[6] Harriss, *Henry V: practice of kingship*, introduction.

Richard II had divided the nation and had paid the price. When, in October 1399, archbishop Arundel, as chancellor, had stated that Henry IV intended to provide good and just rule,[7] he had meant that the new king would no longer rule by his singular will, but with those whose mature advice he could trust. Henry IV, however, never quite fulfilled this undertaking. The trust of his people, which he might have won by meeting the crisis of confidence head on, was never achieved.

A proper understanding of how his contemporaries viewed Henry thus requires us to appreciate that, for them, he was a figure of hope, whose accession to power could mark better days. There exist many signs of this, some more explicit than others.[8] Thomas Hoccleve, the clerk to the privy seal office whose work, *The Regement of Princes*, was dedicated to the Prince in 1412, stressed the need for a king to keep his coronation oath – and all that that implied.[9] Popular versifiers, on their part, demanded a more vigorous application of the rule of law and a purge of those who brought disorder to the country.[10] In parliament, the chancellor, Henry Beaufort, stressed the need for the new king to take advice before acting.[11] More veiled, and more effective for being so, were the words uttered by William Stourton, Speaker in the first parliament of the new reign, that the king knew full well that although the Commons had more than once had their request for proper government granted by his father, little had been done to achieve this.[12] Such expressions went beyond the normal urgings which might be expected on the accession of a new ruler. What men were seeking was a firm commitment to a break with the often negative practices of the past.

There is thus clear evidence of a widely felt hope that Henry would turn out to be a 'positive' king, a man of action. It was the need to portray him in this light which lay behind the descriptions of the sudden change which allegedly came over Henry on his accession.[13] We are in no position to judge the truth of the stories regarding the

---

[7] '. . . bone et jouste Governance' (*RP*, iii, 415).

[8] See how contemporaries discussed the portents of the weather on Henry's coronation day (*St Albans Chronicle*, p. 69 and ch.4 above).

[9] *Regement of princes*, pp. 80–1.

[10] *Twenty-six poems*, pp. 56–8. One is struck by how accurately the versifiers pinpointed the problems which came to demand the new king's attention: the weakness of the law; the difficulties experienced by those living on England's borders or by those whose occupation took them to sea; the divisive effect and the danger to the crown of the activities of the pseudo-Richard (ibid., pp.xvii–xviii).

[11] He spoke to the text 'Ante omnem actum, consilium stabile' (*RP*, iv, 3).

[12] Ibid., iv, 4.

[13] On these 'legends', see, for example, *Brut*, ii, 593–5; *First English Life*, pp. 17 and xx–lvi; Kingsford, *Henry V*, ch.6.

Prince, unable to influence events at the end of his father's reign and impatiently awaiting the time when he would take over the government in person. Did he mix with unsavoury associates, lie in wait to ambush his own receivers, brush with senior officers of the law, try on the crown taken from his father's bedside as he lay asleep? There is never smoke without fire. Yet the important point is that, collectively, these tales represented what Henry put behind him on becoming king. The emphasis is upon change, upon the future and what it would bring. The myth of the 'new man' reflected his subjects' hopes and aspirations for better things to come; equally it emphasized Henry's determination to break with the immediate political past (the night which he spent immediately upon his accession in the company of a holy hermit, unburdening himself of his sins, had both a spiritual and a symbolic significance), for he wanted to improve the relationship between the crown and its subjects so that they could face future problems together. The past was to be left behind and a new start made. Gone, now, would be the days of division. In their place would grow harmony, peace and, above all, unity within the community of the realm.

In 1413 the hopes of the nation in its new king were based on reasonable foundations. The Welsh rebels (the use of the word 'rebel' in this context is significant) had been defeated, and order was in the process of being restored in Wales. At home, Henry already had experience of government and of working with others in council. He had ideas, too, about finance, an area in which his father had been conspicuously lacking. The intervention in France which he had inspired in 1411 had been successful. What people had seen gave them confidence that the future might bring the end of the divisions which plagued early fifteenth-century English society.

The image of Henry as a man of action was to be carefully nurtured and sustained in parliament, where he was portrayed in a favourable light by his two chancellors, Henry Beaufort and Thomas Langley. These used the opening addresses presented at the beginning of each parliament to convey an image of a king concerned for the 'bon governance' of his people. Beaufort, in particular, was anxious to present a contrast between Henry IV's somewhat indecisive and colourless rule and the more vigorous search for the common good which could be expected from his son. From the very first, there was a strong emphasis on the king maintaining the promises made in his coronation oath, and problem areas, which required action, were at once identified. Quite quickly, the image of a king who acted for his people's advantage, whether in protecting trade, preserving law and order, or doing justice as any monarch should, was built up. This was a time for setting things right. If order and religion were threatened by Lollardy, then the king could be expected to take action. Likewise, if the French denied him his just claims, he could be counted upon to assert his rights. By the success won at Agincourt, seemingly against the odds, Henry stood vindicated.

Views expressed in parliament immediately after Agincourt correspond closely to those recorded in other texts. The news of the victory had reached London just as parliament was due to meet. The occasion gave Henry Beaufort the chance of emphasizing the principles which lay behind the king's rule: the establishment of justice in England and the recovery of his right in France (justice in another context), which could be achieved by following the biblical precept 'Fight for justice, and the Lord will fight for you'.[14] It was for this reason that he had sought to capture Harfleur; and while on their way to Calais, by the grace and help of God, the English had defeated the might of France, the greatest advantage ever achieved by the kingdom in so short a time. As the king had done for his people, Beaufort went on, so they must do for him, and be prepared to help him in any way they could. In practice, this meant providing the king with financial support.

In so doing parliament reflected another view which was finding common acceptance at this moment: the need to further co-operation between king and people for their joint good and honour. The king, the chancellor claimed, had gone to France to seek justice denied him by the French even though he did not have the financial backing he needed, pawning his jewels to obtain money, and relying upon the help of God and the justice of his cause to bring him success. His strength of character had brought him victory, to the honour of the crown, to his own personal reputation and to the advantage of his loyal subjects. In such circumstances, it would be wrong, Beaufort implied, for the country not to support its king. The vote of several taxes, including those of tunnage and poundage for life, was intended to reflect this happy state of union between crown and country.

By late 1416 Beaufort could look back on a period in which the king's early promise had been fulfilled; war should now be continued on a solid basis of success, a point underlined by Thomas Langley, who, in the autumn of 1417, followed his predecessor's lead by stressing the king's successes against all rebels and lawbreakers. In the parliaments of 1419 and 1420 the same theme of success (in the form of conquest) was maintained, as was another, the need for the people to support their king in his enterprises. The emphasis was very much on concerted action carried out jointly by ruler and subjects, to the

---

[14] 'Certa pro justicia, & Dominus pugnabit pro te' (*RP*, iv, 62).

benefit of both. This point was underlined by the use made of texts, mostly taken from the Old Testament, to act as exhortatory influences upon those who heard the chancellors speak in parliament. In a number sufficient for it not to have been a coincidence, the texts chosen were concerned with the need to achieve justice, with the use of force if required, and with the absolute requirement to have faith in the support of the Lord, acting through his deputy, the king. While in 1413 the need was essentially that of taking stock and deciding on a course of action,[15] and in early 1414 it was the application of the law of the land which assumed first importance,[16] by the end of that year Beaufort could exhort parliament (in Henry's presence) to seek out what was just and to fight for it to the death,[17] a clear reference to the king's determination to seek his rights in France. Thereafter, the emphasis was to be on the need to give support to Henry in all that he did and to enable him to follow the path which the victory at Agincourt had opened up.[18]

These ideas were being expressed in public in 1416. Within months of them being uttered, the anonymous author of the *Gesta Henrici Quinti*, a member of the king's private chapel and a man well versed in the thinking of the court, was at work on an account of the main events of Henry's reign as so far unfolded, an account which had much in common with the spirit which lay behind Beaufort's perorations before parliament. Like Beaufort, the anonymous chaplain strongly emphasized the ability of the king himself to shape events; his narrative had the king at its very centre, as its chief motivating force. The aim was to create an impression of organized rule by a man with a vision of what he wanted to achieve. If this meant war, it was not war which stemmed from the king's ambition to dominate, but from his desire to see justice done. The war was really God's war for justice, and Henry and the English army were merely his instruments.[19]

Things turned out this way because the king was blessed by God, as the *Gesta* was written to show. Here was the man who put down heresy, which was both a cause and a sign of division. In recognition, God brought him through that trial, through the trap laid for him at Southampton, and then came to his help at Agincourt. In so doing, God was also showing his support for the English nation, several

[15] Ibid., iv, 63.
[16] 'Posuit cor suum ad investigandas leges' (ibid., iv, 15).
[17] 'Usque ad mortem certabis pro Justicia, et quod justum est prosequere' (ibid., iv, 34).
[18] 'Ipse fecit nobis ita et nos ei faciamus' (ibid., iv, 62); 'iniciavit vobis viam' (ibid., iv, 70).
[19] *Gesta* pp. 17–19, 93.

times referred to as God's people,[20] a nation likened to Israel,[21] specially protected by divine power, led by an almost Moses-like figure of
faith and hope to whom God accorded direct assistance in time of
need.[22] It was by God's will that the passage over the river Somme
was found; and it was his will, too, to pronounce a 'divine sentence'
against the French at Agincourt.[23] God answered petitions, in particular those of the Virgin Mary, whose dower England was, and on the
feast of whose Assumption (15 August 1416) the naval victory against
the French and their allies had been won.[24] Closely associated with
the Virgin was St George, England's military patron and favourite
symbol of national awareness, who, along with God, had secured the
defeat of the French at Agincourt,[25] thus earning him the recognition
of being 'the special patron and protector of the English nation' from
archbishop Chichele in 1416.[26]

The public reception of Henry and his army in London was
recorded by the author of the *Gesta* as an integral part of his work,
complementing the success recently won in France. The events may
be seen in more than one historical context. They may have derived
inspiration from the ancient traditions of military triumphs granted
to victors in battle.[27] In the reign of Edward I there had been trium-
phalist celebrations to acknowledge the victory won against the Scots
at Falkirk in 1297; after the battle of Poitiers, in 1356, the Black
Prince had come home with his prisoners to be met with a tumultuous
reception.[28] There was much of that in the events which took place
in London on 23 November 1415. Another, more recent, context was
that of the monarch's formal entry into either his capital or other
important cities of his realm, a practice with very precise political
overtones since it enabled the king to establish his authority over a
city and to be seen doing so in conditions and circumstances which
emphasized the outward trappings of monarchy.[29] Richard II had

[20] Ibid., pp. 49, 121, 147, 151, 155.

[21] Ibid., p. 99.

[22] Ibid., p. 79. Similar comparisons had already been made in the heady days of
Edward III's early victories against the French (W.M. Ormrod, 'The personal
religion of Edward III', *Speculum*, 64 (1989), 849–50.

[23] Gesta., p. 125.

[24] Ibid., pp. 145, 151.

[25] 'And thus Almyghti God and Saint George brought our enymys to grounde and
gaf vs that day the victori' (*Brut*, ii, 379).

[26] *Register of Henry Chichele*, iii, 8–10; *St Albans Chronicle*, p. 70.

[27] E. Kantorowicz, 'The King's advent and the enigmatic panels in the doors of
Santa Sabina', *Selected studies* (New York, 1965), pp. 37–65.

[28] *The Anonimalle Chronicle 1333–1381*, ed. V.H. Galbraith (Manchester, 1927), p. 41;
R. Barber, *Edward, prince of Wales and Aquitaine*, (London, 1978), p. 152.

[29] On the growth of this practice in France, see *Les entrées royales françaises de 1328
à 1515*, ed. B. Guenée and F. Lehoux (Paris, 1968).

made two such symbolic entries into London, the first in 1377 (a relatively simple affair), the second (very much more elaborate) when he had been reconciled to the people of the capital in 1392.[30]

The celebrations of 1415 had something of the character of both these forms of ceremony. Richard II appears to have been the first to enjoy such a reception twice during his reign. There are indications, however, that he may not have been the last. We know almost nothing of Henry V's coronation, but contemporary accounts refer to the 'steynyng and peynting' of a giant to be placed by London Bridge, as well as the payment for other works and the provision of singers for the coronation day.[31] Was this part of the ceremonial, or part of a more formal 'entry' into London associated with that occasion? It is almost impossible to tell. What is clear, however, is that the reception of November 1415 was more than a formal 'entry', although a comparison of the account found in the *Gesta* with that of Richard's entry in 1392 shows certain points in common between the symbolism employed on both occasions. In 1415 the emphasis was to be on two things. London wished to be associated with the recent successes won in France, successes which had been made possible by the large loans which the city had granted the king in the past year or so. London also wished to honour the victor of Harfleur and Agincourt, and to make plain the message that Henry had also depended upon divine aid for the successes which he had achieved.

Certain elements in the reception were intended to emphasize this. Henry was depicted as a David who had just slain a Goliath ('who might appropriately be represented by the arrogant French'), the scene being enacted over the statement 'Welcome Henry ye fifte, Kynge of Englond and of Fraunce'.[32] Another scene involving Henry receiving wafers of bread and wine was compared by the author with the reception of Abraham by Melchizedek 'when he returned with victory from the slaughter of the four kings'.[33] The king was thus being seen in Old Testament terms as a figure favoured by God. Switching to the New Testament, the idea was sustained and developed. The Latin text refers to the eagerly awaited day of Henry's

[30] G.Kipling, 'Richard II's "Sumptuous Pageants" and the idea of the civic triumph', *Pageantry in the Shakespearean theater*, ed. D.M. Bergeron (Athens, Georgia, 1985), pp. 84–5.
[31] Corporation of London RO, Bridge House accounts I, p. 26.
[32] *Gesta*, p. 111; *Chronicon Adae de Usk*, pp. 129, 312.
[33] *Gesta*, pp. 107–11. See K. Schnith, 'Musik, Liturgie, Prozession als Ausdrucksmittel der Politik Heinrichs V. von England', *Festschrift Rudolf Bockholdt zum 60. Geburtstag*, ed. N. Dubowy and S. Meyer-Eller, p. 46. According to the compiler of BL, Harley Ms 565, the mayor addressed the king as 'thou conquerour' (fo.112).

'arrival', or 'adventus', in London.[34] In one sense, the word meant just what it said. In another sense, however, it took on a deeper significance: Christ's entry into Jerusalem was described as his 'adventus'. *Mutatis mutandis*, this 'arrival' was that of a Christ-like king into his capital, London, accompanied by the singing of the 'angelic anthem', 'Blessed is he who comes in the name of the Lord', the whole made all the more appropriate by the fact that the event itself took place only a week before the beginning of Advent which marked the season of preparation for the birth of Christ at Christmas.[35]

Other aspects of the reception merit attention. Notice has already been drawn to the comparison between England and Israel. On the ramparts of the artificial tower set up in Cornhill stood a group of prophets, their white hair wrapped and turbaned with gold and crimson, who sang a psalm which included the line 'he has done wonderful things'.[36] These had their New Testament counterparts in a group of twelve apostles who, together with twelve kings of the English succession and a group of martyrs, sang the psalm, so appropriate for the occasion, 'You have saved us from those who harmed us and have defeated those who hated us'.[37] The ambiguity of such lines, which could refer to either God or the king, whose motto was 'In God is my salvation', is obvious. However, this was not an attempt to give Henry alone the credit for recent successes in France: such a credit would have been uncharacteristic of the king. Instead, it is likely that he wanted it to be acknowledged that he and his people owed much to their heavenly 'protectors', notably that constant patron, St George, but also two other English saints, both kings, St Edmund the Martyr and St Edward the Confessor, whose arms, together with those of England, hung from the tower of the conduit on Cornhill.[38]

The reception brought honours to Henry and, through him, to the crown. So much was intended. It also brought fame to London, his capital, associated in his success. London, a legend inscribed on a wall announced, was the 'city of the king of justice'[39] or, as in two other legends, the 'city of God'.[40] By implication, too, London was the capital of Israel, Jerusalem, a point underlined by the psalm 'Blessed is he . . .' which had been said of Christ as he entered that

[34] *Gesta*, pp. 101–3.
[35] Ibid., pp. 104–5, 191–2; Kipling, 'Idea of civic triumph', p. 92 seq. See also Powell, *Kingship, law and society*, pp. 131–2.
[36] Ps.97.
[37] *Gesta*, pp. 107–9 (Ps.43:7).
[38] Ibid., pp. 105, 107.
[39] Ibid., p. 103.
[40] Ibid., pp. 105, 109.

city.[41] Much of the visual imagery created for the reception of 1415 had probably been on display for Richard II's civic triumph of 1392, which itself was based on the vision of the New Jerusalem of the Book of the Apocalypse. The angels, the towers (one covered in profusion with the city's arms), the wine spouting as if miraculously from a conduit which normally carried only water, all were symbols that London was the capital of a land which had found favour with God. The king's prayer that God should protect London was likely to be heard.[42]

Henry was to see the giant at London Bridge on a third occasion, that of the reception given to him and Katharine on their arrival in February 1421. Although in a lower key than that of 1415, the gains of such an occasion were shared by all who took part. London would benefit again from the return of the king after an absence of more than three years; the king, by his presence and that of his wife, could expect to arouse support for the war and for the demand for loans and subsidies which he was about to make. According to the *Brut*, some 30,000 or more men, including the mayor and the aldermen, went out to Blackheath to greet the couple as they came to London from the royal manor at Eltham where they had been resting.[43] The crowd went with them towards the capital, music accompanying the procession all the way. At London Bridge the giant, probably with a new head, which it had taken two days to make (work done on Henry's express orders), would have confronted him as he entered the city.[44] What other pageants were organized, it is difficult to tell. It is likely that they were quite complicated, since work on them had begun in the first half of January, while early in February teams of carpenters had been hired to work by the week, some of them, it was said, working night and day.[45] Angels featured in the reception, as did nineteen virgins who met the king on the bridge, where a painter had been employed painting an 'image' over the gate for the king's arrival.[46] On the next day, having spent the night in the Tower, Katharine was taken through London, many of whose houses were decorated with tapestries and cloth of gold, 'the beste that myght be gotyn',[47] to her coronation at Westminster. Once again the arrival of royalty in London had led to public demonstration, to underline the city's solidarity with the king and his queen.

[41] Ps.118, and John 12, in which Christ is called the king of Israel by the crowd.
[42] BL, Harley Ms 565, fo.112.
[43] *Brut*, ii, 426.
[44] Corporation of London RO, Bridge House accounts I, pp. 457, 458.
[45] Ibid., pp. 457, 460.
[46] Ibid., p. 464.
[47] *Brut*, ii, 426.

The development of national awareness could be encouraged by
turning people towards the past to see whence they had come. In
common with several other countries, England shared the tradition
that she was descended from Troy, through the person of Brutus, who
had come to Albion and founded Troja Nova, the New Troy, which
was to become London, as well as bequeathing his name to the
country (Britain), the people (Britons) and its history (the *Brut*). This
was the tradition which Geoffrey of Monmouth had taken up and
used in the twelfth century, a tradition whose days were yet far from
numbered: Henry V, while still Prince, had commissioned John Lydgate, monk of Bury St Edmunds, in 1412 to render into English Guido
delle Colonne's history of the siege and destruction of Troy 'By-cause
he wolde that to hyghe and lowe / The noble story openly wer knowe /
In oure tonge, aboute in every age, / And y- writen as wel in oure
langage / As in latyn and in frensche it is; / That of the story the
trouth we nat mys / No more than doth eche other nacioun: / This
was the fyn of his entencioun'.[48] That intention, as Lydgate went on
to explain, was not only to recall the great deeds of the past but to
fulfil one of the tasks of the writer, to ensure that each generation
should have the opportunity of reading of the events of the past which,
if they were not recorded, would be dimmed in the human memory
by the passing of time. The survival of at least twenty-three manuscripts, most of them quality copies meant for display rather than for
reading, reflects the reputation which this translation, and the tradition which it carried, was to enjoy.[49]

A long history (and no nation was worth its salt unless it had a
long history) had to be created if it were not known to exist. In 1320
the Declaration of Arbroath had claimed that Scotland had been
ruled in unbroken line by 113 kings of royal stock.[50] More recently,
propagandists in the service of the kings of France had stressed the
long line of Christian kings by whom the country had been led for
almost a thousand years.[51] Henry V would not have been unaware of
the importance of trying to emphasize the length of royal descent
in England, and the importance of legitimate succession. Both

[48] *Lydgate's Troy Book, A.D. 1412–20*, ed. H. Bergen (EETS, London, 1906), i, 4,
ll.111–18.
[49] R.F. Green, *Poets and princepleasers. Literature and the English court in the late middle
ages* (Toronto, 1980), p. 197; C.D. Benson, *The history of Troy in middle English literature*
(Woodbridge, 1980), pp. 40, 136; L. Lawton 'The illustration of late medieval secular
texts, with special reference to Lydgate's "Troy Book"', *Manuscripts and readers in
fifteenth-century England*, ed. D. Pearsall (Woodbridge/Totowa, 1983), pp. 52, 55–6.
[50] A.A.M. Duncan, *The Nation of Scots and the Declaration of Arbroath* (London, 1970),
p. 35.
[51] C. Beaune, *Naissance de la nation France* (Paris, 1985).

Edward III and Richard II had shown their consciousness of the growing sense of English achievement which was developing in the second half of the fourteenth century, and which culminated, in literature, in the writings of, among others, Geoffrey Chaucer and John Gower. It is notable that, among the figures to appear in the London reception of 1415, alongside the twelve apostles, were 'twelve kings of the English succession, martyrs and confessors . . . with sceptres in their hands, crowns upon their heads, their emblems of sanctity plain to see'.[52] Here, clearly, was an attempt to show what sort of a country England was, a land ruled from of old by kings, many of whom had found particular favour with God. A few years after Henry V's death, the themes would be taken up again by John Lydgate. Between Brutus and Alfred, he claimed, 224 other kings had ruled (thus putting the Scottish claim in the shade!), while the verses which he wrote in praise of England's rulers from the time of the great ninth-century king emphasized, where possible, their devotion to God, their generosity to the Church and their association with saintly figures, in particular, in the case of the tenth-century kings, with the figure of the Benedictine monk and archbishop, St Dunstan.[53]

Historical longevity was one matter. Another was that a people must be considered holy, as the Scots declared themselves to be in the Declaration of Arbroath, and as the French kings, who claimed descent from Clovis (thought of as a saint), regarded themselves.[54] For this reason, in the fourteenth and fifteenth centuries the cult of the country's early saints, particularly those of the Anglo-Saxon period, came to assume considerable significance. It was proof of two things: that England was Christian, and that she had been so for many centuries. Richard II, as the Wilton Diptych shows, had St Edmund, the ninth-century martyr-king of East Anglia, and Edward the Confessor, founder of the abbey of Westminster where his relics were enshrined (and where Richard himself would finally find rest), among his patrons as he was presented to the Virgin. These two pre-Conquest kings (along with St George, whose standard an angel carries on the diptych) were widely regarded as the country's chief spiritual patrons.[55] Both were much in favour at the Lancastrian

[52] *Gesta*, p. 107.

[53] *The minor poems of John Lydgate*, ed. H.N. MacCracken (EETS, London, 1934), ii, 710 seq.

[54] C. Beaune, 'Saint Clovis: histoire, religion royale et sentiment national en France à la fin du moyen age', *Le metier d'historien au moyen age. Études sur l'historiographie médiévale*, ed. B. Guenée (Paris, 1977), pp. 139–56.

[55] E.A. Danbury, 'English and French artistic propaganda during the period of the Hundred Years War: some evidence from royal charters', *Power, culture, and religion in France, c.1350-c.1550*, ed. C.T. Allmand (Woodbridge, 1989), pp. 93–7. It may also

court: Henry IV's chantry chapel at Canterbury was dedicated to St Edward;[56] Henry V ordered that his own chantry be placed as close as possible to the Confessor's shrine at Westminster; while Henry VI had a special devotion both to St Edward and to St Edmund, and was a patron and visitor to the great Benedictine abbey dedicated to the latter at Bury.[57]

In these matters royal influence and support were important. Thomas Walsingham reported that it was at the particular request of Henry V himself that the feasts of St George and St Dunstan were raised to the rank of 'greater double', that of St George, as Adam of Usk put it, meriting a holiday from work.[58] George, a patron of soldiers and very much the saint of chivalry, would easily have found favour with the king. Dunstan, who died in 988, was a native saint. He had also been a Benedictine monk, archbishop of Canterbury, as well as a strong supporter of the monarchy of his day, to which could be added his significant role as a reformer. Was it in Dunstan that Henry was to find the inspiration to reform the Benedictine order in 1421?

These were not the only saints to find favour in Henry's reign. Could it have been on a visit to Chester while still Prince that Henry was introduced to the shrine, at nearby Holywell,[59] of the seventh-century nun, Winefride? Her feast day, 3 November, had already been celebrated for some years throughout the province of Canterbury (which included Wales), when, along with that of the Mercian saint, Chad, it was raised in status in 1416 by archbishop Chichele.[60] Another Anglo-Saxon saint to be favoured was the eighth-century monk-bishop, John of Beverley, on the feast of whose translation Henry had won his victory at Agincourt, after prayers had been offered for his intercession.[61] A much more recent saint who found special favour with the king was St John of Bridlington,[62] the Austin canon who had died in 1379; he was a firm favourite with the Lan-

---

be noted that the angels in the diptych bear Richard's personal badge of the white hart.

[56] I owe this information to Dr Nigel Ramsey.

[57] Lydgate wrote a 'praier' to him (*Minor poems*, i, 124–7). See also 'De Sancto Edmundo: Ave, rex gentis Anglorum, miles regis Anglorum' (Trinity College, Cambridge, Ms B.11.7, fo.25).

[58] *St Albans Chronicle*, p. 70; *Chronicon Adae de Usk*, pp. 127, 310.

[59] He certainly went there in 1416 (*The Oxford dictionary of saints*, ed. D.H. Farmer (Oxford, 1978), p. 408); *Chronicon Adae de Usk*, pp. 129, 313.

[60] London, Guildhall Library, Ms 9531/4, fos 162v-163v.

[61] Ibid., fos 167v-168.

[62] *St Albans Chronicle*, p. 25; *Four English political tracts of the later middle ages*, ed. J.-P. Genet (Camden 4th series, 18, London, 1977), pp. 45–6. Thomas Beaufort was also a visitor to Bridlington in 1417 (*St Albans Chronicle*, p. 114). See above, ch.2, n.79.

castrian dynasty, a man regarded as an example of monastic observance as well as a man of prayer and the giver of practical advice. It was while Henry was on a visit to the shrines, both in Yorkshire, in April 1421 that the news of the death of his brother, Clarence, was brought to him.

The deliberate encouragement of the cult of these English saints of earlier centuries, done to promote the idea that England was, indeed, an island of saints,[63] also reflects the king's desire to honour men and women whose Christian example he wished to follow. Another saint, unlike many from England widely recognized in Christendom, was Thomas of Canterbury, at whose shrine in that city many notable persons, including Henry and the emperor Sigismund, 'offered' as they passed through. It is noticeable that the account of events at the council of Constance given by Ulrich Richental records that on 29 December 1415, and again a year later, the English delegation to the council celebrated the feast of this great English saint with much public ostentation.[64]

Later events in the history of the council forced the English to blow their trumpet even louder on behalf of their country. It had been the absence of a Spanish delegation at the assembly which had allowed the English to take their place as a 'nation'. Once the Spaniards came to be incorporated, the English position became difficult to justify. Early in March 1417 Jean Campan, a member of the French delegation, tried to register a protest against the English. Although interrupted, he was able to submit the text of his speech to the authorities, who had it copied into the official record. England, he claimed, was not really a 'natio principalis', only a 'natio particularis', a term which, translated, meant a kingdom. England, he was saying, was a relatively small country which should be incorporated into the larger German 'nation'. It compared unfavourably with France: for that country's 101 sees and eleven ecclesiastical provinces, England had only two provinces (Canterbury and York) and twenty-five sees, and could not even control the church in either Wales or Scotland. Furthermore, was it right that a country with only a small number of sees (out of a total of about 735) should have one vote out of the four or five which decided the affairs of Christendom at the council?

[63] On English saints, see G. Schmidt, 'Two unknown English horae from the fifteenth century', *Burlington Magazine*, 103 (1961), 48, n.6. Other Anglo-Saxon saints to be referred to in 'historical' texts are St Erkenwald (*Chronicon Adae de Usk*, pp. 129, 312) and St Edith, on whose feast day, 16 September, Henry V was said to have been born. It is worth stressing that Edward III had also used the cult of English saints for political reasons (Ormrod, 'Personal religion', 858–60).

[64] Loomis, *Council of Constance*, pp. 138, 146. See Devon, *Issues of the Exchequer*, pp. 321–2 for evidence of the king's regard for the saint.

England should be forced to return to its more traditional membership of the German 'nation', or votes should be given to nations in accordance with their size. Either decision, with its clear political implications, would be to the advantage of France.[65]

The task of replying to this attack was undertaken by Thomas Polton, one of the council's official notaries and later Henry's proctor at the papal court. Since the French wanted to cause trouble, he, Polton, felt that he must defend the most Christian king, Henry, his lord, who was king of both England and France.[66] He was particularly concerned that men should realize that those who had compiled the Church's law had never intended 'to define the English nation as part of the German nation'. England was a 'nation' on its own, and it included not only Wales, Scotland and Man, but four kingdoms within Ireland, making a total of eight in all.[67] Spiritually, the English 'nation' encompassed ecclesiastical provinces and 110 sees, sixty of which, all 'spacious' were in Ireland. As for the idea that the spiritual affairs of Wales were not controlled from Canterbury, this was non-sense. And although Polton admitted that Scotland was not altogether under English control, the fact remained that it was part of Britain.

Turning to the Christian history of the 'glorious kingdom of England', Polton could claim that it was at least as honourable as that of France in antiquity, faith and dignity. The first to bring Christianity to Britain had been no less a person than Joseph of Arimathaea, who had taken down Christ's body from the cross; he had come (significantly) with twelve companions, had converted the people, and had been well received.[68] The French, however, as Polton emphasized, had been obliged to await the arrival of St Denis to receive the faith:[69] he failed to take account of the tradition that Mary Magdalen, Martha and Lazarus had brought Christ's teaching to the coastal lands of southern France.[70] Anxious to show how influential Britain had been in very early years, Polton recalled that the daughter of King Coel was St Helena, mother of the emperor Constantine, who was born in York. The conversion of the Empire to the Christian religion, the

[65] Genet, 'English nationalism', 65–6.
[66] Crowder, *Unity, heresy and reform*, p. 111.
[67] Ibid., p. 116.
[68] Henry was interested in the link with Joseph of Arimathaea, and he may have been responsible for encouraging excavations at Glastonbury in 1419, which, it was doubtless hoped, would produce, in the form of an identifiable coffin containing bones, evidence of the link between Britain and the Holy Land of apostolic times. (I am grateful to Professor James Carley, of York University, Toronto, for allowing me to see the typescript of his paper, 'A Grave Event: Henry V, Glastonbury Abbey, and Joseph of Aramathea's Bones'.)
[69] Crowder, *Unity, heresy and reform*, p. 119; Genet, 'English nationalism', 67.
[70] Genet, 'English nationalism', 72.

building of the first church dedicated to St Peter in Rome, and the finding of the True Cross could therefore be attributed to members of an English royal family and its descendant. Not surprisingly, with such remarkably Christian kings to lead it, Britain was certain to be a land of faith. While France had scarcely 6000 parish churches, England had more than 52,000, all well endowed, in addition to a host of other notable churches, including cathedrals, monasteries and hospitals.[71]

Before finishing, Polton turned to a further matter, what he called 'the chief and surest proof of being a nation': language. That of France, he claimed, was understood, more or less, by all Frenchmen. In the English 'nation', however, there were five languages: English, used by the English and the Scots; Welsh; Irish; Gascon; and Cornish, none of which was understood by the others. Such, Polton argued, was the strength of the English nation. For him, language was proof of the power of a 'principal nation' to stand with others in its own right at the council. England had played an important role in past councils of the Church; it could scarcely be denied the right to play it again in modern times.[72]

Polton was addressing an audience drawn from all corners of Christendom, few of whom would be aware of the details of British history or the accuracy of his claims. Skilfully he let drop names which might be known or might impress: Helena and Constantine, for example. But, unlike the French, he could appeal neither to a long line of Christian kings nor to a cult of monarchy. Nor could he stress too much the 'nationalist' argument against the French: Henry V saw himself not as the enemy of France, but as its king by lawful descent.[73] All that was open to him to claim was that England was at least as important, as holy, as ancient as France claimed to be – and to leave it at that. The significant factor, however, is that in 1417, with its claim to act as a 'nation' at the council challenged, England could produce an argument in which elements of history (real and imaginary) were mixed with an appeal to the significance of language as a distinguishing mark of nationality to claim that she was deservedly as famous as any other country in the Europe of the time.[74]

The year 1417, that of Polton's defence of English claims before the council, was also to be one of great significance in the development of one of the main props of his argument, the English language. As Polton implied, language was the sign of a people. This had been

[71] Crowder, *Unity, heresy and reform*, pp. 118–19.
[72] Ibid., pp. 121, 125–6.
[73] Genet, 'English nationalism', 75.
[74] Crowder, *Unity, heresy and reform*, p. 125.

shown when, in 1344, Edward III had emotively declared that an attack planned by the French was aimed at destroying the king, his people, their lands and their language.[75] The idea was to be taken up again in July 1400 when Henry Percy, justiciar of Chester, wrote in the Prince's name to summon archers to resist the Scots who proposed 'to make war against the language and people of England',[76] while a text (dated 1407) refers to the intention of the Welsh 'to destroy the English tongue as far as they can and turn it into the Welsh tongue'.[77]

Was it to draw attention to the growth of the language and to the threats levelled against it that, in 1363, 1364 and in 1381, the proceedings at the opening of parliament were recorded in English? Nevertheless, French and Latin remained the strongly dominant languages in this particular matter until well into the fifteenth century, there being only four entries in English, two for each of the years 1414 and 1421, for the entire reign of Henry V. The language of the petitions presented to parliament certainly showed a marked reluctance to abandon French and Latin until the second decade of the fifteenth century. There are two before 1400; none between 1401 and 1410; eight between 1411 and 1420; while the decade 1421–30 saw the number jump dramatically to sixty-three.[78]

There are important indications that, in these years, English was being accepted more and more as the norm of written communication, and that Henry's role can be observed in twin developments which helped bring this about. The king, son of cultured parents, appears to have enjoyed reading. He himself had books in Latin, French and English, but it is the active encouragement which he gave to translators, mainly into English, which must receive emphasis here. Thomas Hoccleve's *Regement of Princes* was a rendering of Giles of Rome's *De Regimine Principum* (and much else), while, as Prince, Henry had commissioned John Lydgate to translate *The Fall of Troy* into English, a task not completed until almost the end of his patron's reign. It was also while Henry was Prince that Edward, duke of York, translated Gaston Phoebus' *Livre de la Chasse* into English for him as *The Master of the Game*.[79]

Henry's personal role must not be overstressed. His brother,

[75] *RP*, iii, 150.
[76] '. . . ad linguam et gentem eiusdem regni debellandum' (PRO, CHES, 2/74, m.15d).
[77] '. . . et ad linguam Anglicanam pro posse suorum destruendam et in linguam Wallensicam convertendam' (Messham, 'County of Flint', 11, 33).
[78] J.H. Fisher, 'Chancery and the emergence of standard written English in the fifteenth century', *Speculum*, 52 (1977), 880, 888.
[79] *Complete Peerage*, xii, 903. On Henry's books, see McFarlane, *Lancastrian Kings*, pp. 116–17, 233–8.

Humphrey, was later to commission Lydgate to translate Boccaccio, and the earl of Salisbury got him to render Deguilevile's *Pelerinage de la Vie Humaine* into English.[80] Likewise, the part being played by other translators, notably John Trevisa and John Walton, and by their patrons, who included members of the Berkeley family, in advancing the use of English as the natural literary language of Englishmen must not be forgotten.[81] None the less, the personal role played by Henry in this work is well in keeping both with the man and the times in which he lived, and cannot be ignored. In governmental circles a move towards the use of English was also in the making. Here, too, Henry had a role to play.[82]

The first surviving royal administrative document written in English is dated, significantly, 1410, when the Prince was at the centre of power; a second occurs in 1414, two more, including a set of minutes, in 1417.[83] Important as this was (minutes are likely to have been drawn up in the accustomed language of those who had attended the meeting and were most likely to read them), it was Henry's personal correspondence which reflected the change to English which, since it was so abrupt, can only have reflected a conscious decision to use the English language as the king's chosen vehicle of communication.[84] It is clear that, as Prince, Henry had used French as the language for the letters which he wrote or were written for him.[85] As king, his signet letters, which formed his most private correspondence, dictated to a clerk before, perhaps, having their style (rather than contents) improved by a secretary, were also in French. In August 1417, when Henry and his army had landed in France on the king's second expedition, a dramatic change came about. From 12 August at the latest Henry had all his signet letters to English subjects written in English, although the address 'De par le roy' rather than 'By the kyng' was still being written in French in a very small number of surviving examples as late as March 1421.[86]

We may speculate on the reasons which made Henry deliberately change his practice to use English rather than French in this form of

[80] D. Pearsall, *John Lydgate* (London, 1970), p. 70.
[81] R. Hanna III, 'Sir Thomas Berkeley and his patronage', *Speculum*, 64 (1989), 878–916.
[82] Green, *Poets and princepleasers*, p. 154; Harriss, *Henry V: practice of kingship*, p. 8.
[83] *PPC*, i, 323–7; ii, 140–2, 236–9.
[84] 'Henry IV was the first king to conduct government business in English, and Henry V the first who preferred to, and made a point of doing so' (D. Pearsall, *Old English and Middle English poetry* (London, 1971), p. 191).
[85] See, for example, those printed in *Anglo-Norman letters*, ed. Legge.
[86] *Signet letters*, ed. Kirby, no.808. See the letter sent to Henry on 25 March 1421 in *Chapters of the English Black Monks*, ii, 104–5.

correspondence. It made sense when he was addressing persons whose language was English, as was the case when he wrote to the people of Bath about the ringing of bells in their city[87] or to those of London from Touques or Caen to report on his successes against these places.[88] Such letters were for general publication, and English, quite naturally, had been used for proclamations and other appeals to public opinion for a good many years. English, too, would be the language calculated to have the most effect in securing active military assistance or the provisions required to feed an army active on French soil. That this was so is shown by the letters exchanged between the king, on the one hand, and the mayor and people of London on the other, in which the replies sent to Henry were also written in English.[89]

The development of the language thus came to depend greatly upon the lead given by the king himself in his correspondence. It was this flow of correspondence (of which the modern editor suggests that perhaps only one tenth survives)[90] which enabled Henry to exert a strong and lasting influence upon the use and development of the English language. This was done in two ways. The signet letters are as close as it is possible to get to letters written by Henry himself: they reflect the king, his ideas and his modes of expression. As one writer has put it, these letters were written in what was literally the 'king's English', enabling Henry himself to have a personal influence on both their style and their linguistic content.[91] Secondly, since a considerable proportion of Henry's signet letters were directed to the chancellor, ordering him to take action on a particular matter which had come to the king's attention, it was through the chancery's English that style and particular linguistic usages came to be developed and, most important, propagated throughout the country. In so far as it is possible to speak of 'standard' English at this period, the English was that of the king's chancery, a language, it has been suggested, which reflected the dialect of part of the central and south midlands, whence many of the chancery's clerks may have come, and whose forms of spelling and, to a certain degree, verbal expression, when transformed into writing, came to be adopted as 'normal' as their usage developed.[92]

Henry's personal written English, remarkably consistent in its form and usage (indicating it was probably his own), may have become a

---

[87] *Signet letters*, ed. Kirby, no.811.
[88] *Book of London English*, pp. 67–8.
[89] Ibid., p. 22 seq. and § III.
[90] *Signet letters*, ed. Kirby, p. 5.
[91] Richardson, 'Henry V, the English chancery, and chancery English', 730, 727.
[92] M.L. Samuels, 'Some applications of middle English dialectology', *English studies* (Amsterdam), 44 (1963), 89, 91, 93.

model for the forms which were to be adopted by chancery.[93] In this respect, the development of the language owes a considerable personal debt to the king. In another sense, too, Henry's contribution must be regarded as important. It is quite evident that his decisive move towards the use of the vernacular language in documents emanating from central government reflected a generally wider use of English in the written word during the second decade of the fifteenth century, in spite of the fear of English when used in religious writings or in translations of the Bible, with its Wycliffite and Lollard associations. In terms of its use in government documents it may possibly reflect a move away from the cultural influence of the clerical class (expressed in Latin) and the noble class (expressed in French) towards a more 'popular', or at least more generally acceptable culture, essentially native and English in character.

In this Henry certainly met a response. It has been noted how, in two of the country's greatest monasteries, St Mary's York and the cathedral priory at Durham, English came to replace French during his reign: 'it was precisely in the second decade of the fifteenth century that the monastic and prior's registers [at Durham] reveal the complete and remarkably abrupt extinction of French as a language of written as well as verbal communication',[94] although Latin still remained in use for written purposes. We have already noted how the corporation of London, when it had need to communicate by letter with the king, did so in English; so did the Benedictine abbot of Bury St Edmunds when he wrote to Henry about his plans to hold a general chapter of the order in 1421;[95] so, likewise, did the royal secretary Robert Caudray when he wrote to Henry (17 June 1421?) about the need of the Parisians to be provided with food held up in Rouen, and promising him a book of Ptolemy's writings which had formerly belonged to the duke of Berry.[96] The best known surviving example of a conscious change to the use of English attributable to the policy of the king is the decision of the London Guild of Brewers, taken before 30 July 1422, to use the English language to record their proceedings. The book in which this was done, a happy survivor of the

[93] 'Even though they are by different scribes, [Henry V's] English letters are remarkably consistent in their forms and usage (indicating that the language was probably his own) and very near to what became Chancery Standard ... So his personal written English may indeed have served as a model for the form adopted by Chancery' (Fisher, 'Chancery and ... standard written English', 898, n.92).

[94] R.B. Dobson, *Durham priory, 1400–1450* (Cambridge, 1973), p. 73; cited by A.C. Baugh and T. Cable, *A history of the English language* (3rd edn, London, 1978), p. 154, n.2.

[95] *Chapters of the English Black Monks*, ii, 104.

[96] BL, Cotton Ms Caligula D v, fo.85.

Great Fire of 1666, was begun by a new clerk, William Porland, in 1418, who wrote his record in French. It was probably in the summer of 1422 that the Brewers decided to 'go English', although, ironically, that decision was recorded in Latin.[97] In their abstract book, however, they set out an English version of the Latin text:

> Whereas our mother-tongue, to wit the English tongue, hath in modern days begun to be honorably enlarged and adorned, for that our most excellent lord, King Henry V, hath in his letters missive and diverse affairs touching his own person, more willingly chosen to declare the secrets of his will, and for the better understanding of his people, hath with a diligent mind procured the common idiom (setting aside others) to be commended by the exercise of writing; and there are many of our craft of Brewers who have the knowledge of writing and reading in the said English idiom, but in others, to wit, the Latin and French, before these times used, they did not in any way understand. For which causes with many others, it being considered how that the greater part of the Lords and trusty Commons have begun to make their matters be noted down in our mother tongue, so we also in our craft, following in some manner their steps, have decreed to commit to memory the needful things which concern us, as appeareth in the following . . .

There follows a record, in English, dated Thursday, 30 July 1422, of the proceedings of that day.[98]

The conscious decision of Henry V actively to encourage the use of English is significant in two ways. It was a practical decision, doubtless guided by the realization that both French and Latin were coming to be understood and used by an ever diminishing section of the population, as the Brewers' statement showed. His lead provided a powerful precedent for the increasingly general adoption of the language for both business and the affairs of government after his death, the 'turning point in the use of English',[99] when the vernacular came to be generally adopted in writing.[100] The encouragement of the vernacular was also part of an emotive appeal to language as the true sign of a nation. Polton had claimed that this was the case. Language was the peculiarity of a people, a mark of its individuality. Henry was anxious to show that his kingdom, and its people, were out of the ordinary, that they could stand on their own feet. The man who commissioned translations and encouraged the more general use of

---

[97] London, Guildhall Library, Ms 5440 (Brewers' accounts, 1418–1440), fo.69v; printed in *Book of London English*, p. 16.

[98] Ibid., pp. 139–42.

[99] See the review, by L.M. Mathieson, of *An anthology of chancery English*, ed. Fisher, Richardson and Fisher, *Speculum*, 61 (1986), 649.

[100] Baugh and Cable, *History of the English language*, p. 154.

the English language was trying to establish his country's cultural independence. These were not the least of the king's contributions towards the creation of a strong spirit of independence which helped to set England apart in the world of the early fifteenth century. It was also a step which helped, in the long term, to create a language proper to the nation. No wonder that Henry V has always been regarded as a very English king. His contribution to the development of the nation's language was a major one by any standards, and, as such, he helped in a crucial and practical way to create an increasingly conscious and successful English nation.

At the start of his reign, Henry had been urged on all sides to work for the unity of his people after the divisions and dissensions of his two predecessors' reigns. It is not the least of his achievements that, by and large, he managed to realize this. In broad terms he did it by being both a conventional, traditional ruler and an innovator. The first reflected his conservative character, but a character which corresponded very much with the needs, mood and desires of the English people of his day. Intelligently, Henry understood what his people wanted of him: order, the rule of peace and truth, proper financial administration, even war abroad if it were fought with success. By providing these, by exploiting publicly the goodwill which he thus achieved, he won for himself the support of a nation now more at peace with itself, readier than for a long time to follow the lead given by the king.

It was as a very English Englishman that Henry caught something of the mood of the day in the encouragement he gave to developments which would have an important bearing upon the future. He used the conflict against France, inherited from his predecessors, as a means of giving to his people the character of a nation blessed by God, favoured because their king was a man who did right. Englishmen should feel proud of being English. To cap this was the vital and, historically speaking, highly significant encouragement which Henry gave to the practical use of the English language. This was now to advance by great strides to become the unifying factor, par excellence, of the English people. Looking back, it provided them with yet another link with their country's Anglo-Saxon past. Looking forwards, it set the language firmly on its way both symbolically, as a sign of the country's unity, and practically, as the instrument through which, increasingly, law and government would come to be administered. In this crucially important matter, Englishmen were to be in no small way indebted to their king.

Chapter 20

EPILOGUE

When, on 22 September 1422, Henry Chichele, archbishop of Canterbury, ordered the bishops of the southern province to urge the faithful to pray for the late king,[1] he was asking them to intercede for the soul of a man whose reign had made a great impression upon his contemporaries. It had covered a decade when, it seemed, the country had been united behind the endeavours of the crown, its powers exercised by one of exceptional talent and energy, who appeared to have achieved what he set out to do. At an early stage, Henry had sought to unite the country behind him by stressing the contrast between his predecessor's style of ruling and his own. He had fully recognized the value of publicity in his effort to underline the nature of his achievement, and it is not unreasonable to suppose that the propagation of some of the anecdotes regarding his youth and the reaction of the French to his demands for territorial concessions may have been deliberately encouraged within his own lifetime. If, by 1422, there were fears about over-involvement in the war against France, it could hardly be doubted that Henry had done much to restore the flagging authority of the Lancastrian monarchy. In a moral sense, Henry VI inherited as good a hand as any player could hope for.[2]

What was done with Henry's thriving historical reputation? Since many of those who directed affairs in the early years of his son's reign had already held positions of high responsibility, it was natural enough that the policies of the late king, used as a means of preserving unity and avoiding 'variance' by stressing their continuation, should have been maintained. Thomas Langley would have had the treaty of Troyes in mind when, speaking as chancellor before Henry VI's first parliament in November 1422, he emphasized that the new king personified the unity of the crowns of the kingdoms of France and England, something which many had long desired and which had

---

[1] See, for example, Worcester, Hereford and Worcester Record Office, b.716.093. BA. 2648/5 (iii) (Morgan's register), pp. 98–9.
[2] C.T. Allmand, 'Henry V the soldier, and the war in France', *Henry V. The practice of kingship*, ed. G.L. Harriss (Oxford, 1985), p. 117; *Brut*, ii, 497.

been finally accomplished as a result of the strenuous endeavours of Henry V and the English people.[3]

Not surprisingly, the memory of Henry and his achievement were to be called upon at moments when the English cause in France appeared to falter. The years immediately following his death witnessed a series of successes and advances into French territory under the leadership of John, duke of Bedford, and Thomas Montagu, earl of Salisbury, both of them loyal followers of the late king. In practice, the undertaking made by Henry in the treaty of Troyes, that those areas of France which did not submit voluntarily would be obliged to do so through the use of force, was being acted upon. With the halting of that advance in 1428, and in particular with the failure experienced by the English in the following year at Orléans, men may have wanted reassurance that the army (and the money) being despatched from England were being used in a good cause. It is probably no coincidence that, at about the same time as Henry VI was being crowned king in England, the blind poet, Audelay, should have written a verse in which he harked back to the glories of the previous reign, notably to the siege of Harfleur, the battle of Agincourt and to the story of the receipt of the tennis balls by the king who used them, metamorphozed, against the French themselves:[4]

> Thus was his fader a conqueroure
> & wan his moder with gret onoure;
> Now may the kyng bere the flour
> Of kyngis & kyngdams in uche cuntre.

The crisis of 1429–31 was overcome, but, with hindsight, things would never be quite the same again. Bedford, who had always striven to maintain English rule in France and, in particular, Normandy, in the way that he imagined his eldest brother would have wished, was in England in 1433 to defend both himself and his policies in France. Although Henry had now been dead some twelve years, it was in terms of the defence of what his brother had initiated in his lifetime that Bedford chose to set out his own political and military achievement:

... howe greete a pitee it were that that noble Reaume, for getyng and

---

[3] '. . . coment de long temps passe, ad este desirez un Roy de les deux Roialmes d'Engleterre, et de France . . . & par la vertuouse & famouse labour de notre nadgairs soverein seigneur, Pier a notre soverain seigneur le Roy q'or est, & de les gens Engloys, sur la conquest del Roialme de France, est la dit desir accompliz en la persone notre dit soverain seigneur . . .' (RP, iv, 197).

[4] Historical poems, ed. Robbins, pp. 109–10, 305.

HENRY V

kepyng of whiche my Lorde that was youre Fadre, to whose Soule God
doe mercy, and other many noble Princes, Lordes, Knightes and Squiers,
and other persones in full greet nombre, have payed hir lyves, many that
been yit on lyve have shedde thaire blode, more precious to hem thanne
eny temporel gode, and spended thaire dayes, and thaire noble and trewe
labours; and as well thai, as in general the Commune of this Lande, have
also spended an infinite goode. . . . [5]

Here was a statement which would appeal to those of all social groups
who had invested time and effort, blood and life, in fighting for and
maintaining Henry's enterprise. Two or three years later, with the
unhappy events of the congress of Arras still fresh in the minds of
Englishmen, the anonymous author of the *Libelle of Englyshe Polycye*
could sing the praises of the man who had so vigorously defended the
interests of the people whose king he was. [6] The appeal of the martial
achievements of Henry's reign was still very strong.

This was to be underlined in the course of the years 1437–40 by
no less a person than Humphrey, the last surviving son of Henry IV.
Humphrey, who had fought at Agincourt and had shown his ability
at the siege of Cherbourg in 1418, had none the less never been given
authority in France, much as he may have desired it. On Bedford's
death in 1435, he had become heir apparent to the throne, and it may
have been this which influenced him to defend English claims in
France with the maximum of publicity. In 1436 he had been able to
capitalize upon strong anti-Burgundian and, in particular, anti-
Flemish sentiment in England by relieving Calais, at the time threatened by siege, and by devastating the country round about.

Contemporary verses suggest that English popular opinion may
have been running very much in Humphrey's favour. [7] To encourage
it, he commissioned Tito Livio Frulovisi, an Italian humanist in his
household, to compose a life (or *Vita*) of his eldest brother, Henry V,
along the classical lines then finding favour in humanistic circles,
placing the king at the centre of the narrative and using his military
exploits (Tito Livio was writing mainly for the nobility) not merely
for didactic purposes but also very much with a political end in mind.
Not only was the young Henry VI invited to imitate his father's
example; the Italian also gave his patron, Humphrey, an inflated
position in his narrative, and described the war very much as he
would have wished. [8]

---

[5] *RP*, v, 436.
[6] *Libelle of Englyshe Polycye*, ll.10, 1010 seq.
[7] *Brut*, ii, 581–4.
[8] A. Gransden, *Historical writing in England: ii. c.1307 to the early sixteenth century*
(London, 1982), 210–12.

Having successfully written a life of Henry V in which the war was idealized as an heroic exploit bequeathed by the late king to his people, Tito Livio was then set a smaller, yet significant, task: the composition of a work in verse in praise of Humphrey himself. This has been seen as a kind of continuation of the *Vita* of Henry V, for while the central figure was no longer the late king but Humphrey (hence its title, *Humfroidos*), the idea of showing him as the continuator of his late brother's exploits was central to the work. A new Henry V, 'as invincible as he', Humphrey took on both Burgundy and France, and, having relieved Calais, carried out a successful raid into Flanders before entering London in triumph. The parallel with the events of 1415 was there for all to see.[9] By 1463 an Italian translation of the *Vita*, made by the humanist, Pier Candido Decembrio, from Tito Livio's original, and dedicated to Francesco Sforza, had extended Henry's reputation beyond the jurisdiction of the two crowns which he had won for his son.[10]

In 1440 Humphrey was to find himself at the centre of a political controversy concerning the royal council's decision to release Charles, duke of Orléans, held a prisoner for the past quarter of a century, in spite of Henry V's express wish that he should not be released unless peace were made. Involved as he had been for many years in a political dogfight with Henry Beaufort, his arch-rival for authority within the council, Humphrey penned a protest (in English) against the projected plan to free Orléans, who had been a prisoner 'of the moost victorious and mighte prince', Henry V, since the day of the triumph won at Agincourt on Saints Crispin and Crispinian's day.[11] Opening up the debate in his defence of 'the kyng of moost blessed memory', he accused Beaufort of having recently urged Henry VI to renounce his use of the title 'King of France'. The young king had given his oath as ruler of France at his coronation in Paris in December 1431, and to protect the royal claim Humphrey said he was prepared to die. If the king no longer used the title, there was a great risk that France would be lost, and the authority of the English crown would suffer accordingly. Such was the view of one of the last survivors of the great days of Henry V's reign. Loyal to the last to his brother, to his achievement and to his memory, Humphrey may not have been moving sufficiently with the pace of events. His rivalry with Beaufort,

[9] R. Weiss, 'Humphrey, duke of Gloucester, and Tito Livio Frulovisi', *Fritz Saxl, 1890–1948. A volume of memorial essays from his friends in England*, ed. D.J. Gordon (London, 1957), pp. 218–25; Weiss, *Humanism in England during the fifteenth century* (2nd edn, Oxford, 1957), pp. 41–3.
[10] J.H. Wylie, 'Decembri's version of the Vita Henrici Quinti by Tito Livio', *EHR*, 24 (1909), 84–9.
[11] *Letters and papers*, II, ii, 441–51.

one of those whose policy and influence he was attacking, would not have helped him to sympathize with those who saw that a change of attitude to the war and to the defence of Henry V's conquest might have become necessary. To Humphrey, any new approach was tantamount to treason. Such was the hold which Henry still had upon his brother some twenty years after his death.

Like Humphrey, the policy-makers could give reasons for their change of view.[12] Peace was badly needed, notably as a means of ending schism within the Church: the release of Orléans was seen as a means of ending the conflict which had lasted 'an hundreth yeeres and more'. There was good precedent for this. For all his successes and conquests, Edward III had found that he could not conquer France, and had been advised to make peace; in his last days Henry V had begun to realize that he was in a similar position, and had been seriously thinking about making peace. Now, nearly twenty years later, England had lost many lives and experienced difficulties similar to those of Edward III; even the people of Normandy desired to live in peace. The French were now willing to come to a settlement, but made the release of Orléans a precondition. In any event, it was against the spirit of the law of arms to keep a man a prisoner for ever.

This last was something with which, it was implied, Henry himself would have agreed. What he would have thought of the remainder of the argument, one can only speculate. Put forward as the expression of realism, it implied an abandonment of the spirit of conquest which had motivated Henry V. Those who make difficult decisions are seldom popular; in this case the decision involved not only the dismantling of a small 'empire' but, worse, the implication (since God had not allowed the English to keep it) that they should never have held it in the first place. The decision to which Beaufort was party showed the man's flexibility. Much had happened since the heady days of Henry's reign when he had strongly justified and encouraged war against France. Humphrey lacked that flexibility. He was not, nor would he have wished to be, in agreement with such decisions. The attitudes of the two men illustrate clearly how the interpretation of the late king's will, and what to do with his political legacy in the very different conditions of 1440, was dividing even the royal family itself.

Yet Henry's memory did not die. New foundations for prayers and masses to be said for his soul were still being established more than thirty years after his death.[13] Some time, probably in the 1440s, a further *Vita* was composed, in all likelihood for Sir Walter Hungerford,

---

[12]   Ibid., II, ii, 451–60.
[13]   *VCH Salop.*, ii, 133.

who had served the late king in many capacities, and had been present at his deathbed. Showing strong evidence of classical influences, and heavily dependent upon the work of Tito Livio, it none the less provides us with valuable information about the last year or two of Henry's life and, hardly surprisingly, details about his death and funeral arrangements.[14] It serves to remind us that, since Henry died at a relatively young age, there were people still active and influential in political and military affairs who were ready to carry the memory of what he had done and stood for into the England of the mid-fifteenth century. Humphrey was to die in 1447 (as was Henry Beaufort), Walter Hungerford in 1449. The deaths of these men may be said to mark the end of the late king's practical influence upon events through those who had actually served with him. In 1450 Normandy once again became French.

The loss of Normandy was later to trigger off a reaction. It was probably in 1452 that William Worcestre, secretary and amanuensis to Sir John Fastolf, composed his *Boke of Noblesse*, a work in which he pleaded for a revival of commitment to war against the French by the English crown. Using a mixture of historical evidence and special pleading from which emotion was not excluded, Worcestre showed how the links between England and Normandy went back to the time of William the Conqueror, and that the achievements of Henry V in conquering the duchy and, more recently, the efforts of Fastolf's patron, John, duke of Bedford, in maintaining the effectiveness of English rule within it were based on a sound historical footing. Henry, 'albeit that it consumed gretlie his peple . . . wanne bothe the saide Duchie of Normandie first and, after, the Roiaume of Fraunce, conqueri'd and broughte in subjeccion and wanne be his grete manhode, withe the noble power of his lordis and helpe of his comonys, and so overleid the myghtie roialle power of Fraunce.'[15] Worcestre's approach was traditional, the stress being on two points. First, Henry was the victor of Agincourt, who achieved his aims with the help of his nobility and people; he was a king of unity. The second was to show how the winning of lands in France, begun by Henry, had been continued after his death. The process of achieving justice had been maintained.

What Worcestre did with his text, almost certainly written in the early 1450s, that is in the immediate aftermath of defeat, remains a mystery. The dedication, such as we have it, is dated June 1475, just at the moment when Edward IV was about to lead an army into

<hr/>

[14] Gransden, *Historical writing*, ii, 213–15.
[15] *Boke of Noblesse addressed to King Edward the Fourth on his invasion of France in 1475*, ed. J.G. Nichols (Roxburghe Club, 1860), p. 16.

France, perhaps, as Worcestre may have hoped, to regain the lands won by Henry V, but since lost. To the Yorkist kings, the Lancastrians were usurpers; in the parliament of 1472 Henry was termed 'late in dede and not in right Kyng of Englond'.[16] This, however, would not have deterred Edward IV from using Henry's achievements in France as a basis for his own territorial ambitions had he so wished. In fact, Edward was to cross the Channel with an army in the summer of 1475, but he soon came to an arrangement with the French king, Louis XI, and withdrew to England. Although Worcestre's work had no influence upon policy in these years, it is of interest mainly for the fact that in the second half of the fifteenth century, when all in France appeared lost, it was thought possible to reanimate interest in reconquest by appealing to past history and, more particularly, to English successes achieved by Henry V and those who had gone over the sea with him.[17]

The visions of the glorious events and achievements of Henry V's reign were to make their influence felt on two further occasions. In the summer of 1513 Henry VIII, who may have harboured ambitions to revive the war against France and to seek glory in this way, invaded north-eastern France, where, at the battle of Guinegate and through the capture of Tournai, he won a respectable degree of glory.[18] Between this time and August 1514, when peace was made with France, an anonymous Translator was at work producing an updated life of Henry V, this time in English. His purpose was to lay before Henry VIII, as he went to war against the common enemy, an account of the 'chivalrous acts of this so noble, so vertuous, and so excellent a Prince, which, so followed, he might the rather attaine to like honnour, fame, and victorie'.[19] Didactic in character and intent, the *Life* was based on the *Vita* of Tito Livio, on the *Polichronicon* published by Caxton (in effect, the *Brut* under another guise), on the work of the Burgundian, Enguerrand de Monstrelet, and on reminiscences provided by the descendants of the Butler earls of Ormonde, one of whom, James, fourth earl, had been a near contemporary of Henry V, whom he had known and accompanied on his campaigns. Some years after Ormonde's death in 1452, another work (perhaps a form of *Vita* of the late king) had been compiled. This work, which included personal memories of Henry recorded by Ormonde, came to be used by the Translator of Henry VIII's reign. Incorporated into this new

---

[16] *RP*, vi, 15.

[17] C.T. Allmand, 'France-Angleterre à la fin de la guerre de cent ans: le "Boke of Noblesse" de William Worcester', *La France anglaise au moyen age. Actes du 111e congrès national des sociétés savantes, Poitiers, 1986* (Paris, 1988), pp. 103–11.

[18] *First English Life*, p. x.

[19] Ibid., p. 4.

work, Ormonde's contributions are somewhat anecdotal in character. Some correspond quite well with what we know from other sources, other stand in their own right.[20] Their value lies in the fact that they add a 'personal' touch to the little we know about Henry as a man; for this reason they cannot be ignored.

A generation later, in the late 1530s, with the war of propaganda against the papacy now being taken very seriously, the memory of Henry's triumph at Agincourt was revived as part of a drive to use drama to encourage patriotic enthusiasm. For this purpose Henry VIII was to be regarded as Moses, who delivered his people out of the hands of the modern Pharaoh, 'the bysshop of Rome'. A parallel was to be drawn with Henry V, to whom God had given assistance in saving his small force from the hands of 'so grate a multitude of the frenshemen at the batell of Agyncourte', an event which 'your noble towne of Caleys and others ther over yerely make a solempne tryumphe, goyng in procession, laudyng God, shotyng gonnes with the noyse and melodye of trumpettes and other instruments, to the great reioysyng of your subiectes beyng aged, the comforte of them that be able men, [and] the encouragyng of yong children'.[21] If celebrations of this nature could take place in Calais (of which Henry V, as Prince, had been captain before becoming king), all the more so should there be processions and bonfires to celebrate the kingdom's liberation from its ties with Rome.

This example emphasizes one thing: that so much of what was associated with Henry V, both in terms of personality and achievement (for did not the second stem from the first?), was used, as it had long been, as 'a valuable asset to the enthusiastic nationalist'.[22] History was being employed for a particular, mainly political purpose, to provide examples from the past for the benefit of the present. Henry VIII wanted to act not only as king (*rex*) but as king-emperor (*rex imperator*), sovereign in his own right, owing allegiance to none. Henry II, for example, was a king to be admired for having tried to stand up to the pope; conversely, Thomas Becket's shrine, a symbol of subservience to the papacy, was to be dismantled. The tale, recounted by the Translator in 1513 on the 'credible report' of Ormonde, that Humphrey of Gloucester had not allowed the emperor Sigismund to land at Dover, when he arrived in May 1416, until he had given an assurance that he would not attempt to exercise imperial rights in England, would have met with a sympathetic response from

[20] Ibid., introduction.
[21] S. Anglo, 'An early Tudor programme for plays and other demonstrations against the Pope', *Journal of the Warburg and Courtauld Institutes*, 20 (1957), 178.
[22] M. McKisack, *Mediaeval history in the Tudor age* (Oxford, 1971), p. 121.

sixteenth-century Englishmen, who would have read it later, in a slightly different version, in Holinshed's *Chronicles*. The theme of most of the history written in the sixteenth century, as that part of it concerning Henry V written in the fifteenth had been, was the glory of Britain. First Robert Fabyan, who died in 1513 and whose work, *The New Chronicles of England and France*, was published in 1516, and, after him, Edward Hall, who died in 1547 and who chose to describe 'the victorious actes of kyng Henry the v', delighted in writing about victories achieved against foreigners.[23]

It was from such writers, and principally Holinshed, that Shakespeare drew facts and stories suitable for his play, published in 1600. By now, however, with a growing public demand for history that was both instructive and entertaining, the development of a form of history which followed certain predetermined lines was coming about. The need to incorporate a didactic approach into historical writing was to be very influential. To Richard Grafton, Henry was 'the noblest king that ever reigned over the realme of England', and he proved this by stressing his great reputation for prowess and martial acts, which led him to victory against the French, thus making him into an ideal patriot. To Samuel David, the king was 'a mirror of vertues'[24] which could be examined for the lessons it might reveal. When Robert Redmayne came to write his *Life of Henry V*, probably about 1575, he was not writing as an authority on the king's life, but mainly to create a character essentially literary and philosophical in nature. In brief, what was emerging looked more like a moral stereotype than a historical figure of flesh and blood.[25] It was what men thought Henry's achievement meant to their generation, rather than any attempt to present a critical picture of a man whose greatness was not in doubt, which met with approval in Tudor England.

Although Shakespeare breathed a new (and living) soul into the character he created, he was still the prisoner of his time. Even if we put aside (as we must) the restrictions imposed by the medium for which he wrote, we are left with the fact that Shakespeare's play is surrounded by much the same constraints (the need to entertain, to instruct, to enlighten, all at once) which restricted the writers of chronicles. Chivalry was far from dead in late Elizabethan England, and Shakespeare made Henry behave in the best chivalric tradition. War, too, was very much in the air in the 1590s, so war, in particular

[23] Ibid., pp. 96, 105, 121.
[24] G. Bullough, *Narrative and dramatic sources of Shakespeare* (7 vols, London/New York, 1957–73), iv, 350.
[25] R.R. Reid, 'The date and authorship of Redmayne's "Life of Henry V"', *EHR*, 30 (1915), 695.

successful war against the traditional (Catholic) enemy, was portrayed on stage. In writing his play, just as other writers had done
when compiling their histories, Shakespeare had to think of what
would sell. His answer to that challenge was to take the most dramatic
aspects of the reign, already given form by the chroniclers, and turn
them into a play.

As he had already done in the case of Richard III, Shakespeare
was to create a Henry V destined to become part of England's cultural
heritage. The person looking to the events of the play for historical
accuracy will be disappointed, although the figure of Henry himself,
based on a century and a half or more of tradition, is, in certain
respects, convincing enough. Shakespeare was more concerned to
create a figure who could be admired not merely for his personal
qualities but also for what he was able to do when he used these for
the benefit of the country over which he ruled, the only fifteenth-
century king in Shakespeare's canon to do this successfully. Essentially, Henry was presented as a soldier, purposeful, determined,
caring for his men's good, able to calm them at times of doubt yet
capable of inspiring them when the moment of test came, much in
the tradition created within Henry's own lifetime by the author of the
Gesta.

The play was also about kingship. Being a good soldier and leader
was one essential part of that function. Another was the ability to
secure obedience to the law and to achieve a state of order in society.
Here Henry the disciplinarian, who hanged those who disobeyed him,
and brought order into the army, was depicted as the leader who was
in control of his men. The French, whose act of withholding what
was English land in France went against the dictates of justice, also
constituted an element of instability. If they could be dealt with,
justice would be restored into the realm of relations between France
and England, and peace would result. For all its excitement and
action, the political and social message of the play was to be neither
ignored nor forgotten. The king, together with his nobles and people,
had restored a measure of order (called since Henry's own day and
even well before by the name of 'justice') to a divided world. That
had been his aim. That is what he was seen to have achieved.

By the time of his death, Henry was regarded as a king who had met
many of his people's aspirations and had fulfilled the ideals of his
office. In 1413 his accession had aroused much expectation. Henry
was already well enough known to offer hope of vigorous yet stabiliz-
ing control of the ship of state by one who knew what he wanted and
was prepared to work hard to achieve it. Henry's contemporaries
understood the young man's impatience to exercise power in his own

right. The stories which came to surround his activities in the last
year or so of his father's reign point to a man, conscious of his own
ability and wanting to make the most of it, faced by a father with
whom he had an uneasy relationship, whose health was not good, and
whose rule was adrift for lack of personal drive and determination to
succeed. Henry stood for something quite different, rule with direction, carried out with drive. As already suggested, the 'new man'
whom Henry became on his accession was a metaphorical way of
stating that, by leaving behind old habits, his reign was going to be
different. Henry IV had not always fulfilled the hopes and promises
of his usurpation and coronation. His son, on the other hand, had a
vision of government. He had, too, the energy with which to deliver
the goods.

The reign was characterized by a marked sense of harmony among
the English people, which was deliberately fostered by the king.[26] The
crises of the Lollard rising and the Southampton plot had to be firmly
dealt with because they undermined both the religious and the political unity of the country. In both cases the king, who personified that
spirit, was said to have been threatened. As a man who valued loyalty,
Henry felt the treason of Oldcastle and, above all, Scrope, both friends
from former years, very personally; his treatment of Scrope in particular was harsh. Both men had been guilty of undermining the unity of
the country – both paid the ultimate penalty for their treachery.

At all times Henry endeavoured to reconcile interests and parties.
The reburial of Richard II late in 1413 was an attempt to close a
chapter in England's history at a moment when a certain political
tension could be felt. Henry wanted to unite, not to cause further
divisions. 'Let us alle row to gedir', urged the preacher before parliament in 1421. The use of the pardon (which he was to be urged to
use by an unknown priest, perhaps bishop Beaufort himself, after
Agincourt) was a sign of strength,[27] as well as of reconciliation. The
way in which pardons and arbitration were used in Henry's name in
May and June 1414 shows the king at his best, more concerned to
bring together those who had offended society than to apply the law

[26] 'Truly, most worthy Prince, it behoveth you not to fear for the subsidies of your
realm . . . because your faithful people so delight in their present happy auspices,
that they offer to you themselves and their goods, and pour out for you unceasingly
their devout prayers . . . [and] heartily desire that you may long reign over them'
(*Letters of queen Margaret*, p. 6, trans. of Latin original). In 1421 the ship of England
was described as being the parts built round the body: 'corpus navis est communitas'
(Haines, 'Our master mariner', 89). The sense of a country united inspires the entire
text: see above, ch.19, p. 405.
[27] Henry was urged to be pious, clement and anxious to pardon (*Letters of queen
Margaret*, pp. 4–5).

rigorously to them. The restoration of the heirs of the earldoms of Huntingdon, Northumberland and Salisbury was also to Henry's credit. In all three cases, the decision was the right one; none was to become involved in any treachery in the years to come.[28]

His success at home rested upon his search for consensus, which is evident in so much of what he did. One of his more notable achievements was to have restored the good relationship between crown and nobility which had suffered so greatly during the reign of Richard II; he consulted the nobility about the war and led them on campaign, rewarding some with the material gains of conquest.[29] Where his father's relationship with parliament had been, at times, an uneasy one, he showed from the very first meeting of the reign that he understood the causes of that unease, so that Henry and his parliaments may be said to have worked together in a cordial atmosphere. The same was true of the persons whose daily life he shared at court. The household was the centre of government, and its members were happy to follow the lead of its head. Masterful personality Henry certainly was; at times he was probably wilful.[30] Yet these were the characteristics recognized as being those of firm and decisive leadership.

A notable feature of his way of ruling was the effort which he made to link his activity and, for example, that of the army when it was in France to the supportive effort of his people.[31] His subjects could help through the payment of taxes, through the settlement of newly gained territory in Normandy, and through their prayers, which associated them directly with the military effort being made in France. They could share in the triumph of Agincourt, in which even those who had remained at home, he believed, had played a part. The image of England as a new Israel, of Englishmen as God's chosen people, and of the king as His knight, whether defending the Church or asserting his claims to justice in France, was one favoured at court. The saints, and in particular the saints of England, were the top-castle of the ship of state.[32] The kingdom might rightly feel more united, more favoured, than it had for many a long year.

That Henry was a fine, indeed a remarkable, soldier cannot be in doubt.[33] Ever since his own day there has been virtual unanimity on this point. He was a natural commander of men, confident in himself, able to inspire in moments of danger and crisis (such as in the days and hours before Agincourt), a firm believer in the virtue of order

[28] Harriss, *Henry V: practice of kingship*, p. 42.
[29] Ibid., ch.2.
[30] '. . . de tres haultain voulloir' (Waurin, 429).
[31] See, for example, *Brut*, ii, 382.
[32] 'Tho topcastel huius navis sunt sancti . . .' (Haines, 'Our master mariner', 89).
[33] Allmand, 'The soldier', Harriss, *Henry V*, pp. 117–35.

and in the need for discipline among all ranks in the army. His moral authority lay at the root of his success. According to Jean Fusoris, the French priest who saw him at Winchester just before the expedition of 1415 set out for France, it was Clarence who looked like a soldier, not Henry, who, the Frenchman reported, had more the air of the priest about him.[34] Looks could easily deceive. As a leader, as a strategist bent on conquest, as an organizer of military power, Henry was highly successful. His contemporaries were right in that regard.

Any consideration of the feasibility of Henry's aims in France poses great difficulties. It can be argued that the invasion of France should be regarded as an integral part of Henry's restoration of English pride and self-awareness. War would do this better than anything else. It can be claimed, too, that war was integral to the revival of monarchy, and that the prestige of the crown demanded war against the old enemy. Henry was also convinced that he had a strong legal and historic claim to the French throne; the war which he chose to wage was certainly not that of a lone megalomaniac, for he had the support of his nobility, and that of his people through parliament, to encourage him. Even at the end of the reign, when parliament had called a temporary halt to taxation for war, there were still many ready to lend him their private financial support.

It is important that Henry's policy be seen both in terms of its short-term aims and its long-term results. Although it is dangerous to rely on such an argument, we should recall that Henry died relatively young. Had he lived even another decade, he might have reacted very differently to developing circumstances. As it was, his death removed his dynamic contribution to the restoration of monarchical prestige and national pride. So much of what he had gained in these respects was lost in the years which followed. In the war against France, the removal of his leadership was to be full of consequences. Henry's powers of decision-making were dead; they could not be replaced by those of a child: even a regent as able as Bedford was hamstrung in France. Decisions were taken by men who, out of loyalty, asked 'what would Henry have done?'. They could not negotiate if this involved making concessions, as to do so would be to deny Henry VI his rights before he ever came to exercise them himself. Furthermore, to do so would have been to undermine one of the central platforms upon which Henry's achievement had been built, namely that, by helping the English to victory, God approved of their conquest. The absence

---

[34] L. Mirot, 'Le procès de Maitre Jean Fusoris, chanoine de Notre-Dame de Paris (1415–1416)', *Mémoires de la Société de l'Histoire de Paris et de l'Ile de France*, 27 (1901), 175.

of Henry in the 1420s and 1430s was, therefore, crucial to the way England responded to the war in those decades. Had he lived, he might have reacted more subtly to events as they developed. That fact must always be borne in mind.

It is too much to ask that Henry should have been able to foresee the final outcome, a whole generation later, of his initiative in France. Yet the signs of difficulties to come were to appear early. By 1416 parliament was already showing opposition to the acceleration of taxation for war purposes. This was one way of complaining of the exceptionally high level of taxation which Henry was exacting for a war which, because it was very different in nature to that pursued by his great-grandfather, Edward III, was proving very expensive. Nor, after 1420, was the answer found in making Normandy itself pay for the war, as Englishmen might reasonably have hoped. In the duchy the effects of the English invasion did not favour the high rates of taxation which the active continuation of the conquest would require. Furthermore (and this is something for which Henry cannot be made to bear any responsibility), the fluctuations in the value of an all-coin currency during the reign (and in particular from 1418 or so onwards) affected the ability of France, as well as of England, to finance the war. It is possible to sympathize with Henry having to deal (as he seriously tried to do) with the instability in money values which affected much of north-western Europe during these years. It is legitimate, however, to enquire how far he would ever have trimmed his plans to suit his financial means.

Lack of money must be allied to lack of manpower, a factor which he fully appreciated by the closing months of his life. By 1421 it was clear to him that the early enthusiasm for the war was waning; the refusal of the gentry of Norfolk to join him in France may not have been entirely typical,[35] but theirs was a warning which could not be ignored. It was one aspect of a wider sense of unease regarding the war, and the king's involvement in it, which was being felt in England from late 1420 onwards. To Henry, the treaty sealed at Troyes in the spring may have appeared as a triumph, a legal triumph, at least. To those at home, it seemed that the king had committed himself to win over by force those areas which remained loyal to the Valois dynasty. This might mean further demands on England's resources. It would certainly make demands upon the king's time and energy; the parliament of December 1420 was clearly unhappy about the long period, by then three and a half years, which the king had spent in France. The need for assurances about this, and about the fear that England could become subject to French law (clear misrepresentation though

---

[35] *PPC*, ii, 246–8; see above, ch.10, n.17.

it was), strongly suggests that there was little public enthusiasm for
the terms agreed at Troyes, even less for a long-drawn-out war.

The treaty of Troyes was, in many respects, the crux of the matter.
Made possible, perhaps even likely, by the murder of John of Burgundy in the presence of the dauphin on the bridge at Montereau on
10 September 1419, it depended too much upon the outcome of that
tragic event. If Henry, by the summer of 1419 already exerting considerable military pressure upon Paris from a north-westerly direction, could make an ally out of the new duke, Philip, together they
might make a political treaty which could resolve many of Henry's
political problems in France at a stroke. In Normandy, Henry had
not received the wide acceptance which he had hoped for. His appeal
to Norman history and traditions (his revival of old ducal institutions
was one way of doing this) had taken too little account of how French
the duchy had become after two centuries of rule from the capital,
and, indeed, of how strong pro-Burgundian sentiment was in certain
towns, notably in Rouen. By allying himself with duke Philip in the
treaty of Troyes, he could be seen as joining the side with which many
Normans felt political sympathy in the context of the civil conflict,
then pitting Burgundians against dauphinists. Yet the use of the same
treaty, which made him heir and regent of the French kingdom, to
give him control of Normandy from Paris might appear as cynical
manipulation by the man who, until then, had appeared as the
defender of Norman particularism and institutions. Henry probably
recognized what the effects of Troyes upon his relationship with Normandy might be. On his deathbed, he insisted that the duchy should
remain under English rule until his successor, his young son, should
take up the French crown and rule every part of France as king.

The question arises, therefore, how good was Henry's political
sense? Did he understand what he was committing himself to in May
1420 when he agreed to the fateful treaty which he sealed with his
marriage to Katharine, the French king's daughter? By then, signs of
impending problems were to be seen everywhere. Did Henry ignore
these and, if so, did he do so because he felt that he could no longer
go back, only forward, regardless of consequences?[36] There can be
little doubt that circumstances had changed since he had first
appeared in France, in 1415, in pursuit of his claim. Perhaps he could
be forgiven if, within sight of a treaty which made him heir to France,

---

[36] 'No man putting his hand to the plough, and looking back, is fit for the kingdom
[of heaven]; but continued effort usually leads to success; and according to Tully
[Cicero] it is the part of true virtue not to look on what has been done, but what
remains to be done; not what a man has, but what he is wanting in' (advice from an
unknown cleric to Henry V, 1415; *Letters of queen Margaret*, p. 5).

he could not see the advantages of settling for less. If he controlled the whole, he controlled the parts, too. And if he could make those who opposed him change their minds (by the use of military force, if necessary) he might one day win effective control of the kingdom to which he could now lay claim by a recently sealed treaty.

Henry failed to take proper account of the political climate and circumstances which produced that treaty. To the French, it was imposed by force, which might, one day, be repudiated. It was also created out of an alliance which Henry had made with only one of the parties in the French civil conflict, an 'unnatural' alliance which might last only as long as the conflict itself lasted. It was, as the French themselves were quick to point out, a settlement basically flawed because in assuming the title of heir to the kingdom of France, Henry had agreed to let Charles VI remain king to the end of his natural life, with the strong implication that he recognized Charles, rather than himself, as the legitimate ruler of France. The act of disinheritance of the dauphin was one which, in the final analysis, few Frenchmen were ready to accept. The principle of inheritance was based on nature; no agreement imposed upon a sick king by the victorious ruler of another country could nullify it. When Charles VI died some six weeks after Henry, in October 1422, the majority of Frenchmen came to see his son, Charles, rather than his English grandson, Henry, as his natural heir. That factor made the conquest of France, formally undertaken in the treaty of Troyes, an even more difficult task than had been foreseen.

In the end, it can be said, Henry made a serious error of judgement, preferring the prospect of the kingdom of France (which would include Normandy) to Normandy either on its own or as part of a wider territorial settlement (perhaps based on the treaty of Brétigny) which he would have been in a position to impose in 1420.[37] Such an agreement would have avoided the political error of altering the succession to the French crown. Yet it is likely that any settlement made in these years of division in France would, one day, have been challenged. Henry was blinded by the fact that his war was being fought to regain territories which he had come to regard as being rightly his. In his eyes, this was the cause of justice. Such a cause had the backing of God, which had been shown during the reign of Edward III and, more recently, at Agincourt and on other occasions, but which the stubborn French refused to recognize.[38] He, in turn, failed to recognize that there were strong forces marshalled against him, however weak the French appeared to be at the time. He did not see that, in France,

[37] Keen, 'Diplomacy', Harriss, *Henry V: practice of kingship*, p. 198.
[38] *Gesta*, pp. 123, 125.

there existed a rapidly growing sense of national spirit and awareness, centred upon the monarch, and inspired by war, a spirit ironically not so very different from that which Henry was trying to encourage in England.[39] Both countries (we can now tell) were looking and moving forwards. By contrast, Henry's appeal was essentially to the past, to what he thought had once been a particular historical situation. He therefore passed on to his son an inheritance which may justly be termed 'damnosa hereditas'.[40]

Henry is best estimated by separating his foreign from his domestic achievements. He saw his invasion of France in search of his right as part of an obligation incumbent upon him as king. The manner in which he portrayed himself as Edward III's successor to certain claims in France underlined that neither of his immediate predecessors, Richard II and his own father, had done much personally to implement them. To renew actively the French war was another way of showing that, under his rule, things would be different. His successes in France were described in terms of the credit which they could bring him, the crown and the people. They served a crucial purpose in helping to unite English society in a common enterprise. Yet, advantageous as this might be in the short term, the French venture was already proving a considerable problem before Henry died. After his death, and during the next thirty or so years, it became an ever increasing political and financial liability for those who ruled England, so much so that Henry VI was eventually to repudiate the enterprise to which his father had devoted so much of his time and energy.

If we base our estimate of Henry more upon his domestic achievement, we are on much safer ground in giving him a favourable verdict. Although he left large debts (normal enough), Henry must be given credit for having seen, at an early age, that forward planning was necessary in organizing the royal finances. In this, he was far ahead of his father. In his relations with his subjects, at all levels, he was markedly successful, achieving a greater degree of political and social harmony than had been known for many years. It was at home that his political skills were seen at their best and at their most effective. Curiously, these achievements were little written about in the chronicles, whereas the more dramatic events of the war received much prominence. Shakespeare was heir to that tradition.

In our own time, with emphasis being placed on different sources and with analysis as well as description being regarded as an essential part of writing history, we take a different view of Henry. While giving

---

[39] See above, ch.19.
[40] Jacob, *Fifteenth century*, p. 202.

him credit for his immediate successes in war and for the personal
qualities which enabled him to achieve them, we look beyond the war
to its possible consequences. It is that view of the future which has
caused some to cast doubts on the real stature of the man. Yet, to
dismiss him as an adventurer,[41] even if that judgement is intended to
apply mainly to his military enterprise in France, is unfair. The
reasons which made Henry invade France were too intricate, too
much rooted in the ideas and assumptions of Englishmen of the time,
to be dismissed so easily.

While we may think of Henry as a 'straightforward' enough character, he was much more complex a figure than may at first appear,
driven less by personal ambition than by what he saw as right, seeking, even in making war in France, to set that kingdom in a harmonious relation with his English one, mainly through him as the ruler of
both. That part of his design was not to last; only in the short term
can he be said to have been successful in France. But in most other
enterprises which he undertook, including the responsible task of helping to bring the great schism to an end, he was successful, to the
advantage of his reputation and to that of his country. Not surprisingly, since his achievement had already won him his people's high
regard, his early death was considered a tragedy. If, in the generations
which followed, the estimation of him was to be based largely on the
military success which he won against the French, later generations
can see him as the king who strove to provide his people with 'bone
et sage governance', thereby seeking to fulfil both their broader hopes
in him and his obligations to them. A careful consideration of his
whole achievement reveals much regarding Henry's stature both as
man and king. From it he emerges as a ruler whose already high
reputation is not only maintained but enhanced.

[41] Ibid., p. 202.

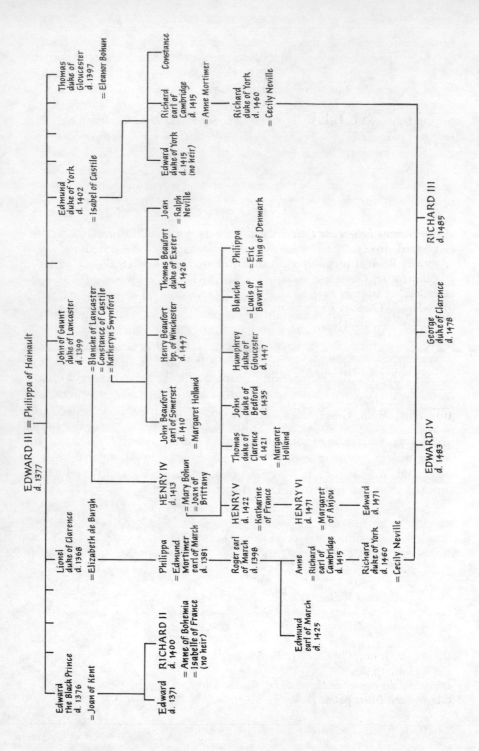

EDWARD III = Philippa of Hainault
d. 1377

Edward
the Black Prince
d. 1376
= Joan of Kent

Lionel
duke of Clarence
d. 1368
= Elizabeth de Burgh

John of Gaunt
duke of Lancaster
d. 1399
= Blanche of Lancaster
= Constance of Castile
= Katheryn Swynford

Edmund
duke of York
d. 1402
= Isabel of Castile

Thomas
duke of
Gloucester
d. 1397
= Eleanor Bohun

Edward
d. 1371

RICHARD II
d. 1400
= Anne of Bohemia
= Isabelle of France
(no heir)

Philippa
= Edmund
Mortimer
earl of March
d. 1381

HENRY IV
d. 1413
= Mary Bohun
= Joan of
Brittany

John Beaufort
earl of Somerset
d. 1410
= Margaret Holland

Henry Beaufort
bp. of Winchester
d. 1447

Thomas Beaufort
duke of Exeter
d. 1426

Joan
= Ralph
Neville

Edward
duke of York
d. 1415
(no heir)

Richard
earl of
Cambridge
d. 1415
= Anne Mortimer

Constance

Roger earl
of March
d. 1398

HENRY V
d. 1422
= Katharine
of France

Thomas
duke of
Clarence
d. 1421
= Margaret
Holland

John
duke of
Bedford
d. 1435

Humphrey
duke of
Gloucester
d. 1447

Blanche
= Louis of
Bavaria

Philippa
= Eric
king of Denmark

Richard
duke of York
d. 1460
= Cecily Neville

Edmund
earl of March
d. 1425

Anne
= Richard
earl of
Cambridge
d. 1415

HENRY VI
d. 1471
= Margaret
of Anjou

Edward
d. 1471

Richard
duke of York
d. 1460
= Cecily Neville

EDWARD IV
d. 1483

George
duke of Clarence
d. 1478

RICHARD III
d. 1485

SELECT BIBLIOGRAPHY

PRINTED SOURCES

Anglo-Norman Letters and Petitions, ed. M.D. Legge (Anglo-Norman Text Soc., Oxford, 1941).

'Annales Ricardi secundi et Henrici quarti', J. de Trokelowe et Henrici de Blaneforde, *Chronica et Annales*, ed. H.T. Riley (RS, London, 1866).

Anonimalle Chronicle, 1333–1381, ed. V.H. Galbraith (Manchester, 1927).

Anthology of Chancery English, ed. J.H. Fisher, M. Richardson and J.L. Fisher (Knoxville, 1984).

Boke of Noblesse addressed to king Edward the Fourth on his invasion of France in 1475, ed. J.G. Nichols (Roxburghe Club, 1860).

Book of London English, 1384–1425, ed. R.W. Chambers and M. Daunt (Oxford, 1967).

Bouchart, Alain, *Grandes croniques de Bretaigne*, ed. H. Le Meignen (Rennes, 1886).

Brut, or The chronicles of England, ed. F.W.D. Brie, ii (EETS, London, 1908).

Calendar of ancient petitions relating to Wales, ed. W. Rees (Cardiff, 1975).

Calendar of Charter Rolls, 1341–1417 (London, 1916).

Calendar of Close Rolls, 1399–1422 (London, 1927–32).

Calendar of early chancery proceedings relating to west country shipping, 1388–1493, ed. D.M. Gardiner (Devon & Cornwall Rec. Soc., new series, 21, 1976).

Calendar of Letter-Books preserved among the Archives of the Corporation of the City of London at the Guildhall, Letter-Book I, c.A.D. 1400–1422, ed. R.R. Sharpe (London, 1909).

Calendar of Patent Rolls, 1399–1422 (London, 1903–11).

Calendar of signet letters of Henry IV and Henry V, ed. J.L. Kirby (London, 1978).

Canonization of Saint Osmund, ed. A.R. Malden (Wiltshire Rec. Soc., Salisbury, 1901).

Capgrave, John, *The Book of the Illustrious Henries*, trans. F.C. Hingeston (RS, London, 1858).

Cartulaire des comtes de Hainaut, ed. L. Devillers (Brussels, 1889).

Charters and letters patent granted to Kingston-upon-Hull, trans. J.R. Boyle (Hull, 1945).

Chartier, Alain, *Poetical Works*, ed. J.C. Laidlaw (Cambridge, 1974).

Chastellain, Georges de, *Oeuvres. I. Chronique, 1419–1422*, ed. K. de Letten-hove (Brussels, 1863).

Chronicle of John Hardyng, ed. H. Ellis (London, 1812).

'Chronicle of John Strecche for the Reign of Henry V (1414–1422)', ed. F. Taylor, *BJRL*, 16 (1932).

Chronicle of London, from 1089 to 1483, ed. N.H. Nicolas and E. Tyrrell (London, 1827).

Chronicles of London, ed. C.L. Kingsford (Oxford, 1905).

Chronicon Adae de Usk, A.D. 1377–1421, trans. E.M. Thompson (2nd edn, London, 1904).

Chronique d'Antonio Morosini. Extraits relatifs à l'histoire de France, ed. G. Lefèvre-Pontalis and L. Dorez, ii (SHF, Paris, 1899).

Chronique d'Enguerran de Monstrelet, ed. L. Douët d'Arcq, ii, iii (SHF, Paris 1858–59).

'Chronique de Gilles de Roy', *Chroniques relatives à l'histoire de la Belgique sous la domination des ducs de Bourgogne*, ed. K. de Lettenhove (Brussels, 1870).

Chronique de Jean le Fèvre, seigneur de Saint-Remy, ed. F. Morand, i (SHF, Paris, 1876).

'Chronique de Normandie de l'an 1414 à 1422', *Henrici quinti Angliae regis gesta*, ed. B. Williams (London, 1850).

Chronique de Perceval de Cagny, ed. H. Moranvillé (SHF, Paris, 1902).

Chronique du Religieux de Saint-Denys, ed. L.-F. Bellaguet, ii (Paris, 1840).

Chronique normande de Pierre Cochon, ed. C. de Robillard de Beaurepaire (Rouen, 1870).

Clanvowe, Sir John, *Works*, ed. V.J. Scattergood (Cambridge/Ipswich, 1975).

Collection générale des documents français qui se trouvent en Angleterre, recueillis et publiés par Jules Delpit (Paris, 1847).

Collection of all the wills now known to be extant of the kings and queens of England, ed. J. Nichols (London, 1780).

Complete Peerage of England, Scotland, Ireland and the United Kingdom, ed. G.E. Cokayne et al. (London, 1910–59).

Concilia Magnae Britanniae et Hiberniae, ed. D. Wilkins, iii (London, 1737).

Contribuables parisiens à la fin de la guerre de cent ans. Les rôles d'impôt de 1421, 1423 et 1438, ed. J. Favier (Geneva, 1970).

Cotton Manuscrit Galba BI, ed. E. Scott and L. Gilliodts-van Severen (Brussels, 1896).

Council of Constance: the unification of the Church, ed. L.R. Loomis (New York, 1961).

Documents illustrating the activities of the general and provincial chapters of the English Black Monks, 1215–1540, ed. W.A. Pantin, ii (Camden 3rd series, 47, RHistS, London 1933).

Documents relatifs au clos des galées de Rouen, ed. A. Merlin-Chazalas (2 vols, Paris, 1977–78).

Dugdale, William, *Monasticon Anglicanum*, vi (London, 1830).

Elmham, Thomae de, Vita et Gesta Henrici Quinti Anglorum Regis, ed. T. Hearne (Oxford, 1727).

English chronicle of the reigns of Richard II, Henry IV, Henry V, and Henry VI, written before the year 1471, ed. J.S. Davies (CS, London, 1856).

English suits before the Parlement of Paris, 1420–1436, ed. C.T. Allmand and C.A.J. Armstrong (Camden 4th series, 26, RHistS, London, 1982).

Entrées royales françaises de 1328 à 1515, ed. B. Guenée & F. Lehoux (Paris, 1968).

Essential portions of Nicholas Upton's De Studio Militari, before 1446, translated by John Blount, Fellow of All Souls (c.1500), ed. F.P. Barnard (Oxford, 1931).

'Extracts from the plea rolls of the reigns of Henry V and Henry VI', ed. G. Wrottesley, *Collections for a history of Staffordshire* (William Salt Archaeological Soc., 17, 1896).

Extrait du registre des dons, confiscations, maintenues et autres actes faits dans le duché de Normandie pendant les années 1418, 1419, et 1420, par Henri V, roi d'Angleterre, ed. C. Vautier (Paris, 1828).

Fabyan, R., *New chronicles of England and France*, ed. H. Ellis (London, 1811).

First English Life of king Henry the Fifth, ed. C.L. Kingsford (Oxford, 1911).

Four English political tracts of the later middle ages, ed. J.-P. Genet (Camden 4th series, 18, RHistS, London, 1977).

Froissart, *Chroniques*, ed. K. de Lettenhove, xvi (Brussels, 1872).

Gesta Henrici Quinti. The Deeds of Henry the fifth, ed. & trans. F. Taylor and J.S. Roskell (Oxford, 1975).

Grands traités de la guerre de Cent Ans, ed. E. Cosneau (Paris, 1889).

Great Chronicle of London, ed. A.H. Thomas and I.D. Thornley (London, 1938).

Gruel, Guillaume, *Chronique d'Arthur de Richemont, connétable de France, duc de Bretagne (1393–1458)* (SHF, Paris, 1890).

Handbook of British chronology ed. E.B. Fryde, D.E. Greenway, S. Porter and I. Roy (3rd edn, London, 1986).

Henrici quinti Angliae regis gesta, ed. B. Williams (London, 1850).

Historical collections of a Citizen of London in the fifteenth century, ed. J. Gairdner (CS, London, 1876).

Historical papers and letters from northern registers, ed. J. Raine (RS, London, 1873).

Historical poems of the XIVth and XVth centuries, ed. R.H. Robbins (New York, 1959).

Hoccleve, Thomas, *Works, i, The minor poems*, ed. F.J. Furnivall (EETS, London, 1892).

——, *iii, The regement of princes, A.D. 1411–12*, ed. F.J. Furnivall (EETS, London, 1897).

Incendium Amoris of Richard Rolle of Hampole, ed. M. Deanesly (Manchester, 1915).

Issues of the Exchequer . . . from king Henry III to king Henry VI inclusive, ed. F. Devon (London, 1837).

Journal de Clement de Fauquembergue, greffier du Parlement de Paris, 1417–35, ed. A. Tuetey, i (SHF, Paris, 1903).

Journal d'un bourgeois de Paris 1405–1449, ed. A. Tuetey (Paris, 1881); ed. C. Beaune (Paris, 1990). See also *Parisian journal*.

Letters and papers illustrative of the wars of the English in France during the reign of Henry the sixth, king of England, ed. J. Stevenson, ii (RS, London, 1864).

Letters of queen Margaret of Anjou and bishop Beckington and others, written in the reigns of Henry V and Henry VI, ed. C. Monro (CS, London, 1863).

Lettres de rois, reines et autres personnages des cours de France et d'Angleterre, ed. J.J. Champollion-Figeac, ii (Paris, 1847).

'*L'honneur de la couronne de France'. Quatre libelles contre les Anglais (v.1418–v. 1429)*, ed. N. Pons (SHF, Paris, 1990).

Libelle of Englyshe Polycye, ed. G. Warner (Oxford, 1926).

Liber regie capelle, ed. W. Ullmann (Henry Bradshaw Soc., 92, London, 1961).

'Le livre des trahisons de France envers la maison de Bourgogne', *Chroniques relatives à l'histoire de la Belgique sous la domination des ducs de Bourgogne*, ed. K. de Lettenhove (Brussels, 1873).

Lydgate, John, *Troy Book, A.D. 1412–20*, ed. H. Bergen (EETS, London, 1906).

——, *Minor poems*, ed. H.N. MacCracken (EETS, London, 1934).

Marcher lordships of south Wales, 1415–1536. Select documents, ed. T.B. Pugh (Cardiff, 1963).

Medical practitioners of medieval England: a biographical register, ed. C.H. Talbot and E.A. Hammond (London, 1965).

Mémoires de Pierre de Fenin, ed. Mlle. Dupont (SHF, Paris, 1837).

Memorials of Henry V, king of England, ed. C.A. Cole (RS, London, 1858).

Memorials of London and London life in the XIIIth, XIVth and XVth centuries, ed. H.T. Riley (London, 1868).

Navy of the Lancastrian kings. Accounts and inventories of William Soper, keeper of the king's ships, 1422–1427, ed. S. Rose (Navy Rec. Soc., London, 1982).

Ordonnances des rois de France de la troisième race, x, xi (Paris, 1763, 1769).

Original letters illustrative of English history, ed. H. Ellis: 1st series, i (London, 1825); 2nd series, i (London, 1827).

Otterbourne, Thomas, *Chronica Regum Anglie, I*, ed. T. Hearne (Oxford, 1732).

Pageant of the birth, life and death of Richard Beauchamp, earl of Warwick, K.G., 1389–1439, ed. Viscount Dillon and W.H. St John Hope (London, 1914).

Parisian journal, 1405–1449, trans. J. Shirley (Oxford, 1968). See also *Journal d'un bourgeois*.

Proceedings and ordinances of the Privy Council of England, ed. N.H. Nicolas, i, ii and iii (London, 1834).

Register of bishop Philip Repingdon, 1405–1419, i, ed. M. Archer (Lincoln Rec. Soc., 57, 1963).

Register of Henry Chichele, Archbishop of Canterbury, 1414–1443, ed. E.F. Jacob (C&YS, 45, 42, 46, 47, 1938–47).

Register of Robert Hallum, bishop of Salisbury, 1407–17, ed. J.M. Horn (C&YS, 72, 1982).

Register of Thomas Spofford, bishop of Hereford (A.D. 1422–1448), ed. A.T. Bannister (Hereford, 1917).

Reports of the Deputy Keeper of the Public Records (DKR), 41 (1880); 42 (1881); 44 (1883).

'Roles normands et français et autres pièces tirées des archives de Londres par Bréquigny en 1764, 1765 et 1766', *Mémoires de la Société des Antiquaires de Normandie*, 3e sér., 23 (1858).

'Rotuli Normanniae ab anno MCCCCXVII ad annum MCCCCXXII, Henrico quinto Angliae rege', *Mémoires de la Société des Antiquaires de Normandie*, 3e sér., 15 (1846).

Rotuli parliamentorum, iii–vi (London, 1767–77).

Rouen au temps de Jeanne d'Arc et pendant l'occupation anglaise (1419–1449), ed. P. Le Cacheux (Rouen/Paris, 1931).

Royal and historical letters during the reign of Henry the Fourth, ed. F.C. Hingeston, i, ii (RS, London, 1860, 1965).

Rymer, T., *Foedera, conventiones, literae, et cujuscunque generis acta publica*, iv (The Hague, 1740).

St Alban Chronicle, 1406–20, ed. V.H. Galbraith (Oxford, 1937).

Sacrorum conciliorum nova et amplissima collectio, cd. J. Mansi, 27 (Venice, 1784).

Select cases in chancery, 1364–1471, ed. W.P. Baildon (Selden Soc., 10, London, 1896).

Select cases in the court of king's bench. Henry V, ed. G.O. Sayles (Selden Soc., 88, London, 1971).

Select documents of English constitutional history, 1307–1485, ed. S.B. Chrimes and A.L. Brown (London, 1961).

Selections from Hoccleve, ed. M.C. Seymour (Oxford, 1981).

Shropshire peace roll, 1400–1414, ed. E.G. Kimball (Shrewsbury, 1959).

Snappe's Formulary and other records, ed. H.E. Salter (Oxford Hist. Soc., 1924).

Statutes of the Realm, ii (London, 1816).

Titi Livii Foro-Juliensis, Vita Henrici Quinti regis Angliae, ed. T. Hearne (Oxford, 1716).

Tree of Battles of Honoré Bonet, trans. G.W. Coopland (Liverpool, 1949).

Twenty-six political and other poems, ed. J. Kail (EETS, London, 1904).

Upton, Nicholas, *De studio militari*, ed. E. Bysshe (London, 1654).

Ursins, J.J. des, *Histoire de Charles VI, roy de France*, ed. J.F. Michaud and J.-J.F. Poujoulat (Nouvelle collection des mémoires pour servir l'histoire de France, ii, Paris, 1836).

Walsingham, Thomas, *Historia Anglicana*, ii, *1381–1422*, ed. H.T. Riley (RS, London, 1864).

Waurin, Jean de, *Recueil des croniques et anchiennes istories de la Grant Bretaigne, a present nomme Engleterre, 1399–1422*, ed. W. Hardy (RS, London, 1868).

SECONDARY AUTHORITIES

ALLMAND, C.T., *Lancastrian Normandy, 1415–1450. The history of a medieval occupation* (Oxford, 1983).

——, *Henry V* (Historical Association pamphlet, 68, London, 1968).

——, 'The Lancastrian land settlement in Normandy, 1417–50', *EconHR*, 2nd series, 21 (1968).

——, 'Henry V the soldier, and the war in France', *Henry V. The practice of kingship*, ed. G.L. Harriss (Oxford, 1985).

——, 'France-Angleterre à la fin de la guerre de cent ans: le "Boke of Noblesse" de William Worcester', *La France anglaise au moyen age. Actes du IIIe congrès national des sociétés savantes, Poitiers, 1986* (Paris, 1988).

ANGLO, S., 'An early Tudor programme for plays and other demonstrations against the Pope', *Journal of the Warburg and Courtauld Institutes*, 20 (1957).

ANSTIS, J., *Observations introductory to an historical essay upon the knighthood of the Bath* (London, 1725).

ASTON, M., *Thomas Arundel. A study of church life in the reign of Richard II* (Oxford, 1967).

——, 'Lollardy and sedition, 1381–1431', *Past & Present*, 17 (1960); repr. in Aston, *Lollards and reformers. Images and literacy in late medieval religion* (London, 1984).

AUTRAND, F., *Charles VI. La folie du roi* (Paris, 1986).

AVERY, M.E., 'An evaluation of the effectiveness of the court of chancery under the Lancastrian kings', *LQR*, 86 (1970).

AVOUT, J. d', *La querelle des Armagnacs et des Bourguignons* (Paris, 1945).

BALDWIN, J.F., *The King's Council in England during the Middle Ages* (Oxford, 1913).

BALFOUR-MELVILLE, E.W.M., *James I, King of Scots, 1406–37* (London, 1936).

BARBER, R., *Edward, prince of Wales and Aquitaine* (London, 1978).

BAUGH, A.C., and CABLE, T., *A history of the English language* (3rd edn, London, 1978).

BEAN, J.M.W., 'Henry IV and the Percies', *History*, 44 (1959).

BEAUNE, C., *Naissance de la nation France* (Paris, 1985).

——, 'Saint Clovis: histoire, religion royale et sentiment national en France à la fin du moyen age', *Le metier d'historien au moyen age. Etudes sur l'historiographie médiévale*, ed. B. Guenée (Paris, 1977).

BECK, R.T., *The cutting edge* (London, 1974).

BELLAMY, J.G., *The law of treason in England in the later middle ages* (Cambridge, 1970).

BENNETT, M.J., *Community, class and careerism. Cheshire and Lancashire society in the age of Sir Gawain and the Green Knight* (Cambridge, 1983).

BENSON, C.D., *The history of Troy in middle English literature* (Woodbridge, 1980).

BETCHERMAN, L.-R., 'The making of bishops in the Lancastrian period', *Speculum*, 41 (1966).

BEVERLEY SMITH, J., 'The last phase of the Glyndŵr rebellion', *BBCS*, 22 (1968).

BOIS, G., *The crisis of feudalism. Economy and society in eastern Normandy, c.1300–1550* (Cambridge/Paris, 1984).

BONENFANT, P., *Du meurtre de Montereau au traité de Troyes* (Brussels, 1958).

BRADLEY, P.J., 'Henry V's Scottish policy – a study in realpolitik', *Documenting the past. Essays in medieval history presented to George Peddy Cuttino*, ed. J.S. Hamilton and P.J. Bradley (Woodbridge/Wolfeboro, 1989).

BROWN, A.L., 'The Commons and the council in the reign of Henry IV', *EHR*, 79 (1964).

——, 'The privy seal clerks in the early fifteenth century', *The study of medieval records. Essays in honour of Kathleen Major*, ed. D.A. Bullough and R.L. Storey (Oxford, 1971).

——, 'The reign of Henry IV', *Fifteenth-century England*, ed. S.B. Chrimes, C.D. Ross and R.A. Griffiths (Manchester, 1972).

——, 'The English campaign in Scotland, 1400', *British government and administration. Studies presented to S.B. Chrimes*, ed. H. Hearder and H.R. Loyn (Cardiff, 1974).

BROWN, R.A., COLVIN, H.M., and TAYLOR, A.J., *The History of the King's Works. i & ii: The Middle Ages* (London, 1963).

BULLOUGH, G., *Narrative and dramatic sources of Shakespeare*, 4 (London/New York, 1962).

BURNE, A.H., *The Agincourt war* (London, 1956).

——, 'The battle of Agincourt, October 25, 1415', *History Today*, 6 (1956).

BURROW, J.A., 'Autobiographical poetry in the middle ages. the case of Thomas Hoccleve', *Proceedings of the British Academy*, 68 (1982).

CARPENTER-TURNER, B., 'Southampton as a naval centre', *Collected essays on Southampton*, ed. J.B. Morgan and P. Peberdy (Southampton, 1958).

CARPENTER-TURNER, W.J., 'The building of the *Holy Ghost of the Tower*, 1414–1416, and her subsequent history', *Mariner's Mirror*, 40 (1954).

——, 'The building of the *Grace dieu*, *Valentine* and *Falconer*, at Southampton, 1416–1420', *Mariner's Mirror*, 40 (1954).

CATTO, J., 'The king's servants', *Henry V. The practice of kingship*, ed. G.L. Harriss (Oxford, 1985).

——, 'Religious change under Henry V', *Henry V. The practice of kingship*, ed. G.L. Harriss (Oxford, 1985).

CHAMPION, P., *Vie de Charles d'Orléans, 1394–1465* (Paris, 1911).

——, and DE THOISY, P., *Bourgogne, France-Angleterre au traité de Troyes* (Paris, 1943).

CHEVALIER, B., 'Les Ecossais dans les armées de Charles VII jusqu'à la bataille de Verneuil', *Jeanne d'Arc. Une époque, un rayonnement* (Paris, 1982).

CHRIMES, S.B., 'The pretensions of the duke of Gloucester in 1422', *EHR*, 45 (1930).

CHURCH, A.J., *Henry the Fifth* (London, 1891).

COLKER, M.L., 'A previously unknown manuscript of the *Gesta Henrici Quinti*', *Revue d'Histoire des Textes*, 12–13 (1982–83).

CRAIG, J., *The Mint. A history of the London mint from A.D. 287 to 1948* (Cambridge, 1953).

CROMPTON, J., 'Leicestershire Lollards', *Trans. of the Leicestershire archaeological and historical society*, 44 (1968–69).

CROWDER, C.M.D., *Unity, heresy and reform, 1378–1460* (London, 1977).

——, 'Henry V, Sigismund, and the council of Constance', *Historical Studies*, ed. G.A. Hayes-McCoy, 4 (1963).

——, 'Correspondence between England and the Council of Constance, 1414–18', *Studies in Church History*, 1, ed. C.W. Dugmore and C. Duggan (London, 1964).

CURRY, A.E., 'Cheshire and the Royal Demesne, 1399–1422', *Medieval Cheshire (Transactions of the historic society of Lancashire and Cheshire*, 128 (1978)).

——, 'The first English standing army? – Military organisation in Lancastrian Normandy, 1420–1450', *Patronage, pedigree and power in later medieval England*, ed. C. Ross (Gloucester/Totowa, 1979).

——, 'Towns at war: relations between the towns of Normandy and their English rulers, 1417–1450', *Towns and townspeople in the fifteenth century*, ed. J.A.F. Thomson (Gloucester, 1988).

DANBURY, E.A., 'English and French artistic propaganda during the period of the Hundred Years War: some evidence from royal charters', *Power, culture and religion in France, c.1350–c.1550*, ed. C.T. Allmand (Woodbridge, 1989).

DAVID, H., 'Du nouveau sur Jean sans Peur', *Annales de Bourgogne*, 30 (1958).

DAVIES, J.D. Griffith, *Henry V* (London, 1935).

DAVIES, R.G., 'Thomas Arundel as archbishop of Canterbury, 1396–1414', *Journal of Ecclesiastical History*, 24 (1973).

——, 'Martin V and the English episcopate with particular reference to his campaign for the repeal of the Statute of Provisors', *EHR*, 92 (1977).

——, 'Lollardy and locality', *TRHistS*, 6th series, 1 (1991).

DAVIES, R.R., *Conquest, coexistence and change. Wales, 1063–1415* (Oxford, 1987).

——, 'Baronial accounts, incomes, and arrears in the later middle ages', *EconHR*, 2nd series, 21 (1968).

——, 'Owain Glyn Dŵr and the Welsh squirearchy', *Trans. Honourable Society of Cymmrodorion* (1968).

DAY, J., 'The great bullion famine of the fifteenth century', *Past & Present*, 79 (1978).

DÉPREZ, E., 'Un essai d'union nationale à la veille du traité de Troyes (1419)', *BEC*, 99 (1938).

DOBSON, R.B., *Durham priory, 1400–1450* (Cambridge, 1973).

DOUCET, R., 'Les finances anglaises en France à la fin de la guerre de cent ans, 1413–1435', *Le Moyen Age*, 2e sér., 37 (1926).

——, 'Livre tournois et livre sterling pendant l'occupation anglaise sous Charles VI et Charles VII', *Revue numismatique*, 4e sér., 29 (1926).

DUNCAN, A.A.M., *The Scots nation and the Declaration of Arbroath* (London, 1970).

DUPARC, P., 'La conclusion du traité de Troyes', *Revue historique de droit français et étranger*, 49 (1971).

EARLE, P., *The life and times of Henry V* (London, 1972).

EMDEN, A.B., *An Oxford hall in medieval times. Being the early history of St Edmund Hall* (Oxford, 1927).

FAVIER, J., *Nouvelle histoire de Paris. Paris au XVe siècle, 1380–1500* (Paris, 1974).

——, 'Une ville entre deux vocations: la place d'affaires de Paris au XVe siècle', *Annales ESC*, 28 (1973).

FISHER, J.H., 'Chancery and the emergence of standard written English in the fifteenth century', *Speculum*, 52 (1977).

FLOOD, F.S., 'The story of Prince Henry of Monmouth and Chief-Justice Gascoign', *TRHistS*, new series, 3 (1886).

——, 'Prince Henry of Monmouth: his Letters and Despatches during the War in Wales, 1402–1405', *TRHistS*, new series, 4 (1889).

FORD, C.J., 'Piracy or Policy: the crisis in the Channel, 1400–1403', *TRHistS*, 5th series, 29 (1979).

FOREVILLE, R., 'Manifestations de Lollardisme à Exeter en 1421?', *Le Moyen Age*, 69 (1963).

FOWLER, K.A., *The Age of Plantagenet and Valois. The struggle for supremacy, 1328–1498* (London, 1967).

——, *The king's lieutenant. Henry of Grosmont, first duke of Lancaster, 1310–1361* (London, 1969).

FURLEY, J.S., *City government of Winchester from the records of the XIV and XV centuries* (Oxford, 1923).

GENET, J.-P., 'English nationalism: Thomas Polton at the Council of Constance', *Nottingham medieval studies*, 38 (1984).

GIVEN-WILSON, C., *The royal household and the king's affinity. Service, politics and finance in England, 1360–1413* (New Haven/London, 1986).

GOODMAN, A.E., *John of Gaunt. The exercise of princely power in fourteenth-century Europe* (London, 1992).

——, 'Responses to requests in Yorkshire for military service under Henry V', *Northern History*, 17 (1981).

——, 'John of Gaunt', *England in the fourteenth century*, ed. W.M. Ormrod (Woodbridge, 1986).

——, 'John of Gaunt: paradigm of the late fourteenth-century crisis', *TRHistS*, 5th series, 37 (1987).

GOODWIN, T., *The history of the reign of Henry the Fifth, king of England* (London, 1704).

GRANSDEN, A., *Historical writing in England: ii. c.1307 to the early sixteenth century* (London, 1982).

GRAY, H.L., *The influence of the commons on early legislation. A study of the fourteenth and fifteenth centuries* (Cambridge, Mass./London, 1932).

GREEN, R.F., *Poets and princepleasers. Literature and the English court in the late middle ages* (Toronto, 1980).

GRÉVY-PONS, N., 'Propagande et sentiment national pendant le règne de Charles VI: l'exemple de Jean de Montreuil', *Francia*, 9 (1980).

GRIFFITHS, R.A., *The reign of King Henry VI. The exercise of royal authority 1422–1461* (London, 1981).

——, *Boroughs of Medieval Wales* (Cardiff, 1978).

——, 'Some partisans of Owain Glyn Dŵr at Oxford', *BBCS*, 10 (1962–64).

——, 'The Glyndŵr rebellion in north Wales through the eyes of an English-man', *BBCS*, 22 (1967).

——, 'Wales and the Marches', *Fifteenth-century England*, ed. S.B. Chrimes, C.D. Ross and R.A. Griffiths (Manchester, 1972).

——, 'Patronage, politics, and the principality of Wales, 1413–1461', *British government and administration. Studies presented to S.B. Chrimes*, ed. H. Hearder and H.R. Loyn (Cardiff, 1974).

GRIFFITHS, W.R.M., 'Prince Henry, Wales and the Royal Exchequer, 1400–13', *BBCS*, 32 (1985).

——, 'Prince Henry's war: Armies, garrisons and supply during the Glyndŵr rising', *BBCS*, 34 (1987).

——, 'Prince Henry and Wales, 1400–1408', *Profit, piety and the professions in later medieval England*, ed. M. Hicks (Gloucester/Wolfeboro Falls, 1990).

GWYNFOR JONES, J., 'Government and the Welsh community: the north-east borderland in the fifteenth century', *British government and administration. Studies presented to S.B. Chrimes*, ed. H. Hearder and H.R. Loyn (Cardiff, 1974).

HAINES, R.M., 'Church, society and politics in the early fifteenth century, as viewed from an English pulpit', *Church, society and politics (Studies in Church History, 12)*, ed. L.G.D. Baker (Oxford, 1975).

——, ' "Our master mariner, our sovereign lord": a contemporary preacher's view of king Henry V', *Medieval Studies*, 38 (1976).

HANNA, R. III, 'Sir Thomas Berkeley and his patronage', *Speculum*, 64 (1989).

HARRISS, G.L., *Cardinal Beaufort. A study of Lancastrian ascendancy and decline* (Oxford, 1988).

——, ed., *Henry V. The practice of kingship* (Oxford, 1985).

——, 'Aids, loans and benevolences', *Historical Journal*, 6 (1963).

——, 'Cardinal Beaufort – patriot or usurer?', *TRHistS*, 5th series, 20 (1970).

HARVEY, M.M., *Solutions to the Schism. A study of some English attitudes, 1378 to 1409* (Sankt Ottilien, 1983).

——, '*Ecclesia anglicana, cui ecclesiastes noster Christus vos prefecit*: the power of the crown in the English Church during the Great Schism', *Religion and national identity (Studies in Church History, 18)*, ed. S. Mews (Oxford, 1982).

——, 'Martin V and Henry V', *Archivum Historiae Pontificiae*, 24 (1986).

HATCHER, J., *Rural economy and society in the duchy of Cornwall, 1300–1500* (Cambridge, 1970).

HAYES, R.C.E., 'The pre-episcopal career of William Alnwick, bishop of Norwich and Lincoln', *People, politics and community in the late middle ages*, ed. J. Rosenthal and C.F. Richmond (Gloucester/New York; 1987).

HEPBURN, F., *Portraits of the later Plantagenets* (Woodbridge/Dover, N.H., 1986).

HERBERT, A.E., 'Herefordshire, 1413–61: some aspects of society and public order', *Patronage, the crown and the provinces in later medieval England*, ed. R.A. Griffiths (Gloucester/Atlantic Highlands, 1981).

HEWITT, H.J., *The organization of war under Edward III, 1338–62* (Manchester/New York, 1966).

HIBBERT, C., *Agincourt* (London, 1964).

HIPPEAU, C., *L'abbaye de Saint-Etienne de Caen, 1066–1790* (Caen, 1855).

HORNER, P.J., '"The king taught us the lesson": Benedictine support for Henry V's suppression of the Lollards', *Mediaeval Studies*, 52 (1990).

HUDSON, A., *The premature reformation* (Oxford, 1988).

——, 'A Lollard sermon-cycle and its implications', *Medium Aevum*, 40 (1971).

——, 'Lollardy: the English heresy?', *Religion and national identity (Studies in Church History, 18)*, ed. S. Mews (Oxford, 1982).

HUNTER, J., *Agincourt* (London, 1850).

HUTCHINSON, H.F., *Henry V. A biography* (London, 1967).

JACK, R.I., 'Owain Glyn Dŵr and the lordship of Ruthin', *Welsh History Review*, 2 (1965).

JACOB, E.F., *Henry V and the Invasion of France* (London, 1947).

——, *Henry Chichele and the ecclesiastical politics of his age* (London, 1952).

——, *Essays in the conciliar epoch* (2nd edn, Manchester, 1953).

——, *The fifteenth century, 1399–1485* (Oxford, 1961).

——, *Archbishop Henry Chichele* (London, 1967).

——, 'Wilkins's *Concilia* and the fifteenth century', *TRHistS*, 4th series, 15 (1932).

——, 'Two lives of Archbishop Chichele', *BJRL*, 16 (1932).

——, 'The collapse of France in 1419–20', *BJRL*, 26 (1941–42).

——, 'The medieval chapter of Salisbury cathedral', *Wiltshire archaeological and natural history magazine*, 51 (1947).

——, 'A note on the English concordat of 1418', *Medieval studies presented to Aubrey Gwynn, S.J.*, ed. J.A. Watt, J.B. Morrall and F.X. Martin (Dublin, 1961).

JOHN, T., 'Sir Thomas Erpingham, East Anglian society, and the dynastic revolution of 1399', *Norfolk Archaeology*, 35 (1970).

JOHNSON, P.A., *Duke Richard of York, 1411–1460* (Oxford, 1988).

JOUET, R., *La résistance à l'occupation anglaise en Basse-Normandie (1418–1450)* (Caen, 1969).

KANTOROWICZ, E., 'The "King's Advent" and the enigmatic panels in the doors of Santa Sabina', *Selected studies* (New York, 1965).

KEEGAN, J., *The Face of Battle* (Harmondsworth, 1978).

KEEN, M.H., *The Laws of War in the late Middle Ages* (London/Toronto, 1965).

——, *England in the later Middle Ages* (London, 1973).

——, 'Diplomacy', *Henry V. The practice of kingship*, ed. G.L. Harriss (Oxford, 1985).

——, 'The influence of Wyclif', *Wyclif in his times*, ed. A.J.P. Kenny (Oxford, 1986).

——, 'English military experience and the court of chivalry: the case of Grey v. Hastings', *Guerre et société en France, en Angleterre et en Bourgogne, XIVe – XVe siècle*, ed. P. Contamine, C. Giry-Deloison and M.H. Keen (Lille, 1991).

KINGSFORD, C.L., *English historical literature in the fifteenth century* (Oxford, 1913).

——, *Henry V. The typical medieval hero* (London/New York, 2nd edn, 1923).

——, 'The early biographies of Henry V', *EHR*, 25 (1910).

——, 'A legend of Sigismund's visit to England', *EHR*, 26 (1911).

——, 'The first version of Hardyng's chronicle', *EHR*, 27 (1912).

——, 'An historical collection of the fifteenth century', *EHR*, 29 (1914).

KIPLING, G., 'Richard II's "Sumptuous Pageants" and the idea of the civic triumph', *Pageantry in the Shakespearean theatre*, ed. D.M. Bergeron (Athens, Georgia, 1985).

KIRBY, J.L., *Henry IV of England* (London, 1970).

——, 'The financing of Calais under Henry V', *BIHR*, 23 (1950).

——, 'The council of 1407 and the problem of Calais', *History Today*, 5 (1955).

——, 'Councils and councillors of Henry IV, 1399–1413', *TRHistS*, 5th series, 14 (1964).

——, 'Henry V and the city of London', *History Today*, 26 (1976).

KNOWLES, D., *The religious orders in England. ii: The end of the middle ages* (Cambridge, 1955).

KNOWLSON, G.A., *Jean V, duc de Bretagne, et l'Angleterre (1399–1442)* (Cambridge/Rennes, 1964).

LABARGE, M.W., *Henry V. The cautious conqueror* (London, 1975).

LAWTON, L., 'The illustration of late medieval secular texts, with special reference to Lydgate's "Troy Book"', *Manuscripts and readers in fifteenth-century England*, ed. D. Pearsall (Woodbridge/Totowa, 1983).

LEFF, G., *Heresy in the later middle ages. The relation of heterodoxy to dissent, c.1250–c.1450* (2 vols, Manchester, 1967).

LEGUAI, A., 'The relations between the towns of Burgundy and the French crown in the fifteenth century', *The crown and local communities in England and France in the fifteenth century*, ed. J.R.L. Highfield and R. Jeffs (Gloucester, 1981).

LINDSAY, P., *Henry V. A chronicle* (London, 1934).

LITTLE, R.G., *The Parlement of Poitiers. War, government and politics in France, 1418–1436* (London, 1984).

LLOYD, J.E., *Owen Glendower* (Oxford, 1931).

MCFARLANE, K.B., *John Wycliffe and the beginnings of English nonconformity* (London, 1952).

——, *Lancastrian kings and Lollard knights* (Oxford, 1972).

——, 'Anglo-Flemish relations in 1415–16', *Bodleian Library Quarterly*, 7 (1932).

——, '"Bastard feudalism"', *BIHR*, 20 (1945).

——, 'Henry V, bishop Beaufort and the Red Hat, 1417–1421', *EHR*, 60 (1945); repr. in McFarlane, *England in the fifteenth century* (London, 1981).

——, 'Loans to the Lancastrian kings: the problem of inducement', *Cambridge Historical Journal*, 9 (1947); repr. in McFarlane, *England in the fifteenth century* (London, 1981).

——, 'A business-partnership in war and administration, 1421–1445', *EHR*, 78 (1963).

MCHARDY, A.K., 'Liturgy and propaganda in the diocese of Lincoln during the Hundred Years War', *Religion and national identity (Studies in Church History, 18)*, ed. S. Mews (Oxford, 1982).

——, 'Religious ritual and political persuasion: the case of England in the Hundred Years War', *International Journal of Moral and Social Science*, 3 (1988).

MCKISACK, M., *Medieval history in the Tudor Age* (Oxford, 1971).

MACLEOD, E., *Charles of Orléans, Prince and poet* (London, 1969).

MCNAB, B., 'Obligations of the Church in medieval society: military arrays of the clergy, 1369–1418', *Order and innovation in the middle ages. Essays in honor of Joseph R. Strayer*, ed. W.C. Jordan, B. McNab and T.F. Ruiz (Princeton, 1976).

MCNIVEN, P., *Heresy and politics in the reign of Henry IV. The burning of John Badby* (Woodbridge/Wolfeboro, 1987).

——, 'Prince Henry and the English political crisis of 1412', *History*, 65 (1980).

——, 'The problem of Henry IV's health, 1405–1413', *EHR*, 100 (1985).

MALDEN, A.R., 'An official account of the battle of Agincourt', *Ancestor*, XI (1904).

MASSEY, R.A., 'The land settlement in Lancastrian Normandy', *Property and politics: essays in later medieval English history*, ed. A.J. Pollard (Gloucester/New York, 1984).

MATTHEW, D.J.A., *The Norman monasteries and their English possessions* (London, 1962).

MATTHEW, E., 'The financing of the lordship of Ireland under Henry V and Henry VI', *Property and politics: essays in later medieval English history*, ed. A.J. Pollard (Gloucester/New York, 1984).

MEDCALF, S., ed., *The context of English literature. The later middle ages* (London, 1981).

MESSHAM, J.E., 'The county of Flint and the rebellion of Owen Glyndŵr in the records of the earldom of Chester', *Flintshire Historical Society publications*, 23 (1967–68).

MIROT, L., 'Le Procès de Maître Jean Fusoris, chanoine de Notre-Dame de Paris (1415–1416). Episode des negociations franco-anglaises durant la guerre de Cent Ans', *Mémoires de la Société de l'Histoire de Paris et de l'Ile de France*, 27 (1900).

——, 'Lettres closes de Charles VI conservées aux archives de Reims et de Tournai', *Le Moyen Age*, 2e sér., 29–30 (1917–18).

MISKIMIN, H.A., *Money and power in fifteenth-century France* (New Haven/London, 1984).

MITCHELL, J., *Thomas Hoccleve. A study in early fifteenth-century English poets* (Urbana, 1968).

MORGAN, M.M., 'The suppression of the alien priories', *History*, new series, 26 (1941–42).

MORGAN, P., *War and society in medieval Cheshire, 1277–1403* (Chetham Soc., Manchester, 1987).

MOWAT, R.B., *Henry V* (London, 1919).

MUDROCH, V., 'John Wycliff and Richard Flemming, bishop of Lincoln: gleanings from German sources', *BIHR*, 37 (1964).

MYERS, A.R., *England in the later middle ages* (Harmondsworth, 1952).

——, 'Parliamentary petitions in the fifteenth century', *EHR*, 52 (1937).

——, 'The captivity of a royal witch: the household accounts of queen Joan of Navarre, 1419–21', *BJRL*, 24 (1940); repr. in Myers, *Crown, household and parliament in fifteenth-century England*, ed. C.H. Clough (London/Ronceverte, 1985).

NEWHALL, R.A., *The English Conquest of Normandy, 1416–1424. A study in fifteenth-century warfare* (Yale, 1924).

——, *Muster and review. A problem of English military administration, 1420–1440* (Cambridge, Mass., 1940).

——, 'Discipline in an English army of the fifteenth century', *The military historian and economist*, 2 (1917).

——, 'The war finances of Henry V and the duke of Bedford', *EHR*, 36 (1921).

——, 'Henry V's policy of conciliation in Normandy, 1417–1422', *Anniversary essays in medieval history of students of C.H. Haskins*, ed. C.H. Taylor (Boston, 1929).

NICHOLSON, R., *Scotland: the later middle ages* (Edinburgh, 1974).

NICOLAS, N.H., *History of the battle of Agincourt* (2nd edn, London, 1832).

ORME, N., *From childhood to chivalry. The education of the English kings and aristocracy, 1066–1530* (London/New York, 1984).

OTWAY-RUTHVEN, J., *The King's Secretary and the Signet Office in the XV century* (Cambridge, 1939).

PANTIN, W.A., *The English church in the fourteenth century* (Cambridge, 1955).

PAYLING, S.J., 'Law and arbitration in Nottinghamshire 1399–1461', *People, politics and community in the later middle ages*, ed. J. Rosenthal and C.F. Richmond (Gloucester/New York, 1987).

PERROY, E., *The Hundred Years War* (London, 1951).

PHILLIPS, J.R.S., 'When did Owain Glyndŵr die?', *BBCS*, 24 (1970–72).

PHILLPOTTS, C., 'The French plan of battle during the Agincourt campaign', *EHR*, 99 (1984).

PLANCHENAULT, R., 'La bataille de Baugé (22 mars, 1421)', *Mémoires de la société nationale d'agriculture, sciences et arts d'Angers*, 5e sér., 28 (1925).

——, 'Les suites de la bataille de Baugé (1421)', ibid., 6e sér., 5 (1930).

POQUET DU HAUT-JUSSÉ, B.-A., 'La renaissance littéraire autour de Henri V, roi d'Angleterre', *Revue historique*, 224 (1960).

POSTEL, R., *Siège et capitulation de Bayeux en 1417. Notes pour servir à l'histoire du Bessin pendant la domination anglaise sous l'occupation du roi Henry V* (Caen, 1873).

POWELL, E., *Kingship, law and society. Criminal justice in the reign of Henry V* (Oxford, 1989).

——, 'The king's bench in Shropshire and Staffordshire in 1414', *Law, liti-*

gants and the legal profession, ed. E.W. Ives and A.H. Manchester (London, 1983).

——, 'Proceedings before the justices of the peace at Shrewsbury in 1414: a supplement to the Shropshire peace roll', *EHR*, 99 (1984).

——, 'The restoration of law and order', *Henry V. The practice of kingship*, ed. G.L. Harriss (Oxford, 1985).

POWICKE, M.R., 'Lancastrian captains', *Essays in medieval history presented to Bertie Wilkinson*, ed. T.A. Sandquist and M.R. Powicke (Toronto, 1969).

PRIESTLY, E.J., *The battle of Shrewsbury, 1403* (Shrewsbury, 1979).

PRONAY, N., 'The hanaper under the Lancastrian kings', *Proceedings of the Leeds philosophical and literary society (literary and historical section)*, 12 (1967).

PRYNNE, M., 'Henry V's *Grace Dieu*', *Mariner's Mirror*, 54 (1968).

PUGH, T.B., *Henry V and the Southampton plot of 1415* (Southampton Record Series, 30, 1988).

——, 'The Southampton plot of 1415', *Kings and Nobles in the later Middle Ages. A Tribute to Charles Ross*, ed. R.A. Griffiths and J. Sherborne (Gloucester/New York, 1986).

PUISEUX, L., *Caen en 1421. Appendice au siège de Caen par les Anglais en 1417* (Caen, 1860).

——, *L'émigration normande et la colonisation anglaise en Normandie au XVe siècle* (Caen/Paris, 1866).

——, *Siège et prise de Rouen par les Anglais (1418–1419)* (Caen, 1867).

——, 'Prise de Caen par les Anglais en 1417', *Mémoires de la Société des Antiquaires de Normandie*, 3e sér., 22 (1856).

PUTNAM, B.H., *Proceedings before the justices of the peace in the fourteenth and fifteenth centuries : Edward III to Richard III* (Cambridge, Mass., 1938).

RAMSAY, J.H., *Lancaster and York: a century of English history, A.D. 1399–1485* (2 vols, Oxford, 1892).

RAWCLIFFE, C., 'The great lord as peacemaker: arbitration by English noblemen and their councils in the later middle ages', *Law and social change in British history*, ed. J.A. Guy and H.G. Beale (London, 1984).

REES, W., *South Wales and the March, 1284–1415. A social and agrarian study* (Oxford, 1924).

REEVES, A.C., *Lancastrian Englishmen* (Washington, 1981).

REID, E.J.B., 'Lollards at Colchester in 1414', *EHR*, 29 (1914).

REID, R.R., 'The date and authorship of Redmayne's "Life of Henry V"', *EHR*, 30 (1915).

RICHARDSON, H.G., 'John Oldcastle in hiding, August-October, 1417', *EHR*, 55 (1940).

RICHARDSON, M., 'Henry V, the English chancery, and chancery English', *Speculum*, 55 (1980).

RICHMOND, C.F., 'The keeping of the seas during the Hundred Years War : 1422–1440', *History*, 49 (1964).

——, 'English naval power in the fifteenth century', *History*, 52 (1967).

ROGERS, A., 'Henry IV, the commons and taxation', *Medieval studies*, 31 (1969).

ROSKELL, J.S., *The commons in the parliament of 1422. English society and parliamentary representation under the Lancastrians* (Manchester, 1954).

——, *The Commons and their Speakers in English parliaments, 1376–1523* (Manchester, 1965).

——, 'The social composition of the commons in a fifteenth-century parliament', *BIHR*, 24 (1951).

——, 'The office and dignity of Protector of England, with special reference to its origins', *EHR*, 68 (1953).

——, and TAYLOR, F., 'The authorship and purpose of the *Gesta Henrici Quinti*', *BJRL*, 53, 54 (1971).

ROWE, B.J.H., 'A contemporary account of the Hundred Years War from 1415 to 1429', *EHR*, 41 (1926).

——, 'Discipline in the Norman garrisons under Bedford, 1422–35', *EHR*, 46 (1931).

——, 'The *Grand Conseil* under the duke of Bedford, 1422–35', *Essays in medieval history presented to H.E. Salter* (Oxford, 1934).

——, 'Notes on the Clovis miniature and the Bedford portrait in the Bedford book of hours', *Journal of the British Archaeological Association*, 3rd series, 25 (1962).

ST JOHN HOPE, W.H., 'The funeral, monument, and chantry chapel of king Henry the Fifth', *Archaeologia*, 65 (1913–14).

SAMUELS, M.L., 'Some applications of middle English dialectology', *English studies* (Amsterdam), 44 (1963).

SANDQUIST, T.A., 'The holy oil of St Thomas of Canterbury', *Essays in medieval history presented to Bertie Wilkinson*, ed. T.A. Sandquist and M.R. Powicke (Toronto, 1969).

SCATTERGOOD, V.T., *Politics and poetry in the fifteenth century* (London, 1971).

SCHMIDT, G., 'Two unknown horae from the fifteenth century', *Burlington Magazine*, 103 (1961).

SCHNITH, K., 'Musik, Liturgie, Prozession als Ausdrucksmittel der Politik Heinrichs V. von England', *Festschrift Rudolf Bockholdt zum 60. Geburtstag*, ed. N. Dubowy and S. Meyer-Eller.

SCHRAMM, P.E., *A history of the English coronation* (Oxford, 1937).

SEWARD, D., *Henry V as Warlord* (London, 1987).

SOMERVILLE, R., *History of the duchy of Lancaster. I, 1265–1603* (London, 1953).

STEEL, A., *The Receipt of the Exchequer, 1377–1485* (Cambridge, 1954).

——, 'Receipt roll totals under Henry IV and Henry V', *EHR*, 47 (1932).

STOREY, R.L., *Thomas Langley and the bishopric of Durham, 1406–1437* (London, 1961).

——, 'Gentlemen-bureaucrats', *Profession, vocation and culture in later medieval England. Essays dedicated to the memory of A.R. Myers*, ed. C.H. Clough (Liverpool, 1982).

STRONG, P. and F., 'The last will and codicils of Henry V', *EHR*, 96 (1981).

SWANSON, R.N., *Church and society in late medieval England* (Oxford, 1989).

TATNALL, E.C., 'The condemnation of John Wyclif at the Council of Constance', *Councils and Assemblies (Studies in Church History, 7)*, ed. G.J. Cuming and L.G.D. Baker (Cambridge, 1971).

THOMPSON, E.M., *The Carthusian order in England* (London, 1936).

THOMPSON, G.Ll., *Paris and its people under English rule. The Anglo-Burgundian régime, 1420–1436* (Oxford, 1991).

——, '"Monseigneur Saint Denis", his abbey, and his town, under the English occupation, 1420–1436', *Power, culture and religion in France c.1350-c.1550*, ed. C. Allmand (Woodbridge/Wolfeboro, 1989).

THOMSON, J.A.F., *The later Lollards, 1414–1520* (Oxford, 1965).

——, 'Orthodox religion and the origins of Lollardy', *History*, 74 (1989).

TURNER, E., 'Description of an ancient castle at Rouen in Normandy, called Le Château du Vieux Palais, built by Henry V, king of England', *Archaeologia*, 7 (1785).

VALE, M.G.A., *English Gascony, 1399–1453. A study of war, government, and politics during the later stages of the Hundred Years War* (Oxford, 1970).

——, *War and Chivalry. Warfare and aristocratic culture in England, France and Burgundy at the end of the Middle Ages* (London, 1981).

VAUGHAN, R., *John the Fearless. The growth of Burgundian power* (London, 1966).

——, *Philip the Good. The apogee of Burgundy* (London, 1970).

VICKERS, K.H., *Humphrey, duke of Gloucester* (London, 1907).

VIDAL, J.M., 'Un recueil manuscrit de sermons prononcés aux conciles de Constance et de Bâle', *Revue d'histoire ecclésiastique*, 10 (1909).

WALKER, D., *Medieval Wales* (Cambridge, 1990).

WALKER, J.A., 'John Holland, a fifteenth-century admiral', *Mariner's Mirror*, 65 (1979).

WALKER, S., *The Lancastrian affinity, 1361–1399* (Oxford, 1990).

WAUGH, W.T., 'Sir John Oldcastle', *EHR*, 20 (1905).

——, 'The administration of Normandy 1420–22', *Essays in medieval history presented to T.F. Tout*, ed. A.G. Little and F.M. Powicke (Manchester, 1925).

WEISS, R., *Humanism in England during the fifteenth century* (2nd edn, Oxford, 1957).

——, 'Humphrey, duke of Gloucester, and Tito Livio Frulovisi', *Fritz Saxl, 1890–1948. A volume of memorial essays from his friends in England*, ed. D.J. Gordon (London, 1957).

WILLIAMS, E.C., *My lord of Bedford, 1389–1435* (London, 1963).

WILLIAMS, G., *Recovery, reorientation and reformation. Wales c.1415–1642* (Oxford, 1987).

WILLIAMS-JONES, K., 'The taking of Conwy castle, 1401', *Trans. Caernarvon Hist. Soc.*, 30 (1978).

WOLFFE, B.P., *The royal demesne in English history. The crown estate in the governance of the realm from the Conquest to 1509* (London, 1971).

——, *Henry VI* (London, 1981).

WYLIE, J.H., *History of England under Henry the Fourth* (4 vols, London, 1884–98).

——, 'Decembri's version of the Vita Henrici Quinti by Tito Livio', *EHR*, 24 (1909).

——, 'Notes on the Agincourt roll', *TRHistS*, 3rd series, 5 (1911).

——, 'Memorandum concerning a proposed marriage between Henry V and Catherine of France in 1414', *EHR*, 29 (1914).

——, and WAUGH, W.T., *The Reign of Henry the Fifth* (3 vols, Cambridge, 1914–29).

WYON, A.B., 'On the great seals of Henry IV, Henry V, and Henry VI', *Journal of the British Archaeological Association*, 39 (1883).

THESES

ALLMAND, C.T., 'The relations between the English government, the higher clergy, and the papacy in Normandy, 1417–1450 (Univ. of Oxford D.Phil. thesis, 1963).

ARCHER, R.E., 'The Mowbray earls of Nottingham and dukes of Norfolk, to 1432' (Univ. of Oxford D.Phil thesis, 1984).

BARRON, C.M., 'The government of London and its relations with the crown, 1400–1450' (Univ. of London Ph.D. thesis, 1970).

BROWN, A.L., 'The privy seal in the early fifteenth century' (Univ. of Oxford D.Phil. thesis, 1954).

CAREY, H., 'Astrology and divination in later medieval England' (Univ. of Oxford D.Phil. thesis, 1984).

CROWDER, C.M.D., 'Some aspects of the English nation at the council of Constance' (Univ. of Oxford D.Phil. thesis, 1956).

CURRY, A.E., 'The demesne of the county palatine of Chester in the early fifteenth century' (Univ. of Manchester MA thesis, 1977).

DAVIES, R.G., 'The episcopate in England and Wales, 1375–1443' (Univ. of Manchester Ph.D. thesis, 1974).

FAGAN, E.H. de L., 'Some aspects of the king's household in the reign of Henry V, 1413–22' (Univ. of London MA thesis, 1935); and *BIHR*, 14 (1936–37).

FRIEL, I., 'The documentary evidence for maritime technology in later medieval England and Wales' (Univ. of Keele Ph.D. thesis, 1990).

GRIFFITHS, W.R.M., 'The military career and affinity of Henry, Prince of Wales, 1399–1413' (Univ. of Oxford M.Litt. thesis, 1980).

HARVEY, M.M., 'English suggestions for the reforms to be undertaken by the general councils, 1400–1418' (Univ. of Oxford D.Phil. thesis, 1964).

HERBERT, A.E., 'Public order and private violence in Herefordshire, 1413–61' (Univ. of Wales MA thesis, 1978).

MCNIVEN, P., 'Political developments in the second half of the reign of Henry IV, 1405–13' (Univ. of Manchester Ph.D. thesis, 1977).

MASSEY, R.A., 'The Lancastrian land settlement in Normandy and northern France, 1417–1450' (Univ. of Liverpool Ph.D. thesis, 1987).

PHILLPOTTS, C., 'English policy towards France during the truces, 1389–1417' (Univ. of Liverpool Ph.D. thesis, 1984).

RICHMOND, C.F., 'Royal administration and the keeping of the seas, 1422–1485' (Univ. of Oxford D.Phil. thesis, 1963).

ROGERS, A., 'The royal household of Henry V' (Univ. of Nottingham Ph.D. thesis, 1966).

SINCLAIR, A.F.J., 'The Beauchamp earls of Warwick in the later middle ages' (Univ. of London Ph.D. thesis, 1987).

THOMPSON, G.Ll., 'The Anglo-Burgundian regime in Paris, 1420–1436' (Univ. of Oxford D.Phil. thesis, 1984).

TYLDESLEY, C.J., 'The crown and the local communities in Devon and Cornwall from 1377 to 1422' (Univ. of Exeter Ph.D. thesis, 1978).

WRIGHT, T.E.F., 'Royal finance in the latter part of the reign of Henry IV of England, 1406–13' (Univ. of Oxford D.Phil. thesis, 1984).

INDEX